Masterworks of 20th-Century Music

Masterworks of 20th-Century Music

The Modern Repertory of the Symphony Orchestra

Douglas Lee

Routledge
New York · London

Published in 2002 by
Routledge
29 West 35th Street
New York, NY 10001
www.routledge-ny.com

Published in Great Britain by
Routledge
11 New Fetter Lane
London EC4P 4EE
www.routledge.co.uk

Printed in the United States of America on acid-free paper.

Cataloging-in-Publication Data is available from the Library of Congress.

ISBN 0-415-93846-5 (hb.) — 0-415-93847-3

For Bev

Contents

❧

Alban Berg

Leonard Bernstein

Benjamin Britten

Aaron Copland

John Corigliano

Peter Maxwell Davies

Manuel de Falla

George Gershwin

Alberto Ginastera

Henryk Górecki

Paul Hindemith

Gustav Holst

Charles Ives

Zoltán Kodály

Witold Lutosławski

Darius Milhaud

Carl Nielsen

Carl Orff

Francis Poulenc

Sergei Prokofiev

Maurice Ravel

Dmitri Shostakovich

Igor Stravinsky

Ralph Vaughan Williams

William Walton

Anton Webern

Preface

～✦～

Considering all that has been written about modern music of the 20th century, one might question the justification for yet another book on the subject. But from the perspective of a new millennium, that era is now behind us and therefore lends itself to some definition. Musical developments are by no means inexorably linked to a turn of the calendar, but much discussion of music focuses on chronological periods, and certainly the usual concept of modern music, however it may be defined, is associated with the 20th century. The first sixty years of that era witnessed more dramatic changes and a wider variety of musical styles than any comparable period in the history of music. Perhaps because of those changes, there have been few times when the work of living composers met the pervasive resistance and often grudging acceptance accorded much modern music.

Those modern works that did receive critical approval on their first appearance still represent a relatively small portion of concert hall repertory. A major part of that neglect stems from lack of audience familiarity with the literature, a condition I hope that this book will abridge. This work is directed toward readers without extended professional training in music, but at the same time, there is much here to engage anyone interested in orchestral music or the activities surrounding it.

My goal is to identify and describe the modern orchestral repertory as it was performed in American concert halls during the last decade of the 20th century. Frequency of performance, rather than personal preference or musical idealism concerning which pieces *should* be included, has been used to determine the selection of works. A focus on music performed during the last decade of the century may seem arbitrary, perhaps restrictive. But music that has endured in the concert hall through the end of the century likely will continue to be played. This is the orchestral music that audiences will continue to hear, the repertory that they will want to know and about which they will seek information. Through the winnowing process of public response, the works addressed here represent the *de facto* repertory of modern orchestral music. This may not support current critical opinions of the most influential works nor, in all instances, those that represent the highest artistic achievement. Nor does it represent an attempt to address any balance between composers according to gender or race. These works represent the actual repertory of modern works played in American concert halls.

This definition of the repertory offered some intriguing problems. In determining what is stylistically modern, the chronology of the calendar and composers' life spans can become a trap. There were important composers, Rachmaninoff and Sibelius among them, whose music assuredly was a part of the 20th-century soundscape but whose musical style was unabashedly rooted in late-19th-century Romanticism. That music deserves informed discussion, but not as part of the modern repertory. On the other hand, three of the most significant musical figures of modern times—Arnold Schoenberg, Olivier Messiaen, and John Cage—loomed large on the scene in the fertility and originality of their thought and influence on younger composers, but, alas, their music does not occupy a prominent niche in the active concert repertory.

The very definition of "modernism," as it applies to music, becomes a thorny question when one attempts to define it unequivocally. I have chosen to consider as "modern" those composers who consciously distanced themselves from the immediate past, specifically from the musical styles and values of the late 19th century. Efforts to create something different from what has preceded have been driving forces in much of modern music and have played important roles in the range of styles embraced. Folk music has influenced many works; others have grown from consciously constructed techniques of composition. Among those should be counted a reliance on materials from the distant, rather than immediate, past, often included within the broad framework of neoclassicism. Bringing these considerations full circle, it is the variety of musical styles that has emerged that lends credence to viewing these works collectively as they continued to surface in the concert hall in the last decade of the century.

This book addresses 119 works by 29 composers. Seven of those composers are native-born Americans; the others have their roots elsewhere, even though a number spent a major part of their productive life in North America. As has been true for all periods of creative endeavor in the arts, a handful of artists produced the majority of the works that have endured. Compositions by Samuel Barber, Béla Bartók, Sergei Prokofiev, Maurice Ravel, Dmitri Shostakovich, and Igor Stravinsky account for slightly more than half the repertory discussed here. Of these six, Stravinsky was the most frequently performed, albeit by the narrowest of margins: one work. Slightly less than one half the repertory is purely symphonic, that is, conceived for and performed by a traditional symphonic ensemble. The remainder is nearly equally divided between works featuring a solo instrument and those whose origins lie in some association with the theater: ballet, movies, popular musical theater, or opera.

The reader will not find detailed technical analysis in these pages. A description of the music based on examination of the score lies at the heart of every essay, but the text is intended to invite and to answer the broader question: What should one hear in this music? Information concerning the origins of a work and conditions bearing upon it derive from primary sources: composers' comments, autobiographical data, correspondence, published interviews involving the composer, contemporary reviews, and comparable data. A succinct Glossary provides clarification of technical terms, and the Recommended Readings list offers sources for further background.

My interest in this repertory grew from years of writing program notes. Some of the works addressed here were included among those earlier efforts, but all essays as they appear in the following pages have been written originally for this publication. The book is organized with ease of reference in mind. Composers are listed alphabetically; multiple items within the work list of each composer appear in the order of symphonies, concertos, other works for orchestra (those classified as neither symphony nor concerto), and works whose roots lie in the theater. A dash following a movement's title indicates that the performance is intended to progress into the next movement without interruption.

Composers on rare occasions indicate the date on which they

began work on a score; with somewhat greater frequency they designate the date of completion. I have avoided the temptation to record these data beyond the month and year framing a work's creation; it is impossible to define the length of time a composer may have ruminated on a composition before putting pen to paper or how many times and to what extent a work was revised following completion of a first draft. Dates of first performances have been gleaned from autobiographical accounts, personal correspondence, or contemporary reviews. Those who are immediately involved with orchestral music will find useful data concerning the instrumentation of each work, taken from perusal of the complete text of the published score.

Assuming most readers will not have score in hand, examples involving musical notation do not appear. On the other hand, some essays include graphic diagrams designed to illustrate the total plan of a work. The reader will also find background information providing historical context for a composition, plus, in most instances, a summary of reviews documenting the reception of a piece following its first appearance.

For a composer, music is a means of communication; for a listener, it is a form of knowledge. In both conditions, music speaks for humanity. Some audiences perceive music in that role, but for most, orchestral music is primarily an indulgent pleasure. It is my wish to enhance that pleasure and to call attention to a body of music representing some of the highest artistic attainments of modern society.

Many generous parties have assisted in the pursuit of that goal. Above all I am indebted to my wife, Beverly Haskell Lee, who read the manuscript at several stages of its development and whose sharp eye and literary acumen contributed immeasurably in both substance and detail. Her perceptive judgment has clarified many otherwise murky passages.

I remain grateful to all those colleagues who expressed continuing interest in this endeavor and prodded it along by stimulating questions. Early in the project, a lengthy discussion with Kenneth Schermerhorn, Music Director of the Nashville Symphony, provided encouragement for the development of an idea and introduced the insight of an experienced conductor. Alex McKay was also an early contributor, and her careful sorting of details concerning editions and revisions illuminated many matters of origin and chronology. Dr. Cynthia

Cyrus offered her own experience as a commentator, and was generous with editorial counsel. To Dale Cockrell, Robin Fountain, Michael Kurek, and Mark Wait, professional colleagues at Vanderbilt University who took time from busy schedules to read portions of the manuscript from the perspective of their own special expertise, I owe more than I can readily repay. David Haas, of the University of Georgia, offered perceptive observations concerning the works of Shostakovich; Malcolm Hamrick Brown, of Indiana University, contributed graciously through his linguistic expertise in Russian.

No project such as this could be contemplated without consistent bibliographic support, and I have enjoyed abundant assistance from the staff of the Jean and Alexander Heard Library at Vanderbilt University, particularly Shirley Watts, former Director of Wilson Music Library, and her colleagues, Roger Coleman and Robert Rich. Robert Byrne, Richard Carlin, and the staff of Routledge have been unfailingly helpful and perceptive in technical matters of publication.

John Adams

❧

b. Worcester, Massachusetts, February 15, 1947

I t is entirely appropriate, as well as alphabetically fortuitous, that a descriptive exploration of orchestral music flourishing in America at the close of the 20th century begins with the music of a composer who has done at least as much as any other to bring late-20th-century developments in modern music into the American concert hall. John Coolidge Adams, usually described as a minimalist, represents a crossover between the hard-core avant-garde and mainstream concert music.

Minimalism, also called "systematic music," "process music," or, with a tinge of cynicism, "trance music," grew from many seeds. One of the most fecund was the element of *process* as that premise existed in the serial music of Anton Webern, a major influence on American composers after World War II. The intricacies of that music turned audiences away in droves, convincing many that all modern music was incomprehensible. At the other end of the spectrum, composers came to view audiences as naïve, if not reactionary, and gradually became inclined to write for professional colleagues more than for the broader musical public.

The composers Terry Riley, Steve Reich, and Philip Glass entered this vacuum, approaching composition with a focus on the reduction of materials and an emphasis on repetitive schemes. Minimalism emerged as an effective alternative to the rigors of serialism and the randomness of indeterminate, or "chance," music. The principal features of this genre are a consistent rhythmic pulse that pervades the entire musical fabric, a simple harmonic vocabulary, and above all, the prolonged repetition of small musical units as a means of expansion. Minimalism may sound dull when described in these objective terms, but what proceeds from an inherently simple formula—music made by repetition—often assumes a near-spiritual character, invoking echoes of non-Western musical practices from India, Bali, and Africa. The cultural and sociological mix that marks American society finds in minimalism a musical voice. When minimalism first appeared, it was greeted by many as a welcome answer to the unresolved aesthetic questions posed by much new music; it now became acceptable to be expressive, however that might be accomplished, and this new genre of modern music began to attract an enthusiastic following.

John Adams entered this arena in the 1970s following relatively conventional early musical training as a clarinetist, a student of composition at Harvard University, and a conductor. He moved to California in 1972 as director of the New Music Ensemble at the San Francisco Conservatory and established a working relationship with the San Francisco Symphony Orchestra, first as new music advisor, later as composer-in-residence. In his creative work, he is more intuitive than formalistic and, in a development that has largely been the domain of American composers, he does not hesitate to incorporate his own responses to the stimuli of American jazz, popular music, gospel singing, and rock 'n' roll. Above all he seems to be concerned with communication between composer and audience, and to that end he is willing to be personally expressive. Nineteenth-century sonorities are reinterpreted in the spirit of contemporary music, giving rise to descriptions of his music as neo-Romantic. Adams acknowledged much of this in a 1986 interview:

> What sets me apart from Reich and Glass is that I am not a modernist. They are, in the sense that they still use very pure, single systems. I am not a pure composer; I embrace the whole musical past, and I don't have the kind of refined, systematic language that they have. . . . I rely a lot more on my intuitive sense of balance. . . . I've stopped worrying about whether intuiting a structure is right or not.[1]

Adams addresses a large audience at the same time that he proceeds from firmly held personal criteria. He writes to satisfy his own ear, and notes that what pleases him also pleases other people. His works have been performed by most major orchestras in the United States, many of them with Adams as conductor, a role he has filled with increasing success in America and abroad.

The Chairman Dances: Foxtrot for Orchestra

Adams composed The Chairman Dances *in 1985; it was first performed as an independent work in Milwaukee on January 31, 1986 by the Milwaukee Symphony, Lukas Foss conducting.*

Instrumentation: *two flutes (both doubling piccolo), two oboes, two clarinets (the second doubling bass clarinets), two bassoons, four horns, two trumpets, two trombones, tuba, timpani, pedal bass drum, snare drum, crotales, sandpaper blocks, high and medium wood blocks, crash cymbal, suspended cymbal, sizzle cymbal, high hat, claves, bell tree, triangle, tambourine, castanets, glockenspiel, vibraphone, xylophone, piano, harp, and strings.*

The Chairman Dances was written to fulfill a joint commission from the American Composers Orchestra and the National Endowment for the Arts; it was at the same time a by-product of Adams's work on the opera *Nixon in China*. Responding to an original concept by director Peter Sellars, Alice Goodman produced a libretto based on President Richard Nixon's 1972 trip to Beijing, the three days of that historic visit being reflected in the three acts of the opera. According to Adams's own account, when he found himself confronted with both the opera and an orchestral commission to fulfill, he decided to "kill two birds with one stone" by writing an orchestral work that would also serve in the opera. The result was *The Chairman Dances*, which quickly became a musical entity in its own right. He later tried to incorporate it in the third act of the opera and found the character of the music appropriate but too much of an independent item to fit the operatic score.

An inscription printed in the score reflects the original scenario underlying the work, a mood intended to be both humorous and nostalgic:

> Chiang Ch'ing, a.k.a. Madame Mao, has gatecrashed the Presidential Banquet. She is first seen standing where she is most in the way of the waiters. After a few minutes, she brings out a

box of paper lanterns and hangs them around the hall, then strips down to a cheongsam, skin-tight from neck to ankle and slit up to the hip. She signals the orchestra to play and begins dancing by herself. Mao is becoming excited. He steps down from his portrait on the wall and they begin to foxtrot together. They are back in Yenan, dancing to the gramophone. . . .[2]

The music unfolds over a complex of ostinatos that maintain their fundamental rhythmic patterns as the music shifts through different colors and textures by means of slowly evolving orchestration. Texture and volume accrue until a climax is reached, the orchestration changes abruptly, and the process begins anew. In this manner, the orchestration itself becomes a structural element in the score. In later sections, hauntingly lyrical melodies, not a typical trait of most minimalist scores, float over the constantly chugging rhythm in a manner to suggest a late-20th-century version of Wagner's unending melody. The total effect becomes hypnotic through the insistent rhythmic pulsation and enigmatic melodic extension. The piano plays the last of these extended melodies as a series of alternating major and minor chords, gradually dissipating while a rustling percussion section quietly extends the music into nothingness.

Much of the initial interest in *The Chairman Dances* may have stemmed from its unusual title and the thoroughly American subject matter of the opera to which it was related. Repeated performances have established this piece as an enduring musical work. The listener is entranced by the changing soundscape, while the composer leaves unanswered provocative questions about whether the music is simple or complex.

Short Ride in a Fast Machine

Adams completed Short Ride in a Fast Machine *in 1986 in response to a commission from the Great Woods Festival intended to mark its inaugural concert. It was first performed in Mansfield, Massachusetts, on June 13, 1986, by the Pittsburgh Symphony Orchestra conducted by Michael Tilson Thomas.*

Instrumentation: *two piccolos, two flutes, two oboes, English horn, four clarinets (the third and fourth optional), three bassoons, contra-*

bassoon, four horns, four trumpets, three trombones, tuba, timpani, large bass drum, pedal bass drum, snare drum, two wood blocks, triangle, crotales, suspended cymbal, sizzle cymbal, tam-tam, tambourine, xylophone, glockenspiel, two synthesizers (optional), and strings.

Adams's titles for his compositions sometimes refer to the genesis of the music or to its musical substance, or derive from wordplay and puns. Adams has whimsically compared the experience of *Short Ride in a Fast Machine* to a ride in a nimble sports car, followed by regrets for the indulgence. We may or may not have been on such a ride, but Adams offers no further explanation for the title.

Short Ride is the second of two fanfares for orchestra Adams completed in 1986. The first, *Tromba lontana [Distant Trumpet]*, is a quiet work featuring two solo trumpets offstage, the whole presented as a quiet reverie. By contrast, *Short Ride* opens abruptly with wood blocks clearly marking the beat, quickly joined by clarinets and one synthesizer playing rhythmic groups of four against three. This rhythmic vitality underlies most of what follows as a common element in the ostinato patterns that gradually build to a climax of texture and volume. The music expands through several sections, each growing from a gradual change in orchestration that changes color much like a musical kaleidoscope. Harmonic shifts combine with altered orchestration to mark the division between sections, all carried out over the insistent rhythmic pulse established at the beginning.

Along with the rhythmic energy and orchestral color, harmony plays an important role in the form of the work. The music is indisputably tonal, although tonal centers are established through repetition more than through acoustically based harmonic relationships. Throughout *Short Ride* harmonic relations and shifts of tonal centers identify the structural guideposts for the work. There are only a few areas where the underlying harmonic materials are not clearly outlined; thus harmony provides a structural underpinning for the entire work.

Adams is less doctrinaire than most other composers when working with electronically produced sounds. Instructions in the score make it clear that the two (optional) synthesizers are to be incorporated into the orchestral texture, their sound never broadcast over an external amplification system, with the volume level adjusted to mix with the rest of the orchestra. He nonetheless regards the synthesizer as a valuable tool in expanding a composer's sonic palette. "When you work with synthesizers you learn about sound in a way you just *don't* as a composition student involved with earlier music—you learn to analyze, to listen in a very critical way to the attack of the sound, the area of resonance in its band width, whether sound is fat or skinny, strident or liquid."[3] Adams's light touch in incorporating this potent sound source into the larger ensemble offers another example of his assimilation of current practices into his own technical arsenal.

Short Ride in a Fast Machine, possibly because it *is* short (about four minutes) and fast, has entered the orchestral repertory with an ease unusual for music espousing a new style, the brevity of its statement (if not the ensemble) much in keeping with the principle of reduction underlying music bearing the minimalist stamp.

Samuel Barber

❧

*b. West Chester, Pennsylvania, March 9, 1910; d. New York City,
January 23, 1981*

In the middle decades of the 20th century, Samuel Barber was one of the best-known American composers, or at least among the most frequently performed. At a time when most young composers were struggling to establish a new musical voice for a changed world, Barber managed to energize traditional forms with his own expressive lyricism.

Barber grew from a child prodigy (as composer, pianist, and singer) to become the most promising member of a musical family that included his aunt, Louise Homer, a prominent opera singer, and her husband, Sidney Homer, a successful composer of art songs. As a charter member of the first class at the Curtis Institute of Music in Philadelphia in 1934, he began to attract attention for his compositions and won the first of many awards that would mark his career well into the middle of the century. While still a student, Barber spent many of his summers in Europe, ostensibly to continue his studies in composition with Rosario Scalero, his mentor at Curtis, but also to satisfy a growing cosmopolitanism and a fascination with the artistic environment of the Continent that never left him.

Barber met the legendary Italian conductor Arturo Toscanini in 1935 and, with considerable trepidation, submitted to him the scores of his *Adagio for Strings* and *Essay for Orchestra*. Toscanini's later introduction of those works with the NBC Symphony proved to be a great boost to Barber's burgeoning reputation as a composer. From that point forward, his reputation grew through a steady progression of increasingly successful works. He introduced a number of his songs himself, and Louise

Homer included several on her concert tours. In his instrumental compositions, Barber quickly learned to work closely with the performer for whom a work was designed, benefiting from the personal rapport with those introducing his works to the public as well as gaining technical advice in adapting his musical ideas to the instrumental medium.

His opera *Vanessa* (1957) was introduced by the Metropolitan Opera, and received the Pulitzer Prize for Music in 1958. Barber received a second Pulitzer Prize for his piano concerto (1962), a work commissioned by his publisher, G. Schirmer, in celebration of the firm's centenary. A second large-scale opera, *Antony and Cleopatra*, met a mixed reception when first introduced (1966), but its later revision gained much wider acceptance. Illness and depression diminished Barber's creative spirits during the last decade of his life.

Those who are prone to establish categories for all things musical frequently describe Barber's works as neo-Romantic because of their direct melodic appeal and engaging sonorities. He developed his own style fairly early and felt little urge to experiment. In 1971 he proposed that the constant search for something new inhibited many composers: "This, in my case, would be hopeless. In fact, it is said that I have no style at all but that doesn't matter. I just go on doing, as they say, my thing. I believe this takes a certain courage."[1] From some composers such a comment might be read as a credo of stubborn independence, but with Barber this stance led to a musical language readily accessible to audiences. Few American composers have heard a comparable portion of their creative work performed and assimilated into the repertory so readily. In a catalogue of works that is by no means exhaustive, there are few items by Barber that have not enjoyed considerable success with audiences both in the United States and abroad.

Symphony No. 1 in One Movement, Opus 9

Allegro ma non troppo—Allegro molto—Andante tranquillo—
Con moto.

The symphony was composed between late summer 1935 and February 1936, revised in 1942; it was first performed in Rome on December 13, 1936, by the Philharmonic Augusteo Orchestra, Bernardino Molinari conducting.

Instrumentation: *piccolo, two flutes, two oboes, English horn, two clar-*
inets, bass clarinet, two bassoons, contrabassoon, four horns, three
trumpets, three trombones, tuba, timpani, bass drum, cymbals, harp,
and strings.

Barber wrote his first symphony while in Italy under the aegis of the
American Academy in Rome, one of several grants he received while still
in his twenties. By the composer's own account, the audience at the premiere was about evenly divided between those applauding and those
hissing. But the work proved to be a major success when it was performed in America by Rudolf Ringwall and the Cleveland Orchestra in
January 1937 and by Artur Rodzinsky and the New York Philharmonic
the following March. Rodzinsky later conducted the symphony at the
Salzburg Festival in July 1937, the first work by an American composer
to be performed in that venue. Reactions to the work following the
1942 revision were still more positive, leading to its first recording by
Bruno Walter on Columbia Records.

This one-movement work encompasses four distinct sections that
approximate the traditional multimovement symphony, but here thematic relationships link these sections in their very substance. In both
the original and revised versions, the opening theme becomes the basis
for the scherzo and for the closing movement as well, a passacaglia with
twelve variations. In a similar vein the second subject, first played by
English horn and viola, returns as the principal theme in the slow
movement. Thus the last three movements derive from thematic material presented in the first. The symphony compresses the traditional
design further in that the exposition in the first movement is not
repeated, and the scherzo movement contains no trio. Considered as a
whole, the design shows several similarities with the seventh symphony
of Jan Sibelius which, Barber's sketchbooks suggest, may have been a
model for this work. It is a moot but nonetheless intriguing question
whether the continuity of a one-movement design suggested the thematic derivations or whether those close relationships suggested the
continuing movement as a matter of performance practice. Beyond
these thematic relationships, the music from beginning to end reflects
those traits for which Barber later became known: long, lyric lines
enhanced by pervasive rhythmic vitality.

Barber's symphony was greeted by reviews that varied only in the degree of their enthusiasm. One of the most reserved came from Olin Downes of the *New York Times*, who wrote: "It is evident that he [Barber] is seeking, and is not writing in a merely imitative manner. His orchestration is clear, if needing now and again a little more body and richness of texture."[2] In later years those qualities of "body and richness of texture" were often recognized as some of Barber's greatest strengths.

Concerto for Piano and Orchestra, Opus 38

Allegro appassionato

Canzone: Moderato

Allegro molto

Barber completed the piano concerto in September 1962; it was first performed at New York's Lincoln Center for the Performing Arts on September 24 with Erich Leinsdorf conducting the Boston Symphony Orchestra and John Browning as piano soloist.

Instrumentation: *piccolo, two flutes, two oboes, English horn, two clarinets, bass clarinet, two bassoons, four horns, three trumpets, three trombones, timpani, bass drum, snare drum, cymbals, suspended cymbal, antique cymbals, tam-tam, low tom-tom, triangle, whip, xylophone, harp, solo piano, and strings.*

Barber was commissioned to write the piano concerto by the publishing firm G. Schirmer in celebration of its centenary in 1961, an event extended to include the inauguration of Philharmonic Hall at New York's Lincoln Center for the Performing Arts in 1962. In spite of his early doubts, Barber was a pianist of considerable skill—he had studied with Isabelle Vengerova at the Curtis Institute in Philadelphia—but for this work he consulted with his personal friend, the American pianist John Browning, who had accepted Barber's invitation to give the first performance of the concerto. According to Browning's account, Barber liked to tailor his compositions for particular soloists and to that end he invited Browning to play for him the repertory with which the young American pianist felt most comfortable. He further quizzed Browning about the Russian school of pianism, in part because that tradition represented Browning's own training and also because Barber regarded highly the pianism of the Russian-born virtuoso Vladimir Horowitz, who had successfully introduced Barber's piano sonata in 1949. As a result of these inquiries, the solo part emerged as a near compendium of late-Romantic piano fioritura.

Barber was also a virtuoso in his mastery of the craft of composition, and by 1962 he seemed to take pleasure in writing for performers of comparable technical expertise. Both the pianist and the solo orchestral players encounter substantial demands on their skills. His craftsmanship is further evident in the manner in which his thematic materials are related; principal themes spawn others, producing a cohesive fabric. From these conditions emerges a work that has come to be recognized as a highly idiomatic, unabashedly virtuoso concerto, extending genuinely original keyboard textures into a thematically integrated whole.

The music begins with a solo cadenza announcing three thematic ideas. The orchestra continues with the second of these, leading to a new melody played by the violin and woodwinds, later to become the most important theme of this movement. Both soloist and orchestra embellish this lyric material before the solo oboe introduces a second and equally lyrical theme that, on its second presentation, is accompanied by a rhythmically compressed version of itself. There follows a thoroughly worked development ending in a second major cadenza, a reprise, and an athletic close.

The slow movement originated as an *Elegy for Flute and Piano* written in 1959 for Manfred Ibel, the dedicatee of the piano concerto. Appropriately titled *Canzone* (a lyrical poem or song, which was a secondary title Barber had applied to the *Elegy*), the music of this movement grows from the original melody for flute, later distributed among flute, oboe, and piano in succession. Some of the original piano accompaniment to the *Elegy* remains in the keyboard part, but most of it is shared by harp and strings. The entire movement projects an eloquent, often wistful lyricism.

An irregular five-eight meter pervades the closing *Allegro molto* and contributes much to the propulsive rhythmic drive dominating the movement. A wide-ranging ostinato played by the left hand of the pianist supports toccata-like writing in the right hand, usually grouped in asymmetric groups of two and three. This is enlivened—perhaps *relieved* is a more appropriate term—by rondo-like interjections of contrasting material from the orchestra, but always the insistent ostinato returns, contributing to an energetic and robust finale.

In a review of the first performance, Harold Schoenberg observed that the concerto was a decided hit with the audience, and predicted a promising future for it, a prediction soon reflected in the enthusiastic reviews of John Bowning's performance of the work. One critic, reviewing a performance in London in 1965, ventured that the concerto "is not a work of any real depth or enduring quality, but as America's answer to Khachaturan it was immediately likeable as a romantic virtuoso piece."[3] But few shared even those reservations, and the concerto's performance history shows that it was quickly assimilated into the standard repertory and performed more than forty times during the following season. The concerto won for Barber his second Pulitzer Prize for Music in 1963 (his first was awarded for the opera *Vanessa* in 1958) and the prestigious New York Music Critics' Circle Award in 1964.

Concerto for Violin and Orchestra, Opus 14

Allegro moderato

Andante

Presto in moto perpetuo

Barber began work on the violin concerto in the summer of 1939 and completed it in July 1940; the first public performance took place at the Academy of Music in Philadelphia on February 7, 1941, with Eugene Ormandy conducting the Philadelphia Orchestra and Albert Spaulding as violin soloist.

Instrumentation: *two flutes, two oboes, two clarinets, two bassoons, two horns, two trumpets, timpani, snare drum, piano, solo violin, and strings.*

Barber's violin concerto was commissioned by Samuel Fels, wealthy soap manufacturer and member of the board of trustees of the Curtis Institute of Music, and intended for Iso Briselli, a young violin prodigy and Fels's adopted son. Barber was to be paid $1,000, half to be advanced at the time of the commission, the remainder to be paid upon completion of the concerto. The details of the events surrounding Barber's completion of the score remain unclear. One version has it that when the first and second movements were submitted, the young violinist complained that they were insufficiently brilliant to show off his technique. Barber promised the third movement would compensate for this perceived weakness, but when the last movement was completed, the violinist complained again, this time claiming the music was technically unplayable. The patron demanded the return of his money, which Barber could not do, because it was already spent. The composer turned to a member of the faculty of the Curtis Institute in Philadelphia who, after several hours' practice, returned and played the closing movement for Barber and several other delighted faculty members, offering further to play it at any speed they desired. Briselli was a violinist of professional talent and skills who made a successful New York debut, raising some doubts about his inability to cope with the technical demands of Barber's third movement. The young violinist's own account, offered several years later, claimed that he considered the first two movements beautiful but thought the finale was too inconsequential to balance them. He suggested some adjustment to bring about a more traditional sonata-rondo form, but the composer declined. Whatever the details, the outcome was that Barber received only half of his commission and the young violinist relinquished his right to the first performance. Barber's attempts to respond to Briselli's changing requests may account for the wide stylistic difference between the first two movements and the finale.

Barber provided to the Philadelphia Orchestra his own notes for the first performance:

> The Concerto for Violin and Orchestra was completed in July, 1940, at Pocono Lake Preserve, Pennsylvania. . . . It is lyric and rather intimate in character and a moderate-sized orchestra is used; eight woodwinds, two horns, two trumpets, percussion, piano and strings.
>
>   The first movement—*allegro molto moderato*—begins with a lyrical first subject announced at once by the solo violin, without any orchestral introduction. This movement as a whole has perhaps more the character of a sonata than concerto form. The second movement—*andante sostenuto*—is introduced by an extended oboe solo. The violin enters with a contrasting and rhapsodic theme, after which it repeats the oboe melody of the beginning. The last

movement, a perpetual motion, exploits the more brilliant and virtuoso characteristics of the violin.[4]

The opening *Allegro* does indeed follow closely the principles of sonata design, although the secondary theme moves from a basic tonic of G major to E minor, the change of mode offering greater contrast than does the tonal level itself. The *Andante* is a broad three-part design offering some striking key centers (C-sharp minor and E Major) for a work built around G, and some clever interchange of rhythmic groupings in the solo line. The closing *Presto* offers such a marked contrast that some commentators have described it as a work representing a completely different facet of Barber's style. The solo violin embarks on a continuing pattern of rapid triplets that dominates the movement as a genuine *moto perpetuo*, a concertante whirlwind in which the soloist leads the orchestra in a frantic chase to the end.

Barber's violin concerto stands as a testament to those qualities that accounted for much of his success: classical order in matters of structure, a neo-Romantic gift for melody at a time when traditional melody was not the norm, and harmonies offering the variety and flexibility associated with music of the 20th century.

Concerto for Cello and Orchestra, Opus 22

Allegro moderato

Andante sostenuto

Molto allegro e appassionata

Barber composed the cello concerto between January and November 1945, revising it around 1947; it was first performed in Boston on April 5, 1946, by the Boston Symphony Orchestra, with Serge Koussevitzky conducting and Raya Garbousova as cello soloist.

Instrumentation: *two flutes, oboe, English horn, two clarinets (the second doubling bass clarinet), two bassoons, two horns, three trumpets, timpani, snare drum, solo cello, and strings.*

The conductor Serge Koussevitzky, noted for his support of contemporary music, set in motion the chain of events leading to Barber's Concerto for Cello and Orchestra. Koussevitzky had championed the

Russian cellist Raya Garbousova since her American debut in 1935, and urged her to commission a work, pointing out that the famous patrons of the past were no more and that it was now the responsibility of performing artists to commission works for their own use. While Garbousova pursued the matter independently, Koussevitzky, for reasons still unknown, commissioned Barber to write a concerto for her to be performed with the Boston Symphony Orchestra. Funds to support the commission came from John Nicholas Brown, a trustee of the Boston Symphony and another patron of Garbousova; it was in recognition of Brown's support that Barber dedicated the concerto to him.

As he would do in later years when writing for a specific soloist, Barber asked Garbousova to play for him all her repertory in order to become familiar with the problems and possibilities in writing for the instrument, but also to study her particular strengths. Composer and performer worked together throughout the gestation period of the concerto as Barber submitted and revised various passages while the work progressed, a working relationship that is reminiscent of the collaboration between Johannes Brahms and Joseph Joachim in the preparation of Brahms's violin concerto. As a youth Barber had studied cello briefly before turning to the piano and may have retained some sense of the instrument from that early experience.

These fortunate circumstances brought forth a concerto that was guaranteed a performance by an established virtuoso with a major orchestra, a work completed, for the most part, while Barber was still a member of the American Armed Forces. Koussevitzky predicted that the concerto would eventually occupy a position in the modern repertory comparable to that enjoyed by Brahms's concerto for violin in the 19th-century concert literature. Certainly the work has become a mainstay of the concerto repertory for the cello; most cellists regard it as one of the most demanding solo works for their instrument.

The concerto received the annual New York Music Critics' Circle Award in New York for 1946, but that recognition did little to inspire cellists to perform it, perhaps because of the demanding solo part. Recording companies were equally cautious until 1951, when Decca of London offered to record the concerto with Zara Nelsova, providing that Barber would conduct. With this development, Barber added to his accomplishments as composer, pianist, and singer that of conductor, a breadth of professional versatility extraordinary in the modern concert hall.

The orchestra opens with a jagged motive of wide leaps and clever rhythmic displacement played in unison, a readily identifiable texture that returns several times throughout the movement and ultimately brings it to a close. The principal theme expands upon the rhythmic pattern known as a "Scotch snap" in a manner resembling a microcosm of the syncopation that will dominate the last movement. Exposition, development, and reprise follow in usual order, with the development and recapitulation separated by an extended cadenza that, in its double stops, surpasses the technical problems already laid before the soloist. A graceful *Siciliano,* played in canon between cello and oboe, opens the second movement and becomes a source for much of the thematic material to follow. As in the first movement, the motive heard at the beginning serves to end the movement as well. Thin and well-devised scoring in the last movement allows the soloist to be heard to good advantage in a tumult of syncopation involving double stops, quick changes of register, and trills to tax the technique of any performer.

Considered in its entirety, the cello concerto presents more dissonance than most of Barber's works written up to 1945, but his penchant for lyric melody survives, and it may be that quality to which the public has always responded with favor. In a review of the premiere, Irving Fine described the concerto as "an effective and attractive piece, the difficult medium handled with skill. . . . Barber is still in the process of evolving a more contemporary style and the stylistic inconsistencies are marked by a certain formal diffuseness, especially in the last movement."[5] Another prominent and successful composer, Ross Lee Finney, writing several years later, described the concerto as "one of the most convincing works that this talented American composer has written and one of the finest concertos for the instrument composed during this century."[6]

Adagio for Strings, **Opus 11**

The work originated in 1936 as the slow movement for Barber's string quartet, opus 11; it was first performed in that version at the Villa Aurelia, Rome, on December 14, 1936, by the Pro Arte String Quartet. The arrangement for strings was first performed in New York on November 5, 1938, by Arturo Toscanini and the NBC Symphony Orchestra.

Instrumentation: *violins I and II, violas I and II, cellos I and II, and double basses.*

Had Barber written nothing beyond the *Adagio for Strings,* he would be a well-known composer because of the prominence of this work on the American soundscape. Its musical substance is sufficiently direct that the listener has no significant stylistic hurdles to overcome. It was played over national radio immediately following the announcement of President Franklin Roosevelt's death in 1945, an exposure that has implanted it indelibly in the memory of many American citizens. It subsequently has become an unofficial American funeral dirge, accompanying the memorial services for Roosevelt, Albert Einstein, John F. Kennedy, and Princess Grace of Monaco, among others. The accessibility and pervasiveness of the *Adagio* have raised it to something approaching a cultural theme, heard as an American musical icon by many outside the United States. In 1957 Barber produced a third version of the same material, a choral work setting the text of the *Agnus Dei* from the Latin mass.

Barber submitted the *Adagio for Strings* and his recently completed *Essay for Orchestra* to Arturo Toscanini early in 1938 in response to that conductor's announced search for American works he could include on his famous broadcasts with the NBC Symphony. The 1937–1938 season progressed to its end, and Toscanini returned the scores without comment. Barber was so annoyed at what he considered a professional discourtesy that he declined to visit Toscanini in Italy during the following summer as planned, urging his friend Menotti to proceed without him. Menotti subsequently reported that Toscanini had already decided to conduct both works, but had no need of the scores because he had already memorized them, and indeed the conductor did not see the music again until the rehearsal before the performance several months later. It is easy to forget, after several decades, what a coup Toscanini's decision represented for the career of any young composer. The orchestra that had been assembled for Toscanini to conduct was one of the top ensembles in the United States at the time. Toscanini's musical discipline in conducting the group, along with his fidelity to the printed score when performing masterworks of the standard repertory, had created a musical aura rarely equalled. The musical stature of Toscanini and his NBC Orchestra provided an extraordinary launching pad for any new work by any young composer of any nationality.

Particular qualities of timbre, harmony, and melody establish a ready identity for the *Adagio*. The strings comprise the most homogeneous choir of the orchestra, thus a work relying on this ensemble throughout presents a consistency of timbre that is in itself notable. Traditional harmony usually progresses through a series of root movements that are four or five notes distant from each other. In the *Adagio*, Barber's harmonies move by step, or at least he develops very clever part-writing that gives the impression of stepwise harmonic motion. The melody strides along in even notes, surrounding a central tone in each phrase much in the manner of a dignified embellishment. This pattern passes from one instrument to another in each phrase, building to an intense climax from which the music returns to the opening material.

The enduring effectiveness of this work lies in its direct simplicity: one timbre, played in unified harmonic motion, with one type of melody. The early and extraordinary success of the *Adagio* generated no small amount of discussion in the musical community of 1938 concerning the direction of contemporary music. Some took Barber to task for writing music of fairly conventional style and making no clear statement that could be called "American" when compared to the new music coming from Europe at the time. Others praised Barber for writing what was perceived to be sincere and heartfelt music, presented in a style that was the composer's own without obeisance to the current stream of music by American composers who had studied in Paris following World War I.

Essay for Orchestra, Opus 12

Andante sostenuto—Allegro molto—Largamente sostenuto

Barber began the Essay for Orchestra *in 1937 but it was not completed until early in 1938. It was first performed in New York on November 5, 1938 by the NBC Symphony Orchestra, conducted by Arturo Toscanini.*

Instrumentation: *two flutes, two oboes, two clarinets, two bassoons, four horns, three trumpets, three trombones, tuba, timpani, piano, and strings.*

Barber wrote three works titled *Essay for Orchestra*. All three one-movement compositions share a title and some structural impetus from the nominally parallel literary genre, but otherwise they exploit different technical procedures and orchestral resources. Barber's lasting interest in literature marked his creative efforts from his earliest years, the Overture to *The School for Scandal* (1931) and *Music for a Scene from Shelley* (1933) offering examples of the interaction between literary works and his own creative impulses. As a teenager he had written three essays for piano which remained in manuscript, so in 1938 the title, at least, was not new to him. "Essay" may derive from the compact brevity of the music, comparable to the literary model, or that brevity may have been designed to reflect the implication of the title. Robert Horan, a poet and close friend who for a time lived with Barber, reported that Barber's interest in a compression of form began with the *Symphony in One Movement* and was particularly addressed in the three *Essays*. By 1938 he wanted to develop a concise two-part form that would avoid the overworked cliche of the three-part design underlying so much modern music.

The specific impetus for this *"First" Essay*, as it came to be identified following the appearance of a second in 1942, came from Arturo Toscanini, who had been searching for appropriate works by an American composer to program with his NBC Symphony Orchestra. Responding to the success of Barber's Symphony in One Movement, he had expressed further interest in Barber's work specifically. Following a rush of activity, Barber submitted the *Essay for Orchestra* and his *Adagio for Strings* to Toscanini in the spring of 1938. (The conductor's quick memorization of the music followed by his noncommittal return of the scores has been described in the discussion of the *Adagio*.) Despite Barber's earlier discomfiture, both works were performed on the same concert, an extraordinary boost to Barber's reputation and to his career as a composer.

Such a prominent performance of these two works as examples of contemporary American music caused considerable resentment among many progressive musicians who regarded Barber as too conservative and too conventional, although both works made a favorable impression on the general public. Of the two, the *Essay* seemed to attract the more acerbic criticism, perhaps because of the atypical title. It was described as a pretty but weak piece of little individual technique, lacking in creativity, a pale copy of other composers, and generally showing very slight content. Considering the difficulties encountered by American composers in obtaining public performances of their creative efforts in 1938, these reactions may be as understandable as they are overstated.

The *Essay* consists of two sections: the principal motive from the first returns at several points in the second and again as the substance for a brief coda. With no real necessity for demonstrating a corollary with a literary essay, the work nonetheless follows the premise associated with that genre in that it grows from the expansion of one musical idea and a closing reaffirmation. The main theme consists of a four-measure phrase of two units, the second of which becomes a pervasive motive. That harmonically rich opening phrase is restated and extended, then given out a third time, leading to a further expansion. The second section of the work, a scherzo in character if not in traditional design, contrasts markedly in its speed and thin texture; parts of the opening phrase return, played in long, sonorous tones by either the horns, cellos, or bassoons. Transition to the closing *Largamente sostenuto* and a final reference to the lush opening material come about through rhythmic augmentation and *rallentando*. The principal theme returns as a seemingly inevitable musical event, reminding the listener of the ultimate unity of the complete work, however brief.

Second Essay for Orchestra, Opus 17

Andante, un poco mosso—Con moto—Molto allegro ed energico—Tempo Io, ma un poco agitato—Più tranquillo, ma sempre muovendo

Composition of the Second Essay for Orchestra *was completed in March 1942. The first performance took place at Carnegie Hall in New York on April 16, 1942, with Bruno Walter conducting the New York Philharmonic Orchestra.*

Instrumentation: *piccolo, two flutes, two oboes, English horn, two clarinets (the second doubling bass clarinet), two bassoons, four horns, three trumpets, three trombones, tuba, timpani, bass drum, snare drum, cymbals, tam-tam, and strings.*

The *Second Essay* was first performed during the months following the entry of the United States into World War II, although it was based on thematic material deriving from several years earlier. The principal theme consists of wide intervals typical of trumpet calls, leading one commentator to describe the theme as "bugle material," implicitly reflecting the atmosphere of war. Barber acknowledged that, while the *Essay* had no program, it was possible to hear in it wartime innuendoes. The perspective of time has pushed any bellicose qualities well into the background, if they ever existed, leaving an orchestral score often compared to the first movement of a traditional symphony.

To the extent that an essay is a discourse on a basic theme, the work at hand is well named. The opening theme is first played by the solo flute (usually not regarded as a particularly bellicose instrument). Following an interruptive fermata for the orchestra, the principal theme returns in the horns, now accompanied by itself in diminution in the timpani and lower strings. At this point one wonders whether the theme was not originally conceived as one that could be played by the timpani and only later adapted for the more traditional melody instruments. A vigorous *fugato* offers a marked change of character, leading to a section where the subject, inverted, is accompanied by another version of itself in augmentation. The technique of accompanying one theme with an altered version of the same material occurs several times in Barber's works; the piano concerto offers another example, but nowhere is the process explored more ingeniously than here. A majestic *fortissimo* return of the main theme comprises a shortened recapitulation, and the *Essay* comes to a close with a homorhythmic chorale ending on a sparkling F major harmony.

True to its nominal literary model, Barber's *Second Essay* presents its subject matter, develops it briefly, then reaffirms those basic materials in a straightforward expository manner, achieving a poignant match between title and substance.

Overture to *The School for Scandal,* Opus 5

Barber composed the Overture at Cadegliano, Italy, during the summer of 1931. It was first performed at a Robin Hood Dell concert on August 30, 1933, by personnel of the Philadelphia Symphony Orchestra, Alexander Smallens conducting.

Instrumentation: *piccolo, two flutes, two oboes, English horn, two clarinets, bass clarinet, two bassoons, four horns, three trumpets, three trombones, tuba, timpani, bass drum, triangle, cymbals, tubular bells, celesta, harp, and strings.*

The literary association implied in the title reflects the composer's personal interest and broad background in English literature more than any direct influence of the dramatic work on the music itself. As a student, Barber had explored literature and languages extensively, an inclination that prevailed throughout his mature years. By his own account, his Overture to *The School for Scandal*, a comedy by Richard Sheridan written in 1777, was a musical reflection of the play's spirit. There was no attempt to represent directly the characters or the events of the stage work through specific musical operations.

Barber wrote the Overture during a summer in Italy while he was studying composition with Rosario Scaleri, his teacher at the Curtis Institute in Philadelphia during the scheduled school year. During the following fall, he copied the parts and attempted to obtain a performance at Curtis, but with no success. In April 1933 the Overture won for Barber his second Joseph Bearns Prize (an earlier award in 1929 was for his violin sonata), a stipend of $1,200 awarded by Columbia University for composition in large forms. This enabled him to spend another summer composing in Italy, but it also meant he was absent from the American premiere of the work in August.

If we consider Richardson's play a ribald farce, we might say Barber's Overture opens with a raucous cackle as the trumpets play a minor chord one half-step above the remainder of the orchestra. This galvanizing dissonance resolves into a short introduction to a fairly straightforward sonata design. The first theme—a fast, skipping pattern covering a wide range—appears sequentially in the first and second violins, shortly thereafter in the lower strings. The solo oboe introduces a second theme, a long-breathed melody in the style of a folk song. The music moves through a development relying primarily on the color resources of a large orchestra to expand upon references to the first theme. That material returns in its entirety to mark the recapitulation, but now the English horn balances the earlier sound of the oboe in presenting the second theme. A rhythmically compressed version of the first theme in stretto serves as a lively coda, the whole terminated by a reference to the trumpet flourish from the opening measures.

Reviews of early performances varied; some were cautious, some praised the obvious craftsmanship and clear ordering of materials, others cited it as a work by a promising young American composer, and at least one described it as essentially Italian, presumably because Barber wrote much of it while residing in Italy. As with so many of Barber's works, it entered the standard repertory quickly and often served as a brilliant opening for orchestral concerts in the late 20th century. European performing ensembles often regard it as the quintessential American orchestral work.

Knoxville: Summer of 1915, Opus 24

Barber completed this cantata in April 1947. The first performance was given in Boston on April 9, 1948, by Eleanor Steber and the Boston Symphony Orchestra, Serge Koussevitzky conducting.

Instrumentation: *flute (doubling piccolo), oboe (doubling English horn), clarinet, bassoon, two horns, trumpet, triangle, harp, solo voice, and strings.*

A slightly revised version prepared for smaller orchestra in 1949 was first performed in Washington D.C. on April 1, 1950, by Eileen Farrell and the Dumbarton Oaks Chamber Orchestra, William Strickland conducting. For more intimate venues, the work is performed frequently in a reduction prepared by the composer in 1947 for piano and voice.

James Agee's nostalgic text, *Knoxville: Summer of 1915*, comes from the closing paragraphs of an autobiographical prose poem that appeared in *The Partisan Reader* in 1946, later to be included in his play *A Death in the Family*. Barber had been discussing with Serge Koussevitzky the feasibility of a work for solo voice and orchestra, possibly something along the lines of a traditional three-movement concerto. The American soprano Eleanor Steber offered to commission the work if an appropriate text could be found. Barber's choice of Agee's text clearly called for an approach different from a concerto, and while the finished work shows multiple sections, they are continuous, related by thematic material, and are neither conceived nor projected as separate movements.

Barber regarded Agee's words as a long lyric poem, leading him to divide the lines of the prose text in a manner that would make the rhythm clear. Apparently he empathized closely with the text. Composer and author were nearly exact contemporaries and, after they met, found they held in common many of the childhood experiences addressed in Agee's poem. *Knoxville* ultimately became a personal statement by the composer, heightened by the lingering illness and death on August 12, 1947, of his father, to whom the work is dedicated.

Responses to the first performance were tentative, but almost without exception *Knoxville* has been hailed as an inherently American work in the years since. Agee's text is a nostalgic reflection on his childhood summers in Knoxville. He writes of the sights and sounds of a warm evening: a horse, a buggy, strollers, a streetcar, his parents, and his beginning search for self-identity. He recalls life in the United States during a more leisurely age, a time before television and air conditioning combined to weave their seductive web of isolation around families on warm summer evenings. The images evoked by this text clearly invite some poignant text painting, but Barber chooses a broader plan, and the impact of the piece develops instead from the juxtaposition of clearly contrasting musical sections marked by tempo indications.

The voice enters to the accompaniment of an arpeggiated pattern in the flute. The orchestra interrupts this suggestion of a rocking motion, for so it seems to be, with a motive in the woodwinds that becomes supporting material for "A streetcar raising its iron moan" and subsequent lines. The intensity of the music gradually subsides until the arpeggio accompaniment returns, now in the harp, to the line "Parents on porches." This idyllic lyricism is interrupted by another change of tempo and a rhythmic exchange between duple and triple patterns to the text "On the rough wet grass of the back yard." While the first of these episodes moved from greater to lesser volume and intensity, the second reverses that process by growing toward a climax identified by wide leaps played by the violins before it, too, returns to the character of the opening and the rocking motive with the lines "After a little while I am taken in and put to bed." The same material prevails through a quiet orchestral coda.

In this mold the complete work approximates a rondo design in which the opening accompaniment pattern serves as the principal theme, interrupted by episodes of relatively greater agitation for orchestra. From a broader perspective, *Knoxville* can best be described as a broadly conceived cantata in which a nostalgic text evokes the past with a musical voice of modern times.

Medea's Meditation and Dance of Vengeance, **Opus 23a**

The score developed from a revision of the orchestral ballet suite Medea *in 1955. It was first performed in New York by the New York Philharmonic Orchestra on February 2, 1956, Dmitri Mitropoulos conducting.*

Instrumentation: *three flutes (the third doubling piccolo), two oboes, English horn, clarinet in E-flat, two clarinets in B-flat, bass clarinet, two bassoons, contrabassoon, four horns, three trumpets, three trombones, tuba, timpani, bass drum, snare drum, tom-tom, triangle, cymbals, tam-tam, whip, xylophone, harp, piano, and strings.*

The music of *Medea* first appeared as a score for thirteen instruments written to fulfill a commission from the Ditson Fund of Columbia University for a ballet for Martha Graham, first danced by Graham and her company under the title *Serpent Heart* at Columbia University on May 10, 1946. Graham revised the ballet for the next season, when it appeared on February 27, 1947, at the Ziegfeld Theater in New York under a new title, *Cave of the Heart.* Earlier in 1947 Barber had rearranged this music into a seven-movement suite for full orchestra (*Parados, Choros—Medea and Jason, The Young Princess, Choros, Medea, Kantikos Agonias,* and *Exodos*) titled *Medea,* op. 23, after the mythic character that formed the center of Graham's choreography. In this format it was first performed by the Philadelphia Orchestra on December 5, 1948, with Eugene Ormandy conducting. Audience response to the section titled *Medea* led Barber to rescore the suite in one continuous movement, in the process renaming the work *Medea's Meditation and Dance of Vengeance,* reducing the length of the earlier orchestral suite by about a third, and expanding the ensemble by adding more winds and percussion. All the different versions retained the dedication to Martha Graham.

The score included a brief preface by the composer concerning the implied subject matter:

> The present version . . . is based on material from the ballet which is directly related to the central character, Medea. Tracing her emotions from her tender feelings towards her children, through her mounting suspicions and anguish at her husband's betrayal and her decision to avenge herself, the piece increases in intensity

to close in the frenzied Dance of Vengeance of Medea, the Sorceress descended from the Sun God.

Barber concludes with a quotation from Euripides' *Medea*, which offers a literary program for the music itself:

Look, my soft eyes have suddenly filled with tears:
O children, how ready to cry I am, how full of foreboding!
Jason wrongs me, though I have never injured him.
He has taken a wife to his house, supplanting me. . . .
Now I am in the full force of the storm of hate.
I will make dead bodies of three of my enemies—
    father, the girl and my husband!
Come, Medea, whose father was noble,
Whose grandfather God of the sun,
Go forward to the dreadful act.[7]

Compared to the earlier suite of ballet music, *Medea's Meditation and Dance of Vengeance* takes most of its material from *Parados* (I), the introduction of the main characters, and *Choros* (IV), the introduction to *Medea* (V) and her dance of obsessive and diabolical vengeance. The work opens with sustained, *pianissimo* harmonics in the violins that provide a background for percussive interjections by the xylophone; the pronounced contrast of textures provides an eerie background for the opening motive in the flutes and piccolo. The music builds with increasing intensity, marked by expressive terms in the score that move from "Broadly, from the distance" through "*piu mosso*" (more motion), "mysterious, moving ahead" and "anguished" to "sombre, with dignity," marking the music of Medea's dance proper. Barber's principal biographer has aptly observed that: "the more independent of the ballet the music became . . . the more Barber was compelled to explicitly designate psychologically oriented expressive markings in the score."[8]

In the original ballet suite, the music of Medea's dance is introduced by harp and piano, closely followed by a languorous solo line played by the English horn; that orchestration is retained in the orchestral version, but with interpolations from the side drum. With the entry of a pronounced ostinato played by the piano the music begins a frenetic crescendo culminating in a demonic finish appropriate to a sorceress descended from the Sun God.

Béla Bartók

❦

b. Nagyszentmiklós, Hungary, March 25, 1881; d. New York City, September 26, 1945

Bartók began his career as a pianist, initiated by early studies with his mother. He subsequently became one of the major piano talents during the first half of the 20th century, and for many years sustained his professional activities through his position on the piano faculty of the Academy of Music in Budapest. He was also an ardent ethnomusicologist, and devoted a major portion of his energies to the preservation of Hungarian folk music. At a time when recording equipment of any kind was in its early stages of development, he traveled through the countryside with portable equipment, recording the music of the country folk as they sang it among themselves. The transcription of this material into written form occupied him intermittently for most of his professional life and produced some of the most important scholarly works of their kind. Even if Bartók had not become an extraordinarily fecund composer, his position in the history of music would be assured through his achievements as performer and scholar.

His compositions have established him as one of the outstanding creative spirits of the modern era. Considered as a body, they share a number of endemic qualities: a debt to a wide range of folk styles; a strong inclination toward symmetry, mirror, and palindrome structures; a pervasive interest in continuing variation; and a distinct awareness of musical timbre as a constructive element separate from other musical parameters. Some of his works include elements of folk music, but more frequently one encounters broad stylistic traits reminiscent of folk materials, rather than specific quotations. His own goal was to create a corpus of music representing the brotherhood of humanity; in that context he did not reject any influence, providing it was, in his estimation, "clear, fresh, and healthy."

The Hungarian music in which he had immersed himself in his field studies as an ethnomusicologist was the influence to which he was closest and that emerged most characteristically. Elements of symmetry affect texture, melody, rhythm, and form, all combining to produce intricate structures that lend a subtle cohesiveness to his music even when they are not aurally apparent. Concerning the process of variation, much of his writing expands upon a fundamental theme, an *ur-motive*, or fundamental musical idea of identifiable dimension that may be expanded in various ways throughout a composition. His penchant for exploiting instrumental textures and colors leads to highly original patterns, some new notation, and techniques of execution that must be heard from the perspective of a broad canvas rather than in matters of detail.

Concerto for Orchestra

Introduzione

Giuoco delle coppie (Game of Pairs)

Elegia

Intermezzo interotto (Interrupted intermezzo)

Finale

Work on the Concerto for Orchestra was carried out between mid-August and early October 1943. It was first performed in Boston on December 1, 1944, by the Boston Symphony Orchestra, Serge Koussevitzky conducting.

Instrumentation: *three flutes (the third doubling piccolo), three oboes (the third doubling English horn), three clarinets (the third doubling bass clarinet), three bassoons (the third doubling contrabassoon), four horns, three trumpets (a fourth trumpet "ad libitum"), three trombones, tuba, timpani, bass drum, snare drum, tam-tam, cymbals, triangle, two harps, and strings.*

Musical works carrying the broad title of "Concerto for Orchestra" flourished during the 17th and 18th centuries and have been well represented in the oeuvres of Hindemith and Lutoslawski in the 20th century. But it is safe to say that Bartók's Concerto for Orchestra is the best-known representation of that genre written during the modern era. It has provided the avenue many have traveled in their first approach to Bartók's music and, in a similar vein, it has opened the doors of 20th-century music to many listeners otherwise disinclined to explore modern art music.

The Concerto's enduring success belies the work's inauspicious beginnings. Bartók had left a flourishing career in Europe to evade the onslaught of World War II, arriving in the United States on October 30, 1940, without most of his luggage, cut off from royalties due him for his published works, denied a small pension from the Budapest Conservatory, where he had taught for many years, separated from friends and colleagues, and incipiently ill with the leukemia that would eventually cause his death. A grant from Columbia University for the continuation of his folk music research and a series of lectures at Harvard provided some funds, but the intensity with which he pursued his research brought him to a state of physical collapse. By 1943 he was hospitalized, without income or prospects.

The American Society of Composers and Publishers (ASCAP), in an attempt to provide assistance but knowing that Bartók would not accept a gift, acted through Serge Koussevitzky to commission a large work that Koussevitzky would perform with the Boston Symphony Orchestra, offering $500 initially, the remainder to be paid upon delivery of the score. In fact, there was little substantial expectation that Bartók would complete the project. To the contrary, the commission revitalized him, both physically and spiritually, and he completed the work in slightly more than seven weeks.

Both audiences and critics were enthusiastic in their response to the Concerto for Orchestra. Following the first performance in Boston, the Concerto was hailed as one of Bartók's masterpieces. The New York premiere a few weeks later brought forth a comparable review in the *New York Times*:

> The score is by no means the nut to crack that other of Bartók's late works have offered. It is a wide departure from its author's

harsher and more cerebral style. There might even be the suspicion with an artist of less sincerity than this one, that he had adopted a simpler and more melodic manner with the intention of an appeal to a wider public.

But that would not be Mr. Bartók's motive. Nor would the emotional sequence of this music, and the care with which it has evidently been fashioned, support such an assumption. What is evident is the courage, which this composer never has lacked, with which he is striking out, in his late years, in new directions. The style is less involved and ingrowing than we have thought much of Bartók's late music to be, and it escapes in a large measure, the pale cast of isolated thought which has brooded over so many of his pages.[1]

Subsequent performances met with comparable reception. The Concerto was presented as the concluding work at the International Society for Contemporary Music Festival in London in 1946, and received at least 72 performances in Europe up to 1950. It was tragic that the composer, dead in New York in 1945, did not witness the great success of one of his last works.

The title "concerto" traditionally suggests a featured instrumental soloist in dialogue with a supporting orchestra, but here the term carries different connotations. In Bartók's own description from 1944:

The title of this symphony-like orchestral work is explained by its tendency to treat the single instruments or instrument groups in a "*concertant*" or soloistic manner. The "virtuoso" treatment appears, for instance, in the *fugato* sections of the development of the first movement (brass instruments), or in the "*perpetuum mobile*"-like passages of the principal theme in the last movement (strings), and, especially, in the second movement, in which pairs of instruments appear consecutively with brilliant passages.[2]

The first movement follows a fairly regular sonata design that expands upon the interval of a fourth, a melodic cell permeating both the introduction and main body of this movement. The theme of the *Allegro vivace* section offers a particularly telling example wherein the opening phrase, built around ascending fourths, is mirrored by its consequent. The statement of this theme itself represents no small amount

of creative ingenuity, and the fourths that appear in the opening measures serve, in retrospect, as a cell from which most of the movement is
built, as in the *fugato* sections for both brass and strings.

The *Giuoco delle coppie* (Game of Pairs) describes literally the basic
procedure of the second movement: the interaction of pairs of instruments. In order to clarify that intent, Bartók later asked the title to be
changed to *Presentando la [sic] coppie* (Presenting the Couples). A fairly
straightforward brass chorale serves as the centerpiece, surrounded by
two sections based on solo pairs of wind instruments of the same timbre playing in parallel motion: bassoons in sixths, oboes in thirds, clarinets in sevenths, flutes in fifths, and trumpets in seconds. The broadly
conceived arch form thus established is affirmed by the hollow sound
of a side drum that opens and closes the movement. Arch forms appear
frequently in Bartók's works, but not always accompanied by the concurrence of theme and timbre found here. The movement represents
the combined interests of Bartók and his publisher, Ralph Hawkes. In
1942 Hawkes had suggested to Bartók a series of concertos for solo
instrument or instruments, and string orchestra, something in the tradition of J. S. Bach's *Brandenburg Concertos*. Bartók's later correspondence indicates that his initial efforts on this project had been
terminated by his protracted illness. Preceding Hawkes's letter, the
composer had been engrossed in a study of Yugoslav folk music, in
which he had encountered some unusual melodies performed in two
parts, that is, two parallel lines. The parallelism of the folk music and
the concerto idea found a fruitful synthesis in this second movement.

The *Elegia* opens with a series of fourths in the basses recalling the
beginning of the first movement, but the body of the movement is
fairly dominated by harp glissandos and flourishes in the woodwinds.
The movement becomes a study in orchestral color, punctuated by
short sections of thematic materials in the strings and interjections of
Bartók's atmospheric "night music." In Bartók's own description:
"These [themes] constitute the core of the movement, which is
enframed by a misty texture of rudimentary motives. Most of the thematic material of this movement derives from the 'Introduction' to the
first movement."[3] Considering that he wrote this movement before the
other four, it probably would be more accurate to say that these thematic materials "are shared with" the first movement.

What may be considered an interruption in the *Intermezzo* is represented in part by a burlesque of a theme from the seventh symphony of Dmitri Shostakovich. According to the composer's son, Bartók heard a broadcast of the Shostakovich work while preparing the Concerto and was so unimpressed that he chose to parody some of the material in his own score. The theme in question, a simple descending scale passage, is played by the clarinet near the end of the interruption, and the violins introduce a humorous parody of the same theme a few moments later, both presentations answered by raucous, cackling trills from the trumpets. But to dwell on Bartók's personal jest is to miss the point of a well-balanced symphonic movement that stands as a musical bridge, or *intermezzo*, between the *Elegia* and the *Finale*.

The Concerto closes with a rousing sonata movement, taking its spirit from the dance, some of its inner workings from the fugue, and much of its thematic material from the tradition of Romanian folk music. These qualities belie their seemingly contradictory nature when handled with the extraordinary imagination and craftsmanship of Bartók. A detailed description of the raw musical materials serves little purpose when the treatment of those materials elevates a work to a much higher plane, as happens here.

At the close of his own explanation of the Concerto for Orchestra, Bartók wrote that "the general mood of the work represents—apart from the jesting second movement—a gradual transition from the sternness of the first movement and the lugubrious death-song of the third, to the life-assertion of the last one."[4] That description, perhaps heightened by a morose personal response, led at least one writer to draw a direct corollary between the Concerto and the progressive stages of death and dying in which the movements represent awareness of death (*Introduzione*), denial (*Giuoco delle coppie*), grief and depression (*Elegia*), anger and resentment (*Intermezzo interrotto*), and life-assertion (*Finale*). Although Bartók was terminally ill when he wrote the Concerto, there remains no documentary evidence that he was consciously working along these lines.

The Concerto for Orchestra will endure as a milestone, wherever and whenever it is played. It stands as an eloquent demonstration of the composer's creative powers. The musical materials and their manipulation are so naturally, economically intertwined that it seems improbable to the casual listener that the music could have been written any other way. It has been recognized as a masterpiece from the time of its first performance and remains one of those works that stands among the major orchestral achievements of the 20th century.

Concerto No. 2 for Piano and Orchestra

Allegro

Adagio—Presto—Adagio

Allegro molto

According to Bartók's notation on the 1937 facsimile of the score, the second piano concerto was written between October 1930 and October 1931. It was first performed in Frankfurt am Main on January 23, 1933, with Hans Rosbaud conducting and Bartók as piano soloist.

Instrumentation: *three flutes (the third doubling piccolo), two oboes, two clarinets, three bassoons (the third doubling contrabassoon), four horns, three trumpets, three trombones, tuba, timpani, bass drum, snare drum, triangle, cymbals, solo piano, and strings.*

Studies of paper types show that the second piano concerto was written in two stages, one encompassing the exposition and development of the first movement, the remainder of the work completed at a different and, presumably, later time. The composer's own designation of the period of origination reinforces that observation. Bartók clearly intended the concerto for his own use and performed it at least eighteen times between the premiere and the completion in April 1937 of a revised facsimile score. Writing of the work in 1939, Bartók noted that he "wanted to produce a piece which would contrast with the First [Concerto]. . . . This intention explains the rather light and popular character of most of the themes of my later concerto: a lightness that sometimes almost reminds me of one of my youthful works, the First Suite for Orchestra, Op. 3 (1905)."[5] At the end of the century the bristling difficulties of the Second Concerto rarely impress performers or audiences as light and popular, but Bartók's comments illustrate his desire to reach the public in those works conceived for his own performance.

Considered as a whole, the concerto represents a large arch form of near-symmetrical proportions. Two fast, vigorous movements that share thematic material frame the slow middle movement comprised of an *Adagio—Presto—Adagio* design in which the slow sections, built of the same material, surround the *Presto* as the center of the concerto. Three identifiable motives comprise the principal theme of the opening *Allegro*, the first played by the trumpet, the second by the piano, the third by the oboes, the last two following quickly at two-measure intervals. The solo piano presents the second theme proper, which offers its own brand of symmetry: each hand plays chords of interlocking fifths, moving in an approximate mirror of each other and arpeggiated in opposite directions (the right hand rolls the chord from bottom to top, the left hand from top to bottom). Throughout most of this movement, Bartók's writing for the piano reflects his own technical prowess. Each hand plays double thirds or octaves with added notes, both fairly common, or patterns of interlocking fifths. The latter require extension of the hand to a ninth, just sufficiently unusual to create difficulty for pianists long accustomed to playing octaves. In the recapitulation, the original motives return in inversion, and again in retrograde inversion in the orchestral crescendo that leads to the solo cadenza. Bartók's themes are highly compressed musical elements that expand during the course of the composition as they reflect both their innate potential for growth and the craftsmanship of Bartók the developer.

With the opening of the second movement, the strings appear for the first time (only winds, percussion, and piano play in the first movement), the violins and basses now playing in mirror fashion a chorale theme of three sections separated by two improvisatory passages by the piano. These five sections offer another facet of symmetry, defined by timbre and texture: strings—piano—strings—piano—strings. The central *Presto* offers its own repertory of unusual features. Here (and in other sections of the concerto) the timpani accompany much of the solo passagework, making the drums a partner in the *concertante* writing with the piano at the same time as they illustrate the kinship between these two percussion instruments. Later the piano plays long passages of very quiet tremolo tone clusters, each hand flat on either black or white keys, providing a shimmering support for the motivic interplay between the orchestral instruments. Bartók had heard demonstrations of tone clusters by the American composer Henry Cowell in London in 1923 and, in an act of artistic integrity, had requested Cowell's permission to incorporate the technique in his own work.

Bartók succinctly described the third movement as a free variation of the first. The rondo theme proper, the only important theme of the movement that is new, is played by the solo piano accompanied by timpani, another example of the percussion instruments' rise to solo status. The intervening episodes derive from the motives originally identified as components of the main theme in the first movement. As in the first movement, themes in the reprise appear in inversion.

These techniques of counterpoint and motivic transformation may be less than obvious on first hearing. Nevertheless, they lend an element of cohesiveness, if the listener does not allow that perception to be impeded by common stereotypes.

Concerto No. 3 for Piano and Orchestra

Allegretto

Adagio religioso

Allegro vivace

Bartók composed most of this concerto in the months before September 21, 1945; it was first performed in Philadelphia on February 8, 1946 by the Philadelphia Orchestra conducted by Eugene Ormandy, with György Sándor as soloist.

Instrumentation: *two flutes (the second doubling piccolo), two oboes (the second doubling English horn), two clarinets (the second doubling bass clarinet), two bassoons, four horns, two trumpets, three trombones, tuba, timpani, bass drum, snare drum, cymbals, tam-tam, triangle, xylophone, solo piano, and strings.*

Bartók evidently had made tentative plans for a third piano concerto long before he set down the work we have come to know by that title. As early as 1940, Ralph Hawkes, of the publishing firm Boosey & Hawkes, wrote to Bartók that he would "expect the third piano concerto by the summer of 1941. My reason for saying this is that you will be wanted as soloist with this work for the New York Philharmonic during its Centennial Season 1941–42."[6] Nothing more was heard of the project, and by the summer of 1945 Bartók, terminally ill, was struggling to complete both a concerto commissioned by the violist William

Primrose and the third piano concerto, a work he intended for his pianist wife, Ditta Pastory Bartók. His protracted illness and attendant decline in creative energy, loss of income from concerts and lectures he had been forced to cancel, and the further loss of income from royalties following the dislocations of World War II combined to place the Bartóks in precarious financial circumstances. In this context, Bartók resolved to leave to his wife, Ditta, a concerto designed for her own pianistic talents, thereby providing her with a means of producing some income at the same time that she continued as an advocate for Bartók's music.

To that end he set aside the viola concerto in order to concentrate on the concerto for piano. His declining health in the late summer of 1945 brought the Bartóks back to New York City from Saranac Lake, New York. Just before he was transferred to the hospital on September 21, Bartók asked his son to draw seventeen bar-lines on the manuscript paper; following that he wrote *vége* (the end). He died five days later, leaving to Tibor Serly, a countryman, violist, and personal friend, the task of completing the orchestration of the final seventeen measures based on the composer's sketches. Some observers have interpreted Bartók's final inscription as an epitaphic gesture, reflecting his aware-ness of the seriousness of his condition. Considering his straightfor-ward approach to life and to music, it seems more likely that it was but a practical notation defining the conclusion of the musical work as it existed on the manuscript paper. The characteristic tempo title for the last movement was lacking, as were several other details of expression marks and tempo indications within the movements. Those annota-tions that were deemed necessary were added by Tibor Serly, Eugene Ormandy, the pianist Louis Kentner, and Erwin Stein of the publishing firm Boosey & Hawkes.

Compared to Bartók's earlier concertos, his third is more accessi-ble, more direct, less dissonant, and more obviously tonal than his other late works. Some sections are poignantly melodious, and most of the writing in the first two movements eschews the subtleties of coun-terpoint that had permeated Bartók's compositions in the preceding decades. The percussiveness of the second concerto gives way to an ele-gant lyricism, with much of the piano part offering a one-line melody, doubled in both hands. Some observers have championed this concerto as the beginning of a new era in Bartók's work, had he lived to continue the direction initiated here. Others have speculated that his debilitating illness suppressed the best of his creative powers, and some have criticized him for making concessions in the rigor of musical thought that had characterized most of his previous works. On the contrary, nothing supports the premise of any artistic compromise by this most uncompromising of composers. Considering other works from his last years, it seems more accurate to view the third concerto as a refinement and distillation of both musical substance and technique. Bartók's mastery enabled him to put forth a work of Mozartean élan and clarity, one that reflects a substantive synthesis between classic design and his own musical sophistication.

The piano introduces the principal theme immediately over a double tremolo in the strings, both solo and orchestra confirming the basic tonic of E. This initial theme first appeared in Bartók's sketches in his field notebook for Arabic music, an association that might suggest some Middle-Eastern origins, but nothing in the theme's treatment supports that supposition. Subsequent thematic material derives from this theme in varying degrees, contributing to a tightly knit design. Most of the piano writing continues the pattern set forth at the beginning: single notes in each hand, doubled at the octave with minimal intrusion from the orchestra.

The term *religioso* in the title of the second movement refers to the serious character of the music rather than to any religious origin or intended application of religious materials. That serious vein is one of several intriguing elements shared with the *Molto adagio* of Beethoven's String Quartet, op. 132. Both movements begin quietly, with imitative entries in the strings interrupted five times by a homorhythmic chorale, in the concerto played by the unaccompanied piano. Beethoven prefaced his work with the inscription: "Holy song of thanksgiving to the divinity after a convalescence," a sentiment that Bartók was certainly in a position to share to whatever degree his physical condition would allow. The concerto movement continues with a midsection of "night sounds" of a sort heard in several of Bartók's slow movements—small motives, melodic gestures, fragments of melody that might be derived from nature—presented against a background of shimmering string tremolo. The *Adagio* returns, accompanied by the piano playing two-part counterpoint that dissolves into short, diaphanous cadenzas at the close of each phrase.

The closing rondo presents as its main subject a rhythmic theme of short-long patterns followed by long-short, a diminutive plan of rhythmic symmetry that belies the underlying three-eight meter. The intervening episodes expand upon a vigorous display of imitation, inversion, and stretto, contrapuntal techniques that are here child's play in the hands of a master.

Concerto No. 2 for Violin and Orchestra

Allegro non troppo

Andante tranquillo

Allegro molto

With many interruptions, Bartók wrote the violin concerto between August 1937 and late December 1938. It was first performed in Amsterdam on March 23, 1939, by the Amsterdam Concertgebouw Orchestra conducted by William Mengelberg, with Zoltán Székely as soloist.

Instrumentation: *two flutes (the second doubling piccolo), two oboes (the second doubling English horn), two clarinets (the second doubling bass clarinet), two bassoons (the second doubling contrabassoon), four horns, two trumpets, two tenor trombones, bass trombone, timpani, bass drum, two snare drums, triangle, tam-tam, two sets of cymbals, celesta, harp, solo violin, and strings.*

Bartók wrote two *concertante* works for solo violin. The first, a two-movement work from 1907–1908, was intended for the violinist Stefi Geyer, a young woman with whom Bartók was much enamored in his youth. When this early liaison ended, he recast the first movement as the first of *Two Portraits for Orchestra* and arranged the second movement for violin and piano. In later personal correspondence he renounced the work in its original version, and it was not published until 1959. The existence of the early concerto has led the work at hand to be identified as "No. 2," although Bartók did not identify the effort by key, number, or date. In Bartók's view, this was his only concerto for violin.

At the time Zoltán Székely commissioned the concerto for his own performance, Bartók was primarily interested in writing a large variation form. Székely insisted upon a more traditional concerto format, to which Bartók ultimately agreed, but the element of variation nonetheless dominated the work in that the third movement is a thematic variant of the first, and the second movement is a straightforward set of six variations. Apparently Bartók was able, or perhaps determined, to follow his original musical inclinations under any guise necessary.

By the 1930s, Bartók had reached that stage in his creative processes for which he has become so highly regarded. He was creating large-scale works marked by elements of symmetry and proportions based upon the venerable Golden Section at all levels, a system of balanced correlations known since classical antiquity and one reflected in many facets of the natural world. Contrapuntal techniques laced the fabric of his scores in a manner that provided a further level of cohesiveness. In the violin concerto, these qualities are enlivened by an extraordinary number of genuinely new instrumental effects, events on the musical surface that are usually perceived more readily than the underlying structural elements.

The first movement opens with the harp strumming the tonic chord of B major, over which the violin plays the main theme, drawing heavily on the style of a Hungarian peasant dance. For a striking second theme, Bartók presents a motive incorporating all twelve tones of the chromatic scale, but in no sense is this an attempt at the twelve-tone row technique that was so much in vogue among progressive composers at the time. Székely recalled that Bartók commented in a joking manner about the theme, pointing out its twelve-tone quality in a manner that has suggested to some that he intended it as a sardonic spoof of a musical procedure that was still controversial; on the other hand, he may have wanted to illustrate that such a pattern could be incorporated into thoroughly tonal music. Quite clearly it was an intentional and pertinent gesture by the composer. Quarter-tones introduce another sound unusual in Bartók's music; here they serve to interrupt the fabric of the music to introduce a fiendishly difficult solo cadenza exploiting double-stops. The close of the movement is marked by other Bartókian effects in the orchestra: his own type of pizzicato (for which he developed his own notation symbol) calling for the string to be plucked in a manner that will cause it to rebound off the fingerboard with a snap, and specific indications for the snare drum to be played near the edge of the head (rather than near the center), producing another unique sound.

The theme of the *Andante tranquillo*, the subject for six connected variations, expands through processes that involve all of its constituent elements. As one would expect, the melody appears with embellishment, but the orchestration, texture, and rhythmic patterns share in this developmental process, leaving only the basic structure of the theme as a constant feature. The movement offers a good example of "character variations," the fundamental musical thought appearing in six different settings.

The third movement offers a design and thematic material similar to the first, with the difference that the themes are embellished and orchestration changed. The significance is that in their parallel designs the first and last movements serve as matching frames for the inner movement. Székely objected to Bartók's original close for the third movement, claiming that the solo part was insufficiently brilliant for a major concerto or for a virtuoso of his capabilities. Bartók eventually concurred and provided a revised ending in which the soloist concludes with a flourish. The original coda, consisting of trombones glissando without solo violin, was retained as an option and published at the end of the full score, offering another example of Bartók's perseverance in sustaining his original creative impulse.

From the time of its first appearance, Bartók's violin concerto was recognized as a masterpiece to be placed alongside those by Beethoven, Mendelssohn, and Brahms. The flavor of Hungarian melodies and scales, representing a long tradition of the central European virtuoso fiddler, finds here an exalted expression in modern style.

Concerto for Viola and Orchestra, Opus posth.

Moderato

Adagio religioso

Allegro vivace

Bartók sketched the viola concerto between January and September 1945 in response to a commission from the violist William Primrose. Tibor Serly deciphered and prepared the sketches for publication between 1947 and 1949; his realization was first performed on December 2, 1949, in Minneapolis by the Minneapolis Symphony Orchestra, Antal Dorati conducting, with William Primrose as soloist.

> **Instrumentation:** *Serly's score calls for three flutes (the third doubling piccolo), two oboes, two clarinets, two bassoons, four horns, three trumpets, two trombones, tuba, timpani, bass drum, snare drum, large and small cymbals, solo viola, and strings.*

Bartók's viola concerto probably appears on more concert programs than any other concerto for that instrument in the current repertory; at the same time, its musical legitimacy has been the subject of much controversy. After hearing Yehudi Menuhin's recording of Bartók's second violin concerto, William Primrose was moved to approach the composer with a commission for a comparable work for viola and orchestra. Bartók was reluctant to accept the commission because, in his own estimation, he knew too little about the viola as a solo instrument. The date of this initial interview remains uncertain, but by January 1945 Bartók had decided to accept the commission of $1,000, the fee he had indicated. He also requested through his publisher, presumably for purposes of study, a score of Hector Berlioz's *Harold in Italy*, an extended work for viola and orchestra. Primrose reaffirmed his enthusiasm for the project early in 1945: "Need I tell you how gratified and thrilled I am to learn . . . that you have so kindly consented to write for me a Viola Concerto. I really am very excited & will contact you immediately I return East in March. Please do not feel in any way proscribed by the apparent technical limitations of the instrument. I can assure you that they belong to the day when the viola was merely a 'penzions instrument,' & no longer, in reality, exist."[7] There was no further word about the project until Bartók wrote to Primrose the following August, a letter that remains only as an incomplete fragment, apparently never posted:

> About mid July I was just planning to write you a rather desponding [*sic*] letter, explaining [to] you the various difficulties I am in. But, then, there stirred some viola-concerto ideas which gradually crystallized themselves, so that I am able now to tell you that I hope to write the work, and maybe finish at least its draft in 4–5 weeks, if nothing happens in the meantime which would prevent my work. The prospects are these: perhaps I will be able to be ready with the draft by beginning of Sept., and with the score by end of the same month. This is the best case; there may be, however, a delay of the completion of the work until end of Oct. So,

about [the] end of either Sept. or Oct. you will get from me a copy
of the orch. and the piano score—if I am able to go through the
work at all. . . .

However embrionic [*sic*] the state of the work still is, the general plan and ideas are already fixed. So I can tell you that it will
be in 4 movements: a serious Allegro, a Scherzo, a (rather short)
slow movement, and a finale beginning Allegretto and developing
the tempo to an Allegro molto. Each movement, or at least 3 of
them will [be] preceded by a (short) recurring introduction
(mostly solo of the viola), a kind of ritornello.[8]

The work apparently was in the forefront of Bartók's attention, for
a little more than a month later he forwarded to Primrose a much more
detailed description of his thoughts about the concerto and its state of
completion:

I am very glad to be able to tell you that your viola concerto is
ready in draft so that only the score has to be written which
means a purely mechanical work, so to speak. If nothing happens
I can be through in 5 or 6 weeks. . . .

Many interesting problems arose in composing this work. The
orchestration will be rather transparent, more transparent than in
a violin concerto. Also the sombre, more masculine character of
your instrument exerted some influence on the general character
of the work. . . .

It is conceived in a rather virtuoso style. Most probably some
passages will prove to be uncomfortable or unplayable. These we
may discuss later, according to your observations.[9]

Travel and professional engagements by Primrose interfered with
the planned conference between composer and violist until late
September, by which time Bartók was dead. It was not until some two
years later that Bartók's widow and son, Peter, transferred thirteen
pages of minimal and disorganized sketches to Tibor Serly with the
request, in Serly's account, that he look over the manuscripts carefully.

The publication in 1995 of a facsimile of Bartók's manuscript, plus
a literal realization in print of these fragments, makes clear what a
daunting task confronted Serly in the realization of this score. He had
been a professional violist with several major orchestras, and more

recently had been active as both composer and conductor. For many years, Serly had been a close friend and disciple of Bartók, although not a student in the traditional sense. In professional and personal attributes he was a natural choice for the task; nonetheless in later years he commented frequently and at length on the difficulties that he encountered. Following the premiere in 1949, the concerto was recorded by Primrose in 1950 and, in his own view, has been an enduring success. Primrose has played the work more than any other concerto, and he has expressed considerable gratification in bringing Bartók to the fore at a time when much of his music was not widely known.

Skeptics of the viola concerto's authenticity base their views not on its musical effectiveness but on the question of how much of it represents Bartók's thoughts and how much Serly's interpretations. We can never know with certainty what Bartók might have written had he lived a few months longer. Obviously the concerto was still in a stage of development, because the sketches offer no clear designation of the four-movement plan he mentioned in his letter of August 5, and as that was not posted, it seems unlikely Serly knew of this earlier intent. The manuscript does contain some indications of orchestration, and through many interviews Serly makes a good case for his accurate deciphering of Bartók's notations in spite of the paleographic difficulties. He had arranged several of Bartók's piano works for orchestra, and had received the composer's approval, suggesting considerable musical rapport between the two. Quite possibly the detractors had no opportunity to examine Bartók's script and based their assessment on comparisons with his works from several years earlier. The completed score of the third piano concerto revealed a change in Bartók's style; thus it is not inconceivable that the viola concerto might also reflect a style different from his earlier works.

So is this Bartók's last work or "one after the last"? Similar questions will endure concerning the completion of Mozart's *Requiem* and Mahler's Tenth Symphony by other hands. Such matters must be addressed, but they do not diminish the musical achievement represented by the existing scores for any of these works. With Bartók's manuscript now available for study, there may be a time when there will be multiple versions of his viola concerto.

Dance Suite

Moderato

Allegro molto

Allegro vivace

Molto tranquillo

Commodo

Allegro

Bartók received a commission leading to the Dance Suite *in April 1923, completing the score in August; it was first performed in Budapest on November 19, 1923, by the Budapest Philharmonic Society, Ernö Dohnányi conducting.*

Instrumentation: *two flutes (both doubling piccolo), two oboes (the second doubling English horn), two clarinets (the second doubling bass clarinet), two bassoons (the second doubling contrabassoon), four horns, two trumpets, two trombones, tuba, timpani, bass drum, snare drum, tenor drum, triangle, bells, cymbals, tam-tam, celesta, harp, piano four-hands, and strings.*

The commission that led to the *Dance Suite* came from the civil authorities of Budapest, who were preparing a festival concert celebrating the 50th anniversary of the merging of Buda, Pest, and Obuda into one city. Colored as it was by civic and national pride, the event called forth works from Ernö Dohnányi, Zoltán Kodály, and Bartók. Bartók responded with a suite not formed from a series of stylized courtly dances but built from a series of movements based upon original material written in the style of native folk dances. In a sense, his *Dance Suite* responded to multiple stimuli: the immediate impetus of a commission, an occasion of considerable nationalistic sentiment (for which Bartók as an individual had long held much sympathy), and his long commitment to collecting and editing central European folk music.

Five dances, or dance moods, culminate in a finale summarizing most of the important thematic material. A *Ritornell*, identified as such in the score, links the first three movements with movements four and

five, and reappears within the finale, in the process providing a thread
of continuity for most of the work. With the *Ritornell* as a connecting
link and the near-constant rhythmic flow from one dance to another,
the suite relinquishes most of its sectional character. Rhythmic flexibility permeates the score through the ebb and flow of the basic pulse,
and the composer often worked from a meter signature that indicates
the actual rhythmic groups (three plus three plus two, for example)
rather than adhering to a traditional metric signature and writing syncopated rhythms in the context of that regularized metric pattern.

In most of his early comments about the suite, Bartók addressed
only the order and character of the movements, affirmed that all
themes were his own but written in the style of folk music, and that all
themes returned in the finale.[10] In 1931 he offered further details about
the *Dance Suite* in notes originally intended for a lecture:

> It [the *Suite*] is made up of six small dance-like movements, one of
> which, the ritornello . . . returns several times in the manner of a
> leitmotif. The thematic material of all the movements is in imita-
> tion of peasant music. The aim of the whole work was to put
> together a kind of idealized peasant music . . . in such a way that
> the individual movements of the work should introduce particu-
> lar types of music. Peasant music of all nationalities served as a
> model: Magyar [Hungarian], Wallachian [Rumanian], Slovak, and
> even Arabic. In fact, here and there is even a hybrid from these
> species. Thus, for example, the melody of the first subject of the
> first movement is reminiscent of primitive Arabic peasant music,
> whereas its rhythm is of East European folk music. . . . The fourth
> movement is an imitation of quite complex Arabic music, perhaps
> of urban origin. . . . The ritornello theme is such a faithful imita-
> tion of a certain kind of Hungarian folk melodies, that its deriva-
> tion might puzzle even the most knowledgeable musical
> folklorist. . . . The second movement is Hungarian in character,
> and the third is alternately Hungarian and Wallachian.[11]

From its opening piano glissando, the first movement unfolds
around a twisting, narrowly contained theme first played by the bassoons.
Interjections by the larger ensemble lead to other short themes that gradually subside in the *Ritornell*, a contrasting solo line initiated by the violin
and answered by the clarinet. The *Allegro molto*, identified by the composer

as Hungarian in character, becomes more agitated, prominent glissandos by the trombones offering an orchestral timbre common in much popular dance music but less usual in the concert hall. The *Ritornell* returns, but with a reversal of instrumentation: it is now introduced by the clarinet and answered by the violin. The third movement goes beyond the first two in its expanded variety of thematic material and orchestral timbres. Harp, piano, and celesta add their own unique sound qualities to what is essentially a rondo design. At one point the piano part calls for two players (four hands) in a short, closely spaced canon with a countersubject in the harp, an unusual combination in any orchestral score and one of striking effect in spite of its relatively quiet dynamic level.

With no reference to the *Ritornell* theme, and following a grand pause, the fourth movement begins quietly with an alternation between the string choir, playing extended chords built on fourths, and a series of languorous thematic statements by the wind instruments. As this dialogue progresses, the wind ensemble grows from two to five parts, increasing in volume, while the remainder of the ensemble becomes quieter until, at the midpoint, the pattern of orchestration begins to mirror itself, the wind ensemble phrase by phrase returning to a two-part texture while the strings play a muted background. The concluding *Ritornell*, much shortened, is now shared by solo violin and celesta. In the movement as a whole, the musical thrust derives from the interaction of instrumental timbres more than from thematic operations.

The last of the five dance movements (*Commodo*) expands upon a short rhythmic pattern played in parallel fourths, these 23 measures serving largely as an introduction to the finale. The interval of the fourth now marks a close series of imitative entries in the string section, rising consecutively from the basses through the first violins. From this point forward, the complete suite is summarized in that thematic materials from all movements but the fourth, plus the *Ritornell*, are synthesized, the whole brought to a close by a vigorous coda.

With the perspective of time, the finale emerges as a musical realization of Bartók's thoughts on the fundamental brotherhood of all people. In a letter to the Rumanian writer Octavian Beu, Bartók expressed his personal credo on the subject:

> My creative work, just because it arises from 3 sources
> (Hungarian, Rumanian, Slovakian), might be regarded as the

embodiment of the very concept of integration so much emphasized in Hungary today. . . . My own idea, however—of which I
have been fully conscious since I found myself as a composer—is
the brotherhood of peoples, brotherhood in spite of all wars and
conflicts. I try . . . to serve this idea in my music; therefore I don't
reject any influence, be it Slovakian, Rumanian, Arabic or from
any other source. The source must only be clean, fresh and
healthy.[12]

Bartók's idealism concerning music as a common voice of humanity, a reflection of nature, and a medium for the expression of timeless
artistic values (his much discussed Golden Section, for example) finds
here one of its early musical expressions. An awareness of that condition may have contributed to the quick and enduring popularity of the
work: it was performed in Germany at least fifty times within the year
following its first appearance, an unusual record for a new composition
of such distinctive characteristics. The work has continued to be
regarded as one of the compositions in which Bartók found his voice.
He later arranged the score for solo piano, presumably for his own concert tours, but it was not heard until György Sándor, countryman and
student of Bartók, first performed the virtuoso piano version in New
York City on February 20, 1945.

Divertimento

Allegro non troppo

Molto adagio

Allegro assai

Bartók composed the Divertimento *during August 1939. It was first
performed in Basle, Switzerland, on June 11, 1940, by the Basle
Chamber Orchestra, Paul Sacher conducting.*

Instrumentation: *five-part strings.*

The *Divertimento* was commissioned by and dedicated to Paul Sacher,
conductor of the Basle Chamber Orchestra, who had also commissioned Bartók's *Music for Strings, Percussion and Celesta* and the Sonata for
Two Pianos and Percussion. Beyond providing the musical and finan-

cial stimulus for the work and guaranteeing its first performance, Sacher also made available his chalet at Saanen, where the composer could work uninterrupted in tranquil surroundings. Bartók claimed the conditions made him "feel like a musician of olden times—the invited guest of a patron of the arts. . . . I have to work. And for Sacher himself—on a commission (something for string orchestra). . . . Luckily the work went well, and I finished it in 15 days (a piece of about 25 minutes), I just finished it yesterday."[13] A similar burst of creativity marked several of Bartók's late works, among them the Concerto for Orchestra, which was completed in seven weeks, and his fifth quartet, which occupied him for one month (August 6 through September 6, 1934). One could attribute this great productivity to the practical support that allowed the composer to concentrate on his work without interruption, but it also reflects a composer much in command of his own style and musical language, not driven to experimentation or to a search for new effects.

The title *Divertimento* usually implies music of relatively less rigor and an absence of serious mein; historically the term has been applied to a series of dance movements, each in binary design, to be played by a chamber group of winds or strings. Because of this early association, Bartók's title is often qualified by a reference to the medium (*Divertimento* for Strings), but that was not a distinction provided by the composer. He turned to 18th-century models for the general character of the work, but the texture resembles the older concerto grosso more than it does any reference to dance music, the last movement offering a possible exception.

The musical structure of the *Divertimento* follows a plan common to many of Bartók's later works: a cycle of three movements in which the first follows the outline of a sonata form, the second reflects in some manner a broad arch design, and the finale expands upon the rondo principle, often coupled with a suggestion of folk dance characteristics. Here and in other scores the internal structure of individual movements is identified by the composer's own description of subsections through timings added to the musical text. Practical experience has shown that these timings often need to be revised, but they nonetheless identify a facet of the composer's musical thought.

The small details of mirror construction and imitation that pepper the first movement often attract more attention than more comprehensive structural designs. The nine-eight meter, traditionally divided three-by-three, appears here in small-scale metric symmetry as eighth-note groups of one-two-three-two-one within each measure; Bartók's interest in symmetrical constructions pervades much of his music, but usually on a scale larger than the individual measure as encountered here. Mirror imitation prevails, not in extended sections but in smaller units of three measures or less. Typical is a section near the beginning of the development, where a figure is introduced by the cello, with imitative entries following in a series of rising fifths through the higher parts of the ensemble. This is interrupted by two measures of symmetrical rhythms as described above, then the violins play the same figure, with entries following in a series of descending fifths through the lower parts of the ensemble. Pitch materials, instrumentation, and rhythm combine in ingenious contrapuntal expansion.

The *Molto adagio* was the last movement to be composed. Bartók cast this in four sections, the first and last based upon corresponding musical materials. The heavily accented short-short-long patterns of the second section produce some of the most intense, morose writing of the entire work, and that quality continues through a third section dominated by double trills in the first violin played over organum-like parallel harmonies in the lower strings. Much of the thematic material of the two inner sections is a type of "night music" as heard in *Music for Strings* and other late works.

In its rondo pattern and vigorous rhythmic drive, the finale suggests a folk dance, although there is no clear reference to folk materials. A written cadenza played by the first violin interrupts the constant rhythmic drive approximately midway in the movement, after which an approximation of the main theme returns, inverted. The busyness of the movement carries the listener to a coda marked by convoluted triplets in the upper strings that, in their beehive simulation, create a tension not resolved until the emphatic pronouncement of the closing measures.

The buoyancy of the *Divertimento* belies the encroaching clouds of war surrounding its creation in 1939. The music is straightforward, accessible to all listeners, and makes no issue of the meticulous attention to detail encountered in many of Bartók's later compositions. In its broadest outlines it fulfills most of the expectation we might hold for a work titled *Divertimento*, and the craftsmanship underlying the music is so complete that it rarely attracts the attention of a casual listener.

Music for Strings, Percussion, and Celesta

Andante tranquillo

Allegro

Adagio

Allegro molto

Music for Strings, Percussion and Celesta *took shape between late July and early September 1936; it was first performed in Basle, Switzerland, on January 21, 1937 by the Basle Chamber Orchestra, Paul Sacher conducting.*

Instrumentation: *timpani, bass drum, side drum with and without snares, cymbals, celesta, xylophone, harp, piano, and two choirs of strings.*

This extraordinary work was prompted by a commission from the conductor Paul Sacher for the Basle Chamber Orchestra's jubilee concert celebrating that ensemble's tenth anniversary in January 1937. Contrary to his usual practice of working from an assembly of sketches, Bartók wrote the work out initially in full score, implying that it had already been well formed in his mind or that he had been working on such a score before receiving the request from Sacher. In a letter to his close friend, the violinist Zoltán Székely, Bartók referred to the commission as "better than nothing and I had been planning something like it for quite a while."[14] In many ways this unusual work has come to be recognized as one of the masterpieces of music in the Western tradition: thematic integrity, mirror structures that permeate the score, balanced proportions that function at several levels, and elements of symmetrical construction combine in a creation of extraordinary subtlety and vitality.

Bartók's own description of the music, while more extensive than those he offered for most of his compositions, was nonetheless very brief and straightforward, giving little inkling of the broad concepts that envelop the work or the many intricacies of structural balance and

proportion. Among the most pronounced of the work's musical qualities is the ensemble itself. In traditional orchestration winds and percussion function together, but here the winds are omitted, the
percussion group in its entirety serving as an element of timbre and
color. The timpani, which normally play a supporting role, frequently
emerge as a solo part. Carrying his awareness for the specificity of timbre and color a step further, Bartók specified a seating plan that placed
the percussion instruments between two groups of strings; one version
of his design customarily appears in study scores.

	Double bass 1	Double bass 2	
Violoncello 1	Timpani	Bass Drum	Violoncello 2
Viola 2	Snare Drum	Cymbals	Viola 2
Violin 2	Celesta	Xylophone	Violin 4
Violin 1	Piano	Harp	Violin 3

Spatial separation becomes a constructive feature of the intended
sound and was probably a part of Bartók's original conception long
before the technical apparatus of stereophonic recordings had been initiated. Extending from the seating and the spatial separation that
results, the music often moves from one side of the ensemble to the
other; for example, the introduction of the fugue is played by the
instruments to the right of center, but the movement ends with instruments on the left.

There is no doubt that Bartók's conception was directed toward the
total work more than to a series of four independent movements. The
first and last movements are centered on A, moving to the tritone E-flat
at their midpoint. The second movement begins and ends on C, moving to the tritone F-sharp at its midpoint, while the third movement
mirrors that tonal plan by beginning and ending on F-sharp, with its
midpoint centered on C. All four movements together form a mirror
relationship around A as a focal point. Moreover, the main theme of the
first movement, treated there as a fugue subject, appears in all the other
movements as an element of reference or in an expanded version, linking the entire work thematically. Similarities of temporal proportions
within the movements reinforce this premise of an architectonic unit.

The first movement is an unusual fugue based on a chromatically
convoluted subject introduced by muted strings. Following the first

statement on A, *pianissimo*, subsequent entries of the subject appear in two series, one a rising sequence of fifths, the other a descending series of fifths, the two coming to a temporary halt on the tritone C–F-sharp. The process expands through a removal of mutes and a continuing crescendo until the climax of the movement on E-flat (a tritone removed from the beginning A), *fortissimo*. From this point, the whole process is approximately reversed through a gradual decrescendo, the fugue subject played in inverted contour, and a return to the original pitch. The marvelously compressed coda of three measures presents the subject in both original and inverted contours, encapsulating in one phrase the pitch pattern of the entire movement.

The broad arch achieved by dynamics (*pianissimo—fortissimo—pianissimo*), by key centers that divide the octave (*A–E-flat–A*), and by melodic contour (the subject played in both original and inverted contours) is enhanced by a plan of proportions in the relative lengths of sections. This plan is based on the sequence of Fibonacci numbers (1:1:2:3:5:8:13:21:34:55:89), a series in which any unit is the sum of the two preceding. This intriguing succession appears many times in the natural world. It describes the number of petals in concentric circles of floral patterns, the growth of some branches and buds on trees, and the ratios in the distances between planets, and it appears as well in some facets of science dealing with atomic particles. It was known as a facet of classic and Gothic architecture and in the physical proportions of works of art, where the smaller of any two consecutive numbers has been described as the "Golden Section" or "Golden Mean" of the larger.

When the same series appears in the music of Bartók, one is tempted to view the operation as some manifestation of a world-encompassing, primordial formula. Here the Fibonacci numbers describe the distribution of musical events in time, representing a broad principle of artistic balance in the proportions of movements in which bars of music become the unit of measure. The opening *Andante tranquillo* contains 88 measures (one short of the Fibonacci number of 89); the climax of volume and texture occurs at the end of measure 55 (the "Golden Section" of 89); at measure 34, the timpani enter for the first time and mutes are removed from the strings; by the end of measure 21, all parts have stated the subject at least once; at the beginning of the fugue, the second entry of the subject occurs at measure 5, the third at measure 8, the fourth at measure 13. In that part of the movement following the climax, the subject is inverted for thirteen measures; in the last twenty measures (one measure less than the Fibonacci number of 21), the mutes are replaced on the strings, and the celesta enters the ensemble.

The intriguing element of balance represented by the Fibonacci numbers also poses some fundamental questions about this composition. Ernö Lendvai's description of the series as it applies to Bartók's works led to a tenuous mathematic analysis of harmonic structures as well as formal proportions. Many listeners have questioned whether the series is relevant if not perceived aurally; nonetheless, the proportions become perceptible with repeated exposure, in the same degree that a perceptive listener will become aware of other underlying musical structures after repeated hearings. Was this plan intended by Bartók or was it an accident of creation? If it was a conscious act, the system represents an extraordinary degree of musical craftsmanship and artistic imagination, but one wonders why, if that were true, the composer did not add an extra measure to extend the movement to the expected number of 89 measures. If the proportions were not the product of conscious design, their existence is even more impressive in the degree to which they represent an inherently natural element of temporal balance and proportion. An awareness of these qualities has begun to reach a wider audience in recent decades; they need to be experienced and digested by a still broader range of the musical public before we can satisfactorily answer these questions.

At the opening of the second movement, the two string groups alternate antiphonally, the second group presenting a principal theme derived from the fugue subject of the first movement. The music expands upon a fairly traditional sonata design, enhanced by many mirror patterns within the ensemble and further variants of the original subject, one of which appears in a *fugato* section during the last half of the development.

The third movement presents a broad arch design, common to much of Bartók's writing, in which the thematic material consists of small motives and detached sounds often described as "night music," after the movement of that name from his *Out of Doors Suite*, in which they appeared so prominently. Rather than melodic, these motives might better be described as atmospheric. Bartók's interest in symmetrical construction finds here a particularly ingenious expression in the design of the total movement. Five sections, musically identified by their different exploitation of color effects, are separated by the four phrases of the subject from the first movement. The first and last sections contain similar material and open and close with an accelerating and then slowing rhythmic pattern played by the xylophone. The second and fourth sections are identified by glissandi in the celesta, harp, and piano. The middle section of this broadly conceived arch adds to this implied symmetry: the point of its climax is marked by several measures that, in their pitch patterns, produce mirror contours.

The closing *Allegro molto* opens with a bonhomie contrasting markedly with the careful calculation that pervades the first three movements. The fugue subject appears again, slightly transformed through widened intervals, but most of the movement follows a broad rondo design that expands upon antiphonal writing for the two groups of strings, punctuated by interjections from the percussion instruments. The chromatic intensity of the first three movements is answered, musically and psychologically, by the diatonic, folk-like *joi de vivre* of this rousing finale.

From the time of its first appearance, many audiences have regarded the inner order of *Music for Strings* as something bordering on the mystic. The complete work can be perceived on many levels, coheres through a variety of musical processes, exploits one fundamental theme in several guises, and still appeals to the uninitiated listener on the basis of its sonorous qualities alone. It endures as Bartók's masterpiece.

The Miraculous Mandarin: Music from a Pantomime by Melchior Lengyel, Opus 19

Music for The Miraculous Mandarin *was probably initiated in 1917, when Bartók first encountered the libretto; it was certainly completed as an assembly of sketches and a four-hand piano score by 1919. Orchestration was begun in April 1924, and the first performance as a stage work took place at the Cologne Stadttheater on November 27, 1926, with Jenö Szenkár conducting. The first concert performance was in Budapest on October 15, 1928, by the Budapest Philharmonic Orchestra, Ernö Dohnányi conducting.*

Instrumentation: three flutes (the second and third doubling piccolo),
three oboes (the third doubling English horn), three clarinets (the second doubling clarinet in D, E-flat, and A, the third doubling bass clarinet), three bassoons (the second and third doubling contrabassoon),
four horns, three trumpets, three trombones, tuba, timpani, bass drum,
snare drum, tenor drum, cymbals, triangle, tam-tam, xylophone,
celesta, piano, harp, organ, and strings.

In its degenerate plot, the stage action that fired Bartók's imagination
for *The Miraculous Mandarin* reflected the social upheaval and deteriora-
tion enveloping Hungary and most of Western Europe in the turmoil
following World War I. The following synopsis of the pantomime
derives from notations in the score originally designed to coordinate
the music with action on the stage.

The curtain rises on a shabby room in a city slum. The first of three
thugs (Bartók called them "apaches") gropes in his pockets for money,
but comes up empty-handed, as does a second thug, who rummages
through the drawer of a table. A third henchman rises from the bed and
roughly orders a girl accompanying them to stand by the window in
order to lure men to the room, where they can be robbed. She refuses,
but, following repeated orders, hesitantly moves to the window for the
first decoy game. The first victim is a shabby old rake, and the second a
timid adolescent to whom the girl is attracted, but the thugs throw both
of them out because of their impoverished circumstances. Again they
turn to the girl, demanding that she attract a suitable victim.
Immediately they see a weird figure in the street and hear his tramp upon
the stairs. The Mandarin enters and stands immobile in the door; the girl
flees in terror from this unnatural figure as the thugs hide. The girl gradually overcomes her repugnance and invites the Mandarin to come closer.
She begins to move, ending in a wildly erotic dance as the Mandarin
watches her with an impassive stare. The girl slips down to embrace him
as he begins to tremble in feverish anticipation, but she shudders as he
approaches her and tries to tear herself from his grasp. She flees as he
chases her ever more wildly. When he finally catches her, they struggle.
The thugs leap from hiding, rob him of his possessions, smother him
under cushions, and run him through with an old sword, but he will not
die. He continues in his fixation on the girl and hurls himself upon her.
They then hang him, but he still lives and begins to emit a strange inter-

nal glow. Only when the girl asks that he be cut down and takes him into her arms do his wounds begin to bleed, allowing him to die.

The music of the concert version ends at the point of struggle between the Mandarin and the girl; except for two short cuts and a revised ending inserted at that point, the music is the same as that accompanying the stage action. Bartók wrote the score with the idea that it would serve both as orchestral accompaniment for the pantomime and as an independent orchestral work. He revised the ending of the chase between the Mandarin and the girl in 1927, after the publication of the original orchestral score, thereby eliminating approximately the last third of the work in its first complete version. He insisted the concert version should be designated "*Music from . . .*" rather than a suite, because it was not a series of excerpts, nor sectional, nor derived from any real choreography. The music matches the stage action on two levels: there are long sections where the orchestra presents a broad characterization of the drama, as when the Mandarin chases the girl around the room to a lively fugue. Others are more specific, such as the three decoy games that are supported by solo woodwinds: clarinet in A for the old rake; clarinet, oboe, and English horn for the adolescent; clarinet and flute for the Mandarin.

Considered in the context of Bartók's other works, this orchestral score is the largest he produced and, in his own estimation, it was his best up to 1927. His notation of quarter-tones by small arrows above the notes first appeared here, and other purely orchestral effects abound. At a time when the symphonies of Mahler were still a recent memory and the orchestral tone poems of Richard Strauss were current fare, Bartók produced a score for large orchestra equal to the most colorful of the era.

Throughout the early history of *The Miraculous Mandarin*, Bartók encountered difficulty in obtaining adequate performances of the work. The length of the score and the orchestral resources required presented practical difficulties for many potential performing groups, but it was the libretto itself that posed the greatest problem. The social significance of the story, reflecting a grotesque and morbid commentary on the materialism of a changing age, did not save the work from accusations of vulgarity. The first performance in Cologne inspired a reaction comparable to the infamous furor over Igor Stravinsky's ballet music for *Le sacre du printemps* some thirteen years earlier in Paris:

From the beginning on, the pantomime . . . roused opposition
from a vast majority of the audience. The commotion, which
broke out in the auditorium, and the disgusting plot caused the
rows in front of the stage to be emptied out before the end. And
as the curtain went down, a hasty retreat ensued from the spaces
that had been profaned by this (to put it mildly) inferior work. . . .
The première of the Bartókian prostitute and pimp play with
orchestral racket would have ended in a calm, noiseless rejection,
if small groups, assigned to different sections of the house, had
not tried through hand-clapping and calling for the author to
twist the incontestable failure of the work into a success. This
roused the indignation of the fleeing public so much that even
women, from whom one normally learns what is proper, took part
in the hand-clapping and calling. The mob stormed back into the
hall. When persistent hisses could not overpower the clapping,
shouts resounded a hundredfold for minutes: "Shame! Vulgarity!
Scandal!" and the applause was nearly subdued. The noise
mounted again when, in spite of the exodus, Mr. Bartók stepped
onto the stage; it was now high time for the fire curtain to be
rung down—which was done to the applause of the large
majority.[15]

The work was withdrawn and the conductor censured by city officials, but Bartók remained uncompromising in his determination to
retain the social commentary of the pantomime and to support it with
appropriate music. In an age that had witnessed the musical orgies of
Salomé, as set by Richard Strauss, and the rites of seduction and sacrifice in Stravinsky's Le sacre du printemps, it seems the dramatic discor-
dance of The Miraculous Mandarin should have been less disturbing to
the audience. Bartók continued to seek performances and revised the
score once again in 1936, but the work was not performed as a stage
work in his native Hungary until 1946, the year after his death. The difficulty of obtaining performances provided such frustration for the
composer that The Miraculous Mandarin remains the last of his dramatic
works and the last large orchestral work he would write without the
support of a commission.

Alban Berg

~~~

b. Vienna, Austria, February 9, 1885; d. Vienna, December 24, 1935

lban Berg's name usually calls to mind two other composers with whom he was closely associated: his teacher, Arnold Schoenberg, and his friend and fellow student, Anton Webern. The trio has often been cited as the nucleus of a school of composers following Schoenberg's twelve-tone row technique. This generalization has some basis in fact but is far too inclusive to accurately describe the works of Berg, who, during the last half of the 20th century, emerged as the most enduring (if not the most influential) of the three composers. His relatively short work list includes items written in a Romantic but still tonal idiom, others that are atonal, and later works that exploit the principles of twelve-tone music but with Berg's individual application of that process. Within these traditions, his music expands on traditional forms adapted to his own individual stamp—symmetrical constructions; tone rows with common and familiar substructures; quotations; numerology; and various types of continuing variations— all underlying music that on the surface appears to carry a very different message. Berg's works show a carefully executed development of musical ideas and principles of design. Nothing is done on impulse. Few passages give the impression of facile creativity, as musical operations are concentrated and distilled through slow and careful composition. Numerology and other references pervade his scores, presumably intended to offer a thread of comprehensibility at a time when musical styles in Vienna were in a great state of flux. These conditions have established for Berg's works a fame based on their musical design and extramusical implications. His stature at the end of the 20th century readily surpasses the considerable renown already accorded him at the time of his death in 1935.

Berg spent most of his life in the environs of Vienna. As a young adult, he was very much a part of the social and intellectual ferment preceding World War I and the events leading to the fall of the Hapsburg Empire. Apparently any systematized training that he had in music was comparably slight until he met Schoenberg late in 1904, the beginning of an association that exerted overwhelming influence on Berg both personally and musically. But in 1911, Berg was left to his own devices when Schoenberg left for Berlin.

The first work Berg wrote on his own, without guidance from Schoenberg, was a collection of songs to texts by Peter Altenberg. At a concert in Vienna in 1913, the performance of only one of these provoked a disturbance in the audience to rival the outcry in Paris at the performance of Igor Stravinsky's *Le sacre du printemps* a few months later; police were called and the remainder of the concert was canceled, leaving Berg's musical self-confidence in a state of disarray. His first international success came with the opera *Wozzeck*, which, coupled with his *Lyric Suite* for string quartet, his violin concerto, the opera *Lulu*, and the works discussed here, assured his lasting presence in art music of the 20th century. He had just completed the violin concerto and was still at work on the opera *Lulu* when he died from complications stemming in part from a series of infections initiated by a severe insect bite.

Concerto for Violin and Orchestra

Part I: Andante—Allegretto

Part II: Allegro—Adagio

Berg composed the Violin Concerto between April and August 1935. It was first performed in Barcelona during the Festival of the International Society for Contemporary Music on April 19, 1936, with Hermann Scherchen conducting, and Louis Krasner as violin soloist.

Instrumentation: *two flutes (both doubling piccolo), two oboes (the second doubling English horn), three clarinets (the third doubling alto saxophone), bass clarinet, two bassoons, contrabassoon, four horns, two trumpets, two trombones, contrabass tuba, timpani, bass drum, snare*

drum, cymbals, tam-tam (low), gong (high), triangle, harp, solo violin,
and strings.

Berg was immersed in the completion of the opera *Lulu* when the
Russian-born American violinist Louis Krasner approached him in
January 1935 with a proposed commission for a violin concerto. Berg
was loath to set aside his work on the opera, but the proposed commission of $1,500 came at a time of pressing financial need. In 1934 the
Nazi government, through its spokesman Hermann Goebbels, had
publicly denounced atonality as evidence of how a Jewish intellectual
"infection" had taken hold of the national body, a proclamation probably aimed at Arnold Schoenberg as the progenitor of twelve-tone row
composition. As a result, the works of all the composers associated with
the serial technique were proscribed from public performance, reducing Berg's income significantly. Nonetheless, the composer did not
respond to Krasner's proposal immediately, in part because of his wish
to complete *Lulu* in its entirety and also because he felt some discomfort in approaching an unfamiliar medium.

Louis Krasner was in the early years of a promising concert career.
He had become enamored of music of the Schoenberg school, was
determined to further its cause before concert audiences, and was
equally convinced that Berg was the composer most likely to produce a
concerto of the necessary lyrical qualities. He had been instrumental in
bringing about a performance of Berg's *Symphonic Sketches from the Opera
Lulu* by Serge Koussevitzky and the Boston Symphony Orchestra, a gesture of professional support that could only help in gaining Berg's
favor. In his own dialogue with the composer he pointed out that the
"criticism of 12–tone music everywhere is that this music is only cerebral and without feeling or emotion. . . . Think of what it would mean
for the whole Schoenberg Movement if a new Alban Berg Violin
Concerto should succeed in demolishing the antagonism of the 'cerebral, no emotion' cliché and argument."[1]

Krasner returned to America, apparently holding only a tentative
agreement with the composer. Matters were not confirmed until the end
of March, when Berg, in response to a telegram from Krasner, responded
that he would write the concerto and that he had already completed
some preliminary work. A more immediate and pressing stimulus came
from the tragic death of Manon Gropius, daughter of Alma Mahler and

the architect Walter Gropius. The seventeen-year-old Manon had already attracted the romantic attention of prominent intellectuals and artists in Vienna when she contracted polio in 1934. She survived with paralysis in the legs for one year, but succumbed on April 22, 1935, to the sorrow of many who were prominent in artistic circles. Berg sought permission to dedicate his new violin concerto "To the Memory of an Angel," much in the spirit of a requiem for the young woman. From that point work progressed quickly, particularly when compared to Berg's usually studied pace of composition. The rapid progress presumably benefited from whatever preliminary work he had completed in March.

The dedication to the memory of Manon Gropius in effect became a program influencing the musical plan on several levels. Preliminary sketches show that at an early stage Berg was thinking of a four-movement cycle divided into two parts of two sections each: Part I: *Andante (Praeludium)—Allegretto (Scherzo)*; Part II: *Allegro (Cadenza)—Adagio* (chorale setting). With the dedication to Manon, the first of these parts took on the semblance of a musical portrayal of the girl and the second a suggestion of death and transfiguration, in the perception of those most familiar with Berg's mode of operation. At some point in the process, Berg decided to quote in the second part a Carinthian folk song, *Ein Vogel auf'm Zwetschgenbaum* (A Bird in the Plum Tree), and the funeral chorale by J. S. Bach, *Es ist Genug* (It Is Enough). With its text of penitent supplication, the chorale fits the context perfectly, but the significance of the folk song is less clear, although later writers have proposed that the text could be an autobiographical reference to events in the composer's earlier personal life.

Beyond its conception as a memorial for Manon, other influences, some of them highly personal, bear upon the score. Berg was convinced of the power of certain numbers, an attitude reflecting the fascination with numerology and paranormal psychology that swept Europe in the early decades of the 20th century. For him the most important number was 23, in part, at least, because he had suffered the first of many serious asthma attacks on July 23 (some suggest the year 1908, when he would have been 23 years old). In a letter of June 10, 1915, addressed to Schoenberg, Berg described in much detail why he considered 23 to be his particular nemesis and how, in its multiples, it dominated his life. The number 23 appears in various manifestations in the violin concerto—not in a manner to be readily grasped by the listener, but it was a significant factor in Berg's creative process. Expression marks added to the score, particularly in the chorale setting near the end of the work, have also been interpreted as references to another personal program as yet not thoroughly understood. However these may have been intended, there were a number of stimuli that elevated Berg's violin concerto to a level of creativity well beyond the terms of the original commission. Berg turned to Krasner himself for assistance with the solo part. In June 1935, Berg invited the violinist to visit him at his home overlooking the Wönthersee and asked him to play not items from his current repertory but free improvisations. When Krasner drifted into established literature, Berg emerged from an adjoining room, insisting on no sonatas or concertos, only freely improvised pre-luding; presumably he wanted to develop a grasp of violin patterns that were natural both to the instrument and to Krasner.

In structural matters, Berg constructed a tone row of overlapping minor and major triads arranged in such a manner that alternate notes of the series coincided with the four open strings of the violin: G-B-flat-D-F-sharp-A-C-E-G-sharp-B-C-sharp-D-sharp-F. The advantages are similar to those of composing in D major, the favorite key for violin concertos, where the open strings coincide with tonic, dominant, and subdominant pitches. Moreover, the chordal outlines, usually avoided in twelve-tone row designs, establish a context for accommodation with the tonal system and thereby a support for the traditional materials: the folk song and the Bach chorale.

The tempo plan of Parts I and II offers a broad element of symmetry in its slow–fast–fast–slow pattern. It is reinforced by the appearance in the opening and closing measures of the same motivic material, a series of rising then descending fifths derived from the alternate notes of the row that coincide with the open strings. Meticulous scoring produces a transparent, often ethereal texture in which all gestures can be heard; little is left to interpretive chance. That trait is particularly well illustrated in both sections of Part II, where the climax is indicated not only by the usual dynamics and scoring for the full ensemble but also by a boldly printed *HÖHEPUNKT* (HIGHPOINT) in the text, not to be missed by any performer studying the score. Considering that Berg completed in six weeks a work manifesting such intricacy and multiple levels of meaning, it is understandable that he could comment to Krasner that "I have never in my life worked with such constant industry, and I have taken increasing joy in it."[2]

The tortuous turn of events surrounding the creation of the concerto was matched by circumstances preceding the first performance. The premiere had been scheduled for the 1937 Festival of the International Society for Contemporary Music, but Anton Webern, as officer of the society and the scheduled conductor, was able to reprogram the introduction for 1936, following more closely upon Berg's untimely death. During preparations for the festival, Webern's personal involvement with the concerto, the last work completed by his longtime friend and colleague, was so intense that he became emotionally unable to manage rehearsals. After much delicate negotiation, Hermann Scherchen was brought in to replace Webern and achieved a successful premiere based on only one rehearsal, bolstered by intense behind-the-scenes consultation with Krasner.

Critical assessment of Berg's violin concerto has produced some of the more substantial discussions about contemporary musical style during the middle decades of the 20th century. For a work based on the principles of serialism and atonality, this concerto atypically expands on elements rooted in the tonal system: a tone row formed from triads and concluded by a whole-tone scale, plus an established folk song and Bach chorale as important quoted materials. Some early commentators proposed that, among Schoenberg's students and peers, Berg pursued serial techniques primarily because of Schoenberg's pedagogical influence. The assumption was that, given time, Berg would have returned to a clearly tonal idiom, a hypothesis apparently based on the premise that tonal music was the preferred course for music to follow. Others have seen that same combination of tonal and atonal idioms as fundamentally incompatible, claiming that by definition a work cannot be tonal and atonal at the same time, and therefore the violin concerto, for all of its extraordinary fecundity and craftsmanship, was destined to be an artistic failure.

Much of this discussion must be considered in light of the broader cultural and political tensions that prevailed during the middle of the 20th century, a contest of systems that pitted communism against democracy. In this contest, the supposed conflict between serialism and tonality that many imposed on Berg's violin concerto cast the serial idiom as an element of musical Bolshevism out to destroy the traditions of German counterpoint established during the past three hundred years. Many early performances in Europe ran afoul of the German press, which regarded anything produced by the Schoenberg-

Berg-Webern school as subversive. Others heard the quotation of folk song and Bach chorale as a gesture toward the amalgamation of tonal materials with atonal techniques, but that view failed to recognize the full range of Berg's achievement. With the perspective of time, Berg has emerged as the most enduringly expressive composer of the Schoenberg school. All was grist for his creative mill, an operation that, through meticulous work, could embrace dissimilar materials in an approach to a higher level of musical expression.

Three Pieces for Orchestra, Opus 6

Präludium

Reigen (Round Dance)

Marsch

The first and third of the Three Pieces for Orchestra *were written in the year between August 1913 and August 1914, the second before August 1915. The first and second pieces were first performed in Berlin on June 5, 1923, conducted by Anton Webern as part of an "Austrian Music Week" celebration. The first performance of the complete cycle took place in Oldenburg (Altenburg), Germany, on April 14, 1930, conducted by Johannes Schüler.*

Instrumentation: *four flutes (doubling on piccolo), four oboes (the fourth doubling English horn), four clarinets (the third doubling clarinet in E-flat), bass clarinet, three bassoons, contrabassoon, six horns, four trumpets, four trombones, contrabass tuba, timpani, bass drum, snare drum, fixed and suspended cymbals, large and small tam-tam, tenor drum, triangle, hammer (with a nonmetallic tone), glockenspiel, xylophone, celesta, two harps, and strings.*

The influence of Arnold Schoenberg on those who studied with him extended well beyond the normal relationship between teacher and student. The consuming force of Schoenberg's intellect and personality contributed to a personal dependence that students often were loath to break and that Schoenberg, by all accounts, was quite willing to exploit. Following Schoenberg's departure from Vienna in 1911, Berg was bursting with ambition to write something big, probably a symphony, but announced his musical independence first with a set of five songs based on picture postcard texts by Peter Altenberg (the *Altenberg Lieder*, op. 4) and *Four Pieces for Clarinet and Piano*, op. 5. In early June of 1913, Berg and his wife traveled to Berlin for a visit with the Schoenbergs that provided both composers an opportunity to discuss recent and continuing composition projects. At some time during this visit, Schoenberg evidently criticized Berg's most recent efforts severely, maintaining that they were deficient in both talent and industry. Upon his return to Vienna, Berg wrote an obsequious and frequently quoted letter thanking Schoenberg for his criticism, promising to begin work on the suite that Schoenberg apparently had recommended as an appropriate endeavor. In a subsequent letter, Berg spoke of his struggles with this new project after it was under way:

> Unfortunately I have to confess, dear Schoenberg, that I haven't made use of your various suggestions as to what I should compose next. Much as I was intrigued from the start by your suggestion to write an orchestral suite (with character pieces), and though I immediately began to think of it often and seriously, and did intend to work it out, nonetheless it didn't come about. Again and again I found myself giving into an older desire— namely to write a *symphony*. And when I intended to make a concession to this desire by beginning the suite with a prelude, I found (upon beginning the work) that it again merely turned into the opening of this symphony. . . . Concurrently though, the plan for the suite is sure to mature to the point where I can actually begin writing it, and then your kind suggestion will be realized— though belatedly.[3]

The result of Berg's effort was neither a suite nor a symphony but a little bit of both: the *Präludium* and *Marsch* of the *Three Pieces for Orchestra*.

Berg worked industriously to complete these pieces by late August 1914 in order that they would be ready as a present for Schoenberg on his fortieth birthday on September 13. He was unable to complete *Reigen* until the summer of 1915; when it was finished, he dedicated the complete set to Schoenberg "in unmeasurable appreciation and love." Berg may have intended the *Three Pieces for Orchestra* as a peace offering to assuage the mild rift that had developed with his former teacher, to redeem himself in matters of musical creativity, to show that he took Schoenberg's criticism to heart—or some combination of all these sentiments. Much to Berg's chagrin, Schoenberg never responded to the dedication.

Although written over a period of more than two years and in a sequence different from their final order, the *Three Pieces for Orchestra* cohere through shared musical elements. Moving from the *Präludium* to the *Marsch*, the amount of musical text, calculated by the number of metrical bars in each piece, expands approximately in the ratio of 1:2:3 (56, 121, and 174 measures). In the matter of duration, a more realistic measure of any musical work, the *Marsch* requires slightly more time than the two preceding pieces taken together. The result is a sense of proportionally increasing weight as one moves through the work.

In a set of analytic notes prepared for the first complete performance in 1930, Berg described the three pieces in terms of a fairly traditional symphonic outline: the *Präludium* was to represent the first movement; *Reigen* contained within it the scherzo and slow movement, in that order; and the *Marsch* was to be considered the finale. For all that, he nonetheless indicated in the published score that the first two movements could be performed together without the concluding *Marsch*. He further spoke of an element of binary design as defined by the mirror imagery in *Präludium*, the suggestion of scherzo and slow movement in *Reigen*, and the juxtaposition of the march-like group and the march itself in the third movement. If Berg felt it necessary to describe the three pieces in terms of a symphony cycle, it must have been because that was a familiar and established entity; these works were sufficiently complex to benefit from any familiar element that might be recognized by audiences in 1930.

On first hearing, one of the work's most striking qualities is the range of color produced by a large and meticulously scored orchestra. The balance of timbre gives to the percussion and brass sections a more important role than usual. There also are many passages for some instruments that exist for their timbre alone. This score features one of the most complex textures in all of Berg's works, produced not only by the size of the orchestra but also through the accumulation of motives massed one on top of the other. At several points motives are exchanged between movements, contributing to a broad element of coherence. Berg realized the problems inherent in creating large forms that did not rely on tonality as a unifying element: motivic and thematic organization became sufficiently important to substitute for tonal orientation and, therefore, for the comprehensibility of the musical statement. As an aid to performers, Berg follows the lead of Schoenberg's *Pierrot Lunaire*, first performed in 1912, in identifying primary and secondary lines through graphic symbols designating the *Hauptstimme* (H, or principal voice) and *Nebenstimme* (N, or neighboring, or secondary voice), notations that have been of great aid to performers introducing these works.

Rhythmic patterns often function independently from the motivic or harmonic material that marked their initial appearance; these patterns frequently become autonomous units that may appear at various points in the music to mark important structural junctures. In essence, rhythm begins to function as a separate element, a technique that achieved its most famous application in *Invention on a Rhythm* in Act III of Berg's opera *Wozzeck*, a score that occupied Berg at the same time that he was working on the *Three Pieces for Orchestra*. Rhythmic and motivic units thus function both together and independently, and both are dispersed through different movements as elements of continuity.

The title *Präludium*, a German form of *prelude*, represents perhaps the most obvious connection with the original idea of a suite, yet there is little here to remind one of a dance or of an improvisatory warm-up. The title may be equally misleading in that, through exchange of motivic materials with the other pieces, it represents an integral part of the whole set much more than a literal prelude or introduction. For many listeners the fine gradations of orchestral sound recall Impressionism, a style Berg found very attractive and one in which he was well versed. The music begins with silence from which emerges scratches of sound in the percussion instruments; these in turn merge into tone, the whole operation occupying an eight-measure introduction clearly separated from the body of the movement by a printed caesura. The substance of these eight measures returns at the end of the movement, but in reverse order, as tones diminish to whispers in the percussion instruments, followed by silence. This implied symmetrical balance sets the stage for a larger arch design encompassing the entire movement, with a climax approximately at the midpoint achieved through dynamics and texture.

It is difficult to identify a clear reflection of the title *Reigen* (Round Dance) in the music of the second piece. One writer has suggested that the "round dance" may refer to the dramatic structure of the play *Reigen* by Arthur Schnitzler, which had opened to considerable public scandal in 1912.[4] From a purely musical perspective, the element of dance comes forth in the designation of one of the interim sections as *"ins langsame Walzer tempo"* (in slow waltz tempo), but here again the dynamics (soft–loud–soft) project a broad arch design with a Grand Pause (silence) shortly after the midpoint.

More clearly than most works, the *Marsch* reflects the influence of Mahler in its rhetoric and in some specifics of scoring, particularly Mahler in his Sixth Symphony. At that point in the score marked *HÖHEPUNKT* (HIGHPOINT), Berg calls for three hammer strokes by a large wooden hammer, initially identified among his list of percussion instruments in the score. Mahler included such hammer strokes in the finale of his Sixth Symphony as part of his representation of a worldview; Berg probably introduced the hammer strokes here as a straightforward sonorous enhancement to a complex score. Surrounding the climax, the music is divided into a number of sections that offer an outline for structural design at the same time as they provide relief from the tension created by a continuing accumulation of motives encountered earlier in the score.

In a description that has come to be a part of the Berg canon, George Perle, one of the leading Berg scholars, has described the *Marsch* as a reflection of the social upheaval that was engulfing Europe during the time Berg was immersed in this work:

> The *Marsch* was completed in the weeks immediately following the assassination at Sarajevo and is, in its feeling of doom and catastrophe, an ideal, if unintentional, musical expression of the ominous implications of that event. Fragmentary rhythmic and melodic figures typical of an orthodox military march repeatedly coalesce into polyphonic episodes of extraordinary density that surge to frenzied climaxes, then fall apart. It is not a march, but music *about* a march, or rather about *the* march, just as Ravel's *La Valse* is music in which *the* waltz is similarly reduced to its minimum characteristic elements.[5]

Of all Berg's works, only the opera *Wozzeck* has attracted analysis and commentary more extensive than the *Three Orchestra Pieces*. Just as the cataclysm of World War I represented a major watershed in Western history, these three pieces represented a departure on paths toward new ways of thinking about music in 1915.

Leonard Bernstein

b. Lawrence, Massachusetts, August 25, 1918; d. New York City, October 14, 1990

eonard Bernstein was a multitalented musician who enjoyed
unusual success as a symphony conductor, composer of works
for the concert hall and for the popular musical theater, educator in the broadest application of that term, and pianist. He was edu-
cated at Harvard University and the Curtis Institute in Philadelphia
and later studied conducting with Serge Koussevitzky before becoming
assistant conductor of the New York Philharmonic Orchestra in 1942.
He burst upon the national musical scene on November 14, 1943, when
he substituted as conductor, on a few hours notice and with great success, for the ailing Bruno Walter on a nationwide radio broadcast. The
success of this unannounced debut launched an extraordinary conducting career that eventually included appearances with at least 72 of
the most important orchestras in the United States, Latin America, and
Europe, chief among them the New York Philharmonic, where
Bernstein served as music director from 1958 to 1969, the Boston
Symphony Orchestra, the Israel Philharmonic, and the Vienna
Philharmonic. As a conductor he did much to introduce audiences to
20th-century music and was a particular champion of American composers, giving first performances of works by Elliott Carter, Aaron
Copland, Charles Ives, Carl Ruggles, Roger Sessions, and many of his
own compositions. In the standard repertory, he did more to bring the
symphonies of Gustav Mahler to the attention of the broader public
than any conductor since Mahler himself.

It was also in his role as conductor that Bernstein reached his
largest audience through the *Omnibus* telecasts from 1954 to 1958. In

his subsequent and enormously popular Young People's Concerts he created lively, informative programs appealing to a wide audience, programs so successful that they continue to circulate in print and on video. His success in these activities led many to describe him as an educator, but perhaps *communicator* is a better term; Bernstein was unusually adept at explaining and illustrating music to nonprofessional audiences. He brought that same articulate demeanor to all facets of human activity that concerned him, art, politics, and religion among them.

Bernstein pursued a parallel career—perhaps two parallel careers— as a composer of works for the concert hall and for the American popular musical theater: the Broadway stage. Considering his work list as a whole, it seems that his creative imagination flourished best when it was sparked by some theatrical or textual association. His concert works often touch upon religious themes or spiritual concerns and frequently incorporate biblical or liturgical texts, as in his Symphony No. 1 (*Jeremiah*, 1943), Symphony No. 3 (*Kaddish*, 1961), *Chichester Psalms* (1965), and a theater piece titled *Mass* (1971) written for the opening of the John F. Kennedy Center for the Performing Arts in Washington, D.C., a score that includes elements of the concert hall, the Roman Catholic mass, popular lyric theater, and social concerns of the late 1960s.

Those scores designed specifically for the musical stage offer an amalgamation of contemporary idioms, jazz, dance, extensive syncopated rhythms, and a high degree of integration between music and stage action, as in *On the Town* (1944), *Candide* (1956), and *West Side Story* (1957). Among these, *West Side Story* is recognized around the world as a landmark in American musical theater. His works for the stage collectively represent his best achievement as a composer in their broad appeal, genuinely American idiom, synthesis of popular and classic elements, and coordination between drama and music. In this venue Bernstein set a standard equaled by few composers since Mozart's comic operas of the 18th century.

For many outside the United States, Bernstein's music has given identity to the musical culture of America in its versatility and amalgamation of popular and classical techniques. His family roots lie in Eastern Europe, but all of his training took place in the United States, although as a conductor he worked with the last generation of musical figures trained in Europe. Nonetheless, his own musical style reflects the multiplicity of influences that permeate American life and music. Acting from a position of wide influence, he became a great musical populist of extraordinary talents whose success in reaching the public as conductor, composer, performer, and musical commentator commanded enduring respect in an age not noted for a substantive dialogue between art music and the public at large. Through the breadth and success of his musical endeavors, Bernstein may be known by name more widely than any musician who was active in the last half of the 20th century.

Serenade (after Plato's *Symposium*) for Solo Violin, String Orchestra, Harp, and Percussion

Phaedras: Pausanias

Aristophanes

Eryximachus

Agathon

Socrates: Alcibiades

Bernstein wrote the Serenade *between the fall of 1953 and August 1954. The premiere took place in Venice on September 12 with the Israel Philharmonic Orchestra, Bernstein conducting, Isaac Stern as violin soloist. The work has been choreographed by Herbert Ross and was first performed as a ballet in Spoleto, Italy, on June 13, 1959, by the American Ballet Theatre, Carlo Franci conducting, Salvatore Accardo as violin soloist.*

Instrumentation: *timpani, bass drum, snare drum, tenor drum, triangle, suspended cymbal, tambourine, Chinese blocks, chimes, xylophone, glockenspiel, harp, solo violin, and strings.*

The *Serenade* was conceived as a concerto for Isaac Stern and described as such by Bernstein in a letter written shortly before the completion of the score in the late summer of 1954. In most of the modern concert repertory, the title *Serenade* implies music played by a string orchestra, designed to be entertaining or at least less pretentious than a symphony; in earlier times the title carried the connotation of evening music, also entertaining and perhaps intended as a musical offering for a fair lady. The five-movement format found here was common in such works, a format that may have suggested the title *Serenade* rather than concerto.

On the day after completing the work, Bernstein added to the score an extended program drawing allusions between the movements of the *Serenade* and speeches comprising Plato's *Symposium*, but also gave the disclaimer that there was no program for the *Serenade*, even though it had been inspired by his rereading of Plato. Plato's text consists of five imaginary speeches defining love, all supposedly delivered at the conclusion of a dinner party given by the philosopher Agathon for Socrates and other friends. Bernstein treats the original text with some freedom: Eryximachus gave the second speech rather than the third, as implied by Bernstein's sequence; and the musical apex of the concerto arrives in the fourth movement, while the longest and summarizing speech in the original text is given at the end by Socrates. Bernstein further describes the music as a series of related statements in praise of love, like the speeches in Plato's text, and offers literary allusions for reference. These allusions call for considerable imagination on the part of the listener, but it is clear that for Bernstein the entire effort was a panegyric to love directed to humanity in its broadest manifestation.

The unaccompanied solo violin opens the work with what sounds, on first hearing, as a soliloquy. This theme is subsequently extended in fugal style by the first violins, later the violas, and finally the full string choir before the music embarks on the main body of the movement. This vigorous section expands through a sonata design based on thematic material from the opening *Lento*. That same trait appears throughout the score: each of the following movements evolves in some manner from the movement that precedes it.

In *Aristophanes,* the soloist plays in a musical style quite different from the strings and harp. Much of the solo part occupies a high, sustained lyrical line that goes its own way while the accompanying strings expand on a number of rhythmic patterns. In a midsection played pizzicato by violin, accompanying strings, and harp, the soloist shares in a dialogue with the lower strings but returns to a separate line for the closing section. Bernstein associates the transparent musical texture with Aristophanes as storyteller, invoking fanciful myths of love.

The solo violin and strings enter into a more clearly defined musical dialogue in the third movement, including passages of statement and response. But the prevailing texture consists of rapid passagework played with much vigorous bowing by both the soloist and the orchestral strings, good humor lying just beneath the surface throughout.

Agathon is cast as a straightforward three-part design; for most listeners, its lyricism and thorough craftsmanship have established this movement as the most memorable in the *Serenade*. Above a continuously moving string accompaniment, the soloist plays sustained, lyrical lines in the upper registers of the violin. The midsection is given over to the string choir plus timpani, concluding with a cadenza in double-stops for the soloist that leads to the return of primary material. Grace, élan, and tonal beauty prevail, suggesting, without much imagination, Bernstein's allusion to "Agathon's panegyric [which] embraces all aspects of love's powers, charms and functions."[1]

Socrates' speech was the longest in Plato's text, and that same quality is found in the musical dimensions of the related movement of the *Serenade*. The slow introduction expands at length upon the midsection of the preceding movement before ending in a brief, meditative cadenza for the solo violin. The orchestra shatters this mood with two emphatic *fortissimo* chords, and the music moves off in a rollicking, freely structured rondo. Jazz-like passages provide their characteristic variety and energy; for Bernstein, jazz was not intended as "anachronistic Greek party-music," but as a contemporary American's reaction to the spirit of that timeless party that is life.

The substantive relevance of the text in the *Serenade* remains open to discussion. The composer considered the literary element sufficiently important to have the entire text printed in the score, so it should not be ignored by either performer or listener. Although the music of the *Serenade* does not follow the general outlines of traditional concertos, it nonetheless was written very much in the spirit of that genre and, with or without reference to Plato, offers an entirely satisfactory musical experience through its musical qualities alone. The fourth movement has been frequently described as one of Bernstein's outstanding achievements, the *Serenade* as a whole one of his most enduring works.

As so frequently happened in the reception of Bernstein's music for the concert hall, audiences were enthusiastic while critics were cool, sometimes condescending. Soon after the American premiere, a New York critic opined that the *Serenade*, although attractive in some places, fell short of expectations. But in Chicago the same work was described as "wonderfully salubrious. . . . The kind of thing Haydn might have written if he had lived in New York City in the 1940s."[2] Setting critical evaluations aside, the *Serenade* enjoys a particular niche among Bernstein's concert works as one of his few compositions for solo instrument and orchestra.

Divertimento for Orchestra

Sennets and Tuckets

Waltz

Mazurka

Samba

Turkey Trot

Sphinxes

Blues

In Memoriam—March: "The BSO Forever"

Bernstein completed the Divertimento *for Orchestra during August of 1980. It was first performed at Symphony Hall in Boston on September 25, 1980, by the Boston Symphony Orchestra, Seiji Ozawa conducting.*

Instrumentation*: two piccolos (the second doubling third flute), two flutes, two oboes, English horn, two clarinets, E-flat clarinet, bass clarinet, two bassoons, contrabassoon, four horns, three trumpets, three trombones, tuba (doubling baritone euphonium), timpani, bass drum, four snare drums, two conga drums, three bongos, set of traps, four temple blocks, cymbals, large cymbals, suspended cymbal, tam-tam, triangle, tambourine, wood block, two Cuban cowbells, sandpaper block, rasp, maracas, chimes, glockenspiel, xylophone, vibraphone, piano, harp, and strings.*

Bernstein wrote the *Divertimento* for Orchestra to fulfill a commission by the Boston Symphony Orchestra celebrating the orchestra's centennial in 1980. As a native Bostonian, he must have taken pride in contributing to this commemoration of an orchestra that had opened the doors to symphonic music to him during his youth. The score carries the inscription "Dedicated with affection to the Boston Symphony Orchestra in celebration of its First Century."

The title, traditions, and musical character of a *divertimento* are most appropriate for a commemorative event. These works have long been associated with diversion, as the name implies, appropriate for entertainment or a festive occasion. Most of the movements present a titular reference to pleasant proceedings or to inherently American traditions. All of them include in some manner the two-note motive B–C, a musical acronym for **B**oston **C**entenary, a subtle musical reference to the event for which the work was commissioned.

The eight-movement sequence is divided into two halves of four movements, each comprising two movements of full orchestra and quick tempo surrounding two inner movements of slower tempos and reduced orchestration. The musical balance is entirely comprehensible and aurally satisfying on the basis of tempo and timbre; the changing musical styles and motivic integration (various manifestations of the rising half-step from B to C) add to this sense of order when perceived but do not detract from it when they are not.

Musical characterization of the individual movements is as concise as the basic motive itself, some of them lasting less than a minute. The title *Sennets and Tuckets*, an archaic term for trumpet fanfares signaling a stage entrance, is well chosen for an opening movement that, in its character, is an extended and jazzy flourish involving full orchestra. The atypical seven-eight meter of the *Waltz*, for strings alone, very likely is a parody of the equally unusual five-four meter of the waltz movement from Tchaikovsky's Sixth Symphony, one of the most successful movements in that work and one of Bernstein's favorites as a conductor. The composer's immersion in Beethoven's Fifth Symphony shows itself near the end of the *Mazurka*, scored for double reeds and harp, when the graceful but morbid harmonies give way to a quotation of the famous oboe solo from the first movement of that work, a tongue-in-cheek gesture addressed perhaps to the performers as much as to the audience. *Samba* closes the first half of the *Divertimento* as the percussion section leads the full orchestra in a salute to Latin dance rhythms. *Turkey Trot* continues the spirit of ethnic dancing with a stylized tribute by full orchestra to American folk dance. With only one phrase for strings and a second for winds, *Sphinxes* maintains the appropriate tradition of mystery for less than sixty seconds. The *Blues* could not be described otherwise, and a languorous solo trumpet pays eloquent tribute to Bernstein's immersion in and facility with American popular idioms. *In Memoriam* and *March* directly address the traditions of the Boston Symphony Orchestra. Three flutes playing a meditation in canon represent conductors Charles Munch, Serge Koussevitzky, and the other personalities no longer present, while the *March: "The BSO Forever"* draws on the works that were a feature of Arthur Fiedler's famous Boston Pops concerts. In keeping with traditions associated with John Philip Sousa and continued in spirit by Fiedler, the piccolo and brass sections are instructed to stand for the rousing finale so that the *Divertimento* concludes with an appropriate flourish of musical *joie de vivre*.

Audiences were delighted by the *Divertimento*, and its popularity has continued in the decades following its first performance. Critics were less impressed and for the most part considered the work an essay in musical entertainment. Some thought the work too much of a trifle for the occasion, but nearly all acknowledged the technical skills inherent in the score and its probable durability in the lighter orchestral repertory, a prophecy that has been fulfilled.

Chichester Psalms

Maestoso—Allegro molto—Dolce tranquillo

Andante con moto—Allegro feroce

Sostenuto molto—Adagio—Lento possibile

This dramatic choral work was composed during April and May 1965 on commission from the Very Rev. Walter Hussey, Dean of Chichester Cathedral, England. It was first performed in New York on July 15, 1965, by the Camerata Singers, conducted by Abraham Kaplan, and the New York Philharmonic Orchestra, conducted by Bernstein, John Bogart, tenor. The first performance of the original version, designed for male chorus, countertenor or boy alto, three trumpets, three trombones, bass drum, snare drum, triangle, wood block, temple blocks, tam-

bourine, three bongos, cymbals, suspended cymbal, whip, rasp, glocken-
spiel, xylophone, chimes, two harps, and strings, took place at
Chichester Cathedral, England, on July 31, 1965, with the combined
choirs of Chichester, Winchester, and Salisbury Cathedrals, plus person-
nel from the Philomusica Orchestra of London.

In a reflection of Britain's long tradition of choral singing, the cathedral choirs from Chichester, Winchester, and Salisbury each year join in a festival featuring choral music both old and new (not to be confused with the better-known Three Choirs Festival, which involves groups from Gloucester, Worcester, and Hereford). Bernstein was commissioned to write the *Psalms* for the 1965 festival at Chichester. The work was dedicated to his personal friend and physician, Cyril Solomon, who had served as intermediary in securing the commission.

In May 1965, Bernstein wrote to Dean Hussey of Chichester Cathedral to describe the work he proposed, explaining a change in title (the original was *Psalms of Youth*) and requesting permission to include the work on an all-Bernstein concert in New York with an adult mixed choir and the New York Philharmonic Orchestra. Apparently permission was granted, or at least it was not refused, so the original version for male chorus and boy's voice was retained for Chichester, although the world premiere of an adapted version took place in New York a few weeks earlier. The distinctive sound of all-male voices in the original version is supported by an orchestra without woodwind instruments, a combination of timbres that contributes much to the unique sonorities of this work.

Bernstein had chosen sacred texts for other major works for the concert hall and in all of these, the *Psalms* included, the interaction of text and music inspired some of his most intensely personal writing. Each of the three movements of *Psalms* includes the Hebrew text of one complete psalm and a portion of another: the first movement begins with Psalm 108, verse 2 and continues with all of Psalm 100; the second opens with Psalm 23 and concludes with two verses of Psalm 2; and the third presents Psalm 131 plus the first verse of Psalm 133.

The musical elements of *Psalms* grew from several roots. During the previous year, Bernstein had taken a leave from his conducting responsibilities with the New York Philharmonic Orchestra in order to revitalize his creative energies and more specifically to come to grips, as a composer, with the questions posed by serial music, a style of composition near or slightly past its apogee in 1964 and 1965. The firm harmonic orientation of *Psalms* has been interpreted as a reaffirmation of his own commitment to tonality, a move heralding the trends in musical style in the later years of the 20th century. Structurally, the work is framed by a motive derived from a melodic pattern in the music for High Holy Days, a descending fourth followed by a major or minor second (F–C–B). This same motive occurs elsewhere in Bernstein's works, giving rise to some debate about its role as a subconscious expression of faith or as an element reflecting Bernstein's craft of composition.

Assuming melodic permutations, the basic motive appears in the opening measures of the first movement in both orchestral and vocal parts, again at the introduction of Psalm 100 (*Hariu l'Adonai kol haarets* [Make a joyful noise unto the Lord]), and in the orchestra in the closing measures. A snappy rhythm with seven quick beats per measure dominates the last part of the movement, offering multiple possibilities of rhythmic groupings that recall some of Bernstein's most characteristic writing for the musical theater. Psalm 100, which provides most of the text for the first movement, is best known to American audiences as the genesis for the psalm tune "Old One Hundredth" in the tradition of American psalmody, a tune widely known and sung throughout the United States.

In the second movement, the shepherd's harp reflects the pastoral qualities of the 23rd Psalm (*Adonai roi* [The Lord is my shepherd]). Even more emphatic text painting marks the entry of the tenors and basses (*Lamah rag'shu goyim* [Why do the nations rage?]), a passage that could give meaning to any expression of anger in music.

The basic motive introduces a sustained chorale to open movement three, and here again an unusual metrical pattern—units of ten—creates considerable rhythmic flexibility. The music continues in a sustained mood until the end, where the unaccompanied chorus sings a variant of the opening chorale (the basic motive once again). The closing folds in upon itself with music and text of noble tranquility (*Hineh mah tov, Umah nayim, Shevet ahim Gam yahad* [Behold how good, And how pleasant it is, For brethren to dwell together in unity]).

Dean Hussey of Chichester Cathedral had suggested to Bernstein that they would be pleased if the commissioned work would show some hint of the musical style of *West Side Story*. As the work emerged, the clergyman received more of American musical theater than he realized. The disruption of the second movement by the tenors and basses singing *Lama rag'shu goyim* (Why do the nations rage?), originated as a chorus cut from the Prologue to *West Side Story* with the text "Make a mess of 'em! Make the sons of bitches pay." Other sections derive from the unfinished musical *The Skin of our Teeth.* Composers have always adapted material designed for one work into another composition when circumstances warranted; the difference here is the contrast of venue for which the musical was intended and that in which it finally came before the public, a condition that again underlines Bernstein's position as a synthesizer of musical styles.

Chichester Psalms met with immediate and widespread acceptance; few of Bernstein's works for the concert hall have weathered critical review so well. Certainly the texts are timeless, and the musical style has proven to be an enduring mix of popular and classical idioms.

Orchestral Works Derived from Music for the Theater

By the middle of the 20th century, American popular musical theater had grown sufficiently in sophistication, technology, and musical traditions that it bore little resemblance to its roots in stage production such as *The Black Crook* (1866) or the musical reviews from the turn of the century. The practice of building a show around a continuing narrative or plot, one developed by writers of considerable stage experience and set to music by composers whose musical skills equaled those heard in concert halls, had produced stage productions that were difficult to define. They were too cohesive to be called *revues,* too serious to be identified as *musical comedy* (although comic scenes were still included), usually less pretentious than *opera,* and too much involved with music to be called *musical plays.* The favored descriptive term that emerged was the *Broadway Musical,* or, in the interests of efficiency, *The Musical,* with uppercase initials appropriate and intended. This popular entertainment had grown into an art form that represented some of the best achievements in musical theater. Many observers drew parallels with the 18th century, when comic opera grew to rival *opera seria* in its success with the public, and found a great champion and model in some of the late works of Mozart.

On October 7, 1956, Leonard Bernstein devoted the fourth of his *Omnibus* telecasts to the subject of American musical theater, claiming

that contemporary conditions were ripe for a modern Mozart to come
forward and forge a new style of musical theater with a new and appropriate name. He was echoing the 18th-century poet Christian Martin
Wieland, who had voiced similar thoughts about the German *Singspiel*
in 1775, before Mozart's most famous essays in that genre had come
into being. With Bernstein the public declaration may have been self-
serving, because two of his major achievements in musical theater,
Candide (1956) and *West Side Story* (1957), were to open in New York
within a year of his *Omnibus* telecast. Bernstein was thoroughly
immersed in the problem of spawning a new type of musical theater
and searching for ways to educate the public, and accomplished all of
this in a thoroughly American endeavor. Most critics agree that
Bernstein's musicals have indeed established a new standard for popular musical theater; certainly they are among the most successful ventures in that direction we have from the 20th century.

Overture to *Candide*

Bernstein began collaborating on a musical setting of Voltaire's Candide
*in 1954, working to a book by Lillian Hellman with lyrics by Richard
Wilbur, John la Touche, Dorothy Parker, Hellman, and Bernstein himself. The first performance took place in Boston on October 29, 1956,
with Samuel Krachmalnick conducting; the first concert performance of
the Overture was given in New York on January 26, 1957, by the New
York Philharmonic Orchestra with Bernstein conducting.*

Instrumentation*: two flutes (the second doubling piccolo), oboe (doubling English horn), two clarinets in B-flat (the first doubling clarinet in
E-flat, the second doubling bass clarinet), bassoon, two horns, two
trumpets (the first doubling cornet), two trombones, tuba, timpani,
bass drum, snare drum, tenor drum, suspended cymbal, crash cymbals,
triangle, high-hat, tambourine, gong, ratchet, whip, two wood blocks,
cowbell, maracas, gourd, bongos, steel drums, brake drums, castanets,
chimes, xylophone, glockenspiel, harp, and strings.*

The Overture to this literary farce turned musical is one of the few parts
of the original score to retain its identity, reflecting a performance history of this musical setting of Voltaire's picaresque tale that could well
become a story in itself. The original setting was not a great success

with the public; it closed in New York after 73 performances. In retrospect it was generally agreed that the show suffered from being too much like an opera for Broadway and too much like popular theater to succeed as opera. Some of the problems probably lay in a plot too sophisticated for audiences expecting facile entertainment, disregarding that such sophistication provided the very core of Voltaire's text. Lillian Hellman's adaptation leaned toward psychological development with undertones of social commentary, while Bernstein was writing witty, ebullient music appropriate for a fast-moving, easily accessible entertainment. To resolve these fundamental problems there were cuts, revisions, and more cuts, with the result that the production lost its focus and became a piecemeal sequence of double-entendre wit set to music ranging from brilliant to superficial. It was unclear whether to expect an opera, an operetta, a parody of opera, a bit of moralizing commentary, or a more traditional Broadway musical, however any of those might be defined. The show contained elements of all these but established identity with none, no matter the creative talents involved. Attempts to salvage both the music and script led to many later reconstructions; by 1990, there had been at least seven different versions of *Candide*, including efforts on both sides of the Atlantic.

Some critics thought the music was the most brilliant Bernstein had written, certainly some of his most original, and the score became the star of the show, the Overture its most sparkling point of light. Apparently conductors agreed, for in its first two years the Overture was performed in concert by nearly a hundred different orchestras. It is now among the half-dozen most frequently performed orchestral works by a 20th-century American composer.

In its musical substance the Overture could best be called a sonatina—a statement of three identifiable themes, a restatement of that same material without significant intermediate development, and a closing coda. The first theme is little more than a fanfare; the second reminds one of a cancan with strident, satirical woodwinds; and the third derives from a lyrical duet between the two principal characters, "Oh Happy We." Following a brief orchestral extension, these same materials return, now in the tonic key. One of the most famous songs from the score, the coloratura aria "Glitter and Be Gay," provides material for a rousing coda.

There is little reason why an overture to any work for the popular

stage needs to follow traditional designs, but the ingenious craftsmanship through which Bernstein creates this small sonatina is so
smoothly exercised that the whole takes on a quality of spontaneity. As
with many musical works, technical mastery by the composer provides
the basis for enduring musical vitality, here carried out so artfully that
the craftsmanship passes unnoticed.

Music for *Fancy Free*

Blues: "Big Stuff"

Enter Three Sailors

Scene at the Bar

Enter Two Girls

Pas de deux

Competition Scene

Three Dance Variations: Galop, Waltz, Danzon

Finale

Blues: "Big Stuff"

Bernstein completed the score for the ballet Fancy Free *in April 1944
to fulfill a commission from Ballet Theatre (now American Ballet
Theatre). Choreographed by Jerome Robbins, it was first performed at
New York's Metropolitan Opera House on April 18, 1944, with the
composer conducting.*

Instrumentation*: two flutes (the second doubling piccolo), two oboes,
two clarinets, two bassoons, four horns, three trumpets, three trombones, tuba, timpani, bass drum, snare drum, cymbals, suspended cymbal, triangle, wood block and cowbell (optional), piano, and strings.*

Fancy Free was Bernstein's first ballet score, spawned during the concert
season of 1943 to 1944 that included so many successes for him as both
conductor and composer. His own scenario set the scene in wartime
New York, 1944. Three sailors explode onto the stage, in town on
24–hour leave and on the prowl for girls. The ballet depicts their adven-

tures as they meet first one girl, then another, fight over them and lose them, only to leave the scene in pursuit of a third.

The music Bernstein produced to complement Robbins's choreography was symphonically conceived, making it possible to present the ballet score as an independent work without revising it for the concert hall. That same quality doubtless contributed to the original success of the ballet with audiences who were accustomed to hearing ballet music in a role subordinate to stage activity. The music continues without interruption throughout and, broadly considered, is noteworthy for both its shape and its musical characterization, "shape" referring to the planned distribution of materials and "characterization" to the distinctive traits of the individual numbers in the ballet. Before the curtain rises a phonograph (or jukebox) plays a vocal blues titled "Big Stuff," its husky lament interrupted by four percussive rim shots. This, Bernstein's own blues song, assimilated the vocal style and harmonic idiom of blues into a compressed combination of the traditional 12-bar blues structure and the A–A–B–A design of American popular music. The jukebox excerpt played at the opening performance had been recorded by Bernstein's sister, Shirley, making her debut in show business with this performance of her brother's blues song. (Several years later, Bernstein included Billie Holiday singing "Big Stuff" in a recording of the *Fancy Free* score by the Ballet Theatre Orchestra for Decca Records, and he sang "Big Stuff" himself in a recording of the work by the Israel Philharmonic.) The song returns at the conclusion of the ballet and serves as the basis for the *Pas de deux*, thus providing an element of integration through references to the same material at the beginning, middle, and end of the score. Principal musical materials from the first dance number also return near the conclusion of the *Finale*, drawing on both musical and choreographic references and confirming the musical shape of the score.

Within this context, separate numbers emerge with considerable individuality, originally conceived to support the choreography but composed in a manner that, separated from the dancing, establishes them as musical character pieces. The entry dance realizes in musical terms the brash swagger of young males out to "do the town." The *Scene at the Bar* and the entry of the two girls change style appropriately, and the *Pas de deux* elaborates on both the structure and melodic material of "Big Stuff." The *Three Dance Variations* offer three pronounced opportunities to develop individual choreography, and in the process the movement introduces three national dance styles—the French *galop*, the German waltz, and the Spanish *danzon*—all highly stylized but all drawing on the musical traits of their models. The *galop*, for example, retains the rapid duple meter that marked it as a fast and furious finale for European balls around the mid-19th century. Variation 2 opens and closes with the graceful triple meter of a waltz, but most of the number is concerned with the quality of grace more than with a literal reproduction of waltz rhythms. The *danzon* reflects its Cuban heritage through unmistakable Latin rhythms, involving frequent shifts between rhythmic groupings of two and three. Continuing in the spirit of national dances, the closing number opens with a headlong rush typical of the Italian *saltarello*, although it is not so identified, with the rapid six-eight meter prevailing until interrupted by quotations from the two opening dances.

The idea for a ballet that would portray the energy of three sailors on leave in New York through stylized social dances originated with Jerome Robbins in 1943. He first approached Vincent Persichetti, also a student at the Curtis Institute in Philadelphia in its early years, but Persichetti was not comfortable with jazz, and Robbins's search ultimately led him to Bernstein. That first meeting must have been electric. According to several accounts (all admittedly originating with the two principals), when Robbins explained his idea, Bernstein countered with a tune he had just that day jotted down while at lunch; he played it for Robbins, who "went through the roof" with enthusiasm, and the ballet *Fancy Free* took root. The two had much in common; both were the sons of Russian-Jewish fathers who were opposed to their sons' careers in the arts, and both were afire with the possibilities of musical theater in an American mold.

Bernstein wrote the music in a matter of months in spite of prior commitments by both parties that required extensive traveling. Much of the score was composed on trains, in restaurants, or wherever and whenever time would allow. Bernstein adopted a plan of recording completed sections in a two-piano version with Aaron Copland, forwarding that recording to Robbins, who would respond with comments, and adjustments would follow accordingly.

Unlike most of Bernstein's creations, *Fancy Free* was an unqualified success with both audiences and critics. "Big Stuff" proved to be a shocking opening in the hallowed atmosphere of the Metropolitan Opera House, but audiences were soon standing in line for admission. The *New York Times* described it as "more than terrific," and *Time* magazine wrote enthusiastically about the variety, energy, and imagination reflected in the dancing. The ballet was presented some 160 times during its premiere year and became a hallmark of Ballet Theatre productions. This enthusiastic reception was all the more noteworthy considering that the overwhelming cataclysm of World War II was then entering its closing stages, a time when the public concern ordinarily would not be focused on any ballet, much less one featuring three dancing sailors. Perhaps a score expanding on jazz rhythms, jazz piano playing, the blues, and American sailors on the streets of New York somehow invoked an inherently native idiom appealing to a public hungry to identify with any facet of America ascendant.

Symphonic Suite from *On the Waterfront*

The music was originally composed as a film score between February and May 1954, and revised as an independent orchestral work in 1955. It was first performed at Tanglewood on August 11, 1955, by the Boston Symphony Orchestra, Bernstein conducting.

Instrumentation*: two piccolos, two flutes, two oboes, four clarinets (including E-flat clarinet and bass clarinet), alto saxophone, three bassoons (the third doubling contrabassoon), four horns, three trumpets, three trombones, tuba, timpani, bass drum, snare drum, three tuned drums, two tam-tams, cymbals, wood block, triangle, chimes, glockenspiel, xylophone, vibraphone, piano, harp, and strings.*

The Symphonic Suite from *On the Waterfront* is much more of a symphonic poem than it is a suite: the music proceeds without interruption from beginning to end and for the most part grows from the metamorphosis of motives heard at the beginning. The score originated as an attempt by Bernstein to save some of the material he had written for Elia Kazan's movie *On the Waterfront* after editing had removed a major portion of the music from the final sound track.

Following his successes in composing music for the stage works *Fancy Free, On the Town*, and *Wonderful Town*, Bernstein had declared disinterest in attempting a film score. Considering that the best music for a motion picture is that which is not consciously heard, he maintained that the medium offered little inducement for an imaginative composer. But at the urging of producer Sam Spiegel, Bernstein attended a showing of *On the Waterfront* and was captivated by the dramatic intensity of the script and the talent displayed by director Elia Kazan and a cast including Marlon Brando, Eva Marie Saint, Lee J. Cobb, Karl Malden, and Rod Steiger. By his own account, he heard music as he watched, and the collective talent of the actors provided even further inspiration to him, so he took the assignment. It was too good to pass up. The scene is centered around a grim and crime-ridden waterfront, the extortion and racketeering that permeated organized labor on the docks, and the challenges facing one longshoreman (Marlon Brando) as he confronted these conditions.

While Bernstein's musical responses to the film came readily, the technical matters of assembling and coordinating the score offered their fair share of difficulties. In his own account of the proceedings at "Upper Dubbing, California," a reference to the dubbing room at Columbia Studios where sound and film tracks were synchronized, Bernstein described the process:

> Sometimes there would be a general decision to cut an entire piece of music out of the picture because it seemed to "generalize" the emotional quality of a scene, whereas the director wished the scene to be "particularized." Sometimes the music would be turned off completely for seconds to allow a line to stand forth stark and bare—and then be turned on again. Sometimes the music, which had been planned as a composition with a beginning, middle, and end, would be silenced seven bars before the end.
>
> And so the composer sits by, protesting as he can, but ultimately accepting, be it with a heavy heart, the inevitable loss of a good part of the score. . . . It is for the good of the picture, he repeats numbly to himself: it is for the good of the picture.[3]

On the Waterfront was shown at the Venice Film Festival in 1954, where the screening was repeatedly interrupted by applause. The film won seven awards from the Academy of Motion Picture Arts and Sciences in 1954, equaling the previous record held by *Gone with the Wind*. Bernstein's music was not among those parts of the film recognized by the Academy. He received $15,000 for his work, and created the Symphonic Suite from materials excised from the film score, but this remained his only essay into film music.

This score remains the longest uninterrupted piece of music in Bernstein's catalogue. Other works may encompass more time, but they are built from a series of clearly articulated sections. The music was symphonically conceived, and most materials follow the chronological flow of the film score. The integration of the whole through the trans-formation of the opening motives creates an entirely unified score, comprehensible in its own dimensions. We hear an opening soliloquy by horn and flute, a virile percussion section for piano and timpani, a long melodious section referring to the opening material, often described as the "love theme," a vigorous *allegro*, and a recall of the opening motives announced by vibraphone and celesta. The motivic unity of the whole work is one of its most pronounced features, most easily grasped following a second or third hearing.

In retrospect, the Symphonic Suite has outlived the film from which it emerged in that it has become a part of the frequently per-formed symphonic repertory. In his enthusiasm for Bernstein the man and for this work in particular, the Russian conductor-cellist-composer Mstislav Rostropovich remarked that the "Suite from *On the Waterfront* I have conducted many, many times, and the music *smells* of the United States. But it is a good smell!"[4]

Symphonic Dances from *West Side Story*

"Prologue"—"Somewhere"—"Scherzo"—"Mambo"—"Cha-Cha"—
"Meeting Scene"—"Cool Fugue"—"Rumble"—"Finale"

West Side Story *grew from an idea by Jerome Robbins realized in the book by Arthur Laurents to lyrics by Bernstein and Stephen Sondheim, their collaboration progressing irregularly from initial discussions in 1949. The completed work was first performed in Washington, D.C., on August 19, 1957. The Symphonic Dances drawn from that score were assembled and orchestrated by Bernstein with Sid Ramin and Irwin Kostal, and first performed in New York on February 13, 1961, by the New York Philharmonic Orchestra, Lukas Foss conducting.*

Instrumentation: *piccolo, two flutes, two oboes, English horn, two clar-inets, E-flat clarinet, bass clarinet, alto saxophone, two bassoons, con-*

trabassoon, four horns, three trumpets, three trombones, tuba, timpani,
bass drum, snare drum, traps, four pitched drums, three bongos, tom-
tom, timbales, tenor drum, cymbals, triangle, gourd, three cowbells,
congas, police whistle, two suspended cymbals, finger cymbals, cas-
tanets, small and large maracas, tambourine, chimes, wood block,
claves, temple blocks, slide whistle, ratchet, gourd, glockenspiel, vibra-
phone, xylophone, piano/celesta, harp, and strings.

It is appropriate that an excerpt from *West Side Story* concludes a discussion of Bernstein's works for musical theater. While it was not the
last of his endeavors in that venue, it topped the others in its popular,
artistic, and commercial success. This was the work that carried his
name around the world as a composer, to an extent that Bernstein more
than once expressed despair that he would be remembered for this
score and nothing else.

Jerome Robbins's initial plans for a contemporary setting of *Romeo*
and Juliet accounted in large part for the central role choreography came
to play as the production took shape. Certainly the subject was viable.
From the time of the classical tale of Pyramus and Thisbe, the tale of
two lovers coming from competing families, known by whatever names,
had been the basis for at least 85 settings as opera or ballet by the time
Bernstein and his companions decided to address the subject. Those
companions comprised a stellar group. All but Stephen Sondheim had
established major reputations in their fields, documented not only by
significant artistic success and the accompanying public visibility but
also by awards from professional groups acknowledging the distinction
of their work. Sondheim was less well known, but his promise was well
fulfilled here and in subsequent works. Robbins acknowledged the
problems inherent in bringing together four talents of this caliber, and
in later years claimed that their purpose was to produce an American
musical, determining in the process whether they could combine their
considerable talents and complete a work on a classical subject in a relevant popular style.

The work encountered significant growing pains. Casting went on
for six months, some performers auditioning as many as twelve times
for one of several roles for which they were qualified by age and physical appearance. The problems lay in identifying applicants who could
both dance and sing. After much experimentation, it was deemed best

to find dancers who could be taught to sing rather than trying to train singers to dance. Bernstein's vibrant music won plaudits from all who heard it, but it did not fit conventional patterns and, combined with the rigorous dance numbers, it required extensive rehearsals. The original title was *East Side Story* but, with the demolition of slum areas on the east side of Manhattan, the title was changed to *Gangway!* and much later to *West Side Story*. As problems loomed, several potential producers turned away; they recognized the artistic promise of the show but anticipated financial failure. Any stage production involving music readily generates problems in production, but *West Side Story* had to surmount more than its share.

In this contemporary setting of the *Romeo and Juliet* story, the Jets, a self-styled American street gang with Tony as one of their older members, confront the Sharks, a rival Puerto Rican gang whose leader, Bernardo, has recently been joined in America by his younger sister, Maria. Doc, the neighborhood druggist whose store sometimes serves as a common meeting ground for the gangs, recalls the character of Friar Lawrence from Shakespeare's setting. Tony and Maria enter into a touching teenage romance but become entangled in the violent street warfare of the Jets and Sharks. The gang conflict leads to the death of Bernardo and, in reprisal, the death of Tony as the final curtain falls. The play closes with Maria's wrenchingly poignant monologue on the futility of such strife.

The reception accorded *West Side Story* produced one of the great successes of mid-century musical theater. The popular press reported the production in detail, conveying clearly that the triumph was largely Bernstein's from opening night forward. The show continued for more than seven hundred performances, then toured nationally before returning to New York for an additional 253 performances. A cinematic version won even greater fame, earning ten awards from the Academy of Motion Picture Arts and Sciences, one of them for best picture of the year. Sales of the sound track from the film set records, and the complete show circulated through countless copies of home videocassettes. The rehearsals for a later recording with professional opera singers were filmed and telecast as a separate program, and the record produced by that effort came to be regarded as a classic.

Many elements contributed to the extraordinary success of *West Side Story*: Jerome Robbins was one of the most effective directors and choreographers of his day; Arthur Laurents produced a book that is still regarded as a model of compressed drama; and the lyrics of Sondheim and Bernstein (the composer collaborated in this part of the venture as well) were topical, idiomatic, and humorous. Nonetheless, Bernstein's musical score remained paramount, to which the Symphonic Dances stand in mute testimony. He was able to bring to bear thoroughgoing technical skills and a depth of experience unusual among other composers for the popular stage. His score is by turns a virtuoso display of rhythmic vitality, harmonic coloration, and poignant lyricism, all connected by a few integral musical motives—among them the interval of the augmented fourth, a calling card for this score—and principal melodies that permeate the score in different shapes.

The youthful cast responded with a level of virtuosity rarely achieved. They successfully executed Robbins's most difficult dances, sang Bernstein's highest notes, and projected one of the theater's most poignant dramas. Bernstein had learned from his experiences with *Candide* that opera and popular musical theater were different venues and were not ready for a synthesis in the 1950s. *West Side Story* expanded the potential inherent in this medium. It set a new model and was much more of a unified whole than most shows before the public. But the prevailing tenor of musical shows has not changed, a few works by Andrew Lloyd Weber notwithstanding, and the genre at large has not yet led to a tradition of vernacular opera. In retrospect, these conditions highlight all the more prominently the artistic achievements of *West Side Story*.

As a collection of excerpts, the Symphonic Dances are well named, considering the importance of choreography in the original production. The music remains unchanged from the original except in the sequential order. "Somewhere" appears near the beginning rather than in its original location before the finale. The contrasts between the dance numbers as they are identified in the orchestral work illustrate another factor in the show's success: the wide range of musical styles presented. The "Prologue" gathers musical momentum and moves toward increasing dissonance as members of the rival gangs gradually gather on stage, the increasing dramatic tension prominently reflected in the music, while the strident sound of the augmented fourth sounds an ominous and central motive. The nostalgic lyricism of "Somewhere" stands in stark contrast to the opening, and becomes one of several key melodies that returns in a transformed guise later in the score. "Mambo" depicts the athletic dancing of the Puerto Ricans at the dance held in the gymnasium, as does "Cha-Cha," which follows, but here we encounter a musical anticipation of Tony's song, "Maria," which later became one of the two or three songs identifying this score for listeners everywhere. "Meeting Scene," a backdrop for the meeting of the two gangs to establish the ground rules for their street fight, also grows from "Maria," identified by the signature interval of a rising augmented fourth. "Cool Fugue" expands on that same motive over suggestions of "Somewhere" in the bass. The music for "Rumble" continues this process of linking musical elements, when material from the "Prologue" and "Cool Fugue" combine as music and action rise to a frenzy.

The Symphonic Dances share with the original score a pervasive unification in that both short motives and longer melodies appear in various transformations in different numbers; at the same time, the dances differ sufficiently in character to provide lively variety.

Benjamin Britten

❧

b. Lowestoft, United Kingdom, November 22, 1913;
d. Aldeburgh, United Kingdom, December 4, 1976

In the context of the 20th century, Benjamin Britten has emerged as a composer who developed his own creative techniques without following a recognized school or the dominant influences of a master teacher. While he could not be described as an iconoclast in any fundamental sense, in the middle decades of the century he was one of the most thoroughly original composers to hold the interest of the musical public. At least some of that originality grew from his thoroughly English musical heritage or, some would say, the lack of it. England had produced several important composers in the early part of the century—Edward Elgar and Gustav Holst are the best known—but the preceding centuries had witnessed no flourishing talents native to England that would match the level of those active in Germany, Italy, France, and the remnants of the Austro-Hungarian Empire centered around Vienna. Britten developed without a direct line of musical tradition and was free, or perhaps forced, to develop his own musical voice. He could draw on any sources suiting his purposes, and in that process he created music that was accessible to audiences around the world.

One of his chief accomplishments was the regeneration of English opera through the success of his works *Peter Grimes* (1945), *Billy Budd* (1951), *The Turn of the Screw* (1954), *A Midsummer Night's Dream* (1960), and *Death in Venice* (1973). Much of his success in the opera house came from his pervasive sense of lyricism and grasp of English prosody. He was by no means a slave to convention in matters of text setting. By his own account he felt that traditional accentuation based on the sense of a text often contradicted stress patterns demanded by emotional content; he therefore did not avoid unnatural stresses if the dramatic situation warranted them. Often his works were written for small ensembles, sometimes because of economic restraints but more frequently generated by the needs of a specific commission. Many of his later compositions were thus inspired, and he was always ready to shape his ideas to meet the needs of the moment. For Britten, each composition represented a special musical problem, often profitably resolved through his musical eclecticism.

Deteriorating political conditions in Europe prior to World War II led Britten to emigrate to the United States in 1939, and it was there that he composed his first major work for orchestra, the *Sinfonia da Requiem*. Perhaps the most important development during his sojourn in America was a confirmed homesickness for his native land and an enduring commitment to things British. He began efforts to return in the fall of 1941, but wartime travel conditions delayed his departure until well into 1942. Upon his return, Britten established his status as a conscientious objector to active participation in warfare and through special dispensation was able to continue appearances throughout England as pianist and conductor. In the postwar years, Britten was occupied with many of the stage works that confirmed his international reputation. His masterpiece was the *War Requiem*, written to celebrate the consecration of the rebuilt Coventry Cathedral in 1962. Another major endeavor was the establishment in 1948 of the Aldeburgh Festival, a yearly event that draws performers and audiences from around the world. Britten's artistic accomplishments and musical contributions to his native land were recognized by many awards, among them a life peerage conferred shortly before his death.

Sinfonia da Requiem, Opus 20

Lacrymosa—Dies irae—Requiem aeternam

Britten fashioned the score of the Sinfonia da Requiem *from April through June of 1940. It was first performed in New York on March 29, 1941, by the New York Philharmonic Orchestra conducted by John Barbirolli.*

***Instrumentation**: three flutes (with doublings on piccolo and bass flute), two oboes, English horn, two clarinets, bass clarinet, two bas-*

*soons, contrabassoon, alto saxophone (*ad libitum*), six horns (fifth and
sixth horns* ad libitum*), three trumpets, three trombones, tuba, timpani, bass drum, snare drum, cymbals, tambourine, whip, xylophone,
two harps (second harp* ad libitum*), piano, and strings.*

Although Britten wrote the *Sinfonia da Requiem* during the time he lived
in the United States, it does not reflect any element of musical
Americana. The work lies well within the traditions of Western concert
music, drawing on traditions of personal expression, carefully executed
musical cohesiveness, and elements of inspiration from the broad character of texts in the Latin mass for the dead.

As England began to come under aerial attack in 1940, Britten
became increasingly worried about the welfare of family members he
had left behind. His concerns were intensified, it seems, by a sense of
guilt over his own absence from his homeland at a time of national
stress. On September 21, 1939, Ralph Hawkes, of the firm Boosey &
Hawkes, Britten's publisher, cabled the composer that the British
Council had inquired about Britten's interest in a commission for a
full-scale orchestral work. Britten affirmed his interest the following
day, with the provision that no jingoism would be required. His personal convictions as a conscientious objector to the war then engulfing
Europe would have given him cause to be wary of any commitment
requiring support for a bellicose foreign policy. In a letter of September
23, Hawkes gave the details of the commission that had been conveyed
to him only a day earlier: the Japanese government had asked that an
English composer write an orchestral work to be performed at a concert
in Tokyo celebrating the 2,600th anniversary of the Japanese Empire.
The requirements were usual and straightforward, including a stipend
ranging from £115 to £540 (a handsome fee for 1939), depending on
the type of work submitted, and the stipulation that the score must
arrive in Tokyo no later than May, 1940. Britten responded in October,
asking that at least a portion of the fee be paid in advance, and saying
that he had "a scheme for a short Symphony—or Symphonic poem.
Called Sinfonia da Requiem (rather topical, but not of course men-
tioning dates or places!) which sounds rather what they would like."[1]
Apparently no further word was immediately forthcoming, because on
December 7, 1939, Britten wrote to Hawkes that he had given up hope
of anything materializing from the proposed commission. For reasons

that remain unclear, there was considerable delay in confirming the agreement, although the Japanese officials announced the event in some detail.

> Promoting international friendship through the medium of music, Europe's leading composers are writing symphonic works which they will dedicate to Japan and in which the 26th centenary of the Japanese Empire will be glorified, it was revealed Saturday night.
>
> Through their diplomatic envoys stationed in Japan, the governments of several nations have expressed the desire to contribute toward the celebrations being held in the course of this year throughout the Japanese Empire, and proposed to have their leading composers write symphonic works for the occasion.
>
> Thus far, it has been decided that Richard Strauss, of Germany; Jacques Ibert, of France; Ildebrando Pizzetti, of Italy; Sándor Fellesz [Veress], of Hungary; and Benjamin Brittain [*sic*], of England, [will] dedicate their compositions to Japan.[2]

Writing of the matter retrospectively the following November, Britten claimed to have communicated a description of the proposed work to his publisher on March 30, 1940. On April 7, he wrote to a friend that the commission from the Japanese government was before him and that he was planning a work with plenty of peace propaganda in it. He soon complained about the pressure of writing a symphony in about three weeks, saying that he "only heard officially on Friday," adding that "I should have written the work anyhow—it is a Sinfonia da Requiem, combining my ideas on war & a memorial for Mum & Pop."[3] All this suggests that Britten may have had earlier plans for some sort of composition combining his antiwar sentiments with a memorial to his parents, and the commission from the Japanese presented an opportunity to carry out those plans.

The symphony was completed before June 11, 1940. After an extended silence, during which it became apparent that all was not well, Japanese officials rejected the *Sinfonia da Requiem* in a diplomatically worded letter forwarded in early November 1940:

> Mr. Benjamin Britten's composition is so very different from the anticipation of the Committee which had hoped to receive from a

friendly nation felicitations expressed in musical form on the 2,600th anniversary of the founding of the Japanese Empire.

We are afraid that the composer must have greatly misunderstood our desire or that we did not understand each other fully enough.

It seems to us that this is a composition in the nature of a "Requiem Symphony" composed in memory of the composer's own parents and does not express felicitations for the 2,600th anniversary of our country.

Besides being purely a religious music of Christian nature, it has [a] melancholy tone both in its melodic pattern and rhythm making it unsuitable for performance on such an occasion as our national ceremony.

We are puzzled and should like to ask that you make further inquiry in this matter. Meanwhile the Committee will hold Mr. Britten's composition.

> Yours very truly,
> Prince Fuminaro Konoye[4]

It remains unclear why the problem would not have come to light earlier. Prince Konoye was the brother of Viscount Hidemaro Konoye, founder of the New Symphony Orchestra of Tokyo, the ensemble that was to perform the ceremonial concert. Viscount Konoye had spent many years in Germany, was well versed in Western musical traditions and literature, and presumably would have been in touch with the Japanese committee through his brother.

The response from Britten and his publishers evidently required considerable effort and several drafts, but Britten replied personally on November 27, 1940, to the Japanese Vice-Consul in New York:

I must say at once that I am grievously shocked and hurt by the contents of the letter. My position in regard to the matter is quite clear.

At no time did the committee give any indication of wishing for some special kind of work, and they were informed of the nature of the work and its titles at the end of March through the British Council in London.

Mr. Konoye objects to the Christian nature of the work. If this is his real objection, it is difficult to understand why the committee ever commissioned a work from a composer who is a member of a Christian nation.

Mr. Konoye calls the work melancholy. This is, of course, a matter of opinion, though I cannot but feel that he has not examined the score very carefully and has possibly been misled by his perhaps false idea of what the title means. An examination of the structure of the music would dispel any doubts as to its real nature. The conflict of the first two movements, one a slow march, the other a desperate dance, moves to a solution in the final movement which is one of peace and quiet rejoicing.[5]

On the same date, Britten wrote to Hawkes describing the substance of his letter, declaring that there had never been any question about the nature of the work. Britten's response irritated Hawkes, who found himself in the midst of a diplomatic brouhaha at a time when relations with Japan were becoming increasingly strained. He described to Britten some of the procedural matters that went awry but took him to task for what he described as a flippant attitude toward the matter and Britten's omission of the appropriate diplomatic courtesies in his letter to the Japanese official.

Britten's later comments offer some insight into his own view of the matter. After the *Sinfonia da Requiem* had been performed in New York, he wrote to his sister describing the premiere. "Well—I have produced my first Symphony (the Requiem one, in memory of Mum & Pop, paid for by the Japanese government—nice touch that—don't you think?). . . ."[6] Still desirous of clarifying the whole affair, Britten described in a published letter his initial response to the Japanese:

The reply to this was definitely in agreement to my conditions, but for six months I waited for the actual contract. When this finally arrived I was working on the "Sinfonia da Requiem," which was a tribute to the memory of my parents. Owing to this delay I was left with something like six weeks in which to complete the required symphony, and I replied that the only work I could provide in the time would be the said "Sinfonia da Requiem." I discussed the suitability of the work with the local Japanese consul, indicating its nature, and telling him that each movement had a Latin title—Lachrymosa, Dies Irae, and Requiem Aeternam. He communicated, I presume, with his ambassador and I was notified that the work was considered entirely suitable. I accordingly completed the score, delivered it to the consul, and for at least six months heard no more.[7]

Britten's account here differs slightly from his description of matters in his early correspondence with several parties, so the composer may have contributed his fair share to whatever misunderstandings developed. Both the Japanese government and the publisher Boosey & Hawkes glossed over the details of the failed commission; the Japanese implied that the score had not arrived in time to be included in the scheduled concert, and the publisher printed only the bare outlines of the matter in a press release issued prior to the first performance in New York.

Even without knowledge of Britten's original conception and the dedication to his parents, the title *Sinfonia da Requiem* suggests something more than an abstract symphony. The Latin titles taken from the Requiem Mass carry with them characteristic moods that serve as a point of departure for the music. The sorrowful anguish of the *Lacrymosa* text, pleading for deliverance on that final day of weeping, speaks with an eloquent voice through the melody and prevailing syncopation of the first movement. Similarly, the agitation of the *Dies irae* texts, addressing the fearsome aspects of the final day of atonement, spawns music best described as controlled chaos, and the eternal rest implicit in texts of the *Requiem aeternam* also finds here appropriate musical expression.

Britten displayed an uncharacteristically casual attitude to the instrumentation, designating use of the alto saxophone, extra horns, and harp as *ad libitum*. In preparation for a concert he was to conduct in Chicago in November 1941, he was delighted with the extra woodwinds that were available to him, and inquired whether the alto saxophone and extra horns could also be provided, although he claimed that they were not absolutely essential. It is not clear whether this accurately reflected his musical intent or whether it was a diplomatic gesture acknowledging the scarcity of extra instruments in a concert supported by the Work Projects Administration in the closing years of the Great Depression. The *ad libitum* designation for the alto saxophone is particularly puzzling because at several places in the score the instrument plays melodic lines doubled by no other unit of the ensemble.

Considered as a whole, the three movements of the symphony offer considerably more than a conventional sonata, scherzo, and finale. They describe a balanced musical arch with two quiet movements surrounding an agitated inner scherzo, all three adhering to the tonal center D. This consistency of tonal reference throughout multiple movements is one of the most successful examples of monotonality among major orchestral works of the 20th century. Triple meter also underlies all three movements, although different tempos and rhythmic groupings avoid any sense of metric repetition.

Following a series of smashing, percussive tonic accents, the *Lacrymosa* embarks on a slow, lugubrious march built around three motives: a syncopated theme of sequential units introduced by the cello; a stately theme harmonized with widely spaced intervals introduced by the horns and woodwinds; and a series of two-note motives exchanged between flutes and trombones. In the *Dies irae,* the flutes play the principal material, incorporating an unusual tremolo figure that Britten advises the winds to play with flutter tonguing whenever practical (again we encounter an "if possible" attitude rather than dogmatic specificity in the scoring). The music progresses through a series of climaxes, the last and most powerful bringing about a dissolution of the musical activity and an uninterrupted flow into the closing *Requiem aeternam,* which, by contrast projects peaceful resolution, even resignation. The flute introduces the principal theme in the opening measures over an undulating figure of wide intervals played by both harps. The strings play an intense, long-breathed, contrasting melody before the flutes return with the introductory motive, which ultimately fades to a whisper in the clarinets.

The complete work incorporates considerable thematic integration. Varied treatments of the principal theme of the *Lacrymosa* appear in some guise throughout the score. The motive played by the saxophone at the close of the first movement returns, much faster and in retrograde, to create the scampering patterns played by the violins through most of the *Dies irae,* and that same motive becomes a part of the flute theme in the *Requiem aeternam.* These subtle musical links, usually perceptible only through careful analysis, are the result of Britten's meticulous craftsmanship.

The *Sinfonia da Requiem* represents one of several touchstones in Britten's career. It was his first large, independent orchestral score. It represented a major step in the melding of his technical skills and creative powers, all put on paper in a relatively short span of time, and therefore became one of several works to which most of his later composition were compared.

Immediate reactions to the *Sinfonia* in the press embraced a curious mix of opinions. Some reviews of the first performance in New York were inconclusive, but one offers an example of the difference in perception between critics and audiences:

> The pronounced weakness of the entire composition was its pitiful lack of emotional warmth. That the instruments wailed and shrieked in the "Lachrymosa" failed to make the music there communicative, because nothing more was suggested than merely the wailing and shrieking of instruments. The "Dies Irae" was conceived as a "Dance of Death," but it was simply wild and noisy, with no suggestion of terror or any other human or superhuman connotation. Piling up climaxes was the chief form of procedure in both movements, climaxes just for their own sake.
>
> The "Requiem Aeternam," the best part of the whole, was in three-part song form, with a placid melody as its chief theme that at times verged on real emotional utterance, but never achieved it. All of the symphony was knowingly contrived and often quite individual in its color effects. And it brought a prolonged ovation for the composer, who bowed his acknowledgement from the platform.[8]

Following several later performances, Britten described to his sister a general response that, in his opinion, had been more positive:

> In every case much applause (three or four calls for me at each performance of the Symphony)—the reaction of the intellectual composers has been bad (I am definitely disliked (a) because I am English (no music ever came out of England) (b) because I'm not American (everything is nationalistic) (c) because I get quite alot [*sic*] of performances (d) because I wasn't educated in Paris—etc. etc.)—the reaction of the press mixed—usually the respectable papers (like the Times) bad or puzzled—the rag papers or picture papers good—funny, isn't it—[9]

Reviews of a performance in Chicago in November described the *Sinfonia* as uninteresting and incomprehensible. Britten described these as "pretty catty," but left no doubt that this was the attitude he expected from American journalists.

Comments in the press following the first performance in England on July 22, 1942, were much more favorable, but with some interesting twists. Critics agreed that Britten demonstrated his mastery of orchestration and the craft of composition, but Jack Westrup, one of the most distinguished British scholars of the time, feared "that the technique had become an end in itself and that invention . . . had been left to take care of itself."[10] This in turn elicited further responses from supporters in praise of Britten's craftsmanship. Nonetheless, the *Sinfonia da Requiem* entered the domain of the concert hall, gaining fairly quickly a popularity with audiences that it retained through the end of the century.

The Young Person's Guide to the Orchestra, Opus 34
(Variations on a Theme of Purcell)

Britten wrote The Young Person's Guide to the Orchestra *during December 1945, completing it on New Year's Eve. It was first performed at Liverpool on October 15, 1946 by the Liverpool Philharmonic Society, Sir Malcolm Sargent conducting.*

Instrumentation: *piccolo, two flutes, two oboes, two clarinets, two bassoons, four horns, two trumpets, three trombones, tuba, timpani, bass drum, snare drum, cymbals, tambourine, triangle, Chinese block, castanets, gong, whip, xylophone, harp, speaker* ad libitum, *and strings.*

Britten's most frequently performed instrumental work was rooted in his earlier work as a film composer. Originally it was composed for the Crown Film Unit's educational documentary, *Instruments of the Orchestra*, produced by the British Ministry of Education and first screened under that title on November 29, 1946, at the Empire Theater, London. For an earlier performance in Liverpool as a concert work, the producer, Eric Crozier, had added a brief commentary. With that spoken text, the work assumed its enduring title, *The Young Person's Guide to the Orchestra*, dedicated to the four children of John and Jean Maud, personal friends of the composer.

The project was initiated at a time when England was commemorating the 250th anniversary of the death of one of her greatest composers, Henry Purcell. It was probably with that event in mind that Britten turned to Purcell's incidental music for the play *Abdelazar, or The Moor's Revenge* (1695) as a source for something that would honor Purcell and provide a platform for Britten's skill as an orchestrator. Without the spoken commentary, *The Young Person's Guide to the Orchestra* was identified on many BBC broadcasts by its structural content, *Variations and Fugue on a Theme of Purcell.* Britten objected consistently and strenuously to this title. The score is properly known by the title *The Young Person's Guide to the Orchestra,* with others sometimes offered as subtitles.

An introductory statement of Purcell's theme by the full orchestra precedes four strophes, one each played by the principal choirs of the orchestra—woodwinds, brass, strings, and percussion—concluded by a full-orchestra reprise of the ten-measure theme. Each of the thirteen variations that follow focuses on specific instruments of the orchestra—piccolo and flutes, oboes, clarinets, bassoons, violins, violas, cellos, double basses, harp, horns, trumpets, trombones and tuba, and percussion—each variation comprising a short character piece that expands on one or more elements from Purcell's theme. Some are miniature masterpieces of design or color. Note the fourth variation, for bassoons, in which the opening motif appears in triadic outline but with jerky rhythms, dissolves into a six-measure dialogue, then returns to the original motif, but now inverted, the whole variation an approximate mirror of itself. The final variation introduces individual members of the percussion battery—timpani, cymbals, bass drum, tambourine, snare drum, wood block, xylophone, castanets, and the whip—presenting the basic material in a kaleidoscope of timbres.

The fugue expands on a subject by Britten drawn from Purcell's theme, the instruments of the orchestra presenting the subject in the same order in which they entered in the variations. This carefully planned counterpoint culminates in a dignified statement of Purcell's theme by the brass, embellished by Britten's fugue subject played by the strings and woodwinds.

The ready accessibility of *The Young Person's Guide to the Orchestra* gave rise to at least three settings as a ballet: *Oui ou Non? (Ballet de la Paix),* by the Association des Amis de la Danse (1949); *Fanfare,* by the New York City Ballet (1953); and the descriptively titled *Variations on a Theme of Purcell,* by Sadler's Wells (1955).

Britten's mastery of orchestration and his abiding interest in the music of Henry Purcell both come to the fore in *The Young Person's Guide to the Orchestra.* The expectations aroused by the title have led some to criticize the work as being too straightforward, even simpleminded, while others, working from the same assumption, have thought the score too sophisticated. It is as much a composer's guide to orchestration as it is a listener's guide to the instruments of the orchestra.

War Requiem, **Opus 66**

Requiem aeternam

Dies irae

Offertorium

Sanctus

Agnus Dei

Libera me

Britten began work on the War Requiem *during the winter or early spring of 1961, completing the compressed draft the following December. It was first performed at Coventry in St. Michael's Cathedral on May 30, 1962, with soloists Heather Harper, Peter Pears, Dietrich Fischer-Dieskau, the Coventry Festival Chorus, City of Birmingham Symphony Orchestra, Melos Ensemble, and the boys' choirs of Holy Trinity, Leamington, and Holy Trinity, Stratford, conducted by Meredith Davies (full orchestra) and Britten (chamber orchestra).*

Instrumentation*: three flutes (the third flute doubling piccolo), two oboes, English horn, three clarinets (the third doubling clarinet in E-flat and bass clarinet), two bassoons, contrabassoon, six horns, four trumpets, three trombones, tuba, timpani (four players), bass drum, two snare drums, tenor drum, tambourine, triangle, cymbals, castanets, whip, Chinese blocks, gong, bells, antique cymbals, vibraphone, glockenspiel, piano, organ, three soloists (soprano, tenor, and baritone), four-part mixed chorus, boys' choir, and strings, with an additional chamber orchestra of flute (doubling piccolo), oboe (doubling English horn), clarinet, bassoon, horn, timpani, bass drum, snare drum, cymbals, gong, harp, and strings.*

Few works composed during the 20th century achieved the immediate and lasting success accorded Britten's *War Requiem* by both critics and audiences. Even before the work had been performed publicly, it was described as a masterpiece by those privy to the compressed vocal score.

These reactions were inspired by the masterful score, created by a composer at the height of his creative and technical strengths. The selection of texts, their subject matter and interactions, all reached audiences at a time when memories of World War II were still vivid and tensions generated by escalating hostilities in Southeast Asia sufficient to raise fears about another global conflict.

The *War Requiem* was written in response to a commission for a major choral work to mark the consecration of the rebuilt St. Michael's Cathedral in Coventry. The city had suffered extensive damage during the Battle of Britain, and the destruction of its famous cathedral loomed in the minds of many British citizens as a stark reminder of the horrors of that experience and the enormity of all war. Britten was first approached in 1958 and readily accepted the commission. For some time he had been contemplating a requiem of some sort. The commission resolved the special musical problems attendant on this venture by providing a specific occasion for its composition; at the same time, it offered Britten a chance to give voice to his personal outlook on war. This would become a requiem for war in general, a plea for the demise of all warfare as well as a memorial to those killed in battle. The printed score carries a dedication to four personal friends of Britten who fought in World War II: Roger Burney, David Gill, and Michael Halliday, all of whom lost their lives in the conflict, and Piers Dunkerley, a survivor who died by his own hand in 1959, at a time when the *War Requiem* was in the planning stage.

In searching for texts that would contrast the pleading of the traditional requiem text with the violence of modern warfare, Britten was drawn to the *War Poems* of Wilfred Owen, an articulate pacifist killed on November 4, 1918, one week before the armistice ending World War I. He added to the title page of the *War Requiem* three lines from the *Preface* to Owen's collection:

> My subject is War, and the pity of War.
> The Poetry is in the pity. . . .
> All a poet can do today is warn.

Owen's *Strange Meeting*, a poem in which the spirit of a British soldier confronts that of a German he has killed in battle, formed a major part of the *Libera me*. The dialogue in the text suggested two male soloists; that decision made, the remaining eight poems by Owen were divided between those soloists (tenor and baritone). Musical balance suggested a female soloist for the other texts, and the boys' choir was added to support the higher *tessitura* of the soprano and to add a musical backdrop of implied innocence. As the work progressed, Britten began to regard the three solo singers as representatives of the three countries that had suffered heavily in World War II: England, Germany, and Russia. He later carried this a step further by creating solo parts for specific performers from those countries: Peter Pears, English tenor and Britten's longtime companion; the famous German baritone Dietrich Fischer-Dieskau; and Galina Vishnevskaya, wife of the Russian cellist Mstislav Rostropovich, with whom Britten had gradually developed a warm personal and professional friendship. Russian authorities would not allow Vishnevskaya to leave the country at the time of the premiere, so the soprano part was first performed by Heather Harper. It was not until a recording session in early January 1963 that Britten was able to hear the work performed by all the singers for whom he had created the solo parts.

The final ensemble, large enough to call for two conductors, creates three planes of musical expression: the calm of the Latin liturgical texts praying for peace after death, sung by boys' choir supported by organ; texts of mourning and supplication, often apprehensive, sung by soprano soloist, large choir, and full orchestra; and poems that cry out against war by those who are its immediate victims, sung by the two male soloists with chamber orchestra. At first glance it would seem that such a division of musical labor would lend itself well to the concertato writing of a concerto grosso, and there is an element of that process in this section. But more important are the texts themselves and the sensitive orchestration that gives them their musical poignancy.

As a purely sonorous unit, the tritone F-sharp—C sounds throughout the *Requiem*. If one wishes to identify a single pervasive motive for the work, this, heard both harmonically and melodically, would be a viable candidate. It appears in the opening measures of the *Requiem aeternam*, returns in imitative entries, becomes a static setting for much of the choral text, appears as a prominent melodic interval in the tenor solo, serves as a consistent point of return played by the orchestral bells, and finally sets up the distinct closing cadence for the first movement, where it unexpectedly shifts to a quiet F major. That same cadence concludes the *Dies irae*. The tritone C-sharp—G reflects the tonal relationships between the introduction to the *Offertorium,* for boys and organ, and the contrapuntal corpus of that movement. For the introduction to the *Sanctus,* the tuned percussion instruments (vibraphone, glockenspiel, antique cymbals, orchestral bells, and piano) play in tremolo the tritone F–sharp–C in support of the tenor's solo incantation. The conclusion of this monumental work, the final cadence of the *Libera me,* repeats the sliding tritone cadence first heard at the end of the *Requiem aeternam.* Rather than a modern "fixed idea," as in Berlioz, or leitmotiv in the tradition of Wagner, the tritone, distinctive in its static neutrality, becomes an element very useful in coordinating the disparities of musical materials and performing resources that comprise the *War Requiem.*

The musical impact of the *Agnus Dei* far exceeds its compact design. The tenor solo, accompanied by chamber orchestra, alternates with the threefold *Agnus Dei* sung by the chorus with full orchestra in a dialogue of text and timbre. The *Libera me* continues this mood, gradually accelerating into an erratic march as the double basses play a slower version of the accompaniment to the first of Owen's poems. The reprise of the closing cadence from the *Requiem aeternam* and *Dies irae* offers a striking summation of the work, its condensed simplicity a marked contrast to the dense scoring of the *Requiem's* closing pages.

Comparisons with earlier settings of the requiem text by Berlioz, Cherubini, and Verdi have become common, and Britten acknowledged the inevitable presence of such historical precedents: "I think that I would be a fool if I didn't take notice of how [earlier composers] . . . had written their Masses. I mean, many people have pointed out the similarities between the Verdi *Requiem* and bits of my own *War Requiem,* and they may be there. If I have not absorbed that, that's too bad. But that's because I'm not a good enough composer, it's not because I'm wrong."[11] Similarities between Verdi and Britten reflect two composers responding with similar musical techniques to the setting of the same Latin text. Beyond that, Britten has expanded both the musical and textual frame of reference by adding, much like medieval tropes, poetry from the modern age to address a modern musical conception.

The reception accorded the *War Requiem* was so enthusiastic that some of those contributing to the avalanche of praise soon began to question their own critical assessment. There had been so much ballyhoo, so many quick references to the work as a masterpiece prior to the first public performance, that many critics began to draw back.

Moreover, it was difficult to separate the music from its subject matter, and who would be willing to be caught in a negative stance against a work decrying war in favor of peace? The first performance at Coventry, and many others at locations of wartime destruction (Dresden, Halle, Tokyo, and London), aroused sentiments that extended well beyond musical responses alone. There were also claims that Britten's technical facility as a composer sometimes substituted for, or in some degree compromised, his musical inspiration. The composer was apparently the victim of his own success!

At an early point in the creative process, Britten claimed that he was writing what would become one of his most important works, and as the *War Requiem* became more widely known, critical sentiment shifted strongly toward the composer's early perception. It quickly entered the repertory, and some critics considered it one of the outstanding musical works to come from England at any time. In its own way, the public was equally eloquent in its response. Upon the release of the first commercial recording by Decca Records in early 1963, it sold more than 200,000 copies in five months, an extraordinary initial sale for concert hall music in any style. The score later became the basis for a film of the same title directed by Derek Jarman, first screened in London on January 6, 1989, to broad acclaim.

There is little question that considerations beyond the purely musical played a role in the enduring success of the *War Requiem* around the world and particularly in England. It is noteworthy that a work that in many ways attacked the establishment in mid-century became, by the end of the century, one of the most frequently performed choral works representing the century as a whole.

Orchestral Works Derived from Music for the Theater

Four Sea Interludes from *Peter Grimes,* Opus 33a

Dawn

Sunday Morning

Moonlight

Storm

Britten began addressing the problems of the libretto for Peter Grimes
*in 1942, but composition of the score was delayed until the period
between January 1944 and February 1945. The completed opera was
first performed in London on June 7, 1945 by the Sadler's Wells
Opera, Reginald Goodall conducting. The* Four Sea Interludes *were
introduced as independent excerpts at the first Cheltenham Festival on
June 13, 1945, with Britten conducting the London Philharmonic
Orchestra.*

Instrumentation*: two flutes (both doubling piccolo), two oboes, two
clarinets (the second doubling clarinet in E-flat), two bassoons, contrabassoon, four horns, three trumpets, three trombones, tuba, timpani,
bass drum, snare drum, cymbals, gong, tambourine, xylophone, bells,
harp, and strings.*

Peter Grimes was another landmark in Britten's career. On the English
musical scene, it represented some return to normalcy following the
disruption of World War II. But perhaps more important, its extraordinary musical qualities and resounding success marked the first of a
series of operas by Britten that would establish a foundation for the
revival of English opera around the world. Since the works by Henry
Purcell in the late 17th century, English opera had faltered and succumbed to the operatic productions of Italy and Germany. The country's own literary classics had been turned into operatic masterpieces by
Verdi, but no English composer had been able to compete.

Britten's first ideas about composing *Peter Grimes* arose during his
years in the United States. Following a performance of his *Sinfonia da
Requiem* by Serge Koussevitzky and the Boston Symphony Orchestra on
January 2, 1941, while Britten was awaiting transportation back to
England, Koussevitzky, always a beneficent champion of new works,
asked Britten why he had written no operas. The composer replied that
he could not undertake such a project while faced with the immediate
necessity of earning a living. The outcome of this exchange was a commission for $1,000 from the Koussevitzky Music Foundation for an
opera, a commission Britten completed almost exactly three years later.

The plot derives from *The Borough*, an extended poem by the 18th-
century English poet George Crabbe, whose works Britten had encountered while visiting in California. (Crabbe's writing in general and the
evocation of the Suffolk coastline in particular would eventually

become major factors in Britten's decision to return to England.) The poem describes life in a small seaside fishing village. Peter Grimes is a brutish, lonely fisherman who stands accused of the maltreatment and, over several years, the successive deaths of two young apprentices. His only supporter in the community is the local schoolmistress, whose friendship he rejects until he can establish respectability in the eyes of the local populace, in his eyes a status to be achieved only through material wealth. In Grimes's hurried preparations to reach a large shoal of fish and the profit it represents, his second apprentice falls to his death from the fisherman's hut by the sea. The villagers form their own conclusions about Grimes's responsibility for this tragedy. They pursue him through the moors and swamps until he is near madness with fear and exhaustion, at which point he is advised by a village elder that there is only one way out: he must take his boat to sea, scuttle it, and go down with the ship.

The libretto by Montagu Slater sets the story in a Prologue and three acts of two scenes each; to cover scene changes and gaps in time, Britten wrote an orchestral Interlude to precede each of the six scenes, the origin of the *Four Sea Interludes*. The first of these, *Dawn*, separating the Prologue and Act I, expands upon three motives: a unison, high-pitched line played by violins and flutes; an arpeggiated figure played by clarinet, harp, and viola; and a chordal passage that follows in the brass. These are repeated and subsequently developed as the overlapping presentations of the first two motives are interrupted by two chordal passages played by the brass, the whole subsiding after sustaining a contemplative mood throughout the music.

Sunday Morning sets the mood for the second act: the schoolmistress sits by the sea with Grimes's second apprentice, urging the lad to describe his difficulties with his master, while in the background the sunlight glistens on the waves and the church choir intones segments of a hymn. The music opens with the horns playing a series of interlocking harmonies, recalling the church bells of a small town, and continues with detached punctuation by the woodwinds. References to the opening motive of *Dawn* return, and the music subsides on a sustained E-flat, as far removed from the original tonic of A as is possible in the context of acoustic harmony. *Moonlight* opens the third act as an evocative orchestral number relying on precise orchestration (notice the echo effects divided between the flutes and harp) that creates a broad arch of sound, beginning and ending quietly with an apex of orchestral texture and volume at approximately its midpoint. Broadly conceived, all the movements are programmatic in that they depict scenes on the stage, but *Storm*, which in the opera appears between the two scenes of the first act, is the most vividly descriptive of the four. Drawing on material from the first scene, the musical intensity expands through climaxes depicting the increasing rage of a coastal storm, ending with a resounding orchestral thunderbolt.

A *passacaglia*, the interlude connecting the two scenes of the second act, also came to assume its own identity as an independent orchestral work, although it appears with less frequency than the *Four Sea Interludes* as they were introduced by Britten a few days following the opera's premiere. Within the context of the opera, the *Interludes* provide dramatic continuity; musically they bind the score together in that they frequently include material already heard or suggest themes that are yet to appear. Thus they are thoroughly integrated with the libretto as well as with the musical score. This quality of integration plays a large part in the high regard the music of *Peter Grimes* has enjoyed since its introduction.

Aaron Copland

❧

b. Brooklyn, New York, November 14, 1900; d. North Tarrytown, New York, December 2, 1990

By his own account, Aaron Copland's early years were very unpromising for the development of a composer. His parents, both Russian immigrants, met in the United States and subsequently established their home in a Brooklyn neighborhood populated largely by other immigrant families. Aaron was increasingly drawn to music through his own discoveries at concerts; by the age of sixteen, he was vaguely aware that he wanted to compose. The strongest influence on his musical development was his departure for France in 1921, initially to study at the American Academy at Fountainbleau and later with the famous pedagogue Nadia Boulanger in Paris.

Copland's return to the United States in 1924 coincided with the gradual emergence of a distinctive school of American composers. Copland proved to be the most articulate propagandist for their mutual cause: recognition by their contemporaries as valid creative artists. It became his goal to establish a connection between music and the life that surrounded him. At the time there existed no established style recognized as quintessentially American, a style that spoke for this nation and no other. Charles Ives had been active up to 1922, but the neglect of his works made them well outside the mainstream of musical discourse, and jazz was still on the musical periphery. It should be acknowledged that America has never been free from musical influences external to her national boundaries, but with Copland's early works American concert hall music found a voice and began to assume an identity as music that represented something of a common denominator for the multifaceted American culture.

To establish his own creative voice, Copland turned to jazz, folk, and hymns, and, to a lesser degree, Latin American dance rhythms. He had discovered jazz while in Europe rather than in his native New York, and the rhythms of this new music began to appear in his concertos for piano and clarinet and some scores for the theater. His travels to Mexico in 1932 and his extended tours of Latin America on behalf of the United States government in 1941 and 1947 brought him into contact with a broader range of American culture, most clearly represented in his popular *El Salón México*. Further, the ballet scores for *Billy the Kid, Rodeo,* and *Appalachian Spring* unabashedly drew on cowboy songs and hymns as indigenous artifacts of American musical life. Some critics chose to interpret these references as a pursuit of popular images and commercial techniques designed as a quick means of currying favor with a broad public. It would be more accurate to say that Copland adjusted his musical language to reflect his environment and the audience he wanted to reach, and that he remained consistent in that quality throughout his creative life.

Copland received many awards, citations, grants, and honorary degrees. From 1951 to 1952, he was invited to present the Charles Eliot Norton Lectures at Harvard University, the first native-born American composer so honored. His notes for those lectures later appeared as one of his widely read books, *Music and Imagination* (1952). During the last half of the 20th century Copland was customarily cited as "The Dean of American Composers," a term of admiration recognizing the corpus of music he had produced, its identity with American culture, and the influence he exerted on other American musicians. For many he is the most significant American composer of the 20th century, an assessment that might be debated but cannot be dismissed.

Third Symphony

Molto moderato—with simple expression

Allegro molto

Andantino quasi allegretto—

Molto deliberato (Fanfare)—Allegro risoluto

Copland composed his Third Symphony between July 1944 and September 1946. It was first performed in Boston on October 18,

1946, by the Boston Symphony Orchestra under the direction of Serge Koussevitzky.

Instrumentation: *piccolo, three flutes (one doubling second piccolo), two oboes, English horn, two clarinets, bass clarinet, two bassoons, contrabassoon, four horns, four trumpets, three trombones (the third doubling tuba), timpani, bass drum, snare drum, tenor drum, tom-tom, cymbals, slapstick, ratchet, anvil, claves, tubular bells, xylophone, glockenspiel, celesta, two harps, piano, and strings.*

When Copland began his Third Symphony, the undertaking represented a turn to absolute music after nearly a decade devoted to music for ballet and films, scores based on extramusical associations. The impetus for this work came from a commission from Serge Koussevitzky, facilitated through the Koussevitzky Music Foundation. Always a champion of young American composers, Koussevitzky's introduction of Copland's Third Symphony was the culmination of twelve such premieres he conducted with the Boston Symphony Orchestra and one of many performances he gave of new American works. It is no surprise that Copland worked to produce a score whose broad outlines he thought would match Koussevitzky's expectations. He acknowledged that he "knew exactly the kind of thing he [Koussevitzky] liked to conduct and what he wanted from me for the occasion. I was determined that this piece be a major work."[1]

Although much of his earlier work had drawn on indigenous American music, Copland made it clear that the Third Symphony contained neither folk nor popular material, and that any reference to folk materials or jazz was unintentional. Beyond that, he offered his own descriptive analysis of the symphony as a broad musical arch in which the two outer movements, linked by shared thematic materials, frame a central portion consisting of two markedly contrasting inner movements: the second movement, following the outline of a scherzo and trio; and the *Andantino*, a much more languid and freely designed slow movement.

The first movement expands on three themes, the first played by the violins in the opening measure, the second presented shortly thereafter by English horn and viola, and the third announced by the trombones over a murmuring string accompaniment. The first and third themes return in the last movement as connective musical references.

There follows a second section that builds on those two themes, not so much a development as a restatement in a different key and with increasingly dense orchestration. A third section serves as a quiet coda, ending with the principal theme played in open octaves as it was in the beginning, a gesture that eventually concludes the symphony.

By contrast, the following *Allegro molto* meets the traditional expectations for a scherzo in both its structural design and its spirited activity. The first theme is much like a fanfare, its opening motive permeating the musical fabric through a number of transformations. A sustained unison on F, marked *sff* for full orchestra, marks the transition to a midsection whose theme exudes an American folk idiom, even though it represents no quotation of a known folk tune. The return to the principal section follows as expected, but this is no literal restatement. The themes are much expanded, accompanied by a machine-like reiteration of the opening harmonies, and lead to a dramatic ending punctuated by the motive that opened the movement.

At the beginning of the *Andantino,* the violins, playing in unison in their high register, present a rhythmic transformation of the third theme from the first movement. This in effect serves as an introduction for several linked sections based on a theme introduced by the solo flute. The music unfolds until the opening returns, now projected by flutes and violin harmonics that lead without interruption into the finale, the longest movement of the symphony and the one that follows most closely the outlines of a customary sonata design. This closing movement opens with a free adaptation of Copland's *Fanfare for the Common Man* (1942), played first by the flutes, restated more loudly by the brass, and, finally, by the full orchestra, emphatically introducing motives that will permeate much of the music to follow. As the music returns to the principal theme, the motives from the opening fanfare mingle with the opening theme from the first movement. The symphony closes with these two musical references clamoring for attention, the fanfare played by the brass instruments, the introductory theme given out by the violins in widely spaced harmonies.

Following Copland's earlier successes, his Third Symphony, the longest orchestral work he produced, was an event much anticipated by the American musical community. The United States had emerged victorious from a war that had consumed the national consciousness, and pride in country and national culture was abundant. The time was ripe for a musical statement by an American composer to reflect these sentiments. It was in that spirit that Copland incorporated material from his *Fanfare for the Common Man,* a work originally commissioned by Eugene Goosens, conductor of the Cincinnati Symphony, as one of several orchestral fanfares intended to honor American fighting forces in 1942. Copland acknowledged that he used the opportunity "to carry the *Fanfare* material further and to satisfy my desire to give the Third Symphony an affirmative tone. After all, it was a wartime piece—or more accurately, an end-of-war piece—intended to reflect the euphoric spirit of the country at the time."[2]

Soon after its introduction, the Third Symphony won the New York Music Critic's Circle Award as the outstanding orchestral composition of the 1946-1947 season. Serge Koussevitzky, who admittedly had a personal interest in the matter, declared it to be the greatest American symphony ever written, and Leonard Bernstein described it as a work full of American qualities: "jazz rhythms, and wide-open optimism, and wide-open spaces, and the simplicity and the sentimentality . . . a noble fanfare, a hymn, everything!"[3] Initially, a few critics considered the work pretentious, fraught with heavy-handed naïveté, a pale imitation of symphonies by Prokofiev and Shostakovich. But in the concert halls of the United States, the symphony has been established as a repertory item, generally regarded as a milestone in American orchestral literature.

Concerto for Clarinet

Slowly and expressively—Cadenza—Rather fast

Copland began the Clarinet Concerto while on tour in Latin America in 1947 and finished it, after several interruptions, in October 1948. The first performance was part of a radio broadcast on November 6, 1950 by the NBC Symphony, conducted by Fritz Reiner, with Benny Goodman as soloist; the first concert performance was given on November 28, 1950 by the Philadelphia Orchestra, Eugene Ormandy conducting, Ralph McLane as soloist.

Instrumentation*: solo clarinet in B-flat, piano, harp, and strings.*

Copland composed the clarinet concerto for a commission from Benny Goodman, a clarinetist best known as the leader of a popular big band

and small jazz groups. In addition to his success as a jazz musician, Goodman wanted to establish some identity in concert hall music, and to that end had commissioned works from Béla Bartók (*Contrasts* for clarinet, violin, and piano, 1938) and Paul Hindemith (Clarinet Concerto, 1947). Copland also had been approached by Woody Herman about writing a work for clarinet without any accompanying strings, something that Herman could play with his own jazz group as a counterpart to the *Ebony Concerto* he had commissioned from Igor Stravinsky in 1945. For reasons unknown, Copland chose to accept the Goodman commission and received $2,000, the same fee Goodman had offered to Bartók and Hindemith, for a work with no prescribed limitations other than Goodman's exclusive two-year performance option.

The concerto occupied Copland while he was on tour in Latin America in the fall of 1947. On October 4, he wrote to a colleague that: "I badly need a fast theme for part 2. The usual thing. I used the 'pas de deux' theme for part 1, and I think it will make everyone weep."[4] The reference to the "pas de deux theme" suggests that the concerto drew on sketches from an earlier dance project. Copland evidently found at least part of the material he needed for the fast movement in a Brazilian popular tune he heard in Rio and incorporated in the closing rondo.

The finished score consists of two parts connected by an extended cadenza for the soloist. The first part is a languorous, tentative waltz appropriate for a *pas de deux*. The orchestra offers quiet, widely spaced harmonies in support of a steadily moving and thoroughly melodious solo line. With his open harmonies and thin texture, Copland achieves maximum effect through a minimum of written notes, an eloquent illustration of the musical economy for which he is recognized. The cadenza grows out of the last bars of the movement through an extension of the soloist's closing motive, thus the transition from the main body of the movement into the cadenza comes through motivic evolution rather than a starkly interruptive cadence. Contrary to most cadenzas, which expand upon material already heard, this extended solo passage introduces thematic sketches that are developed in the following rondo. The rapid scale leading from the cadenza into the second part is matched at the end of the concerto by a long glissando for the clarinet, in effect framing the movement in similar gestures by the soloist. Copland wanted the cadenza as a whole to be played close to the way he had written it, "but it is free within reason—after all, it and the movement that follows are in the jazz idiom. It is not ad lib as in cadenzas of many traditional concertos; I always felt that there was enough room for interpretation even when everything is written out."[5] He later referred to the second part as a fusion between elements of North and South American popular music, represented most clearly by allusion to dance rhythms, slapping pizzicato basses, and the reference to the Brazilian popular tune.

Copland sent to Goodman a tape recording of the concerto arranged for two pianos; initial rehearsals between composer and performer used another version for clarinet and piano that proved to be so effective that it was published and performed independently. The autograph score shows some changes to the original musical text, accompanied by Copland's annotation "(too difficult for Benny Goodman)," a comment some subsequent observers have magnified into a major issue. Goodman had requested a short break before launching into the cadenza, and Copland accommodated this reasonable request by inserting two iterations of the soloist's closing motive in the harp, all duly noted as an option in the score. In similar spirit, Goodman also requested that a few of the highest notes at the end of the cadenza and again at the close of the concerto be lowered, because, as he explained, he could comfortably reach those notes when playing jazz for an audience but might find them difficult when recording. These were practical alterations requested by a musician thoroughly familiar with the demands and pitfalls of public performance on a reed instrument. Copland recognized this, and in his account of the rehearsals commented that he agreed to the requested change. It is highly unlikely that his written comment about the difficulty of the solo part represented any implied criticism of Goodman's technical skills.

Initial responses to the concerto were mixed, largely because there were so few similar works available for comparison. A legion of clarinet players took the score to heart and assured its survival so emphatically that the work has become one of Copland's most frequently performed creations. Jerome Robbins used the music for his ballet *The Pied Piper* (1951), a venue in which the score has enjoyed great success. When Leonard Bernstein and the New York Philharmonic Orchestra performed the concerto on their tour of Japan in 1970, the soloist Stanley

Drucker was called back for eight curtain calls and eight minutes of uninterrupted applause.

By contrast, at least one American critic felt that the work lacked substance:

> Copland didn't deliver in this work. Although the clarinet is kept busy throughout, the piece . . . is flat and bare. There are no musical ideas of any interest that I could hear, and I wondered at the thinness of the music. . . . After the long cadenza, the clarinet is roused to a kind of false gaiety and darts foolishly around while the orchestra gives itself over to Latin-American jazz impulses. Quite a business is made of slapping the bass, whacking the frame of the harp, and going through other frenetic substitutes for genuine animation, and I'm afraid they're all as empty as the squeal and yelps that issue from a third-rate Cuban band.[6]

In a lighter vein, a British writer described the concerto as "an exciting hotchpotch of unpretentious tomfoolery."[7]

Critical reactions aside, with jazz idioms permeating the second part, enhanced by a Brazilian popular tune, Copland's clarinet concerto endures as an emphatically American work.

El Salón México

Copland made the initial sketches for El Salón México *in 1933. It was first performed on October 11, 1935, in New York at the New School for Social Research by John Kirkpatrick and the composer in a version for two pianos; the orchestral version, completed in 1936, was introduced on August 27, 1937, in Mexico City by the Orquestra Sinfónica de México, Carlos Chávez conducting.*

Instrumentation*: piccolo, two flutes, two oboes, English horn, clarinet in E-flat, two clarinets in B-flat, bass clarinet, two bassoons, contrabassoon, four horns, three trumpets, three trombones, tuba, timpani, bass drum, snare drum, cymbals, tambourine, Chinese blocks, wood blocks, gourd, xylophone, piano, and strings.*

Copland's broad concept of American music, economic conditions of the Great Depression, and his close friendship with Carlos Chávez, a composer and leading figure in musical circles in Mexico whose career and musical goals closely paralleled his own, combined to draw Copland to Mexico several times during the 1930s. Chávez accompanied him to a popular dance hall in Mexico City called *El Salón México,* where Copland was captivated by the color and vitality of the dancing. A tourist guidebook in which Copland first learned of the dance hall described the establishment as a "Harlem type night-club for the peepul, grand Cuban orchestra, Salón México. Three halls: one for people dressed in your way, one for people dressed in overalls but shod, and one for the barefoot."[8]

Copland's impressions of his experience led to a sketch of the musical work: "All that I could hope to do was to reflect the Mexico of the tourists; because in that 'hot spot' one felt . . . a close contact with the Mexican people. It wasn't the music that I heard, but the spirit that I felt there, which attracted me. Something of that spirit is what I hope to have put into my music."[9] He adapted several Mexican themes for the score, not tunes he had heard in the dance hall itself, but melodies he found in published collections of Mexican folk music. *Cancionero Mexicano,* edited by Frances Toor (1931), provided *"El Palo Verde"* (The Green Stick) and *"La Jesuista"* (The Little Jesus), and from the collection by Ruben M. Campos, *El Folklore y la Musica Mexicana* (1928), he took *"El Mosquito"* (identified by Copland as The Fly) and the indigenous dance tune *"La Malacate."* These and a few others were treated freely and juxtaposed in a musical collage overlapping in both complete and partial statements in various parts of the ensemble. Copland managed to assemble fairly commonplace themes into a new setting that speaks to an audience far beyond the cultural milieu of the original material.

Appropriately for music derived from dance, of whatever style, most of the work's interest lies in its rhythmic facets. The metric displacement permeating the score results from the different groupings of common rhythmic units: eight notes divided into two groups of four (traditional), groups of five and three (in either order), or groups of three and two (in any order). In a similar manner, six notes are grouped into units of three or units of two. All of these rhythms are applied to the permutations of the folk melodies that permeate the score. *El Salón México* is not an easy work to perform. The shifting rhythms posed problems for a number of conductors, among them Serge Koussevitzky, one of the work's early champions.

Beyond the Latin rhythms and specifically Mexican folk tunes, the folk-like dance music attracted much attention for its orchestration, praised by both conductors and other composers for its colorful variety. One of the most vital facets of Copland's score was a percussion section that included a Chinese wood block, a guiro (a properly prepared gourd), and cymbals played with wire brushes, sounds not common to symphony orchestras of the 1930s. The availability of a guiro, in particular, posed problems in early performances of the work in both North America and Europe.

El Salón México was an immediate success. At the final rehearsal before the first performance in Mexico City, the orchestral players interrupted their work on a Beethoven symphony to applaud Copland as he entered the hall, a gesture Copland rightfully interpreted as a statement of the musicians' pleasure that a foreign composer had found interest in their national music. In the year following its publication, it was performed by 21 orchestras, sixteen in the United States and five in other countries, an unusually favorable reception for any orchestral work in a contemporary idiom in the 1930s. It was the first work by Copland to achieve international popularity, the first to successfully represent his ideal of writing in a direct manner that could and did reach a broad public audience, and was in no small degree responsible for initiating his long association with the publishing company Boosey & Hawkes. In an abbreviated arrangement, *El Salón México* became the background music for the 1947 movie *Fiesta*, starring Esther Williams and Ricardo Montalban. As music derived from dance, it has provided the background for choreography by José Limón (1943) and for ballets by Maurice Béjart (*Chapeaux*, 1957) and Eliot Field (*La Vida*, 1978). Beyond its widespread popularity, *El Salón* established Copland's credentials as a composer of music for dance, leading indirectly to commissions for his American ballets *Billy the Kid* (1938), *Rodeo* (1942), and *Appalachian Spring* (1944). In this American venue, his success has been compared to the ballets of Igor Stravinsky from the early 20th century. The crux is the "American" element; with *El Salón México,* music from the New World firmly established its hold on audiences everywhere.

Orchestral Works Derived from Music for the Theater

One of Copland's earliest extended works was the ballet *Grohg*, written during his student days in Paris but never published in its entirety. His next venture in the arena was *Hear Ye! Hear Ye!* (1934), a combination of contemporary popular dances and a social commentary on the American judicial system. His three American ballets—*Billy the Kid*, *Rodeo*, and *Appalachian Spring*—represent quite a different story. They were acclaimed when they first appeared and have continued to be among Copland's most popular compositions, whether danced in the theater or presented as purely orchestral works in the concert hall. His last complete ballet, *Dance Panels* (1959), was revived in 1962, and reflects Copland's efforts to adapt his ballet writing to changing musical styles.

The ballets on distinctly American themes inspired musical scores imbued with nationalistic materials that caught and retained the fancy of the American public, scores that have contributed as much as any works toward Copland's reputation as a musical voice speaking with some hint of the American vernacular.

Suite from *Appalachian Spring*

Copland composed the ballet score between June 1943 and June 1944. It was first performed during the Coolidge Festival at the Library of Congress, Washington, D.C., on October 30, 1944, by the Martha Graham Company, Louis Horst conducting, with Martha Graham and Erick Hawkins in the principal roles.

Instrumentation: flute, clarinet, bassoon, piano, two first and two second violins, two violas, two cellos, and double bass.

In the spring of 1945 Copland expanded the ensemble of a shortened version into an orchestral suite introduced in New York on October 4, 1945, by the New York Philharmonic Orchestra, Artur Rodzinsky conducting.

Instrumentation: two flutes, two oboes, two clarinets, two bassoons, two horns, two trumpets, two trombones, timpani, bass drum, snare drum, tabor (long drum), triangle, wood block, cymbals, claves, xylophone, glockenspiel, harp, piano, and strings.

Copland's score for what would become *Appalachian Spring* was the result of a commission from Elizabeth Sprague Coolidge. As one of its original provisions, the request from Mrs. Coolidge asked that the score include "not more than ten or twelve instruments at the outside

... a small orchestra with one instrument of each kind, both wind and strings with piano."[10] Beyond that, the physical limitations of the auditorium at the Library of Congress, the venue of the Coolidge Festival, would not accommodate a large ensemble.

The early success of the ballet music prompted the orchestral suite in which Copland deleted from the original score three sections representing choreographic interests only. Subsequent arrangements and revisions have produced an often confusing multiplicity of versions. In addition to the original score, which Copland had stretched to thirteen instruments, one can encounter a revised version of the complete ballet music for both orchestra and for chamber group, a suite for both orchestra and chamber group, an expanded suite for thirteen instruments, and sets of variations on the tune of the famous hymn "Simple Gifts" for band and for orchestra.

Martha Graham and Copland had discussed the possibility of a musical and dance collaboration several times. The plan put forth by Graham and Coolidge called for music from Copland and from Carlos Chávez. Material from Chávez was very slow in coming and, when it did arrive, it did not meet expectations, so Paul Hindemith was approached as a substitute. Later, Darius Milhaud was included as well, so Copland was in company with two of the best-known composers of the time, both then resident in the United States. Hindemith produced the music for *Mirror before Me* (*Hérodiade*) and Milhaud wrote *Jeux de Printemps* (titled *Imagined Wings* by Graham), but apparently it was Copland's score, at first called simply and tentatively *Ballet for Martha*, which attracted most of Graham's attention.

As choreographer, Martha Graham proposed a script for the ballet titled *House of Victory*, a drama originally involving biblical quotations, allusions to the Civil War, and references to the Shaker sect, a broadly conceived scenario that went through many transformations during the process of rehearsals. It was this script for which Copland fashioned a musical score; Graham subsequently developed the choreography to match the music as she received it piecemeal from the composer. This process ultimately produced a different scenario and choreography centering on a house-raising in Western Pennsylvania in the early 19th century in which a young farmer-husband and his bride-to-be enact their emotions as they contemplate the future: the joy and apprehension invited by their new partnership; confident determination to

counter a neighbor's warnings about the rocky road ahead; and contemplation as a wandering revivalist reminds them of the frightening
aspects of human fate. Finally, the couple remains alone, firmly established in their new house.

When Copland arrived for final rehearsals, he was surprised to find
that many of the physical movements were quite different from those
he had indicated in the music. He also found that Graham had changed
the title to *Appalachian Spring*, taken from Hart Crane's poem "The
Dance," where the line "O Appalachian spring. . ." refers to a natural
fount rather than to springtime, as it came to be identified in the ballet. Recalling that we often hear in a piece what we want to hear,
Copland frequently recounted that: "nowadays people come up to me
after seeing the ballet on stage and say, 'Mr. Copland, when I see that
ballet and when I hear your music I can just *see* the Appalachians and
just *feel* spring.'"[11] If it worked well Copland was not perturbed by dancing contrary to his original conception, nor was he substantially concerned about the title, as long as it evoked the broad appeal for which
he was striving. That the Shakers were not known to have settled in
Pennsylvania was a factual discrepancy, but details of geography were
subservient to the much broader concept of a musical statement evoking the American vernacular.

The composer acknowledged that both Martha Graham's personality and her choreographic style influenced his conception of the
music. Much of Graham's previous work had treated American subjects, and a wish to create an American style of dance, distinct in its
character from inherited European traditions, permeated most of her
endeavors. Copland responded with a score reflecting his own efforts to
reach a broader public. The original ensemble of thirteen instruments
produced a thin, often transparent texture that allowed every level of
musical activity to be heard. Through judicious orchestration, Copland
managed to preserve much of this quality in the orchestral suite. A basi-
cally diatonic harmonic scheme eschews most aspects of any substantive harmonic complexity. Modulations pass quickly and clearly, even
though Copland's harmonic vocabulary focuses on fundamentally
straightforward triads, rarely more complicated than the sonorities
produced by the brief overlapping of two related chords. The open
intervals outlining those chords had long been a Copland trademark,
and here that quality carries over into angular melodies based on widely

spaced intervals outlining fundamental harmonies. Rhythm offers some of the most pronounced effects. Patterns of syncopation often ensue from quick interchanges between three-four (thrice two) and six-eight (twice three) meters, the whole based on a quick and constantly reiterated pulse. In a similar rhythmic displacement, measures of four beats are transformed by displaced accents into units of three, as in **one**-two-three, **four**-one-two, **three**-four-one, **two**-three-four, and so on. Organization on a broader scale is bound up with activities on stage, but the quietly plaintive clarinet figure from the opening measures returns at the end to frame the complete work, just as a slightly longer motive introduced a few measures later by the flute serves as a loosely configured motto theme for much of the musical score.

The quotation of the tune from the Shaker hymn "Simple Gifts" near the end is by far the most familiar element, a melody and text that—through its simple appeal extended in several arrangements, by Copland and by others—has become a part of the American soundscape. Copland found the tune in Edward D. Andrews's study of Shaker hymns, *The Gift to Be Simple* (1940), where "Simple Gifts" is traced to the 1840s and the singing of the church elder Joseph Brackett. The text sets forth the Shaker view of life and carries within it much of the spirit underlying *Appalachian Spring*:

> 'Tis the gift to be simple, 'tis the gift to be free,
> 'Tis the gift to come down where we ought to be,
> And when we find ourselves in the place just right,
> 'Twill be in the valley of love and delight.
> When true simplicity is gain'd,
> To bow and to bend we shan't be asham'd,
> To turn, turn will be our delight,
> 'Till by turning, turning we come round right.[12]

Copland expands upon the tune through five variations and a coda. The popularity of this segment of the ballet led to the subsequent sets of variations for band and orchestra and one item within Copland's first set of *Old American Songs*.

The ballet as a whole has always evoked a patriotic resonance in the United States. It appeared when World War II was approaching some of its darkest hours, and the scenario addressed values from the nation's past at a time when those values were facing formidable challenges from abroad. Copland's music, with its illusions to space so important to the imagination of dancers, brought forth images of America's open spaces and fundamental simplicities, a comparison no less valid for all of its tenuousness.

Appalachian Spring earned a Pulitzer prize for Copland, coincidentally announced in the same issue of the *New York Times* that heralded the end of World War II in Europe. A few weeks later, the Music Critic's Circle of New York gave its annual award to *Appalachian Spring* as the outstanding work in dramatic composition. Rarely, if ever, has any modern composer been so expressly honored. The work confirmed Copland as a leading figure in American music, and it was a capstone for Martha Graham's career as a choreographer. None of Copland's works is so closely linked with his name as *Appalachian Spring* and none has generated a comparable number of arrangements and excerpts.

Suite from *Billy the Kid*

"Introduction: The Open Prairie"—"Street in a Frontier Town"—"Prairie Night (card game at night)"—"Gun Battle"—"Celebration (after Billy's capture)"—"Billy's Death"—"The Open Prairie Again"

Copland composed the original ballet music during the summer of 1938 in response to a commission from Lincoln Kirstein of Ballet Caravan. The ballet was first produced in Chicago on October 6, 1938, the score played on two pianos by Arthur Gold and Walter Hendl, with Eugene Loring in the title role. Copland arranged the orchestral suite during 1939; it was first performed in New York on November 9, 1940, by the National Broadcasting Company Symphony, William Steinberg conducting.

Instrumentation: *piccolo, two flutes, two oboes, two clarinets, two bassoons, four horns, three trumpets, three trombones, tuba, timpani, bass drum, cymbals, wood block, sleigh bells, gourd, slapstick, xylophone, glockenspiel, harp, piano, and strings.*

The ballet music for *Billy the Kid* grew from the efforts of Lincoln Kirstein, founder of Ballet Caravan (a predecessor of the New York City Ballet), outspoken commentator on contemporary dance, and ardent champion of dance in America and American dancers. From his position of influence, he was trying to move American ballet away from established Russian tradition toward a more indigenous style, an effort similar to Copland's musical goals. He had commissioned several one-act ballets on American themes with music by American composers. With *Billy the Kid,* it was his intent to establish a working partnership between Copland and one of his principal choreographers, Eugene Loring. He asked Loring to develop choreography around W. N. Burns's *Saga of Billy the Kid* (1925) and for musical impetus gave Copland two collections of cowboy songs to peruse. To the composer's disclaimer of any familiarity with the Wild West, Kirstein pointed out that if Copland could assimilate Mexican tunes into a work as effective as *El Salón México,* he could at least explore some native American material for a ballet. Loring provided a plot sufficiently detailed that it included timings for various sections, and Copland set to work to produce the musical score for *Billy.*

The final scenario, as outlined by Copland, drew on scenes from the life of Billy the Kid (born William A. Bonney, November 23, 1859, died July 13, 1881) as they have come down to us through a mixture of legend and fact. The ballet opens on a street in a frontier town popu-lated by cowboys and frontier figures. A lively dance by some Mexican women is interrupted by a drunken brawl. Billy and his mother are part of the crowd that gathers. As tempers flare, shots ring out and, through some unexplained misfortune, one of them kills Billy's mother. In a fury, Billy grabs a knife from a cowhand and stabs his mother's killers, thus beginning his own career as a killer. In following episodes from his life, we see him at night on the open prairie, in a card game with his fel-low outlaws. He is hunted by a posse led by his former friend, Pat Garrett. A colorful gun battle ensues and Billy is captured, leading to a drunken celebration among the townspeople. The suite omits the music for Billy's imprisonment and escape, moving on to the conclud-ing scene in the desert where Billy, hunted and tired, rests with his Mexican girlfriend. Awakened from a sound sleep, Billy senses move-ment around him. It is the posse; Billy's escapades are at an end.

The plot represents in large part Loring's response to the romanti-cized version of Billy the Kid's life as described in Burns's *Saga,* where Billy at first is the victim of circumstances and later becomes a symbol for the disappearance of the Western frontiersman as he is overcome by an encroaching and corrupt civilization. A 1934 collection of American folk ballads contains a "Ballad of Billy the Kid," which ends with a verse expressing the popular sentiment surrounding this legendary antihero:

> There's many a man with a face fine and fair,
> Who starts out in life with a chance to be square,
> But just like poor Billy he wanders astray,
> And loses his life in the very same way.[13]

Copland's music reflects the Western ambience through a number of folk tunes; the substance of the drama develops through musical characterization. The most strident music is associated with the settlers and lawmen, particularly in the celebration following Billy's capture. By contrast, Billy in the desert with his card-playing buddies and Billy alone with his love are scenes supported by some of the most engaging music in the score.

The suite opens with an evocation of the lonely prairie. Open fifths played by clarinets, and later by strings, lend an aura of homespun simplicity to music designed to reflect the open, often deceptive simplicity of the prairie landscape. Piano and double basses suggest the irrevocable forces of nature through a recurring pedal point stated as a syncopated, descending fourth.

With "Street in a Frontier Town" the piccolo (replaced by a tin whistle in stage performances) plays a modified version of the folk song "Great Granddad." Other folk tunes follow, converted to Copland's own style: the strings play an agitated version of "The Old Chisholm Trail" as an interruption to the melodic character that has prevailed, followed shortly by a brief reference to "Git Along Little Dogies" by two trombones. The Mexican dance at the end of this scene opens with a version of "Come Wrangle Yer Bronco" cast in five-eight meter (two plus two plus one), and the scene concludes with a melodious presentation of "Goodbye Old Paint."

A lone oboe provides the transition to "Prairie Night," which expands on an eloquent setting of "O Bury Me Not on the Lone Prairie." The mournful melody is appropriate for the situation confronting Billy; the inevitability of his fate is further suggested by a continuing series of rising scales played by cellos in the manner of a freely treated pedal point.

In the exciting "Gun Battle," Copland creates a technical study limited to the elements of thundering percussion (bass drum, harp, and piano) reinforced by the interval of a major third (low strings), both interrupted by rat-a-tat-tat interjections from trumpets and snare drum. From these simple materials Copland portrays a vivid suggestion of a running gun battle, complete with gunshots and other sounds of combat.

In response to Billy's capture, the people embark on a wild celebration marked by garish dance hall tunes and lurching dance rhythms. The general debauchery finds appropriate musical expression in the clash between the keys of C in the melody instruments and C-sharp played by the bass instruments. The resulting dissonance implies more about the inherent venality of Billy's captors, on the surface hardworking frontier folk and lawmen, than could any amount of choreography.

A sustained note by the trumpet leads to "Billy's Death," a relatively short, quiet interlude marked by gently descending arpeggios that lead directly into the epilogue, "The Open Prairie Again." Material from the opening measures of the score recalls the tranquility of the open prairie and serves as a musical frame for the complete score. As the music swells to a thunderous conclusion, the pedal point from the first section returns, invoking a strain of inevitability in the denouement of Billy's escapades.

Incorporating folk tunes, or melodies in the style of folk tunes, into a symphonic score poses fundamental problems in balancing two very different idioms. Maintaining the natural lilt of a folk tune while setting it to fresh harmonies is difficult; moreover, folk tunes do not always fit the development processes common to an orchestral score. Beyond both concerns lies the need to keep the music in proper balance with the events on stage. Much of Copland's success in the music for *Billy the Kid* derives from his graceful rapprochement of these disparate elements.

John Corigliano

b. New York City, February 16, 1938

S ince gaining international attention with his Clarinet Concerto in 1977, John Corigliano has championed a set of musical values that have challenged many accepted norms and have won for him a broad-based popularity. At a time when contemporary art music still gropes for a common language, he offers something for all listeners. Communication with an audience is one of his major concerns. He rejects the premise of the composer as misunderstood artist, affirming that it is the responsibility of composers to reach out to audiences with any means at their disposal and that communication should be the primary goal of music-making. In this context, he recognizes no clear line of demarcation between serious and popular music, maintaining that it is all serious and all popular, in varying degrees.

To reach these ends, he has been more concerned with the substance of his musical material than with any consistency of style:

> If I have a style, it's unknown to me. Most people think of style as something to latch onto and continue doing. I find that limiting, and I think it's a leftover of that horrible 19th-century originality complex—the idea that the ultimate goal is to sound like no one else. . . . That's no goal. The goal is to write music, and good material, not style, is what holds a piece of music together.[1]

Reflecting that view, each of Corigliano's compositions is a world unto itself, created for the medium and the musicians who will be playing it or have commissioned it. He adapts techniques and materials from the world around him, fashioning these in whatever manner he thinks most appropriate to his end. He often draws on sounds from scores by Aaron Copland and Leonard Bernstein, at one time sardonically declaring that he should sign his scores "Aaron Bernstein" as an acknowledgment of the music that influenced him.

Music was a part of Corigliano's environment from his early years; his father was concert master of the New York Philharmonic from 1943 to 1966, his mother an accomplished pianist and established teacher. That heritage gave him a natural ear for music, but not the support for a career. He pursued music professionally against strong paternal objections. His mother offered one piano lesson, but the two became embroiled in an argument and that was the end of maternal music instruction. Corigliano describes himself as largely self-taught, learning orchestration by listening to records while following the score and indulging his fascination for musical analysis. His first major recognition came after he won the chamber music prize at the 1964 Spoleto Festival with his Sonata for Violin and Piano. He had written the work for his father, who casually set it aside with the comment that he saw music all day long and didn't want to be bothered with more on his time off. In his own perception, the younger Corigliano found his creative voice with his Clarinet Concerto (1977), a work whose premiere brought excited shouts of approval from New York audiences. That was followed by solo concertos for piano and oboe, other major orchestral works, film scores, and successful operas. Awards from the Guggenheim Foundation and the National Endowment for the Arts, and election to the American Academy and Institute of Arts and Letters represent only a sample of the honors awarded Corigliano for his creative accomplishments.

Symphony No. 1 for Orchestra

Apologue: Of Rage and Remembrance

Tarantella

Chaconne: Giulio's Song—

Epilogue

Corigliano composed the Symphony No. 1 in response to a commission from the Chicago Symphony Orchestra; that ensemble gave the world premiere in Chicago on March 15, 1990, Daniel Barenboim conducting.

Instrumentation: piccolo (doubling fourth flute), three flutes (second and third doubling piccolo), three oboes, English horn, three clarinets in B-flat (the third doubling clarinet in E-flat and contrabass clarinet), bass clarinet, three bassoons, contrabassoon, six horns, five trumpets, four trombones, two tubas, timpani, two bass drums, snare drum, tam-tam, three tom-toms, three roto-toms, field drum, tenor drum, sus-pended cymbal, finger cymbals, three temple blocks, tambourine, anvil, metal plate, brake drum, triangle, flexatone, police whistle, whip, ratchet, crotales, glockenspiel, vibraphone, xylophone, marimba, two sets of tubular bells, harp (doubling offstage piano), and strings (two stands of second violins doubling mandolin).

Between 1987 and 1990, Corigliano was the first composer-in-residence with the Chicago Symphony, an appointment leading to the commission and premiere of his Symphony No. 1 for Orchestra. Beyond that, the symphony was generated by the composer's personal loss of several friends to AIDS and was offered as a memorial to them. The first three movements relate to three of those friends specifically, and the third recalls still others through a pastiche of short melodies. Many traditional orchestral works offer the plan of a large three-part design embracing a fast dance movement, an expressive slow movement, and a lively finale. Corigliano's symphony follows the broadest outlines of that pattern except for the last movement, *Giulio's Song*, which closes with a quiet *Epilogue* reflecting on the music that has gone before. His concern for specific acoustic effects produced a revised seating plan for the orchestra in which all brass instruments are placed at the outer perimeter of the ensemble, surrounding the wind, strings, and percussion. The trumpets sit at rear center with three horns on the right and left, two trombones and tuba continuing the pattern along the sides.

The first movement is a large A–B–A design alternating between bittersweet nostalgia and anger, as the composer memorializes a concert-pianist friend lost to AIDS. (Broadly conceived, the entire symphony becomes an *Apologue*, a musical allegory offering a testament to personal loss.) The music begins with an open-string A in the violins and violas, twice building to a percussive interruption by the orchestra. The full ensemble enters to the accompaniment of a slow timpani beat that lays the foundation for a series of orchestral crescendos. Individual choirs of the orchestra interject their own chattering commentary, leading to a massive, widely spaced tone cluster whose slow pulsations increase in volume and speed until it explodes in a burst of sound, leaving the gossamer thread of a solo violin to carry on into the midsection. Here an offstage piano plays a nostalgic transcription of a tango by Isaac Albeniz, a favorite piece of Corigliano's pianist friend. The opening section does not return in the traditional manner; it accrues through the gradual reappearance of brass motives that culminate in an overwhelming dissonance as in the first section. This repeats with maddening intensity until it gradually slows to a stop, dying of its own mass. Original materials return, the offstage piano plays a bit of the tango, and the movement closes on a solitary A as it began, now two octaves higher.

The *Tarantella* was written in memory of an executive in the music industry, also a pianist, for whom Corigliano had earlier written a tarantella as one item in a set of small piano pieces. In Italian folklore, dancers perform the tarantella at increasingly faster speeds until they achieve a hypnotic state, supposedly effective in neutralizing the poisonous bite of a tarantula spider. Corigliano's score starts the dance at a lively tempo, but as the music progresses the pitches waver and aleatoric sections suggest the loss of focus one might experience in a hypnotic condition. The dance returns, increasingly insistent drumbeats recall the "heartbeat" of the first movement, and flexible pitches offer further references to some sort of musical dementia. The end comes with an orchestral scream, sharpened by a police whistle. The contrasts between lucidity and disorientation throughout the movement became particularly ironic for the composer, because his friend eventually succumbed to dementia.

Chaconne: Giulio's Song juxtaposes a series of chords appearing throughout the movement (the chaconne) with melodic fragments taken from an improvisation recorded earlier by the composer and a cellist friend, Giulio Sorrentino. The wavering harmonic passage opens the movement, followed by the solo cello playing a melodic fragment that grows into a soliloquy presenting the principal thematic material. Short melodies introduced by other solo instruments are identified in the score with names of personal friends lost to AIDS, a symbolic gesture by Corigliano that will slip by a listener without score in hand. A second solo cello takes up Giulio's song, followed by different wind instruments as the strings provide a continuing background with the chaconne harmonies. Instruments gradually join the activity to form an all-encompassing tone cluster, only to end abruptly, leaving the solo cello to sustain the interminable A that opened the symphony. This tenuous sound leads directly into the closing *Epilogue*. In an atmosphere of quiet contemplation, muted brass instruments provide a harmonic background that accumulates its mass by adding successively lower pitches. Against this careful scoring, the two solo cellos play their own commentary until only one is left, sustaining quietly the same A with which the symphony began.

Materials from the slow movement have been expanded into an independent composition, *Of Rage and Remembrance,* for solo voices and chorus, with texts by William Hoffman. The premise of a musical memorial extends to including unassigned names chanted by members of the chorus "who have lost friends and wish to remember them."

Honors have been heaped on Corigliano for this symphony. In 1991 it received the Grawemeyer Award for Music Composition as well as two Grammy awards. The Chicago Symphony recorded the work, and it has been performed by many other orchestras across the United States. Some critics have described it as the great American symphony of the modern era. There is no doubt that Corigliano achieved his goal of communication, because the symphony conveys a dramatic and personal statement to audiences.

Peter Maxwell Davies

❧

b. Near Manchester, United Kingdom, September 8, 1934

Peter Maxwell Davies is one of the most important figures in British music who remained active at the end of the 20th century. His wide range of compositions includes works for nearly every medium and for venues of church, chamber, theater, and schools. A penchant for the materials and techniques of early music permeates much of his writing, a characteristic that takes a particularly British bent with his interest in the music of John Dunstable, from the 15th century, and the life and music of John Taverner, from the 16th. The processes of serialism in his earliest works have sometimes found compatible expression with the medieval techniques of *talea* and *color*, qualities that by extension have caused many observers to compare him with Olivier Messiaen, who reverted to similar techniques. What appears on first encounter to be an element of musical eclecticism in his creative activity becomes, with scrutiny, a consistent dedication to music remarkably well suited to any performer or venue for which it is intended. Some of his works grow from a subtle platform of social commentary; not infrequently they border on the irksome to those not prepared to accept the music objectively.

Davies studied at Manchester University, where he came to be identified with a coterie of progressive young musicians known as "New Music Manchester," or simply "The Manchester Group," comprised of composers Harrison Birtwistle and Alexander Goehr, conductor and trumpeter Elgar Howarth, and pianist John Ogdon, an active faction committed to the avant-garde music of the 1950s. Davies wrote his first acknowledged works as a member of this group before continuing studies with Goffredo Petrassi in Rome and Roger Sessions at Princeton University. An early appointment as music master of Cirencester Grammar School in England introduced him to the need for music accessible to children, a situation he met by composing some works in an uncomplicated style and arranging for children many works from the standard repertory. With Birtwistle he formed the Pierrot Players in 1967, an ensemble imitating the instrumentation of Arnold Schoenberg's *Pierrot Lunaire,* plus percussion, later regrouped as the Fires of London. For those ensembles, or for their constituent soloists, he wrote many of the works that have become the basis for his international reputation. In the 1970s Davies took up residence on a remote part of the Orkney Islands north of Scotland. He quickly established a strong rapport with this striking environment, and from that point forward much of his music has reflected a broad range of Orkadian influences.

An Orkney Wedding, with Sunrise

An Orkney Wedding *was composed in 1984 and 1985 and first performed in Boston on May 10, 1985, by the Boston Pops Orchestra, John Williams conducting.*

Instrumentation: *two flutes, two oboes, two clarinets (the second doubling bass clarinet), two bassoons, two horns, two trumpets, two trombones, timpani, pedal bass drum, snare drum, large tambourine, cymbals, suspended cymbals, crotales, four wood blocks, Swanee whistle, slapstick, marimba, glockenspiel, solo bagpipes, and strings.*

With highlands bagpipes as a solo instrument and a title that inevitably piques curiosity, *An Orkney Wedding, with Sunrise* turns out to be a straightforward example of program music that carries on in the best spirit of the Boston Pops Orchestra, which commissioned it. Davies claims the music depicts a wedding he witnessed on Hoy, in the Orkney Islands. Guests arrive at the hall, braving very bad weather. Following the processional, they are received by the bride and groom and offered the first glass of whisky. The dance band tunes up and, as the assembled parties begin to feel the influence of the alcohol, the vigorous dancing becomes ever wilder, until the lead fiddler can no longer control the music. As the evening's festivities wane and guests finally depart into the cold night, with music of the processional echoing in their memories, the sun rises in a glorious dawn, represented in all its majesty by the arrival on the scene of the highlands bagpipes.[1]

In concert presentations, the piper enters the auditorium at the rear and progresses toward the performance platform while playing with the orchestra. The intonation of the bagpipes, acoustically different from the tempered scale of most orchestral instruments, plus the typical asperity of chanter and drone, create a marked contrast between orchestra and bagpipes, usually to the great delight of audiences. Carrying the ribaldry of the music a bit further, some performances have included a bit of clowning in which a bottle (presumably representing one of Scotland's famous exports) is passed among the players with exaggerated and humorous results as the performance deteriorates.

Davies builds much of the music on a theme taken from his *Sinfonietta Academica*, written in 1983. That title refers to the commission from Edinburgh University that generated the piece rather than to any academic musical materials or procedures. With all its boisterous gaiety, the tune effectively does double duty for both the *Sinfonietta*, and *Orkney Wedding* and has become by far Davies's best-known creation.

Manuel de Falla

❧

b. Cadiz, Spain, November 23, 1876; d. Alta Gracia, Argentina,
November 14, 1946

Manuel de Falla (Matheu) was a composer whose works spoke eloquently for his native Spain. At a time when Bartók in Hungary, Vaughan Williams in England, and Janáček in Czechoslovakia were drawing heavily on native folk material in the development of their musical style, de Falla was producing scores that reflected his own folk traditions by projecting the spirit of Spanish music rather than by quoting directly identifiable folk material. His continuing search for brevity and purity of expression later induced an element of self-criticism that produced scores of great efficiency at the same time that they restricted his output to a list of compositions less extensive than many of his contemporaries.

Confronted with the necessity of earning a living at the end of his student years, de Falla turned to the composition of *zarzuelas*, the Spanish popular musical theater. Soon thereafter he studied for a short time with Felipe Pedrell, a composer, musicologist, and folk song collector, whose studies of Spanish liturgical music became a seminal influence in the general awakening of Spanish musicians to the music from the 16th and 17th centuries, the heyday of Iberian influence. The impact of Pedrell's technical instruction was probably slight, but his knowledge of Spain's musical heritage, both cultured and vernacular, exerted an immediate and lasting impact on de Falla.

A move to Paris in 1907 brought de Falla into close contact with the major representatives of Impressionism and, more importantly, brought about his own first successful publications, which were heavily influenced by that style. Settling in Granada in 1920, he entered a period of introspection that led him more deeply into his examination of native Spanish music. For a time he was immersed in the study of *cante hondo* (*jondo*), a generic style of singing based on folk melodies, gypsy influences, and musical materials ranging from Domenico Scarlatti in the 18th century to the flamenco dancing and guitar playing of de Falla's childhood. He wrote a pamphlet on this native genre that remains one of the most informative sources on the subject. Continued withdrawal and self-criticism marked his later years. During the disruptions of the Spanish Civil War, de Falla decided to move to Argentina in 1939, where he spent his last years in seclusion and ill health.

De Falla was not a revolutionary composer, but his works are in line with 20th-century traditions in their projection of musical nationalism through the techniques associated with the broader panorama of Western music.

Nights in the Gardens of Spain

In the Generalife

Distant Dance—

In the Gardens of the Mountains of Córdoba

De Falla completed Nights in the Gardens of Spain *in the spring of 1915, based on sketches begun in Paris in 1909. The finished work was first performed in Madrid on April 9, 1916, by the Orquesta Sinfónica de Madrid, Enrique Fernández Arbós conducting, with José Cubiles as pianist.*

Instrumentation: *piccolo, two flutes, two oboes, English horn, two clarinets, two bassoons, four horns, two trumpets, three trombones, tuba, timpani, celesta, harp, solo piano, and strings.*

Shortly after de Falla's four *Pièces espagnoles* for solo piano were published in 1909, he began work on three nocturnes for the same medium. At the urging of Parisian friends, particularly Isaac Albeniz, he expanded his original concept into the symphonic impressions for piano and orchestra known as *Nights in the Gardens of Spain*. A planned fourth movement was to be a nocturne recalling his native Cadiz, but that music did not take shape until it was later assimilated into the *Pantomime* of *El amor brujo*.

Contrary to its treatment by some performers, the piano part in *Nights* was not intended as a solo instrument in the tradition of a virtuoso concerto. It is instead a part of the orchestral ensemble that offers a different, though admittedly prominent, element of orchestral texture. De Falla had studied piano as an entrée into the musical world and was himself a proficient performer on the instrument. The pianistic writing, often reminiscent of passages from Franz Liszt, reflects the composer's original conception and his own facility at the keyboard.

The title of the first movement recalls the famous Generalife garden at the Alhambra in Granada. A theme that will dominate most of the movement sounds immediately in the violas and harp, the strings producing a buzzing tremolo as they play *sul ponticello* (near the bridge of the instrument). The theme itself undulates within a narrow range, finding no clear point of repose. The first entry of the piano takes up this same line, but now inverted and decorated by coruscating arpeggios that, in their turn, lead into brilliant passagework for the pianist. From this point, the music expands on the initial theme until most of the movement becomes a loosely configured metamorphosis, first in the violas, then in the full orchestra. The piano introduces a different but closely related theme, restated by full orchestra as the piano launches another barrage of glittering arpeggios. This new theme appears once more in the violas before the original material returns to dominate the music: first in a passage for the piano, written to recall the sound of the guitar; subsequently by the full orchestra in inversion; then by the brass with accompanying piano glissandos, all brought to a close by a final quiet statement in the horn.

The *Distant Dance* opens with a pedal figure in the lower strings to which the woodwinds add a rhythmic motive of distinctive dance character. The piano enters with that same figure, soon answered by the cello, before the piano embarks on further rapid-fire passagework, clearly intended to suggest guitar figurations. The orchestra interrupts with a new theme, later assumed by the piano in one of its few genuinely solo passages. In a much-reduced tempo, the opening rhythmic motive and the new theme intertwine in a series of exchanges involving all sections of the orchestra. A delicately orchestrated coda begins with a shimmering tremolo in the violins as wind instruments and celesta play the opening motive in a transition to the vivacious dance music of the finale.

The *Gardens of the Mountains of Córdoba* is much easier to describe in character than in technical matters. The movement invokes the spirit, if not the literal material, of one or more Spanish dances. John Brande Trend, de Falla's biographer and close associate during the composer's later years, described the closing movement as a *zambra*, a term of Moorish origin referring to nocturnal revelry involving lively conversation punctuated by occasional dancing with instrumental accompaniment. Emerging from these origins, the term was applied to the music of such gatherings and, in some instances, the musical ensembles typical of them. These events have not come down to us in defined patterns of music or dance, but de Falla's closing nocturne lends itself well to the imagined atmosphere of such an event. The strings and piano, in order, play a heavily accented dance melody. Horns and piano then share a theme of two contrasting strophes, each of which, in the following development, manages to preserve its original identity. The alternation of refrain and episode resembles a loosely defined rondo, punctuated by the interjection of dance rhythms shifting between rhythmic groupings of two and three. For all of its vigor and vitality, the movement closes quietly, fading away under a series of hauntingly extended appoggiaturas.

Nights in the Gardens of Spain as a whole reflects the Spanish idiom that permeates most of de Falla's music. He acknowledged that it was also intended as a tribute to the techniques of French Impressionism, possibly owing to its conception in Paris and the collegiality de Falla enjoyed with Debussy, Ravel, and Dukas. The composer has offered his own perspective to serve as a closing word on this score:

> If these "symphonic impressions" have achieved their object, the mere enumeration of their titles should be a sufficient guide to the hearer. Although in this work . . . the composer has followed a definite design, regarding tonal, rhythmical, and thematic material . . . the end for which it was written is no other than to evoke [the memory of] places, sensations, and sentiments. The themes employed are based (as in much of the composer's earlier work) on the rhythms, modes, cadences, and ornamental figures which distinguish the popular music of Andalucia, though they are

rarely used in their original forms; and the orchestration frequently employs, and employs in a conventional matter, certain effects peculiar to the popular instruments used in those parts of Spain. The music has no pretensions to being descriptive: it is merely expressive.[1]

Orchestral Works Derived from Music for the Theater

Some of Manuel de Falla's first compositions were the *zarzuelas* of Spanish popular theater. He continued his interest in combining music with a text or with a theatrical setting throughout his productive years, in the process creating some of his most enduring music.

Suite from *El amor brujo*

Introduction and Scene—In the Cave—Song of Love's Sorrow—The Apparition—Dance of Terror—The Magic Circle—Midnight—Ritual Dance of Fire—Scene—Song of the Will-o-the-Wisp—Pantomime—Dance of the Game of Love—The Bells of Morning

De Falla composed the original ballet music for singer, reciter, and eight instruments to a scenario by Martínez Sierra, between November 1914 and April 1915. Its first performance took place in Madrid at the Teatro Laro on April 15, 1915, with Moreno Ballesteros conducting and Pastora Imperio as featured soloist. Following several revisions for both concert and staged settings, the present orchestral suite came into being sometime before May 22, 1925, when de Falla conducted a staged performance in Paris.

Instrumentation*: two flutes (one doubling piccolo), oboe, English horn, two clarinets, bassoon, two horns, two trumpets, timpani, glockenspiel, piano, soprano voice, and strings.*

The Spanish title does not lend itself readily to English translation. Neither "The Love Wizard" nor "Love the Magician" describes the subject matter appropriately, so the original El amor brujo *has been retained in most common references.*

The impetus for this colorful score came from Pastora Imperio, member of a gypsy family and famed for her beauty and dancing. She asked Martínez Sierra for a work by himself and de Falla in which she could both sing and dance. Through Imperio's mother, Rosaria la Mejorana, herself a renowned dancer, Sierra and de Falla were introduced to many legends and much folklore on which they drew for the project at hand. The resulting *gitaneria* (gypsy dance) in one act of two scenes, in which the principal figure, Imperio, both danced and sang, fit no pattern of traditional stage works and met with a cool reception in Madrid. But the people of Pastora Imperio's family understood and responded with enthusiasm. A revised version appeared in 1916 with the orchestra expanded and the order of dances changed. Other revisions followed, written for various ensembles, until the present score emerged sometime in 1922.

The synopsis of the scenario published with the orchestral score outlines a tale of love thwarted by a spirit from the past, a theme found elsewhere in European folklore. Candelas, young and passionate, still mourns her dead lover, a jealous, demanding, and dissolute gypsy. She is held in thrall by her memories, both fascinated and fearful. Still, she is young, spring comes, and so does a new love, in the person of Carmelo. Candelas is willing to be won, but memories of her former lover prey upon her, and when Carmelo approaches her, the specter of the dead lover appears, prohibiting their kiss of perfect love. Knowing the wiles and ways of the man when living, Carmelo appeals to his weakness for women by soliciting the aid of Lucia, a young and pretty gypsy girl who is also a friend of Candelas. The prospect of flirting with the ghost of one who was so vigorous in life appeals to Lucia, so she assumes her post. When Carmelo returns to Candelas, the specter appears as before, but vanity prevails and he succumbs to the coquetry of Lucia. Carmelo succeeds in convincing Candelas of his love, and with the spirit transfixed by Lucia's pretty face, the lovers can exchange their perfect kiss, sealing the fate of the spirit forever.

To accompany these scenes, de Falla drew on the spirit of Andalusian folk materials plus the rhythms and scales often associated with music of the gypsies. The music assumes a life of its own through varied references to two themes introduced at the beginning, creating a continuing metamorphosis of thematic material. In the *Introduction and Scene,* the orchestra introduces the first of two main themes, a dramatic fanfare theme on E. That tonal point of reference is emphasized by a brief shift to a semitone above before the music returns to the beginning pitch. *In the Cave* introduces the second theme, a dark and ominous rumbling from the lower strings and brass, concluding with a Moorish plaint by the oboe, all standing in marked contrast to the fanfare theme. The muted trumpet plays an inversion of the second theme as the main feature of *The Apparition*, and in the following *Dance of Terror* that same theme is divided between different instruments of the orchestra. The simulation of twelve bells in the orchestra marks the witching hour of *Midnight*, a prelude to the *Ritual Dance of Fire*. This is the number audiences await, recognized as the most familiar part of the score. The second theme continues through the following *Scene* and *Song of the Will-o-the-Wisp*. With the *Dance of the Game of Love,* the opening motive of the second theme provides a background for the voice, representing Lucia, as she sings to the evil spirit, accusing it of having accepted undeserved love and proclaiming "I am the voice of your destiny, I am the fire in which you burn, I am the wind in which you sigh, I am the sea in which you drown." The suite closes with *The Bells of Morning* (orchestral bells, horn, and piano) as Candelas sings in exaltation of the approaching dawn and her glorious happiness.

Through his usual attention to details of composition, de Falla managed to mirror the elements of mysticism, passionate love, and irony comprising the plot. The locale is not specified, but the title of the second number, *In the Cave*, reflects de Falla's recollection of a cave traditionally occupied by gypsies in the vicinity of Granada. Others close to the composer claim that the intended venue was somewhere around the Bay of Cadiz, a proposal supported in part by the reference to the fishermen in the subtitle of *The Magic Circle*.

Early critics denigrated *El amor brujo* as a folk opera, although it contained no literal quotation of known folk materials and took as much of its life from dance as from dramatic elements. The characteristic turns of phrase common to gypsy music surely were in de Falla's ear, but again, one can search in vain for any direct borrowing. The work quickly gained favor as a concert number, and in that venue it has enjoyed consistent and widespread success. The subtle transformation of two principal themes links the scenes through purely musical means, enabling the score to stand independently from any association with dance. Associations with the original stage setting fade further into the background when, as often happens, the vocal solos are played by an orchestral instrument. With the inimitable vitality of Spanish dance for its animation, and the coherence of two themes in permutation for its musical logic, the suite from *El amor brujo* endures in the concert hall as a unique expression of the Spanish idiom and one of de Falla's most frequently performed compositions.

Suites from *The Three-Cornered Hat*

Introduction

Part I: Afternoon—Dance of the Miller's Wife (Fandango)—The Corregidor—The Miller's Wife—The Grapes

Part II: Dance of the Neighbors (Sequidillas)—The Miller's Dance (Farruca)—Final Dance (Jota)

De Falla composed the ballet music for The Three-Cornered Hat *between 1917 and 1919. It first appeared in a concert version in Madrid on June 17, 1919, played by the Orquesta Filarmónica de Madrid, Bartolómé Pérez Casas conducting; the complete ballet was first performed in London on July 22, 1919, by the Ballets Russes, conducted by Ernst Ansermet, choreography by Leonide Massine, sets and costumes by Pablo Picasso.*

Instrumentation: *three flutes (the first and second doubling piccolo 1 and 2), two oboes (the second doubling English horn 2), English horn 1, two clarinets, two bassoons, four horns, three trumpets, three trombones, tuba, timpani, bass drum, snare drum, castanets, triangle, cymbals, tam-tam, tubular bells, xylophone, glockenspiel, celesta, piano, harp, mezzo-soprano voice, mixed stage voices, hand clappers, and strings.*

Suite No. 1: "Scenes and Dances from Part I," *but with reductions in the* Introduction *and* Dance of the Miller's Wife.

Instrumentation: *two flutes (the second doubling piccolo), two oboes (the second doubling English horn), two clarinets, two bassoons, two horns, two trumpets, timpani, suspended cymbals, bells, xylophone, piano, harp, and strings.*

Suite No. 2: "Three Dances from Part II," *with a major cut in* The Miller's Dance.

Instrumentation: *piccolo, two flutes, English horn, two clarinets, two*

bassoons, four horns, three trumpets, three trombones, tuba, timpani, bass drum, cymbals, castanets, triangle, tam-tam, tambourine, xylophone, celesta, piano, harp, and strings.

The music of *The Three-Cornered Hat* is represented in the orchestral repertory by three independent items. The ballet music is often played in full; the two suites consist of different musical excerpts from that larger score.

The story had long been a part of Spanish folklore, generally known as *El corregidor y la molinera* (The Governor and the Miller's Wife) before it achieved literary status at the hands of Pedro Antonio de Alarcón in the late 19th century with the title *El sombrero de tres picos* (The Three-Cornered Hat). Alarcón claimed to have heard the story from a number of minstrels, all versions varying in details that he tried to reduce to their common elements. He set the plot in 1805, and it was his setting that Hugo Wolf adapted for his opera, *Der Corregidor*, in 1895. G. Martínez Sierra used the same material for the scenario of a pantomime, to which de Falla added a score for eleven instruments in 1916. It was this stage work that de Falla introduced to producer Serge Diaghilev and choregorapher Leonide Massine of the Ballets Russes while the troupe was exiled in Spain during World War I. All three agreed that the story and music offered much potential for a full-length ballet, although de Falla protested that he would need to study native dances further before he could transfer them into an appropriate idiom. The creative flurry that followed was very much a collaborative effort between Massine and de Falla, with many irritating intrusions by Diaghilev. Whatever difficulties those conditions generated, the result was a score that has remained one of the most successful among many famous ballets introduced by Diaghilev's Ballets Russes.

The synopsis published with the full score tells of an elderly governor's advances toward the pretty young wife of a miller; his badge of office, the archaic three-cornered hat, becomes a symbol for his frustrations and a title for the modern plot.

The miller and his wife are tending grapes, drawing water from the well for their garden, and generally enjoying the fullness of their life together. The elderly governor (*corregidor*) approaches with his retinue, his flirtation with the pretty miller's wife cut short by the irritation of his own wife. He later returns and finds the wife partially responsive to his advances—implied by her seductive dance with a bunch of grapes—but his lunge for a kiss leaves him sprawled on the ground. The miller and wife feign sympathy for the elderly rake, and as he leaves in a huff, they continue their celebration of life with the completion of the *fandango*.

In the second part, the neighbors celebrate as they dance *seguidillas*, and the miller responds with his own extended solo dance. Proceedings are interrupted by the governor's bodyguards, come to arrest the miller on obscure charges. Thinking the coast is clear, the governor returns, bent on amorous adventure, but instead awkwardly falls into the stream. The miller's wife is indignant at his continued intrusions, they quarrel, and after she runs off he hangs his wet clothing and three-cornered hat on the bedpost to dry and retires to the miller's bed. That worthy gentleman returns, draws his own conclusions on seeing the governor's clothing hung by his bed, and plots his revenge. He exchanges his clothing for the governor's and departs, determined to repay in kind the bumbling official for his assumed dalliance. At the final dance, the governor hurriedly dons the miller's clothes, but is seized by his own men, who mistake him for the escaped miller. There follows a general melee with the governor and miller in exchanged identities, both wives defending their (supposed) husbands, as neighbors return to view the general uproar. As the miller and his wife are reconciled, the senescent Lothario is revealed in his true identity and playfully buffeted by the crowd as they toss him in a blanket.

De Falla's introduction to the ballet proper is an extended fanfare for timpani, mezzo-soprano, stage voices, and castanets, written at the insistence of Diaghilev to provide an opportunity for the audience to survey Pablo Picasso's colorful fore-curtain. The musical score itself is closely related to the choreography throughout, providing well-defined illustrations for events on the stage. Birdcalls played by the wind instruments illustrate the miller's playful interaction with a pet blackbird, and two piccolos plus violin harmonics become the musical embodiment of a squeaking well wheel. The governor, in most appearances, is announced by an awkward passage in the solo bassoon, the buffoonery associated with that instrument (rightly or wrongly) offering a match for his general ineptitude. Music for the *fandango* danced by the miller and his wife expands on the major/minor ambivalence associated with that dance, interrupted only once by the quixotic *corregidor's* theme in the bassoon.

In Part II, the *seguidillas* danced by the neighbors introduce an element of musical autonomy in the theme first played by the violins. This returns throughout the opening number, played by various instruments, as a thread of musical continuity. The *farruca* of *The Miller's Dance* intermittently invokes the strumming of guitars by vigorous bowing in the strings, *sul ponticello*. Leonide Massine, who created the role of the miller, has written of his hypnotic immersion in this extended solo, a performance that became a highlight of the original choreography and did much to establish his reputation as a solo dancer. The miller's celebration is interrupted by the bodyguards knocking at the door—to the orchestral accompaniment of the "fate" motive from Beethoven's Fifth Symphony—before they take him away, leaving his wife alone, as a voice in the distance sings that as the cuckoo calls, married couples should bolt their doors, for the devil is not sleeping. The concluding *jota* cleverly incorporates a broadly conceived sonata design as it reflects the choreographic denouement on stage. The increasingly colorful orchestration reflects the arrival of more and more dancers on the stage, punctuated by guitar effects and rhythmic interplay between duple and triple meter.

The *seguidillas* of Part II offer one of the few examples of a direct quotation of folk melody in de Falla's works. According to Massine, he and de Falla were returning from the Alhambra in Granada one afternoon when they encountered a blind beggar singing a melody that seemed to consume the composer's interest. He listened for several minutes with eyes closed before writing the beggar's tune in his notebook. It became a part of *Dance of the Neighbors*. At other points, de Falla includes snippets of tunes known to a Spanish audience, but these are fleeting references only, worthy of mention only because of their rarity.

By the time of its London premiere, the ballet was apparently identified interchangeably as *The Three-Cornered Hat* and *Le Tricorne*. Under either name it was a great success, bringing that season of the Ballets Russes to a triumphant close. One commentator compared the work to Stravinsky's *Petrushka* as a landmark ballet, describing the collaboration of de Falla and Picasso as a triumph of quality over quantity. Rarely have two artists of comparable stature joined forces in a manner so focused on one bit of dramatic material. In spite of the talents represented, responses to early performances in Madrid were mixed. The conservative press criticized the artistic license exercised by composer, painter, and choreographer in the depiction of a thoroughly Spanish subject, claiming that the production cast traditional Spanish values in an unfavorable light. By the end of the century, the success of the music in the concert hall, whether represented by the complete ballet music or by either of the two suites drawn from it, eloquently testified to the vitality and color of de Falla's score.

George Gershwin

b. Brooklyn, New York, September 26, 1898; d. Hollywood, California, July 11, 1937

The music of George Gershwin is probably known to more people around the world than are the creations of most other American composers. Before the term "crossover" was common currency, he established himself and his music in the venues of both popular and symphonic music. His popular songs have become so well known that they approach folk material, their chord changes perpetuated by jazz musicians of every style, and his symphonic compositions grace orchestral programs wherever symphony orchestras perform.

Born Jacob Gershvin to Russian immigrant parents, he left high school to become a song plugger for Remick Music Company, where he spent hours every day demonstrating popular songs to potential sheet-music customers. From this early experience he moved on to writing his own songs (Al Jolson's recording of *Swanee* in 1919 sold hundreds of thousands of copies and gave Gershwin his first hit song when he was 21) and at least 29 Broadway shows and musical reviews. One of his most popular stage works, *Of Thee I Sing* (1932), was the first Broadway musical to receive a Pulitzer prize (in drama). His work list includes more than eight hundred songs, many of them written with brother Ira as lyricist. After 1930 he began to write for films as well, expanding his already widespread popularity and financial success. His masterpiece was *Porgy and Bess* (1935), a summit in the annals of American opera.

Throughout his career, Gerhswin expressed the wish to produce symphonic works; in that arena his reputation rests on six compositions produced in a span of ten years: *Rhapsody in Blue* (1924); Concerto in F

(1925); *An American in Paris* (1928); *Second Rhapsody* (1931); *Cuban Overture* (1932); and *Variations on "I Got Rhythm"* (1934). For all of their popularity, a reliable and accurate version of these larger orchestral works remains in question, because most of them were altered by editors or conductors who, with genuinely good intentions, often felt it necessary to "improve on" Gershwin's original scores. His untimely death from a brain tumor cut short a musical career unequalled on the American scene.

Conditions beyond Gershwin's music contributed in varying degrees to his success. He was perceived, by himself and by others, as a musical spokesman for America of the 1920s in the same way that Johann Strauss and his waltzes represented late-19th-century Vienna. The terms "highbrow" and "lowbrow," with their mildly derisive connotations, were current at the time and doubtless reflected an element of self-consciousness where music was concerned. Gershwin's music effectively challenged the common belief that concert hall music, with its attendant traditions, was superior to popular music, with its reliance on the performer as creator. His symphonic works offered a partial answer to the modernism emerging abroad. Although modern European composers and their music continued to represent the avant-garde, Gershwin's music was clearly rooted in the soil of American popular music, a characteristic form of expression in the United States.

At the time of his death, the regard that Gershwin enjoyed in the eyes of his fellow musicians spoke eloquently of his musical stature. Arnold Schoenberg, a personal friend of Gershwin and one of the most influential composers of the century, spoke of him as an artist and composer who expressed new musical ideas in a new way. Arturo Toscanini, the international lion of orchestral music during the middle decades of the century, wrote in 1944 that he considered Gershwin's music the only real American music. Such an evaluation might be considered hyperbole today, but it reflected the prevailing view of Gershwin and his accomplishments in the years shortly after his death.

Concerto in F

Allegro

Adagio—Andante con moto

Allegro agitato

Gershwin composed the Concerto in F between July and November 1925. The first performance took place at New York's Carnegie Hall on December 3, 1925, with the New York Symphony, Walter Damrosch conducting, Gershwin as piano soloist.

Instrumentation: *piccolo, two flutes, two oboes, English horn, two clarinets, bass clarinet, two bassoons, four horns, three trumpets, three trombones, tuba, timpani, bass drum, snare drum, cymbals, triangle, bells, gong, wood block, slapstick, xylophone, solo piano, and strings.*

Paul Whiteman's famous concert, titled "Experiment in Modern Music," which introduced the *Rhapsody in Blue* on February 12, 1924, attracted an audience containing many luminaries, among them Walter Damrosch, musical director for the New York Symphony Society. About a year later, Damrosch asked Gershwin to write something he could play with the New York Symphony. A contract was signed on April 17, 1925, specifying that Gershwin was to "play his own composition, New York Concerto, for piano with orchestra and this will be the first performance of the work in New York."[1] Although this was to be the first "public" performance of the work, Gershwin often shared bits and pieces of a score as it came into being with his wide circle of friends and colleagues. True to form, he had already played bits of the concerto for his friends.

Gershwin had many musical irons in the fire, and shortly after signing the contract he left to oversee the London production of *Lady, Be Good*. It was while in London that he reportedly acquired several books on musical structure to explore what was meant by concerto form, an account which, if true, may have reflected his awareness of his lack of formal training. It seems just as likely that the story was intended as good press copy, as were so many comments attributed to Gershwin by journalists who documented his every move. By the time he returned to New York in June, he had sketched some ideas for the score. Constant interruptions interfered with concentrated work on the concerto until late July, when Ernest Hutcheson, Dean at the Juilliard School and central figure at the Chautauqua Institute in western New York, offered Gershwin a private studio at Chautauqua where he could work undisturbed.

According to dates in the original two-piano score, the first movement was completed in July, the second in August and September, and the third also in September. He then turned to the orchestration, which was completed by November 10, all dates supporting his later statement to the press that it took him three months to compose the concerto and another month to complete the orchestration. Two weeks before rehearsals with the New York Symphony began, Gershwin hired a group of musicians, obtained use of the Globe Theater, asked his friend William Daly to conduct, and played through the concerto as a test. Walter Damrosch and others attended this preliminary hearing and possibly offered some suggestions about technical matters. Daly suggested several cuts, some of which Gershwin heeded, but from all available accounts it seems that the concerto sounded as Gershwin intended. He later recalled that hearing the score performed for the first time was one of the greatest joys he had experienced with any of his works.

The press distributed Gershwin's own description of the concerto, now titled simply Concerto in F, either in response to mounting curiosity about the work or as effective preconcert publicity:

> The first movement employs the Charleston rhythm. It is quick and pulsating, representing the young, enthusiastic spirit of American life. It begins with a rhythmic motif given out by the kettledrums, supported by other percussion instruments and with a Charleston motif introduced by bassoon, horns, clarinets, and violas. The principal theme is announced by the bassoon. Later, a second theme is introduced by the piano.
>
> The second movement has a poetic nocturnal atmosphere which has come to be referred to as the American blues, but in a purer form than that in which they are usually treated.
>
> The final movement reverts to the style of the first. It is an orgy of rhythms, starting violently and keeping the same pace throughout.[2]

Gershwin follows tradition in the fast-slow-fast sequence of three movements common to most concertos, but within each of these he adapts convention to his own ends, creating unique designs that only approximate common practice. The "Charleston motif" creates a snappy introduction, but the "second theme" introduced by the piano ultimately becomes the most important tune for this movement. A number of fertile themes appear, expand, and return, resembling but not reproducing in detail the classic exposition, development, and reca-pitulation of more traditional concert works. In this score, Gershwin often works with multiple themes simultaneously, one of the most pro-nounced departures from the common practice of composing medleys of tunes as in many Broadway scores. Rapid changes of key, often achieved through passagework or brief cadenzas by the solo piano, lead to unexpected tonal centers, until the timpani motive from the opening measure leads to the majestic return of the main theme, now played by full orchestra.

The slow movement reflects the blues more in its character than in its structure. It unfolds through the manipulation of four-bar phrases, with the half-step melodic inflections common to blues, but these phrases do not coalesce into the common twelve-bar pattern found in blues compositions since the mid-'20s. The solo trumpet introduces a languid tune that sets the mood for most of the movement. The piano interrupts this soliloquy with a more spirited blues tune, later expanded by the orchestra and piano together. An improvisatory cadenza returns to the earlier languor as the flute assumes the line orig-inally played by the solo trumpet. The sophisticated possibilities inher-ent in the blues expand within a broader A–B–A–C–A design, the whole contributing to the effect of a broadly conceived and atmospheric orchestral nocturne. Gershwin lavished much attention on this slow movement, in the process producing one of his most polished works.

The closing *Allegro agitato* owes much to Gershwin's own pianism. At some point in his pianistic growth, he developed a facility for rapid repeated notes in keyboard patterns divided between the hands. These patterns generated much of the music for one of twelve preludes for solo piano that Gershwin had planned. The set was never completed, but the prelude fragment titled "January, 1925" became the basis for the last movement of the concerto. The orchestral introduction to this orgy of rhythm is taken up by the piano and returns a number of times in rondo fashion. Following the soloist's first episode, the main theme from the first movement returns in the orchestra, only to be inter-rupted by more machine chatter from the piano and xylophone, until a resounding orchestral gong brings everything to a halt. Confirming Gershwin's concern for formal unity, the big theme from the first movement returns, this time more expansively, until the piano inter-rupts with its toccata-like passage to close the movement.

By all accounts, the premiere must have been a stunning feat of piano playing, for it drew sincere praise from the violinist Jascha Heifetz and pianists Sergei Rachmaninoff and Josef Hoffmann, reigning concert artists of the day. The capacity audience responded to the performance with thunderous applause. Some of the enthusiasm grew from well-planned advance publicity that included a glib introduction attributed to the conductor, Walter Damrosch:

> Various composers have been walking around jazz like a cat around a plate of hot soup, waiting for it to cool off, so they could enjoy it without burning their tongues, hitherto accustomed only to the more tepid liquid distilled by cooks of the classical school. Lady Jazz, adorned only with her intriguing rhythms, has danced her way around the world. . . . But for all her travels and her sweeping popularity, she has encountered no knight who could lift her to a level that would enable her to be received as a respectable member in musical circles.
>
> George Gershwin seems to have accomplished this miracle. He has done it boldly by dressing this extremely independent and up-to-date young lady in the classic garb of a concerto. Yet he has not detracted one whit from her fascinating personality. He is the Prince who has taken Cinderella by the hand and openly proclaimed her a princess to the astonished world, no doubt to the fury of her envious sisters.[3]

Reactions from professional critics were mixed. Nearly all recognized Gershwin's youthful talent as both pianist and composer, the natural spontaneity of his themes, and the contemporary tone of the concerto, while at the same time they pointed out his technical deficiencies in composition. One of the most balanced reviews appeared several months following the first performance:

> Mr. Gershwin has written not only a very courageous, but also a very creditable work—creditable especially because his jazz-concerto does not contain a trace of the vulgar. There are inevitably stretches that reveal a lack of experience and resourcefulness, others that are uninteresting and made of stuff as mediocre as any well-behaved and dry-as-dust conservative can roll off by the yard. The merit and the promise of this composi-

tion lie in the portions that are distinctly poetical; in the orchestral coloring, that is often piquant without ever being offensive; but chiefly in the general tenor, which is unquestionably new of a newness to be found nowhere except in these United States. If the dance-rhythms employed by Mr. Gershwin occasionally fail to excite the listener, it is because they are a trifle too persistent, or not reckless enough. In themselves these rhythms have nothing that should bar them from marrying into the proud old family of the concertos and symphonies, which are inclined to forget conveniently their early and somewhat low-born origin. An addition of a little red blood has often saved the weakened blue.[4]

In spite of mixed reviews at home, the concerto spread rapidly to other musical centers. Following a Paris performance in May 1928 by the pianist Dimitri Tiomkin, Gershwin was introduced to Sergei Prokofiev and the next day played for the Russian composer and virtuoso pianist. Prokofiev was cool toward the concerto, describing it as an assembly of 32 bar phrases, but he was intrigued by its pianistic inventiveness. After hearing Gershwin play, he commented that the American would go far if he could evade the dollars and dinners that surrounded Gershwin wherever he traveled.

Beyond the satisfaction of at last writing a major symphonic work, Gershwin himself was typically objective about the concerto. He professed to be uncomfortable with the jazz label, maintaining that he had only developed some jazz rhythms along symphonic lines. In his view it was a straightforward concert piece.

Rhapsody in Blue

Gershwin composed Rhapsody in Blue *between December 1923 and late January 1924. Its sensational premiere took place in New York's Aeolian Hall on February 12, 1924, with Paul Whiteman and his dance orchestra, Gershwin as piano soloist.*

Instrumentation*: the original score, prepared by Ferde Grofé for Whiteman's expanded orchestra, included three reed players (collectively doubling on flute, oboe, E-flat soprano clarinet, B-flat clarinet, alto and bass clarinets, soprano, alto, tenor, and baritone saxophones, heckelphone, two trumpets (doubling on flugelhorns), two horns, two* *trombones (doubling on euphonium and bass trombone), tuba/string bass, timpani and a set of traps, banjo, two pianos, eight violins, and solo piano.*

Rhapsody in Blue was the result of an invitation to Gershwin extended by Paul Whiteman, leader of a prominent and highly successful dance orchestra, sometime after November 1, 1923. Whiteman requested from the composer something that could be included in a concert illustrating the growth of jazz, which he was planning for an indefinite date in the future. From this point forward, the story of the genesis of the work is colored by the great publicity machine that centered around the young composer. Much of the preserved commentary about *Rhapsody in Blue*, by Gershwin and others, originally served for good publicity copy as much as a factual account of events.

Gershwin's description of the circumstances surrounding the first sketches for *Rhapsody in Blue* is typical:

> At this stage of the piece I was summoned to Boston for the premiere of *Sweet Little Devil*. I had already done some work on the rhapsody. It was on the train, with its steely rhythms, its rattley-ty-bang that is often so stimulating to a composer. . . . I frequently hear music in the very heart of noise. And there I suddenly heard—and even saw on paper—the complete construction of the rhapsody, from beginning to end. No new themes came to me, but I worked on the thematic material already in my mind, and tried to conceive the composition as a whole. I heard it as a sort of musical kaleidoscope of America—of our vast melting pot, of our unduplicated national pep, of our blues, our metropolitan madness. By the time I reached Boston I had a definite *plot* of the piece, as distinguished from its actual substance.[5]

Sweet Little Devil opened in Boston on December 20, 1923, so Gershwin's train trip would have taken place shortly before that date. Biographers agree that the next reference to the work came late in the evening of January 3, 1924, when Ira Gershwin called George's attention to an article in an early edition of the next day's issue of the *New York Herald Tribune*. Whiteman's concert was announced for February 12 in Aeolian Hall, with the further information that a panel of judges, to include Sergei Rachmaninoff, Jascha Heifetz, Efram Zimbalist, Alma

Gluck, and Leonard Leibling, would decide "What Is American Music," and the further news that Gershwin was working on a jazz concerto. Burdened by continuing rehearsals for *Sweet Little Devil* and a forthcoming recital with the singer Eva Gauthier, Gershwin tried to withdraw from the project. Whiteman's own enthusiasm for the concert, plus his offer of Ferde Grofé's services as arranger, prevailed. Soon thereafter—on January 7, if the inscription on the first page of score represents the starting date—Gershwin began work on the project in earnest.

According to Grofé's account of events, he visited the Gershwin home daily while work was in progress, taking from the composer each day the music just completed and arranging it for Whiteman's orchestra, often abbreviating the score by nominal reference to the individual players whose sounds and styles he knew so well. Gershwin produced a two-piano score, with one part for the solo piano, the other for the accompanying orchestra or, in this instance, a jazz band. Gershwin later claimed that he completed the score in ten days, and at another time reported that it occupied him for no more than three weeks. As an experienced theater composer accustomed to meeting deadlines, Gershwin maintained a notebook of tunes to be used as needed, and we have noted above that he had formed a conception of the music during the previous December. Thus in early January of 1924 he could have moved forward quickly with materials at hand. In the process, the original title of *American Rhapsody* was abandoned, legend has it, at the urging of brother Ira, who had recently spent some time studying the paintings of James McNeil Whistler. Impressed by the painter's objective titles, such as "Nocturne in Black and Gold" and "Arrangement in Grey and Black" (the famous "Whistler's Mother"), he suggested *Rhapsody in Blue* as a useful title for the composition. The endeavor probably came to its first stage of completion around January 24 or 25, when Gershwin became heavily involved with the daily production problems of *Sweet Little Devil*. Grofé's orchestration was completed on February 4, approximately one week before the scheduled performance.

The announced purpose of Whiteman's concert was to demonstrate how jazz had developed since it first appeared. But the real goal was to feature the Paul Whiteman Orchestra, capitalizing on the group's recent and highly successful tour to London. Whiteman's musical reputation relied on skilled arrangements of popular dance tunes designed for his own players much more than it did on the spontaneity of jazz. For all of this, the popular bandleader was a master of publicity; he invited influential members of the press to rehearsals, distributed complimentary tickets, solicited advice from some critics he thought might be cool to the undertaking, and above all ensured, through one means or another, the attendance of luminaries such as John Philip Sousa, Walter Damrosch, Leopold Stokowski, Mischa Elman, Fritz Kreisler, and Ernest Bloch. In what may have been a self-conscious attempt to justify the whole undertaking as a cultural experience, a preconcert lecture described the event as purely educational, designed as a stepping stone toward public appreciation of symphony and opera.

The program itself hardly addressed those stated goals. Through more than twenty numbers the orchestra presented a variety of popular tunes in various styles, all of which began to sound much alike. *Rhapsody in Blue* was the penultimate number on the program, and by all accounts the performance saved the day at the same time that it launched Gershwin's national reputation as composer and pianist. The opening clarinet glissando and the "quacking" phrase that followed, introduced by Ross Gorman in jest at an early rehearsal, galvanized attention, brought early leave-takers back from the exits, and focused attention on Gershwin, who, as an athletic performer and fluent improviser, created a furor of excitement with his playing. It remains difficult to determine which aroused the greater enthusiasm, Gershwin's performance or the music itself, but many were convinced they were witnessing an epochal landmark in music. The work apparently met the expectations of an audience in search of a resolution to the questions then posed by much contemporary music.

Much of the credit for the success of *Rhapsody* on its first airing has been given to Ferde Grofé's orchestration. Reports originating with Grofé that Gershwin was unable to handle the orchestration grew out of the frequent meetings between the two at Gershwin's home, during which Gershwin peppered Grofé with questions about instrumentation. He was certainly familiar with the standard pit orchestra, although Whiteman's band offered far more resources than most theater groups could muster. Gershwin had studied elemental orchestration during his years working with Edward Kilenyi, and he was an avid student of modern scores, so he could not be considered a complete novice in matters of orchestration. As an unusually busy composer, Gershwin could not have completed the orchestration in the time available to him in January, and he would have been far less familiar than was Grofé with the personnel of Whiteman's band. Gershwin reportedly regarded composition and orchestration as separate activities, or else he probably would not have relinquished to a second party the score of *Rhapsody*, which was far more venturesome than his usual Broadway scores. There is no doubt about Grofé's skills; the recording of *Rhapsody* made in June 1924 preserves a wide and colorful range of instrumental timbre coming from Whiteman's orchestra, all of which provides a varied background for Gershwin's freewheeling piano playing. It is in this juxtaposition of the sweet and the raucous that the music shows its closest connection to the jazz traditions of the time.

In spite of the title *Rhapsody*, implying a free form, some critics searched for a discernible and conventional design, thereby imposing on the work a quality never intended. Not finding one of the expected structures, they sometimes found the music deficient. Gershwin frequently claimed that when he wrote *Rhapsody* he began with the "blues" and constructed an expanded, more serious form. Without further elaboration that plan is difficult to identify, but one can discern that *Rhapsody* grows from five basic themes, all based on some multiple of the eight-bar structure common to popular song in the Tin Pan Alley tradition. These themes are usually open-ended; they do not close with a firm cadence, allowing them to be organized in variable sequence. Within these themes, or frequently as a link between them, one encounters the four-note tag so common to the vaudeville stage (D–E–D–F), usually identified with the jocular text "Good evening friends." This motive must have been on Gershwin's mind, for it became the nucleus for one of his most popular songs, "The Man I Love," written later in 1924 and intended for (but not included in) the show *Lady Be Good*. Another unit that appears in various guises is a rhythmic group of eight notes that replaces the usual grouping of four-plus-four with a pattern wherein the fourth and fifth notes are tied, as in the familiar *Andante moderato* theme, an excerpt quoted so frequently that it has assumed a life of its own.

These melodic units appear with a consistency sufficient to produce a score more tightly knit than most auditors realized on first hearing, a quality which no doubt has contributed much to the durability of the work. Key centers sometimes change abruptly, but the work closes with a clear affirmation of the original tonic, so there is little question about tonal orientation. Above all, *Rhapsody in Blue* is melody, so clearly stated that, for most listeners, any one part can represent the whole.

There is a fundamental problem in discussing *Rhapsody*: its very identity. Immediately following the first performance, two versions existed: Gershwin's two-piano score, and Ferde Grofé's orchestration specifically designed for Whiteman's orchestra. From these Gershwin's publishers created versions designed for commercial success, apparently with Gershwin's blessing. In the process, much of the score was edited according to prevailing conventions of harmony, phrasing, and dynamics, as arrangements were made for a wide variety of instrumental combinations. The recording from June 1924 (Victor 55225-A) is probably closest to the original sound, if not the original musical text. Gershwin was within four months of the premiere, so his playing was likely closer to the original performance than in later recordings. When a second recording was made in April 1927, designed to take advantage of new electronic technology (the microphone), Whiteman's band featured new and different musicians and therefore a different mix of instrumental timbre. A much-expanded orchestration by Grofé from 1942 has become the most frequently heard version, but there are others based on piano rolls by Gershwin. Many of these and other versions delete different segments, making it difficult to establish an unequivocally authentic musical text.

Beyond the excitement it aroused at the first performance, *Rhapsody* continued to generate discussion in the press for several weeks. One of the typical assessments appeared the day following the concert:

> This composition shows extraordinary talent, just as it also shows a young composer with aims that go far beyond those of his ilk, struggling with a form of which he is far from being master. It is important to bear both these facts in mind in estimating the composition. Often Mr. Gershwin's purpose is defeated by technical immaturity, but in spite of that technical immaturity, a lack of knowledge of how to write effectively for piano alone or in combination with orchestra, an unconscious attempt to rhapsodize in the manner of Franz Liszt, a naiveté which at times stresses something unimportant while something of value and effectiveness goes by so quickly that it is lost—in spite of all this he has

expressed himself in a significant, and on the whole, highly original manner.[6]

Another critic claimed:

the title of *Rhapsody* was a just one, suitable for covering a degree of formlessness. . . . But the beginning and ending of it were stunning; the beginning, particularly, with a flutter-tongued, drunken whoop of an introduction which had the audience rocking.[7]

But there were others who held a more conservative point of view:

How trite and feeble and conventional the tunes are, how sentimental and vapid the harmonic treatment, under its disguise of fussy and futile counterpoint. . . . Recall the most ambitious piece on yesterday's program . . . and weep over the lifelessness of its melody and harmony, so derivative, so stale, so inexpressive. And then recall, for contrast, the rich inventiveness of the rhythms, the saliency and vividness of the orchestral color.[8]

Gershwin felt that he had achieved one of his major goals: a musical illustration that jazz was more than the stereotypical song and chorus, a style capable of a more substantive musical statement. The success of the work has been consistently supported by the public. Some perceived it as an inchoate piano concerto in the Romantic tradition and applauded it accordingly, but in fact it assimilated the timbre of jazz groups and melodic patterns from popular song under a title and format common to the concert hall. In that context, it has remained before the public as a work expressing both European and American sensibilities. Its artistic success was matched by financial success. With Gershwin and other pianists, Whiteman played *Rhapsody* 84 times in 1924 alone, and the first recording of 1924 sold more than a million copies. Gershwin earned more than $250,000 from records and other commercial ventures based on the music, $50,000 alone in 1930 for allowing it to be used in the movie *The King of Jazz*, starring Paul Whiteman, and it continued to be a major asset in Gershwin's estate long after his death.

Aside from the immediate popularity generated at Whiteman's concert, *Rhapsody in Blue* represented one step toward filling a vacuum in American concert halls. During the preceding year, New York audiences had been excited by performances of Arthur Honeggar's *Pacific 231*, Darius Milhaud's ballet incorporating jazz, *La création du monde*, and, less than two weeks before the concert in Aeolian Hall, Igor Stravinsky's *Le sacre du printemps* (January 31, 1924). *Rhapsody in Blue* represented to the public a musical rejoinder that was inherently American, addressed to a widely diverse audience, and created by a native composer of indisputable talent and promise.

An American in Paris

Gershwin began focusing his efforts on An American in Paris *early in 1928 and completed the orchestration in November. It was first performed at New York's Carnegie Hall on December 13, 1928, by the New York Philharmonic Orchestra, Walter Damrosch conducting.*

Instrumentation: *three flutes (the third doubling piccolo), two oboes, English horn, two clarinets, bass clarinet, two bassoons, three saxophones (alto, tenor, and baritone), four horns, three trumpets, three trombones, tuba, timpani, bass drum, snare drum, triangle, cymbals, large and small tom-toms, four taxi horns, wood block, wire brush, bells, xylophone, celesta, and strings.*

Gershwin's success as a composer of popular songs and Broadway shows continued with little interruption from the time of *Rhapsody in Blue* (1924) until his untimely death in Hollywood (1937), but during those years he sustained his interest in writing for the concert hall. Following the success of his Concerto in F, he promised Walter Damrosch—who was now affiliated with the New York Philharmonic Orchestra—that his next symphonic work would be written with Damrosch in mind. Gershwin had long wanted to write a work projecting his own impressions of Paris; as early as April 11, 1926, he had written out a theme on a photograph inscribed to his friends Bob and Mabel Schirmer, which would become the opening of *An American in Paris*. He began to assemble this and other ideas in January 1928.

For the purpose of refreshing his impressions of the city and finding uninterrupted opportunity to compose, Gershwin left for a Paris vacation on March 10, 1928, accompanied by several family members. After a stop in London, he arrived in Paris on March 25 with sketches for the planned orchestral work in piano score. He went on an extended shopping expedition to find the taxi horns that would later become a musical signature for the work, and throughout the creative process he played fragments of the score for friends and admirers. By the time the Gershwin party returned to New York on June 18, enough of the music had been committed to paper that the composer could complete the entire score by August 1, turning then to the orchestration, which occupied him until November 18.

Meanwhile, the *New York Times* had announced on June 6 that Gershwin's new work would be played by Damrosch and the New York Philharmonic the following season. While in Europe during the summer, Damrosch had attempted to meet with Gershwin to discuss the new work, but with no success. The conductor continued his efforts to see the score he was to conduct, writing to Gershwin on May 5, August 5, and again on August 21, urging Gershwin to visit and bring the score with him. By November 5, Damrosch had not yet seen the music and continued to be concerned about the matter, asking Gershwin to visit him and play the score to establish tempos. If Gershwin's usual mode of operation prevailed, Damrosch probably did not see the score until after the orchestration was completed, some three weeks prior to the first performance.

An advance description of the score, attributed to Gershwin, appeared in the late summer of 1928:

> This new piece, really a rhapsodic ballet, is written very freely and is the most modern music I've yet attempted. The opening part will be developed in typical French style, in the manner of Debussy and the Six, though the tunes are all original. My purpose here is to portray the impressions of an American visitor in Paris as he strolls about the city, listens to the various street noises, and absorbs the French atmosphere. As in my other orchestral compositions, I've not endeavored to present any definite scenes in this music. The rhapsody is programmatic only in a general impressionistic way, so that the individual listener can read into the music such episodes as his imagination pictures for him.[9]

Gershwin's reference to "Debussy and the Six" should be taken with some reservation. The styles of American popular music and Impressionism, with Debussy as its principal representative, were mutual influences, but Impressionism is not a dominant feature of

Gershwin's score. The six French composers to whom he referred comprised an artistic group identified only through journalistic convenience; if their music contributed anything to *An American in Paris*, it lies in the realm of insouciant satire.

In the playbill for the first performance, Deems Taylor expanded on Gershwin's original description with a much more detailed program, which, for better or worse, has largely replaced the composer's original description. Gershwin probably knew about (and tacitly accepted) Taylor's romanticized prose, and there is no doubt he had some program in mind, because he later acknowledged that it was a program piece. At the same time, he stoutly defended it as abstract music created from representative themes. The discrepancy may represent Gershwin's own struggles with his financial success versus his aspirations for what he and others considered artistic success.

Without encumbering the music with more specific associations, the score offers several salient points of reference. The first theme, in retrospect usually identified as the "walking theme," is an expansion of the photographic inscription Gershwin had offered to his friends, the Schirmers, in 1926. The taxi horns soon make their entry, and the progressive permutation of the walking theme offers listeners ample opportunity to exercise their imagination. A seductive violin cadenza leads into a blues section identified by a languid trumpet solo. This markedly different material goes through several orchestral transformations before another violin solo introduces an unmistakable jazz section. The blues theme returns, much faster and with a music hall accompaniment, before the walking theme reappears piecemeal, and the whole comes to a close with an expansive restatement of the blues music.

These infectious themes are often linked by transitions closely related to them; the resulting musical integration marks another level of mastery in Gershwin's rapid growth following *Rhapsody*. Another strength of *An American in Paris* is that it can be heard in several ways: the walking theme may suggest a returning rondo design (the usual analysis); the whole work might be described as a broad three-part design with the blues providing a midsection and coda; or one can simply follow the musical depiction of the inferred program. Any of these approaches will sustain its own sense of musical logic.

Perhaps it was the success of the composition itself that once again led to questions about Gershwin's abilities as an orchestrator. It was openly recognized by all that Ferde Grofé had orchestrated *Rhapsody in Blue*. Proceeding from that, some questioned the authenticity of Gershwin's orchestration of Concerto in F, in part because it had advanced so far beyond *Rhapsody in Blue* in a relatively short period of time. There was no substantive reason to doubt that the concerto was Gershwin's own effort. But by 1932, Allen Langley—composer and violist in the Musicians' Symphony Orchestra assembled for an all-Gershwin concert—was sufficiently disenchanted by what he considered artistic misrepresentation that he accused Gershwin of offering as his own a score that had in fact been orchestrated by the conductor William Daly. Gershwin was understandably outraged and contemplated a lawsuit, but did not pursue legal action because of his many commitments, leaving the refutation of Langley's accusation to Daly. This Daly did eloquently and with dispatch, affirming that he had never written or orchestrated any portion of Gershwin's symphonic works. The entire issue might be dismissed as one of those experiences that often plague famous people, except that Gershwin was a composer active in the concert hall and on the popular stage, bridging whatever gap existed between the two with extraordinary popular and commercial success. Throughout his later years, there existed a mild controversy among friends and associates over whether he should continue to focus his talents on popular theater or on music for the concert hall. Langley's accusation brought much of this to a head, and Daly's response seemed to have laid the matter to rest, at least in the mind of the public.

As with most of Gershwin's symphonic music, audiences were delighted with *An American in Paris*, the critics divided. A review of the December 13 concert was devoted almost entirely to Gershwin's composition:

> If it is necessary to discuss this amusing piece analytically, it may be recorded that it contains too much material, too many ideas, for its best good. But Mr. Gershwin has developed in his technical knowledge of composition and orchestration too. He has woven into his piece some modern harmony and has now and again combined melodic fragments with genuinely contrapuntal results. . . . The music at least escapes pompous classic formulas. The composer seeks a new form of his own working, germane to the nature of his ideas. If these ideas are fragmentary, they are spontaneous, melodic,

characteristic of Mr. Gershwin. He does not always join smoothly . . . the different parts of his piece, but there is a material gain in workmanship and structure over the two earlier works that have been mentioned.[10]

A week following the concert, Oscar Thompson, distinguished editor and encyclopedist, described the first performance as one in which the audience "found the musical buffoonery of Gershwin's *An American in Paris* good fun in spite of, or perhaps because of its blunt banality and its ballyhoo vulgarity. . . . To conceive of a symphonic audience listening to it with any degree of pleasure or patience twenty years from now, when whoopee is no longer even a word, is another matter."[11] By contrast, Leonard Bernstein, who has been one of the work's enthusiastic interpreters, claimed that the good points were irresistible, and: "If you have to go along with some chaff in order to have the wheat, it's worth it."[12]

With the perspective of time, the viability of *An American in Paris* has been documented by its appearance in venues outside the concert hall. It was first recorded on January 9, 1929, the first of Gershwin's works to be so preserved without cuts or alteration. Florence Ziegfeld adapted the music for a ballet segment in *Show Girl* (1929), but the work received its broadest dispersion as part of the score for the movie *An American in Paris* in 1951. Gene Kelly and Leslie Caron revived Gershwin's original ballet concept in colorful scenes that many listeners will forever recall when hearing this music. The movie was voted best film of the year by the Academy of Motion Picture Arts and Sciences, and Oscars were granted to six of the participants in the cinematic effort. The popularity of Gershwin's tone poem remained undiminished through the end of the 20th century, an era whose spirit it describes faultlessly for many audiences.

Cuban Overture

Gershwin composed Cuban Overture *during July and August 1932. It was first performed at New York's Lewisohn Stadium on August 16, 1932, by the New York Philharmonic Orchestra, conducted by Albert Coates.*

Instrumentation: *three flutes (the third doubling piccolo), two oboes, English horn, two clarinets, bass clarinet, two bassoons, contrabassoon,*

four horns, three trumpets, three trombones, tuba, timpani, bass drum,
snare drum, cymbals, Cuban sticks (claves), gourd, maracas, bongos,
Cuban tom-tom, bells, xylophone, and strings.

Gershwin's musical portrayal of an American visitor to Paris was in part the result of several years planning that came to fruition during his own visit to that city during 1928. There is no record that his vacation trip to Havana in May 1932 was based on a similar plan, but he nonetheless was very impressed by the music he heard in the Cuban capital and determined to write something reflecting that experience. He was particularly impressed by the exoticism of Latin rhythms and the percussion instruments associated with them. To be certain that his chosen instruments would receive the attention he wished, he added to the title page of his score a "Conductor's note" in which he drew pictures of the "Cuban sticks," bongos, gourd, and maracas in miniature and a diagram of their position on the stage: directly before the conductor at the front of the orchestra. The original title, *Rumba,* was in keeping with all of this, leaving no doubt about the Latin roots of the music.

The concert at which *Rumba* was introduced represented a high point in Gershwin's career. He wrote to a close friend, George Pallay, on the day following that it had been the most exciting concert of his own works he had experienced, not only for the music, but also because the attendance broke the record for stadium concerts. According to Gershwin there were 17,845 paid customers and another 5,000 turned away at the gates, immensely gratifying attendance for any composer. At a second concert at the Metropolitan Opera House on November 1, by the Musician's Symphony, held as a benefit for unemployed orchestral players, Gershwin renamed the work *Cuban Overture,* the title under which it was published after his death and continues to be known.

The structural elements reflected Gershwin's increasing command of the techniques of composition and, by his own account, represented the manner in which he hoped to work in the future. Sometime early in 1932, he began studying with Joseph Schillinger, a composer and theorist who had developed a systematic, mathematical approach to composition. The *Cuban Overture* represents the first manifestation of Schillinger's techniques in Gershwin's music. The composer offered a stilted description of the music for inclusion in the program: "In my composition I have endeavored to combine the Cuban rhythms with my own thematic material. The result is a symphonic ouverture which embodies the essence of the Cuban dance. It has three main parts."[13]

The "three main parts" follow a fast-slow-fast design common to other Gershwin instrumental works. The difference lies in the contrapuntal elements and the Latin rhythms that underlie the whole score. The consistent gusto of the percussion instruments played against other materials—rhythmic or melodic, or both together—in the other sections of the orchestra produces a broadly conceived contrapuntal fabric in which one orchestral choir competes with another, each of them operating with some independence. On a more intricate scale, the first part concludes with the opening vamp in the higher instruments, answered in inverted canon in the lower-pitched instruments, the whole supported by the same motive in the basses played in notes of double value. As if once were not enough, the same passage returns in the third part, only now played twice as fast. Considered together, these sections represent a sophisticated handling of canon, inversion, augmentation, and diminution at one stroke. Carefully executed thematic references reflect a similar degree of conscious structure. The clarinet cadenza that links the first and second parts of the overture, moving from a lively dance to a plaintive blues, expands on the motive from the opening measure, which in turn becomes a main constituent of the blues to follow, and the same material returns shortly before the close of the third part. Rhythmic patterns associated with the rumba (three plus three plus two, or the retrograde, two plus three plus three, in various manifestations) permeate the score, creating a lively crosscurrent of rhythmic activity. From the accumulation of these materials, *Cuban Overture* emerges as a complex work whose boisterous energy obscures polished technical processes, for the most part the result of Gershwin's work with Schillinger or, if not that, at least the type of creative effort Schillinger's system would suggest to any student of his theories.

The responses to *Overture* followed a pattern common to the introduction of many of Gershwin's orchestral works. Audiences cheered, while the professional critics responded with polite disdain. Howard Taubman claimed that despite the addition of the Cuban instruments, the work was merely the old Gershwin enlivened by some new effects. The perspective of time plus familiarity with the score suggest that it was instead a new Gershwin, writing with a subtle sophistication well beyond most of his earlier ventures.

Alberto Ginastera

॰॰॰

b. Buenos Aires, Argentina, April 11, 1916; d. Geneva, Switzerland,
June 25, 1983

The 20th-century movement toward music as an expression of national character found in Alberto Ginastera an eloquent spokesman. His works reflect the Latinization of urban Argentina in their indebtedness to the French Impressionists and Stravinsky's *Le sacre du printemps*. Even more pronounced was his sense of nationalism, which led him toward music of the gaucho and all the traditions associated with that hard-riding herdsman of the pampas.

Ginastera described his own evolution as a composer in three broad periods. "Objective nationalism" was his term for those early works drawing fundamentally on gaucho music or materials from the native people of Argentina. Representative works created during this period include the ballets *Panambí*, which marked his emergence as a major figure in Argentina, and *Estancia*, based on scenes from the daily life on a cattle ranch. His second period, which he described as "subjective nationalism," began in the 1950s and included the *Variaciones concertantes* and those other works conceived for an international audience but still showing elements of Argentinean folk materials. His later years, for him an era of neo-Expressionism, showed a turn toward greater dissonance, techniques borrowed from serialism, and large-scale symmetry.

In the composer's opinion, there are no firm "boundaries" marking the change from one period to another. Rather, one work leads to the next, showing a continuing process of growth and assimilation. From a still broader perspective, the works by which Ginastera was best known at the end of the century—extending from the ballet *Panambí* (1937) to his opera *Beatrice Censi* (1971)—show an overriding concern with the reconciliation of folk-inspired materials and rigorous designs of musical structure.

Ginastera described the corpus of his work as an attempt to revive the transcendental facets of the pre-Columbian world. At the same time, he proclaimed that he wanted to be a contemporary figure. "I want to be in the society of my age as an artist and a composer. . . . Each of my works, in one way or another, should bear the stamp of my own spirit."[1] He further described himself as a classicist, based on the permanence he wanted his works to achieve. Those aspirations offer a comprehensive view of Ginastera's style: the expression of musical elements from his native land through technical processes of universal appeal.

His accomplishments brought Ginastera wide renown, particularly in the United States, where he received major awards from the Guggenheim, Fromm, and Koussevitzky foundations, among others. He was also a visiting professor at many universities in the United States and was highly regarded as a lecturer, teacher, and articulate representative of the mainstream of modern music. In Europe, his works won a strong and loyal following for their technical mastery. His First Piano Sonata (1952) quickly became a repertory piece, included in competitions as a representative contemporary work for piano. His string quartets and operas have been hailed as masterpieces to be included among the most important additions to the modern repertory from the mid-20th century.

Variaciones concertantes, Opus 23

Tema per Violoncello ed Arpa

Interludio per Corde

Variazione giocosa per Flauto

Variazione in modo di Scherzo per Clarinetto

Variazione drammatica per Viola

Variazione canonica per Oboe e Fagotto

Variazione ritmica per Trombe e Trombone

Variazione in modo di Moto perpetuo per Violino

Variazione pastorale per Corno

Interludio per Fiati

Ripresa dal Tema per Contrabasso

Variazione finale in modo di Rondo per Orchestra

Ginastera completed the Variaciones concertantes *in March 1953. It was first performed in Buenos Aires on June 2, 1953, by the Orchestra of the Association of Friends of Music, Igor Markevitch conducting.*

Instrumentation: *two flutes (the second doubling piccolo), oboe, two clarinets, bassoon, two horns, trumpet, trombone, timpani, harp, and strings.*

A note published with the score indicates that the work was commissioned by the Association of Friends of Music of Buenos Aires and dedicated to Mrs. L. H. de Carabello and Igor Markevitch, who were also responsible for the first performance. Ginastera also described the ensemble as a chamber orchestra, presumably based on the reduction to one each of oboe, bassoon, trumpet, and trombone.

The variations offer a good example of Ginastera's self-proclaimed "subjective nationalism" in their combination of nationalistic materials with relatively conventional structural procedures. The title accurately reflects the prevailing texture of the music, for each variation features a different "concerted" instrument. These solo instruments emerge from and return to the total orchestral fabric, in the process producing a continually shifting timbre when heard in the context of the complete work. Thus orchestral color becomes a major feature of the musical design. Two solo instruments introduce the basic material. An interlude by strings, based on that theme, precedes the body of variations, concluded by a balancing interlude for winds, also based on the theme. The theme is stated again by two solo instruments, similar to its first appearance, and the whole concludes with a dance-inspired finale for full orchestra. The symmetrical plan embracing variations I through XI reflects a quality found with increasing frequency in Ginastera's later works.

Variation I	Theme	Harp and cello
Variation II	Interlude	Strings
Variations III-IX		Various solo instruments
Variation X	Interlude	Winds
Variation XI	Theme	Harp and bass
Variation XII	Finale	Full orchestra

Considered collectively, the variations comprise far more than a series of decorative elaborations on one theme. They represent instead a metamorphosis in which musical elements of the theme are extracted and through development coalesce into something new.

Tema per Violoncello ed Arpa The theme consists of three sections, closely related by several motives that are expanded in the following variations. As a support for the theme in the cello, the harp plays a symbolic "guitar chord," an arpeggio outlining the open strings of the guitar. (A similar gesture is made in Ginastera's First String Quartet, in the Piano Sonata, and in his *Malambo* for solo piano. In referring to the guitar, the typical instrument of the gaucho, Ginastera recalls a whole tradition of music on which he drew for much of his life.) The following phrase continues with an inversion of the theme, ending the first section. The cello then continues with an extension of the opening motive, supported by the harp's simultaneous chords. The closing section returns to the guitar chord, as the cello plays another inverted version of the theme. Thus, within the first seventeen measures, Ginastera has already introduced several variants of the theme, while establishing a link with Argentine culture.

Interludio per Corde The first violins assume the final E of the cello and carry it into an extended version of the theme, imitated by the second violins and violas. Several statements of the initial semitone of the theme, inverted, provide a succinct coda.

Variazione giocosa per Flauto The original three-part structure of the theme becomes the focus of attention, producing an A–B–A design framed by two statements of a four-measure fanfare.

Variazione in modo di Scherzo per Clarinetto The lively orchestral patterns are answered by one of the most demanding clarinet parts in the orchestral repertory. Both orchestra and solo clarinet draw on the basic theme, in both original and inverted contours, following an A–B–A design with coda.

Variazione drammatica per Viola The three-part design of the theme remains. The strings play in imitation in the first section and the winds follow suit in the third, with the two sections separated by an intense cadenza by the solo viola.

Variazione canonica per Oboe e Fagotto The oboe extends the opening theme, imitated by the bassoon in strict canon a fifth lower. After an intermediate cadence, these roles reverse, with the bassoon playing the theme, answered by the oboe in strict canon a fifth higher.

Variazione ritmica per Trombe e Trombone Trumpet and trombone appear as soloists in the first two of three roughly parallel sections, culminated by the headlong rush of the full ensemble in the third.

Variazione in modo di Moto perpetuo per Violino The solo violin scampers about without interruption, as indicated by the title, while fragments of the principal theme support this brilliant passagework. The detached bowing of the violin at the beginning of this movement is answered by the flutes in its closing section, which play the same material, but now *legato*.

Variazione pastorale per Corno The horn plays lyrical variations on the midsection of the theme. The expansion of one motive by imitation among the winds in the closing section refers briefly to the opening, the whole being dominated by harmonies built of fourths.

Interludio per Fiati Just as the first *Interludio* followed the theme, the second precedes its return; balanced orchestral timbres support the symmetrical arrangement.

Ripresa dal Tema per Contrabasso In one of the most eloquent solos in the orchestral repertory for a solo contrabass, the theme returns in a low string instrument, embellished by the guitar chord in the harp. The three-part design remains, with the bass and harp concluding on the E of the first presentation.

Variazione finale in modo di Rondo per Orchestra Rhythmic activity and the interplay of orchestral choirs comprise most of the musical substance of this brilliant close. The opening motive of the theme provides a point of departure for the ritornello sections, and the full ensemble participates in the rhythmic contrasts between duple and triple patterns.

The variations were a pronounced success with both audiences and critics on their first appearance. They were quickly disseminated to the broader musical community when Igor Markevitch included them as part of his course in conducting at the Salzburg Festival in 1954. The Music Critics' Circle of Buenos Aires cited the work as the best composition introduced in 1953. Four years later, the score received the Cinzano award for the best orchestral work of the past ten years. The music later became the inspiration for several ballet settings: *Tender Night* (New York City Ballet, January 20, 1960); *Variaciones concertantes* (Ballet del Teatro Colón of Buenos Aires, May 22, 1960); *Surazo* (Ballet Nacional Chileno, July 13, 1961); and *La Chapeau* (Ballet du Grand Théatre Municipal de la Ville de Bordeaux, February 13, 1965). Critics have varied in their perception of the music, some describing it as Romantic, several others referring to it as Impressionistic. Judged by any criteria, the variations represent a major contribution to modernism. More important than any stylistic classification is the musical logic in both large- and small-scale design of the variations, a quality that should assure it a lasting position in the orchestral repertory.

Orchestral Works derived from Music for the Theater

In Ginastera's view, it was the ballet *Panambí* that marked the beginning of his career as a composer. By this time, he had discarded a number of earlier compositions—among them a piano concerto, his first symphony, and a sonatine for harp—feeling that they did not represent a mature effort, but this stage work apparently met his standards. He would go on to write other major works for the theater, among them *Don Rodrigo, Bomarzo,* and *Beatrix Cenci,* operas that have established Ginastera as one of the most effective dramatic composers of the 20th century.

Dances from *Estancia*, Opus 8a

Los trabajadores agrícolas *(The Land Workers)*

Danza del trigo *(Wheat Dance)*

Los peones de hacienda *(The Cattle Men)*

Danza final *(Malambo)*

Ginastera wrote the ballet music for Estancia *in 1941. The suite of four dances was first performed in Buenos Aires on May 12, 1943, by the Orchestra of the Teatro Colón, Ferruccio Calusio conducting.*

Instrumentation: *two flutes (the second doubling piccolo), two oboes, two clarinets, two bassoons, four horns, two trumpets, three timpani, bass drum, snare drum, tenor drum, cymbals, triangle, tambourine, castanets, tam-tam, xylophone, piano, and strings.*

Lincoln Kirstein, the dedicatee, commissioned the work for the Ballet Caravan company (a predecessor of the New York City Ballet), following a suggestion by the choreographer George Balanchine. The suite of dances was performed soon after Ginastera completed the score, but the ballet itself did not come into being until it was mounted by the Teatro Colón of Buenos Aires in 1952.

Both the scenario and music of *Estancia* reflect Ginastera's early penchant for nationalistic materials. The plot presents various aspects of life on an *estancia* (Argentine ranch) in a dawn-to-dawn vignette. A country girl despises the man from the city until he proves that he can perform the tasks associated with the rural environment, including, it seems, some vigorous dancing. The music reflects the composer's images of the plains, their imaginary vistas punctuated by the vigorous dances of the gauchos:

> Whenever I have crossed the pampa or have lived in it for a time, my spirit felt itself inundated by changing impressions, now playful, now melancholy . . . produced by its limitless immensity and by the transformation that the country undergoes in the course of the day. . . . From my first contact with the pampa, there awakened in me the desire to write a work that would reflect these states of my spirit. Already in some moments of my ballet *Estancia*

the landscape appears as the veritable protagonist, imposing its influence on the feelings of the characters. Nevertheless, my wish was to write a purely symphonic work, ruled by the laws of strict musical construction, but whose essence would partake of my subjective feeling.[2]

The repetitious banging of *The Land Workers* would fit well with any music designed to describe rigorous physical labor. The percussion instruments, led by the piano, hammer out a rapid pattern of six notes per measure, their rhythms shifting constantly between groupings of two, three, and four in various combinations. The rest of the orchestra soon joins in this sonorous bombast, making this opening dance an exercise in rhythmic propulsion that carries all before it.

The *Wheat Dance* offers a welcome respite in this otherwise hyperactive suite. The flute and two horns share a lyrical melody played high above an accompaniment of pizzicato strings. In the midsection, the lower strings turn to bowing in support of a sustained line played by violin and winds. This slowly moving line becomes increasingly static until it expires on a sustained D, leading to a reprise of the first section. Now the violins and horns provide the melody, as the lower strings return to their pizzicato accompaniment before the gossamer fabric fades away to nothing.

The rhythmic drive of the first movement returns in *The Cattle Men*. A continuing stream of eighth-notes divides into varying groups of two or three, the multiple meter signatures notwithstanding. The relentless energy of the underlying pulse never relaxes, drawing the full ensemble into an insistent rhythmic propulsion. The result is much like a rhythmic *moto perpetuo* for full orchestra.

Elements of Argentine rural dance come to a climax in the final *Malambo*. This is the gaucho's traditional competition dance, in which he strives to demonstrate his dominance by "dancing down" his male partner. Two gauchos face off; one begins to dance, then stops and his competitor continues. The dancers improvise steps of increasing complexity as the bystanders cheer on their favorite, the event sometimes lasting for hours. In Ginastera's setting, a prevailing six-eight meter shifts between the traditional three-plus-three and a contrasting pattern of four-plus-two. He enlivens this rhythmic interplay with tone clusters and harmonies built of fourths, creating an increasingly static harmonic vocabulary that casts the rhythmic element into ever sharper relief. Coupled with a general crescendo from beginning to end, the dance, and the suite, come to a breathless conclusion.

Ginastera wrote *Malambo* for solo piano the year before he wrote *Estancia*, and the character of this vigorous dance appears in other works by him. Traditions of rural dance and urban concert music cross in these movements, both drawing on the strengths of the other and making *Estancia* a milestone in the *gauchesco* tradition in the music of Argentina. On a broader scale, it also illustrates the role of music in the expression of national character in the 20th century.

Henryk Górecki

❦

b. Czernika, Poland, December 6, 1933

Górecki's early penchant for music was marked by stubborn perseverance on his part far more than by recognition of childhood talent or encouragement from a supportive family. His first formal instruction in composition began with Boleslaw Szabelski at the High School of Music in Katowice in 1955. As a composer, his provincial isolation proved to be something of a boon, for he was free to develop his craft relatively unencumbered by prevailing political dogma. He turned first to advanced serialism, the vogue in the 1950s, but by 1958 he had developed a style based upon the manipulation of timbre, texture, and register. From that point forward recognition came quickly, represented by a first prize from the Polish Composer's Union in 1960, three prizes from the Polish Ministry of Culture (1965, 1969, 1973), and first prize at the UNESCO competition in Paris in 1973.

Much of Górecki's early reputation was associated with music designed to confront the prevailing political mores, represented by scores that expressed a musical rebellion comparable to the political turmoil gripping Poland at the time. He, Krzysztof Penderecki, and Kazimierz Serocki were recognized as a musical troika credited with much of the impetus behind Poland's musical renaissance. Górecki's later works are noted for their intense personal expression, often symbolic, sometimes growing out of liturgical texts, which evolve from slowly shifting masses of timbre and texture that are deceptively simple in concept even when intricately complex in execution.

The attention showered on Górecki by the public, particularly through the Third Symphony, stands in marked contrast to his reserved personal demeanor. At times he has been the center of mass-media attention on a scale usually reserved for stars of the entertainment industry. A review of his published works suggests that the public has much yet to hear from this introspective composer.

Symphony No. 3, Opus 36 (*Symphony of Sorrowful Songs*)

Lento

Lento e largo—Molto lento

Lento—Lento e largo—Molto lento—Largo ben tenuto

At the end of his autograph score for the Third Symphony, Górecki inscribed the dates "30.10—30.12.76," implying that the symphony was written during the last two months of 1976, but at least a part of the third movement had been sketched in 1973. The complete work was first performed during the International Festival of Contemporary Art and Music in Royon, France, on April 4, 1977, by the commissioning body, the Orchestra of the Southwest German Radio, conducted by Ernest Bour, with Stefanie Woytowicz as soprano soloist.

Instrumentation: *four flutes (the third and fourth doubling piccolo), four clarinets, two bassoons, two contrabassoons, four horns, four trombones, harp, piano, soprano soloist, and strings.*

The addition of a text to a work identified as a symphony cannot be regarded as extraordinary in the late 20th century, particularly after the eloquent precedent set by the works of Gustav Mahler. In Górecki's Third Symphony, it is the subject matter of the texts rather than their single authorship that provides the thread of continuity: the three different texts address, in broad terms, a common theme of maternal grief over the loss of a child.

The original order of composition differed from the final plan. The first text that Górecki set became the focus of the last movement, an extended lament in which a mother mourns the disappearance of her son during a political uprising. She assumes he is dead and wails that she doesn't know his burial site, at the end praying that flowers may blossom around his grave to grant him peaceful repose. The source of the text remains unclear, but it is thought to have originated around 1919 to 1921 in response to anti-German uprisings in Silesia. At first, Górecki had difficulty composing an appropriate setting for this text, so he set the work aside while he searched for other texts with a comparable spirit and sense of humanity. He found one such text in a published account of Gestapo atrocities around Zakopane, Poland, during World War II. In a guesthouse that had been used as a prison, Polish researchers found graffiti left by prisoners. One of them, eighteen-year-old Helena Wanda Blażusiakówna, imprisoned on September 25, 1944, inscribed a simple prayer to her mother and to the Mother of God: "Oh Mama do not cry—Immaculate Queen of Heaven support me always. Hail Mary, dear and glorious." It was the simple but meaningful brevity of the text that appealed to Górecki, and it became the focus of the second movement. For a third text, ultimately to be incorporated into the first movement, Górecki chose a verse from a mid-15th-century Polish lament in which the Virgin Mary begs to share the suffering of her dying Son and pleads for a last word from Him as she mourns His passing. The three texts thus offer a dramatic balance as they speak from mother to child, child to mother, and mother to child. As poignant laments, they offer partial explanation for the prevailingly slow tempos and lugubrious character of the symphony. There is little doubt that they provided the basis for many later interpretations of the work as a testament to the horrors of war in the 20th century, but that interpretation has not been consistently supported by the composer.

Other than the pathos of the texts, it is the sequence of three slow movements in succession that makes the strongest impression on most audiences. In the traditional repertory, two movements in slow or moderate tempo may follow in succession, but to present more than fifty minutes of music in abidingly slow tempos represents a musical conviction, even a degree of courage, that few composers have embraced. Nonetheless, this very quality has given the Third Symphony an aura that comprises its greatest attraction for many listeners.

The duration of different performances will vary, but in any event the first movement will occupy close to one half the performance time required for the whole symphony. This carefully constructed statement opens with double basses whispering a theme adapted from a fragment of a Kurpie folk song. The progressive accumulation of parts, low to high, contributes to a crescendo without break in pulse or forward motion, mesmerizing the listener with seamless polyphony until the *fugato* unwinds and the parts combine and quietly come together on a unison E, the same pitch on which the exercise began. The entry of the soprano with the same E–F-sharp–G motto first played by the basses marks the beginning of a midsection, with her text unfolding before a background of slowly shifting dyads punctuated by gong sounds from the piano and harp. The soprano's solo moves to its conclusion through a series of interlocking motives based on the opening theme, ending on a broadly spaced D major harmony. The introductory canon returns, but now in reverse order, so that the music concludes with the murmur of the double basses with which it began. The movement thus represents a broad arch, with the pertinent text at its center surrounded by two sections of counterpoint in mirror design.

In a 1977 lecture, Górecki described the second movement as one of "a highland character. . . . I wanted the girl's monologue as if hummed . . . on the one hand almost unreal, on the other towering over the orchestra. . . ."[1] To this end the orchestra provides shifting masses of two-note chords allocated to each section, the voice moving above these in long-breathed phrases. The movement fades away, much in the spirit of the opening, to a sustained dyad of B-flat–D-flat.

The third movement deals with a multiversed folk text, the longest of the three involved. It expands to the accompaniment of simple orchestral repetition alleviated by one shifting tone within the static framework of the musical interval A–F. Even when the pitch center changes, the two-unit harmonic undulation continues until the close of the movement, where an insistent A major harmony dominates roughly 23 pages of score. Some listeners hear this as a final and uplifting apotheosis, while others describe the effect as a mind-numbing reversion to convention. In response to those who criticized this ending as reactionary, Górecki proposed that the prolonged repetition of the A major triad was as valid and as effective as the infamously repeated C major triad at the close of Beethoven's Fifth Symphony!

The festival at Royon, France, was not an auspicious venue for the introduction of a new work that was more personal than it was iconoclastic. The festival traditionally courted works firmly anchored in modernism and creative expressions considered the cutting edge in art and music. Górecki's symphony, expanding on undulating and long-sustained triadic harmonies, did not meet those expectations. Early reviewers maintained that Górecki had strayed from the avant-garde and was merely trashing what was truly modern, that the symphony was a noncomposition in pursuit of childish simplicity. But critics in Poland praised the work, in part because they were aware of its tortuous path of artistic development, in part because the texts addressed suffering of a sort all too familiar to Poles in the aftermath of two world wars that had raged across their land. Beyond that, the similarity between the opening of the third movement and the opening of the *Mazurka*, op. 17 no. 4, by Chopin, the most famous Polish musician of all, was sufficient to confirm Górecki and his symphony as an instrument of Polish national pride.

Following the introduction at Royon, the life of the Third Symphony was extended through recordings, rather than the usual means of concert performance, which became a story in itself. It was first taped in Poland but was not released on record until 1982, when a new recording, made in Germany, was distributed throughout Western Europe and the United States. Interest began to mount, the work was incorporated as background music in the Maurice Pialet film *Police*, and the original Polish recording was reissued by the British label Olympia (OCD 313). In 1992, Elektra Nonesuch issued a disc (79282–2) featuring Dawn Upshaw, soprano, with David Zinman conducting the London Sinfonietta, which caught the public's attention, setting records for sales of classical music recordings on both sides of the Atlantic. During most of 1993 the symphony was listed among the top-selling recordings in Britain and, soon thereafter, in the United States. The record became a major success on the popular charts, and among classical recordings it surpassed existing records for a single disc of concert hall music. The Elektra Nonesuch recording alone has sold more than a million copies, surpassing existing records for the sale of one recording by a living composer. The unparalleled success of this recording inspired concert performances, a reverse of the usual relationship between those arenas.

The symphony has been used as background for at least three films and one movie for television; portions of it have been choreographed by at least three ballet companies, one of these settings dedicated to the environmental tragedy of the Exxon Valdez oil spill in Alaska. A performance in Lincoln, Nebraska, was dedicated to AIDS victims, and in 1995 a Santa Fe art gallery mounted an exhibition of paintings that had been inspired by Górecki's work.

The tragedy implied in the texts, or the tenor of the times, or more likely the two together have led some to regard Górecki's Third Symphony as a musical memorial to the Holocaust, although the composer has not endorsed this interpretation. He instead stresses his focus on a broader scale of suffering and holds specific associations in abeyance. References to the Holocaust have nonetheless been emphasized in concert performances and in some of the adaptations for film, based largely on the emotional response the work has elicited from audiences. In attempting to explain this phenomenon, some writers have drawn a corollary between the period of the symphony's greatest popularity, 1989 to 1995, and the fiftieth anniversaries of the beginning and ending of World War II. Disregarding any association with the human tragedy of the Holocaust, there is little doubt that the work has assumed its own aura of solace and quiet grace, eliciting personal reactions sometimes approaching states of ecstasy.

Paul Hindemith

❧

b. Hanau, Germany, November 16, 1893; d. Frankfurt, Germany,
December 28, 1963

In the period between the two world wars, Paul Hindemith was one of the leading composers in Germany and an articulate spokesman for the values of discipline, technique, and communication in music. He began his career as a violinist at the conservatory in Frankfurt in 1908; by 1915 he was the leader of the Frankfurt Opera Orchestra. Following military service, he returned to the Frankfurt Opera, but was now playing the viola, the instrument on which he would later develop a reputation as a major virtuoso. He began to attract notice as a composer in 1922, leading to an appointment at the Hochschule für Musik in Berlin in 1927. Some of his lurid one-act operas and naive political statements brought him into conflict with the Nazi regime in Germany. As a result, the work generally considered to mark the establishment of his mature style, the opera *Mathis der Maler*, met with a government boycott in 1934. The issue became a *cause célèbre*, marked by a public letter from the conductor Wilhelm Furtwängler in defense of Hindemith and responding to public condemnation from Chancellor Adolf Hitler and his minister for cultural affairs, Joseph Goebbels. Hindemith emigrated to Switzerland in 1938, later moving to the United States where, with his lively intellect and fresh ideas, he exerted considerable influence as professor of music at Yale University from 1940 to 1953. Following his return to Germany, he became increasingly involved in conducting, particularly concerts of his own works.

Hindemith moved beyond German nationalism and wrote in an international style, an idiom addressed to the broader musical community of Western Europe and North America. In this growth, he made use of the corpus of collected works and historical sets of earlier music that appeared after World War I. He was one of the most articulate proponents of playing old music on historically authentic instruments and expected his students to participate in the performance of both old and new music. "Participation" is a key word, because Hindemith stressed the practical skills necessary to make use of musical materials from the past as well as the present. He was also a champion of music for the nonprofessional and at one point set for himself the goal of writing duo sonatas (with piano) for most of the orchestral instruments. He identified most of the works written in this spirit collectively as *Sing und Spielmusik* (Music for Singing and Playing). This effort did not imply simple or pedagogical pieces but music that was often written for a specific purpose other than formal concerts: music for radio, film, and above all, chamber music. His approach came to be labeled *Gebrauchsmusik* (useful or practical music), a term that Hindemith disliked but one that, in the view of the broader musical community, represented his objective approach to music.

As a means of conveying his own values, and partially to counter the serial techniques of Schoenberg and his followers, Hindemith developed his own theoretical system around a hierarchy of pitches and intervals founded on natural acoustics. Movement through these series progressed systematically from consonance to dissonance, providing a rational means of creating and assessing those qualities. He outlined a number of rules that established a framework in which musical activity could flourish, rather than a set of prescriptions intended to be applied literally and consistently. A still broader intent was the establishment of a technical basis on which future generations could build; if he did not succeed in that effort, he at least proposed a system designed for positive expansion rather than one based on the dissolution of existing theories. All of this he set forth in several volumes under the collective title, *The Craft of Musical Composition,* one of the theoretical touchstones of modern music. In a period when the dissolution of tonality was a major topic of conversation, Hindemith was a champion of the major triad, maintaining that music, at least for him, would always proceed from and return to that acoustic basis.

From 1949 to 1950, Hindemith was invited to present the Charles Eliot Norton Lectures at Harvard University, later published as *A*

Composer's World. Here he offered a view of musical creativity reaching far beyond technical matters, approaching a broad social consciousness holding music as its common tongue: "A German proverb says: *Böse Menschen haben keine Lieder* (bad men don't sing). It is not impossible that out of a tremendous movement of amateur community music a peace movement could spread over the world. . . . People who make music together cannot be enemies, at least not while the music lasts."[1]

Hindemith's ideas represented a comprehensive approach to music based on a firm technical mastery. He was able to apply these to his own composition with extraordinary facility, sometimes completing a composition within days. He was a musician's musician, one of the few who could address the general public as eloquently as he addressed professional musicians.

Symphony, *Mathis der Maler*

Angelic Concert

Entombment

Temptation of St. Anthony

Hindemith began work on the opera Mathis der Maler *in the summer of 1933, but wrote the three movements of the eponymous orchestral score between November and the following February. The first complete performance was given in Berlin on March 12, 1934, by the Berlin Philharmonic, Wilhelm Furtwängler conducting.*

Instrumentation: *two flutes (the second doubling piccolo), two oboes, two clarinets, two bassoons, four horns, two trumpets, three trombones, tuba, timpani, bass drum, snare drum, large and small cymbals, triangle, glockenspiel, and strings.*

From the early part of 1933, perhaps earlier, Hindemith had been focusing his attention on an opera that would match his earlier success with *Cardillac* in 1926. With much encouragement from his publisher, Willi Strecker of B. Schotts Söhne, he finally chose to write his own libretto based on events in the life of Mathis Grünewald (d. 1532), one of Germany's most famous painters from the early 16th century.

Grünewald is best known for his work for the monastery at Isenheim (now on display in Colmar), an altarpiece comprised of paintings showing him to be an artist of fervent passions expressed with bold imagination. Hindemith's libretto casts Grünewald as a protagonist in the peasant uprising of 1524, first as a champion of the people, later as a reluctant participant who realizes that his greatest contribution will be through his art. Ultimately, he must suffer isolation to achieve the artistic expression he seeks. The psychological drama thus generated has usually been considered a close parallel to Hindemith's own artistic struggles in Nazi Germany after 1933: the conflict between dedication to artistic expression and the responsibilities of a creative artist in a troubled society.

Hindemith eventually produced a libretto of seven acts, all to be illustrated by musical preludes and interludes. To fulfill a different request from the conductor Wilhelm Furtwängler for an orchestral work, he decided to incorporate these musical segments into an independent suite. As work progressed, the music came to be associated with individual panels from Grünewald's altarpiece. In January 1934, Hindemith wrote to Strecker that he was forwarding the music for *Angelic Concert* and *Entombment*, and that the "other pieces" would soon follow. Work did not progress rapidly, and at one point Hindemith considered ending the orchestral work with only those two items. By February, he had resolved whatever creative problems he had faced and was promising to have *Temptation of St. Anthony* completed by the middle of the month. In fact, it was not completed until shortly before the scheduled performance in March.

After completing the three movements, only later to be identified as a symphony, Hindemith refocused his attention on the opera. Thus the independent orchestral work emerged from and yet was completed before the operatic endeavor that spawned it. *Angelic Concert* served without change as the overture for the opera; *Entombment* became an interlude between scenes 1 and 2 of Act Seven. Most of *Temptation of St. Anthony* appeared in Act Six, but some segments were omitted, others placed in different sequence, and some paraphrased. The distribution of materials and Hindemith's letters during the course of composition make it clear that this movement gave him the most trouble.

Hindemith completed his sketches for the opera in the late summer of 1934, but it was not to meet the same reception as the first performances of the symphony. His music had frequently been castigated by the conservative political forces gaining ascendancy in Germany. At about this time, remarks attributed to him roused the ire of public officials to the point of open public criticism of the composer. With the best of intentions, Wilhelm Furtwängler, who had recently conducted a successful premiere of the work now called a symphony, wrote an open letter supporting Hindemith that was printed in the *Deutsche Allgemeine Zeitung* of November 25, 1934. Government officials were placed on the defensive, and the opera faced a national boycott. In protest, Furtwängler resigned from his positions as vice president of the State Music Office and director of the Berlin Philharmonic and Berlin State Opera. The opera was not performed until May 28, 1938, in Zurich, Switzerland.

The symphony fared much better. It was well received throughout Germany and North America. Even Hindemith's critics hailed it as a return to a harmonic style more comprehensible than that found in many of his earlier works. Further, the association of individual movements with one of Grünewald's most famous works created an element of programmatic illustration, a musical expression familiar to German audiences. For Hindemith, *Mathis* represented a synthesis of past musical efforts on which he would draw heavily in the years ahead. Critics and audiences often describe his stylistic development by dividing his works into categories of those appearing before and after *Mathis*, with the years 1933 to 1935 as a chronological watershed. Historically and musically, the work looms large in Hindemith's musical legacy.

Two chorale tunes anchor the first and last movements of the symphony. The first appears near the beginning, following a brief introduction by strings and woodwinds; the second comes near the end, followed by a comparably brief *Alleluia* played by brasses. Between these two extended movements, *Entombment* sounds as an interlude, the same role it played in the last act of the opera.

Angelic Concert opens quietly over a sustained G played by the horns. Against this the winds play a melodic fragment punctuated by widely spaced, resonant major chords. The chorale "*Es sungen drei Engel*" (There Were Three Angels Singing) draws on the panel of Grünewald depicting three angelic figures playing idealized string instruments while cherubs hover in the background. It is repeated three times, each time a third higher, until the introduction concludes with material from the opening measures. The main body of the movement starts with a lively main theme answered by three chords in the brass, three times, leading to a second theme also stated three times. The flute plays a closing theme, ending with three quiet chords in the strings. (Obviously, the number three plays a central role in this work.) First and second themes become entangled in an elaborate contrapuntal development until the "Three Angels" tune leads into a compact recapitulation and emphatic close on bright major chords.

Grünewald's painting, from which the slow movement takes its name, is a graphic portrayal of Christ's body being laid to rest. Muted violins play a quiet melody that soon gives way to a contrasting theme played by woodwinds. Following little more than an introduction of this new theme, the full orchestra returns with a loud and emphatic restatement of the opening to create a terse three-part design. A widely spaced major chord, played *fortissimo*, ends the movement, only to be followed by a portion of the second theme as an afterthought.

The scenes of personal torment in which Grünewald painted the martyr St. Anthony, in turn provided the inspiration for an elaborate symphonic movement of seven sections. Hindemith added to the beginning of the score a Latin epigraph taken from the Isenheim altarpiece, sung in the opera by St. Anthony at the height of his torment: *"Ubi eras bone Jhesu / ubi eras, quare non affuisti / ut sanares vulnera mea?"* (Where were you, good Jesus, where were you? Why have you not healed my wounds?) The orchestral score begins with a unison recitative, punctuated by the now-familiar major chords. The various sections of the orchestra compete for attention in an energetic tumult much less complicated than it seems. Throughout the score, Hindemith rarely presents more than three musical lines: a clearly stated melody, a contrasting countermelody, and a third line offering harmonic support. Through various manifestations of this texture, he carries us through the longest movement of the symphony until, over the full ensemble, the horn floats Hindemith's version of the second chorale melody: *"Lauda Sion Salvatorem"* (Zion, Praise the Savior). The brass section summarizes events, both musical and psychological, with a majestic *Alleluia* of three regal phrases.

Symphonic Metamorphosis of Themes by Carl Maria von Weber

Allegro

Turandot Scherzo

Andantino

March

Hindemith completed this score in June and August of 1943, based on sketches originating in 1940. It was first performed in New York City on January 20, 1944, by the New York Philharmonic Orchestra, conducted by Artur Rodzinski.

Instrumentation*: piccolo, two flutes, two oboes, English horn, two clarinets, bass clarinet, two bassoons, contrabassoon, four horns, two trumpets, three trombones, tuba, timpani, bass drum, snare drum, tenor drum, tambourine, tom-tom, triangle, small and large cymbals, small gong, wood block, tubular bells, glockenspiel, and strings.*

The *Symphonic Metamorphosis of Themes by Carl Maria von Weber* was one of Hindemith's first major orchestral works to emerge after he settled in the United States. He had worked with the choreographer Leonide Massine on a very successful production of the ballet *Noblissima visione* in 1938, and had completed the musical score for a second ballet, based on a scenario inspired by the paintings of the 16th-century Flemish artist Pieter Breughel. Massine subsequently proposed another ballet to music by Weber, and met with Hindemith in March 1940 to outline the project. In a letter to his wife, Hindemith expressed reservations about the idea: "He [Massine] thinks of it only as a plain ballroom dance . . . with good people milling around with bad people. He has some funny ideas about the music but I will write what I want to write, namely, music based on those charming piano duets by Weber."[2] Working quickly, Hindemith completed two of the pieces and forwarded them on March 31, but Massine was not pleased, saying that Hindemith's treatment of Weber's music was "too personal." Further negotiations accomplished little; it seems that Massine wanted little more than a straightforward orchestral arrangement of Weber's music. Hindemith was insulted that the choreographer expected nothing more from him than an orchestration, and when Massine further proposed that Salvador Dali prepare the scenic designs, Hindemith was happy to use another commission, this time from George Balanchine, as a reason to withdraw from his contract.

But his efforts were not lost, for in the fall of 1942 he wrote to a colleague that he was contemplating a *Weber Suite*, a project that came to fruition in the summer of 1943 as the *Symphonic Metamorphosis of Themes by Carl Maria von Weber*. In this form, the work is essentially a paraphrase of principal thematic fragments from several of Weber's piano duets. Hindemith maintained these excerpts in their original shape, adding to them further material to expand their musical character according to his own creative impulses. The result was four movements that were genuinely new compositions, taking Weber's themes as points of departure.

The title raises the obvious question: Which themes by Weber? When asked, Hindemith jovially declined to identify his sources, inviting his inquisitors to find out for themselves. We now know that the first, third, and fourth movements are based, respectively, on Weber's *Eight Pieces for Piano Duet*, Opus 60, no. 4; Opus 10, no. 2 (not Opus 3, as sometimes reported); and Opus 60, no. 7. The musical genealogy of the second movement is more complex. Weber took the melody from Jean-Jacques Rousseau's *Dictionnarie de musique* (1768), where it was cited as an example of Chinese music, which Rousseau in turn had quoted from a lengthy cultural study of the Orient by Jean-Baptiste de Halde (1735). Weber incorporated the tune in an *Overture Chinesa* (1804) that he later revised as incidental music for J. A. Schiller's adaptation of the drama *Turandot*. Thus a tune transmitted by missionaries returning from the Far East became a dictionary item in France in the 18th century, was then assimilated into a stage work in Germany by Weber in the early 19th century, and later became the basis for variations and a jazzy fugue by Hindemith working in America in the 20th century!

The opening *Allegro* expands on excerpts from Weber's piano duet through four autonomous sections. The first and third are repeated, both quoting thematic fragments from Weber. The second and fourth sections sustain the vigorous march character, and the fourth alludes to Weber's theme stated at the beginning, offering a reprise of sorts before ending with a nod to the closing measures of Mahler's Ninth Symphony.

Turandot Scherzo offers a more sophisticated example of the composer's craft. It encompasses several different musical techniques arranged in a way to create a musical statement comprehensible on multiple levels. In a compact introduction, Hindemith presents the two phrases of Weber's theme, each stated twice to create an A–A–B–B thematic structure. The flute introduces each phrase, followed by a second statement with piccolo and clarinet. From the first four notes, F–D–C–A, Hindemith creates a motto, one note being played by the glockenspiel before each of the four phrases comprising the full theme. The introduction closes with a brief interlude for the percussion instruments.

At this point, Hindemith has succinctly presented the ideas that he expands throughout the movement: a basic theme; a four-note motto; articulating interludes for percussion; and orchestration coordinated with these structural elements. There follows a series of seven variations, the orchestration expanding with each phrase of the theme until reaching a climax that dissolves into a rippling murmur in the first violin. Above this, a syncopated version of the opening phrase appears, to be expanded as a fugue with three consecutive countersubjects. Another percussion interlude brings this to a close, with the glockenspiel playing the basic motto in long notes while the timpani taps it out in diminution. A reprise of the opening phrase in its original shape introduces another set of variations, now limited to the first phrase and, like the opening variations, expanding the orchestration with each statement. The percussion section once again brings the process to a close, with the motto F–D–C–A played by glockenspiel and timpani. Punctuated by sputtering interjections from winds and strings, the music closes with a coda matching the introduction in its basic materials.

The following graphic outline of the *Turandot Scherzo* illustrates the salient features of a balanced structure that extends the musical elements presented in the introduction. The comparison with a sonata design does not imply a direct connection with that tradition, but it does reveal a plan of comparable aesthetic balance exploiting seminal elements of Weber's theme.

F (glockenspiel) → phrase a (flute)	INTRODUCTION
D (glockenspiel) → phrase a (piccolo, flute, clarinet)	
C (glockenspiel) → phrase b (flute)	
A (glockenspiel) → phrase b (piccolo, flute, clarinet)	

Percussion interlude

Seven variations: expansion of   EXPOSITION
    orchestration with each statement
    of the theme

Cadence: transition to fugue
    Fugue: subject based on phrase a,   DEVELOPMENT
    three countersubjects

Percussion interlude: F–D–C–A
    (glockenspiel and timpani)

Variations: phrase a, expansion of   REPRISE
    orchestration with each statement

Percussion close: F–D–C–A (glockenspiel   CODA
    and timpani)

Andantino offers immediate respite in its simple A–B–A design, the first theme played by clarinet and other woodwinds, the second by cellos and violas. At the reprise, the solo flute adds an extended arabesque that is one of the more elaborate passages for that instrument in the orchestral repertory. A short trumpet fanfare taken from Weber introduces the closing *March,* and the martial mood continues to the end. Four sections are clearly defined by contrasting thematic material and changing orchestration, much as in the opening *Allegro.* The different choirs of the orchestra present their own material, sometimes together, sometimes in alternation. The vigorous march rhythm eventually reintroduces the opening fanfare to produce a brilliant finale.

The score finally fulfilled its original conception as ballet music when George Balanchine successfully choreographed it in 1952. More important is the popularity the *Symphonic Metamorphosis* has enjoyed in the concert hall, where it continues to be one of Hindemith's most frequently performed works. The review of the New York premiere set a tone that did much to establish the work as a repertory item:

As for what Mr. Hindemith, who was present, has done with the themes of Weber, he must take the full responsibility. He has remarked that since these are by no means the best of Weber's themes, he has felt the freer to treat them as he pleases! . . . But we must also confess to finding the music diverting and delightful. Its wit and its mastery alike intrigue us, and suggest a fresh if not a new departure by this composer. . . . This metamorphosis employs counterpoint as a matter only incidental to the gay development of the ideas, and there is sunshine in every nook and cranny of the transparent, debonair score.

It is music, one would say, that has gained by human contacts. It is without pompousness or dead weight. The Chinoiserie of the second movement . . . is patent and intentional absurdity, with waggish nonsense of percussion instruments, from summoning bells to thuds of drums and clucks of xylophones.

For quite a while there is no fugue, but of course Hindemith has to come to a fugue before he has gone too far without one and the fugal business in this movement does not cease to be diverting. His Andante is in singing style, with broad developments and proper contrast to the other movements. His final March has a humor and gusto which does not come as an anticlimax after all the capital fooling and perspicacious music-making which has preceded. How delightful is learning carried in these pages![3]

The element of "learning" obviously refers to the craftsmanship Hindemith displayed in creating so much music out of so little material. That craftsmanship represented at least a part of the legacy Hindemith wanted to leave to following generations.

Gustav Holst

❧

b. Cheltenham, United Kingdom, September 21, 1874;
d. London, United Kingdom, May 25, 1934

ustav Holst was one of the most widely performed British composers in the decades surrounding World War I. Son of a long
line of continental musicians, he began his career as a pianist.
The neuritis that would plague him throughout his life brought that
activity to an end, and Holst turned to conducting (leading village
choirs, in which he was most happy) and composition. When he arrived
in London from the West Country in 1893, he made no great impression; he was still laboring under the influence of Richard Wagner's
music dramas, as were most young composers, and had not yet found
his own creative voice. He made ends meet by playing trombone in theater and resort orchestras, and then took a number of modest teaching
posts of the sort that would support him for most of his life.

In spite of his reluctance as a pedagogue, Holst's success at St.
Paul's Girls' School in Hammersmith led to the addition of a new
music wing, where he was able to establish a soundproof room that
would become the locus of his creative efforts. It was here that he composed *The Planets* between 1914 and 1916, a work whose popular success never ceased to dismay him. Publishers and recording companies
began to pursue him. He came to be much in demand as a conductor
of his own works, *The Planets* in particular, but his programs included a
very respectable catalogue of vocal and instrumental works as well. The
acclaim that his works received created in the mild-mannered composer an attitude of reticence bordering on bewilderment. He received,
and consistently declined, offers of honorary degrees from universities

in Britain and abroad. Conducting was another matter. He was genuinely pleased to accept conducting engagements in the United States at The University of Michigan (1923), Yale (1924), and Harvard (1932).

The decline of Holst's reputation in his later years was in some degree the result of the unusual popularity of *The Planets,* which overshadowed all his subsequent works. He had become typecast by audiences and critics, underrated by most of them, and therefore overlooked by scholars. As a result, much of his later productivity was relegated to undeserved neglect. His continued efforts to develop a musical style different from the ever-popular *Planets* were regarded by most audiences as austere, even sterile, an evaluation that Holst's own diffidence toward the public in general did nothing to dispel. He received a concussion from a fall in early 1923 from which he apparently recovered, but as time passed it became clear that his creative spark was dampened, leading him into deepening introspection and further withdrawal from the public, all of which cast an even darker shadow over his later works.

The Planets, Opus 32

Mars, the Bringer of War

Venus, the Bringer of Peace

Mercury, the Winged Messenger

Jupiter, the Bringer of Jollity

Saturn, the Bringer of Old Age

Uranus, the Magician

Neptune, the Mystic

Holst composed The Planets *between 1914 and 1916. Support from the patron Balfour Gardinor brought about the first (private) performance of excerpts in London on September 29, 1918, by the New Queen's Hall Orchestra, Adrian Boult conducting.*

Instrumentation*: female chorus (offstage, last movement only), four flutes (the third doubling piccolo 1, the fourth doubling piccolo 2 and alto flute), three oboes (the third doubling bass oboe), English horn,*

three clarinets, bass clarinet, three bassoons, contrabassoon, six horns,
four trumpets, three trombones, tenor tuba, bass tuba, timpani (two
players), bass drum, snare drum, cymbals, triangle, tambourine, gong,
bells, glockenspiel, xylophone, celesta, two harps, organ, and strings.

In 1913, Holst became acquainted with the madrigals of Thomas
Morley, an experience he described as changing his musical outlook for
all time. In July he heard the London performance of Stravinsky's *Le
sacre du printemps*, fresh from its famous premiere in Paris, and not
much later heard Arnold Schoenberg's *Five Pieces for Orchestra*. The flexible rhythms of the Elizabethan madrigal, the overwhelming orchestral
power and rhythms of Stravinsky's ballet music, and the kaleidoscopic
play of color in Schoenberg's score prompted Holst to bring together
many ideas he had long nurtured. Thus it was that in *The Planets* he first
found his own voice as a composer.

An abiding interest in personal horoscopes and astrology provided
a focus for Holst's creative energies. He consistently maintained that
the suite was not programmatic but a series of "mood pictures" depicting the subtitles he added to each movement by way of definition.
Writing to a friend, he claimed that:

> I dislike analytical programs and have not any of the Planets on
> me. Two things I would ask you to avoid. 1) The names have
> nothing—or little—to do with classical gods and goddesses. The
> music was suggested by the astrological attributes [of the Planets]
> and these are suggested by the sub-titles "Bringer of War." Mars
> was *NOT* suggested by the Great War! It's too bad of some really
> good critics to take this for granted. . . . As far as I can remember I
> had the scheme of the Planets roughly worked out in my mind by
> Easter 1914 except Mercury which was added later. I work
> extremely slowly and if the production of anything of mine seems
> to fit some event in the outward world you can be fairly sure that
> I began thinking about the music anything [*sic*] from 3 to 15
> years before the event happened.[1]

In support of Holst's declaration, note that the order of movements does not follow the order of the planets, and the order of composition differed from the sequence of movements as it was finally
established: *Mars* was completed before August 1914, *Venus* and *Jupiter*

later that year; *Saturn, Uranus,* and *Neptune* were written in the summer
and fall of 1915, in that order; and *Mercury* was finished in early 1916.
Each movement is autonomous, with any preconceived programmatic
elements lying in the realm of musical metaphor based on the characterizations Holst added to each movement.

In purely musical matters, Holst was concerned with unconventional tonal relationships, expanding upon the possibilities inherent in
the intervals of the semitone, major third, and tritone in lieu of the conventional fourths and fifths underlying traditional tonality. Eschewing
those usual harmonic relationships moved him away from many conventional formal structures, and the musical characterizations of the
zodiac may have comprised a subjective substitute for the comprehensibility normally provided by traditional structural plans.

Orchestration accounted for much of the musical success of *The
Planets.* The sounds of an alto flute (identified as a bass flute in the original score), bass oboe, and tenor tuba added colors not common to the
orchestral palette in 1914, and the organ, in spite of its brief appearances, added a further touch of novelty. Holst was a thoroughly practical musician in his scoring, knowing from his years as a trombonist in
theater and civic orchestras what combinations would be effective.
Apparently he conceived his musical materials with the orchestral timbres in mind and wrote them down as they came to him, undeterred by
technical niceties of notation. Consider the passages at the conclusion
of *Mars* and again in *Uranus* where he writes *ffff*, an exaggerated dynamic
level that, however impractical, nonetheless gets the attention of
orchestral players and emphatically conveys his intent. His scoring was
undeniably effective, leading many of his contemporaries to claim that
he had no superior as an orchestrator, high praise at a time when Ravel
and Stravinsky were raising the art of orchestration to new heights of
refinement.

Mars, the Bringer of War is probably the least complex movement of
the suite and, for many listeners, the most effective. The chief musical
ingredients are a five-four meter shifting between three-plus-two and
two-plus-three, a descending melodic second, and a driving rhythmic
ostinato introduced in the opening measure. Holst organizes these into
an A–B–A design, the outer sections defined by the ostinato. The relentless drive and blaring harmonies create a gripping effect, which the
composer declared should be both unpleasant and terrifying.

Venus, the Bringer of Peace offers a dramatic contrast in its prevailingly mellifluous character. Solo horn and violin play prominent melodies against a background of shifting harmonies from the woodwinds. One of the harps plays harmonics, a timbre that will return frequently in the following movements. The whole movement becomes a study in orchestral color, which ultimately fades away to infinity.

The prevailing character of *Mercury, the Winged Messenger* is speed, a quick and airy dialogue between the winds that exploits the tritone in the manner of a melodic ostinato, making the whole texture more of an "activity" than it is any "theme-with-accompaniment" or a series of returning sections. The tritone emerges from one of Holst's essays into bitonality, because much of the material derives from a combination of scales built on B-flat and E. In the context of the traditional orchestral repertory, *Mercury* reflects the spirit of a swift-footed scherzo.

Along with "jollity," *Jupiter* introduces a number of tunes familiar beyond the orchestral suite. The headlong rush introduced by winds and strings breaks off to introduce a fanfare that has been quoted many times, and at the *Andante maestoso* we hear a tune known to many under a different title. When Holst was asked to set to music the hymn "I Vow to Thee, My Country" in 1921, he was so overwhelmed with work that with much relief he followed a suggestion from Ralph Vaughan Williams that he use this excerpt from *Jupiter;* it fit the text and saved Holst from producing a completely new composition. The setting has since found its way into at least one edition of the *Methodist Hymnal* under the title *Thaxted*, the country village where Holst maintained a residence during most of the time he was working on *The Planets*.

Saturn, the Bringer of Old Age is another movement expanded by an ostinato, here a melodic element distributed throughout the orchestral fabric. The opening theme, played by the basses, returns as a closing reference before the two harps close with a cascade of arpeggios. There is little here to illustrate old age, unless a ponderous tempo and terminal *diminuendo* stand as hallmarks of maturity.

Uranus, the Magician opens with a four-note fanfare played by the trumpets and trombones, quickly restated by tubas and timpani in increasingly smaller note values. This motive reappears in various permutations before the music works itself up to a thundering climax, only to be thwarted by an unexpected glissando by the organ. In a flash, all is over.

The suite closes with *Neptune, the Mystic*, where Holst directs the orchestra "to play sempre [*sic*] *pp* throughout, dead tone, except for Clarinet and Violin. . . ." For Imogen Holst, the composer's daughter and principal biographer, this is "not the dead hush of despair: it is the intense concentration of a prolonged gaze into infinity."[2] Shimmering harmonies played by harps and celesta create a background over which woodwinds and a textless women's chorus superimpose haunting melodies. Holst was equally explicit in the effect he wanted from the singers; they were to be placed in an adjoining room and the connecting door was to be slowly and silently closed during the concluding measures. This muffled chorus repeats the last two measures, ever more softly, until the sound fades away completely.

Holst's early disclaimers about *The Planets* having a "program" should be regarded in the context of an era when the tone poems of the late 19th century still occupied the attention of audiences. Compared to the literal representation found in works by Richard Strauss and Frederick Delius, *The Planets* stands as a relatively abstract statement. But certainly the bellicose character of *Mars*, god of war, finds good representation in the first movement, and the fleet-footed Mercury is well described in the movement of that name. Still, the psychological program is more important for the suite as a whole. Characterizations on a broad scale move from the aggressiveness of *Mars* to the serenity of *Neptune*; *Venus, the Bringer of Peace* follows immediately upon *Mars, the Bringer of War*; and *Jupiter, the Bringer of Jollity* (youth?) is answered by *Saturn, the Bringer of Old Age*. Reflecting on the suite as a whole, each of the movements is an autonomous tone poem built around its own musical processes, but all are assimilated into a larger musical statement.

The early problems of performance centered around the difficulties in assembling a sufficiently large ensemble, owing to the economic stresses of World War I, and the reluctance of orchestras to program the complete suite instead of excerpts. Early responses were mixed, ranging from high praise to near condemnation. Most negative reviews were the result of piecemeal performances. Many programs offered *Mars, Venus, Mercury, Saturn*, and *Jupiter*, a decision apparently based on musical contrasts. Another format was the sequence of *Mars, Venus, Mercury*, and *Jupiter*, suggested by its similarity to symphonic fare that traditionally offered a major three-part opening movement, a slow movement, scherzo, and a concluding movement in sonata design. The first public performance of the full suite took place in London on November 15, 1920, with Albert Coates conducting the London Symphony Orchestra. This initiated a decade of near-unstinting critical praise for *The Planets*. In the United States, the Chicago Symphony and the New York Philharmonic competed vigorously for the first performance in North America, resolving the dispute by agreeing to play the work at the same time on the same evening (time zones giving New York a slight edge). By the end of the century *The Planets* had gone through several cycles of popularity, in the process serving as the first enduring introduction to music of the modern age for many audiences.

Charles Ives

❧

b. Danbury, Connecticut, October 20, 1874; d. New York City, May 19, 1954

The outstanding quality about Charles Ives, man and musician, was his original and independent thought on all matters that concerned him; he was not one to compromise his personal beliefs or his creative impulses to match the prevailing mores. As an independent thinker on social issues, he vigorously proposed a twentieth amendment to the Constitution of the United States in favor of more direct public participation in government. During the years before the entry of the United States into World War I, when the isolationists were in full cry, Ives was a determined and articulate supporter of a "People's World Nation," ultimately realized in the United Nations; in support of that principle, he was quite ready several years later to write to President Franklin Roosevelt, urging him to support legislation that would work toward that end. As a musician he marched to his own drummer, composing many pages of music to reflect his own experiences and imagination. None of these activities were driven exclusively by egocentricity; they represented instead expressions of personal conviction and an uncommon independence. His music is the most enduring manifestation of those qualities.

Ives grew up in Danbury, Connecticut, a thoroughly New England town where he was surrounded by the hymns, gospel singing, band marches, and Stephen Foster songs common to late-19th-century America. His father was the town bandmaster, a progressive musician who energetically proposed that music should be allowed to grow along its natural lines. He was interested in polyphony of more and wider scales, new tonal combinations, and a wider variety of rhythms. These beliefs led him to the exploration of bell tones, spatial separation of performing groups, and other experiments that many of his contemporaries regarded as crankish eccentricities. The elder Ives provided Charles with a rigorous grounding in traditional theory but also taught him to be comfortable with multiple keys and rhythms, and encouraged his son's youthful experiments in reproducing on the piano sounds from the local bandstand. In this environment, as a teenager Charles was already writing fugues in four keys at once. His musical experiments playing hymn tunes in his role as church organist (from 1888 to 1902) were often a source of dismay to those around him.

As a student at Yale, the young Ives studied composition with the German-trained Horatio Parker, gaining much in technical discipline but quickly learning as well that his iconoclastic creative efforts would receive little support from the established musical community. Following graduation, he consciously chose a career in the insurance business, partly from a sense of economic responsibility, but even more because he would thereby be less constrained in pursuing his own path in musical matters. His creative imagination flourished in both fields; in later years he maintained that his business career had helped his work in music, and his musical activities had helped him in business. His considerable success in insurance enabled him to retire in 1930, primarily to accommodate health problems that had plagued him since 1918. Most of his energy in the last 36 years of his life was directed toward assembling, collating, completing, or otherwise revising the works he assigned to the years between 1898 and 1918, the repertory by which he is generally known today.

These continuing revisions, a facet of Ives's creative process, have contributed to questions about an accurate chronology of his compositions and thereby their iconoclastic qualities in their original form. The young Elliott Carter met Ives several times and observed the older man's procedures in 1929:

> He was working on, I think, *Three Places in New England*, getting the score ready for performance. A new score was being derived from the older one to which he was adding and changing, turning octaves into sevenths and ninths, and adding dissonant notes. Since then, I have often wondered at exactly what date a lot of the music written early in his life received its last shot of dissonance and polyrhythm. . . . I got the impression that he might have fre-

quently jacked up the level of dissonance of many works as his tastes changed.[1]

Studies of Ives's manuscripts have shown that, in the process of revision, original dates of composition were often retained, even when the music had been changed substantially; there are examples of earlier dates being superimposed on an original that was several years later. These conditions detract nothing from the musical substance of such scores, but they have created problems, as yet incompletely resolved, about the stylistic chronology of many works.

Most discussions of Ives's music focus on the frequent quotation of borrowed materials, themes drawn from the soundscape that surrounded Ives throughout his life: hymns, college songs, marches, popular tunes, and excerpts from the European classics. These references are better described as paraphrases, because Ives rarely stated a borrowed theme in its original form, preferring to embellish, change rhythms, expand or diminish intervals, or otherwise place his own stamp on the music. These materials lie at the very core of Ives's creative process, providing the musical substance, often a programmatic commentary, plus rhythmic and harmonic structures that become grist for his musical mill. They may provide autobiographical references and sometimes humorous puns for the listener who is familiar with the originals. Fundamentally, they represent Ives's view that all experience was valid as a subject for his musical expression.

Recognizable musical fragments offer any listener a comfortable thread of identity, a sense of familiar ground. At the same time, they pose problems if relied upon too heavily. Many of the tunes familiar to Ives are now unfamiliar to some audiences and therefore do not carry the same connotations they held for the composer. Often it is unclear whether a familiar snatch of music derives from an earlier source or comes to us as a musical coincidence. Once aware of the process of quotation, the temptation is to search for all possible references to other music, as in a musical jigsaw puzzle, thereby missing the larger impact of some very imaginative scores. Further, the detailed search for musical paraphrase often attributes to identified fragments associations irrelevant to the substance of the music. Ives's choice of material was based on its fundamental musical qualities: the rhythms, harmonies, melodic contours, and motivic fragments of borrowed material fit their musical context. These musical characteristics were more of a determining factor in their inclusion than were matters of original text or other extramusical associations.

The broad scope of American vernacular music from which Ives borrowed most of his quotations has established him as one of the most American of all composers. If that were not his immediate goal, it was an emphatic result. He was well acquainted with the Germanic musical traditions of the 19th century and sustained many of them but moved beyond them in favor of following his own muse. When his music was compared to that tradition as a model, it was sometimes found wanting, but in the 20th century, vernacular music has been added to Western art music in an expansion of the musical canon. In this context, Ives has gradually come into his own as a harbinger of modern music in the United States. At the same time, his use of vernacular idioms has appealed to international audiences at least as eloquently as to his countrymen, and accounts in large part for the attention his music has received outside his own country.

During the 1930s, Ives's works began to be performed with increasing frequency. He was elected to the National Institute of Arts and Letters in 1946, and in 1948 received the Pulitzer prize in music for his Third Symphony, parts of which were composed in 1904. At the close of the 20th century, his star was still rising.

A Symphony: *New England Holidays*

Washington's Birthday (Winter)

Decoration Day (Spring)

The Fourth of July (Summer)

Thanksgiving and Forefather's Day (Fall)

Ives dated these four movements, or portions of them, between 1897 and 1933. The symphony was first performed in its entirety in Minneapolis on April 9, 1954, by the Minneapolis Symphony Orchestra, Antal Dorati conducting.

Cumulative instrumentation: *two or three fifes (optional), piccolo (a second piccolo optional), two flutes (a third flute optional), two oboes,*

*English horn, two clarinets in B-flat (a third clarinet in E-flat optional),
two bassoons (a third bassoon optional), contrabassoon, four horns (a
fifth horn optional), four trumpets (one doubling cornet), three trombones, tuba, six Jew's harps, timpani, bass drum, snare drum, cymbals,
high-medium-low bells, church chime, low chime, glockenspiel, xylophone, celesta, piano, strings, three extra violins, mixed chorus, plus an
offstage ensemble of contrabassoon, four horns, and trombone.*

In 1897, Ives wrote an organ Prelude and Postlude for a Thanksgiving
service, a work he later described as his first really good piece that did
not follow the rules laid down by Prof. Parker at Yale. He later orchestrated this organ work under the title *Thanksgiving and Forefather's Day,*
and while copying out the score came up with the idea of a *Holidays
Symphony* in which each movement would be based on the memories of
childhood holidays. *Thanksgiving* ultimately became the last movement
of that symphony, preceded by *Washington's Birthday, Decoration Day,* and
The Fourth of July. Certainly Ives did not work on the *Holidays Symphony*
consistently between 1897 and the completion of the score for
Thanksgiving in 1933, but returned to the project from time to time,
expanding, editing, and changing it according to his usual practice.
Most of the music presumably came into being between 1904 and 1913.

Beyond their references to national holidays, the movements at
some point became associated with the seasons of the year, later
included as subtitles. Ives changed his mind frequently on such matters; at various times, the symphony was also identified as "4 New
England Holidays," "IV Symphony (or Set for Orchestra sharp1)," "1st
Orchestral Set," "Set of Pieces for Orchestra—'Holidays in New
England,'" "Holidays in a Connecticut Country Town," and a few other
titles in similar vein. It was Ives's intent to portray by musical means
events in the lives of common people in the rural communities. Even
though collectively identified as a symphony, he still thought of the
movements as separate pieces that could be performed independently.
They are to some degree autobiographical in their reference to events
Ives recalled from his youth. *Decoration Day* and *The Fourth of July* in particular draw on his experiences with the town band, directed by his
father, serving as a memorial to the man who was so much a part of the
composer's early musical experience and training.

Washington's Birthday incorporates some barn dance tunes first written down in 1909, but, according to Ives, the music assumed its basic shape in 1913 and was revised in the 1920s. He brought together several instrumentalists from a theater orchestra to play the piece in 1913 or early 1914; in spite of an incomplete ensemble, they apparently managed to get through the work fairly well and performed it at the Globe Theater in New York in 1914 and 1915. Several years later, another group drawn from the New York Symphony played through the score in a private hearing. In Ives's view "they made an awful fuss about playing this, and before I got through, this had to be cut out, and that had to be cut out—and in the end the score was practically emasculated."[2] Conducting an ensemble assembled expressly for the purpose, Nicolas Slonimsky introduced *Washington's Birthday* in San Francisco on September 3, 1931.

The ensemble for this movement has often been described as a chamber orchestra, consisting of flute/piccolo, horn, Jew's harps (or two clarinets), percussion, and strings. Ives advised that six to a hundred Jew's harps would be needed to recall his own experiences of country dances where "about all the men would carry Jew's harps in their vest pockets or in the calf of their boots, and several would stand around on the side of the floor and play the harp more as a drum than as an instrument of tones."[3]

He outlined a more specific program in a Postface to the full score in which he first quotes a portion of the poem "Snowbound" by John Greenleaf Whittier, then describes the winter holiday he envisions in greater detail:

> But to the younger generation, a winter holiday means action!— and down through "Swamp Hollow" and over the hill road they go, afoot or in sleighs, through the drifting snow, to the barn dance at the Centre. The village band of fiddles, fife and horn keeps up an unending "breakdown" medley, and the young folks "salute their partners and balance corners" till midnight. As the party breaks up, the sentimental songs of those days are sung, and with the inevitable "adieu to the ladies" the "social" gives way to the gray bleakness of the February night.[4]

The music reflects his narrative through three sections: a slow opening depicting the bleak New England winter; an *Allegro* built around energetic fiddle tunes to represent the barn dance; and a concluding

Andante representing the dissolution of the evening's activities. The first section conveys the impression of a cold and frozen landscape with slowly moving, dissonant chords articulated by brief references to "Old Folks at Home" and, later, "Turkey in the Straw"; other borrowed materials are less easily observed as the music fades to a whispered ending. The *Allegro* interrupts this mood abruptly with the lively fiddling of the barn dance. Other dance tunes enter the musical fray, and once again the music offers a snatch of "Turkey in the Straw," followed by hints of "Sailor's Hornpipe" and "Camptown Races," and the flute plays a bit of "For He's a Jolly Good Fellow" before everything melds into a general melee at the entry of the Jew's harps. Fragments of other tunes can be found in the score, but they become lost in the bustling orchestral activity. All this comes to a sudden end, replaced by the *Andante* and a long, lyrical melody played by the first violins. As the festivities wind down and dancers leave, a fragment of the traditional "Good Night, Ladies" mixes with echoes of the fiddle tunes still sounding in the dancers' heads as they depart into the "gray bleakness of the February night."

Decoration Day evolved over a period of nearly twenty years, its early stages marked by conceptions for a brass band and, at one time, a sonata for violin and piano. Ives first mentioned *Decoration Day* in 1911; in an early list of his works cited in his *Memos* he attributed the work to 1913, in a later list he gave the date 1912; the surviving sketches were made on paper that can be dated no earlier than 1915. He recopied the score in 1919 for an open rehearsal in 1920 and revised it further in 1931. Disregarding questions about what represents an authoritative version, this process of continuing revision was typical of Ives's musical creativity.

The New Symphony Orchestra of New York first performed *Decoration Day* in May 1920, as part of an open rehearsal for which the orchestra had solicited manuscript scores by native composers. After receiving the parts, the players at first reneged because they thought it too difficult to read. Ives related that he wrote to them saying that he expected them to play it, and would hold the orchestra to the bargain, because the public notice had said nothing about any accepted level of difficulty. His account of the public rehearsal describes a sorry state of affairs in which the players were unable, or perhaps stubbornly unwilling, to cope with the unfamiliar music. The conductor, Paul Eisler, returned the score with the peremptory comment that "There were limits to musicianship." Ives wanted to respond that the greatest limitation was the conductor's musicianship! The premiere of record took place in Havana on December 27, 1931, with the Orquestra Filarmónica de la Habana, conducted by Amadeo Roldán.

As with *Washington's Birthday*, Ives appended a postface to the score of *Decoration Day* offering a program for the music based on his recollection of the holiday (now Memorial Day) from his childhood. He described the holiday atmosphere, the events of the traditional Memorial Day parade, and services at the local cemetery. The music corresponds to his description of events in well-defined sections. An original motive played by the English horn identifies the gathering of floral tributes; as people come together on the square, phrases of "Marching through Georgia" sound in the wind instruments. The procession to the cemetery takes place to an organum-like setting of *Adeste Fideles*, which in Ives's youth was more frequently associated with the text "How Firm a Foundation" than with the Christmas hymn "O Come All Ye Faithful." References to "Tenting on the Old Camp Ground" and "The Battle Cry of Freedom" reinforce the somber mood, and "Taps" sounds quietly as a concluding gesture. With the return to town, the music moves smoothly into the vigorous *Second Connecticut March* (*Second Regiment Connecticut National Guard March* [1877] by D. W. Reeves), which, at 56 measures, is the longest quotation of borrowed material in all of Ives's works. Clarinets and oboes play a fragment of "The Battle Hymn of the Republic" before the march reaches its final cadence, a sonic climax suddenly replaced by a muted chord that serves as a background for one last statement of the flower-gathering motive and a barely audible reference to "Taps," played by the bells and solo viola.

The program outlined in the postface apparently held a particular meaning for Ives; in his *Essays before a Sonata*, written in 1919 and 1920, he describes the same experience:

> In the early morning of a Memorial Day, a boy is awakened by martial music—a village band is marching down the street—and as the strains of Reeves' majestic *Seventh* [sic] *Regiment March* come nearer and nearer—he seems of a sudden translated—a moment of vivid power comes, a consciousness of material nobility—an exul-

tant something gleaming with the possibilities of this life—an
assurance that nothing is impossible, and that the whole world
lies at his feet. But, as the band turns the corner, at the soldiers'
monument, and the march steps of the Grand Army become
fainter and fainter, the boy's vision slowly vanishes—his "world"
becomes less and less probable—but the experience ever lies within
him in its reality.[5]

The personal element in this text and in his Postface has led many
observers to consider *Decoration Day* as a memento of Ives's boyhood,
implicitly a memorial to the father whose loss continued to pain him.

The Fourth of July occupied Ives over a number of years. At one time
he indicated that it came from around the period 1905 to 1906. In an
early work list he assigned it to 1912, in a later list he expanded that to
1912 to 1913, and some parts of the final version were completed in the
1920s. Thus it is safe to say that *The Fourth of July* emerged from the long
gestation and extensive revision common to most of Ives's larger works.
Nicolas Slonimsky conducted the premiere in Paris on February 21,
1932, leading a group of players drawn from the Orchestre
Symphonique de Paris in a concert sponsored by the Pan American
Association of Composers. *The Fourth* was the centerpiece in a three-
movement suite that opened with *In the Cage* and closed with *In the
Night*, both drawn from the *Set for Theatre Orchestra* (1906–1911).

Ives provided multiple versions of a program for this work. It was
not included as a postface, but appeared in his *Memos* several years after
an early version of the score had been completed. For Ives, the work was
both program music and abstract music:

> It's a boy's 4th—no historical orations—no patriotic grandilo-
> quences by "grownups"—no program in his yard! But he knows
> what he's celebrating—better than most of the county politicians.
> And he goes at it in his own way, with a patriotism nearer kin to
> nature than jingoism. His festivities start in the quiet of the mid-
> night before, and grow raucous with the sun. Everybody knows
> what it's like—if everybody doesn't—Cannon on the Green, Village
> Band on Main Street, fire crackers, shanks mixed on cornets,
> strings around big toes, torpedoes, Church bells, lost finger, fifes,
> clam-chowder, a prize-fight, drum-corps, burnt shins, parades (in
> and out of step), saloons all closed (more drunks than usual),

baseball game (Danbury All-Stars vs Beaver Brook Boys), pistols, mobbed umpire, Red, White and Blue, runaway horse,—and the day ends with the sky-rocket over the Church-steeple, just after the annual explosion sets the Town-Hall on fire. All this is not in the music,—not now.[6]

True to his words that "All this is not in the music," the association between the program and the music is far more general than in the preceding movements. Literal portrayals of the memories Ives described rely on the listener's perception at least as much as on the musical events in Ives's score.

The movement opens and closes with brief, quiet passages, tentative at the beginning, reflective at the end. The main body of the music expands upon "Columbia, the Gem of the Ocean" and other tunes, but portions of "Columbia" finally coalesce into a complete statement. The tune, one of Ives's favorites, first appears in the basses immediately after the introduction, rhythmically altered but clearly recognizable. As it continues to emerge piecemeal, it is accompanied at various times by snippets of "The Battle Hymn of the Republic," "Sailor's Hornpipe," "Reveille," "Marching through Georgia," "Yankee Doodle," "Katy Darling," and other tunes that add a fleeting counterpoint as "Columbia" gathers force. The first of three sonic explosions engages the full ensemble playing *fff, Con furore,* as the violins and violas play streams of tone clusters. At the second climax, the strings return to that mode, while trumpets and trombones intone "Columbia" to the accompaniment of "Yankee Doodle" from the xylophone, different phrases of "Battle Hymn of the Republic" from flutes and oboes, and "Katy Darling" played by the piccolo. The complexity of the score at this point offers a major challenge to both conductor and audience. A brief pause interrupts the melee before one last explosion that is itself abruptly terminated, leaving the three muted violins to play a closing reverence.

In composing *The Fourth of July,* Ives drew on an earlier sketch inspired by the sinking of the steamboat *General Slocum* in the East River of New York in 1904. To achieve the desired effect of bands playing and people singing, all overwhelmed by deadly explosions, he expanded on a combination of different rhythmic patterns, all played simultaneously to establish several strata of music that contributed to the accumulation of sound leading to the orchestral climaxes. The entire score was constructed in a spirit of musical independence in which Ives indulged his own whims in matters of musical material, thinking the piece would never be played. In a famous note to his copyist he directed: "Please don't try to make things nice! All the wrong notes are <u>right</u>. Just copy as I have—I want it that way. . . ."[7] If he were not aware of the probable reactions to the music, there were many who would so advise him. Edgar Stowell, a conductor who first performed a portion of *Washington's Birthday*, described the score as the best joke he had seen in a long time, and inquired of Ives whether "anybody would be fool enough to try to play a thing like that?"[8]

Many ensembles have since been "fool enough" to play the work, and with considerable success. Reactions to the first performance in Paris were mixed, although several critics admired the orchestral writing in the final climax. One described Ives as a composer whose works stood out at the concert:

> His art is at times coarse and clumsy, but in him there is genuine strength and inventiveness, thematically as well as rhythmically, in no way taking fashion or authority into consideration. Ives's suite *The Fourth of July* . . . is based on national motifs; in this regard Ives is, perhaps, the only one of the composers of North America whose work is profoundly national, and in him there is something reminiscent of Walt Whitman.[9]

If *The Fourth of July* was not readily accepted in all quarters, clearly there were some in the musical community who recognized Ives as an American original.

Ives wrote *Thanksgiving and Forefather's Day* over a period extending from 1897 to 1933. Some parts of the music originated as an organ prelude and postlude Ives wrote for Thanksgiving Day services at Center Church, New Haven, in 1897, making this the only part of the *Holidays Symphony* to be written while he was still a student at Yale. In his *Memos* he recalls incorporating the organ compositions into a single orchestral work around 1904, at which time he conceived the idea of a symphony celebrating national holidays. His sketches show that he continued to work on the project between 1907 and 1919, but the complete score was not finished until 1933. *Thanksgiving* was first performed in Minneapolis on April 9, 1954, by the Minneapolis Symphony Orchestra, Antal Dorati conducting, as the concluding movement for the premiere of *A Symphony: New England Holidays.* Thus portions of *Thanksgiving* were among the earliest parts of the symphony to be composed and the last to be performed, just weeks before Ives's death.

Thanksgiving is less personal than the previous movements, concerned with a more universal appeal and lacking specific program elements. It does, however, expand on borrowed materials and follows a structural plan open to more than one interpretation. The movement opens quietly, with the orchestra sounding very much like a large organ playing a solemn hymn tune. The music continues in this vein, gradually adding instruments and presenting portions of the hymn tunes "Federal Street" and "Duke Street." A midsection expands on two presentations of the gospel song "Shining Star," played by the strings, separated by a reference to "In the Sweet Bye and Bye." The music continues to build into a closing section based on "Duke Street," now set for chorus and full orchestra to the text "God, beneath Thy guiding hand, Our exiled fathers crossed the sea; And when they trod the wintry strand, With prayer and praise they worshipped Thee," words written in 1833 to celebrate the founding of New Haven. To this moving climax the trombones play, as *fortississimo* counterpoint, the melody of "Federal Street," first heard at the beginning. The movement follows a loosely scripted three-part design, defined by different statements of "Federal Street" and "Duke Street" surrounding a smaller three-part exposition of "Shining Star." At the same time, the order in which these borrowed materials appear approximates a symmetrical pattern, with "In the Sweet Bye and Bye" at its center.

The four movements comprising A Symphony: *New England Holidays* lead a double life: they are performed as independent works as well as constituent parts of a larger cycle. They offer no intrinsic musical connection other than their titular assimilation under the umbrella of national holidays, but considered from a broader perspective they encompass Ives's productive years and represent his style and musical aesthetics in a comprehensive statement. There is nothing quite like this symphony in the modern repertory.

Orchestral Set No. 1: *Three Places in New England*

The "St. Gaudens" in Boston Common (Col. Shaw and his Colored Regiment)

Putnam's Camp, Redding, Connecticut

The Housatonic at Stockbridge

*According to Ives's records, the three movements were completely scored
by 1914 from materials composed between 1903 and 1912. They were
first performed in a version for chamber orchestra before the American
Committee of the International Society for Contemporary Music meeting in New York on February 16, 1930, conducted by Nicolas
Slonimsky, and the first public performance of that score was presented
in New York on January 10, 1931, by the Chamber Orchestra of
Boston, also conducted by Slonimsky. A version prepared in 1972 and
1973 by James Sinclair was first performed in New Haven on February
9, 1974, by the Yale Symphony, John Mauceri conducting.*

Instrumentation (chamber orchestra version): *flute (an added piccolo optional), oboe (doubling English horn), clarinet, bassoon, horn,
trumpet, trombone, tuba, timpani, bass drum, snare drum, piano,
celesta (optional), organ (pedals 16' and 32'), and strings.*

Three Places in New England emerged through a circuitous path. Ives
referred to this score as his *First Orchestral Set* about as frequently as
Three Places in New England, and at other times as *A New England
Symphony* and *Three New England Places* as well.

In 1903 he wrote a "Country Band March" and an "Overture and
March: 1776," probably intended for a stage work planned by his uncle
Lyman Brewster. These were later incorporated into *Putnam's Camp*. In
1908 he sketched the music that would become *The Housatonic at
Stockbridge* and four years later wrote a "black march" designed as a trib-
ute to the first African-American regiment in the Union Army during
the Civil War. Fully orchestrated, this became the substance of *The "St.
Gaudens" in Boston Common*. At that point, he created *Putnam's Camp* out
of the earlier "Country Band March" and "Overture and March: 1776,"
and between 1913 and 1914 completely orchestrated *Putnam's Camp* and
Housatonic to form collectively the basis of *Three Places in New England*.
Ives revised this score in 1929 for Slonimsky's early performances with
chamber orchestra; that version was the first major orchestral work by
Ives to be published in its entirety. Later performances by full orchestra
used this chamber orchestra version with expanded instrumentation,
until James Sinclair pieced together a semblance of the original from a

diffuse collection of earlier manuscripts, essentially the music of the chamber orchestra version but with the instrumentation from 1914. This has come to be the generally accepted musical text.

The New York performance of 1931 was one of few given in Ives's presence. He was delighted with what was reportedly a rather ragged performance, and enthusiastically confided to Slonimsky that it was "Just like a town meeting—every man for himself. Wonderful how it came out."[10] The music was in part autobiographical in its recollection of places and causes close to the composer's heart, building on his own memories and past experiences. The individual movements gave musical substance to his personal sense of time and place.

The *"St. Gaudens" in Boston Common* refers to a statue commemorating Col. Robert Shaw and the 54th Regiment of Massachusetts, a unit of all-black volunteers that met a disastrous defeat at Fort Wagner in South Carolina during the Civil War. Colonel Shaw was one of the first to die, and the Confederates unceremoniously buried him and all the dead from his unit in one mass grave. August St. Gaudens was a prominent American sculptor, best known for his design of some American coins. He responded to a commission for a memorial to Shaw and his regiment with a monument highlighting Shaw on horseback, with his weary and dispirited soldiers marching in the background, thus the subtitle *Col. Shaw and his Colored Regiment.*

In its opening moments the music offers a quiet dirge representing Ives's personal reaction to the monument and all it represents. That which follows resembles an unbalanced arch. A motive from "Old Black Joe" opens the work and appears in a number of transformations, some in the melodic foreground, others more subtly incorporated as part of a pedal point in the basses. Material drawn from "Marching through Georgia" comes to the fore, supported by a new pedal figure and a simple street beat in the timpani and drums to suggest the marching element. A fragment of "The Battle Cry of Freedom," played by the trombone, leads to the climax on a resounding major chord, after which the musical tension gradually subsides, as the materials from the first part of the movement return in reverse order. Fragments of "Old Black Joe" lead to a whispered ending, as though the marchers had disappeared in the distance.

Putnam's Camp offers all the musical trappings of a battle piece, recalling the trials of colonial soldiers during the War for Independence.

Ives provided a commentary recalling a Fourth of July celebration, a part of which is the musical representation of two bands playing different tunes as they parade toward the center of town, reaching a climax of polyharmony and polyrhythms before they recede in the distance. Nicolas Slonimsky established a reputation as a virtuoso conductor in performing this movement; he directed one part of the ensemble playing four measures in the same span of time that another section was playing three, leading one group with his right hand, the other with his left. The music incorporates materials from two earlier marches, the "Country Band March" and "Overture and March: 1776," and the influence of two contrasting elements is reflected throughout the score. It was in this movement that some critics claimed to hear elements of Stravinsky, but Ives claimed that it was "written before Stravinsky wrote the *Sacre* (or at least before it was first played), and came direct from the habit of piano-drum-playing."[11] The texture offers a quintessential illustration of the polystrata, or layered textures, described earlier.

The third movement had its roots in an experience from Ives's honeymoon near Stockbridge with Harmony Twitchell Ives:

> We walked in the meadows along the river, and heard the distant singing from the church across the river. The mist had not entirely left the river bed, and the colors, the running water, the banks and elm trees were something that one would always remember. Robert Underwood Johnson, in his poem, *The Housatonic at Stockbridge,* paints this scene beautifully.[12]

Ives quoted Johnson's poem as a preface to the score, and arranged the music as a song for voice and piano in 1921. The music starts quietly, growing consistently in texture and volume until it reaches its climax on a *fortississimo* tone cluster containing all twelve chromatic tones of the octave. In typical Ives fashion, this is abruptly curtailed, leaving the strings to intone a quiet hum to the end.

The first performance of all three movements in New York attracted little notice, but another in Boston on January 25, 1931, elicited comments about the "lunatic fringe" of modern music, the thick and "monotonously dissonant" first movement, and complaints that the music bore no observable relation to the subject implied by the title and that the conclusion of *The Housatonic at Stockbridge* suggested that noble river was caught up in an ice jam. Yet another critic thought that the same movement contained measures that were genuinely beautiful, offering moments of nostalgic melancholy, and described *Putnam's Camp* as "an ingenious and sometimes humorous parody of the efforts of a country band."[13]

Later the same year, Slonimsky conducted the work in Paris in the first of two programs devoted to American music. The reviewer Henry Prunières was perceptive, if not entirely accurate:

> I cannot say that these concerts have been a very great success. The first left a terrible impression of emptiness, which the second succeeded in effacing only in part. If it be true that Charles Ives composed his "Three New England Scenes" before acquaintance with Stravinsky's "Le Sacre du Printemps," he ought to be recognized as an originator. There is no doubt that he knows his Schönberg, yet gives the impression that he has not always assimilated the lessons of the Viennese master as well as he might have. The second part, with its truculent parody of an American march in the Sousa vein and the unloosing of its percussion achieves a picturesque effect. The third part presents a typical American theme with pretty orchestral effects. The composer is manifestly a musician.
>
> I should like to be able to say as much about the other names inscribed on the program.[14]

It seems clear that Prunières considered Ives and *Three Places in New England* superior to other parts of the program. Ives, always sensitive to criticism, regarded the review as a negative commentary, and went to some pains to refute what he perceived to be misinformed journalism, pointing out that he had heard nothing of Stravinsky until 1923 or 1924 and emphatically rejecting the probability of any influence by Arnold Schönberg. The following year Paul Rosenfeld described *The Housatonic at Stockbridge* as "the hero of the suite and easily one of the freshest, most eloquent and solid orchestral pieces composed in America, transmitting in polyrhythms the movement of the great river in its vernal expansiveness."[15]

Time has vindicated Rosenfeld's perception and Prunières's closing assessment of Ives. At the end of the 20th century, *Three Places in New England* held an established position as one of Ives's eloquent essays in musical Americana.

The Unanswered Question

This is one of several innovative works Ives attributes to 1906. The first performance of record was at Columbia University in New York on May 11, 1946, by students from the Juilliard Graduate School conducted by Erick Schenkman (onstage) and Theodore Bloomfield (offstage).

Instrumentation: *four flutes, solo trumpet, and strings.*

Ives wrote a number of experimental pieces reflecting efforts to expand his creative procedures at least as much as they represented practical experiments in matters of performance. In his *Memos*, he recalled that some of them were tried out by friends, the experiments usually ending in some sort of confrontation, a response to which he would become accustomed in the years to follow. The title of *The Unanswered Question* probably came from Emerson's poem *The Sphinx* (1841): "Thou art the unanswered question; / Couldst see thy proper eye, / Always it asketh, asketh; / And each answer is a lie."[16] Most performing groups present the work as an independent composition, but during its early history it was included as one movement within several larger cycles. Ultimately it appeared as the first of two *Contemplations* under the title *A Contemplation of a Serious Matter* or *The Unanswered Perennial Question*, followed by its complement, *A Contemplation of Nothing Serious* or *Central Park in the Dark in "The Good Ole Summer Time."* The experimental quality reflected in these various combinations surfaced in the choice of instruments as well. Ives indicated that the third and fourth flutes could be replaced by oboe and clarinet if available, the solo trumpet line could be performed by English horn, oboe, or clarinet, and the contrabass was an optional part of the string choir.

In the foreword to the published score, Ives described the strings as "The Silences of the Druids—Who Know, See and Hear Nothing," the trumpet was to represent "The Perennial Question of Existence," its inquiries answered by the winds as "The Invisible Answer." He asked that the strings play *ppp* throughout, offstage or at least distant from the trumpet and winds. Against their sustained, slowly changing harmonies the trumpet intones its question seven times, each presentation the same except for the last note that alternates between B and C. Original sketches showed a B-flat for the end of the last phrase, but the published version, based upon copyists' work that Ives approved, maintained the B–C alternation. Several recent editions and recordings offer both versions of the trumpet part. Winds respond to each trumpet call with increasingly agitated answers until they finally disperse in confusion, allowing the trumpet to offer its last inquiry, while the Sphinx-like strings hum on into eternity.

In technical matters, the work raises questions of time different from any found in the music of Ives's predecessors. The barring for the strings and winds does not coincide at all points, and the string parts move so slowly that they offer no strong sense of metric organization. The trumpet becomes an intermediary between two strata of activity, one measured and atonal (winds), the other rhythmically free and tonal (strings). The spatial separation created by the offstage strings both draws upon and enhances this temporal division. Ives may have recalled his father's experiments with spatial separation and planned to expand upon them. Certainly the effect pleased him, because he incorporated the same technique into *Central Park in the Dark* and again into his Fourth Symphony. Some historians consider Ives's work in this manner as a model or inspiration for efforts by Karl-Heinz Stockhausen and John Cage later in the century.

Comparing further the musical notation and Ives's instructions in his Foreword to the score, there emerges a quality of intended random coordination among the musical lines. From his own comments, and from descriptions by associates of his performance of his own scores at the piano, it seems clear that Ives was not deeply concerned that his music be performed exactly as written, although he was consistent in his arguments to retain the notation as he presented it. It seems that he wrote the music as a philosophical proposition; if a performance did not follow the score exactly, it was no great problem, because he, as composer, had made his statement.

By the time of its first public performance, *The Unanswered Question* no longer aroused the antagonism reported by Ives following its introduction, and by the end of the century it was well established as Ives's most frequently performed orchestral work. It has provided an introduction to his music for listeners in America and abroad; for many it is a favorite work in Ives's catalogue. The idea is straightforward, the form clear, the musical effect eloquent and provocative.

Zoltán Kodály

✥

b. Kecskemét, Hungary, December 16, 1882; d. Budapest, Hungary,
March 6, 1967

During the first half of the 20th century, Kodály was in the van-
guard of contemporary musical thought in his rejection of
late-19th-century styles, his desire to build an identifiable
corpus of music based on his own national culture, and the incorporation of those native musical elements into his own creative works. He
succeeded in these efforts through his activities as a scholar of folk
song, an educator who played a seminal role in redefining music
instruction in Hungary and around the world, and a composer who
summarized in his works for the school and concert hall many centuries of European music.

Kodály was born to parents who were themselves musical, and as a
youth he heard and participated in much chamber music in his own
home. Between 1885 and 1892 he attended school in Galánta in western Hungary (later Czechoslovakia), where he first became acquainted
with the singing of the Hungarian country folk and the music of a
small gypsy band. Precocious in both music and academic studies, he
pursued his formal education in Budapest, earning diplomas in composition (1904) and teaching (1905) and a Ph.D. in philology (1906)
with a thesis on the stanzaic structure of Hungarian folk song. There
followed many expeditions to collect and catalogue folk songs, in the
course of which he joined efforts with Béla Bartók. The two formulated
a plan for the systematic collection and study of Hungarian folk song
that ultimately grew to become one of the most far-reaching ethnomu-
sicological ventures of the century. For the remainder of his life, Kodály

embarked on similar field trips, publishing many collections of music and scholarly studies designed to preserve a tradition he feared was fading away, and at the same time establishing a genuinely national music culture.

Kodály became convinced that the musical training of schoolchildren should draw on more substantial materials than were commonly used at the time. He became heavily involved in reforming music instruction and singing in the schools of Hungary, introducing into the curriculum folk materials from his own collection. These efforts eventually came to fruition following World War II, and the Kodály System for music education became widely recognized throughout Europe, the United States, and Japan. For these efforts, Kodály was recognized by many honorary degrees, government awards, titles, several national festivals celebrating his birthday, and the formation of the International Kodály Society to carry on his work.

Kodály composed music throughout his life. It is not surprising that many of his works reflected stylistic elements of the Hungarian folk songs in which he was so thoroughly immersed. As a result of his ethnic studies, he became convinced that no folk song text could be adequately interpreted without the melody to which it was sung, and that many times the melody was paramount. Reflecting this conviction, many of his compositions were dominated by a melodic approach. His mildly unorthodox harmonies drew much criticism from his countrymen in his early years, but his music never approached atonality as it was recognized in the 1920s and later. His most consistent musical traits are a free, quasi-improvisatory melodic line (frequently based on pentatonic or modal pitch patterns), a firm control of form, and repetitive rhythmic patterns. Above all, his style was consistently enriched by his commitment to producing scores reflecting the musical traditions of the Hungarian countryside and music that would be accessible to all people.

Dances of Galánta

Kodály wrote the Dances of Galánta *in the summer of 1933 as a work to celebrate the eightieth anniversary of the Budapest Philharmonic. The score was first performed in Budapest by that orchestra on October 23, 1933, with Ernó von Dohnányi conducting.*

Instrumentation: *two flutes, two oboes, two clarinets, two bassoons, four horns, two trumpets, timpani, snare drum, triangle, bells, and strings.*

Kodály often referred to his early years in Galánta as among the happiest of his life. It was there that he first encountered genuine Hungarian folk music. The difference between that experience and his later encounters with so-called "Hungarian" music that was performed in the cities aroused an interest that grew to dominate his professional life. He was particularly enthralled by the *verbunkos* music of a local gypsy band, vivid dance music that originated as part of military recruiting activities during the 18th century. In this tradition the Hussars of the imperial army collaborated with itinerant musicians, usually gypsies, in improvised dancing intended to attract recruits through its robust enthusiasm. The impression left by these musical encounters drew Kodály back to Galánta in 1905 on his first field trip. The tunes he collected there provided the inspiration, if not the thematic substance, for his orchestral *Dances of Galánta*.

The *Dances of Marsszék*, written for piano in 1927 and orchestrated in 1930, had been introduced by the New York Philharmonic Orchestra under Arturo Toscanini with considerable success, setting the stage for Kodály's composition of the *Dances of Galánta* in 1933. Both scores are orchestral settings of characteristic *verbunkos* dance music, with the emphasis on the spirit of the music rather than on specific dance types. For much of the thematic material in the *Dances of Galánta*, Kodály drew on two existing collections of music arranged for keyboard (*Ausgesuchte Ungarische Nationaltänze im Clavierauszug von verschiedenen Zigeunern aus Galantha* and *Originelle Ungarische Nationaltänze für das Clavier*), both published in Vienna in 1804, and a later collection from Central Transylvania prepared by Lászlo Lajtha and Zoltán Kallós.

The *Dances* unfold continuously, the ebb and flow of improvisation reflected in constantly changing tempos, the rhythmic vitality of the *verbunkos* represented by dotted rhythms and sharply articulated syncopation. Kodály gave these his own stamp through a wealth of melody, pungent harmonies, and colorful orchestration. An Introduction and Coda frame a basic rondo design in which five dances and the interludes separating them are often linked by exchange of themes. The Introduction grows from the solo cello's initial theme, agitated interjections by the strings separating restatements by other instruments, the whole ending with a brief cadenza by the clarinet. The clarinet continues its languorous solo into Dance I, until the flute introduces Dance II with a theme derived from the Introduction. This in turn is interrupted by a full-orchestra interlude based on Dance I. The oboe now introduces Dance III, interrupted again by an orchestral interjection of portions of Dance I. Dances IV and V continue in similar vein, each brought to a close by an Interlude for full orchestra. The first of these introduces new material, the second offers an extension of Dance IV. The Coda returns to the theme from Dance I and includes a second cadenza for clarinet before closing with a rousing reference to Dance V.

Introduction	Solo cello followed by other solo instruments, separated by orchestral interjections and closing clarinet cadenza
Dance I	Clarinet solo
Dance II	Solo flute, followed by other instruments
Interlude (from Dance I)	Full orchestra
Dance III	Solo oboe
Interlude (from Dance I)	Full orchestra
Dance IV	Strings, pronounced syncopation
Interlude (new theme)	Clarinet, grazioso
Dance V	Full orchestra
Interlude (from Dance IV)	Full orchestra
Coda	Flute, accompanied by string tremolo, leading to clarinet cadenza and full orchestral close with theme from Dance V

Much of the folk music Kodály catalogued included an element of shared material, because many longer folk melodies were extended by varying a primary tune. That was particularly true in the *verbunkos* music, so that an extended series of dances shared common material growing from the traditions of improvisation that spawned them. The orchestral *Dances of Galánta* reflect a similar procedure in the distribution of common thematic material throughout the work, a procedure Kodály continued with equal success in several later scores: the *Variations on a Hungarian Folk Song* (The Peacock, 1939); the *Concerto for Orchestra* (1939), and his Symphony (1961). He described the process succinctly in his "Introduction to the Performance of the Peacock

Variations": "Variation is the most natural development of folk music, for folk music itself is nothing but an endless series of melodies developing from each other and changing from one to the other in unnoticeable transitions."[1] Thus it seems that Kodály found his voice as an orchestral composer with *Dances*, his continuation in later compositions of techniques found in that score perhaps reflecting the work's popularity as much as influences from national culture.

Soon after publication of the score in 1934, the conductor Heinrich Jalowetz in Vienna wrote an appreciative summary:

> I think this is a gift in which the orchestra may find pleasure. Kodály's invention springs so deeply from the soul of instruments that with him even the simplest musical phenomenon assumes a special sparkle. This is an exceptionally fresh and transparent orchestral texture, marked by the musical joy of sound and an absolute certainty of acoustical vision.[2]

Orchestral Works Derived from Music for the Theater

Aside from incidental music for plays, Kodály wrote three works for the musical stage. His purpose was to introduce original Hungarian folk songs to the theater, to awaken in the Hungarian people an awareness of their own musical heritage. The first of these efforts, *Háry János*, won an early and lasting success in Hungary as an epic drama drawing on national folklore and music.

Suite from *Háry János*

Prelude—The Fairy Tale Begins

Viennese Musical Clock

Song

The Battle and Defeat of Napoleon

Intermezzo

Entrance of the Emperor and his Court

Kodály wrote the music for Háry János *in 1925 and 1926. It was first staged in Budapest on October 16, 1926, with Nánder RéKay conduct-*

ing. *The Suite was prepared soon thereafter and first performed in*
Barcelona on March 24, 1927, by the Pablo Casals Orchestra, Antal
Fleischer conducting.

Instrumentation: *three flutes (all doubling piccolo), two oboes, two*
clarinets in B-flat (one doubling E-flat clarinet), two bassoons, alto sax-
ophone, four horns, three trumpets, three cornets, three trombones,
tuba, timpani, bass drum, snare drum, tam-tam, triangle, cymbals,
tambourine, glockenspiel, tubular bells, xylophone, piano, celesta, cim-
balom (Hungarian dulcimer), and strings.

Béle Pauline and Zsolt Harsányi prepared the libretto for *Háry János*
from the 19th-century comedy *The Veteran*, by János Garay. Háry János
was a historical figure, a potter by trade. In the opera, he is a grizzled
veteran of the wars who returns to his native village of Nagyabony and
regales the townsfolk with embroidered accounts of his life as a soldier,
much to their delight and general skepticism. He operates much like a
storytelling poet who plays to his audience, with both raconteur and
listeners recognizing the narration as a fable but nonetheless taking
much pleasure in the event.

At a gathering in the village inn, Háry tells of his adventures on the
frontier, where he thwarts the stubbornness of sentries and, by himself,
opens the border to travelers. One of these is the Princess Marie Louise,
who rewards Háry by enrolling him in the imperial guard. Our hero
accepts the appointment, but not before eliciting several important
guarantees, among them proper food for his horse and the company of
his fiancée, Örzse, as he travels to the capital. At the glittering court in
Vienna, Marie Louise takes a fancy to Háry, who by now has further
ingratiated himself by recommending suitable treatments for the
emperor's illness. Rivals send Háry off at the head of an army to meet
Napoleon and his army, both quickly dispatched by Háry singlehand-
edly. Emperor and princess fall at Háry's feet, the whole scene marred
only by the stubborn presence of Örzse. Preparations are under way for
the wedding of Háry and Princess Marie Louise, but Háry, feeling out
of place in the sumptuous court, returns to his hometown fiancée,
finds a suitable mate for the princess, and wrests from the emperor a
guarantee that he will not oppress the Hungarian people. Háry remains
a hero to the end!

In Kodály's musical setting, a distant chorus offers a prologue and epilogue based on a folk song summarizing the spirit of the drama: "Nagyabony has only two towers, Milan's thirty-two outnumber ours. Milan's churches all could be forgot, for our little church is worth the whole lot." This musical reference surrounds four (originally five) adventures, and the action is carried forward largely by spoken dialogue punctuated by folk songs and composed instrumental numbers. That format has led writers to describe the work variously as a *Singspiel, opera buffa, vaudeville*, ballad opera, folk opera, or simply a play with songs. Setting those distinctions aside, the popular success of *Háry János* on the stage invited a sequel, leading Kodály to draw from his score a suite of instrumental dances that has done far more to disseminate the music of *Háry János* than did the original creation for the stage.

The order of movements in the suite differs slightly from the sequence in the stage work, reportedly as the result of a suggestion from Bartók. In their musical characterization, movements one, three, and five establish a background for the opera, while movements two, four, and six illustrate particular events. The contrasts between folk music and composed instrumental numbers may be compared to the contrasts between the village and the court, between rusticity and sophistication. When Kodály describes the world in which the characters are strangers, he projects a sardonic, mocking quality. When the characters are themselves the subject, his pervasive rapport with folk music comes forth in a more straightforward musical statement. Thus the plot of the opera contributes much to the musical sense of the suite and, subjectively, to the character of individual movements.

The *Prelude* opens with a marvelous orchestral wheeze, representing a fit of sneezing by one of Háry's skeptical listeners as a commentary on the questionable veracity of the storyteller. With one gesture the music transports the listener from reality to the world of fancy. Low strings introduce the motive that provides thematic substance for the whole movement, and soon the woodwinds introduce cascading arpeggios invoking a fairytale atmosphere. An abrupt halt and long silence interrupt this fantasy, before the flute and oboe quietly recall a portion of the basic motive, supported by muted horns.

Orchestral bells introduce the *Viennese Musical Clock*, and their four notes are soon taken up by the piano as background for the woodwinds' presentation of the principal theme, a shepherd's tune Kodály had recorded in 1912. An eight-bar period sharply divided into four two-measure phrases proceeds with the regularity of clockwork, its repetitions interrupted by three episodes to form a clearly defined rondo. The precise regularity of these contrasting sections, the square-cut phrase structure of both theme and episode, and the sudden shifts of orchestration contribute to the irresistible humor of the movement.

In the following *Song*, Kodály adapts one of the folk songs from the opera as a reference to Háry's devotion to his beloved Örzse. Unaccompanied violas play the complete melody before the orchestra joins with a colorful tremolo built around the cimbalom. This typically Hungarian instrument, unusual in orchestral scores, contributes to a shimmering background for subsequent tender statements of the "song" by oboe, horn, and cello.

Notes provided by Kodály for the first American performance by the New York Philharmonic in 1927 offer a succinct program for the fourth movement, *The Battle and Defeat of Napoleon*:

> Háry, as general in command of the Hussars, confronts the French army. He brandishes his sword and lo! the French begin to fall before him like tin soldiers! First, two at a time, then four, eight, ten, and so on. Finally, there are no more soldiers left, and Napoleon is forced to engage in person the invincible Háry. Háry's fantasy pictures a Napoleon made in the image of his own burly peasant imagination—an immensely tall and formidable Napoleon who, shaking in every limb, kneels before his conqueror and pleads for mercy.[3]

Bass drum and cymbal set a march tempo supporting a sardonic theme blatted out by trombones and trumpets. The augmented fourth that concludes the phrase, pathetic sighs by the saxophone, and an out-of-tune trumpet call together reflect a ludicrous state of affairs on the stage. A contrasting midsection capitalizes on the humorous effect produced by trombone and tuba glissandos, still supported by percussion, and this in turn sets the stage for a concluding funeral march. In mock seriousness, continuing glissandos from the low brass are answered by hiccups from the saxophone and a steady rattle from bass drum and tambourine. The musical humor will elicit a sardonic smile from any listener.

The *Intermezzo* quickly establishes a very different character through its classic three-part structure, combined with the spirit of the

Hungarian *verbunkos*, the 18th-century military recruiting music so prominent in many of Kodály's later orchestral works (see *Dances of Galánta*). The melody has been attributed to an early 19th-century piano method book by István Gáti, but there is nothing inherently pianistic in the sharply articulated rhythms and repeated sections. The clear design and characteristic spirit of this movement have made it one of the most popular in the suite, reflected in frequently performed transcriptions for violin/piano or solo piano.

Levity returns with the *Entrance of the Emperor and his Court* through the grotesque pomposity of themes patently unsuitable for such a dignified event. The full orchestra plays throughout most of the movement, but even that ensemble sounds as though it were playing tongue-in-cheek. That is, after all, the spirit in which the tale of Háry János began.

Háry János as a stage work is a whimsically mendacious tale. As a bit of musical theater, most of its success has been confined to Hungary, but the instrumental suite has been played around the world with much success. The music projects vigor and humor through a full complement of techniques that were progressive for 1926. At the same time, and perhaps more important, Kodály speaks for his national culture in a musical voice readily understood by all audiences.

Witold Lutosławski

❧

b. Warsaw, Poland, January 25, 1913; d. Warsaw, February 9, 1994

The lack of a consistent musical language was an enduring problem for Western art music in the 20th century. Any composer whose works offered the possibility of an amalgamation of the different styles in vogue attracted attention as a possible master who might bring forth a new classicism. Witold Lutosławski was such a composer. He left a relatively short catalogue of orchestral works, but among them are many important compositions. In the modern age, his music represents one of the most important contributions to the European musical heritage.

The repression of creative artists in the Soviet Union, starting in 1948 (see the discussion of music by Prokofiev and Shostakovich), echoed through Poland and other satellite countries in the years following. Lutosławski had completed his First Symphony in 1947, only to see it quickly banned under the politically motivated edict against formalism. He then poured his creative energies into utilitarian music intended for the radio, much of it drawing on folk materials. The musical style for which he became best known derived from his adaptation of aleatoric processes as he encountered them in the music of John Cage. A broadcast performance of Cage's Piano Concerto (1957–1958) introduced Lutosławski to a new world of possibilities. By the time of his *Venetian Games* (1961), he had developed a style he called "controlled chance," a process in which a number of performers play *ad libitum* simultaneously, without specific coordination through meter or tempo. At least a part of the impetus leading him in this direction was his search for a means of sound production not limited by the acoustic properties of traditional instruments. He was searching for capabilities of complete chromaticism as well as new instruments to produce new sounds. At the same time, he maintained that playing traditional instruments in nontraditional ways was not an effective means of expanding the orchestra's tonal palette. Several of his later compositions drew on his own design of "chain form." In this process, multiple strands of music are played simultaneously, but they neither begin nor end at the same time, drawing their energy from the shifting combinations produced by these "strands" as they enter and leave the musical fabric independently.

Lutosławski's stylistic development was unusual in that he became ever more modern as he matured, rather than consolidating the musical ventures of his youth. At various times he drew inspiration from different musical procedures recognized as facets of 20th-century style: folk elements, dissonant counterpoint, and chance procedures. He saw his own line of development extending from Debussy and early Stravinsky but a more important influence was the music of Bartók, some of whose techniques reverberate in the Concerto for Orchestra.

Concerto for Orchestra

Intrada: Allegro maestoso

Capriccio notturno e arioso: Vivace

Passacaglia, Toccata e Corale

The Concerto for Orchestra occupied Lutosławski from 1950 until August 1951. It was first performed in Warsaw on November 26, 1954 by the Warsaw National Philharmonic Orchestra, conducted by Witold Rowicki.

Instrumentation: *three flutes (the second and third doubling piccolo), three oboes (the third doubling English horn), three clarinets (the third doubling bass clarinet), three bassoons (the third doubling contrabassoon), four horns, four trumpets, four trombones, tuba, timpani, bass drum, snare drum, tenor drum, three drums (soprano, alto, tenor) without snares, three cymbals (two crash and one suspended), tam-tam, tambourine, xylophone, glockenspiel, celesta, piano, two harps, and strings.*

The Concerto for Orchestra was commissioned by the conductor of the Warsaw Philharmonic Orchestra, Witold Rowicki, who requested a work that would be within the capabilities of his new ensemble but still allow the group to show its best qualities. As work progressed, the composer became increasingly immersed in the project, eventually dedicating the finished score to Rowicki, who also had the honor of giving the first performance. Lutosławski later described the Concerto as a unique work in his oeuvre, written during his "folk song" period:

> Of course, there is one single piece in which I used a technique that is essentially different from my personal technique of writing music. It consists of using simple diatonic tunes—mainly folk tunes—accompanied and combined with some sophisticated harmonies and sometimes even atonal—or non tonal—counterpoint. This combination of very simple diatonic tunes with such counterpoints and harmonies formed the style that is present in all of my functional music. The only piece that is not functional but is written in this language is the Concerto for Orchestra.[1]

He later went to some pains to point out that the folk elements served only as the raw material for an extended multimovement work, and that there were several folk motives that commentators had overlooked in their repeated analyses. Those folk materials that have been identified come from the area around Warsaw. They appear not as direct quotations but as germinal motives that Lutosławski expanded into a larger framework.

Lutosławski's acknowledged admiration for Bartók, his references to ethnic sources, and an identical title have generated many comparisons between this work and Bartók's Concerto for Orchestra from 1943. Beyond the title, both include an internal reference to a chorale, and one can find some intriguing similarities in techniques of motivic extension and sequence, but there is no substantial evidence that Lutosławski patterned his efforts after Bartók's famous Concerto. Bartók drew on folk songs for thematic material or constructed original themes reflecting ethnic character, whereas Lutosławski expanded on ethnic sources in the fundamental structure of his music. Bartók composed a work of five autonomous movements designed to display the orchestral instruments; Lutosławski created a large work divided into three movements that grow organically from beginning to end,

combining timbre, texture, dynamics, and tempos as integral components of the musical statement.

In his early struggles to form his own musical style, Lutosławski
had formulated a basic two-movement design for his major works in
which the first movement prepares for all that is to follow, thus shifting the expressive weight of a composition from the beginning toward
the end:

> The first [movement] is meant only to interest, to attract, to
> involve, but never to fully satisfy the listener. During the first
> movement the listener is supposed to expect something more
> important to happen, and may even grow impatient. This is
> exactly the situation when the second movement appears and
> presents the main idea of the work. This distribution of the musi-
> cal substance over time seems natural to me, and conforms with
> the psychology of the perception of music.[2]

In the Concerto for Orchestra, this premise is expanded to embrace
three movements, the third looming as the most important and
encompassing more time than the first two taken together. The sense
of continuing growth derives from and contributes to Lutosławski's
shift of emphasis toward the conclusion of the work.

Beyond these qualities, a tonal plan based on third relationships
underlies the three movements and their subsidiary sections. The
Intrada is built around the pitch F-sharp. The *Capriccio notturno* is based
on B-flat, with a brief return to F-sharp for the *Arioso* that intervenes
before the return of the *Capriccio*. A theme firmly maintaining D major
provides the core for the *Passacaglia*, and the *Toccata* continues the cycle
of thirds to F-sharp, with intermediate reference to E-flat for the *Corale*
before returning to F-sharp for the final statement of the *Toccata*. The
juxtaposition of tonal centers a third apart was not new in 1954, but it
is another facet of a comprehensive design underlying the complete
score.

The Baroque titles of individual movements reflect Lutosławski's
interest in form as a process more than an attempt to resurrect earlier
models. The title *Intrada* identifies both the character and function of
the opening movement. It consists of three distinct sections, the first
and last built on a common theme, the second offering a broadly based
contrast in both theme and character. Above an ominous F-sharp pedal

played by basses, bassoons, and harp, the cellos introduce a folk tune that expands its range with each iteration.[3] Progressively wider intervals comprise an element of internal growth that becomes a fundamental part of the theme's character. Subsequent entries played by viola, second and first violins, and finally woodwinds occur in a pattern of fifths rising to F-sharp, arriving finally at a tonal concurrence with the pedal point that has been maintained from the beginning. The closing section mirrors this plan as the F-sharp pedal appears in the higher instruments while the original theme is played by the woodwinds in a series of tonal centers descending by fourths, moving downward from D to F-sharp, ultimately matching the pedal played in the high register of the celesta. The pattern of fifths mirrored by fourths offers a well-conceived structural plan that Lutosławski reinforces through his orchestration; strings are answered by winds, and the pedal point reverses its location from the bottom to the top of the orchestral texture.

Two contrasting thematic units form the midsection. The first (*b* in the diagram below) derives from the rising semitone of another folk tune and returns in the closing *Toccata*. The second (*c*) is new, marked by emphatically articulated descending sixths. These units alternate in a near-symmetrical pattern, but each section expands on the one preceding until the closing grows to an imposing climax.

First section:	Theme *a*
entries on	D ↗ A ↗ E ↗ B ↗ F-sharp
	vc va vn2 vn1 fl/ob, over an F-sharp pedal
Midsection:	Themes b c b c b
Closing section:	Theme *a*
entries on	D ↘ A ↘ E ↘ B ↘ F-sharp
	fl ob clt Eng. hn clt, below an F-sharp pedal

The *Capriccio notturno e arioso* fills the role of an orchestral scherzo in its character and structural outlines. Muted violins scamper about in passagework marked *mormorando* (murmuring) and punctuated by sharply articulated minor chords played by the woodwinds at the end of each phrase. Short interlocking mirror passages in the woodwinds bring this rapid interplay to a halt on a *Grand Pause*, after which the *Capriccio* is repeated on G-sharp, one whole-tone lower than the initial B-flat. The *Arioso*, serving in lieu of a traditional trio section, continues that tonal descent to F-sharp. In contrast to the muted chattering of the *Capriccio*, the trumpets announce the *Arioso* theme *ff* until the full orchestra reaches a climax from which the music subsides, ultimately dwindling to a combination of trills and tremolos supporting one last statement of the *Arioso* theme. A compressed version of the *Capriccio* progressively dilutes the texture until only the basses and percussion remain for a whispered coda, now restored to the original tonal center of B-flat.

The last movement brings the Concerto to a grand and tumultuous conclusion. Each of the three sections—*Passacaglia, Toccata*, and *Corale*—draws on Baroque titles and traditions to which Lutosławski gives a vigorously modern treatment. The *Corale* is a section within the *Toccata*, giving the listener the aural impression of two major parts, the *Passacaglia* and the *Toccata*, with the *Toccata* as the musical climax for the entire Concerto. The *Passacaglia* is based on eighteen presentations of an eight-measure theme introduced by the basses. The first and last statements serve as introduction and conclusion, leaving sixteen full presentations for the body of the movement. As the music unfolds, doubling of the theme at the upper octave accrues until at one point it is spread over six octaves. From this point, the lower parts gradually drop away, leaving the theme in the highest register of the orchestra. The process has some kinship with the transfer of the F-sharp pedal from a low to a high part of the orchestra in the outer sections of the *Intrada*. As the orchestration expands and contracts, it provides a basis for episodes in contrasting style that rarely coincide with the restatements of the *Passacaglia* theme. These changing orchestral combinations offer variety to the stolid unity of the *Passacaglia,* at the same time that the overlapping of the bass theme and the episodes produces a push and pull to propel the music forward.

In the *Toccata,* the strings begin with a vigorous fanfare introducing the agitated music that dominates this section. Over fast and propulsive repeated notes, the folk-tune theme from the midsection of the *Intrada* returns, played high above the orchestra by the first violins and much extended in range and duration. A *diminuendo* leads to the *Corale*, played in turn by woodwinds, brass, and strings. The *Toccata* returns, its resounding climax interrupted by an emphatic statement of the *Corale* by the brass instruments before a breathtaking coda brings all to a close.

Folk materials have provided the substance for many works in the modern repertory, but few of those orchestral essays have drawn on ethnic tunes as extensively or as subtly as does Lutosławski's Concerto. That his treatment transforms these folk elements beyond ready recognition detracts little from the character they impart to his music. Even more impressive is the sense of coherence he achieves through his formal structures of both large and small scale based on folk elements.

The Concerto for Orchestra confirmed Lutosławski's position as the leading composer in Poland. On July 22, 1955, he received from the government the State Prize, class I, and Order of Labor, class II, for the musical achievement represented by this work. It stands today as one of the masterpieces for orchestra from the last half of the 20th century.

Darius Milhaud

b. Aix-en-Provence, France, September 4, 1892; d. Geneva, Switzerland,
June 22, 1974

For Darius Milhaud, composing was a part of daily life. He wrote
music as naturally and as consistently as eating, breathing, and
sleeping. This regimen produced a catalogue of at least 443
works, a fecundity that may have hindered the widespread recognition
that Milhaud might otherwise have been accorded, because few people
have as yet assumed the task of thoroughly perusing such a volume of
music. Among these works one can find a number of masterpieces.
There are others that are routine, but all are marked by a fertile imagination expressed through masterful craftsmanship.

Milhaud began his formal training at the Paris Conservatory as a
violinist, but by 1910 had shifted his energies to composition and was
already writing works for the stage. Between 1916 and 1918, he served as
secretary to the poet Paul Claudel, who was serving in Rio de Janeiro as
French minister to Brazil. The native music Milhaud heard there generated two important works that appeared shortly after his return to
France, the ballet *L'homme et son désir,* and a collection of dances titled
Saudades do Brazil. In the 1920s Milhaud was included in the group
known as *Les Six,* a band of young composers named due to journalistic
convenience far more than any shared philosophy or musical technique.
Milhaud enjoyed the renown accorded the group in the press but pursued his own interests, which, in the years following, extended from the
United States to Russia and the Middle East. Milhaud escaped the
repression directed at Jews during World War II by accepting an appointment at Mill's College in Oakland, California, a position he held until ill

health forced him to resign in 1971. After 1947, he held a concurrent appointment as professor of composition at the Paris Conservatory.

Beyond the eclecticism that reflected the influence of his travels, Milhaud's music is dominated by melody in all its ramifications. From about 1915 onward, he was much interested in polytonality, a trait that for many listeners became a hallmark of his music. Both qualities combine in the prevailingly transparent textures that have contributed much to the enduring accessibility of his music.

La création du monde, Opus 81

Milhaud composed music for the ballet La création du monde *during May and June of 1923. It was first performed in Paris on October 25, 1923, by the Swedish Ballet, Vladimir Golschmann conducting the orchestra of the Théâtre des Champs-Élysées in support of a scenario by Blaise Cendrars, choreography by Jean Börlin, and scenery by Fernand Léger.*

Instrumentation: *two flutes, oboe, two clarinets, bassoon, horn, two trumpets, trombone, piano, three timpani, two small timpani, pedal bass drum with cymbal, snare drum, tenor drum, tambourin (narrow two-headed drum with or without snares), tambourine, metal block, woodblock, suspended cymbal, two solo violins, E-flat (alto) saxophone, cello, and double bass.*

La création du monde is one of several works from the early part of the 20th century drawing heavily on jazz for materials and inspiration and one of relatively few such works to survive on its musical merits alone. Milhaud first encountered jazz in 1918 when he heard some New York jazz bands in Paris. His interest was further stimulated in 1920 when he heard Billy Arnold's band in London, an experience described both perceptively and enthusiastically in his autobiography:

> The new music was extremely subtle in its use of timbre: the saxophone breaking in, squeezing out the juice of dreams, or the trumpet, dramatic or languorous by turns, the clarinet, frequently played in its upper register, the lyrical use of the trombone, glancing with its slide over quarter-tones in crescendos of volume and pitch, thus intensifying the feeling; and the whole, so various yet not disparate, held together by the piano and subtly punctuated

by the complex rhythms of the percussion, a kind of inner beat,
the vital pulse of the rhythmic life of the music. The constant use
of syncopation in the melody was of such contrapuntal freedom
that it gave the impression of unregulated improvisation, whereas
in actual fact it was elaborately rehearsed daily, down to the last
detail. I had the idea of using these timbres and rhythms in a
work of chamber-music, but at first I had to penetrate more
deeply into the arcana of this new musical form, whose technique
still baffled me.[1]

Milhaud advanced his interest on a trip to New York in 1922, when
he confounded reporters by declaring that American music—in this
instance, jazz—was exerting a strong influence on European music. The
subsequent newspaper headlines announcing that jazz was dictating
the future of European music were perhaps overstated, but won for
Milhaud the sympathy of African-American musicians and paved the
way for his visits to Harlem to hear what probably was some of the most
vital jazz of the day:

> The music I heard was absolutely different from anything I had
> ever heard before, and was a revelation to me. Against the beat of
> the drums, the melodic lines criss-crossed in a breathless pattern
> of broken and twisted rhythms. A Negress whose grating voice
> seemed to come from the depths of the centuries . . . sang over
> and over again . . . the same refrain to which the constantly
> changing melodic pattern of the orchestra wove a kaleidoscopic
> background. . . . Its effect on me was so overwhelming that I could
> not tear myself away. . . .
>
> When I went back to France, I never wearied of playing over and
> over, on a little portable gramophone shaped like a camera, "Black
> Swan" [an American record label that featured blues and jazz artists]
> records I had purchased in a little shop in Harlem. More than ever I
> was resolved to use jazz for a chamber-music work.[2]

In later writings, Milhaud described the difference between the jazz
he heard played by white Americans (written down and rehearsed) and
that by black Americans (largely improvised). He also distinguished
between the quarter-tone in jazz, which was the result of expressive
melodic inflection, and the quarter-tone as it was being explored in

Central Europe, which was based on division of the twelve-note chromatic scale. Above all, he admired the musical skills of the jazz musicians, declaring that they had created "absolutely new elements of tone and rhythm of which they are perfect masters. . . . These magnificent orchestras need a concert repertoire."[3]

Shortly after Milhaud returned to France, Rolf de Maré, director of the Swedish Ballet in Paris, proposed to him a ballet involving the collaboration of Blaise Cendrars, librettist, Jean Börlin, choreographer, and Fernand Léger, stage designer. Cendrars had recently published a collection of African stories collected from a missionary, and these provided a fertile plot. Léger's costumes and scenery were similarly taken from African art. The premise was to depict creation as traditionally described in African culture, and this led to an avant-garde production in which the dancers and scenery moved together in a staged mobilization.

The ballet opens with three deities in consultation as they circle a formless mass on the stage. A tree begins to grow, drops a seed from which another tree sprouts, and a fallen leaf gradually becomes an animal. A dancer bursts forth from other animals as they appear, circling the three deities until two torsos emerge from the mass: man and woman, standing upright. As the couple performs a ritual mating dance, all the creatures gradually join the choreography, leading to a frenetic general dance. The frenzy subsides and figures disperse in small groups as the couple stands apart from the action in an embrace. Thus spring breaks forth upon the world.

The Swedish Ballet was scheduled to leave for a tour of the United States in November 1923 with *La création du monde* as one of the most important works in its repertory. Lack of a sufficiently large stage in the theaters available to them forced the deletion of the ballet from their programs, but in retrospect the combination of artistic forces offered much promise. What better opportunity for Milhaud to create a score drawing on jazz in order to depict a scenario and stage designs drawn from African elements and designed for audiences in America:

> At last in *La Création du monde*, I had the opportunity I had been waiting for to use those elements of jazz to which I had devoted so much study. I adopted the same orchestra as used in Harlem, seventeen solo instruments, and I made wholesale use of the jazz style to convey a purely classical feeling.[4]

Milhaud's claim that he wrote for the orchestra he heard in Harlem may raise some questions about the orchestra he had in mind. The ensemble assembled for the ballet resembled a theater or hotel dance orchestra more than the smaller groups traditionally associated with jazz in 1922. As he had projected, he did reflect chamber music traditions in that all instruments play one to a part, but one wonders how Parisian theater musicians in 1923 reacted to the variety of percussion instruments covered by one performer. The saxophone replaces the viola in the traditional string choir, a reasonable substitution considering the comparable range and mellow tone of both instruments.

The overture consists of four sections, all of which expand on material introduced in the opening measures. Over a constant thud from the bass drum, later to be joined by timpani and bass, the saxophone plays a melancholy lament supported by an undulating line from the piano and strings. A syncopated countermotive from the trumpet and short glisses from the trombone eventually expand to match the prominence of the saxophone until, with the return of the opening material, the music gradually subsides to a fermata, the musical cue for the rise of the stage curtain.

As the choreography unfolds, the string bass introduces a jazzy fugue marked by pronounced syncopation and the vacillation between major and minor thirds often associated with the blues. It should be noted that Milhaud is writing jazz-inspired music more than he is creating an authentic jazz sound; the fugue subject clearly draws on jazz styles, but the closely spaced imitative entries in trombone, saxophone, and trumpet reflect a European process based on a jazz theme. The initial motive (D–E–D–F) permeates much of American popular music, recognizable as the stereotypical "Good evening, friends" from vaudeville or the opening motive of Gershwin's *Rhapsody in Blue* (which appeared a few months after Milhaud's ballet). This motive, the pronounced syncopation, chromatic inflection, and slides return in varied guise throughout much of the music to follow, in the process creating a subtle musical link and contributing to a continuity of style.

Scene II offers a dramatic change of pace. In both structure and melodic/harmonic style the music draws on the blues. Three sections in an A–A–B relationship mirror, on a larger scale, the similar pattern of phrases within the classic twelve-bar blues pattern. The first of those sections itself consists of three twelve-bar units. More noticeable is the wavering blue note in the oboe's solo line, accompanied periodically by motives from the overture and a variant of the fugue subject.

Another high point is the solo clarinet in the fourth scene as it plays a representation of an improvised jazz solo against stop time accompaniment by piano and winds. Portions of the overture interrupt this mood before the trumpet assumes the clarinet's line, and both clarinet and trumpet carry on a lively jazz dialogue. Materials derived from the overture and the blues section mingle in the background before the fugue subject returns to close the complete work with an exquisite coda, a shimmering tremolo played by the winds as figures on the stage disperse into the wings.

La création du monde was very much a mirror of contemporary artistic trends. The scenario reflects the contemporary fascination with primitivism and in that context has invited comparison with Stravinsky's *Le sacre du printemps* of ten years earlier. Like that score, the music endured as a separate entity long after the choreography and stage setting were forgotten. Unlike *Le sacre*, Milhaud's score invokes the legends of Africa, whereas Stravinsky was drawing stories from the Slavic people of Central Europe. The infusion of jazz reflects Milhaud's own fascination with that musical tradition in 1923, also addressed by Stravinsky in his *L'histoire du soldat* and *Ragtime for 11 Instruments*, both from 1918, and by Ravel's two piano concertos from 1929 to 1931. The solo instrumentation and Milhaud's own reference to "a purely classical feeling" offer an element of neoclassicism, whether by design or by happenstance.

Critical response to *La création du monde* was mixed. Some audiences were shocked, but at least one critic thought that the music did not go far enough when compared with the libretto and stage design: "A scenario by Blaise Cendrars and the costumes of Fernand Léger seemed to have made of this evening an audacious manifestation of the avant-garde. It was nothing like that. The technique of Milhaud, which never has been fundamentally revolutionary, becomes more learned day by day. . . ."[5] Reflecting on the matter in his autobiography, Milhaud observed that "the critics decreed that my music was frivolous and more suitable for a restaurant or dance-hall than for the concert-hall. Ten years later the self-same critics were discussing the philosophy of jazz and learnedly demonstrating that *La Création* was the best of my works."[6] The assessment of *La création du monde* as one of Milhaud's masterpieces has endured to the present.

Carl Nielsen

❧

b. Nørre-Lyndelse, Island of Fyn, Denmark, June 9, 1865;
d. Copenhagen, Denmark, October 3, 1931

T he works of Carl Nielsen experienced a continuing ebb and flow of popularity in the last half of the 20th century, with each surge of interest moving them toward wider favor and recognition. Nielsen was regarded as a national hero in Denmark at the time of his death, recognized as a musical figure equal to his direct contemporary in Finland, Jan Sibelius. The dominance of German and Italian music in Denmark made the native son's artistic achievements all the more noteworthy. He brought Denmark into the 20th century by rejecting the subjectivity of Romanticism, emphasizing instead his own veneration for nature and thorough craftsmanship. That outlook led him to propose that music should appeal to all through its natural and uncomplicated melody. He was active in both art and popular music, producing many songs to Danish texts that his countrymen quickly took to heart. "Music is Life" became a mantra for Nielsen, realized in both his music and literary works. A collection of essays titled *Levende musik* (*Living Music*, 1925) affirmed that expression in many contexts, and in *Min fynske barndom* (*My Childhood*, 1927) Nielsen described his lifelong fascination with the natural world and his fellow human beings as a part of it. During Nielsen's early student years, he was a fan of Richard Wagner. Nielsen later objected to the extravagance of such music with the admonition that "the only cure for this sort of taste lies in studying the basic intervals. The glutted must be taught to regard a melodic third as a gift from God, a fourth as an experience, and a fifth as supreme bliss."[1]

During his early years, Carl Nielsen's musical talents emerged in spite of menial jobs as shepherd and grocer until, under some duress and with last-minute cramming for an audition, the fourteen-year-old was appointed bugler for a regimental military unit in Odense. This marked the beginning of a promising student career that led to the award of the Anckert travel scholarship, which allowed him to travel to the musical centers of Europe to experience all that was new in the musical world of the late 19th century.

It was during these travels that Nielsen's compositions began to attract attention outside Denmark. In 1891 in Paris he married Anne Marie Brodersen. This union was to be both a strain and a support for Nielsen. In the ensuing years, Anne Marie pursued her own career as a sculptor with determination and considerable success, living apart from her husband for long periods. As recompense, it was her income that often provided support for the Nielsen's three children while Carl was struggling to establish a musical career, first as orchestral violinist in the Danish Royal Orchestra, later as an occasional conductor of that group, and in the Copenhagen Music Society, where he flourished as a conductor of his own works.

In 1901, Nielsen received a government stipend to support his creative work, and shortly thereafter he entered into an undertaking with Thomas Laub (1852–1927) that eventually produced two volumes of Danish songs and a songbook for the folk schools. Here Nielsen could illustrate his convictions about the impact of simple melody cast in a natural setting. He produced his most important works after 1914: the Fourth and Fifth Symphonies; the concertos for flute and clarinet; several larger works for piano; and his published collections of popular songs and hymns. By the 1920s, he was widely recognized as both composer and conductor. Overwork and prolonged stress contributed to a series of heart attacks that ended the composer's life in 1931; his passing was marked by a state funeral and formal tributes from the governments of Denmark, France, Germany, Iceland, Italy, Norway, and Sweden.

Nielsen worked against the prevailing currents of his own time, eschewing both the excesses of late-19th-century Romanticism and the fabricated systems designed by his contemporaries, who were searching for a new musical style. Throughout his adult years he explored literature, painting, and sculpture, finding in them stimulation and common grounds for his own concept of music. He described his aesthetic views in long letters to friends and colleagues, espousing naturalness, integrity of expression, and mastery of the craft of composition. His view that "a fresh, live awkwardness is far better than a brilliant but over-ripe perfection"[2] is typical of his often homespun philosophy. In pursuit of his goals he produced scores embracing the simple and the sophisticated, art and popular music, vocal polyphony and dissonant modernism, modal and tonal melodies, all melded into a distinctive personal style.

Symphony No. 4, Opus 29 (*The Inextinguishable*)

Allegro—

Poco allegretto—

Poco adagio quasi andante—

Allegro

Nielsen composed his Fourth Symphony between 1914 and January 1916. It was first performed in Copenhagen on February 1, 1916, with Nielsen conducting the Music Society Orchestra.

Instrumentation*: three flutes (the third doubling piccolo), three oboes, three clarinets, three bassoons (one of them doubling contrabassoon), four horns, three trumpets, three trombones, tuba, two timpanists (stationed on opposite sides of the orchestra), and strings.*

In a preface to the published score, Nielsen offered a partial explanation for the title *The Inextinguishable*:

> Under this title the composer has endeavoured to indicate in one word what the music alone is capable of expressing to the full: *The elemental Will of Life*. Music *is* Life and, like it, is inextinguishable. The title . . . might therefore seem superfluous; the composer . . . has employed the word in order to underline the strictly musical character of his subject. It is not a programme, but only a suggestion as to the right approach to the music.[3]

Shortly after starting work on the symphony, he wrote to the opera singer Emil Holm about his first efforts. "I can tell you that I have come a good way on a new, large orchestral work, a kind of symphony in one movement, which would describe everything one feels and thinks by the concept we call Life or, rather, 'Life' in its inmost meaning."[4] After the symphony was well under way, he wrote to Julius Röntgen, Dutch composer and personal friend, telling of his progress and offering further details about his musical intentions:

> I shall *also* soon have a new symphony ready. It is very different from my other three and there is a specific idea behind it, that is, that the most elementary aspect of music is Light, Life, and Motion, which chop silence to bits. It's all those things that have Will and the Craving for Life that cannot be suppressed that I've wanted to depict. *Not* because I want to reduce my art to the imitation of Nature but to let it attempt to express what lies behind it. The crying of birds, the wailing and laughter of man and beast, the grumbling and shouting from hunger, war, and mating, and everything that is called the most elementary—I see well that my words cannot explain, for one can rightly say, "Shut up, and let us hear the thing when it is finished."[5]

For all of Nielsen's many other declarations favoring objectivity in music, he describes the Fourth Symphony as a subjective depiction of the irrevocable processes of nature, reflected in the struggles between contrasting elements in the score.

One of the most obvious of those struggles is the dialogue between the two timpanists. Nielsen designates that the second timpanist be placed at the edge of the orchestra, toward the audience, enhancing the musical opposition with spatial separation. Timpani I punctuates the opening measures with an accented tritone, an interval the ancients called *diabolus per musica*. The devil himself would enjoy the battle (no other term seems adequate here) between the two timpanists and the orchestra that develops in the last movement, with both players hammering away at different tritones while the orchestra continues with its own material. The symphony grows internally through conflicting tonalities, sometimes producing much dissonance, but in such a manner that the conflict of keys, or the motion from one tonal center to another, becomes the substance of Nielsen's musical dialectic. This continuing tonal evolution permeates the symphony, leading to an uninterrupted tonal fabric, and the four movements are played without interruption.

The first movement erupts with contrasting harmonies of C (in the strings) and D (in the winds), with the tritone A–E-flat in the timpani adding to the general harmonic instability. The calm lyricism of a second theme, played by the clarinets, offers marked contrast to the violent opening, and becomes a frequent point of reference. It returns near the movement's end in an emphatic declamation by bassoons and brass instruments over a reiterated E in the timpani, which then becomes the musical link with the following *Poco allegretto*. This graceful three-part intermezzo serves the role of a traditional scherzo movement. Much of it is written for the woodwinds, the orchestral timbre that was associated with most of the stable points of reference in the first movement. Continuing that reference, clarinets end the movement with a series of plaintive, descending thirds. The combination of implied harmonies in C and G leave the question of key unresolved, particularly when the following *Poco adagio quasi andante* abruptly moves off toward E, introducing a mediant relationship to C and G. The quiet character gradually gives way to increasing agitation that subsides only slightly before closing with an abrupt *con anima* for strings.

A *Grand Pause* offers both players and audience an opportunity to catch a collective breath before the full orchestra bursts forth with the closing *Allegro*. The timpani erupt again in their bellicose dialogue, responding to a note in the score advising them that they should maintain a menacing character through the end of the movement, even when playing quietly. References to the clarinet theme from the first movement appear frequently until it finally returns, emphatically, in the home key of E. The final arrival at the basic key of the work introduces a forceful element of stability that continues to the end of the symphony.

Reactions to the first performance of Nielsen's Fourth Symphony in 1916 were swallowed in the enormity of events surrounding the war then engulfing Europe. In later years, the intensity of the work often jolted audiences. Even if listeners are unaware of the tonal operations, the music largely speaks for itself, with the conflicts involving key, theme, and instrumentation producing a dramatic musical statement.

Symphony No. 5, Opus 50

Tempo giusto—Adagio non troppo

Allegro—Presto—Andante un poco tranquillo—Allegro (Tempo I)

Nielsen began work on his Fifth Symphony early in 1921, completing the score in January 1922. It was first performed in Copenhagen on January 24, 1922, by the Music Society Orchestra, Nielsen conducting.

Instrumentation*: piccolo, two flutes, two oboes, two clarinets, two bassoons (the second doubling contrabassoon), four horns, three trumpets, three trombones, tuba, timpani, snare drum, cymbals, tambourine, triangle, celesta (in a revised version by friends of Nielsen), and strings.*

From 1914 through the completion of his Fifth Symphony in 1922, most of Nielsen's public life was given over to conducting orchestras in Copenhagen and Gothenberg. On March 4, 1921, he told his wife that the first movement of a new symphony was completed, but complained of his slow progress. Over the following months he moved from his winter quarters to a summer house, then to the home of friends, and finally to Gothenberg in the autumn to fulfill conducting duties, working on the symphony all the while, often in sessions extending through the night. He later claimed that the work was the most arduous task he had set for himself up to that time.

The symphony carries no descriptive title, as do his Second, Third, Fourth, and Sixth Symphonies. Responding to inquiries on this matter, Nielsen claimed that the other titles were essentially little more than different terms applying to one underlying principle: the contrast between passive and active forces. Unable to find an appropriate title to convey that concept as it applied to the Fifth Symphony, he simply offered no title at all. In several commentaries published after the symphony's early success, Nielsen was willing to elaborate in greater detail, offering that the two movements were complementary, representing "the division of dark and light, the battle between evil and good. A title like 'Dream and Deeds' could maybe sum up the inner picture in front of my eyes when composing [this work]."[6]

Nielsen's image of "Dream and Deeds" gave rise to two movements, both reflecting this composer at the height of his creative powers. Those talents were directed toward his own solution to many of the problems confronting European society, and music as a reflection of that society, after World War I. Some composers developed new technical procedures, of which Arnold Schoenberg's system of atonality is probably the best known. Others turned to an objective treatment of acoustics or revived traditions of the past in neoclassicism. Nielsen addressed the problem by original conceptions of form and sound in his orchestral scoring. He assimilated symphonic elements of the past—sonata design and the four-movement symphony—into his own mold, with an inherent logic drawn from his cultural roots and tempered by hard-won craftsmanship.

The musical fabric of his Fifth Symphony grows from the contrast between the orchestral choirs. Ostinatos and pedal points of different kinds penetrate the mass of sound to define musical sections or to maintain continuity. These ostinatos may be a sustained tone, a trill or tremolo, or a repeated pattern of melodic or rhythmic material. Solo instruments may be assigned a cadenza or given intentionally disruptive sounds to play, to disrupt the overwhelming drive of the full ensemble; both strategies are illustrated by the feisty clarinet and snare drum in the first movement. Tonal centers underlie most of this activity, although they may not be established by traditional means. At times a part of the ensemble becomes obsessed with one pitch or key, and the obsession gradually expands to include other parts of the orchestra, a process often described as "emerging tonality" in Nielsen's music. Whether by design or by default, most important melodies appear in the upper part of the orchestral fabric. When different choirs present simultaneous melodies, as often happens, the effect is a type of counterpoint, with each group supporting its own melodic component. Melodies in the first movement rely heavily on the intervals of a semitone and minor third, while the second movement contains many themes built around a perfect fourth. This may reflect the division between the "Dream and Deeds" that Nielsen claimed as his inspiration, or it could be the melodic consistency of a careful composer.

These broad musical traits come together in a structural design both original and assertive. The first movement is built from relatively autonomous sections identified by thematic material, an ostinato, or both. The *Tempo giusto* opens with a tremolo in the violas that becomes a supporting ostinato for the introductory passage played by the bassoons. That same tremolo figure continues as a background until it is replaced by a short rhythmic ostinato played by the snare drum, an element that comes to dominate the movement. The music expands with other themes, now accompanied by warbling figures from the flute and clarinet, the side drum rattling away insistently. At the point when one might expect a reprise of earlier material, an *Adagio non troppo* introduces a markedly different character—a lyrical intermezzo played by violins and bassoons, supported by horns and lower strings. But this eventually returns to more warbling in the winds, and the snare drum returns, ever more insistent, until it is given a free cadenza, played *ad libitum* against the full ensemble. The timpani undergird the increasingly busy score with a long pedal point on D that becomes the dominant for the final resting point on G. The solo clarinet closes the movement with an introspective cadenza as the accompanying tattoo of the snare drum fades into silence.

In this work, the traditional first and slow movements have fused into one unit, the whole sharing the dry chatter from the percussion section. Most listeners will recall this movement with a lasting impression of wailing woodwinds, particularly the clarinet, and an obstinate snare drum. This departure from traditional symphonic timbres created a minor scandal at a performance in Stockholm in 1924. Much of the audience rushed for the exits, while many of those remaining tried to overpower the sound of the drum with hissing. Such is the road to be traveled by a composer with the courage to introduce new sounds into a traditional venue!

The second movement extends the principle of compound structures to encompass four clearly defined sections. The opening *Allegro* robustly sets forth a theme marked by displaced phrasing, played by the violins over pedal points in the woodwinds and double basses. A dramatic *Grand Pause* introduces a declamatory second theme, played by full orchestra and extended through competition between orchestral choirs. Dynamics and texture eventually subside to introduce the *Presto*, a gigue-fugue that builds to its own climax before subsiding to a long pedal on D-flat, the introduction to the *Andante un poco tranquillo*. Here a second fugue begins, based on a rhythmic permutation of the principal theme from the opening *Allegro*. Nielsen expands this material contrapuntally until the *Allegro* returns, now compressed and restating the principal thematic materials in a different order. This in turn elides into an emphatic coda, brought to rest by sustained trills on the final tonic of E-flat.

The structure of this extraordinary movement lends itself to multiple interpretations. The four sections offer the first and most obvious level of comprehensibility, with the fugues creating contrast through contrapuntal texture. Explored further, the movement can be considered a broad sonata design in which the opening *Allegro* presents the principal thematic material, while the closing *Allegro* represents a slightly altered reprise. In this context, the fugues serve as a development, a role heightened by the permutation of the opening theme in Fugue II. From still another perspective, the four sections might be compared to the outline of a one-movement symphony consisting of an opening fast movement, scherzo (Fugue I), slow movement (Fugue II), and finale. Note these comparisons in the following schematic diagram of the main features of the symphony.

Four Sections	As a Sonata	As a One-Movement Symphony
Allegro (three themes)	Exposition	Opening *allegro*
Presto (Fugue I)	Development	Scherzo
Andante un poco tranqillo (Fugue II—derived from *Allegro*)		Slow movement
Allegro (three themes)	Recapitulation	Finale

If these multiple levels of interpretation are not apparent on first hearing, they nonetheless comprise a subtle element of communication to which audiences have responded warmly.

The first performance of the Fifth Symphony was well received by both critics and audiences, the aforementioned hullabaloo in Copenhagen apparently being an exception. Any new work will have its detractors, but most audiences recognized this symphony as Nielsen's crowning achievement in this idiom. Nielsen himself was somewhat circumspect in his own view of the work:

> They tell me my new symphony isn't like my earlier ones. I can't hear that. But maybe they're right. I do know that it's not so easy to grasp, nor so easy to play. . . . Some have even said that now Schoenberg can pack his bags with his dissonances. Mine are worse. But I don't think so.[7]

Nor have audiences thought so in the years since. The symphony has particularly benefited from the advent of LP and CD recordings. By the close of the century, it had been recorded by many of the major orchestras in Europe and North America, by far the majority made after its successful performance at the Edinburgh Festival in 1950.

Concerto for Flute and Orchestra

Allegro moderato

Allegretto—Adagio ma non troppo—Allegretto—Tempo di marcia

The Flute Concerto was completed in Florence in October 1926. The premiere took place at the Salle Gaveau in Paris on October 21, with Emil Telmányi conducting the Paris Conservatory Orchestra and Holger Gilbert Jespersen, the dedicatee, as soloist. Nielsen soon thereafter revised the ending to produce the version known today, first performed in Oslo in November 1926.

Instrumentation*: two oboes, two clarinets, two bassoons, bass trombone, timpani, solo flute, and strings.*

After his symphonies, Nielsen's most important orchestral works are the concertos for violin (1911), flute (1926), and clarinet (1928). The wind concertos were inspired by the success of his woodwind quintet as played by the Copenhagen Wind Quintet in 1922. Nielsen was so pleased with the group that he resolved to write a concerto for each player that would display their individual musical skills and, to the degree possible, their personalities.

The Flute Concerto was to be introduced at an all-Nielsen concert in Paris, which also included the overture to the opera *Saul og David*, the Violin Concerto, the Fifth Symphony, and five pieces from his opera *Aladdin*, with the conducting duties shared by Nielsen and his violinist son-in-law, Emil Telmányi. Illness interrupted Nielsen's work on the concerto and eventually caused him to relinquish all his conducting responsibilities to Telmányi. Faced with the deadline of an important concerto, Nielsen sent portions of the score to the flutist, Holger Gilbert Jespersen, as he completed them. Even with these efforts, it was necessary to submit a makeshift ending, and it was for that reason that Nielsen revised the concerto (really completed it) so soon after the first performance. The manuscript apparently reflected the haste in composition. In a Foreword to the published score, Telmányi points out discrepancies between ink and pencil notations in the composer's hand, plus further editorial corrections, also presumably added to the score by Nielsen following early performances.

Except for their tonal wanderings, Nielsen's compositions generally draw on classical models. The Flute Concerto follows that practice, but Nielsen bends those models to his own purpose. Many other features of the concerto derive from Nielsen's famous sense of humor and the musical personality of the intended soloist. Jespersen was a refined Francophile of fastidious musical and personal habits. Nielsen contrasted his polished playing with a chamber orchestra in which the soloist enters into competitive dialogues with clarinet and bassoon, clarinet and violin, timpani, clarinet alone, bassoon alone, horn and violas, and above all, the bass trombone, a musical antipode of the flute.

The music bursts forth with a clash between E-flat and D minor, finally settling into E-flat minor, when the soloist plays the first theme to orchestral accompaniment. Three subsequent statements of that material by the soloist and violins lead to a relaxed second subject, introduced by the violins and soon taken up by the flute. A cadenza for flute, violin, and clarinet in dialogue leads to an expressive statement of the second theme to open the development. Here the bass trombone and timpani embark on music of a very different character, with the flute scampering about in the upper register as though trying to find an escape from its rambunctious orchestral brethren. The woodwinds introduce a new and long-breathed theme that prevails until interrupted by another cadenza, this time for flute alone, leading gracefully into the recapitulation of the main theme in the lower strings. An extended cadenza for the soloist, starting over an extended pedal point in the timpani and concluding with a dialogue between flute and clarinet, leads to the close. Nielsen has adapted a flexible sonata design, punctuated by cadenzas to conclude each of the major sections. Virtuoso display becomes an inherent part of the musical fabric, offering opportunities for the soloist to shine but integrating that trait, traditionally associated with concertos, into the larger musical statement.

The *Allegretto* is more traditional, in its outline of a rondo that returns to G for each large-scale ritornello. The *Tempo di marcia* offers one of the most delightful of these reference points, skipping along until it is disrupted by the bass trombone. What follows can best be described as humorous blathering, the trombone apparently trying to disconcert the dignified solo instrument but, not succeeding, venting its frustrations at the end of the movement in caustic glissandos, their incongruity gaining the last word.

The Flute Concerto has remained in the repertory as one of the most accessible and endearing of Nielsen's works. His choice of a chamber orchestra was probably a gesture toward highlighting the tone of the solo flute, but it was also in keeping with the smaller ensembles of neoclassicism that flourished in the 1920s. Audiences in both Paris and Copenhagen responded to the concerto with favor. Nielsen later referred to the Paris concert as one of the greatest experiences of his life. What composer would not feel gratified following a concert devoted to his works in one of Europe's major capitals? The French government awarded Nielsen the *Legion d'Honneur* the following day, not specifically because of the premiere of the Flute Concerto but to acknowledge his broader contributions to modern music.

Carl Orff

❦

b. Munich, Germany, July 10, 1895; d. Munich, March 29, 1982

The music of Carl Orff stands apart from the main currents of musical development during the 20th century. In his mature works he came to regard music as part of a broad spectacle that found its natural outlet in the theater. Since the appearance of *Carmina burana* in 1937, that has been the venue for most of his creative activity.

Orff came from a family with a long tradition of military service, but his own youthful inclinations clearly indicated that music would be his career. His first serious compositions were songs based on his own poems, reflecting a penchant for combinations of music and text that would dominate most of his creative efforts. Church works and small-scale music dramas followed, as Orff was drawn ever more intensely toward the theater. In 1915 he was appointed conductor of the Munich Kammerspiele and at about the same time turned his attention to early music, an interest that led to his recasting of works by Renaissance and Baroque masters, particularly Claudio Monteverdi. It was in the modern realization of the older *stile rappresentativo* (representative style) that he developed his skills in compressed musical drama.

With dancer Dorothee Günther, he founded the Güntherschule in 1924, a program of instruction that introduced the premise of teaching music to young children through coordinated body movement. For this purpose, he designed a range of percussion instruments that have since been widely used with children in Germany, England, Russia, and the United States. He set forth his pedagogical principles in five volumes titled *Schulwerk*, basing his musical designs on folk music, repetition, and ostinato patterns. Those same traits were carried over into his more avowedly artistic works, most of which continued to call for extensive performing resources focused on dramatic presentation in the theater.

In Orff's mature works, physical movement, expressed through dance or patterned stage movements, dramatic texts, and extraordinary instrumental textures (usually drawn from percussion instruments), came together in large works based on dramatic Greek subjects, of which the best known are *Antigone* (1949), *Oedipus der Tyrann* (1954), and *Prometheus* (1966).

It was his success as an innovative educator and music dramatist that distinguished Orff from his contemporaries. In 1961 a center was established at Salzburg for the propagation of his ideas about school music. Perhaps his most enduring legacy will be the body of high-quality musical instruments he designed for students, still in use around the world. His larger musical works addressed to the broader public also occupy a unique niche as modern expressions of total theater. For these accomplishments, Orff received many awards, among them honorary degrees from the universities of Tübingen and Munich, and election to the Bavarian Academy of Fine Arts.

Carmina burana

Fortune, Empress of the World

In Springtime and On the Meadow

In the Tavern

Court of Love

Fortune, Empress of the World

Orff composed this "scenic" cantata between 1935 and 1937. It was first performed by the Municipal Theater of Frankfurt am Main on June 8, 1937, with Bertil Wetzelsberger as musical director.

Instrumentation: *three flutes, (the second and third doubling piccolo), three oboes (the third doubling English horn), clarinet in E-flat, two clarinets in B-flat (one doubling bass clarinet), two bassoons, contrabassoon, four horns, three trumpets, three trombones, tuba, timpani (five drums), bass drum, snare drum, tambourine, castanets, rattle, jingles*

(sleigh bells), triangle, two antique cymbals, four large cymbals, tam-
tam, three chimes, tubular bells, three glockenspiels, xylophone, celesta,
two pianos, three soloists (soprano, tenor, and bass), large and small
mixed chorus, boys' choir, and strings.

As a title, Carmina burana initially identified the 1847 edition of a collection of medieval poetry and music taken from a manuscript discovered in the early 19th century at the Benedictine abbey of
Benediktbeuren, south of Munich. *Carmina* is an old term for song,
burana, the vernacular term for the locale of the monastery where the
manuscript was found. Thus a reasonable translation is "Songs from
Burana" or "Songs from Benediktbeuren." This collection represents
one of the major sources of poetry by the German Goliards and early
Minnesingers, young men and boys with some clerical training who, in
their wandering between universities or monastic communities, celebrated their lifestyle in verses both pious and bawdy. The manuscript is
noteworthy both for its size and for the rudimentary music notation
that, to those already familiar with the poems, served as a mnemonic
device in recalling appropriate tunes to accompany the texts. The
specifics of that notation are lost to us today, but in the 13th century
there was sufficient interest in the material to induce several professional scribes to copy with meticulous care a manuscript obviously
intended for posterity.

Most of the poems follow simple rhyme schemes, easily remembered and often the product of improvisation. Many of them derived
from church festivals and provided the source for early Passion Plays;
others reflected their authors' thoroughly secular interests in wine,
women, and song, not substantially different from the preoccupations
of young men throughout history. Light of purse and full of youthful
vitality, these wandering minstrels produced trenchant rhymes reflecting the pain and pleasure of their lives, satirizing vice and authority in
equal measure, accepting both when they had no choice.

Orff's experience in reviving early dramatic works had focused his
attention on musical settings reduced to their fundamental elements
for maximum dramatic impact. Working in that vein, he selected from
Carmina burana texts divided into four groups, providing them with the
subtitle *Cantiones profanae cantoribus et choris cantandae comitantibus instru-*
mentis atque imaginibus magicis (Secular Songs for Soloists and Chorus,

Accompanied by Instruments and Magic Images). An embittered acceptance of the goddess Fortune, Empress of the World, "changeable as the moon, . . . always either improving or deteriorating," opens the work as the force ultimately determining all life. The three sections that follow, the core of the work, address man's encounter with nature (springtime and its attendant pleasures in the meadow); the fruits of nature (wine and the pleasures of the tavern); and man's role in courtly love (a paean to womanhood ranging from idealized homage to ribald lust). The opening plaint addressed to the ever-turning Wheel of Fortune returns at the close, framing Orff's text design.

Within this impressive arch, Orff sets individual poems separately, changing the ensemble as well as the musical material from poem to poem. Multiple stanzas within a poem receive the same musical setting, leading to repetition within each section in lieu of development. Most sections expand upon a relatively short unit of one or two measures presented over an ostinato figure; thus the music expands from a minimum of material, enabling a ready grasp of Orff's technical procedure.

The most important element is the orchestral fabric, which is dominated by percussion instruments. Its rhythmic power introduces an elemental primitivism, an accumulation of sound eliciting a response from the most basic level of our consciousness. This percussion-dominated orchestration finds its best outlet in rhythmic ostinatos, a basic feature in Orff's music. The whole effect is intentionally simple, grasped subliminally if not consciously, although it is difficult to imagine any listener being unaware of the array of percussion instruments.

As generally defined, harmony becomes relatively less important, and one hears little modulation. Melody, too, occupies a role less important than could be expected in a major choral work, but this quality changes from one poem to another. Orff creates different melodic styles for different languages; Latin and Old French texts tend to generate a relatively lyrical line, particularly when compared to the more jagged contours associated with German texts.

The music nonetheless contains some poignant moments. *"Veris leta facies"* (The smiling face of spring), the first number in *Springtime*, offers a sensitively colored setting celebrating the renewal of the earth, and the cadenzas for the Baritone solo in *"Dies, nox et omnia"* (Day, night, all things are against me) give telling expression to the travail of a frustrated lover. Such cogent expression reaches a high point in the setting of *"Dulcissime, totam tibi subdo me"* (Sweet one, I give myself to you totally), when the solo soprano combines resignation and excitement in a four-measure cadenza supported only by a sustained chord played by the strings.

Carmina burana was first presented as a dramatic stage production, much in the spirit of those works by Monteverdi that had earlier occupied Orff's attention. Subsequent performances included a variety of settings involving staging and music. Some audiences maintained that Orff was returning to the ideals of the 17th-century Italian *camerata*, the essence of the early simplicity now couched in a modern orchestral idiom. Others regarded the work as a solution to some of the problems posed by contemporary music through its straightforward and dramatic demand for attention. Shortly after the work appeared, Orff commented to his publisher that everything he had written to that date could be destroyed, because his true style began with *Carmina burana*.

Francis Poulenc

b. Paris, France, January 7, 1899; d. Paris, January 30, 1963

F rancis Poulenc came from a comfortably affluent family whose home was a center of music-making as well as a venue frequented by persons active in literature, the theater, and the fine arts. This background established Poulenc's contact with a Parisian society that became the audience for most of his early works and in turn elicited from him a penchant for insouciant music presented in a straightforward manner, designed primarily to draw approval from those whose company he enjoyed.

Following early piano instruction with his mother, Poulenc moved on to study with the Spanish pianist, Ricardo Viñes, supplemented by a comparatively short period of theoretical study with the French composer and scholar Charles Koechlin. In later years Poulenc would claim to be largely self-taught, although many observers have noted that his inclination to borrow from other composers was a major factor in his musical development. In 1914 he heard an orchestral performance of Igor Stravinsky's *Le sacre du printemps* that initiated a lifelong admiration for Stravinsky's music. Stravinsky responded by arranging for Poulenc's early *Rapsodie nègre* to be printed by his own publisher, Chester Music of London.

In 1920, while still in military service, Poulenc was included in a group of six young French composers destined to be known in the history books as *Les Six*. The music critic Henri Collet, in a purely journalistic gesture, posed the names of Georges Auric, Louis Durey, Arthur Honegger, Darius Milhaud, Poulenc, and Germaine Taillefere as a Gallic counterpart to the "Mighty Five" among Russians composers from a generation earlier. Poulenc and his French colleagues shared little more substantial than an interest in music of their own day and their attempts to establish themselves as composers, but the name stuck and has been enshrined in the annals of music history.

As the 1920s blossomed in Paris, Poulenc emerged as one of the most frequently performed of the group, a young composer comfortable with his own homosexuality and the social circles in which he moved. He appeared frequently as pianist in performances of his own works and after 1934 began a long and fruitful association with the singer Pierre Bernac. The two had much success in introducing Poulenc's art songs to an ever-widening audience and, in the years following, texted vocal music became Poulenc's most successful medium. In his steady stream of finished works Poulenc also created ballet, piano music, chamber music, and concertos, but his masterpiece was the opera *Dialogues des Carmélites*, first performed as an Italian opera at La Scala in Milan on June 26, 1957. This was closely followed by a short solo opera for soprano based on a dramatic text by Poulenc's personal friend Jean Cocteau, *La voix humaine*, introduced in Paris in February 1959.

In all of his works, Poulenc wrote with much creative élan. The clear tonal orientation of his music remained unaltered by many passing dissonances and quick shifts of key. Melody was his greatest strength and a major factor in the success of his songs and works for the musical stage. He often suffered from the image of a playboy composer who composed with great facility. This stereotype ignored the careful craftsmanship underlying most of his scores and his considerable skill as a pianist. In the years between the two world wars, many critics did not take Poulenc's work seriously, confusing the absence of complexity with a lack of musical substance. Attitudes changed slowly, and by the end of the 20th century Poulenc had established his niche in the concert repertory as a thoroughly accessible composer of wit and eloquence.

Concerto in D minor for Two Pianos and Orchestra

Allegro ma non troppo

Larghetto

Finale: Allegro molto

Poulenc wrote the Concerto for Two Pianos and Orchestra between the fall of 1931 and August 1932. The premiere took place during the Festival of the International Society for Contemporary Music in Venice on September 5, 1932, with Désiré Defauw conducting the Orchestra of La Scala, with Poulenc and Jacques Février as soloists.

Instrumentation: *two flutes (the second doubling piccolo), two oboes (the second doubling English horn), two clarinets, two bassoons, two horns, two trumpets, two trombones, tuba, small drum and military drum without snares, snare drum, bass drum, castanets, tambourine, triangle, two solo pianos, and strings.*

If Poulenc's aristocratic contacts in Parisian society gave him great personal satisfaction, they undoubtedly led to many professional opportunities as well. The Princess Marie-Blanche de Polignac introduced the composer to her aunt by marriage, the Princess Edmond de Polignac, one of the most prominent patrons of the arts in France. Born Winaretta Singer, she was the daughter of the American sewing-machine industrialist I. M. Singer. After the death of her husband, she created a salon that became a center of artistic activity in Paris. For this venue she commissioned works from a number of promising composers, Ravel, Stravinsky, and Satie among them. Her offer of a commission to Poulenc was direct and to the point:

Dear Sir and Friend:

I regret that I did not see you before your departure, in order to inquire whether you could envisage the possibility of writing a work for my "collection" [of contemporary scores] which comprises, as you know, *Renard, Les Tréteaux de Maître Pierre, Socrate,* etc. . . . This work ought to take the form of a piano piece, in the manner of the Landowska Concerto, arranged if possible for 3 pianos: one solo and two secondary.

The work, which should be dedicated to me, would be reserved to me up to the premiere at my salon (from the point of view of execution). The author should deliver the manuscript to me.

May I propose that you accept for this work a sum of 20,000 francs, 5,000 more for the performance which would take place this winter or next spring at my salon in Paris. I will be so pleased to add your name to those of Stravinsky, Faure, Falla, and Satie who have written for my "collection" the most beautiful pages, as you know.[1]

The result was the Concerto for Two Pianos and Orchestra, the third of five keyboard concertos included in Poulenc's work list. The first of these, the *Concert champêtre*, for harpsichord and orchestra, was introduced in May 1929 by Wanda Landowska and was doubtless the "Landowska Concerto" cited by the Princess de Polignac. Later that same year, Poulenc introduced the ballet *Aubade*, a *Concerto chorégraphique* for piano and eighteen other instruments, commissioned by another set of friends, the Vicomte and Vicomtesse de Noailles. Poulenc's response to the Princess de Polignac's commission was thus a reflection of his own recent experience: his skill as a pianist had introduced him to Parisian audiences, he had recently completed two successful keyboard concertos, and the princess had demonstrated a fondness for piano concertos at her concerts, presenting three during one evening's program in October 1930. Poulenc was matching his proven skills to known audience tastes.

Although his patron referred to a concerto "arranged if possible for 3 pianos: one solo and two secondary," Poulenc's references to his work on the score imply that from an early date he was thinking of a work featuring two solo pianos, possibly expanding on sketches of a sonata for that medium. Those same references suggest that the total effort may have occupied him longer than the two and a half months he claimed. On October 6, 1931, he described the concerto to Marguerite Long as something that would amuse her because "the piano is treated in two timbres."[2] He wrote to Mme. de Noailles on July 6, 1932, saying that he still had to finish the concerto. On August 10, he claimed to be "crazy from work. After a month of formidable labor I have finished . . . the Venetian Concerto." Perhaps not, for on August 26 he wrote once again, saying "concerto finally finished [I] am dead but not dissatisfied."[3] It would not be unusual for a composer to adapt a commission to ideas already in ferment, and the princess's letter was not firm about the matter of three pianos. Whatever Poulenc's original plans were, it was the commission from the Princess de Polignac that provided the stimulus for completion of the concerto in its final form.

In preparation for the undertaking, Poulenc had consulted piano concertos by Mozart, Liszt, and Ravel. With that music as background and his awareness of the sophisticated society his composition was to address, he produced a score of neoclassical clarity suffused with wit and energy. Development of musical materials is not a prominent feature, and the solo parts require versatile facility more than a thoroughgoing keyboard virtuosity. After an opening of toccata-like passagework for the soloists, the first movement proceeds with a theme built around a four-note motive exchanged between soloists and orchestra, perhaps the "two timbres" Poulenc had in mind when he described the concerto to Marguerite Long. Two subsequent themes suggest dance hall music and lead to a slow midsection in which the soloists play some of the most lyrical passages of the concerto. The quick tempo of the beginning returns, but now all is much compressed, and the movement closes with a coda written in imitation of the Balinese gamelan music Poulenc had heard at the Colonial Exposition in 1931.

The opening of the *Larghetto* closely resembles the slow movement of Mozart's *Coronation Concerto*, K. 537, in both melodic line and title, an affinity Poulenc acknowledged:

In the Larghetto of this concerto, I allowed myself, for the first time, to return to Mozart, for I cherish the melodic line and I prefer Mozart to all other musicians. If the movement begins *alla* Mozart, it quickly veers, at the entrance of the second piano, toward a style that was standard for me at that time.[4]

In drawing on the musical style of an earlier composer, Poulenc was following the model of Stravinsky, who had earlier turned to the music of Bach (Concerto for Piano and Winds, 1924), the style and materials of the 18th century (*Pulcinella*, 1920), and Tchaikovsky (*Divertimento*, 1928). Poulenc's historical reference was perhaps a nod toward a contemporary he held in high esteem as much as it was an expression of his own tastes.

The *Finale* has been described as a rondo, but the variety of thematic materials and their shifting juxtaposition bring the music closer to the character of a fantasia. Themes and figuration based on them meld in a fast-paced collage of sound, the sheer effervescence of the music carrying all before it. The Balinese music from the first movement returns briefly, before the two soloists share an antiphonal cadence of chromatic chords to close the concerto.

Shortly after the premiere, Poulenc described the concerto to Paul Collaer as one of his major accomplishments:

You will see for yourself what an enormous step forward it is from my previous work and that I am really entering my great period.

You will also recognize that the germs of this progression are in the *Concert champêtre* and in *Aubade*, which were two essential stages in my development. It is possible that, in these two concertos, my concern for technical perfection—especially in the orchestration—might have diverted me from the true nature of my music; but it was necessary, and you will see for yourself with what a "precise" pen I have orchestrated *Le Bal* and the Concerto, which I assure you are absolutely pure Poulenc.[5]

The initial performance at Venice confirmed Poulenc's high opinion of the work, because, in both his account and in the reviews of major critics, it was a great success. Poulenc and Jacques Février had been performing together since childhood, the orchestra of La Scala had been trained by Arturo Toscanini, and the conductor, Désiré Defauw, would go on to establish a reputation as an interpreter of modern music. This fruitful combination of performers no doubt contributed much to a successful first performance, described by the French critic Henry Prunières:

> The success was worth the wait, thanks above all to the *Concerto for Two Pianos and Small Orchestra* of Francis Poulenc which was, in the symphonic domain, the grand event of the Festival.
>
> If I had little taste for the *Larghetto*, which imitated a little too directly the style of Mozart, I liked very much the first and third movements. The initial *Allegro* belongs to the best vein of Poulenc. One finds here that fresh melodiousness which combined the charm of his first compositions with a harmonic and orchestral facility which has long been in default. The execution by Poulenc, Jacques Février and an ensemble of soloists from La Scala under the direction of Désiré Defauw was absolutely marvelous.[6]

Not all critics were equally impressed, for a review following an early New York performance claimed that "nothing of his [Poulenc] has given him claim to be taken seriously. . . . If we deduct from the concerto all that is cheap and undistinguished, nothing remains. . . ."[7] Other writers have found borrowings in Poulenc's score, but most have at the same time credited his writing with great verve enhanced by colorful harmony and orchestration.

Poulenc did not approach composition with furrowed brow, as an essay in profundity, but neither was he as flippant as some have charged. He was concerned above all with communication. If the audience he addressed, at least in his younger days, was inclined toward quick and witty music, he was prepared to write in a style that would appeal to them. In his own view, that goal did not require him to be a musical iconoclast: "I am well aware that I am not the kind of musician who makes harmonic innovations, like Igor [Stravinsky], Ravel or Debussy, but I do think there is a place for *new* music that is content with using other people's chords. Was this not the case with Mozart and with Schubert?"[8] Indeed it was!

Sergei Prokofiev

~~~~

b. Sontsovka, Ukraine, April 23, 1891; d. Moscow, Russia, March 5, 1953

The larger part of Prokofiev's creative effort focused on music for the theater—opera, ballet, and film music—but he also contributed substantially to the genres of symphony, concerto, and piano music. In all of those works he acknowledged as part of his catalogue, he showed a strong sense for fundamentally classic structures, usually enlivened by a sense of irony and humor that often became a burlesque of common musical practices. He was a master of the grotesque musical gesture that was intended as a humorous rather than a caustic statement. To these ends, his music often projects a frenetic intensity created by propulsive rhythms, sudden harmonic shifts, violent contrasts, quick changes of direction, and elements of youthful enthusiasm. Prokofiev incorporated these traits within the bounds of his own concept of musical tradition. He maintained that the new and original materials alone would not survive, because they could be copied by others; at the same time, he believed that any composer who had nothing new to offer would soon be forgotten.

In his later years, Prokofiev described his compositions in terms of four different lines—classical, modern, toccata, and lyrical—broad concepts that, for him, represented the genesis or character of a work. A fifth line, grotesque, was urged on him by others, but Prokofiev maintained that this was nothing more than a deviation from the four lines given here, if it existed at all. Disregarding some initial shock on the part of some of his contemporaries, his works have proven to be tonal, accessible, and widely popular.

Prokofiev's musical training extended from early piano lessons with his mother through a brilliant student career at the St. Petersburg Conservatory. His First Symphony was performed to much acclaim in 1918 and indirectly enabled him to gain an exit visa for travel to the West. The official in charge of issuing such documents cited him as a revolutionary in music just as the new government was revolutionary in human affairs, and assumed, it seems, that as he traveled abroad Prokofiev could be a voice for the new order in Russia. The young pianist-composer left Petrograd in 1918 and arrived in the United States by way of Japan. For the next decade he was industriously engaged in giving concerts to establish his own reputation, striving to expand his earlier successes to encompass international concert circles. From 1927 he began to visit Russia periodically for concerts as composer and pianist, finally establishing residence in Moscow as a Soviet citizen in 1936.

Critics have differed in their assessment of the music Prokofiev wrote following his return to Russia, but on November 19, 1945, he achieved the *ne plus ultra* of public attention in the United States: his picture on the cover of *Time* magazine. The supporting article described him as Russia's greatest living musician. Following the end of World War II, the Soviet government under Joseph Stalin turned its attention to the ordering of internal affairs with unswerving rigor, leading to several political purges, show trials, and other repressive acts. On February 10, 1948, the Central Committee of the Communist Party, acting under the leadership of Andrei Zhdanov, issued a resolution criticizing the opera *The Great Friendship*, by Vano Muradeli. This statement included a sweeping indictment of works by Prokofiev, Shostakovich, and most other Russian composers who were thought to be tainted by formalism—the pursuit of cerebral procedures in composition—or by any semblance of Western influence:

> Particularly bad are the conditions in symphonic and operatic production, with reference to composers who adhere to the formalistic anti-national movement. This movement has found its fullest expression in the works of composers such as Comrades Shostakovich, Prokofiev, Khachaturian, Shebalin, Popov, Miaskovsky, and others, in whose music formalistic distortions, and anti-democratic tendencies which are alien to the Soviet people and its artistic tastes, are represented with particular obvious-

ness. The characteristic features of this music are the negation of basic principles of classical music; the preachment of atonality, dissonances and disharmony, supposedly representative of "progress" and "modernism" in the development of musical forms; the rejection of such all-important concepts of musical composition as melody, and the infatuation with the confused, neuropathological combinations which transform music into cacophony, into a chaotic agglomeration of sounds. This music is strongly reminiscent of the spirit of contemporary modernistic bourgeois music of Europe and America, reflecting the dissolution of bourgeois culture, a complete negation of musical art, its impasse.[1]

Too ill following a heart attack to attend a later meeting at which composers attempted to defend themselves and their works, Prokofiev wrote an extended letter in which he acknowledged, as was expected of him, some digressions from accepted artistic dogma. Increasingly poor health restricted Prokofiev's work in the years following, although he completed several works for the stage plus the Symphony-Concerto for Cello and Orchestra and his Seventh Symphony. He died on the same day as Joseph Stalin, an irony that, under other circumstances, likely would have elicited trenchant comment from the composer.

Symphony No. 1 in D, Opus 25 (*Classical*)

Allegro

Larghetto

Gavotte: Non troppo allegro

Finale: Molto vivace

Prokofiev assembled his First Symphony from the summer through September of 1917 from sketches made in 1916. The symphony was first performed in Petrograd (St. Petersburg up to 1914, Leningrad after 1924) on April 21, 1918, with Prokofiev conducting the former Court Orchestra.

Instrumentation: *two flutes, two oboes, two clarinets, two bassoons, two trumpets, two horns, timpani, and strings.*

The February Revolution of 1917 in Russia at first exerted little impact on those in the musical and artistic community, many of whom considered the arts independent from the surrounding social turmoil. As a young man, Prokofiev claimed to care nothing about politics; he claimed that art was removed from the political world and that he disassociated himself from political ideology when composing. During the summer of 1917, he took refuge in the country, intentionally leaving behind a piano, his usual tool for composition, relying instead on his musical ear and his established craftsmanship as a composer for the creation of his First Symphony:

> I deliberately did not take my piano with me, for I wished to try composing without it. Until this time I had always composed at the piano, but I noticed that thematic material composed without the piano was often better. At first it seems strange when transferred to the piano, but after one has played it a few times everything falls into place. I had been toying with the idea of writing a whole symphony without the piano. I believed that the orchestra would sound more natural. That is how the project for a symphony in the Haydn style came into being: I had learned a great deal about Haydn's technique from [Nicolai] Tcherepnin, and hence felt myself on sufficiently familiar ground to venture forth on this difficult journey without the piano. It seemed to me that had Haydn lived to our day he would have retained his own style while accepting something of the new at the same time. That was the kind of symphony I wanted to write: a symphony in the classical style. And when I saw that my idea was beginning to work I called it the "Classical" Symphony: in the first place because that was simpler, and secondly for the fun of it, to "tease the geese," and in the secret hope that it would prove me right if the symphony really did turn out to be a piece of classical music.[2]

His incorporation of sketches from 1916 for the first, second, and fourth movements no doubt facilitated the creation of this work. For the third movement, he took over in its entirety his completed Gavotte in D.

Prokofiev's *Classical* Symphony is a witty satire, combining his iconoclastic turns and twists with the traditional outlines of the late-18th-century symphony. On first encounter, the work might seem to be an early manifestation of the neoclassicism that marked much music in the decades following World War I. But Prokofiev refers to styles of an earlier time in a spirit of sardonic irony, offering a witty burlesque of music from the classical period, whereas the neoclassicism of the 1920s was more nearly an attempt to revive the spirit, substance, and clarity of line associated with the 18th century. For all that, Prokofiev's designation "Classical" has proven to be well founded, because the score does indeed follow outlines of a classical symphony, and its established niche in the repertory is "classical" in that it has come to represent much that is typical in 20th-century music.

The symphony opens with a modern version of the 18th-century "Mannheim Rocket" theme, an ascending rush, with crescendo, through the tonic chord. Following its initial appearance, the main theme returns for a second strophe, not in the expected dominant key but a whole-tone lower (in C major), and the harmony has already shifted to a distant key. An elegantly different second theme sounds in the dominant key, as any polite and proper second theme should, but leaps of two octaves introduced the pointillism that became a prominent melodic trait of much modern music. In a typical classical symphony, both themes would return in the tonic key; Prokofiev begins his recapitulation in C major, then, reversing the harmonic plan of the beginning, restates that theme a step higher, in D major, to return to the home key for the conclusion of the movement. Tradition has not been set aside completely, just given a quick and clever nudge.

The *Larghetto* outlines a broad three-part design that would have been familiar to Haydn, but the violins play the principal theme so high that it sounds more ethereal than lyrical, perhaps an intended jest in carrying lyricism to extremes of range.

For the third movement, Prokofiev inserted his Gavotte in D. The tradition of the classical dance movement remains, but the graceful triple meter of the minuet gives way to the more heavy-footed duple meter of the older gavotte, always beginning on the second half of the measure. Prokofiev was so fond of this music and its original shifts of harmony that he incorporated an extended version of it in his ballet music for *Romeo and Juliet*, and invited conductors to insert that version in the symphony, an invitation rarely, if ever, accepted. The *Finale* continues the tradition of Haydn in its ebullient high energy, marked by sudden shifts of harmony and quixotic twists the listener has by now come to expect from Prokofiev.

The *Classical* Symphony quickly became Prokofiev's first unqualified success. Even those who had castigated his earlier works recognized here a clarity and lyricism that have continued to appeal to
audiences. One critic noted the absence of what he called grimaces and
outrageous chords: "It is all chaste and pure, clear, simple, and reminiscent of the best youthful inspirations of Haydn and Mozart."[3]
Another praised the young composer for "striving to give up his artistic flippancy and buffoonery, his attempts to settle down, to delve more
deeply, to become more serious, even if it should imperil his reputation
for originality, that is, for grotesquerie."[4] In large measure, time and
public favor have confirmed the substance of these early reactions.

Symphony No. 5 in B-flat, Opus 100

Andante

Allegro marcato

Adagio

Allegro giocoso

*Prokofiev composed his Fifth Symphony during the summer of 1944,
completing the orchestration that November. He performed the piano
score at the Central House of Composers in October, and conducted the
orchestral premiere in Moscow on January 13, 1945, with the Moscow
State Philharmonic Orchestra.*

Instrumentation: *piccolo, two flutes, two oboes, English horn, clarinet
in E-flat, two clarinets in B-flat, bass clarinet, two bassoons, contrabassoon, four horns, three trumpets, three trombones, tuba, timpani, bass
drum, snare drum, triangle, cymbals, wood block, tambourine, tam-
tam, piano, harp, and strings.*

In many ways, the Fifth Symphony is the most conventional of the seven
Prokofiev composed. For that reason alone, it cannot be considered his
most characteristic, because his penchant for originality, expressed as a
young man, continued to dominate his compositions. Most audiences
familiar with the work regard it as the greatest among his symphonies,
coming at the apex of his career. He had long been hailed as one of
Russia's most gifted composers, his works had enjoyed several decades

of success in the West, and his physical vitality had not yet been diminished by the ill health that dominated the last years of his life. For the composer, the symphony was apparently a highly personal statement, intended as a hymn in praise of the nobility of the human spirit. The cataclysm of World War II, with all of its horrors and hardships for the Russian people, was approaching its end, Russian forces were routing the enemy, a swelling tide of national pride in all things Russian was in the air, and Prokofiev was regarded by many as one of the voices best equipped to express the joy of national survival. The symphony quickly became a standard item in the orchestral repertory, and was one of the few works by Prokofiev not condemned in the Central Committee's resolution of 1948. Indeed, in his response to that criticism, Prokofiev had cited the Fifth Symphony as one of those works in which he had, in his view, succeeded in suppressing elements of formalism and other undesirable traits purportedly found in his later works.

During the summer of 1944, Prokofiev and other established composers were evacuated to the government-operated Composer's House near the small town of Ivanovo, some fifty miles from Moscow. Prokofiev became a central figure in this small community as he organized recreation and established a daily meeting of the composers at which each was to present the results of his day's labors, presumably for collegial discussion and criticism. Under these conditions, Prokofiev composed his Fifth Symphony and the Eighth Piano Sonata in slightly more than a month.

Although frequently cited as one of the Russian "War Symphonies," the Fifth Symphony reflected little of the events surrounding that struggle. Prokofiev had produced works inspired by the war: the *Ballad of an Unknown Boy* (1942–1943), a cantata based on the story of a young boy who avenges the death of his father at the hands of the Nazis; *Ode to the End of War* (1945); and other quasi-patriotic works. His approach to abstract symphonic composition in 1944 came several years after his last essays in this genre, the Third (1928) and Fourth (1930) Symphonies, both based on materials originating in works for the theater. One could expect any Russian citizen to be affected by the death and destruction that permeated the country in 1944, but those events find no identifiable expression in the score at hand.

The first performance in the Grand Hall of the Moscow Conservatory was a musical and political triumph. National sentiments were running high; shortly before the concert, the Red Army had crossed the Vistula River in a rout of the Germans. As described by many who were present, when Prokofiev raised his baton, the sound of artillery erupted in the distance. The composer remained still with upraised baton until the din subsided, and then began the symphony. Many listeners felt that the event was replete with extramusical significance, because the mood of elation over the progress of the war and its anticipated end permeated all activities. The symphony met with unreserved praise for its ennobled expression and ready accessibility.

The plan of the four movements follows a slow—moderate—slow—fast design. The opening *Andante* is usually performed in a moderate tempo, but when compared to the fast tempos that are traditional for the opening of a major symphony, it seems comparatively slow. The subject of relative tempos in this work has generated continuing discussion among conductors and critics, because the second and third movements also rely on an unhurried pace to realize their planned acoustic effect. As another type of relationship between movements, the monumental theme that opens the *Andante* returns in the *Allegro giocoso,* linking these two movements as a frame for a broader orchestral statement that at times approaches epic grandeur.

This epic theme serves as the basis for a straightforward sonata design that unfolds at a dignified pace in the opening *Andante.* Low brass instruments play a prominent thematic role, and much of the orchestration achieves its singular effect from the doubling of principal melodic lines several octaves apart, usually involving instruments of markedly different range or timbre. The opening, for example, is played by bassoon and flute an octave apart, with interjections by the low strings some two octaves lower. Prokofiev's orchestration underscores his belief in the importance of originality in contemporary works. The opening theme returns with sufficient frequency to become a basic motto. In its slightly altered statement at the beginning of the coda, punctuated by bass drum and piano tremolos, it assumes a markedly different character that expands in heroic proportions until the majestic bang of the final chord.

The second movement is a scherzo following a broad three-part design with the outer sections marked by an ostinato pattern in the strings. The midsection offers a more open texture, usually characterized by one clear melodic line, often doubled in wide-spaced octaves, over a syncopated accompaniment. This accelerates to a return of the principal theme, but now calling for the full ensemble, punctuated by quips from the lower brass. The movement provides a perfect illustration of Prokofiev's typical orchestral sound.

Rhythmic vacillation between different treatments of triple meter pervades the *Adagio*. At some points this is realized as a constant shifting between thrice two and thrice three (three-four versus nine-eight), at others, it is a matter of both patterns acting together in rhythmic counterpoint. Beyond that, the dominant character of the music is its restrained and deliberate presentation of declamatory themes surrounded by masses of orchestral color.

In spite of the quick tempo in the *Allegro giocoso*, the melodic lines, written in comparatively larger note values, stand out in a stately manner, as in the reference by the string choir to the opening theme of the first movement. Prokofiev organizes his material along the lines of a sophisticated sonata-rondo design that here suggests an element of symmetry (introduction-A B A C A B A-coda). Through much of the movement, the low brass instruments play principal thematic material in long notes against tumultuous passagework in the violins and woodwind instruments. The coda becomes a *perpetuum mobile* as the music rushes along under its own momentum, arriving precipitously at a thunderous close.

Doubtless the initial success of Prokofiev's Fifth Symphony owed something to the atmosphere of elation ensuing from military victories, but subsequent assessments have sustained the original response of the audiences at premieres in Moscow, Paris, and Boston during 1945. Following an early performance in New York, the symphony was described as "one of the most interesting, and probably the best, that has come from Russia in the last quarter-century. It is unquestionably the richest and most mature symphonic score the composer has produced. There are new spiritual horizons in the serenity of the opening movement and wonderful development that come later."[5]

Concerto No. 1 for Piano and Orchestra in D-flat, Opus 10

Allegro brioso—Andante assai—Allegro scherzando

Prokofiev began the First Concerto for Piano in the summer of 1911, completing it in February 1912. It was first performed in Moscow's

Sokolniki Park on August 7, 1912, with Konstantin Saradzhev conducting and Prokofiev as soloist.

Instrumentation: *piccolo, two flutes, two oboes, two clarinets, two bassoons, contrabassoon, four horns, two trumpets, three trombones, tuba,
timpani, bells, solo piano, and strings.*

Prokofiev was just gaining notice as a composer when he began his First
Piano Concerto. He had convinced the publishing firm P. I. Jurgenson to
publish several of his smaller works for solo piano, and, to Jurgenson's
surprise, these works sold rather well. Prokofiev's outlook on life and
music was that of an angry young man with a musical chip on his shoul-
der. Still a student, he was chafing under what he considered to be reactionary musical values at the St. Petersburg Conservatory. He was eager
to establish his reputation, and he was always a vigorous exponent of
originality and simplicity in all things. He developed his own system of
spelling, which he considered more efficient in that all vowels were
omitted (he spelled his name PKFV), and in a similar vein he began to
write all his orchestral music in C score, that is, he wrote for all the
instruments at their sounding pitch, leaving to the copyists the necessary adjustments for transposing instruments as they prepared the performance parts. As a pianist, he was already known for his athleticism,
physical strength, and technical speed; apparently he enjoyed the shock
effect he was able to create with these skills at the instrument. Thus it
was that he turned to a work for piano and orchestra, originally conceived as a concertino but later expanded into a one-movement work of
several clearly identified sections and presented as a solo vehicle, to display his wares as both pianist and composer.

Summer concerts in Sokolniki Park near Moscow had been established as a forum for contemporary music by a group of modernists led
by the editor of the magazine *Muzyka*, Vladimir Derzhanovsky.
Prokofiev's supporters presented the young musician to this group as
one who should be heard. Prokofiev, in his first appearance as soloist
with an orchestra, brilliantly performed his First Piano Concerto, a
musical debut that quickly polarized the musical community in
Moscow. Derzhanovsky and his cohorts praised the work for its brilliance, imagination, and originality, one writer hesitantly prophesying
that Prokofiev would take his place in a line of musicians extending
from Glinka through Rimsky-Korsakov. Others were vehemently nega-

tive, decrying the young composer as a madman, not a real talent, but a purveyor of cacophonous confusion. Prokofiev apparently enjoyed all the furor, making the most of the tributes and responding to his critics with ridicule. It seems that here, as later in his career, these controversies appealed to his innate competitive instincts.

The First Concerto became the focus of attention again in 1914 when Prokofiev graduated from the St. Petersburg Conservatory. He had completed the course in conducting and, left to his own resources because of the illness of his piano teacher, he decided to complete the piano course and to enter the Rubinstein Competition, a student contest that offered a piano as first prize. In keeping with his iconoclastic ways, for the required classical concerto he submitted his own. Recalling the event later, Prokofiev observed that:

> while I might not be able to compete successfully in performance
> of a classical concerto, there was a chance that my own might
> impress the examiners by the novelty of technique; they simply
> would not be able to judge whether I was playing it well or not!
> On the other hand, even if I did not win, the defeat would be less
> mortifying since no one would know whether I had lost because
> the concerto was bad or because my performance was faulty.[6]

The jury was reluctant to accept his proposal of an unknown concerto, but finally agreed with the stipulation that each examiner would receive a copy of the score a week before the competition. At that point Prokofiev besieged the publisher Jurgenson with requests to publish the work in time for the competition, or he would be unable to compete. The score was published just in time and duly distributed to all twenty members of the jury. At one stroke, Prokofiev had fulfilled his need for a contest piece and brought out his first major orchestral publication. His performance won for him the Rubinstein first prize, a Schroeder piano, and a performance of the concerto at graduation exercises.

The Russian-born American composer Vernon Duke [Vladimir Dukelsky] heard Prokofiev perform in 1914 and recorded his own impression of the young composer's appearance on stage:

> The strangely gauche manner in which he traversed the stage was
> no indication of what was to follow; after sitting down and
> adjusting the piano stool with an abrupt jerk, Prokofiev let go

with an unrelenting muscular exhibition of a completely novel kind of piano playing. The prevailing fashion in those days was the languorous hothouse manner of a Scriabin or the shimmering post-Debussy impressionist tinklings of harp and celesta. This young man's music and his performance of it reminded me of the onrushing forwards in my one unfortunate soccer experience— nothing but unrelenting energy and athletic joy of living. No wonder the first four notes of the concerto, oft-repeated, were later nicknamed "*po cherepoo*" ("hit on the head"), which was Prokofiev's exact intention. . . . There was frenetic applause, and no less than six flower horseshoes were handed to Prokofiev, who was now greeted with astonished laughter.[7]

The success that attended his First Concerto established Prokofiev as both pianist and composer, with published works and a notebook full of reviews to support a burgeoning career. In later years, he regarded the concerto as his first mature work, and it became a mainstay of his career when he first traveled outside Russia as a professional musician. On his first tour of the United States in 1918, he performed the work in Chicago on December 6 and 7 and again in New York four days later. The musical traits of the work came to be those that, for most listeners, identified Prokofiev's music in general: a volcanic musical temperament marked by sharp swings in mood and thematic materials; an unabashed pleasure in his own prodigious technical skills at the keyboard; and a "steely tone" (a term often appearing in early reviews, particularly in America), which stood well apart from the relatively mellifluous fabric of the prevailing musical style of the late 19th century. Russian music in general and Prokofiev's works in particular were now considered a revolt against musical traditions comparable to the political revolt that had transformed Russia.

One can interpret the musical plan of this concerto in several ways. It is a one-movement work of several contrasting sections played without interruption in which the main theme appears at the opening, near the midpoint, and again at the close. The distinctive qualities of this opening theme provide continuity and the intervening materials offer considerable variety in timbre and tempo. The work can also be heard as a more traditional three-movement plan performed without break, in which the brief *Andante assai* serves as a second, slow movement. Still more traditional is a view of the entire work as an expanded sonata design in which the return of the main theme at the midpoint of the concerto represents the beginning of a development section, with the return of that theme at the end serving as a coda. Prokofiev's own description offers some further insight:

> The conception is expressed, firstly, in some of the means used for combining piano and orchestra, and secondly in the form: a sonata Allegro with the introduction repeated after the exposition and at the end; a short Andante inserted before the development; development in the form of a Scherzo and a cadenza to introduce the recapitulation. True, this form was criticized on the grounds that the concerto consisted of a succession of unrelated episodes. But these episodes were held together quite firmly.[8]

The main theme appears immediately, with much of the orchestra playing in unison and reinforced by octaves in the upper range of the piano. Two contrasting themes follow, introduced by the piano, and the orchestra presents a third while the piano contributes glittering passagework. The main theme returns, played by the full orchestra while the pianist plays octaves, but now it is ingeniously redistributed between the pianist's hands. Following a Grand Pause, the *Andante assai* continues in a key one whole-tone lower than the basic tonic. Whether this serves as a separate movement or as part of a development, the unusual key, the lyrical writing for the piano, and the muted strings set it apart from the remainder of the concerto. The *Allegro scherzando* follows immediately, marked by rhythmically propulsive passagework for the piano that carries all before it through its sheer exuberance.

Both performer and listener find here an intriguing musical statement open to multiple interpretations. In that multiplicity, the concerto finds one of its greatest strengths.

Concerto No. 2 for Piano and Orchestra in G minor, Opus 16

Andantino—Allegretto—Andantino

Scherzo: Vivace

Intermezzo: Allegro moderato

Allegro tempestoso

Prokofiev composed his Second Concerto for Piano during the winter of
1912 and 1913, later reconstructing it in 1923. The original version
was first performed in Pavlovsk on September 5, 1913, by an orchestra
conducted by A. P. Aslanov, Prokofiev playing the solo part. Prokofiev
was again the soloist in the first performance of the reconstructed ver-
sion in Paris with Serge Koussevitzky and his orchestra in May 1924.

Instrumentation*: two flutes (the second doubling piccolo), two oboes,*
two clarinets, two bassoons, four horns, two trumpets, three trombones,
tuba, timpani, bass drum, snare drum, cymbals, tambourine, solo
piano, and strings.

The echoes of Prokofiev's First Concerto for Piano had barely subsided
when he began to assemble earlier sketches into a new work that he proposed would be more substantial than his initial essay in this genre.
First word about the project came from his fellow student and close
friend Nicolai Miaskovsky, who wrote that "Serge Prokofiev is finishing
his Second Piano Concerto in four movements. It is very fresh and
interesting, and in a more intimate vein than the First, but also more
difficult. He played some of it for me—there are wonderful bits, quite
novel and most intriguing."[9] At some point soon after the early performances, the concerto score was accidentally burned. Prokofiev
reconstructed it from memory in 1923, but we cannot know how that
reconstruction, the version known today, compares with the original,
because Prokofiev acknowledged that he revised the text slightly in the
process of re-creating it. Miaskovsky's description of the work having a
sense of "intimacy" in comparison to the composer's First Concerto is
not upheld by the work as we know it, but it is impossible to know if
the original version had a more intimate character. In Prokofiev's own
comparison of the two concertos, he considered the First as a nearly
equal partnership between soloist and orchestra, while in the Second
the solo part was dominant. That becomes apparent following even the
briefest encounter with the Second Concerto. The piano writing is as
demanding as any written by Prokofiev up to this time, incorporating
much original passagework showing a complete and inventive mastery
of the technical and acoustic properties of the instrument.

The first performance in Pavlovsk attracted many people from both St. Petersburg and Moscow who were curious about Prokofiev and his music following the critical attention he had received with his First Concerto. There were many attempts to place him within one or another of the musical styles emerging at the time, but reviews of the performance suggest that audience dismay and irritation were more common than substantive comprehension:

> The debut of the pianistic cubist and futurist Prokofiev has brought excitement in the public. In the train going to Pavlovsk, one hears on all sides: "Prokofiev, Prokofiev, Prokofiev . . . a new star of the piano!"A youngster appears on the podium. It is Sergei Prokofiev. He sits at the piano and proceeds to make motions as though he were dusting the keys or tuning the instrument. All this he does with a sharp dry touch. The audience is puzzled. Some are outraged. A couple leaves and runs for the exit: "This kind of music will drive you crazy!" "What is this? A deliberate persiflage?!" After the first exits, other listeners begin to leave their seats. Prokofiev is now playing the second movement of his Concerto. Once more, a rhythmic jumble of sounds. The more audacious members of the audience begin to hiss. The hall is gradually emptying. Finally, with a mercilessly dissonant combination of brass instruments, the young artist concludes his Concerto. Most listeners react by booing. Prokofiev bows defiantly, then plays an encore. The public flees. On all sides one hears, "To the devil with this futurist music! My cat can play like that!" Prokofiev's Concerto is cacophony which has nothing to do with cultural music. His cadenzas are insufferable. The *Concerto* is filled to overflow with musical mud, produced, one may imagine, by accidental spilling of ink on music paper.[10]

The critic Vyacheslav Karatygin was one of the few who spoke in support of Prokofiev: "The audience hissed. This is in the order of things. Some ten years from now it will expiate these hisses by unanimous applause for Sergei Prokofiev, famous composer with a European reputation."[11] Karatygin would have the satisfaction of seeing his projected timetable for Prokofiev's success met almost exactly.

Considering the social conditions in Russia in 1913 and the audience that would have been in the majority at a concert held at a summer resort—members of the aristocracy and their minions—their reaction should not be surprising. Russia was on the threshold of a wrenching social change; any voice that challenged the increasingly tenuous hold of the established social order was destined to meet with critical rebuttal from those who saw their world threatened.

A later performance in Petrograd before the Russian Musical Society on February 19, 1915, gained wider acceptance. Although there remained much divergence of opinion about Prokofiev as a musical iconoclast, there was wide agreement that the Second Concerto represented the work of a major talent. Prokofiev continued to be in demand as a performer of his own works, and his Second Concerto became an important part of his repertory. Several years later in Paris, he played the work for the impresario Serge Diaghilev, who, impressed by Prokofiev's obvious talent, envisioned a ballet that would be performed while Prokofiev played the concerto in the pit (the undertaking was not successful). Another Paris performance in 1924 with Serge Koussevitzky and his orchestra was a pronounced success and helped confirm Prokofiev's international stature as both pianist and composer.

The nervous morbidity of Russia in 1913 found expression in this concerto's melancholy lyricism and many of its extravagant stylistic effects, all compounded by the staggering technical demands of the solo part. Prokofiev had developed a style of writing for the piano that often surrounds a melodic line in the middle range of the instrument with coruscating figuration above and below, the passagework demanding a distribution of labor wherein individual notes of the line are played by the hands in alternation. The intensity generated in the solo part prevails throughout the concerto, because the plan of tempos over the four movements (moderate-fast-fast-fast) offers no slow movement for respite or repose.

After only the suggestion of an introduction, the piano plays the main theme of the *Andantino* in ringing octaves, marked *narrante* (in the style of a narrative). The laconic mood prevails through the following graceful passagework until the piano embarks on a long solo section that expands upon the main theme through the process of recapitulation and development. The orchestra returns for a brief coda invoking the opening measures. One can easily impose the outline of a sonata design on this movement, but it is the logical treatment of clearly stated materials that comes forth most clearly in Prokofiev's search for originality in his adaptation of classic procedures.

The *Scherzo* is a breathtaking *perpetuum mobile* in which both hands of the pianist play in parallel motion throughout, the orchestra adding support and intermittent punctuation. The writing represents the toccata line as Prokofiev described it in his assessment of his musical style; indeed, it has often been compared to his Toccata for Piano, op. 11, completed shortly before he began work on the Second Concerto. The unremitting sixteenth-note pattern challenges the stamina of the soloist as a performer at the same time that it underscores the imagination of the composer in maintaining interest in the face of a nearly monorhythmic solo part. A heavy-footed ostinato introduced at the beginning of the *Intermezzo* permeates most of the movement. The piano assumes this pattern in its prominent solo sections, expanding the original intervals more than two octaves but maintaining the original marchlike character.

The primordial force of the *Finale* inevitably calls to mind the primitivism of Igor Stravinsky's *Sacre du printemps*, first performed in Paris only a few months before Prokofiev's Second Concerto was heard in Russia. The design is interrupted twice by quiet, sustained chords in the piano that bring the headlong rush to a temporary halt. The first of these interruptions serves to introduce a haunting, folklike melody that becomes the subject of some complex variations; the second leads to further development; both interruptions serve as a freshening of the rhythmic drive more than for any harmonic purpose. The movement closes with a return to the main theme, played with clangorous abandon. The juxtaposition in the coda of markedly unrelated harmonies may have been an attempt to shock the audience one last time as much as it was a gesture of harmonic originality.

Musical works offering new techniques are often rejected by audiences comfortable only with the familiar repertory. Few of those compositions have enjoyed a transition from general rejection to popular acceptance comparable to that accorded Prokofiev's Second Concerto for Piano.

Concerto No. 3 for Piano and Orchestra in C, Opus 26

Andante—Allegro

Andantino

Allegro ma non troppo

Prokofiev completed the Third Concerto from earlier sketches during the summer of 1921. It was first performed in Chicago on December 16, 1921, by Frederick Stock and the Chicago Symphony Orchestra, with Prokofiev as piano soloist.

Instrumentation: *two flutes (one doubling piccolo), two oboes, two clarinets, two bassoons, four horns, two trumpets, three trombones, timpani, bass drum, castanets, tambourine, cymbals, solo piano, and strings.*

Prokofiev's Third Concerto for Piano has been more popular than any of his other concertos. Its three-movement design is the most traditional of all his works, and the balance of musical materials has appealed strongly to audiences. It was the only concerto Prokofiev was invited to record; since his performance of the work with the Koussevitzky Orchestra in Paris in 1922, the work has been a major item in the repertory of most professional pianists.

Prokofiev wrote the concerto in a small town on the coast of Brittany, where he had established residence as an escape from his busy life of traveling and concerts. Most of the work coalesced through the assembly of materials he had written over several years. From his childhood, Prokofiev had been in the habit of recording both musical and personal thoughts on a daily basis, a methodical approach characteristic of most facets of his life. Much of the musical material became the substance for his current compositions, but from his own accounts we learn that much was also held back for later use. So it was that the Third Concerto derived from materials he had jotted down over a long span of time; the amalgamation of originally disparate materials into an organic whole looms as one of the greatest achievements in this concerto.

The composer described the first performance in Chicago as a qualified success, but performances in New York a few weeks later were a different matter. In his own view, the negative response from New Yorkers was tied to their earlier dislike of his opera *The Love of Three Oranges*. He claimed that "in Chicago there was less understanding than support. . . ; in New York there was neither understanding nor support."[12]

After several decades of familiarity, it is difficult to understand why the Third Piano Concerto would find difficulty making its way with either audiences or critics. In many ways its harmonies and keyboard patterns are the most conventional of the three piano concertos he had composed to this date. The first movement follows a recognized sonata design, and perhaps is most noteworthy for some of its keyboard patterns. The piano introduces the first theme through parallel writing between the hands, much in the manner of the *Scherzo* from Prokofiev's Second Concerto. The passage of ascending triads near the end of the movement, originating in 1911, bears no thematic connection to the rest of the movement, but it proves to be a striking pianistic device: the right hand plays on the black keys, the left hand on the white, the two alternating as in mallet strokes. Here the physical configuration of the keyboard becomes the genesis for original and effective passagework.

The principal theme opens and closes the *Andante*, with the surrounding five variations offering an unusual mix of piquant simplicity and vigorous instrumental display. The theme follows a straightforward A–B–A¹ design, its character and structure reminiscent of a stylish dance. The variations quickly depart into an imaginative treatment of the underlying harmonies, but the theme itself becomes little more than an afterthought until it returns at the conclusion, reminding the listener of its underlying presence.

The closing *Allegro ma non troppo* opens in the character of a march, albeit in triple meter, and the orchestra continues in that character through a rondo with virtuoso embellishment in the solo part. The second episode introduces a melancholy tune that expands to become a majestically soaring theme, played by winds and strings, embracing in its nobility all the activity the ensemble can generate; here, Prokofiev's lyricism rises to its most memorable levels. The return to the elements of the opening march builds toward a sparkling close.

For many listeners, the Third Concerto stands as a genuinely Russian statement, and perhaps that quality contributed to the later success the concerto enjoyed. At the first orchestral performance in Russia in 1925, with Samuel Feinberg as soloist, it created a sensation and has since been recognized around the world as one of the great concertos of the modern era.

Concerto No. 1 for Violin and Orchestra in D, Opus 19

Andantino

Scherzo: Vivacissimo

Moderato—Allegro moderato

Prokofiev composed the First Violin Concerto between 1915 and the summer of 1917. It was first performed in Paris on October 18, 1923, by Serge Koussevitzky and his orchestra with Marcel Darrieux as violin soloist.

Instrumentation: *two flutes (the second doubling piccolo), two oboes, two clarinets, two bassoons, four horns, two trumpets, tuba, timpani, snare drum, tambourine, harp, solo violin, and strings.*

Prokofiev's concertos for violin and his approach to the violin as a solo instrument differ significantly from his other works. His First Concerto for Violin offers a near-compendium of violin techniques as generally practiced in 1917, producing a musical fabric ranging from intimate tunefulness to vigorous evocations of a gypsy dance. At times the high tessitura of the solo violin and the refined orchestration create an ethereal atmosphere, interrupted only by Prokofiev's inimitably pungent harmonies. In this framework, the music is less a contest between soloist and orchestra than it is a broadly conceived concerted work in which the solo gradually emerges as leader, urging the ensemble forward to ever more colorful effects. Of virtuosity there is plenty, but it tends to be a virtuosity exploiting technical feats with studied restraint. The three movements follow a slow–fast–slow plan rather than the more traditional fast–slow–fast, and there is no cadenza. All these qualities impress the listener as atypical of concertos in general and of concertos by Prokofiev in particular, a condition that probably would appeal to this composer's penchant for originality.

The discussion of the Second Concerto for Piano identified four lines of creativity that Prokofiev attributed to his own music: lyric, classic, modern, and toccata style. In the First Violin Concerto, the opening theme played by the soloist could hardly be a better illustration of his lyric bent; indeed, he cited that theme as an illustration of his skill as a melodist when defending himself against charges of formalism in 1948. The second theme stands well apart through its quirky ornaments, fragmentation, and discontinuity, offering an element of thematic contrast that becomes a secondary feature of the movement. That contrast erupts again near the end of the development with vigorous pizzicato chords in the solo violin; otherwise, the orchestration, designed to highlight the soloist, makes for a prevailingly thin texture. The recapitulation offers a memorable illustration when the muted solo violin and harp combine to produce a gossamer background for the return of the principal theme in the upper register of the flute, a closing passage of striking tranquility.

Prokofiev cast the *Scherzo* in a rondo design similar to the plan of the last movement of his Third Piano Concerto, but less extensive. The solo part calls for a variety of technical effects: pizzicato interspersed with bowing, harmonics, double stops, glissandos, and lurching dotted rhythms.

The finale is a three-part design with an extended coda. The movement opens in the character of a lyrical march, identified by a "walking" pattern in the strings. The following *Allegro moderato* offers contrasts of tempo and double stops before a return to the distinctive accompaniment, now graced by gliding scales from the solo violin. The extended coda becomes the most interesting section of the concerto; it combines the main theme of the finale, in the winds, with the lyrical opening of the first movement, now played by the soloist. Thus the coda serves not only as a close for the finale but also as a summation of the entire concerto, the principal theme arching over the entire work from beginning to end. For all the potency of this thematic synopsis, the music fades away to a shimmering *pianissimo*.

Reflecting on the concerto in the context of Prokofiev's oeuvre, his four lines (styles) of composition are well represented in the lyric element of the main theme; the classic element of the first movement's sonata allegro design; the modern harmonies that pervade the score; and the clear toccata element in the accompaniment for the main sections of the *Scherzo*.

Prokofiev initially imagined the work as a concertino (a small concerto, or any work that was less ambitious than a concerto but still featuring solo instruments), but as so often happens, the work grew with the maturation of the composer's ideas. The first performance of the concerto was scheduled for November 1917, but events in Russia disrupted concert schedules, and the First Concerto was not heard in public until 1923, when Koussevitzky and his orchestra introduced it in Paris. Most critics considered the concerto disappointingly tame, chastising Prokofiev for its conservative traits and apparently expecting something more in keeping with his reputation as a musical iconoclast. Joseph Szigeti played the concerto at a festival of modern music in Prague in 1924 with great success and in the years following he performed the work consistently as one of its greatest champions. In his autobiography, Prokofiev described an early performance by Szigeti in Paris:

> When he came to Paris and I expressed the desire to attend the rehearsal his face fell. "You see," he said, "I love that concerto and I know the score so well that I sometimes give pointers to the conductor as if it were my own composition. But you must admit that under the circumstances the presence of the composer would be embarrassing for me." I agreed and went to the concert instead. Szigeti played superbly.[13]

Concerto No. 2 for Violin and Orchestra in G minor, Opus 63

Allegro moderato

Andante assai

Allegro, ben marcato

According to Prokofiev, he worked on the Concerto No. 2 for Violin from the spring through August 1935. The first performance took place in Madrid during a Festival of the International Society for Contemporary Music on December 1, 1935, by the Madrid Symphony conducted by Enrique Fernández Arbós, Robert Soëtens as soloist.

Instrumentation*: two flutes, two oboes, two clarinets, two bassoons, two horns, two trumpets, bass drum, snare drum, triangle, cymbals, castanets, solo violin, and strings.*

The Second Concerto for Violin was one of the last major works Prokofiev completed before reestablishing his home in Russia in the spring of 1936. Nearly all commentators have nonetheless grouped the Second Concerto with those works that marked a new style associated with, and presumably reflecting, the composer's return to his homeland. By his own account, Prokofiev wrote the concerto in response to a request from a number of admirers of the French violinist Robert Soëtens. He had already accumulated some sketches of a work for violin and orchestra, and focused those earlier efforts by searching for an original title for the piece. He eventually returned to the simple generic title, but still wanted the work to be quite different from the First Concerto.

In an interview published many years later, the violinist Soëtens offered his own recollections of how the piece was created. In his account, no group of friends approached the composer on his behalf. Instead, Prokofiev, who had known Soëtens for some time, initiated the project, because he admired Soëtens and wanted to write a work for him. Soëtens claimed that the work was completed in Paris by late March, and that he followed Prokofiev to Russia later in the summer, from whence they embarked on an extended tour that eventually took them to Madrid, where they gave the first performance of the concerto. As documentary evidence to bolster his report, Soëtens has preserved a letter from Prokofiev requesting editorial suggestions from Soëtens before sending the score to the printer:

> I beg you to sacrifice a half-day to review the solo part of the concerto, especially the bowings, slurs, the dots, the accent marks, etc. Put in as few fingerings as possible, indicating only those which represent a real find or which tend to change the sonorities. If you have any doubts, put them on a sheet of paper and give it to Madame Prokofiev who is in Paris now. . . . I'll look at them when I correct the proofs. Then, give the violin part to the publisher for copying. Ask my former secretary who works there now to copy it himself. Don't give the piano part to anybody. I've made a perfect version which I'll send them one of these days.
>
> Excuse me for bothering you in this way and don't delay: the printers are so slow and the sending of the proofs to Moscow will take so much time that I don't think the keyboard [part] can come out before late autumn.[14]

Following the Madrid premiere, Soëtens wanted to continue with other performances, but letters from Prokofiev indicated that he was under pressure from Soviet authorities that a Russian premiere should involve a Russian violinist, so B. Fischman introduced the concerto to Moscow audiences in 1936. Soëtens was still able to exercise his presumed right of first performance in Paris in 1936, and in London and Amsterdam in 1938.

A number of questions arise when comparing these accounts, but it should be noted that one comes from the composer, written a few years after the event, the other from a performer, relating events nearly sixty years later. At best, the discrepancies could be simple memory slips on the part of either composer or performer. At worst it could be an attempt on the part of Soëtens to establish a relationship between himself and Prokofiev for which there is little corroborating evidence. Neither condition changes the musical stature of the G minor Concerto.

Prokofiev's self-described classical line is manifest in the clear separation between the exposition, development, and recapitulation of the sonata design in the first movement; equally clear is the lyric element in the solo line throughout the movement. The concerto opens with the unaccompanied solo violin playing the principal theme in a straightforward manner to maximize the rhythmic structure of five-beat phrases. Considering the frequency of similar phrase structure in the music of other Russian composers (the *Promenade* in Modest Mussorgsky's *Pictures at an Exhibition* and the second movement of Pyotr Tchaikovsky's Sixth Symphony come to mind), this may be one of the traits that many listeners interpret as a distinct Russian element in this concerto. The main theme carries its lyricism throughout the movement when it returns in the recapitulation and again in the coda, the last time in canon with low strings, solo violin, and bassoons.

The accompaniment patterns of the *Andante assai* suggest a siciliano rhythm (twelve-eight, or four beats of three notes each), but the solo line stands apart through its prevailing duple meter. Even more important for the projection of the solo is a continuation of the lyrical writing heard elsewhere in the concerto, a quality that contributes much to the serenity of the movement.

The closing *Allegro* incorporates some wide-ranging solo pyrotechnics in a sonata design based on three themes. The most prominent musical qualities are rhythmic energy, often dancelike in its vitality, and scoring that always gives free reign to the solo line. The orchestral ensemble consists of the strings plus woodwinds in pairs typical of a classical orchestra, but the distribution of materials reflects the originality that Prokofiev continued to pursue in this work. On first encounter, the clarity of design in the opening *Allegro moderato* and the economical orchestration suggest something of the neoclassicism in vogue during the 1930s, but those traits derive more directly from the ideal of simplicity that Prokofiev was championing for himself and for other Soviet composers, an attempt to project a clarity of time that would speak directly to the people.

Reviews of the premiere were laudatory and, according to Prokofiev, reflected the enthusiasm of the audience. Echoing the arch-conservative tastes of fascism, the Spanish critic Antonio Las Heras praised what he perceived as a return to the classical style of Vivaldi, especially welcome, in his view, in light of contemporary developments in music. Another critic wrote simply: "This Prokofiev doesn't scare us; he delights us."[15]

Compared to the First Concerto for Violin, the Second is more melodic, consistently more inviting in its sonorous properties, and more modest in its extremes, leading some to refer to it as a work of philosophic, even intimate character. Many of these qualities reflect subjective evaluations, but they also betoken a concerto with ready appeal to a broad audience. Critics and biographers have frequently characterized these attributes as a manifestation of Prokofiev's return to Russia, of the renewed contact with his cultural roots, and of the ideology of Soviet aesthetics, disregarding that at least a major portion of the Second Concerto for Violin, if not all of it, was written before he had reestablished his residence there. As a matter of political propriety, those speaking for the Soviet system would attribute qualities of mature clarity to a superior artistic climate in Russia. Prokofiev may have benefited from these conditions—he could hardly have said anything else—but this maturation could also ensue from normal technical and musical development, conditions that could well have come about through the growth of an industrious creative faculty. Beyond that, problems in the composer's personal life after he returned to Russia, exacerbated by his ill health after 1944, were sufficiently severe to effect a change in his personality and thereby in any personal artistic expression. In any event, the change in Prokofiev's style was under way before he returned to Russia as a Soviet citizen, and the Second Concerto for Violin stands as a testament to that condition.

Symphony-Concerto for Cello and Orchestra, Opus 125
(*Sinfonia concertante*)

Andante

Allegro giusto—Andante—Allegro assai

Andante con moto—Allegretto—Allegro marcato

Prokofiev produced the Symphony-Concerto between 1950 and 1952 as a restructuring of his Concerto for Cello of 1934 to 1938. The new work was first performed in Moscow on February 18, 1952, by the Moscow Youth Orchestra conducted by Sviatislov Richter, Mstislav Rostropovich as soloist.

Instrumentation: *two flutes (the second doubling piccolo), two oboes, two clarinets, two bassoons, four horns, three trumpets (the third optional), three trombones, tuba, timpani, bass drum, snare drum, cymbals, tambourine, triangle, celesta, solo cello, and strings.*

The hybridized title "Symphony-Concerto" is often replaced by the more familiar *Sinfonia concertante*, but in Western traditions that Italian title suggests a genesis different from the work at hand. Moreover, *Sinfonia concertante* is an inexact translation of Prokofiev's original *Simfonia-Kontsert*. The confusion derives from the relationship between this work and Prokofiev's earlier Concerto for Cello, Opus 58, commissioned by Gregor Piatigorsky, sketched during 1933 and 1934, and completed in Moscow on September 18, 1938. This original concerto was not well received upon its first performance, possibly because of some structural problems but almost certainly because of attendant performance difficulties. Sviatislov Richter, later to be recognized as one of Russia's outstanding pianists, participated in early rehearsals prior to the first Moscow performance and reported that the soloist, identified only as L. Berezovsky, had little sympathy for the work and that the performance itself was a complete failure. Prokofiev later became convinced that the concerto needed revision and promised to do so, writing in September of 1938 that he felt there were obvious seams between the episodes and that not all the music was of equal value. Beyond that, his close friend, the composer Nikolai Miaskovsky, had expressed reservations about the effectiveness of the music, so Prokofiev had ample stimuli to revise the score. A substantially revised version was introduced in the United States by Gregor Piatigorsky in 1940.

After hearing the young Mstislav Rostropovich play the concerto, Prokofiev was convinced of the need for further revision. Rostropovich became heavily involved in the process, advising on idiomatic writing for the solo instrument, distribution of thematic materials, and orchestration. In its new version, the work was first identified as a Second

Concerto for Cello, but following still further revision in early 1952, Prokofiev applied the title Symphony-Concerto, with a new opus number and a dedication to Rostropovich. Thus the new work responded to ideas from two brilliant performers, Rostropovich and Richter, and from a trusted friend and composer, Miaskovsky. For all the revision, Prokofiev did not reject the earlier cello concerto, accurately describing Opus 125 as a reworking of the earlier composition. Perhaps in self-defense, perhaps out of conviction, he railed against critics of the cello concerto, saying they should be more responsible in their comments. He asserted that the work was very close to the Second Concerto for Violin (which had been a marked success), and that indifference to Opus 58 was mere stupidity, words that recalled the tenor of his trenchant responses to critics of his earliest compositions.

In the breadth of its musical conception, the originality of the writing for both soloist and orchestra, and certainly the consummate virtuosity required of the solo part, the Symphony-Concerto stands as the major accomplishment of Prokofiev's last years. In a span of nearly forty minutes, he presents three movements of markedly different character: a weighty sonata movement formed around an extraordinary solo cadenza as a centerpiece, preceded by a broadly paced *Andante*, and followed by an ingeniously designed set of variations.

The *Andante* opens with a series of emphatic chords played by full orchestra, soon subsiding to a steadily pulsing accompaniment that prevails through most of the movement. Four themes in an approximate pattern of ab/cdc/ab suggest a design of three sections, but that structural plan becomes less important than the steady march of the orchestral accompaniment that supports a solo part ranging from colorful figuration to long-breathed melodic lines. The coda concentrates on a quiet and reflective return of the second theme, its essence played by the high woodwinds in counterpoint to a busy but diminishing flourish from the soloist.

The second movement is the longest of the three. It expands on a broadly conceived sonata design in which an extended virtuoso cadenza introduces the development by expanding on portions of the opening themes. We have no confirmation that this represents the influence of the cellist Rostropovich, but without doubt the cadenza represents the efforts of a performer thoroughly conversant with the musical possibilities of unaccompanied passagework. Here and

throughout the movement, the cello exploits its total range, incorporating a virtuoso's catalogue of double-stops, scales, and harmonics.
Above all, it is the originality with which these effects are presented that
raises this writing above the level of technical display alone.

One of the oldest techniques in music, a process of theme and variation, underlies the last movement. Variations on two themes intermin-
gle with another cadenza, this time near the beginning of the movement,
in a manner that brings the music to a climax on a straightforward
statement of the theme first played by the cello in the opening measures.
The whole ends with a coda based on this theme plus a fragment from
the second movement, all concluded by the soloist's closing passagework,
which seems to play itself out from sheer dissolution of energy.

When Prokofiev returned to Russia in the 1930s, many critics
described a change in his musical style that allowed more room for lyricism, more concern for the idiomatic qualities in instrumental music,
and a personal bow to sensuality. Some cited these traits as a sign of
declining creativity, musical impoverishment, or an acquiescence to
political aesthetics in Russia. Observers from outside Russia in particular, noting the general favor Prokofiev enjoyed following his return,
chose to interpret these changes of style as illustrations of what was
and was not acceptable in Soviet aesthetics, a point of view that found
resonance in the international politics growing from the tensions
between Russia and the West. It now seems more likely that these traits
were natural developments in the work of a mature composer who was
a master of his craft, secure in his reputation, and no longer inclined to
shock audiences through iconoclastic gestures. The old and the new in
Prokofiev stand side by side in the Symphony-Concerto, the old represented by acrid harmonies, harsh contrasts of timbre, and the dis-
jointed character of some passagework, the new by idiomatic writing
for specific instruments (particularly the solo cello), and long lyrical
lines for both soloist and orchestra. Attempts to politicize these musical qualities fade in the face of an unbiased hearing of the work.

The history of the Symphony-Concerto reflects Prokofiev's passion
for revision and reworking of material, a trait further illustrated in his
suites based on music originally intended for the theater. It also speaks
of his commitment to fulfill the musical potential of any work he has
created. These qualities eventually established the Symphony-Concerto
as one of his crowning achievements, on a level with the Third Piano

Concerto and the music for *Romeo and Juliet*. When Rostropovich introduced the work to audiences outside Russia, it was greeted with near
universal acclaim.

Orchestral Works Derived from Music for the Theater

Throughout his life, Prokofiev revised or adapted his stage works into
orchestral settings that could stand independently from the dramatic
action with which they were originally associated. At least 21 independent orchestral works came into being through this process, including
those that have enjoyed the most enduring popularity: *Lieutenant Kije* and
Alexander Nevsky both derive from film scores, and the ballet *Romeo and
Juliet* provided the music for three separate orchestral suites. Prokofiev's
reasons for recasting this music are unknown, but they might include the
desire to reach an audience wider than that attracted to the theater, a
wish to make the greatest use of his creative product, or an attempt to
enhance whatever economic gain possible. But it seems likely that a more
fundamental impulse was the breadth of his musical conception,
wherein musical ideas transcend the specificity of any given medium and
therefore lend themselves readily to more than one venue.

Music of Socialist Realism was not readily marketable outside
Russia. Western audiences had little interest in the musical glorification
of political leaders, the Red Army, or the rural collective. Music for films
was one prominent exception, and both Prokofiev and Dmitri
Shostakovich invested their talents generously in this medium. Silent
films relied on the personal musical resources of a house pianist or
organist for accompanying musical effects; the advent of sound films at
first brought about a collage of excerpts from known repertory, but the
unsatisfactory discontinuity of that process meant that the art of film
music had to be developed. Russian cinematography was in the van-
guard in this process, because Soviet music and the Soviet film industry
were born at about the same time and grew side by side. As a result, from
the earliest years Soviet film composers were a more integral part of the
cinematic process than were their counterparts in other countries.

Prokofiev viewed the cinema as one of the most viable of the new
art forms, one that offered:

> new and fascinating possibilities to the composer. These possibilities
> must be utilized. Composers ought to study and develop them,

instead of merely writing the music and then leaving it to the mercy of the film people. Even the most skilled sound engineer cannot possibly handle the music as well as the composer himself.[16]

Acting on that premise, Prokofiev created scores for at least eight films. Several remain unrealized or unpublished, but the suite from *Lieutenent Kije* and the cantata *Alexander Nevsky* mark the arrival of the symphonist as a composer of film music and remain high and enduring standards for the combination of film and music.

Alexander Nevsky, Opus 78

Russia under the Mongolian Yoke

Song about Alexander Nevsky

The Crusaders in Pskov

Arise, Ye Russian People

The Battle on Ice

Field of the Dead

Alexander's Entry in Pskov

Prokofiev composed the music for Alexander Nevsky *during 1938 as the score for the film of that title, first screened in Moscow on December 1. The cantata, a reworking of that music with texts by Prokofiev and V. Nugovsky, was completed during the early months of 1939 and first performed in Moscow on May 17 by the Moscow Philharmonic Orchestra conducted by Prokofiev, V. Gagarina as mezzo-soprano soloist.*

Instrumentation: *piccolo, two flutes, two oboes, English horn, two clarinets, bass clarinet, tenor saxophone, two bassoons, contrabassoon, four horns, three trumpets, three trombones, tuba, timpani, bass drum, snare drum, tambourine, maracas, wood block, triangle, cymbals, low-pitched bell, tam-tam, tubular bells, xylophone, chorus, mezzo-soprano soloist, and strings.*

The Grand Duke Alexander Yaroslavich of Vladimir (1220–1263) was given the popular name Nevsky following his great victory over invading Swedes at the Neva River on July 15, 1240. In early April of 1242, he triumphed in an even greater battle against the invading Teutonic knights in the defense of Novgorod on Lake Peipus, near Pskov. The struggle reached its peak on the frozen lake when the overwhelming weight of the heavily armored Teutons and their horses broke the ice, engulfing the invaders in a frigid grave. The film and subsequent cantata commemorate this event, a battle of great importance for the eventual consolidation of a country that at the time was neither powerful nor unified, a land occupied in the south by Mongols who tolerated scattered duchies in the north, leaving them responsible for their own defense against marauding Swedes and Teutons. As the subject of a hagiographic biography, Nevsky came to be viewed as the founder of a dynasty that would lead to the Dukes of Muscovy and from them to the Tsars. Thus in 1938, when Russia once again faced an imposing threat of Teutonic origins, the earlier triumph of the 13th century appealed to a broad public as well as to creative imaginations.

Prokofiev was delighted when invited by the noted film director Sergei Eisenstein to produce music for the film *Alexander Nevsky*. He considered the cinema a fertile medium for composers, and his mode of composition had proven to be particularly well suited to film music. By all accounts, the success of the undertaking was due in large part to the extraordinarily effective coordination between the music and events on the screen, and this in turn ensued from the mutual high regard between Prokofiev and Eisenstein. As a filmmaker, Eisenstein was much impressed by Prokofiev's meticulous attention to detail, his willingness to participate in all facets of the production, and his systematic approach to the musical tasks at hand. He was particularly impressed by Prokofiev's work habits:

> We leave the small projection room, and even though it is now midnight, I feel completely calm. For I know that at exactly 11:55 A.M. a small, dark blue car will come through the gate of the film studio. Sergei Prokofiev will get out of it. In his hands will be the next piece of music for *Alexander Nevsky*. At night we look at a newly filmed sequence. In the morning the new musical sequence will be ready for it. Prokofiev works like a clock. The clock isn't fast and it isn't slow.[17]

Prokofiev was pleased to note that Eisenstein respected music sufficiently that he was prepared to adjust the sequence of action so as not to upset the balance of a musical episode. Under such conditions, elements of history, national pride, and compatible creative efforts driven by current political events fused to produce a film of immediate and lasting success.

In composing music to support action on the screen, Prokofiev attempted to incorporate music that might have been known to the original combatants. His efforts to find examples of appropriate medieval music led him to some early choral works, never specifically identified, which he considered too remote and emotionally alien to stimulate the imagination of modern audiences. He therefore decided to produce music representing his own concept of early sounds and textures. We have no way of knowing what musical sources he consulted nor anything about their authenticity, but it is intriguing to speculate how Prokofiev might have responded to the achievements of the early music movement as it developed in the last half of the 20th century. With Prokofiev's efforts to provide music to fit the cinematic action, the contrasts between the invading Teutonic knights and the defending Russians led to marked contrasts in thematic materials and in the orchestral palette. No listener could hear the music written for the invaders as anything but ominous, nor could one hear the music of the Russians as anything but heroic. When recast for the cantata, this element of contrast extends to the scoring, producing an alternation between instrumental and choral numbers, so the essence of the dramatic action assumes a musical configuration.

The cantata is much more than an assembly of episodes drawn from the film. The stringent time element that bore on the film score was no longer a determining factor, enabling the music to expand along sonorous lines as needed. Prokofiev had provided much of the text himself, and adapting some of the choral passages from the film required changes in the balance of orchestration. Moreover, the novel recording techniques that had contributed so much to the impact of the film score were not applicable to a live performance with chorus. As a result, the music of the film score needed to be completely reorchestrated for the cantata. Now musical settings representing opposing forces became more pronounced in their contrast: the invaders are depicted by austere timbres, open harmonies, and ponderous rhythm, while the mellifluous sounds of strings, chorus, and mezzo-soprano speak for the Russian patriots through legato lines of noble dignity.

Twenty-one separate numbers from the film score were reduced or compressed to seven movements for the cantata in a type of choral-symphonic program music.

The opening movement, *Russia under the Mongolian Yoke*, sets an ominous musical stage through widely spaced instrumentation—oboes and bass clarinet playing parallel lines several octaves apart—and a pervasive quality of musical stasis. The music comes from the opening scenes of the film showing the countryside as ravaged by the Mongols, a land marked by heaps of bones, broken weapons, empty fields, and burned villages. The *Song about Alexander Nevsky* introduces the chorus singing about the hero's victory over the Swedes. The simple tune, sung in unison, suggests folk music without actually drawing on any known folk materials. To portray *The Crusaders in Pskov*, Prokofiev writes biting harmonic dissonances as the trombone and tuba, playing in open octaves, provide guttural commentary on the advance of the crusaders. The chorus sings a brief Latin text suggesting the hypocritical righteousness of the Christian knights—"*Peregrinus, expectavi, pedes meos in cymbalis*" (A pilgrim, I expected my feet to be covered with cymbals)—but the character of the music belies any altruistic intent. *Arise, Ye Russian People* offers a response to the first movement. The *Song about Alexander Nevsky* related events of the past, but now we hear an ardent call to battle in defense of the future. The chorus sings the text "Arise to arms, ye Russian folk" to martial music undiluted by any expressive sentimentality, and the final cadence on a ringing major chord seems to speak of unfettered optimism in anticipation of a patriotic triumph.

The principal elements of this dramatic scenario, as film or cantata, come together in the fifth movement, an extended musical portrayal of the battle on the frozen lake pitting heavily armed Teutonic knights against Russian folk equipped more with courage than with instruments of war. *The Battle on Ice* is the most extensively developed movement of the cantata. The low brass fanfare representing the Crusaders, first heard in the third movement, mingles with thematic elements from the fourth movement, *Arise, Ye Russian People*. The chorus sings again the "*Peregrinus*" text from the third movement plus another representing the Crusaders' salute to their arms, "*Vincant arma crucifera! Hostis pereat!*" (Victory to arms marked by the Cross! Death to the enemy!), as the battle, and the musical activity, mount to an apex of intensity. All this gives way to a section of clangorous harmonies and sweeping scales played antiphonally between strings and winds. The temptation to draw a direct parallel with images of icy waves engulfing the invading forces is strong, but must be left to the imagination of the listener. The movement closes with a quiet coda as muted violins play an eerily sustained treatment of the theme from the middle of movement four, one that accompanied the text "In our great Russia, no foe shall live."

Field of the Dead is a plaintive aria sung by the mezzo-soprano soloist, depicting a lonely girl searching for the body of her lover on the wasted field of battle. The poignancy of this simple melody offers a telling antidote to the musical furor of the *Battle on Ice*. The seventh and concluding movement, *Alexander's Entry into Pskov*, relies heavily on themes heard earlier in the cantata as a musical and dramatic summation. The sound of bells, historically an identifying feature of the Russian soundscape, reflects the joy of a festival and the justifiable frivolity of a people saved from destruction.

Presented as a cantata, the seven movements sustain their own musical logic based on the distribution of thematic materials alone. Movements one through four introduce the main themes; the fifth movement, *Battle on Ice*, resembles a development in the manner in which themes from movements three and four are expanded, fragmented, and intermingled. From this melange, the solo aria from *Field of the Dead* emerges as a musical foil for the battle music, an interlude that itself recalls a portion of the third movement, and the last movement emerges as a free recapitulation of the principal thematic materials of the cantata. Whether dictated by the dramatic program or by Prokofiev's mastery of composition, this plan adds one more level of comprehensibility to an already colorful programmatic work.

The film and cantata were both presented throughout Russia. Eisenstein and Nikolai Cherkasov, the actor who portrayed Nevsky in the film, received the Order of Lenin, and Soviet officials praised Prokofiev's music lavishly. Only one voice demurred. Dmitri Shostakovich wrote to Prokofiev that in spite of some amazing music, he did not care for the work. For Shostakovich, the loud, illustrative music exceeded aesthetic norms. Audiences were not troubled. *Alexander Nevsky* quickly became one of Prokofiev's most enduringly popular compositions.

Suite from *Lieutenant Kije*, Opus 60

Kije's Birth

Romance

Kije's Wedding

Troika Song

Kije's Burial

The music for Lieutenant Kije *was composed as a film score during the spring of 1933 and recorded as a sound track later that year. From that material Prokofiev completed the symphonic suite on July 8, 1934 and conducted the first performance for a radio broadcast in Moscow on December 21.*

Instrumentation: *piccolo, two flutes, two oboes, two clarinets, two bassoons, tenor saxophone or baritone voice, four horns, cornet, two trumpets, three trombones, tuba, bass drum, snare drum, triangle, cymbals, tambourine, sleigh bells, celesta, piano, harp, and strings.*

At the court of Tsar Paul during the last years of the 18th century, a textual error in transmitting the names of a list of officers submitted to the pompous ruler for approval produced the apocryphal name "Kije." The unusual name attracted Paul's attention and he quixotically demanded to know all about this young officer. Fearing to acknowledge their error, court functionaries fabricated for the nonexistent Kije a career, sent him into Siberian exile to keep him out of sight, later promoted him through the ranks, married him to a bride who explains dryly that Kije has no "presence," and saw that he was killed. All of this was carried out through bureaucratic machinations.

The plot appealed to Prokofiev's innate sense of ironic humor and social satire in pointing a finger at an inflated bureaucracy. The setting provided another opportunity to expand upon elements of classicism in an original manner, and for a composer who was in the process of returning to his native Russia, the assignment offered a chance to address Soviet audiences through a medium designed for mass appeal. Beyond those considerations, he was enthusiastic about the future of the cinema as a new medium of expression, photography had always fascinated him, and he was intrigued by the technology required to coordinate a music score with cinematic action. From the beginning, Prokofiev requested information in great detail about the music expected of him. Rather than producing music as a supplemental commentary for scenes on the screen, he felt that the music should be considered an integral part of the complete production. The film score that emerged consisted of sixteen musical segments, each written after the filming and each projecting its own musical idea.

Whatever effect this may have produced when combined with film, the music has been best known through the suite bearing the title *Lieutenant Kije*. Prokofiev reworked the film score extensively. The suite presented more problems than the film music itself, because he had to find an appropriate form, reorchestrate the score, and combine some of the thematic materials. The result is a suite of five movements, two offering the option of a vocal solo, all following their own design and benefiting from Prokofiev's piquant orchestral scoring.

Kije's Birth opens with a tentative fanfare played by the cornet *à piston*, which will become Kije's leitmotiv as the suite progresses. The second movement focuses on a solo line played by tenor saxophone, that instrument whose tone so closely resembles the human voice. Prokofiev patterns the theme on a sentimental ballad incorporating the poem "The Little Grey Dove Is Cooing," a text that in alternate versions of this movement is sung by baritone voice. At *Kije's Wedding* the cornet returns, with its subdued military character, playing a wedding march that, as it moves through several reorchestrated permutations, sounds more satirical than nuptial. A graphic portrayal of a troika, a three-horse sleigh, dominates the fourth movement. As a foil for the second movement, the main theme derives from a Hussar song played by tenor saxophone or bassoon, or both together. *Kije's Burial* opens with a return of the hero's motive, first heard in the opening measures of the suite. From that point forward, themes from all movements return and mingle in symphonic development until the music gradually dies away, to be brought to a conclusion by one last statement of Kije's motive.

Much of the musical success of the suite derives from the sense of order established through the distribution of musical materials. Kije's motive frames the first and last movements, and those together embrace the suite as a whole. Movements two and four incorporate popular melodies, and both offer the option of a vocal solo with texts of immediate if not familiar appeal. At the center lies *Kije's Wedding*, a joyous celebration with its own theme and colorful scoring for full orchestra.

At a time when a composed film score was a new development in a medium intended for mass appeal, Prokofiev established an early and high standard. Following performance of the suite in the United States by several major orchestras, he was pursued with lucrative offers from several Hollywood directors, but his attentions were increasingly turned toward his native Russia.

Suites from *Romeo and Juliet,* Opera 64, 101

Suite No. 1, Opus 64b

Folk Dance

Scene

Madrigal

Minuet

Masks

Romeo and Juliet

The Death of Tybalt

Suite No. 2, Opus 64c

The Montagues and the Capulets

Juliet, the Young Girl

Friar Laurence

Dance of the Five Couples

Romeo and Juliet before Parting

Dance of the Maids with the Lilies

Romeo at Juliet's Tomb

Both suites were prepared in 1936. Suite No. 1 was first performed in Moscow on November 24, 1936, by the Moscow Philharmonic Orchestra, Georg Sebastian conducting; Prokofiev conducted the premiere of Suite No. 2 in Leningrad on April 15, 1937.

Instrumentation: *piccolo, two flutes, two oboes, English horn, two clar-inets, bass clarinet, tenor saxophone, two bassoons, contrabassoon, four horns, two trumpets, cornet, three trombones, tuba, timpani, bass drum, snare drum, triangle, tambourine, cymbals, glockenspiel, xylo-phone, piano, harp, and strings. The Second Suite adds celesta and viola d'amore* ad libitum *(often played by a solo viola).*

Suite No. 3, Opus 101

Romeo at the Fountain

Morning Dance

Juliet Prepares for the Ball

The Nurse

Aubade—Dawn of Juliet's Wedding Day

The Death of Juliet

Prokofiev revised the score for a Third Suite during 1944. It was first performed in Moscow on March 8, 1946.

Instrumentation: *piccolo, two flutes, two oboes, English horn, two clar-inets, bass clarinet, two bassoons, contrabassoon, four horns, three trumpets, three trombones, tuba, timpani, bass drum, snare drum, wood block, triangle, tambourine, cymbals, glockenspiel, celesta, piano, harp, and strings.*

The plot of William Shakespeare's *Romeo and Juliet* has sparked the cre-ative imagination of many composers. A complete list of musical set-tings of this drama would include at least 28 operas and eleven ballets, not counting the most successful and famous scores by Prokofiev. For all of its prominence in the history of theater music, and notwith-standing its stature as one of Prokofiev's greatest achievements, his music for the ballet *Romeo and Juliet* suffered unusually prolonged birth pangs marked by a number of aborted productions.

Sergei Radlov, director of the Kirov Theater in Leningrad, first sug-gested the project to Prokofiev in 1934. Soon thereafter Radlov was replaced by a director more acceptable to government authorities, and the project was dropped, but Prokofiev continued working on the music through 1935, finishing the orchestral score of three acts by April 1936.

He subsequently signed an agreement with the Moscow Bolshoi Theater, but the music was dismissed as undanceable, and that contract was broken as well. Frustrations with these ventures led Prokofiev to prepare the first two orchestral suites in 1936, but the ballet itself was first performed at the Municipal Theater of Brno, Czechoslovakia, on December 30, 1938, which surely must have generated some embarrassment within the Russian performing arts community. A new choreographer, Leonid Lavrinsky, was appointed at the Kirov Theater in 1938. He reopened musical discussions with the composer and, with the continued assistance of Radlov and the critic and playwright Adrian Piotrorsky, the now-famous Russian production took place in Leningrad on January 11, 1940.

Descriptions of the production in Prokofiev's autobiography and in a sympathetic account by Galina Ulanova, the ballerina who built her career around the role of Juliet, indicate that the undertaking was a struggle for all parties involved. Prokofiev's treatment of the famous tragedy extends over three acts occupying one evening's performance, a setting requiring that dancers act as well as dance and sustain a continuing thread of action throughout. The emphasis on extended dramatic continuity rather than on technical virtuosity required an approach not appreciated by all members of the ballet troupe. Another problem was Prokofiev's orchestration. Often sparse and carefully written to complement the dramatic elements, it was considered too quiet by dancers accustomed to a full orchestra playing with clearly defined rhythmic accents. Ulanova has described a rehearsal during which the dancers asked that Prokofiev join them on stage in order to convince him that they could not hear the orchestra. He responded irritably that they wanted drums rather than music. He nonetheless recognized the practical problem and agreed to revise the music at that point. Prokofiev's fluctuating rhythms also confused the dancers, primarily because the shifting patterns differed from the regularity to which they were accustomed. This was compounded by a pervasive distrust of the composer, whom the dancers feared as a cold and haughty personality, one who apparently held little respect for their art or for their immediate problems in working with an unfamiliar musical style. Beyond all this, Prokofiev had created a small furor among the dramatists by writing a happy ending in which Romeo arrives just a few minutes earlier than in Shakespeare's original and finds Juliet alive, and all ends well. He pointed out that his reasons for changing the traditional ending were purely choreographic: living people could dance, the dead and dying could not. But once again, the dancers intervened and convinced the composer that they could portray death through choreography, and the ending was revised to correspond to its original tragic close.

The concern of the performers was so great that as late as two weeks prior to the Russian premiere the orchestra players met and, to avoid what they were convinced would be an embarrassing failure, voted to cancel the performance. Fortunately, other forces prevailed. To the surprise of many, the ballet was an unqualified success with both audiences and critics. At a private party following the performance, Galina Ulanova proposed a toast ending with lines quoted many times since: "Never was a tale of greater woe than Prokofiev's music for *Romeo*."[18] Prokofiev reportedly enjoyed the jibe as much as anybody.

Once established, *Romeo and Juliet* became a landmark in the lofty tradition of Russian ballet. At least some of the ballet's success derived from Prokofiev's knack for portraying through musical means the flashes of earthy humor that pepper an otherwise tragic tale. *Romeo and Juliet* is not an unrelieved tragedy, for Shakespeare was very much a practical dramatist who never forgot that, for survival in his own venue, he had to address an audience with a broad spectrum of tastes. Prokofiev's quick wit and sardonic humor superbly match Shakespeare's flashes of ribaldry through both thematic materials and orchestration. The contrasting dramatic elements give rise to contrasting musical designs that propel the music forward in both the original ballet score and the suites derived from it. The comic and the tragic, the commonplace and the lofty, the frivolous and the poetic find an idiomatic counterpart in Prokofiev's musical language. The very essence of dramatic energy finds here a thoroughly compatible musical expression.

The movements comprising the suites follow their own musical plan rather than their order in the ballet score. Some numbers were taken from the ballet music directly, others were reworked and compiled from diverse materials. In the first suite, four movements represent dance episodes that describe the background against which the drama unfolds: *Folk Dance*, depicting the folk festival at the opening of the second act; *Scene*, a street scene, insouciantly described by bassoon and oboe; *Minuet*, the ballroom scene at the mansion of the Capulets; and *Masks*, subdued music to accompany the arrival of Romeo and his kin as masked guests. These contrast with three dramatic episodes: *Madrigal*, a dialogue between violins and flute that, with little imagination, comes to represent a conversation between the two young lovers; *Romeo and Juliet*, taken from the famous balcony scene; and *The Death of Tybalt*, an amalgamation of episodes from the second act depicting the duel between Tybalt and Romeo, Tybalt's death, and a musical reference to his funeral procession.

The second suite offers a musical portraiture of several main characters: *The Montagues and the Capulets*, opening with very dissonant harmonies appropriate to the discord between the rival families; *Juliet, the Young Girl*, with much skittish, playful music appropriate to the adolescent whimsies of the child-woman; and *Friar Laurence*, as quiet, reserved, and lugubrious as the solemn monk himself. These stand in contrast to two dramatic episodes: *Romeo and Juliet before Parting*, an extended *pas de deux* from the ballet, and *Romeo at Juliet's Tomb*, a solo trumpet crying discordantly against the rest of the ensemble. Beyond these descriptions, most of the movements present a musical substance appropriate to their titles. The suite served to bring the music before the public in spite of the early difficulties in achieving a complete performance of the ballet.

Prokofiev prepared the third suite in connection with the first postwar revival of the ballet in December 1946, a performance for which he also wrote some new musical numbers. As with the earlier suites, the movements came from different parts of the ballet score. There is no discernible reason for the presence of six rather than seven movements as in the suites of 1936. Perhaps the most noteworthy movements are *Aubade—Dawn of Juliet's Wedding Day*, where plucked strings reminiscent of the accompaniment of a serenade underlie most of the movement, and *The Death of Juliet*, a musically poignant ending to one of the world's most tragic love stories.

In many later performances of all three suites, movements have been extracted or reassembled to meet the exigencies of specific concerts or the tastes of individual conductors. The music of *Romeo and Juliet* must have been close to Prokofiev's heart. He compiled a collection of ten pieces from the ballet that he arranged for solo piano and performed in Moscow in 1937; these were published as his Opus 75 in 1938. When defending himself and his music before the Central Committee of the Communist Party in 1948, he cited *Romeo and Juliet* as one of those works in which he had freed himself from the corruption of Western formalism.

Maurice Ravel

~~~

b. Ciboure, France, March 7, 1875; d. Paris, France, December 28, 1937

Most of Ravel's productive years coincided with *la belle époque*, that period following Victor Hugo's death in 1885 that saw art, music, and literature flourish in France as they had not since the days of Louis XIV. After the death of Claude Debussy in 1918, Ravel was one of the most prominent French musicians in the artistic ferment associated with the era. From about 1899 until the early 1930s, he produced a steady stream of compositions demonstrating unusual lucidity, sophistication, and polished craftsmanship.

Born in a seacoast village on the French-Basque border, Ravel was always a Frenchman, but his Basque and near-Spanish roots often influenced his later compositions. By the time he reached musical maturity, he was a member of *Le Club des Apaches*, a rowdy group of devotees of the avant-garde who championed progressive artistic ventures in Paris between 1902 and World War I. He lent to the group his stature in the musical community, while he broadened his own horizons by participating in the long disputations for which the *Apaches* were famous. The conservative bureaucracy of the Societé Nationale de Musique, founded to promote the cause of French music in general, led Ravel to organize the rival Societé Musicale Indépendante to support contemporary music specifically.

Ravel's unwavering commitment to matters of artistic principle often led him into confrontations with convention and authority. In 1905, nearing the age limit of thirty, he made his fifth and last unsuccessful attempt to win the coveted *Prix de Rome*, an award that enabled promising young composers to spend a year in Rome, free to devote their energies to composition. The public controversy that developed over Ravel's failure to qualify became a *cause célèbre* in the French press and musical community. In 1920, he created another uproar by declining his nomination as Chevalier of the Legion of Honor, refusing, as a matter of principle, to be decorated with one of his country's highest honors. He maintained that for a man of true merit, such decorations were superfluous, and for one of less merit, no such award could lend true distinction. It's clear that Ravel marched to his own drummer!

A four-month tour of North America in 1928 introduced him to American musical theater, jazz, and George Gershwin, whose still-novel *Rhapsody in Blue* elicited Ravel's genuine admiration. He appeared coast to coast as conductor, pianist, and guest composer, enjoying a reception that surpassed the considerable accolades he had already received in his native France. In 1933, the symptoms of a neurological disorder, ultimately diagnosed as ataxia and aphasia, became more pronounced; his condition worsened in the following years and gradually entirely halted his ability to compose. Ravel bore his increasing isolation with something akin to stoicism, but on one occasion he lamented to a friend. "I still have so much music in my head, I have said nothing. I have so much more to say."[1] He died following brain surgery, three days after Christmas in 1937.

The piano played an important role in Ravel's creative process; he was a proficient pianist and habitually composed at the keyboard. Many of his orchestral works originated as piano compositions that he later transcribed for the larger ensemble. He outlined still more fundamental facets of his working methods in a lecture presented during his American tour:

> In my own work of composition I find a long period of conscious gestation . . . necessary. During this interval, I come gradually to see, and with growing precision, the forms and evaluation which the subsequent work should have as a whole. I may thus be occupied for years without writing a single note of the work—after which the work goes relatively rapidly; but there is still much time to be spent in eliminating everything that might be regarded as superfluous, in order to realize as completely as possible the longed-for final clarity.[2]

Similar procedures characterize the work of many composers, but to this approach Ravel added an overriding pursuit of technical perfection. He acknowledged this as an unattainable ideal but maintained that it was important to come as close as possible to its realization. The self-criticism resulting from such an idealistic approach ultimately produced highly polished scores, and accounts in part for Ravel's comparatively modest work list, for the continuing refinement of technical detail is not conducive to voluminous productivity.

Concerto for the Left Hand, for Piano and Orchestra

Lento—Andante—Allegro

Ravel wrote this one-movement concerto during 1929 and 1930. The first public performance was given in Vienna on January 5, 1932, by the Vienna Symphony Orchestra, Robert Heger conducting, with Paul Wittgenstein as soloist.

Instrumentation*: three flutes (the third doubling piccolo), two oboes, English horn, clarinet in E-flat, two clarinets in B-flat, bass clarinet, two bassoons, contrabassoon, four horns, three trumpets, three trombones, tuba, timpani, bass drum, snare drum, cymbals, triangle, wood block, tam-tam, harp, solo piano, and strings.*

Except for the song cycle *Don Quichotte à Dulcinée*, the two concertos for piano were the last major works Ravel completed. He was occupied with the composition of both concertos during the same period of time, contrary to his usual practice of concentrating intensely on one project. This procedure is even more surprising in light of the markedly different character of the two works. He had been contemplating a concerto for his own use since 1928, but by 1929 the project had not progressed beyond the stage of preliminary sketches. At this point a commission from the Austrian pianist Paul Wittgenstein, who had lost his right arm as a result of injuries suffered in the early years of World War I, posed challenges that stimulated Ravel's creative energies. For Ravel the perfectionist, the fear of difficulty was never equal to the pleasure of overcoming it.

Dismissed from military service because of his amputation, Wittgenstein aggressively worked to revive what had been a promising solo career by building a repertory of works for the left hand alone. Ravel had many projects requiring attention but acceded to

Wittgenstein's request largely because of the technical challenges it posed, much in the same spirit he had approached the composition of *Boléro*. He set to work immediately and by August 1929 wrote to a cousin, rather crudely, that he was gestating a concerto, and at that moment was "at the vomiting stage." He eventually introduced the concerto to Wittgenstein by playing the solo part, with both hands, followed by a piano reduction of the orchestral score. Wittgenstein was not impressed and apparently voiced his reservations. He later acknowledged that Ravel's pianism, in his opinion not professionally polished, negatively influenced his original perception and that it was not until he had studied the score extensively that he recognized the stature of the work his commission had inspired.

Ravel was unable to attend the premiere on January 5, 1932, but did travel to Vienna soon after to perform the G major concerto with Marguerite Long. Wittgenstein arranged a dinner to be followed by an evening musicale in which he played the left-hand concerto with a supporting piano accompaniment in order that Ravel could hear the complete work. According to Marguerite Long's personal account, Ravel responded to the performance with increasing agitation as he became aware of the adjustments Wittgenstein had made in the distribution of material between the solo and orchestra parts. He was sufficiently disturbed that he confronted Wittgenstein immediately following the performance and in a short but heated exchange affirmed the primacy of his views as the composer. Several months later, Ravel wrote to Wittgenstein, alluding to the infringement of the musical text and asking for a commitment that it would henceforth be played as written. Wittgenstein demurred and declined to play the concerto in Paris under the strictures Ravel imposed. Differences between composer and performer eventually were resolved to the extent that Wittgenstein, who held exclusive performance rights to the concerto for six years, introduced the concerto in Paris on January 17, 1933, with Ravel conducting.

Ravel's prominence as the leading contemporary French composer plus the novelty of a full-blown piano concerto for the left hand generated considerable interest in the work. To this Ravel responded with several frequently quoted commentaries comparing the Concerto for Left Hand and the Concerto in G, introduced in Vienna and Paris within weeks of each other:

The Concerto for the left hand alone . . . contains many jazz
effects. . . . In a work of this kind, it is essential to give the impression of a texture no thinner than that of a part written for both
hands. For the same reason, I resorted to a style that is much
nearer to that of the more solemn kind of traditional Concerto. A
special feature is that after a first section in this traditional style, a
sudden change occurs and the jazz music begins. Only later does
it become manifest that the jazz music is built on the same theme
as the opening part.[3]

In the hands of a lesser composer, the conditions imposed by the use
of only one hand would be a limitation; but Ravel was stimulated to create keyboard patterns that would provide melody, harmony, and counterpoint in a style that could be executed in that manner. To prepare himself
for the task, he perused etudes and transcriptions for the left hand by Carl
Czerny, Valentin Alkan, and Alexander Scriabin that, collectively, had significantly expanded the level of left-hand technique in piano playing. The
piano part Ravel produced demands much of the left hand, but in a manner that is thoroughly idiomatic and within the capabilities of any professional pianist. The sustaining pedal plays an important role, maintaining
harmony or long melody notes while the hand moves to other materials;
at other times it facilitates the blend of one harmony into another. The
left thumb probably is most crucial, its strength and accuracy frequently
exploited to project a melody line at the top of extended chordal patterns.

Ravel's frequent references to jazz elements in this concerto have
aroused audience expectations that are less than fully realized in the
music, at least for those familiar with the jazz idiom. There is no question that Ravel was fascinated with jazz, and that in his own perception
jazz styles were assimilated into several of his later works, the two piano
concertos in particular. However, jazz is only thinly represented here by
some mild syncopation, traditional chords with notes altered and
added, and fairly extensive dotted rhythms.

The music consists of two major sections preceded by an extended
slow introduction. Half the basses and cellos sustain a long pedal point
while the remaining basses play quiet arpeggios. Above this the contrabassoon plays the principal theme in dotted rhythms, giving audiences
(and bassoon players as well) a welcome opportunity to hear this
instrument in its lyrical register. The introduction slowly builds to the

first climax, followed by an extended cadenza for solo piano that expands on the opening theme. The following section is much like an improvisation, incorporating elements of jazz. This expansion on the theme introduced by the contrabassoon is set off by a languid second theme played by the piano, soon interrupted by restatements of the main theme by winds as the soloist turns to colorful arpeggios.

The *Allegro* interrupts this lyrical mood with a rapid passage of descending chords from the piano, and the music sets off on a rollicking scherzo as the pianist plays some slippery chord passages before embarking on a one-finger dance pattern. Ravel's mastery of orchestration comes to the fore as harp and winds play thematic material while the piano provides harplike arpeggios. A bit later the solo bassoon returns with a sustained, syncopated line that gives the impression of moving at one half the speed of the accompanying strings. A second solo cadenza ranges over the entire keyboard, this phenomenal passagework culminating in a dramatic return of the principal theme supported by broad arpeggios. The orchestra gradually joins the soloist in order to close with a cracking five-measure coda.

The Concerto for the Left Hand offers a side of Ravel not common in his other works. The composer of sparkling orchestral fantasy created here one of his most dramatic statements, focusing an unusual type of instrumental virtuosity on the development of limited thematic materials. The darker character of the work derives largely from technical matters. The left hand of the piano ranges over the entire keyboard, but much of the writing understandably takes place in the lower part of the piano range. Maintaining a musical balance between piano and orchestra led Ravel to favor the lower register of the orchestra as well (note the opening solo for contrabassoon), so the score as a whole assumes a somber quality because of the prevailingly lower tessitura. The contrasting clarity and sparkle of the G major concerto, occupying Ravel's attention at the same time, casts this quality into even greater relief.

Concerto in G Major for Piano and Orchestra

Allegramente

Adagio assai

Presto

> The Concerto in G was composed between 1929 and November 1931. The premiere took place in Paris on January 14, 1932, with Ravel conducting the Lamoureux Orchestra, and Marguerite Long, the dedicatee, as piano soloist.
>
> **Instrumentation**: *piccolo, flute, oboe, English horn, clarinets in E-flat and B-flat, two bassoons, two horns, trumpet, trombone, timpani, bass drum, snare drum, cymbals, triangle, tam-tam, wood block, whip, harp, solo piano, and strings.*

Ravel's tour of North America in 1928 was so successful that he immediately began plans for a world tour. For this he needed a concerto, preferably one in which he could be featured as soloist. Another impetus came from a proposed commission from Serge Koussevitzky for a work to celebrate the fiftieth anniversary of the Boston Symphony Orchestra in 1930. Ravel first considered a rhapsody on Basque themes with piano solo. Several conditions combined to delay the completion of that effort, chief among them the commission from Paul Wittgenstein for the Concerto for Left Hand. He also immersed himself in practicing the *Études* of Chopin and Liszt in order to develop his keyboard proficiency to cope with the concerto he planned for himself, all of which brought on a state of exhaustion undermining his creative activity. On December 5, 1929, Ravel wrote to a friend that he had been ordered to rest and was forced to acknowledge that the concerto would not be ready during that season. He next planned a premiere for March 9, 1931, in Amsterdam, but that, too, had to be set aside. Interruptions for public appearances, work on the Concerto for the Left Hand, and continuing performances of his other works took their toll, leading Ravel to complain to a friend that "I am not dead, although in the last four months I wish I were. I had to stop all my work completely. I had hoped that fifteen days of rest would be enough. Now I have hardly begun working on the Concerto again, but this time I have to be careful."[4] Eventually he offered the concerto to the French pianist Marguerite Long, who was enthusiastic about Ravel's offer and honored that he dedicated the concerto to her. She received the score from Ravel on November 11, 1931, and rushed to prepare the work for its Paris premiere, to be conducted by Ravel on January 14, 1932. Within days following the first and highly successful performance, Ravel and Long set off on an extended tour of twenty European cities, performing the concerto with unqualified success.

Sparkling clarity plus striking contrast between the *Adagio assai* and
the movements surrounding it comprise the salient features of the
Concerto in G. A crack of the whip (slapstick) in the orchestra sets the
piano off on a continuing pattern of bitonal arpeggios, recalling for
some listeners a similar pattern in Stravinsky's music for the ballet
Petrushka. Ravel claimed that this opening theme came to him during a
train trip between Oxford and London. (Accepting that, one is tempted
to draw another comparison with a well-known work that Ravel
admired, for George Gershwin reported that parts of his *Rhapsody in
Blue* were suggested by the sounds of the train as he traveled from New
York to Boston.) Ravel further described the concerto as one written
"very much in the same spirit as those of Mozart and Saint-Saëns. The
music of a Concerto should, in my opinion, be light-hearted and brilliant, and not aim at profundity or at dramatic effects. . . . I had
intended to entitle this Concerto 'Divertissement.' Then it occurred to
me that there was no need to do so, because the very title 'Concerto'
should be sufficiently clear."[5] These comments carry no inference of
copying or intentional borrowing. Ravel was highly sensitive to the
sounds around him, whether encountered in Spain, in the concert hall,
or while traveling, and his fertile imagination assimilated these aural
experiences into his creative process.

Above the scampering passagework played by the piano, the piccolo introduces a theme drawn from Basque folk tradition, a remnant
from Ravel's original plan for a Basque rhapsody plus an enduring element from his own cultural heritage. A permutation of that material
leads into a brief interlude for the piano that draws even more heavily
on Moorish influences, recalling Ravel's fondness for the Iberian penin-
sula and its music. The clarinet theme that follows is the first of three
drawing on jazz; two others are introduced in short order by the piano,
recalling the blues in their melody and languorous tempo. The solo
cadenza offers some of this same quality, but the opening measures are
marked by trills notated with unusual specificity: Ravel designates the
extra note of each trill, sometimes above, sometimes below the main
note.

The *Adagio assai* comes from a different world. The orchestra is so
subordinate that the music gives the impression of a piano solo, with
a languid horn obligato added for the last half of the movement. A
rhythmically displaced waltz accompaniment introduced by the left

hand of the pianist in the opening measures continues relentlessly throughout the movement. The conflict of twice three in the left hand against thrice two in the right creates a subtle cross-rhythm that sustains one of the most extended lyrical passages to be found anywhere in Ravel's music. When Marguerite Long commented on the natural flow of this long melody, Ravel responded that he had worked on it bar by bar, and that it had, in his words, nearly killed him! As is so often true, a musical passage that seems inherently natural was in fact the result of much studied effort. To another close friend Ravel claimed that he wrote the *Adagio* two bars at a time, with Mozart's Clarinet Quintet close at hand for consultation. Rather than borrowing material directly from a composer Ravel venerated as a model, this was a matter of creating a solo line comparable in its clarity to that achieved by Mozart. The languid horn solo that dominates the last half of the movement is supported by murmuring filigree in the piano, ultimately fading away on a long trill.

The *Presto* disrupts this quiet mood with a rollicking outburst from both orchestra and soloist. Trombones punctuate the driving passage-work with some jazzy smears, but the two-handed toccata style of the piano part prevails to the end.

The concerto met with success wherever it was performed and quickly became a repertory item. It is a concerto growing from the brilliance of the solo piano, its gaiety belying the labors of the composer. In her many performances of the work, Marguerite Long was asked to repeat the last movement so frequently that it became a near-normal occurrence. The music figured prominently in a television documentary on Ravel's life by Radio-Television Belgium broadcast in 1975, and by the end of the century the work was one of the most frequently performed concertos in the modern repertory.

Tzigane: Rapsodie de Concert for Violin and Orchestra

Ravel completed Tzigane *for violin and piano in April 1924, shortly before the premiere in London on April 26 by Jelly d'Aranyi, violin, and Henri Gil-Marchaux, piano. The version for violin and orchestra was finished by the following July and first performed in Paris on November 30, 1924, by the Colonne Orchestra conducted by Gabriel Pierné, again with Jelly d'Aranyi as soloist.*

Instrumentation: *two flutes (the second doubling piccolo), two oboes, two clarinets, two bassoons, two horns, trumpet, snare drum, cymbals, triangle, celesta, harp, solo violin, and strings.*

Tzigane means "gypsy," or at least a musical evocation of gypsy music as it was understood in the early 20th century. Following an evening musicale in London in July 1922, where he heard his Sonata for Violin and Cello performed by Jelly d'Aranyi and Hans Kindler, Ravel asked the Hungarian violinist to play some gypsy melodies. He requested another, and another, until gypsy melodies continued on into the early hours of the morning. Ravel's imagination was stimulated. Not long thereafter, he called on his friend and neighbor, the violinist Hélène Jourdan-Morhange, for advice about writing for the violin, asking her to come quickly, bringing the Paganini *Études* for reference. Thus from its inception, it seems, *Tzigane* grew from Ravel's concept of gypsy violin-playing, enhanced by the virtuosity represented in the *Caprices* of Nicolo Paganini.

It was not until the spring of 1924 that Ravel wrote to d'Aranyi with more specific plans: "This *Tzigane* must be a piece of great virtuosity. Certain passages can produce brilliant effects, provided that it is possible to perform them—which I'm not always sure of. If there is no other way, I will submit them to you by mail. Obviously, this would be less convenient."[6] Ravel must have been working on the score until a few days before the scheduled premiere. Reportedly, d'Aranyi received the music only two days before the performance, and word of her quick mastery of the score added substantially to the great success she enjoyed with the work at her performance on April 26. D'Aranyi brought to the music a long tradition of Hungarian violin-playing. She was a niece of the 19th-century violinist Joseph Joachim, a pupil of the Hungarian Jenö Hubay, and a well-known interpreter of Béla Bartók, whose First Violin Sonata she was performing, with the composer at the piano, when Ravel first met her in Paris in 1922. Ravel often tailored a composition to specific performers, and d'Aranyi's playing obviously figured in the creation of *Tzigane*.

The work represents a technical *tour de force* for the violinist. Harmonics, double-stops, pizzicato, and extended trills combine in a rhythmic ebb and flow sufficient to tax the skills of any performer. References to the so-called "Hungarian" or "gypsy" scale of alternating minor and augmented seconds (C–D–E-flat–F-sharp–G–A-flat–B–C) give a distinctive harmonic character to the music as the frequent changes in tempo lend an aura of impassioned improvisation. Ravel presents these qualities in two sections: the first, for unaccompanied violin, offers a pastiche of themes; the second, for violin and accompanying chamber orchestra, expands on a few of those themes but continues in the manner of a musical collage embellished by extravagant violin passagework.

Ravel also prepared a third version of *Tzigane* calling for a lutheal, an attachment to the piano intended to approximate the sound of the Hungarian cimbalom. The Belgian organ builder George Cluetens patented the device in 1925, but it had no lasting vogue.

Tzigane proved to be a great vehicle for violinists who could dispatch its technical difficulties with aplomb. Its musical qualities drew less favorable reviews. An anonymous critic reporting on the first performance described the musical plan and recognized that d'Aranyi had played the work with amazing assurance. Comments about the music were less enthusiastic:

> One is puzzled to understand what Mr. Ravel is at. Either the work is a parody of all the Liszt-Hubay-Brahms-Joachim school of Hungarian violin music . . . or it is an attempt to get away from the limited sphere of his previous compositions to infuse into his work a little of the warm blood it needs.[7]

It seems more probable that Ravel, always the perfectionist, created in *Tzigane* a colorful response to music of the gypsies as he understood it, a response so carefully conceived and highly polished that the technical mastery of conception and execution sometimes go unnoticed by those who hear only the soloist's virtuosity.

Alborada del gracioso

Ravel originally composed Alborada del gracioso *for piano during 1904 and 1905; in that format it was first performed in Paris on January 6, 1906, by Ricardo Viñes. He recast the work for large orchestra in 1918; this version was introduced in Paris on May 17, 1919, by the Pasdeloup Orchestra, conducted by Rhené-Baton [René Baton].*

Instrumentation: *piccolo, two flutes, two oboes, English horn, two clar-*

inets, two bassoons, contrabassoon, four horns, two trumpets, three
trombones, tuba, timpani, bass drum, snare drum, triangle, crotales,
tambourine, castanets, cymbals, xylophone, two harps, and strings.

The *Alborada del gracioso* offers another example of the Spanish element
in Ravel's music. An *alborada* is a morning song, also known as *alba* or
albora, tracing its roots to the earlier troubadour and trouvère tradition,
where the *alba* portrayed the parting of two lovers at dawn, their plaint
traditionally accompanied by a double-reed instrument (dulzaina) and
small drum (tamboril). *Gracioso* stands for the classic genial buffoon of
Spanish comedy. Thus the best English equivalent of the title becomes
"A Jester's Morning Song," but that conveys only in part the connotations of the original.

In the original piano version, *Alborada* was the fourth in a set of five
pieces collectively titled *Miroirs*, each item intended as a musical mirror
of external elements depicted in the music and each dedicated to a
member of the *Apaches*, that group of Ravel's cohorts informally established in 1902. *Alborada* came to be the best-known item of the set
because of its colorful musical qualities and the challenges it offered to
pianists. The double-note glissandi and rapid repeated notes for which
the piano version is famous offer technical challenges infamous among
pianists who have performed the work. But whatever success *Alborada*
enjoyed as a piano work, it gained still wider recognition in its orchestral setting.

The principal rhythmic and melodic materials underlying *Alborada*
appear in the opening measures. Rhythmic patterns shift quickly
between six-eight and three-four meter (twice three versus thrice two) in
support of a Moorish theme introduced by the bassoon. The orchestra
develops these materials through several climaxes until a midsection
offers a pronounced contrast with a bassoon solo interrupted by guitar-
like chords played by the strings. The prominent solo by this double-reed
instrument could be a simple matter of effective orchestration, but it
could as well be a reference to the dulzaina that traditionally accompanied works with this title. A compressed version of the opening section
returns, culminating in an extended accumulation of orchestral effects.
Double glissandi by the harps and rapid repeated notes by the winds provide a brilliance and sense of jest so natural to the medium as to suggest
that *Alborada* might have been conceived with the orchestra in mind.

Rapsodie espagnole

Prélude à la nuit

Malagueña

Habanera

Feria

Ravel wrote the Habanera *for two pianos in 1895; the* Prélude, Malagueña *and* Feria *were added in 1907, the whole arranged for piano four hands and performed at a concert of the Societé Nationale de Musique in October by Ravel and Ricardo Viñes. The orchestral version was first performed in Paris on March 15, 1908, by the Orchestre Colonne, Edouard Colonne conducting.*

Instrumentation: *two piccolos, two flutes, two oboes, English horn, two clarinets, bass clarinet, three bassoons, sarrusophone, four horns, three trumpets, three trombones, tuba, timpani, bass drum, snare drum, triangle, tambourine, castanets, tam-tam, xylophone, celesta, two harps, and strings.*

Contrary to his usually studied pace of composition, Ravel reportedly wrote the three new movements of *Rapsodie espagnole—Prélude, Malagueña,* and *Feria*—in a period of thirty days, urged on by his knowledge that Claude Debussy was working on his own *Iberia,* another orchestral piece based on evocations of Spain. Ravel had been obliquely accused of plagiarizing Debussy in the recent past and perhaps wanted to bring forth his own Spanish piece in time to preclude further problems with the critics. There is little question that he completed the score under the pressure of time, because on March 3, 1908, he wrote to his sometime-student, Ralph Vaughan Williams, that he had an enormous amount of work, fretting that the *Rapsodie* was to be performed on March 15, but at the moment he had completed the orchestration for only the last movement. The inscription of February 1 on his autograph score implies some stage of completion on that date, but the substance of his letter to Vaughan Williams, which we have no reason to question, suggests that the score was completed not long before the premiere.

In its finished state, the *Rapsodie* marked an important point in Ravel's career. It was his first major orchestral work and illustrated his mastery of orchestration, which would be a feature of many later compositions. It also eloquently expressed his interest in the music of Spain and his knack for suggesting Spanish elements without relying on quoted folk materials. He was not alone in this inclination: Emanuel Chabrier's *España* and Rimsky-Korsakov's *Capriccio espagnole* had enjoyed much success, but neither of these projected the Spanish idiom with a naturalness equal to the *Rapsodie espagnole*. Manuel de Falla, a contemporary of Ravel and the most outstanding Spanish composer since the 16th century, declared that the *Rapsodie:*

> surprised me by its genuinely Spanish character. In absolute agreement with my own intentions (and diametrically opposed to Rimsky-Korsakov in his *Capriccio*) this "Hispanization" is not obtained merely by drawing upon popular or "folk" sources . . . but rather through the free use of the modal rhythms and melodies and ornamental figures of our popular music, none of which has altered in any way the natural style of the composer. . . .[8]

De Falla observed that Ravel's mother was from the Basque country, spoke Spanish fluently, and had spent some of her early years in Madrid. During Ravel's childhood, she serenaded him with songs known to her from her years in Spain, particularly the *habanera*, a type of song that was much in vogue while she lived in Madrid. It is by no means unusual for a mother to sing to her child songs from her youth. But Ravel was particularly attached to his mother. She represented the only abiding emotional tie of his life, and he never became completely reconciled to her death. If the Spain Ravel knew was an idealized image known primarily through songs from his childhood, it was no less realistic when he portrayed it in the musical works of his maturity.

Orchestration plays a major role in this colorful characterization. Ravel had studied the tone poems of Richard Strauss thoroughly, along with the textbook from his conservatory days, Charles-Marie Widor's *Technique de l'orchestre moderne*. He took note of the "safe" and "dangerous" ranges of the instruments as described by Widor and deliberately explored their dangerous possibilities, often asking performers to produce effects beyond their instruments' traditional repertory of sounds. Combined with his constant search for technical perfection, this grounding produced a mastery of scoring new to both performers and audiences. At a time when the art of orchestration had already reached new heights in the works of Rimsky-Korsakov, Strauss, and Mahler, Ravel's *Rapsodie* projected a sinuous transparency of instrumental color carrying that art to still higher levels of finesse.

The *Rapsodie* as a whole might be described more appropriately as a suite because, with the exception of the first movement, the music expands on stylistic elements of Spanish dances cast in a free idiom. An expanded percussion section recalls dance rhythms, and the sarrusophone, a brass double-reed instrument that here replaces the contrabassoon, offers a timbre found more frequently in French orchestras than elsewhere. The *Prélude à la nuit* provides an atmospheric opening, its dynamic level never rising above *mezzo-forte*. It opens with a descending four-note motto (F–E–D–C-sharp) that continues throughout the movement and returns in the second and fourth movements as a thread of continuity. The first thematic material added to this, a short phrase played by the clarinets, also returns in the *Feria*. The ensemble continues to build on the motto theme until interrupted by a cadenza for the clarinets; the motto returns, cut short by another cadenza, this time played by two bassoons. Once again the motto appears quietly as a closing gesture, its last sigh preparing for the following movement.

Many composers have incorporated the *malagueña* from southern Spain into works large and small. Ravel maintains the typical rhythmic interplay between duple and triple meter throughout; above this the trumpets introduce the principal theme, a squib of material soon taken up by the violins and horns in turn. As the orchestra builds to the first tutti we have heard, a meditative soliloquy played by the English horn interrupts the forward motion. As this haunting interlude dies away *pianississimo*, the motto theme from the *Prélude* returns; shortened by one note, it leads to a quiet ending.

Ravel had written the *Habanera* in 1895 as the first of two movements in the *Sites auriculaires* for two pianos. He added the earlier date to the orchestral score as a supplement to the title, possibly to establish its chronological precedence over Debussy's *La soirée dans Grenade* (1903) and thereby resolve any remaining questions of plagiarism involving the two works, both of which expand on the traditional habanera rhythm. The fabric of the music is marked by a rhythmic division of each measure into a three-plus-two pattern and a sustained C-sharp–D-flat pedal tone that passes from one section of the orchestra to another through all but a few measures. The uncomplicated technical structure allows the sophisticated orchestration to make this movement one of Ravel's most happy achievements.

The *Feria* is by far the longest movement of the four, its length nearly equal to the other three movements combined. As the portrayal of a festival or carnival, it is also the most robust and vigorous. It follows a three-part design in which two vigorous sections for full orchestra surround a slower interlude featuring the distinctive timbre of the English horn. One can count at least five themes throughout the movement, but more important are the musical effects achieved by chord streams, whole-tone scales, and glissandi creating great surges of orchestral sound. The clarinet theme from the *Prélude* returns in the closing section, and the opening motto establishes another link with the beginning shortly before the cumulative orchestral forces bring the work to a brilliant close.

As often happens with musical works that break new ground, the *Rapsodie* met with a mixed reception. At the first performance, the *Malagueña* was enthusiastically received by the listeners in the upper gallery, but an encore drew murmurs of dissent from the orchestra seats. At that point Florent Schmitt, winner of the *Prix de Rome* in 1900 and a member of the *Apaches*, called from the top gallery for a second encore for the benefit of those in the audience who were unable to grasp the music, or at least were reserved in their response! The professional critics varied in their comments, one calling the *Rapsodie* one of the most exciting works of the season, another describing it as slender, inconsistent, and fugitive. Following a performance in London in 1909 the critic of *Era* wrote that:

> Mr. Ravel throws tiny little dabs of color in showers upon his canvas. There is not an outline nor an expanse in the sketch; everything is in spots. In the third [*sic*] part, a fête, the first violins, literally mewing like a rather deep-voiced tom-cat, brought laughs from the audience.[9]

In later years Ravel declared himself satisfied with the work, except for the *Habanera*, which he claimed was badly orchestrated. When asked to explain, he would comment only that the orchestra was too large for the number of bars, reflecting once again a self-criticism born of his search for his own ideal of perfection.

Le tombeau de Couperin

Prelude

Forlane

Menuet

Rigaudon

Ravel composed Le tombeau de Couperin *as a six-movement suite for piano between July 1914 and November 1917, a period that included interim military service during World War I. It was first performed in Paris on April 11, 1919, by Marguerite Long. Ravel completed the orchestration of the four-movement orchestral suite by June 1919. This was introduced in Paris on February 28, 1920, by the Pasdeloup Orchestra, Rhené-Baton [René Baton] conducting.*

Instrumentation*: two flutes, oboe, English horn, two clarinets, two bassoons, two horns, trumpet, harp, and strings.*

On September 26, 1914, Ravel wrote to a friend that he was working on two projects, a French suite for piano and another work entitled *Nuit romantique*. Only the suite was completed, ultimately titled *Le tombeau de Couperin*. François Couperin was the leading French composer of the late Baroque, best known for his keyboard works and chamber music. By Ravel's own account, the *tombeau* bearing the earlier composer's name was an homage to the heritage of 18th-century French music more than a memorial to the composer Couperin, although Ravel did copy the rhythm that pervades the *Forlane* from one of the suites included in Couperin's *Concerts royeaux*. When the suite first appeared as a piano work, each movement carried a dedication to one of Ravel's friends lost in World War I. In addition to the title *Tombeau*, those dedications led many to regard the entire work as a memorial honoring country and comrades. But Ravel's plans for a suite preceded the outbreak of hostilities, and most of the composition took place during July 1914; thus the music was not war-inspired, and the dedications must be regarded as later additions.

Le tombeau has also been cited as a gesture toward neoclassicism, but on reflection, that term fits the suite less perfectly than it would seem on first encounter. It is, indeed, a salute to musical traditions of the Classic era in France, but the orientation is more nationalistic than historical. The idea of a modern suite of dances in the modern style was not new; Ernest Chausson in *Quelques danses* (1896) and Claude Debussy in *Pour le piano* (1901) had set well-known precedents. In its musical qualities *Le tombeau* rejects the excesses of the *fin de siècle* in matters of exaggerated color and virtuosity. This may represent a search for a new musical language, but one based on the continued refinement of Ravel's creative processes more than on the projection of an aesthetic doctrine. If there are elements of neoclassicism in the suite, it is likely that they lie in the realm of retrospective interpretation more than in the genesis of the music.

In transcribing the original piano music for orchestra, Ravel was acting in response to a request from his publisher, in the process creating a score that, for many listeners, improves on the original. In coaching the French pianist Vlado Perlemuter, Ravel often spoke of melodic lines in terms of orchestral timbres, advising Perlemuter to play some passages while imagining one or another orchestral instruments. Thus one can speculate that he may have had the orchestra in mind from the beginning for this work. By 1919, orchestration had become something of a game for Ravel, a process in which he was so adept that he often pursued it as a pleasurable exercise. In preparing the orchestral suite, Ravel omitted the *Fugue* and *Toccata*, and changed the order of the *Rigaudon* and *Menuet*, to produce the four-movement sequence of *Prelude, Forlane, Menuet,* and *Rigaudon*. Ravel claimed an economy of means as one of his goals in the orchestral work, in keeping with his concept of the music as an evocation of the 18th century.

A gentle perpetual motion dominates the *Prelude*, carried forth by patterns of triplets in nearly every measure until shortly before the end. They appear as part of the main theme, as accompaniment for a secondary theme, and as a constituent of colorful harp arpeggios. The quick tempo carries the listener along at a rollicking gait until the music of the introduction returns, only to be terminated by a brief pedal point and quixotic trill in the strings.

Of the four dances, the *Forlane* offers the most direct reference to the music of Couperin. Nominally, the *Forlane* derives from the Italian *forlana*, a dance with roots in northern Italy. As a French court dance, it was traditionally marked by dotted rhythms and robust choreographic innuendo. Ravel expanded on the dotted rhythm he found in Couperin's piece, creating a jerky pattern pervading the movement. The musical plan is a rondo in which four statements of the refrain surround three episodes, each episode built from multiple sections. With no reference to historical background, rhythm, or structure, the lighthearted snap of the music evokes the dance more cogently than any other movement of the suite.

The outlines of the *Menuet*, with *Musette* (trio), follow the classic A–B–A design associated with such movements since the 18th century. The trio moves from G major to G minor as the woodwinds introduce a dolorous new theme; this same theme extends through the midsection until it reaches the dynamic apex of the movement on D-flat, the harmonic level furthest removed from the original tonic of G. At the point of reprise, comfortably back in the original key, the opening theme sounds above the theme from the trio section, the two together overlapping for eight measures as the minuet proper returns. As a closing gesture toward classical balance, the head-motive provides the substance for a well-defined, eight-measure coda.

The *Rigaudon* offers the lively duple rhythm and regular phrasing of music designed for the dance. A midsection, marked *moins vif* (less lively), sets the English horn, oboe, and flute against the accompaniment of the strings and harp. Surrounding this are two contrasting sections of similar material, each introduced by an emphatic head-motive that returns to close the movement. The total effect invites sympathetic foot-tapping from both performers and listeners.

Considered within Ravel's works list, *Le tombeau* is but one more ramification of his abiding interest in dance music. *La valse*, several minuets, the *Rapsodie espagnole*, and two habaneras all reveal this natural inclination in their vibrant assimilation of music associated with choreography. The *Forlane, Menuet,* and *Rigaudon* were mounted by the Swedish Ballet on November 8, 1920, so successfully that Ravel himself was invited to conduct the hundredth performance in 1923. At least one more transcription took place when Gunther Schuller transcribed the four movements for the Metropolitan Opera Orchestra Woodwind Quintet in 1947. The French critic Pierre Lalo, who rarely lost an opportunity to diminish Ravel's successes, offered one of the rare dissenting comments on the work when he wrote that *"Le Tombeau de Couperin* by Mr. Ravel, that's nice. But how much nicer would be a *Tombeau* of Mr. Ravel by Couperin!"[10] Lalo's caustic quip has done nothing to suppress the popularity of Ravel's monument to the 18th century.

La valse

Ravel completed the orchestral score of La valse *in the spring of 1920. It was first performed in Paris on December 12, 1920, by the Lamoureux Orchestra, Camille Chevillard conducting.*

Instrumentation: *three flutes (the third doubling piccolo), two oboes, English horn, two clarinets, bass clarinet, two bassoons, contrabassoon, four horns, three trumpets, three trombones, tuba, timpani, bass drum, snare drum, tambour (side drum), triangle, cymbals, tambourine, castanets, tam-tam, crotales, two harps, and strings.*

La valse emerged after a long gestation marked by protracted interruptions. Ravel began to plan the undertaking in 1906 as an homage to Richard Strauss; by 1914 he was referring to the project as a symphonic poem to be titled *Wien*, expanding on the dance for which that city was famous. Military service interrupted Ravel's work, and he had much difficulty in reviving his creative spark after being dismissed from the army due to ill health. By 1919 the title had changed to *La valse*, with the added description of "choreographic poem," implying a conception for the stage. Further impetus for completion came from discussions with Serge Diaghilev about a work for the 1920 summer season of the Ballets Russes. In December 1919, Ravel wrote to a friend that he was working on the score at full speed and was at last able to get into a productive mood. Early in January 1920 he reported that he was "waltzing madly" and had started orchestration on December 31. By January 16, he claimed that he was preoccupied with *Wien* (he was still using the titles *Wien* and *La valse* interchangeably), which he felt had to be finished by the end of the month. Evidently he prepared versions for solo piano and for two pianos at about the same time, because on July 3 he wrote to a friend that the two-piano score would arrive at his publisher's office within a week, at the same time alluding to the orchestral score as though it were a *fait accompli*.

It remains unclear whether there was a firm commission from Diaghilev, but Ravel proceeded on that assumption and prepared the score accordingly. When Diaghilev first heard the music in a two-piano version, he pronounced it a masterpiece as a musical work but only a sketch of a ballet. In short, he didn't like it. Francis Poulenc, present at the audition, reported that Ravel quietly folded his score and walked away, initiating a breach between composer and impresario that would never be healed. Ravel and Alfredo Casella performed the work on two pianos in Vienna on October 23, 1920, preceding the orchestral premiere by several weeks. *La valse* was not performed in Paris as a ballet until May 23, 1929, when it was presented by the Ida Rubinstein troupe.

In its early performance history, Ravel wanted programs to mention that the "choreographic poem" was written for the stage; but it became established in the concert hall as an independent orchestral work long before it was mounted as a ballet. Many of Ravel's works have been conditioned by dance music, and from its inception *La valse* grew from the composer's sympathy for "those wonderful rhythms." In search of a more subtle intent, commentators have described *La valse* as a symbol of Vienna, the crumbling Austro-Hungarian Empire, and a way of life that was disappearing from Europe following the vicissitudes of World War I. From this, they chose to hear an element of tragedy, a death wish expressed in music. Ravel offered quite a different interpretation:

> It doesn't have anything to do with the present situation in Vienna, and it also doesn't have any symbolic meaning in that regard. . . . I changed the original title "Wien" to *La valse*, which is more in keeping with the aesthetic nature of the composition. It is a dancing, whirling, almost hallucinatory ecstasy, an increasingly passionate and exhausting whirlwind of dancers, who are overcome and exhilarated by nothing but "the waltz."[11]

Ravel thought of the work as an apotheosis of the waltz, the large intervals and angular melodic lines of the Viennese dance providing a specific model, perhaps initiated by his original conception of the work as an homage to Richard Strauss.

The plan of the music serves its own purpose: the birth, growth, and decay of one musical genre. In that frame of reference *La valse* continues the tradition of the 19th-century symphonic poem, but without a literary inspiration; it focuses instead on a purely musical presentation. Ravel added to the frontispiece of the published orchestral score a summary of his own thoughts about the music:

> Through turbulent clouds, waltzing couples can be faintly seen. The clouds dissipate bit by bit; one can see at [rehearsal] letter **A**

an immense hall peopled with a whirling crowd. The scene becomes progressively more clear. The light of the chandeliers bursts forth *ff* at [rehearsal letter] **B**, revealing an imperial court, around 1855.

The music consists of two segments: the first presents an introduction followed by at least eight waltz themes; the second is built around a nearly unaltered reprise of those themes, two tutti climaxes, and coda. The first portion of the work approximates a Golden Section for the entire composition, likely reflecting Ravel's innate sense of balance more than a planned proportion in the distribution of materials. Within this series of waltzes the orchestra moves from one tutti to another through a continuing variety of passages for smaller ensembles. In the second and smaller segment that same effect is compressed; and the dynamic levels of the two climaxes are increased accordingly. The first theme gradually emerges over a quiet rumble in the low strings. Once under way, phrases follow dance tradition in their regularity of two, four, or eight measures.

Critics who were accustomed to finding in Ravel's works a near-classical balance in form and structure were disappointed by this work, accounting in part for their attempts at programmatic interpretation. Ravel demonstrated that the waltz was not just a rhythm but a style, subject to the permutations applicable to any comparable parameter of music. In the process, he provided one of the most unusual resolutions to the questions of musical coherence posed by challenges from the avant-garde of the time.

Orchestral Works Derived from Music for the Theater

Many of Ravel's works appeared in more than one guise. In that process, several scores were created for the ballet and now appear in both theater and concert hall. The works included here are those Ravel originally conceived for stage production, their later and more frequent appearance on concert programs notwithstanding.

Boléro

Ravel composed Boléro *between July and October 1928. The ballet premiere took place in Paris on November 22, 1928, Walter Straram*

*conducting, costumes and decor by Alexander Benois, choreography by
Bronislava Nijinsky, with Ida Rubinstein as principal dancer. The first
independent orchestral performance took place in Paris on January 11,
1930, with Ravel conducting the Lamoureux Orchestra.*

Instrumentation: *piccolo, two flutes, two oboes (the second doubling
oboe d'amore), English horn, clarinet in E-flat, two clarinets in B-flat,
bass clarinet, two bassoons, contrabassoon, three saxophones, four horns,
piccolo trumpet in D, three trumpets in C, three trombones, tuba, timpani, two snare drums, cymbals, tam-tam, celesta, harp, and strings.*

Boléro is Ravel's most straightforward composition in any medium. It
builds continuously on one rhythm and a single theme of two sections,
supported by a constant orchestral crescendo accomplished primarily
through an accumulation of orchestral timbre; the maniacal repetition
and crescendo are relieved only by a brief shift from C to E major and
back shortly before the end. The comprehensive design is not a matter
of statement and development but a calculated exercise in orchestration built on control of rhythm and dynamics.

Ida Rubinstein had asked Ravel to transcribe excerpts from the
Iberia of Isaac Albeniz for use with her dance troupe in the fall of 1928.
Before starting on the project, Ravel learned that most of that material
had been orchestrated previously by the conductor Enrique Arbós and
was covered by copyright laws. His plans for a pleasant summer exercise
in orchestration thwarted, Ravel realized that he would need to compose his own ballet score. Originally titled *Fandango*, the score he produced bore the performance direction *Tempo di Boléro moderato assai*,
eventually shortened to *Boléro*, although the music shows only the most
tenuous relation to the true Spanish dance of that name.

Ravel's conception of the stage design was an open-air setting with
a factory in the background, the machine elements of the factory
reflected in the relentless mechanical repetition underlying the music.
Other composers had drawn inspiration from the machine age, most
notably Arthur Honegger in his *Pacific 231*, so in this basic premise
Ravel was thoroughly abreast of musical fashion. At the first performance, a different scenario proposed by Rubinstein and her choreographer prevailed, showing a vast cabaret in which a lone woman
(Rubinstein) moved with abandon, arousing the men around her to
join in her increasingly erotic dancing.

Responding to the quick popularity the music achieved when introduced into the concert hall, Ravel many times made it quite clear that *Boléro* was an objective study in the expansion of limited musical materials not requiring subjective interpretation from conductors:

> I am particularly desirous that there should be no misunderstanding as to my "Boléro." It is an experiment in a very special and limited direction, and should not be suspected of aiming at achieving anything different from, or anything more than, it actually does achieve. Before the first performance, I issued a warning to the effect that what I had written was a piece lasting seventeen minutes and consisting wholly of orchestral tissue without music—of one long, very gradual *crescendo*. There are no contrasts, and there is practically no invention except in the plan and the manner of the execution. The themes are impersonal—folk-tunes of the usual Spanish-Arabian kind.
>
> Whatever may have been said to the contrary, the orchestral treatment is simple and straightforward throughout, without the slightest attempt at virtuosity. . . . It is perhaps because of these peculiarities that no single composer likes the "Boléro." From their point of view they are quite right. I have done exactly what I set out to do, and it is for listeners to take it or leave it.[12]

In later years, Ravel continued to emphasize this original dictum, describing *Boléro* as "a dance in a very moderate tempo and absolutely uniform with regard to the melody, harmony, and the rhythm, which is marked unceasingly by the snare drum. The only element of variety is provided by the orchestral crescendo."[13] Ravel did not hesitate to express his conviction about the performance in his comments to conductors who, in his opinion, did not take his instructions literally. He advised the famed conductor Arturo Toscanini, who was rehearsing *Boléro* with the New York Philharmonic, that he was performing the work too fast and accelerating before the end. When Toscanini persevered in his own interpretation at the concert that followed, Ravel was incensed and refused to stand at the conclusion of the performance to acknowledge the enthusiastic response of the audience. When Ravel later confronted the maestro with his musical indiscretions, Toscanini replied that Ravel did not understand his own music, and that the response of the audience vindicated the conductor's views. The

"Toscanini affair" was not put to rest until Ravel wrote a diplomatically worded letter to the conductor, evading the issue of tempo and decrying the malice of the press. In a letter to friends, however, Ravel made it quite clear that he was not overwhelmed by exalted reputations and that he remained committed to his original concept for *Boléro*.

The carefully constructed orchestral crescendo of *Boléro* incorporates within it some unusual effects. Many times the melody is doubled at the fourth and fifth, creating a parallelism common to chord streams in the impressionistic style. Ravel evokes the sound of guitars by writing pizzicato for the strings, often over a widely spaced, four-note chord. The three saxophones reflect his encounter with jazz during his recent tour of America; at one time or another, all three instruments play the theme, introducing a relatively new color into the orchestral palette of 1928. At one point, the flutes, piccolo, celesta, and horn play the theme in octaves, another unusual combination that must have sounded exotic on first encounter. The sudden shift to E major fourteen measures before the end provides a striking but welcome relief from the incessant tonic center on C that has prevailed from the beginning, but Ravel adroitly leads the music back to the original key after only eight measures.

Some commentators have described the concentration on limited materials as a precursor of the minimalism that developed later in the century. The outward trappings of *Boléro* may resemble that technique, but one must keep in mind that for Ravel, the emphasis was on the kaleidoscopic changes in orchestration; the consistent thematic repetition was a means of casting that process in the most bold relief.

Upon completing the score, Ravel claimed that no orchestra would be interested in performing *Boléro* in the concert hall, so the immediate and enduring success of the work with audiences came as a great surprise. In later years he acknowledged that it was the only work in which he succeeded in fully realizing his idea, and at another time sardonically observed that "I have written only one masterpiece. That is *Boléro*. Unfortunately, it contains no music."[14]

The perspective of time offers some possible explanations for the popularity of this work that makes so much of so little. First, it capitalizes on Ravel's recognized mastery of orchestration. He described it as a study in orchestral timbres from the beginning, and that process comprises the only foil to the constant repetition of melody and rhythm. His original task in providing music for Ida Rubinstein was one of orchestrating existing materials (Albeniz's *Iberia*), so it may be that when he decided to produce an original score, the process of orchestration remained foremost in his mind. His planned summer exercise in orchestration was not thwarted, after all! Second, Ravel had demonstrated a penchant for assimilating dance music into his concert works, illustrated by earlier compositions that included the minuet, pavane, forlane, rigaudon, habanera, malagueña, and waltz. The work at hand is not a true Spanish boléro, but it does expand on a characteristic dance rhythm. Third, he had previously demonstrated a knack for capitalizing on elements from Spain, and the theme that pervades *Boléro* is, by his own intent and design, a tune of Spanish character. When these strengths coalesce in one work, its success becomes more readily understandable.

That success finds further expression in the proliferation of recordings, arrangements, and performances in venues outside the concert hall. *Boléro* has been set for dance orchestras, theater orchestras, harmonica, accordion, organ, and likely for other media that have escaped notice. It has formed the basis for at least two films bearing the title *Boléro* (1934 and 1941) and part of the sound track or plot for others, and has been used as supporting music for competitions in both ballroom dancing and ice skating.

Suite No. 2 from *Daphnis et Chloé*

Lever du jour—Pantomime—Danse générale

Discounting the possibility of some early sketches, Daphnis et Chloé *was composed between 1909 and April 1912. It was first performed in its entirety in Paris on June 8, 1912, by the Ballets Russes, Pierre Monteux conducting, choreography by Mikhail Fokine, costumes and scenery by Leon Bakst, with Vaslav Nijinsky and Tamara Karsavina in the title roles.*

Instrumentation: *piccolo, two flutes, alto flute, two oboes, English horn, clarinet in E-flat, two clarinets in A, bass clarinet, three bassoons, contrabassoon, four horns, four trumpets, three trombones, tuba, timpani, bass drum, snare drum, military drum, tam-tam, triangle, tambourine, traditional and antique cymbals, castanets, wind machine,* *glockenspiel, xylophone, celesta, two harps, strings, and wordless chorus offstage.*

In its final form, the scenario of this ballet consists of three tableaux treating the trials of two lovers, Daphnis and Chloé, on the island of Lesbos. In the first and second tableaux, pirates invade the island and abduct Chloé, then hold a celebration and force her to dance for their pleasure. The god Pan sends satyrs and flames against the pirates, who flee. The third tableau, which provides the music for Suite No. 2, opens with daybreak after the pirates' night of revelry. Daphnis awakens, begins his search for Chloé, and the lovers embrace upon their reunion. In scene two, they pantomime Pan and Syrinx. Daphnis disappears among the reeds, fashions a flute, and plays a plaintive melody, inducing Chloé to come forth, dancing to his music with increasing animation. Daphnis swears his love, a group of young bacchantes arrives on the scene, and all participate in the concluding general dance.

By 1911 enough of the score was completed that the *Nocturne* from the first tableau and the *Interlude* and *Martial Dance* from the second were performed at the Théâtre du Chatelet in Paris on April 2, Gabriel Pierné conducting. Today those materials comprise Suite No. 1. Suite No. 2 was a later excerpt, consisting of all but the opening measures of the third tableau, and has become the more popular of the two in the concert hall.

The genesis for this score was the Russian impresario, Serge Diaghilev, who had taken Paris by storm with his exhibitions of Russian artworks and, above all, his Ballets Russes. He commissioned Ravel to provide the music for a new stage spectacle, but accounts from various parties close to the scene differ substantially in their details. According to Roland-Manuel [Roland Alexis Manuel Lèvy], friend and biographer of Ravel, Diaghilev engaged Ravel as one of the most talented among the French composers and introduced him to choreographer Mikhail Fokine, who in turn described his ideas for *Daphnis et Chloé*. While Ravel was eager to write for the Ballets Russes, he thought Fokine's plot feeble and obtained permission to modify it himself.[15]

M. D. Calvocoressi, Parisian critic and enthusiastic propagandist for Russian music, described a different state of affairs. In his account, Diaghilev had been casting about for both subjects and composers. Various libretti were outlined and submitted to Ravel, but the decision for *Daphnis* was finally reached through an intense meeting in Diaghilev's private quarters between Ravel, Diaghilev, Fokine, Bakst, and others. Fokine finally assumed responsibility for the libretto, following many suggestions from those assembled, and cast it to Ravel's satisfaction.[16]

Fokine offered a still different story. He reported in his memoirs, written several years after the event, that Diaghilev asked him for a libretto in the summer of 1910. Diaghilev liked Fokine's suggestion of the Daphnis legend, and then approached Ravel. In Fokine's view, he and Ravel disagreed on only one scene; on that issue, Fokine relented but later regretted that he had not maintained his position more strongly.[17]

Ravel's comments on the matter are more succinct, but outline yet another view of the proceedings:

> *Daphnis et Chloé*, a choreographic symphony in three parts, was commissioned from me by the director of the Ballets Russes, M. Serge de Diaghilev. . . . My intention in writing it was to compose a vast musical fresco, concerned less with archaism than with fidelity to the Greece of my dreams, which follow closely enough those scenes which have been imagined and depicted by the French artists from the end of the 18th century. . . .[18]

Ravel and Diaghilev reportedly first met in 1906; thus there could have been some preliminary discussion or work on the subject prior to 1909.

From all reports, resolution of problems stemming from different conceptions of the libretto and staging produced rehearsals that were so rancorous and combative that they jeopardized the entire production. Anticipating that the score would be prepared by 1910, Diaghilev had engaged the ballerina Karsavina for the role of Chloé. But the score was not completed until 1912, owing to Ravel's many revisions, especially those involving the finale. Diaghilev became dubious, hesitating to produce the ballet because of the problems already at hand. He was convinced to proceed only through the efforts of Ravel's publisher and Serge Lifar, one of the French dancers. In matters of production, Ravel's vision of Greece was quite different from the scenery of Leon Bakst and the choreography of Fokine. Many heated discussions took place, the disagreements eventually leading to a permanent break between Fokine and Diaghilev. Further, the corps de ballet experienced much difficulty in mastering the quintuple meter of the finale, a problem they attempted to resolve by dancing to the five-syllable chant "Ser-guei-Dia-ghi-lev." Ravel wrote to a friend that "I've just had an insane week: preparation of a ballet libretto for the next Russian season. Almost every night I was working until 3 A.M. What complicates things is that Fokine doesn't know a word of French, and I only know how to swear in Russian. Despite the interpreters, you can imagine the flavor of these discussions."[19] His exhaustion continued into the late summer, because on August 5 he wrote to Ralph Vaughan Williams that *Daphnis et Chloé* had left him in such a sorry condition that he felt it neccessary to withdraw to the country to recover.

In the composer's own terms, the score was "constructed symphonically, according to a very rigorous tonal plan by means of a small number of motives whose development assures the homogeneity of the work."[20] The depiction of sunrise at the beginning of Suite No. 2 is still celebrated as some of the most colorfully descriptive writing for the modern orchestra. Winds and harps cascade through burbling arpeggios to portray dew flowing from rocks into murmuring streams as birds twitter (piccolo) and shepherd's pipes sound in the distance (E-flat clarinet). When Daphnis and Chloé find each other, they embrace to the expressive love motive (strings), which had been heard in earlier parts of the score. The two lovers pantomime the adventures of Pan and Syrinx (oboes and English horn), and Chloé dances to the sound of the flute before falling into the arms of Daphnis to a cascade of scales (piccolo, flute, and alto flute). At the entrance of the bacchantes and the beginning of the general dance, the orchestra embarks on a gradual increase of activity that eventually carries all before it. Annotations in the score describe the stage events, but the descriptive qualities of the music are so colorful that the listener's imagination can serve quite well without specific illustrations.

The irritations that attended rehearsals for the first performance assumed another form when the ballet was presented in London in 1914. Diaghilev proposed to perform the work without the offstage chorus, which he considered unnecessary. Ravel had agreed to provide an alternate version, omitting the only solo choral section to facilitate performance in smaller venues with few performing resources, but with the understanding that the full score would be performed in productions in larger cities. When he learned of Diaghilev's plan, he protested in an open letter to London newspapers:

My most important work, *Daphnis et Chloé*, is to be produced at
the Drury Lane Theatre on Tuesday, June 9. I was overjoyed; and
fully appreciating the great honor done to me, considered the
event as one of the weightiest in my artistic career. Now I learn
that what will be produced before the London public is not my
work in its original form, but a makeshift arrangement which I
had accepted to write at Mr. Diaghilev's special request, in order
to facilitate production in certain minor centres. Mr. Diaghilev
probably considers London as one of the aforesaid "minor centres," since he is about to produce at Drury Lane, in spite of his
positive word, the new version, without chorus.

    I am deeply surprised and grieved, and I consider the proceed-
ings as disrespectful towards the London public as well as towards
the composer.[21]

Diaghilev replied, dismissing the composer's complaints, but Ravel
continued his protest in the press with enough success that a written
agreement was drawn up that bound Diaghilev and others to include
the chorus in all major productions. Ravel frequently identified *Daphnis
et Chloé* as his most important work; its costs to him were in proportion
to the level of its musical achievement.

    The first stage performance of *Daphnis* met with mixed reactions,
and the ballet was performed only twice during its first season. The
problems that had plagued the corps de ballet during rehearsals were
not completely resolved; most accounts agree that the orchestra was
prepared but the dancers were not. That the choreographer, stage
designer, and composer were not of one mind became apparent in the
disparity of conceptions that continued to exist. Further, *Daphnis* was
but one part of an evening's program, and most people were more
interested in the graphic and controversial movements of Nijinsky in
Debussy's *Prélude à l'après-midi d'un faune*, which appeared on the same
program. Comments on *Daphnis* from the professional critics ranged
from unstinted praise to caustic criticism. Some thought the music
stirring, marked by élan and a firm control of form. Others who were
customarily critical of Ravel found the rhythm feeble, giving the
impression of marking time.

    The perspective of time has confirmed *Daphnis et Chloé* as one of
Ravel's most impressive works. Nothing in his oeuvre approaches the

closing pages of this score in its combination of rhythmic propulsion and orchestral color.

Suite from *Ma mère l'oye*

Pavane de la Belle au bois dormant

Petit Poucet

Laideronnette, Impératrice des Pagodes

Les entretiens de la Belle et de la Bête

Le jardin féerique

Ravel wrote the five pieces of Ma mère l'oye *for piano four hands between 1908 and April 1910. They were first performed in Paris at the opening concert of the Societé Musicale Indépendant on April 20, 1910, by Jeanne Leleu and Geneviève Durony. Ravel transcribed the suite for orchestra in 1911 and later, in response to a commission from Jacques Rouché, he incorporated that score into a ballet by adding his own scenario, a* Prélude *and* Danse du Rouet, *plus connecting interludes. This version was first performed in Paris at the Théâtre des Arts on January 28, 1912, with Gabriel Grovlez conducting, decor and costumes by M. Dresa, and choreography by Jeanne Hagard.*

Instrumentation*: two flutes (one doubling piccolo), oboe, English horns, two clarinets, two bassoons (the second doubling contrabassoon), two horns, timpani, bass drum, triangle, cymbals, tam-tam, xylophone, glockenspiel, celesta, harp, and strings.*

All three settings of *Ma mère l'oye* (piano four hands, orchestra, and ballet) are played today, but the orchestral version appears on concert programs most frequently, while commercial recordings generally focus on the complete ballet music. In any setting, these charming pieces reflect Ravel's fascination for things in miniature and his abiding fondness for the world of children. Many accounts tell of this sophisticated composer leaving a party of adults to play with the hosts' children, an indulgence exercised in complete and natural sincerity. As a composer, he had demonstrated that he was often guided by the tenet of creating much out of the least material. *Ma mère l'oye* offers another example of that same creative impulse, but here it is high artistic achievement couched in the least complicated of textures. It is this characteristic of "artistry reduced to essentials" that led Ravel to describe *Ma mère l'oye* as one of his most important works.

The original suite was created for and dedicated to Mimie and Jean Godebski, children of Ida and Cipa Godebski, two of Ravel's closest personal friends. He wrote the piano parts with the technical skills of these children in mind, hoping they would play the first public performance. The young Godebskis apparently were not overwhelmed by Ravel's gesture, so two students, ages six and ten, drawn from piano classes at the Paris Conservatory, introduced the work to the public. In the composer's own account, his plan of evoking poems from childhood led him to simplify his manner and reduce his writing to its elements. The sparse texture of the music was in the same vein as the orchestral version of *Le tombeau de Couperin*; both works have been viewed as a gesture toward neoclassicism. More than that, the set of five pieces stands as a spiritual and aesthetic kin to works like Debussy's *Children's Corner* and Robert Schumann's *Kinderszenen*, collections of miniatures whose musical substance extends well beyond their compact outlines.

Ravel took his title from Charles Perrault (1628–1703), whose *Contes de ma mère l'oye* (Tales from Mother Goose) first appeared in 1697. Perrault also provided the story behind the *Pavane de la Belle au bois dormant* (Sleeping Beauty) and *Petit Poucet* (Tom Thumb). The *Pavane* is an essay in melody, a compact balance of form and orchestration encompassing only twenty measures in which the simplicity of the musical structure and the balance of orchestral forces create their own musical world in miniature.

Petit Poucet carries a text describing Tom Thumb's adventures in the forest as he drops bits of bread along the way in order to find his way home but is dismayed when he cannot retrace his steps because birds have eaten all the trail markers he left behind. A consistent pattern of eighth notes defines the first episode, at first cast in a constantly changing metric plan reflecting Tom's uncertainty as he embarks on his journey. The middle episode reaches its apex with high trills and succinct flourishes by flutes and violins, sounding much like the songs of the feeding birds, until a compact reprise of the original walking theme brings both music and story to a rounded close.

The story of *Laideronnette, Impératrice des Pagodes* (The Ugly One, Empress of the Pagodes) comes from a tale by Marie-Catherine, Comtesse d'Aulnoy (d. 1705). The text added to the score describes the empress disrobing and entering her bath, where she is soon serenaded by *pagodes* (small creatures from fairyland) singing and playing on instruments: theorbos of walnut shells and viols of almond shells, all in proportion to their size. Ravel claimed that the pentatonic scales and other oriental effects were derived from Java, possibly through his earlier contacts with gamelan music.

Marie Leprince de Beaumont (1711–1780) provided the tale of *Les entretiens de la Belle et de la Bête* (Conversation of Beauty and the Beast), a classic story illustrated in the score by a snippet of dialogue between Beauty and the Beast, ending with the transformation of the beast into a handsome prince. The music opens with a discreet waltz, its repetition interrupted by guttural rumblings by the contrabassoon as a midsection. The waltz and contrabasson motive combine for the reprise, the two themes merging happily at the end.

Le jardin féerique (The Fairy Garden) carries no illustrative text. It opens with a solemn sarabande that, in its musical character, seems to contradict the implications of the title. The music moves from a quiet beginning, through accumulated orchestration, to a final fanfare graced by shimmering glissandos.

The reduced musical dimensions of *Ma mère l'oye* stand in marked contrast to the torrential flow of harmony and orchestral color found in most other works Ravel created for the orchestra. This childlike élan restored melody to an importance it had not held for some time in his scores. This reduced statement brought praise from critics, who lauded Ravel for offering something natural rather than attempting to overwhelm the audience with his orchestral opulence.

Valses nobles et sentimentales

Modéré

Assez lent

Modéré

Assez animé

Presque lent

Assez vif

Moins vif

Epilogue: Lent

Ravel completed the Valses nobles et sentimentales *for solo piano in
1911. They were first performed in Paris at a concert of the Societé
Musicale Indépendante on May 9, 1911, by Louis Aubert, to whom
they are dedicated. Ravel orchestrated the set for a ballet of his own
design in March 1912 for a performance by the troupe of Natasha
Trouhanova in Paris on April 11, 1912, Ravel conducting the
Lamoureux Orchestra, with decor and costumes by Jacques Drésa, choreography by Ivan Clustina. The first independent orchestral performance took place in Paris on February 15, 1914, with Pierre Monteux
conducting the Orchestre de Paris.*

Instrumentation: *two flutes, two oboes, English horn, two clarinets,
two bassoons, four horns, two trumpets, three trombones, tuba, timpani, bass drum, snare drum, cymbals, tambourine, triangle, celesta,
glockenspiel, two harps, and strings.*

In a brief reference to the *Valses nobles et sentimentales* in his autobiographical sketch, Ravel made it clear that the title reflected his intent to
write a series of waltzes in the spirit of Schubert. His models were
doubtless Schubert's twelve *Valses nobles*, D. 969, and 34 *Valses sentimentales*, D. 779. Ravel treated these titles collectively in his own set of seven
waltzes, followed by an eighth as an epilogue.

The concert at which the piano version of the *Valses* was introduced
was an unusual event for the Societé Musicale Indépendante—a program of works listed without authors. As a group founded to provide a
venue for all that was new and progressive in music, the organization
appealed to the musical erudition of the audience. Ballots were distributed on which listeners were asked to identify the unknown composers
based on their recognition of musical styles. Ravel's *Valses* were greeted
with whistles and catcalls, some of the composer's closest friends decrying what they considered silly music. In Ravel's own account of the incident, he observed dryly that his authorship was identified by only a
feeble majority of those assembled, several people attributing the

dances to Eric Satie or Zoltán Kodály. It is ironic that members of an organization Ravel had helped start as a foil to established conservatism should have such difficulty recognizing works by one of its own founders.

The dancer Natasha Trouhanova was quite taken with the music, and it was at her urging that Ravel produced in two weeks both the orchestration and scenario for the ballet *Adelaïde, ou le langage des fleurs*. This was unusually fast work for Ravel, who was given to revising a score for an extended time until he achieved his desired state of polish and refinement. The ballet was performed only four times when introduced, but the orchestral score assumed a life of its own that continued through the remainder of the 20th century. Ravel described the music as a clear kind of writing "which crystallizes the harmony and sharpens the profile of the music."[22]

The unresolved dissonances of the opening fanfare, marked *très franc* in the original piano score, probably contributed much to the original criticism aimed at the whole set. Most of this dissonance ensues from appoggiaturas that do not resolve until several beats after they appear, but by that time their relationship to the expected note of resolution has been lost. The structural plan is a basic A–B–A design in which the reprise is preceded by an eight-measure harmonic progression as complex as any to be found in Ravel's works, casting the opening dissonance of the return into a role of relative stability. In waltzes 2 through 6, three-part designs prevail. Otherwise, most of the musical interest derives from rhythmic interplay between duple and triple meter, with the addition of much chromaticism for harmonic color.

Ravel described the seventh waltz as "the most characteristic," but whether that means "most typical" or "favorite" remains unclear. This is the longest of the eight waltzes, also cast in a clear ternary design. Ravel described the music as an extension of a secondary dominant, and referred to Beethoven's Sonata for Piano, Opus 31/3, based on the same harmony, as a musical precedent.

The *Epilogue* emerges as a musical summary in that it quotes materials from most of the preceding waltzes. Snatches of melodies and rhythmic patterns weave in and out of the fabric, recalled just long enough to remind the listener of their earlier appearance before the ending fades away through a haze of harmonics played by harp and strings.

The *Valses nobles et sentimentales* were a particular favorite of the composer, leading one to wonder about his thoughts when the piano version was greeted so derisively and whether the ballet's short life may have been a comparable disappointment. Ravel's sophisticated harmonic palette may have been ahead of its time, because he acknowledged in a personal letter that the *Valses* were among the most difficult of his works to interpret.

Dmitri Shostakovich

❧

b. St. Petersburg, Russia, September 25, 1906; d. Moscow, Russia,
August 9, 1975

Shostakovich was one of the first major Russian composers to spend his entire career working under the Soviet regime. That system intruded upon all facets of life in Russia, intellectual and artistic endeavors among them, and rarely have any composer's works been so colored by political dogma in the perception of his audience as were Shostakovich's compositions. He was highly prolific in many genres, but his fifteen symphonies have established his reputation as arguably the most important symphonist in the 20th century. The political ramifications of these works, however defined, do not alone ensure their durability, but political considerations cannot be ignored, because the ebb and flow of this composer's success approximated a mirror of the rise and fall of totalitarianism in Russia under the Soviets. It is difficult to explore the music of Shostakovich without being drawn into an inquiry into the political manipulation of culture in Soviet Russia, a condition that raises a number of unresolved questions. Discussions of his music and musical life in Soviet Russia have appeared in a wide range of printed sources, not the least of them the prefatory material in the volumes of his *Collected Works*. The situation has been confounded by the publication of the composer's memoirs in an edited version that generated heated debate in the musical community outside Russia. This frequently self-contradictory text suggests that Shostakovich was not the pawn of a government bureaucracy, despite the evidence from his own behavior. The debate over the accuracy of the memoirs centers around the authenticity of Shostakovich's comments versus the role of one or more editors in preparing the published text. Until more information becomes available, it is difficult to know what represented the composer's own thinking.

This precocious youth was introduced to music by his mother, a professional pianist. He completed the piano course at the Petrograd Conservatory in 1923 and the composition course in 1925. Following his father's death, financial conditions led him to employment as a movie house pianist between 1922 and 1925. Shostakovich entered the International Chopin Competition in Warsaw in 1927, receiving honorable mention among the finalists, and embarked briefly on a tour as concert pianist. Through all these early years, composition remained his main interest; his graduation exercise at the conservatory, his First Symphony, achieved an unusually quick and far-reaching success, bringing Shostakovich to the attention of the musical public within and outside Russia. The Soviets' need for an articulate spokesman on the international scene during their early period of political consolidation bolstered the early achievement represented by his First Symphony. Shostakovich followed that student work with two more symphonies, both bearing politically correct subtitles, and the opera *Lady Macbeth of Mtsensk* (1934), a work that was performed frequently in Leningrad and Moscow in its first two seasons. The opera was a triumph by any standard, hailed as a work representing the best traditions of Soviet culture.

On January 28, 1936, everything changed. *Pravda*, the government-supported newspaper, printed a review of *Lady Macbeth* titled "Muddle Instead of Music." The critic condemned this already well-known opera, saying that audiences were bewildered by it, and that singing was replaced by screaming. The work was further described as a negation of opera; it was bedlam instead of music, and good music was sacrificed to formalist cerebralism.[1] The fact that the writer was anonymous made it clear that this was an official aesthetic judgment aimed primarily at Shostakovich and, by inference, extending to all Russian composers. Shostakovich's Fifth Symphony (1937), another popular success, temporarily restored his good standing, until he was once again attacked in a resolution on music issued by the Central Committee of the Communist Party in 1948, a document criticizing Shostakovich and other Russian composers for "formalistic distortions" and an "infatuation with confused, neurotic combinations that transform music into cacophony."[2] Shostakovich responded as he was expected, acknowledging his musical transgressions and expressing appreciation to those who pointed out his deficiencies. His outward "conversion" was demonstrated in the years following, when he often played the role of musical spokesman for the Soviets, traveling to Europe and the United States as a musical emissary.

Nonetheless, many of Shostakovich's later works continued to be the subject of debate concerning the verity of their artistic expression versus their political response to Soviet ideology. His Symphony No. 13 (1962), incorporating excerpts from the poem "Babi Yar" by Evgeny Evtushenko, was an oblique criticism of past Soviet policies. After a successful premiere, the score was withdrawn for revision of the text, as this and other late works often existed under a cloud of politically generated suspicion.

For all the political difficulties he confronted, Shostakovich still produced important scores that endure as staples of the 20th-century repertory, meeting with popular as well as professional favor. With the perspective of time, he stands as a sometimes lonely figure who managed to express his publicly professed acceptance of political dogma while maintaining his own high standard of musical integrity.

Symphony No. 1 in F minor, Opus 10

Allegretto—Allegro non troppo

Allegro

Lento—Largo

Allegro molto—Lento—Allegro molto—Largo—Presto

Shostakovich composed his First Symphony between July 1923 and July 1925. It was first performed in Leningrad on May 12, 1926, by the Leningrad Philharmonic Orchestra, Nicolai Malko conducting.

Instrumentation: *piccolo, two flutes, two oboes, two clarinets, two bassoons, four horns, two trumpets, contralto trumpet (a valved trombone resembling a large trumpet), three trombones, tuba, timpani, bass drum, snare drum, cymbals, triangle, tam-tam, bells, piano, and strings.*

The term applied most aptly to the Shostakovich First Symphony is *precocious*; it was written as a student work while the composer was eight-

een years old, and first performed when he was nineteen. By all
accounts the first performance created a sensation; the audience called
for the second movement to be repeated, and all present were amazed
that such a work could be written by one of such youthful appearance.
The early success in Leningrad was followed by performances in Berlin
by Bruno Walter (1927), in Philadelphia by Leopold Stokowski (1928),
and in New York by Arturo Toscanini (1931). It marked Shostakovich's
graduation from the conservatory and at the same time was praised as
an achievement heralding a genuinely new talent; it was also the composer's introduction to substantial ideological conflict. The Russian
Association of Proletarian Musicians found in the score influences of
Tchaikovsky, a composer they described as a bourgeois individualist,
and urged Shostakovich to write for the working class. A rival group,
the Association of Contemporary Musicians, argued that he should
instead modernize his techniques or face early obsolescence. These conflicting evaluations were a mild harbinger of the responses that were to
greet many of Shostakovich's later works.

One of the salient musical features of the First Symphony is the
pervasive thematic integration—the reappearance throughout the work
of related thematic materials. One of several illustrations is the opening
theme, first played by the trumpet, then quickly transformed by the
clarinet. A second theme group also derives from the initial trumpet
motive, and these materials return later in the movement to serve as the
musical frame for a sonata-allegro design.

The second movement projects the character and broad design of a
scherzo and trio, but with repetitions written out fully. Thematic materials in the opening section of this three-part design are reminiscent of
a dance in their rhythmic vitality, and the marked contrast offered by
the somber flute theme of the midsection serves to heighten that quality. The piano plays an important role here, its articulated passagework
scampering about the orchestral fabric with exuberance to spare.

The hauntingly beautiful slow movement exploits the colors of the
woodwinds by contrasting them with the strings, frequently punctuated by a rhythmic motive first played by the trumpet but soon
repeated by other instruments, another manifestation of thematic integration. The movement dissolves into a sustained roll on the snare
drum that leads directly into the closing *Allegro molto,* where the growth
of the music seems to be generated by natural evolution of thematic

materials more than by traditional formal structure. We encounter a profusion of themes, the piano emerges once again in an important role, and the timpani perform a prominent solo based on the rhythmic motive from the third movement. The work closes on a percussive F that gains much of its impact from the preceding interplay between A-flat minor and F major.

A retrospective view of the First Symphony shows a binary division of the four-movement cycle through the pairing of movements one and two, and three and four. The two opening movements project a quality of infectious, sometimes boisterous humor cast in traditional designs. The two closing movements are more introspective, sharing thematic material in the short rhythmic motive introduced by the trumpet; they are further linked by the long snare drum roll, bridging if not obliterating the separation between them. Both follow structural plans that, if not free, at least are much less conventional than those prevailing in the first half of the symphony. It was the distinctive character of the last half of this symphony that the politicized musical groups identified and that formed the basis for their criticism of Shostakovich's early effort.

Symphony No. 5 in D minor, Opus 47

Moderato

Allegretto

Largo

Allegro non troppo

The Fifth Symphony was composed between April and late July of 1937. The premiere took place in Leningrad on November 21, 1937, with the Leningrad Philharmonic Orchestra, Yevgeni Mravinsky conducting.

Instrumentation: *piccolo, two flutes, two oboes, piccolo clarinet in E-flat, two clarinets in B-flat, two bassoons, contrabassoon, four horns, three trumpets, three trombones, tuba, timpani, bass drum, snare drum, triangle, cymbals, bells, tam-tam, xylophone, celesta, piano, two harps, and strings.*

Nearly a year passed from the time Shostakovich completed his Fourth Symphony until he began work on his Fifth. During that time, he had existed in a state of semi-seclusion marked primarily by his frustrations with the Fourth Symphony and its aborted premiere. The terror instilled in the Russian populace by the Stalinist purges, show trials, and the duty to inform on one's neighbor propagated by the Soviet Criminal Code of 1926 led to a situation where normal social intercourse was systematically stifled, to be replaced by unquestioning allegiance to policies originating within the government. Arrest and transportation to labor camps, or worse, comprised an everyday fear confronting people at every level of Russian society. That Shostakovich would even attempt to vindicate himself, following the *Pravda* attack of 1936, by the composition of another major work was in itself an act of courage. Had he wanted only to placate the authorities, he could have written some large texted work extolling the party line or an extended programmatic essay illustrating the triumphs of the Soviet regime. But he chose instead to write a thoroughly abstract symphonic work, relying on musical elements alone for his response.

The audience at the first performance was tense with anticipation in a hall filled to capacity, including leaders from the artistic community and government functionaries. Beyond the immediate interest in a new work by one of Russia's most promising young composers, there was much concern over the response the symphony might elicit from authorities. The performance was a resounding success and the symphony has continued to be regarded as one of Shostakovich's masterpieces. It contains the traditional four movements, the scherzo movement second in order, the slow movement third. The jagged leaps of the opening theme, played as call and response between the low and high strings, comprise a basic motive for the first movement. As the opening leaps subside, the violins play a mournful, lyric melody that could hardly be more different from the aggressiveness of the opening. The second theme, when it enters over a consistent long–short–short rhythm in the lower strings, proves to be a derivative of the opening motive, but now played in long notes, *espressivo* and *piano*. Thematic integration, one theme deriving from another, becomes a trait of this movement; for example, note the mournful melody first played by the violins, later played as a march by the trumpets, or the dactylic rhythm from the second theme, now played by the tam-tam.

The *Allegretto* is too aggressive for a minuet, too piquant for an orchestral scherzo, but it does follow the broad three-part design shared by both those traditions, its playful character serving as an effective foil to the intensity of the opening movement. Tunes enter and remain in our consciousness, often returning as a pleasant reminiscence long after the sound has dispersed. Throughout the movement, Shostakovich rarely writes more than two musical lines, one a principal melody, the other an accompaniment or countermelody. This same quality appears throughout most of the symphony, a facet of the direct appeal and apparent simplicity that caught the fancy of both officialdom and popular audiences in 1937.

The third movement is a small sonata design marked by four principal themes. Violins play the first two, flutes (accompanied by harp) and oboe present the others. For many listeners, this movement represents the apex of the symphony in orchestral color and timbre.

The closing movement was intended as a triumphant finale. Shostakovich was replying to the criticism directed at him by a repressive political system. In *Testimony*, his much-disputed memoirs, the composer is quoted as saying:

> I think it is clear to everyone what happens in the Fifth. The rejoicing is forced, created under threat. . . . It's as if someone were beating you with a stick and saying, "Your business is rejoicing, your business is rejoicing," and you rise, shaky, and go marching off, muttering, "Our business is rejoicing, our business is rejoicing." What kind of apotheosis is that? You have to be a complete oaf not to hear that.[3]

From the opening brass fanfare, played over timpani *ff*, to the final statement of that same theme, now played over 32 measures of A repeated *fff*, there is no question that the music stands as a rousing affirmation of positive mien.

In the Soviet Union, praise came from all quarters, almost as a collective wish to atone for some of the severe criticisms that had been leveled at the composer in the recent past. Performances outside the Soviet Union have met with near-unqualified success, establishing the Fifth Symphony as one of Shostakovich's most frequently performed orchestral works. The lasting achievement of this symphony is that it manages to speak to and for a body politic while maintaining a basic premise of artistic integrity and musical discipline. The work occupies a unique niche in the works of Shostakovich and in the history of music in the Soviet Union during the 20th century.

_____

Symphony No. 6 in B minor, Opus 54

Largo

Allegro

Presto

Shostakovich wrote the Sixth Symphony between April and October 1939. The first public performance was given in Leningrad on November 5, 1939, by the Leningrad Philharmonic Orchestra, Yevgeny Mravinsky conducting.

Instrumentation*: piccolo, two flutes, two oboes, English horn, piccolo clarinet in E-flat, two clarinets in B-flat, bass clarinet, two bassoons, contrabassoon, four horns, three trumpets, three trombones, tuba, timpani, bass drum, snare drum, triangle, tambourine, cymbals, tam-tam, celesta, xylophone, harp, and strings.*

If one were to attempt to describe all fifteen symphonies by Shostakovich, variety (expressed by any number of terms) would inevitably come to the fore. There are marked differences in character between most chronologically adjacent works, the Second and Third Symphonies excepted. Considering the grandiose proportions of his Fourth Symphony, followed by the clearly presented and widely acclaimed Fifth, the Sixth Symphony emerged as a work that presented a character and format different from all his major symphonic works up to 1939.

Following the success of his Fifth Symphony, Shostakovich was urged to continue his creative efforts in a similar vein. In response he announced a symphony honoring Lenin, but, as he approached the subject, various sketches came to nothing and the project was apparently dropped. What finally emerged was a score eschewing any reference to Lenin; it was not a political statement, nor did it follow what many regarded as established norms. The composer created a symphony with three movements instead of four, in a slow–fast–faster sequence. He created one mood or character for each movement, a characteristic trait that would increase in later works by Shostakovich. A slow movement followed by two consecutive scherzo movements represented an element of creative individuality not in favor with prevailing dogma; on aesthetic grounds, the two fast movements were heard as satire, witty and thoroughly crafted but nonetheless jocular and a far cry from a musical tribute to Lenin.

The proportions of the score are atypical. The first movement is nearly half as long again as the second and third taken together, and its markedly different character and tempo produce the effect of a symphony in two parts, with the opening *Largo* balancing the closing *Allegro* and *Presto*. The proportions as described present fundamental problems for any successful performance. The *Largo* has been read with much flexibility by different conductors, producing different balances in matters of duration. An intense, portentous theme in the low strings and winds promises great things, and the element of promise continues throughout the movement. The solo English horn plays a second subject that, here and throughout the movement, wavers between major and minor harmonies. The music never moves far from one or the other of these two themes; much of their interaction is supported by sustained trills serving as pedal points, maintaining a sense of activity without significant harmonic motion.

In contrast to this static busyness, the *Allegro* serves as a scherzo in character and in its general plan of principal song–midsection–principal song. In the closing *Presto,* this same rhythmic drive becomes a propulsive, breathtaking dash through a loosely constructed rondo design. The speed becomes a self-generating force, and led many critics to describe the movement as satirical frivolity, but perhaps an emulation of the 18th-century operatic *buffo* aria is a better description. The orchestration becomes a constructive factor in the mercurial expansion of basic materials, as Shostakovich asks the orchestra to play 67 pages of score in slightly less than four minutes. Meeting that expectation calls for vigorous playing; if it be satire, it must be heard with a heady sense of humor.

The Sixth Symphony met with mixed reactions and considerable speculation. Was Shostakovich withholding another slow movement, which would normally come third in this series of four movements, or a traditional sonata-allegro that would have become the first movement? If so, why? Shostakovich liked the last movement, claiming that he had at last learned to write a finale. Some critics praised the craftsmanship, the orchestration, and the witty music of this finale, while others made much of the imbalance of the three movements and the juxtaposition of two scherzos. At least one dutiful Soviet apologist explained the first movement as a portrayal of life under the Tsars, the third movement as a reflection of postrevolutionary exuberance! Most problems of reception confronting this work derive from expectations that a composition bearing the title "symphony" should necessarily match predetermined models, expectations often inconsistent with this composer's creative imagination.

Symphony No. 7 in C major, Opus 60 (*Leningrad*)

Allegretto

Moderato (poco allegretto)

Adagio

Allegro non troppo

The Seventh Symphony was composed between July and December 1941. The first performance was given in Kuibyshev on March 5, 1942, by the Bolshoi Theater Orchestra, Samuil Samosud conducting.

Instrumentation: *three flutes (the second doubling alto flute, the third doubling piccolo), two oboes, English horn, three clarinets (the third doubling clarinet in E-flat), bass clarinet, two bassoons, contrabassoon, four horns, three trumpets, three trombones, tuba, plus an additional brass group of three trumpets, four horns, and three trombones, timpani (five drums), bass drum, snare drum (two more suggested), triangle, tambourine, cymbals, tam-tam, xylophone, piano, two harps, and strings.*

Shostakovich was working on materials that were to be incorporated into his Seventh Symphony at the same time that he was composing the Sixth. This new work was publicly described, once again, as his symphony in honor of Lenin with an appropriate concluding chorus, but in its completed form it came to be dedicated to the city of Leningrad and identified by that dedication. Shostakovich did not attach the name himself, other than through the dedication, but neither did he countermand the title. As with so many things attributed to Shostakovich that he did not deny, the title has endured and for many listeners has come to be affirmed by tacit approval.

However identified, the Seventh Symphony has generated lasting controversy. It has often been described as one of Shostakovich's "war" symphonies, included with Symphonies No. 8 and No. 9 as the first of a trilogy reflecting Word War II as that conflict affected the Russian people. Any direct and musically defined connection to wartime events is difficult to document in all three of these symphonies. However, circumstances surrounding the composition of the Seventh Symphony in particular caught the popular imagination, and for several years following its first performance, this work and its composer were among the most famous items on the musical scene.

Germany invaded the Soviet Union on June 22, 1941. Shostakovich began concentrated work on the Seventh Symphony in mid-July, and the Germans launched their attack on Leningrad on August 29, an operation that marked the beginning of an eighteen-month siege that exacted a terrible toll on both sides. Under the stress of bombs and air raids, Shostakovich must have worked in the white heat of inspiration, because he completed the first movement on September 3 and, by his own account, originally intended the work to stand as a one-movement symphony. Something, perhaps the surrounding chaos, led him to regard the single movement as incomplete, and he continued with the score, completing the second movement on September 17 and the third on September 29. Rarely has a score of these dimensions been composed more quickly or under more harrowing circumstances. As conditions in Leningrad deteriorated, Shostakovich and his family, along with other creative artists, were evacuated to Kuibyshev, a city far to the east that was declared the temporary Russian capital. Here he completed the fourth movement on December 27, inscribing it "To the City of Leningrad," his hometown and place of employment, the locus of the symphony's origins, and a city then the center of world attention because of its desperate military encirclement.

Among the extraordinary efforts of the Soviets in the face of the German invasion was a government-sponsored program to convince the Russian people that all was not lost, that life continued in spite of the worsening conditions. Shostakovich himself at one time spoke to

the Russian people over the radio, testifying that his creative work continued and represented an element of normalcy. In this vein, the
Bolshoi Theater Orchestra, also billeted in Kuibyshev, began rehearsing
the Seventh Symphony in February 1942, leading to a premiere performance that, by all accounts, elicited an emotionally charged reaction
from those assembled.

From this point forward, it becomes difficult to separate fact from
fiction in matters surrounding the Seventh Symphony because this
work, created in a war-torn city and first performed in the spirit of cultural defense against an overpowering enemy, appealed to widespread
popular imagination. The intense interest generated by the circumstances surrounding the symphony's creation led to the transfer of the
score on microfilm through covert channels to the United States, where
a performance by Arturo Toscanini was broadcast on July 19 to an
audience of millions. The symphony was soon played worldwide, making Shostakovich the most famous composer of the day, documented
by that modern testimony to fame—his picture on the cover of *Time*
magazine, issued on July 20, 1942, showing him wearing a firefighter's
helmet over a grim and determined countenance. Still under siege, the
work's Leningrad premiere in August drew players from the front lines
in order to staff the orchestra; military action was reportedly directed
specifically toward enemy guns in a timely manner to allow the performance to take place without interference from artillery.

Much of the discussion surrounding this symphony, hailed as a
musical phoenix rising from the ashes of a terrible conflict, has been
clouded by some of the composer's own statements. In *Testimony*, the
collection of memoirs attributed to Shostakovich, we read: "I wrote my
Seventh Symphony, the 'Leningrad,' very quickly. I couldn't not write it.
War was all around. I had to be with the people, I wanted to create the
image of our country at war, capture it in music." A later statement
seemingly contradicts this: "The Seventh Symphony had been planned
before the war and consequently it simply cannot be seen as a reaction
to Hitler's attack. The 'invasion theme' has nothing to do with the
attack. I was thinking of other enemies of humanity when I composed
the theme." Still later in the memoirs, Shostakovich (reportedly) states:
"I have nothing against calling the Seventh the Leningrad Symphony,
but it's not about Leningrad under siege, it's about the Leningrad that
Stalin destroyed and Hitler merely finished off."[4] These inherently con-

tradictory comments cast as much doubt on the true creative impetus for the symphony as they do on the accuracy of the memoirs as they appear in *Testimony*.

Accounts by personal acquaintances relate that Shostakovich originally assigned the titles "War," "Memories," "My Native Field," and "Victory" to the four movements of the symphony but later suppressed them. In their place he is reported to have added a more generalized commentary:

> *Allegretto*: War breaks suddenly into our peaceful life. . . . The recapitulation is a funeral march, a deeply tragic episode, a mass requiem. . . . *Moderato (poco allegretto)*: A lyrical intermezzo . . . no program and fewer "concrete facts" than [in] the first movement. *Adagio*: A pathetic adagio with drama in the middle episode. *Allegro non troppo*: Victory, a beautiful life in the future.[5]

It is difficult to untangle the romantic myths that have engulfed the work, given the conflicting comments by Shostakovich himself and the events surrounding the symphony's origins. Popular wisdom would have it that the music portrays events connected with the war around Leningrad, but that reality depends upon the content of the music. As a *pièce d'occasion*, the Seventh Symphony has not sustained the same attention in the West that it garnered following its first appearance in the Soviet Union. But one must consider that Shostakovich, a major creative talent, confronted daily and at first hand the tragedy and horrors of war. Death, destruction, and the very real danger of national annihilation were part of his immediate experience. Any evaluation should consider the circumstances that generated the work and what it meant to the audience for which it was intended. Lacking clear programmatic elements and any consistent statement from the composer, listeners must hear in this symphony what they choose.

The *Allegretto* opens with unison scoring typical of Shostakovich, a texture that continues until a second theme group of two notes enters as accompaniment for a lyrical but rambling melody played by the first violins. The development introduces a march tune so simple as to be banal, the whole played over a two-measure rhythmic figure from the snare drum that continues incessantly for 46 pages of score. Played first by pizzicato strings, this simple march is repeated eleven times consecutively with no intervening material, each time louder and with more instruments. The hypnotic effect of constantly increasing volume and tension is not relieved until the first theme returns *fff* in a gesture toward recapitulation. The setting of this theme has generated much of the discussion of this symphony, some insisting that the march represents the tramping feet of an invading army, the composer's disclaimer notwithstanding. On its first appearance, this skeletal theme hardly seems sufficiently robust to portray an invading army that had swept across most of Europe with unprecedented speed and ferocity. If the march theme reflects war conditions in any way, it seems more likely that it refers to a gradual move from the innocence of peace to the horrors of war. It quickly became the most famous part of a famous symphony, described as either insipid or inspired. Béla Bartók was so unimpressed by what he considered the banality of this tune that he parodied it in the *Interrupted Intermezzo* of his *Concerto for Orchestra* (1943), where each of the two statements of the quoted material is followed by a raucous trill in the trumpets as a caustic musical raspberry. The substitution of what amounts to a set of variations for an expected development section has also fueled some of the criticism directed toward this work. We should recall that Shostakovich originally conceived this as a one-movement symphony intended to conclude with a chorus singing a text by Shostakovich himself, a plan that reduces the expectation of a traditional sonata form.

The second and third movements make their effect through original and imaginative scoring, showing little evidence of the titles originally applied to them. The finale may be a "victory" in its stately and dignified opening; the whole leaves the impression of a gloriously majestic progression from C minor to C major. If one wishes to consider C major as a neutral key (no sharps or flats) appropriate for triumphal music, the last pages of this movement will offer ample illustration.

Some critics in the West later dismissed the work as musically inconsequential, but there is no denying that the conditions surrounding its creation and first performances made it a galvanizing musical experience for Russian audiences. Setting aside the matter of any specific program, Shostakovich's *Leningrad* Symphony ultimately stands as a testament to the irrepressible creativity of the human spirit. That a composer could write a work of these proportions under wartime conditions, and that his countrymen could respond to it as they did, offers proof of that condition.

Symphony No. 8 in C minor, Opus 65

Adagio—Allegro—Adagio

Allegretto

Allegro non troppo—

Largo—

Allegretto

The symphony was composed between July and late September 1943. It was first performed in Moscow on November 4, 1943, by the USSR Symphony Orchestra, conducted by Yevgeny Mravinsky, to whom the symphony was dedicated.

Instrumentation: *four flutes (third and fourth doubling second and first piccolo), two oboes, English horn, clarinet in E-flat, two clarinets in B-flat, bass clarinet, three bassoons (the third doubling contrabassoon), four horns, three trumpets, three trombones, tuba, timpani, bass drum, snare drum, tam-tam, cymbals, xylophone, and strings.*

The initial response to the Eighth Symphony of Shostakovich was more mixed than usual. Following the triumph of the Seventh Symphony, audiences were puzzled by a work that met neither their musical nor their political expectations. Reviews in Russia ranged from the dubious to the rigorously hostile, as did the later reputation of the symphony, which ranged from complete oblivion to praise as one of the composer's greatest achievements. Severely negative criticism ensuing from the Zhdanov resolution on music in 1948 caused the symphony to disappear from the repertory for a time, not to be revised until the 1960s, when it began to attract interest among audiences who did not know or had forgotten the musical scene in the Soviet Union of earlier decades. Many of the ambiguous descriptions derive from the unusual format of the work, the widely different types of musical materials it encompassed, the strikingly original orchestration, and a prevailing moroseness at a time when enthusiastic optimism was expected. These conditions have given rise to commentaries that have often reflected the subjective responses of their authors more than the music itself.

As he would two years later in the Ninth Symphony, Shostakovich set forth a plan of five movements, here in a slow–fast–faster–slow–fast sequence, the last three movements played consecutively. The opening *Adagio* comprises nearly half the symphony, followed by two marches, a somber *Largo*, and a compressed finale that, instead of rallying the troops, steals away to infinity. Many have pointed out the influence on Shostakovich of Mahler's symphonies, but in 1943 the Mahler symphonies were much less familiar than they have since become, and the order of movements set forth by Shostakovich in the Eighth Symphony was disconcerting to many listeners. The distinctly different types of musical timbre and texture may lead an attentive listener to think that there must be some associated program, but no specific musical associations were intended; the music must be heard on its own terms.

The opening measures closely resemble the beginning of the Fifth Symphony in their dramatic texture and instrumentation, but now the music quickly turns to an expected first theme group expanding upon an inversion of the opening motive in the first violins, supported by a sustained string accompaniment. The midsection emerges suddenly as a raucous march, the low brass blaring the first theme in even notes against a tramping ostinato played by full orchestra. A series of full orchestra sonorities, trilled *fff* and connected by rolls in the percussion section, marks the climax of the midsection and a return to the original *Adagio*, a pronounced change of character enhanced by a languorous soliloquy for English horn that must be the most trenchant solo for that instrument since Dvořák's *Symphony from the New World*. The movement closes quietly with a statement of the two principal themes in reverse order. Collectively, these musical events create a broad arch form identified most prominently by the dramatic contrast between the central *Allegro* and the framing *Adagio* sections, reinforced by the mirror order in the reprise of principal themes. Beyond that, the contrast of unusual timbre and texture—the massed orchestral sonorities of the midpoint, connected by percussion, or the subdued *sul tasto* bowing of the first theme—presents the listener with sharply defined differences in orchestral color that become constructive elements for the movement as a whole.

Each of the following fast movements might be described as a march in the spirit of a scherzo. The second movement exploits the shrill cry of the piccolo and clarinet in E-flat, both instruments adding their piercing sound to the string choir. As in the first movement, an instrument usually serving as a color element—in this movement the piccolo—is featured in a prominent and extended solo. The exploitation of instrumental color continues in the third movement, in that the music is not so much a presentation and development of themes as it is an accumulation of colorful sonorities and dynamic stress. A constant rhythmic pattern underlies all of this, the consistently driving pulse relieved only by instrumental screams from the winds and higher string instruments.

A sustained roll on the side drum connects an inexorable *ffff* climax with the following *Largo*, a movement in G-sharp minor that becomes a *passacaglia* based upon a nine-measure theme introduced by cellos and basses. Here a subtle and polished expansion on the bass theme serves as a foil for the brute force of the preceding march. The prevailing rhythm of the theme derives from the first theme of the opening *Adagio*, one of several traits that ultimately link these otherwise disparate movements. Continuing passagework or extended solo lines in the higher-pitched instruments covers the junctions between thematic repetitions, creating a continuing fabric held together by the recurring bass theme. The transition to the finale occurs through an enharmonic spelling too clever to overlook: each of the statements of the bass theme ends on the leading tone of G-sharp minor (F-double-sharp), which is suddenly written as G natural, dominant for the basic tonic of C in the last movement. The finale bursts forth before the listener can be aware of the harmonic operations.

Once the *Allegretto* is under way, the solo bassoon plays the opening motive from the main theme of the *Adagio*, which itself was derived from the introductory measures of the symphony. Unusual scoring continues to dominate the orchestral fabric. At first it is a long solo for double reeds; later the bass clarinet plays an extended and exposed solo that affords a unique opportunity to hear this instrument. As a closing reminiscence, the music eventually subsides to support the melodic motive first heard at the opening of the *Adagio* some sixty minutes earlier.

More than in most of the other symphonies by Shostakovich, niceties of instrumentation and sound effects generate a broad vocabulary of orchestral sonorities. Instruments that normally play a supporting role or serve to add shades of color play significant solo passages, their relatively unfamiliar timbre demanding the listener's attention. Massed chords played as trills, something resembling a static agitation, create a nervous excitement without rhythmic or harmonic motion. According to Yevgeny Mravinsky, the conductor to whom the work was dedicated and who was responsible for the premiere performance, Shostakovich possessed an unusually sensitive ear and could hear all of his orchestral scores in great detail. With any new score, everything had been heard in advance, experienced in the composer's imagination and thoroughly calculated. It is the colorful combinations of timbre and color throughout this score that contribute to the expectation of a program more than does any other quality.

As one of three symphonies composed between 1941 and 1945, the Eighth has often been considered the second part of a trilogy of war symphonies. Certainly the Seventh Symphony, written during the siege of Leningrad, appealed to audiences as a dramatic response to military events. The Ninth Symphony, appearing shortly after the close of hostilities, proved to be something quite different from the expected musical apotheosis of the triumphs of the people, but it has since found its niche based on its own pleasing musical traits. Between these two works, the Eighth Symphony remained a curiosity. It presents an unusual plan of movements and orchestration not easily matched by existing preconceptions. Some observers have cited the Seventh Symphony as a description of specific events in the Great Patriotic War, and the Eighth as a contemplation of its horrors. In searching for some extramusical stimulus that will explain this score, one is left with the impression of a highly original work that may be the most personal and profound of the three war symphonies.

In order to account for the absence of gay and uplifting music in the Eighth Symphony, expected as a reflection of the Soviets' improving fortunes of war in 1943, the authorities posed the idea that it was a musical memorial to the dead of Stalingrad. This supposition has endured in Russia, although it is not frequently encountered in the West nor readily supported by Shostakovich.

The work became the focal point for much of the criticism aimed at Shostakovich and other Soviet composers in the Communist Party's resolution on music in 1948. Andrei Zhdanov, leader of the cultural purge and presuming to speak for The People, maintained that the Eighth

Symphony could in no way be called a composition, that it had no connection with the art of music. He and other detractors further railed
against it as an example of "extreme subjectivism, unrelieved gloom, and
willful complexity." The symphony was indeed a work of unique design
and musical effects, whereas the authorities desired music that would
represent more clearly the enforced optimism of socialist realism as conceived by the Central Committee. By the end of the century, the musical
elements of the Eighth Symphony had triumphed over the political turmoil for which it temporarily served as a scapegoat.

Symphony No. 9 in E-flat, Opus 70

Allegro

Moderato

Presto—

Largo—

Allegretto

*Shostakovich composed the Ninth Symphony between July and
September 1945, incorporating some sketches from 1944. It was first
performed in Leningrad on November 3, 1945, by the Leningrad
Philharmonic Orchestra, Yevgeny Mravinsky conducting.*

Instrumentation: *piccolo, two flutes, two oboes, two clarinets, two bassoons, four horns, two trumpets, three trombones, tuba, timpani, bass
drum, snare drum, cymbals, triangle, tambourine, and strings.*

Compared to earlier symphonies by Shostakovich, his Ninth presents a
clarity of line and fundamental animation of spirit that recalls the
youthful freshness of his first essay in this genre. Here he rarely calls for
the full ensemble, and those sections of reduced scoring are further
thinned to one primary line or melody supported by sparse accompaniment. Proceeding from this transparent texture, the harmony also
avoids the complexity of many of his earlier symphonies. Melodies
stand apart from this relatively simply harmonic support to a pronounced degree, and rhythmic structures are so regular as to invite
comparison with dance music.

Shostakovich follows these broad traits through five movements, the last three played without interruption. In the opening *Allegro*, Shostakovich follows a classical sonata design to the point that he ends the exposition with a formalistic repeat, an usual feature in his symphonies. Violins play the first theme in a triadic outline; the second theme seems to mock that material by the combination of orchestral polarities, with the trombone bleating out a two-note call while the piccolo chirps away several octaves higher. At no point in the *Moderato* does the entire ensemble come into play. Clarinets introduce a melancholy theme over sparse accompaniment, establishing a texture that prevails throughout the movement.

The *Presto*, the first of three movements played consecutively, offers to the listener the character of a scherzo but without the stereotypical repeated sections. The *Largo* is so short that it will sound to any first-time listener like an introduction to the finale; here the trombones are followed by a bassoon cadenza, the low brass returns, only to be interrupted by a second soliloquy by solo bassoon, and the strings close with a harmonic benediction. The closing *Allegretto* continues the sparse scoring that has prevailed up to this point, but gradually accumulates texture and rhythmic intensity until it reaches a symphonic burlesque in the character of music hall satire, the whole driving forward to a breathtakingly abrupt ending.

Many commentators have debated Shostakovich's intent in writing a symphony so different in character from his earlier works. Whatever his motives, there is no doubt that he was aware of the differences and that they were thoroughly calculated. He observed that, in contrast to the tragic and heroic character of his Seventh and Eighth Symphonies, the Ninth was dominated by an airy, serene mood. Anticipating some of the response to this unusual score, he predicted that musicians would love to play it and that critics would delight in blasting it, a prophecy that proved to be thoroughly accurate.

As the tide of battle in World War II began to shift in favor of the Soviets, Shostakovich as early as 1944 had alluded to a symphonic work that would celebrate the final victory as well as the triumph of the Soviet system as that was embodied in Joseph Stalin. During the summer of 1945, working at the state-operated House of Creativity on a table made from a board nailed to stakes driven into the front yard, he completed the Ninth Symphony in about six weeks. With the fall of

Berlin, expectations built that Shostakovich would create a major work that would comprise the third panel of a musical triptych celebrating the Russian victory, one topping the Seventh and Eighth symphonies. Such a work would be expected to be scored for huge orchestra, choir, and soloists, standing as a sequel to the last symphonies of Beethoven and Mahler and equal to them in musical dimensions. What came was a dramatic disappointment to those directing cultural activities. It was likely that only the international fame of Shostakovich protected him from severe retribution. In the memoirs attributed to Shostakovich, he remarked that he knew what to expect when he wrote the Ninth. Stalin was offended by the absence of a chorus and soloist; it did not meet expectations of epic performing resources. The spare, often quixotic music was so contrary to expectation that many in the Party regarded it as an insult. Authorities accused Shostakovich of being subversive; his music was declared trivial and not recommended for performance.

From a musical stance the score might best be regarded as a satire, but not all parties then or now can see the humor implicit in it. Many in Russia confused satire and triviality, depending upon their position in government circles. Outside Russia, the Ninth Symphony has become one of Shostakovich's most frequently performed and recorded works, in part because of its accessible and witty music, in part because of curiosity about a work that successfully evaded heavy-handed government authority.

Symphony No. 10 in E minor, Opus 93

Moderato

Allegro

Allegretto

Andante—Allegro

The final score was composed between June and late October 1953, possibly based on material prepared in 1951. The premiere took place in Leningrad on December 17, 1953, with the Leningrad Philharmonic Orchestra conducted by Yevgeny Mravinsky.

Instrumentation*: piccolo, two flutes (the second doubling second piccolo), three oboes (the third doubling English horn), piccolo clarinet in*

E-flat, two clarinets in B-flat, two bassoons, contrabassoon (doubling third bassoon), four horns, three trumpets, three trombones, tuba, timpani, bass drum, snare drum, triangle, tambourine, cymbals, tam-tam, xylophone, and strings.

The repressive cloud that hung over Soviet musical circles following the Central Committee's resolution of 1948 did not lift until the death of Joseph Stalin in March 1953. In the thaw that followed, Shostakovich turned his attention to many of the ideas and musical works he had suppressed in the intervening five years, including material that would become his Tenth Symphony, which he completed during the late summer and early fall of 1953. Even acknowledging the speed of composition for which Shostakovich was known, the completion of these large movements in this short time period would have been extraordinary without drawing on some existing material. The symphony shares some materials with other works from earlier years, among them the Violin Concerto, lending credence to the suggestion that this imposing work may have grown in part from earlier sketches.

Musicians in the Soviet Union were divided in their response to the Tenth Symphony. Nonetheless, in 1954 Shostakovich was awarded the title "People's Artist of the USSR," the highest honor awarded by the Union of Soviet Composers, and in New York the symphony received the Music Critics' Circle Award as the "Work of the Year." In the spring of 1954, responding to Soviet bureaucracy, Shostakovich appraised his own composition before a meeting of the Union of Soviet Composers in a detached, self-effacing manner. He noted that he had not yet succeeded in writing a true symphonic *allegro* in the first movement, that the second movement was too short, and that the third movement was too long in some places and too short in others, without identifying the sections or materials he thought deficient. Yet he later made no attempts to revise the score to meet any of these described shortcomings, raising questions as yet unanswered about the true spirit of his self-evaluation.

For most audiences, the Tenth Symphony stands as the highest achievement of Shostakovich in this genre. In most of his orchestral works the context and function of the thematic material is more important than the absolute nature of those themes, but here the musical substance and its setting achieve a parity, one growing from the other.

Shostakovich exploits the woodwinds to an unusual degree, as in the piccolo duet that ends the first movement, the combination of oboes plus piccolo clarinet at the start of the *Allegro*, the interplay of oboe, flute, and bassoon near the opening of the last movement, and the bassoon supported by percussion and low strings at the beginning of the final coda. These unusual textures vitalize the musical fabric at the same time that they give the impression of being completely natural for the presentation of this thematic material.

The symphony follows an unconventional plan: a long opening movement is followed by a scherzo, an intermezzo, and a finale with a slow introduction that comprises at least half the time of the entire closing movement. In spite of the disparate lengths of the movements, shared materials link several of them. The first three movements open with the same figure, three notes ascending to fill in a minor third, and a motive derived from the composer's name (D-S-C-H, represented by D–E-flat–C–B) permeates movements three and four.

At the opening, the low strings present a motive that, in varying guise, also opens the second and third movements. Above an extension of this pattern, the solo clarinet plays a theme quoted, consciously or not, from the fourth movement of Gustav Mahler's Second Symphony, where it accompanies the contralto text *"Der Mensch liegt in grösster Noth"* (Mankind lies in greatest need). Many commentators have described Mahler as a pervasive model for Shostakovich, and no composer of symphonies in the early 20th century could ignore Mahler's achievement in this genre, but there is no evidence to show that Shostakovich was consciously aware of this brief quotation or, if he were, what purpose was to be served. Three themes presented in the exposition expand to a climax in volume and intensity marking the apex of a broadly conceived arch form, from which point the music subsides to the duet between the two piccolos, one of them dropping out to leave the gossamer thread of one small flute fading away to nothingness.

The sustained qualities of the first movement contribute to a tension gratefully released by the burst of energy at the opening of the *Allegro*, a perpetual motion that becomes an unremitting, headlong rush from beginning to end. Shostakovich referred to this as a scherzo, a term that applies well to the broad character of the movement if not to the consistent duple meter. The speed of the music brings us to the end in short order, the whole being less than one fifth the length of the first movement. In his remarks before the Union of Soviet Composers, Shostakovich had cited the movement as too short, but any imbalance in length is more than accommodated by the vitality that prevails throughout, ending on a dramatic *sffff*.

In those memoirs attributed to him in *Testimony*, Shostakovich described this movement as a portrayal of the recently deceased Stalin, but any specific characterization must be of the most general sort. One wonders how this impetuous dash could relate to a dictator such as Joseph Stalin. Perhaps the most important point is that, following Stalin's death, the political climate began to relax sufficiently that a composer might claim to portray the leader of the Soviets in any manner whatever without swift and severe retribution.

The unrelenting energy of the *Allegro* is followed by an *Intermezzo*, or second scherzo, of very different character, expanding on three thematic units in a manner sometimes graceful, sometimes tentative. The violins play the first of these, a quiet theme introduced by the same three-note pattern heard at the start of the preceding movements. This expands through canonic imitation until we arrive at one of the composer's most personal statements, a motive derived from the musical equivalents in the German spelling of his name: *D*mitri *SCH*ostakovich: D is taken literally; S becomes E-flat through the phonetic equivalent in German pronunciation; C is also a literal transfer, and H refers to the old German text for a capital B, meaning B-natural, thus D–E-flat–C–B. This motive was not new with this work; Shostakovich had incorporated it earlier in the first violin concerto (1947-1948), and it would latter appear in his String Quartet No. 8 (1960). Nor was the process of building a theme from a surname new: J. S. Bach and Robert Schumann had also expanded on the musical equivalents of letters in their names.

On reexamining the first measures, we see that the opening theme is also a derivative of the composer's musical calling card, one that will return throughout the movement in a variety of transformations and transpositions. The solo horn plays the third motive, a pattern that appears eleven times throughout the movement as a gentle interruption of the musical dialogue, always answered in the orchestra by characteristically different material. These three musical units interact with increasing efficiency until all else drops away, leaving the D-S-C-H motive alone for three clearly articulated statements. The structural plan of the third movement is a design unto itself in which the three principal ideas gradually come to the fore. Here, the prominence of the D-S-C-H motive in the final measures, preceded by many emphatic repetitions, becomes a stamp of personal identity to which Shostakovich returns later in the symphony.

The introductory *Andante* in the finale offers several languid themes played by solo woodwinds. The last of these, first played by the clarinet, becomes the head-motive for the principal theme of the concluding *Allegro*. Here again the music expands in a frenetic whirlwind, until the full orchestra comes together in a unison statement of D-S-C-H, *fff*, accented and sustained. This, we are to understand in no uncertain terms, is the point of the music! The pace resumes by extending the clarinet theme through furious passagework, mingled with D-S-C-H in various permutations, to arrive breathlessly at a closing blaze of E major.

Beyond the masterful craftsmanship revealed throughout the score, Shostakovich's creative enterprise becomes a concerted affirmation of personality that ultimately dominates the music. In this symphony, the composer emphatically speaks for himself.

Concerto No. 1 for Piano, Trumpet, and Strings in C minor, Opus 35

Allegro moderato

Lento

Moderato—

Allegro con brio

Shostakovich composed his First Concerto between March and July 1933. It was first performed in Leningrad on October 15, 1933, by the Leningrad Philharmonic Orchestra, Fritz Stiedry conducting, with Dmitri Shostakovich, piano, and Alexander Schmidt, trumpet.

Instrumentation: *solo piano, trumpet, and strings.*

The instrumentation of this concerto has given rise to different titles, not necessarily conflicting but sometimes confusing. Shostakovich initially conceived the work as a concerto for trumpet. His difficulties in writing for that instrument led to the introduction of his own instrument, the piano. The work progressed in this format, but the piano ultimately eclipsed the trumpet. It was the First Concerto for Piano by Shostakovich, under which title it is commonly known, but the trumpet remains as a prominent solo instrument and is often included in the title. To evade the question whether to identify it as a concerto for piano or for trumpet, or for trumpet and piano together, the work is frequently identified simply as Concerto No. 1.

Fresh from his early success with the opera *Lady Macbeth of Mtsensk* and still dividing his energies between piano performance and composition, Shostakovich felt the need to reaffirm his pianistic credentials and wrote this concerto for his own performance and for the specific skills of the solo trumpet player of the Leningrad Philharmonic Orchestra. In the early performances, the trumpeter was placed at the front of the ensemble alongside the piano, the physical arrangement reflecting the composer's original thoughts about the balance between the two solo instruments and supporting the more inclusive title listed above.

The musical plan includes four movements rather than the traditional three, but the third movement leads directly into the fourth, serving as an introduction to the closing *Allegro con brio* more than as an independent movement. Shostakovich addresses the element of contrast—the genesis of a concerto—by the marked difference in character between the outer movements and the melancholy *Lento*. Both outer movements are peppered with references to familiar works by Shostakovich or by other composers, with themes that sound as though they should be familiar even though they are quite original, and with unexpected turns of phrase that frustrate obvious expectations. In the opening *Allegro moderato*, we hear a first theme reminiscent of Beethoven's "*Appassionata*" sonata, which ultimately leads to a gentle cadence preparing the listener for an effulgent melody in the manner of Rachmaninoff, but the music frustrates our well-founded expectation by a quick and saucy inversion of the first theme. Later one hears references to Tchaikovsky and, in the last movement, a solo passage that takes as its point of departure Beethoven's *Rondo a capriccio*, Opus 129 (*Rage over a Lost Penny*).

Accepting all this as inspired musical comedy, one is tempted to add the adjective *buffoonish* because of the high energy and general ebullience that prevail. Shostakovich claimed that the concerto was influenced by American folk music, but it seems American musical theater would be a more apt model and possibly the one he intended. This is music intended to draw a chuckle, the mirth to be shared by performers and audience alike.

Concerto No. 1 for Violin and Orchestra in A minor, Opus 77 [99]

Nocturne: Moderato

Scherzo: Allegro

Passacaglia: Andante

Burlesque: Allegro con brio—Presto

The Violin Concerto was composed between July 1947 and March 1948. The first performance was given in Leningrad on October 29, 1955, by the Leningrad Philharmonic Orchestra, Yevgeny Mravinsky conducting, with David Oistrakh, soloist.

Instrumentation: *piccolo, two flutes, three oboes (the third doubling English horn), three clarinets (the third doubling bass clarinet), three bassoons (the third doubling contrabassoon), four horns, tuba, timpani, tambourine, tam-tam, xylophone, celesta, two harps, solo violin, and strings.*

Following the end of World War II, the heavy-handed policies of the Soviet Union in cultural matters seemed to relax for a time, but soon resumed on an intensified scale. On August 14, 1946, the Central Committee of the Communist Party issued a resolution containing guidelines for literary activities; on August 26, a similar resolution concerning theater appeared, and on September 4 a comparable document addressed filmmaking. After a pause, its causes not entirely clear, the hammer fell on music on February 10, 1948, in the *Resolution of the Central Committee of the All-Union Communist Party (Bolsheviks)*. Vano Muradeli's opera *The Great Friendship* became a pretext for an extended application of many of the charges first directed at Shostakovich in the *Pravda* article of 1936. The leading Russian composers, Shostakovich among them, were specifically named as those who were guilty of formalism, failure to speak for the masses, and contamination by Western musical decadence.

In subsequent meetings among composers, most of them trying to protect themselves and their work, the accusations became so vitriolic that in 1958 the Party retracted, or at least mollified, the vehemence of its original charges, but by that time irreparable damage to careers and livelihoods had been done. Shostakovich, for example, temporarily lost his position at the Leningrad Conservatory. According to some accounts, the stress under which he was placed drove him to contemplate suicide, but he managed to sustain himself by turning his public attention to the film scores *The Young Guard, Meeting on the Elbe,* and similar politically correct efforts. As he had in the past when confronted with official censure, Shostakovich withheld several creative projects whose reception he questioned, among them the song cycle *From Jewish Folk Poetry* and the First Concerto for Violin. The song cycle reflected his concern for the anti-Semitism that had become increasingly apparent during the later years of World War II, and some melodic characteristics of Jewish music, though no literal quotations, are intimated in the Violin Concerto as well. Shostakovich was at work on the concerto at the time of the Central Committee's resolution. In spite of the severe criticisms directed against the very substance of his musical style, he completed the last movement of the concerto in March 1948, but it was not until two years following Joseph Stalin's death in 1953 that he felt it possible to bring the work before the public. Thus it was that the Violin Concerto first appeared with the opus number 99, representing its chronological order of appearance, while the number 77, which the composer later supported, represented the chronology of its creation.

The cultural purge enveloping Shostakovich was under the direction of Andrei Zhdanov, an articulate minister for the reformation of Soviet cultural affairs whose name came to identify the cultural witchhunts of the late 1940s. In a public speech Shostakovich expressed much appreciation for the criticism directed at him, promising to be more aware of such admonitions in the future. All composers were placed in a precarious situation; failure to follow the party line could mean exile, imprisonment, or worse, but acquiescence presented artistic problems for those with a strong sense of aesthetic integrity. Zhdanov and his supporters, of which there were many, were projecting a music for the masses in which all music would have to speak to and for all facets of Soviet society.

Although somewhat alleviated, the aura of political repression was still in the air when David Oistrakh first performed the Violin Concerto in 1955. The premiere was much anticipated and, as a major musical event, met with great success. But public reaction in the weeks following remained subdued. People were awaiting some official response from the government before committing themselves to any position or evaluation. Oistrakh was the first to break the silence in an analytical article in *Sovetskaya Muzyka,* in which he praised the work in both technical and artistic matters. He included the concerto on his American tour later in the year and performed it with great success in New York on December 29, 1955, later recording it on Columbia Records (ML 5077). Thus the concerto was firmly launched.

Shostakovich was most productive in the symphony and string quartet; the genre of concerto attracted less of his interest, but here that medium is the basis for one of his most original works. It is cast in a cycle of four movements, as with his First Concerto for Piano, but each movement carries its own characteristic title in addition to the traditional tempo marking. The titles *Nocturne, Scherzo,* and *Burlesque* refer to the broad character of the movements they identify, however that may be interpreted by a performer; *Passacaglia* indicates an older type of variation in which a defined melody is repeated in a number of different guises. Broadly speaking, this is a thoroughly symphonic work much more than it is a virtuoso vehicle, although the technical demands of the solo part will surely test the skills of any performer.

In a thoroughly serious *Nocturne,* the solo violin extends long melodic lines to their maximum. If the title holds any significance for the character of the music, it lies in the prevailing tranquility, uninterrupted by any rhythmic distortion or harmonic dissonance worthy of note.

The *Scherzo* typifies comparable works by Shostakovich, a headlong rush from start to finish that embraces in its journey much sardonic humor and rhythmic vitality. The second area is marked by a transposed but clearly stated D-S-C-H motive (see Symphony No. 10). Possibly it was this subtle reference to individuality, for those who could recognize it, that Shostakovich thought would be unacceptable in the Zhdanov era.

The *Passacaglia* is the most tightly knit of the four movements and becomes the focus of the concerto. Continuing variation of the seventeen-measure theme leads into an extended solo cadenza that alludes to the

D-S-C-H motive in some of its passagework. Solo glissandos introduce the closing *Burlesque*, in effect another breathtaking scherzo that borders on the strident and bizarre, fulfilling the implications of the movement's title. It seems that this closing movement, completed shortly after the resolution by Zhdanov, might be heard as the quintessence of the type of music to which the Soviet regime objected. Artistically, it is a marvelous release of the tension formed by the tightly knit *Passacaglia* and the appended cadenza.

At the time of the cultural purge, the Soviets apparently wanted something to depict the unqualified and unrealistic joy of the Russian people in the monolithic society projected by Stalin. In contrast, the First Concerto for Violin is not an overt political statement but seriously conceived art music showing a high level of ordered craftsmanship in the tradition of classical music as that genre differs from the imposed tastes of socialist realism.

Concerto No. 1 for Cello and Orchestra in E-flat, Opus 107

Allegretto

Moderato—

Cadenza—

Allegro con moto

Shostakovich composed his cello concerto between July and early September 1959. It was first performed in a reduction for piano and cello in Moscow on September 21, 1959, by the dedicatee, Mstislav Rostropovich, cellist, and Shostakovich. The first orchestral performance was given in Leningrad on October 4, 1959, by the Leningrad Philharmonic Orchestra, Yevgeny Mravinsky conducting, with Rostropovich as soloist.

Instrumentation: *two flutes (the second doubling piccolo), two oboes, two clarinets, two bassoons (the second doubling contrabassoon), horn, timpani, celesta, solo cello, and strings.*

It is difficult to measure the influence that Mstislav Rostropovich exerted on the composition of this concerto. He and Shostakovich had performed together many times; they had recorded Shostakovich's

Cello Sonata, Opus 40, and had shared many personal and musical experiences. With all that, the only record of the cellist offering any specific suggestions comes in an account in which the composer acknowledged Rostropovich's cleverness, but responded that "If I do it [your way] you'll be the only one who can play it; but I write for everybody, you know."[6] Nonetheless, Rostropovich lent his considerable talents to the introduction of the concerto in Russia and abroad, and his performances became the model for all those following.

In its broadest outline, the concerto follows a plan similar to that of the highly successful First Concerto for Violin; excluding the violin concerto's opening *Nocturne*, we encounter a vigorous fast movement, a slower movement leading to an extended cadenza, and a rapid finale. Here the cadenza is identified as a separate movement, although the music proceeds from the *Moderato* through the *Cadenza* to the *Allegro con moto* without interruption. The cello concerto also shows some affinity with those works by Shostakovich that expand upon his personal D-S-C-H motive (see Symphony No. 10 and First Violin Concerto) in its focus on another motto theme, in this work an original theme introduced in the first measure by the solo violin. This five-note motive permeates all of the *Allegretto*, appears briefly for some development midway in the *Cadenza*, and returns prominently in the closing movement. In the composer's view, he had taken a simple little theme and developed it. This cyclic technique was prominent in the Tenth Symphony, completed several years earlier, and here contributes greatly to a compact and highly integrated work fusing material and medium.

Following the introduction of the motto theme, the orchestra responds with an accompaniment that later becomes a rhythmic unit in its own right, relegated to the orchestra and often serving as a punctuation to the solo part. That process prevails in the second theme area, where a more sustained line in the cello is supported by the orchestra's rhythmic motive from the opening. Throughout much of a fairly straightforward sonata design, the solo horn, the only brass instrument in the score, takes up the motto theme in the manner of a shadow soloist, which, on first hearing, creates some uncertainty about which instrument leads and which follows.

The slow movement should be considered among the most intensely lyrical in the Shostakovich repertory. Simple but imaginative

scoring enhances that quality, contributing to a movement of winning
sensual appeal. A striking example is the melodic dialogue near the end,
repeated several times, between cello harmonics and celesta. Images of
an eerie wind whistling in from the Siberian plains come to mind, or
perhaps a gossamer communion from some other world. Listeners may
indulge their own imagination on hearing these evocative timbres. The
music moves directly into a *Cadenza* that has been given the autonomy
of an independent movement. Thinly veiled references to the motto
theme from the first movement provide a point for further development, not overwhelmed by the virtuosity of the solo passagework.

We have come to expect a Shostakovich finale to be an energetic
rush of instrumental virtuosity carried forth with breathtaking speed.
That energy is apparent in the closing *Allegro con moto*, but now it is
leashed by much more certitude in thematic material and orchestration. The motto theme returns in triple meter, orchestra and soloist
engage in comprehensible musical dialogue, and the concerto ends
with the head motive and original rhythmic pattern in the orchestra,
comprising a near-mirror of the opening measure. The music has come
full circle.

In retrospect, the salient feature of the work is its musical integration supported by an element of conviction more emphatically stated
than in most earlier works by Shostakovich. Satire and sardonic wit
have given way to an impression of certainty in the composer's sense of
himself and of his music.

Festive Overture, Opus 96 (*Festival Overture* or *Holiday Overture*)

Shostakovich wrote the Festive Overture *in late October or early
November 1954 for a performance in Moscow on November 6, 1954,
by the Bolshoi Theater Orchestra, Alexander Melik-Pashayev conducting.*

Instrumentation: *piccolo, two flutes, three oboes, three clarinets, two
bassoons, contrabassoon, four horns, three trumpets, three trombones,
tuba, timpani, bass drum, snare drum, triangle, cymbals, and strings.*

The *Festive Overture* was intended for ceremonies in honor of the thirty-
seventh anniversary of the October Revolution, although in the
Editor's Note to volume 11 of Shostakovich's *Collected Works*, it is pre-

dated to 1947 as part of the celebration for the thirtieth anniversary of that event. A similarly casual approach in identifying the work has introduced *Holiday Overture* as an alternate title, often interchangeable with the original *Festive Overture*.

According to a report by Lev Nikolayevich Lebedinsky, the *Overture* was commissioned by Vasili Nebol'sin, conductor at the Bolshoi Theater in Moscow, who was responsible for producing musical works for public holidays and commemorative events. The choice of works was apparently determined by much political discussion before the assignment of any commission, and Shostakovich was one of few prominent composers who had never been tapped for this financially lucrative assignment. In 1954 no work suitable for the celebration of the October Revolution was ready, and as time for ceremonies approached, Nebol'sin turned to Shostakovich in desperation. With the concurrence of Shostakovich, he proposed to send a courier to the composer's apartment to collect pages of score as soon as they were completed, forwarding them directly and immediately to copyists for the preparation of performance parts. Lebedinsky vividly described how the piece was created:

> Then he started composing. The speed with which he wrote was truly astounding. Moreover, when he wrote light music he was able to talk, make jokes and compose simultaneously, like the legendary Mozart. He laughed and chuckled, and in the meanwhile work was under way and the music was being written down. About an hour or so later Nebol'sin started telephoning:
>
> "Have you got anything ready for the copyist? Should we send a courier?"
>
> A short pause and then Dmitri Dmitriyevich answered, "Send him."
>
> What happened next was like the scene with the hundred thousand couriers out of Gogol's *Government Inspector*. Dmitri Dmitriyevich sat there scribbling away and the couriers came in turn to take away the pages while the ink was still wet—first one, then a second, a third, and so on. Nebol'sin was waiting at the Bolshoi Theater and kept the copyists supplied.
>
> Two days later the dress rehearsal took place. I hurried down to the theater and I heard this brilliant effervescent work, with its vivacious energy spilling over like uncorked champagne.[7]

We should recall that Shostakovich was always known for his speed in composing, and many composers of exceptional talent and mature technique have demonstrated that the feat described here is possible. The process was facilitated in some small degree in that a portion of the opening fanfare, little more than the first page of the score, was based on the piano piece "Birthday," the seventh and last item in the composer's *Children's Notebook*, Opus 69 (1944–1945).

The musical result was a colorful score of nearly six minutes, written in a readily accessible musical style. Brilliant fanfares by the brass instruments open and close the overture, surrounding an interior section approximating a ternary design, the whole gaining much in effect through the contrast between busy passagework and a broad lyric theme first stated by the cellos and horns.

Igor Stravinsky

❧

b. Lomonosov, near St. Petersburg, Russia, June 17, 1882;
d. New York, April 6, 1971

Igor Stravinsky maintained a prominent position on the musical scene from the time of his first widely circulated orchestral work, *Feu d'artifice* (1908), until his death more than sixty years later. Throughout this period, his works captured the musical community's attention; each of them was eagerly awaited and much discussed. He was a multinational composer, Russian in his heritage and musical style, but one who also established residence in Switzerland during World War I, later in France, and after 1939 in the United States, where he became a naturalized citizen on December 28, 1945. The external features of his musical style changed frequently but always reflected his unique creative voice. He responded to influences that surrounded him and in turn exercised considerable influence on other composers and performers. If the panorama of musical styles in the 20th century could be represented by one composer, Stravinsky would be a likely candidate. However they may be considered, his works represent one of the mainstreams of music in the modern era.

Stravinsky's international recognition began with the scores he provided for Serge Diaghilev's Ballets Russes in their Paris performances in the years prior to World War I: *L'oiseau de feu* (1910), *Petrushka* (1911), and *Le sacre du printemps* (1913). These are the works most closely identified with his Russian period in their melodic traits and, to a lesser degree, in their subject matter. Diaghilev's ballets were the embodiment of the avant-garde at the time of their appearance, and Stravinsky benefited from and contributed to that modernity.

Stravinsky produced a number of works from World War I through the completion of his opera *The Rake's Progress* (1951) that have come to be called "neoclassical," a descriptive sobriquet that needs to be addressed if for no other reason than its ubiquity in the Stravinsky literature. This is Classicism as an opposite of Romanticism broadly understood, an orientation toward economic organization, refinement of detail, and clarity of statement, all carried out with a presumed objectivity. In his own works thus labeled, Stravinsky reflected a broad realization of these qualities. He was not attempting a revival of classical style but was drawing on styles of an earlier time from a strong sense of discipline and tradition in his writing. With the perspective of several decades, one can see that these qualities were fundamental to all his works before and after the interwar period. He differed from other composers who also built on earlier models (Beethoven on the works of Haydn and Mozart, Bach on the works of Vivaldi) in that the tradition to which he referred was removed by several centuries rather than by several decades. It is possible that the descriptive term "neoclassicism" also developed from an attempt to categorize Stravinsky's works in a manner that would make them more comprehensible to an increasingly puzzled public.

Still later in his career Stravinsky embraced his own adaptation of the serial process. Again, at least as much as in his neoclassical works, Stravinsky imposed his own musical stamp on an established musical process. For many years these changes of approach to composition were regarded as a stylistic inconsistency, an evaluation usually loaded with negative innuendo. With the perspective of time and exposure, most listeners have come to sense a far-reaching stylistic consistency in which each of these phases reflects instead a continuing expansion in Stravinsky's development of his technical skills and creative imagination.

Above all, Stravinsky was original in the distinctive timbres and textures he achieved through his masterful command of orchestration. His studies with Rimsky-Korsakov doubtless contributed to these qualities in his early works, but throughout his oeuvre an imaginative palette of musical sound formed an inherent part of his musical thought. He was particularly fond of the wind instruments, because of their defined timbre, and often wrote for woodwinds in the extremes of their register, where they assume an even more distinctive color. Strings *divisi*, string harmonics, and expanded percussion added further to his range of orchestral effects.

Many of Stravinsky's thoughts on music, filtered through the literary skills of others, have been preserved in written sources that have established him as a frequently quoted figure in the literature of modern music. In his autobiography, ghostwritten in 1936 by Walter Nouvel, he proposed to resolve the misunderstanding that had come to be associated with his music and his person. His *Poetics of Music* (1947) originated as a translation of six lectures he delivered as the Charles Eliot Norton lecturer at Harvard University during 1939 and 1940. The work has been considered a monograph by Stravinsky, but the text was in fact written by Roland-Manuel [Roland Alexis Manuel Lévy] based upon extended discussions between Stravinsky and that littérateur on the substance of the planned lectures. Stravinsky's own notes for these lectures and, presumably, for his discussions with Roland-Manuel have been preserved in outline form and project some of Stravinsky's opinions on the art of music and his own approaches to it. One theme he addressed here, and at many other times in his career, was the premise that some self-imposed limitation was necessary for his creative process to function:

> My freedom will be so much the greater and more meaningful the more narrowly I limit my field of action and the more I surround myself with obstacles. Whatever diminishes constraint diminishes strength. The more constraints one imposes, the more one frees one's self of the chains that shackle the spirit.[1]

The specifics of this self-imposed discipline may vary among compositions, but in some form it comprises the core of Stravinsky's creative endeavor.

More widely read than either of these works is the series of books that Stravinsky produced in cooperation with Robert Craft, a young conductor who served as his assistant and amanuensis starting in 1948. These publications, at least nine at the time of this writing, take the form of interviews, correspondence, dialogues, narrative conversations, and diaries, written by Craft but assembled and published in a manner to suggest that they were executed with some knowledge and control by the composer. In 1958, Stravinsky wrote to his publisher's agent that the book then under discussion should be titled *Conversations with Igor Stravinsky by Robert Craft*. He asserted that the text was by Craft and that, in effect, Craft had created the substance of the document. Despite some controversy over their accuracy, these conversation books have come to be regarded as a commentary by Stravinsky on his life and music; considered collectively, they offer, through the eyes and language of his closest collaborator, an unusual view into Stravinsky's mode of operation.

Stravinsky's works have been sufficiently important to become the focus of major studies that have influenced the entire discipline of theoretical and aesthetic analysis of 20th-century music. Other composers have described their creative procedures, a few have changed style during their lifetime, and many have proposed new techniques for making music, but in the length of his creative life and in the breadth and variety of his musical styles, there has been no career quite like Igor Stravinsky's.

Symphony in C

Moderato alla breve

Larghetto concertante—

Allegretto

Largo—Tempo giusto, alla breve

Stravinsky composed the movements of his Symphony in C in several stages separated by time and place. He began the first movement in Paris in the fall of 1938, completing it in Sancellmoz, Switzerland, in April 1939. He composed the second movement between April and July while in Switzerland and the Allegretto *at Cambridge, MA, during the winter of 1939 and 1940; the fourth movement was completed in Beverly Hills, CA, in August 1940. The first performance took place in Chicago on November 7, 1940, with the Chicago Symphony Orchestra, Stravinsky conducting.*

Instrumentation: *piccolo, two flutes, two oboes, two clarinets, two bassoons, four horns, two trumpets, three trombones, tuba, timpani, and strings.*

Stravinsky completed the Symphony in C in response to a commission from the American patron Mrs. Robert Woods Bliss, who, with her husband, had a year earlier commissioned the *Dumbarton Oaks* Concerto. Through the efforts of Mrs. Bliss, the symphony was presented to the Chicago Symphony Orchestra in honor of its fiftieth anniversary, the wording of the dedication following the pattern of his dedication of the

Symphony of Psalms to the Boston Symphony in 1930: *"Cette symphonie composée à la gloire de DIEU est dediée au 'Chicago Symphony Orchestre' à l'occasion du cinquantenaire de son existence."*

The initial stages of the symphony were written during an unusually stressful period in the composer's personal life. He had been diagnosed with a serious lung ailment but, contrary to medical advice, went to Paris and, according to his own testament, surmounted the malady by immersing himself in composition. At about the same time, he lost three members of his family in short order: his daughter Ludmilla on November 30, 1938, his wife Catherine on March 2, 1939, and his mother on June 7, 1939. Stravinsky claimed that he had survived these personal traumas by concentrating on the composition of the Symphony in C. This quality of artistic objectivity marks Stravinsky's works in general, often described as a facet of his highly developed sense of discipline. This is not the sort of self-control that would drive him to compose a specified amount of music on any given day or week; instead, it represents an artistic focus on the craftsmanship necessary to resolve any set of creative problems according to parameters the composer had established for a given work.

While his personal problems may have been submerged during his work on the score, he reportedly acknowledged that major changes of location were reflected in the music:

> The world events of 1939–40, though happily not tragic in their bearing on my personal life, did disrupt the tenor of the Symphony. The third movement, composed in Boston, and the fourth movement, stapled together in California . . . are very different in spirit and design from the "European" movements, and they have seemed to many to divide the Symphony down the middle. This schism is especially marked, of course, in the domain of rhythm. The metrical and tempo changes in the third movement are the most extreme in the whole inventory of my work, and they follow a second movement with a steady *ductus* and a first movement with no variation of meter at all.[2]

Stravinsky further claimed that some measures in the third movement would never have occurred to him in Europe, and that others would have been impossible without experiencing California from a speeding automobile! Some observers have added another dimension to this bifurcation of the symphony, claiming that it represented the stylistic separation of his European and American periods, though this is difficult to define based on musical qualities alone.

The first movement, one of Stravinsky's most clearly defined sonata designs, albeit with a compressed development and recapitulation, expands on a motto theme heard in the opening measures. This later becomes a part of the main theme proper and returns in the last movement, contributing a thread of cohesiveness. From a different perspective, the first movement offers a near-symmetrical structure, with the development serving as the pivotal section. The intriguing factor is that either approach makes good sense to the attentive listener. The second movement is most clearly recognizable for its contrasts between the string choir and small groups of wind instruments, both ensembles sharing in the presentation of thematic materials. The uninterrupted transition between the second and third movements is cleverly executed by the continuation of the closing motive of the *Larghetto* in the first measure of the *Allegretto*. Reflecting on the composer's own concerns about the division of the symphony at this point, one wonders whether this was a retrospective attempt to minimize that supposed division. The closing movement continues by expanding on the motive from the opening *Moderato alla breve*, ending the symphony with a quiet and comprehensive summation.

Beyond the disruption during its composition and any derivative changes in style, the Symphony in C represents a departure from Stravinsky's usual procedures. He followed symphonic tradition by expanding a multimovement score through the development of thematic materials, whereas most of the work for which he was famous up to this time had been formed from a series of more or less static musical statements, each fairly independent from the others. The Symphony in C was, in effect, a cohesive and cyclical work.

Responding to reports from visitors to his residence, Stravinsky acknowledged that scores of Haydn, Beethoven, and Tchaikovsky were on his desk during the early stages of his work on the symphony and that those works had provided a broadly based musical stimulation. But this does not represent an attempt to write a symphony in the style those masters would have produced had they lived in modern times. The Symphony in C represents an assimilation of the traditions established by earlier composers, expressed through Stravinsky's own language and aesthetic values. The clarity and coherence of the work aroused considerable interest and enthusiasm, and Stravinsky's fans claimed that the score represented the apex of his compositions for orchestra alone. As it projected a clarity and discipline comparable to works from the 18th century, many came to view the symphony as a neoclassical work with a new voice.

Conductors did not always have an easy time with the score, as Stravinsky anticipated. Writing to his publisher on September 3, 1940, he noted that he had based all of his conducting engagements for the following season on the new symphony, maintaining that he should be the one to establish a tradition for its interpretation. His concerns in the matter were apparently well founded, at least in his own perception, because he complained bitterly about technical inaccuracies in a performance conducted by Leopold Stokowski in a radio broadcast of 1943. There is no reason to believe that such performances were the norm, but the incident implies that many players and conductors were unfamiliar with Stravinsky's musical idiom, and early performances likely suffered as a result.

The decade after 1930 was a period of consolidation in which Stravinsky established an enduring international reputation and successfully assimilated into his own style many of the established forms of the past. At the end of the decade it seemed that his musical language had stabilized, or at least the public seemed more comfortable with the style and procedures of his music. As we reflect on these achievements at the end of the 20th century, the Symphony in C and the Symphony in Three Movements stand out as his most pronounced gestures toward a long tradition of symphonic music. Most of the musical community has come to regard these works as musical statements drawing upon the long tradition of the sonata idea interpreted according to Stravinsky's own creative muse.

Symphony in Three Movements

♩ = 160

Andante—

Interlude: L'istesso tempo—Con moto

Composition of the Symphony in Three Movements extended from April 1942 to August 1945. It was first performed in New York on January

24, 1946, by the New York Philharmonic Orchestra, Stravinsky conducting.

Instrumentation: *piccolo, two flutes, two oboes, three clarinets (the
third doubling bass clarinet), two bassoons, contrabassoon, four horns,
three trumpets, three trombones, tuba, timpani, bass drum, piano,
harp, and strings.*

A combination of events in Stravinsky's professional activities plus the
widespread disruption of World War II caused the composition of the
Symphony in Three Movements to be interrupted by a number of other
projects. One result was that the three movements grew from different
stimuli, reflected in the musical character of the symphony as it gradually coalesced. Stravinsky later remarked that a more exact title for the
work would be "Three Symphonic Movements," implying that he recognized at least some degree of heterogeneity among the movements.
He reported that the first movement was originally conceived as a concerto for orchestra, and *concertante* writing prevails throughout the
score, although the solo piano did not appear in early sketches. The
slow movement, or at least a portion of it, was written in response to a
request from Franz Werfel for music to accompany the film *Song of
Bernadette*. Stravinsky acknowledged that he was attracted by the script,
but felt the situation was too heavily slanted in favor of the film producer. He did compose some music for the "Apparition of the Virgin"
scene, which became the symphonic *Andante*, but it remains a matter of
conjecture whether that original intent contributed directly to the
prominent role of the harp in the orchestral score. It seems likely that
concertante writing, so pervasive in the first movement, was continued
here and found realization in the solo harp.

The straightforward title and the format it implies are much in
keeping with the tradition of the classic symphony, but, as always,
Stravinsky gives this his own twist. A seven-measure interlude, titled as
such, connects the second and third movements, all designated to be
played without interruption. Small ensembles emerge from the symphonic texture repeatedly (the *concertante* element cited earlier), not in
the manner of a concerto grosso, because the combinations of instruments vary, but as groups that take their turn at presenting a variety of
materials. As a part of this process, the piano emerges as an important
instrument in the first movement, functioning sometimes as an orches-

tral instrument, sometimes as a soloist. The harp fills a similar role in the *Andante*; the colorful glissandos generally associated with this instrument give way to thematic material integral to the musical substance of the movement. With inherent musical logic, both instruments flourish together in the last movement.

The first movement opens with a dramatic rush and motto theme, played by the full orchestra and arriving at a collective D-flat; this returns before the closing cadence to frame a broadly conceived sonata design. The concertino groups diverge at the development and regroup for the recapitulation, where the main themes return in reverse order of their original appearance. Pedal figures play an important role in some sections, serving as points of reference and identification. Several of these resemble rhythmic techniques Stravinsky had incorporated with such success into his earlier ballet music: a two-note pattern cast in triple meter or groups of three notes distributed over a duple metric pattern.

The harp, as the instrument of contrast in the slow movement, at times accompanies the winds, later takes the lead in small wind ensembles, and finally joins with the other strings. The whole movement follows a straightforward A–B–A design, the midsection marked by an increase in tempo and a concertino group of harp and woodwinds.

The third movement begins with a vigorous march for full orchestra, refers to the opening motto from the first movement several times before returning to the march, now played by the woodwinds, and then embarks on an expanded version of the march that is interrupted by several abrupt pauses. These cut through the accumulating orchestral texture and offer the listener (and the player) an opportunity to catch a breath before returning to the increasingly energetic forward motion. The sudden shift to D-flat at the final cadence initially comes as a surprise until we recall that this key was introduced by the motto theme at the opening of the symphony, more than twenty minutes earlier. The music has now come full circle through three movements of contrasting character.

For the first performance in New York, Stravinsky provided a note that, he emphasized, did not comprise a program but that nonetheless offers some perspective on his thoughts at the time:

> The Symphony has no program, nor is it a specific expression of any given occasion; it would be futile to seek these in my work. But

during the process of creation in this our arduous time of sharp
and shifting events, of despair and hope, of continual torment, of
tension and, at last, cessation and relief, it may be that all these
repercussions have left traces in this symphony. It is not I to judge.[3]

These or similar thoughts probably generated Stravinsky's frequent reference to the work as his "war symphony."

Several years later, he responded to an inquiry about the influence
of world events on the symphony with a much more detailed program,
but maintained his disclaimer about literal representation of those
events in his music:

> I can say little more than that it was written under the sign of
> them [current events]. It both does and does not "express my feelings" about them, but I prefer to say only that, without participation of what I think of as my will, they excited my musical
> imagination. And the events that thus activated me were not general, or ideological, but specific: each episode in the Symphony is
> linked in my imagination with a concrete impression, very often
> cinematographic in origin, of the war.
>
> The third movement actually contains the genesis of a war
> plot, though I recognized it as such *only after completing the composition* [emphasis added]. The beginning of that movement is partly,
> and in some—to me wholly inexplicable—way, a musical reaction
> to the newsreels and documentaries that I had seen of goose-
> stepping soldiers. The square march-beat, the brass-band instrumentation, the grotesque *crescendo* in the tuba—these are all
> related to those repellent pictures.[4]

Stravinsky continues by comparing some portion of the third movement to the downfall of the Nazi regime in Germany in 1945, when he
was completing the symphony, and then offers a similar background
for the first and second movements, concluding the description with a
reaffirmation that the symphony is not programmatic!

The Symphony in Three Movements was initially accepted more
readily by audiences than by critics. A review of the premiere by Olin
Downes was less than enthusiastic:

> This music is inorganic in its effect. It does not convey the impression of a unified form, but of fragmentary and shortbreathed

ideas, alternated and in places monotonously repeated. . . . Any of the movements could stop at various places and the listener be neither surprised nor worse off for the cessation. The Symphony does not add to Stravinsky's reputation.[5]

Downes's perception of an inorganic quality may have derived from the number of small ensemble sections in the first movement, where the juxtaposition of contrasting instrumental groups is more obvious on first hearing than is its thematic integration. This trait, plus the frequent ostinato passages, led many to compare the symphony with Stravinsky's earlier and more widely known *Le sacre du printemps*, ballet music formed to support choreography more than integrated thematic development.

It may have been some sense of this quality that led Jerome Robbins to express an interest in choreographing the symphony, but Stravinsky was against it. As a composer who had written both ballets and symphonies, he expressed artistic discomfort with symphonic forms as a basis for stage works. In his view, the two were incompatible. Nonetheless, the music has served the ballet stage many times since its introduction as a concert work.

No purely orchestral score by Stravinsky written after the Symphony in Three Movements was of equal scale or intensity. It was his *dernier cri* in the genre of the symphony as that tradition had been inherited from the late 18th century.

Dumbarton Oaks: Concerto in E-flat for Chamber Orchestra

Tempo giusto—

Allegretto—

Con moto

Stravinsky began work on the Dumbarton Oaks *Concerto on July 1937 and completed it during March of 1938. It was first performed at the private residence known as Dumbarton Oaks, near Washington, D.C., on May 8, 1938, Nadia Boulanger conducting.*

Instrumentation: *flute, clarinet, bassoon, two horns, three violins, three violas, two cellos, two double basses.*

Near the end of a concert tour of the United States and Canada in 1937, Stravinsky was a guest of Mr. and Mrs. Robert Woods Bliss at their residence, Dumbarton Oaks, near Washington, D.C. During the course of this visit, he was offered a commission for a concerto to celebrate his hosts' thirtieth wedding anniversary. Upon his return to Europe, Stravinsky forged ahead with work on the concerto, but when he received no deposit from Mrs. Bliss he asked Nadia Boulanger—composer-theorist, personal friend, and famous Parisian pedagogue—to telegram Mrs. Bliss on his behalf: "Stravinsky desires to know should begin composition for you suggest 2500 dollars accepts compose music Brandenburg Concerto dimensions."[6] The reply was apparently positive, because Stravinsky completed the work and it was performed on schedule, with Boulanger conducting in place of the composer because of Stravinsky's ill health at that time.

The concerto was named after the Bliss residence—later to become famous as a conference center, art museum, and library—but what might appear to be a straightforward sobriquet has received many twists that sometimes cloud the identity of the work. The title on Stravinsky's autograph score reads: *Dumbarton Oaks / 8-5-38 / Concerto in Mib / pour petite orchestre*. To at least some degree this was in response to the preference of Mrs. Bliss for the title *Dumbarton Oaks* rather than a formal dedication. On May 26, Stravinsky wrote to his publisher, Willi Strecker of B. Schotts Söhne, saying explicitly that the work should be called "Dumbarton Oaks Concerto in E-flat," but Strecker demurred, countering that "no one outside of America will understand the designation or be able to pronounce it, and stupid remarks may even be made about the name, since it resembles duck or frog sounds in French and German pronunciation."[7] When Stravinsky conducted the first public performance in Paris on June 16, the work was programmed as "Concerto," without reference to its origins. In further correspondence on July 25 with Strecker concerning publication of the score, Stravinsky referred to the work as "my Concerto in E flat (do not forget the flat in the contract, please!). . . ."[8] Since that time various combinations of genre, key, ensemble, and original title have surfaced, but in his personal correspondence in later years Stravinsky consistently referred to it as the "*Dumbarton Oaks* Concerto," a practice followed in the remainder of this text.

Stravinsky indicated in his telegram to Mrs. Bliss that he was proposing a work along the lines of Bach's Brandenburg Concertos, and as the work unfolded those models became more firmly established. Stravinsky's use of models has been much discussed, and some have implied that he was a composer bereft of sufficiently original ideas of his own. That view overlooks a fundamental premise underlying Stravinsky's approach to composition: he was constantly searching for new solutions to problems emerging from his perpetually inquisitive musicianship, and these models were essentially the partial solutions to those creative problems he set for himself. *Dumbarton Oaks* is not a literal copy of any of Bach's concertos but Stravinsky's response to the musical spirit of those works as identified by solo instrumentation, contrast of movements, and the character of some of the thematic material. As a work that responds in contemporary idiom to the style of earlier music, the concerto lies within the parameters of Stravinsky's neoclassical endeavors in the same sense as the Symphony in C that was to follow.

Stravinsky's gesture toward Bach's Brandenburg Concertos finds as one of its most direct realizations the independent treatment of the fifteen solo instruments, but all are assimilated into a larger ensemble; there are solo passages, but no cadenzas to highlight an individual performer. Three movements in the traditional fast–slow–fast sequence are linked by a continuing musical flow and the strikingly tonal cadences that define them: the first movement closes on an F octave that serves as a dominant leading to the B-flat of the second movement, and that slow interlude in turn concludes on a clearly stated B-flat harmony that becomes dominant for the E-flat of the last movement.

The texture and thematic material in the opening measures of the first movement offer one of the closest similarities to the music of Bach, but the remainder does not expand on an alternation of tutti and ritornello passages in the manner of an earlier concerto grosso. From this opening contrapuntal interplay, a motive emerges that expands upon the interval of a fourth in the same way that it appears in the Symphony in C, a score that was in its germinal stages at about the same time. This motive ultimately becomes the subject for a loosely construed fugue marking the central part of the movement.

The *Allegretto* offers a study in timbre and texture. The main theme alternates among violins, violas, and clarinet in a manner that in its visual impression resembles some of the "open" scores of contemporary serial composers. A midsection involving the full ensemble creates marked contrast, and when the theme returns for the third part of this A–B–A' design, the flute plays a florid arabesque above the dialogue between strings and clarinet.

The theme and character of the third movement become a march reaching one of several climaxes with a cleverly constructed fugue presenting the subject in both overlapping entries and inversion. This contrapuntal intricacy might be considered as another gesture toward the perceived traditions of Bach's music or as a balance to the fugue in the first movement, or both. The march closes with a Stravinsky trademark: a rhythmic pattern of two beats shifting in and out of synchronization with measures of duple and triple meter.

When the *Dumbarton Oaks* Concerto was heard in Europe, many criticized Stravinsky severely for what they perceived as stylistic imitation. Borrowing of thematic materials from earlier sources was a long-established practice, but the musical reference to Bach's Brandenburg Concertos struck both critics and some fellow composers as creative sterility. With the benefit of a longer perspective, it seems that in this work Stravinsky had begun to come to terms with traditions of concert hall music, maintaining his own musical language while writing in a format compatible with the repertory of traditional concert programs in which he was appearing as conductor with increasing frequency. One reason for any modern composer to follow a model is that a perceptible exemplar offers to the listener a comprehensible frame of reference for something that otherwise might leave the uninformed at sea. When original musical thought is couched in a recognizable mold, the listener has the best of both worlds, the old and the new. So it is with the *Dumbarton Oaks* Concerto.

Concerto for Piano and Wind Instruments

Largo—Allegro—Maestoso

Largo

Allegro

Stravinsky composed the Concerto for Piano and Wind Instruments between July 1923 and April 1924, revising it in 1950. It was first per-

formed in Paris on May 22, 1924, by Serge Koussevitzky and his orchestra, with Stravinsky as piano soloist.

Instrumentation: *piccolo, two flutes, two oboes, English horn, two clarinets, two bassoons (the second doubling contrabassoon), four horns, four trumpets, three trombones, tuba, timpani, solo piano, and six contrabasses.*

The development of Stravinsky's Concerto for Piano and Wind Instruments followed a circuitous path. Following the completion of the full score in 1924, he prepared a two-piano arrangement that was performed privately prior to the orchestral premiere at the Koussevitzky Concerts in May. The two-piano version was published in 1924, the full score in 1936, and a revised version in 1950. Most of the revisions followed those found in the two-piano arrangement, largely because Stravinsky used the keyboard score as a working draft that he changed piecemeal as the work evolved. In its early stages, he did not conceive the work as a piano concerto. Only during the creative process did he gradually realize that the musical material lent itself most effectively to the piano. At a time when the musical substance of most concertos was generated by the capabilities of the solo instrument, the primacy of the musical material over the medium was a fundamental reversal of procedure.

The choice of an orchestra of wind instruments reflected a wider array of influences. In other important works—*Le sacre du printemps* and *Symphony of Psalms* in particular—Stravinsky favored wind instruments for their sharply contrasting colors and natural quality of aspiration, the latter an element he came to regard and exploit as a characteristic expressive feature. Further, he felt that a wind ensemble would provide a better contrast to the percussiveness of the solo instruments as well as complementing the natural decay of the piano sound. And in a still broader context, he was working to counteract the prevailing opulence of the orchestra as it existed in his earlier works: "Orchestration has become a source of enjoyment independent of the music, and the time has surely come to put things in their proper places."[9] The implied clarity of line and texture was also much in keeping with musical elements of neoclassicism that have been held up as traits of this period in Stravinsky's life.

The concerto marked the beginning of a period when Stravinsky was heavily involved with the piano as both composer and performer. As a composer he habitually worked at the piano, and the physical properties of the keyboard often influenced some of his distinctive musical structures; the famous *Petrushka* chord and the polychord underlying the *Augurs of Spring* in *Le sacre du printemps* are among the best-known examples. *Petrushka* originated as an attempt at an earlier piano concerto, and his arrangement for solo piano of three movements from that score, dedicated to Artur Rubinstein, has become a staple of 20th-century piano literature. Shortly before he began the Concerto for Piano, Stravinsky had completed *Les noces* (1923), four choreographic scenes calling for a percussion orchestra centered around four pianos. In an interview published in 1926, he claimed that in the context of other works he was attempting to restore the piano to its proper role as a percussion instrument. Shortly after the concerto, he produced his Sonata for Piano (1924), the *Serenade en La* (1925), and a few years later the Capriccio for Piano and Orchestra (1929) and the Concerto for Two Pianos (1935).

As a performer, Stravinsky reserved the solo part of the piano concerto for himself for five years, during which time he played the work at least forty times, working with some of the most prominent conductors of the era. In his student days, Stravinsky had developed his pianistic skills to the point of performing Felix Mendelssohn's G minor Concerto and sight-reading opera scores, and he had frequently appeared as accompanist for some of his own works. The prospect of performing his own concerto was not part of his original plan; reportedly it was Koussevitzky who suggested that he assume the solo role (Artur Rubinstein later also laid claim to the same persuasive influence). Stravinsky hesitated in this venture, questioning whether he could develop the technique and endurance necessary to perform a work requiring sustained effort and concentration.

To prepare himself, he began practicing exercises by Carl Czerny (the *sine qua non* of rudimentary piano technique), which, by his own account, was a task to which he had to devote many hours a day. As a soloist on the concert platform, Stravinsky struggled with the problems common to most performers: stage fright and the necessity of maintaining a polished technical edge in the execution of passagework. In later years, he described his experience at the premiere when he could not remember the beginning of the slow movement and had to rely on hummed cues from Koussevitzky to begin the opening passage. Similar problems continued over the years, and Stravinsky came to doubt that he had the mechanical memory necessary for solo performance. His view of the demands placed upon a solo pianist compared to those of conducting were reflected in the fees he requested: $1,000 for a performance in the piano concerto, $500 for appearance as a conductor. Those same figures may explain in part his perseverance in the role of solo pianist. Later in life, he acknowledged that at the time it was necessary to continue performing in order to earn a living.

The element of contrast that traditionally supports concerto writing is expressed through contrasting timbres more than through contrasting themes. The traditional three-movement plan encompasses two movements of nearly equal length followed by a finale dominated by patterned figuration for the soloist. Dotted rhythms of a stately march frame the first movement, suggesting the character of a Baroque overture. In the first movement, an exact reprise of the principal material approximately midway in the *Allegro* suggests a sonata design, but the statement and extension of materials introduced by the soloist are more obvious to a listener than any established formal plan. Throughout this movement, the prevailing motoric drive and extension of motivic patterns have reminded many listeners of music by Sebastian Bach, a perception both deriving from and contributing to the premise of neoclassicism often ascribed to Stravinsky's music of this period.

The *Largo* offers marked contrast through the lyricism of both the solo piano and supporting winds, particularly the horn. Two cadenzas divide the movement into an approximation of a three-part design, while at the same time they offer the most noticeable examples of traditional pianistic flourishes found anywhere in the concerto. The closing *Allegro* quickly establishes and maintains passagework for the solo piano that seems to regenerate itself through its own momentum. At a few points this subsides into patterned figuration in support of a solo wind instrument, but the prevailing character builds in intensity until a march, reminiscent of the opening measures of the concerto, interrupts the energetic flow before the whole concludes with a short, precipitous coda.

The Concerto for Piano and Wind Instruments found greater favor with most audiences than it did with professional musicians and critics. One of the first of the musical figures to comment was the Russian composer Nikolai Medtner. He attended the premiere in Paris, admitted to enjoying the three prewar ballets that shared the program, but described the concerto with sardonic wit:

> But then the composer appeared with his new concerto and gave me such a box on the ear for my silly sentimentality that I couldn't bear to stay until the end of *The Rite of Spring*. . . . I walked out. But the public . . . steadfastly withstood every slap in the face and every humiliation, and what is more, rewarded the composer with deafening applause. . . .[10]

A few months later, Sergei Prokofiev described the work as an affectation of neoclassicism that he found misdirected: "Stravinsky's Piano Concerto is fashioned after Bach and Handel, and that doesn't particularly appeal to me. . . . Here and there contemporary syncopated dance rhythms appear, which considerably freshens the scratched-up Bach."[11]

Reactions in the press became increasingly negative during the five-year span of Stravinsky's performances, and by 1929 vitriolic comments had become usual. An unidentified writer for the *Sunday Times* (London) thought that "the pleasure of seeing the composer of *Petrouchka* again was equaled only by the pain of hearing the composer of the piano concerto. It was sad to think that the one-time man of genius had degenerated into the manufacturer of this ugly and feeble commonplace."[12] These responses may have been the result of Stravinsky's dry, finely articulated performance, a texture unfamiliar in piano concertos and unexpected by those still consumed by the sensuous scores of the late 19th century that enjoyed current favor. As the clarity of line and texture associated with neoclassicism achieved greater understanding, Stravinsky's Concerto for Piano and Wind Instruments came to occupy a singular niche in the repertory of both the piano and the wind ensemble.

Concerto in D for Violin and Orchestra

Toccata

Aria I

Aria II

Capriccio

With many interruptions for concert engagements and the relocation of his residence, Stravinsky composed the Violin Concerto between October 1930 and late September 1931. It was first performed in Berlin on October 23, 1931, by the Berlin Radio Orchestra, conducted by Stravinsky, with Samuel Dushkin as violin soloist.

Instrumentation: *piccolo, two flutes, two oboes, English horn, piccolo clarinet in E-flat, two clarinets in B-flat, three bassoons (the third doubling contrabassoon), four horns, three trumpets, three trombones, tuba, timpani, bass drum, solo violin, and strings.*

The impetus for the Violin Concerto came from Willi Strecker of B. Schotts Söhne, publisher of several Stravinsky scores. Strecker suggested to Stravinsky that the young American violinist, Samuel Dushkin, already an established soloist with a flair for contemporary music and a personal friend of Strecker, would be a sympathetic collaborator in such a venture. Stravinsky hesitated because he felt that, as he was not a violinist himself, he would have difficulty resolving problems posed by a major concerto for the instrument. His reservations led him to contact Paul Hindemith, one of the best violists of the era as well as a prominent composer who began his career as a violinist. Hindemith assured Stravinsky that his lack of familiarity with the violin could well be an asset rather than an impediment, in that habitual finger patterns would not condition the flow of musical ideas. Stravinsky eventually took further comfort from his earlier successes in writing for the solo violin in *Petrushka* and *L'histoire du soldat*, and the prospect of a commission carried its own allure.

As the project developed, the concerto was commissioned by Blair Fairchild, an American composer and musical expatriate in Paris, who had adopted Dushkin, and the young violinist himself came to work with Stravinsky on a regular basis. The prospect of working with a virtuoso further concerned Stravinsky, because he was well aware of the penchant of most audiences for bravura display in concertos and the inclination of young soloists to fulfill those expectations. Fortunately, in Samuel Dushkin he found a musically sympathetic partner who was a born violinist, broadly cultured, and willing to place his talents at the service of the music. During most of the time Stravinsky was working on the concerto, he conferred with Dushkin on a near-daily basis as the violinist experimented with newly composed passages and offered suggestions on idiomatic writing for the solo violin while he was learning the work. The two musicians developed a lasting rapport and, according to Dushkin's account, Stravinsky often included the violinist's practical suggestions in the score. This interaction between composer and performer resembled similar exchanges between Mendelssohn and Ferdinand David or Brahms and Joseph Joachim in the preparation of those composers' concertos, and for the same reason: the composers, primarily pianists themselves, were relying on the practical skills of performing violinists in their efforts to create a work well suited to the instrument.

Stravinsky also prepared for the task by studying the violin concertos of the standard repertory (particularly Vivaldi, Bach, Beethoven, and Brahms), although he later claimed that they offered him no satisfactory model because, in his opinion, they did not represent the best achievements of their creators. He began promoting the work well before any part of it was completed. On December 25, 1930, he wrote to Strecker in agitation that the premiere had been promised to the Berlin Radio Orchestra, while he (Stravinsky) had made a similar promise to the Amsterdam Concertgebouw Orchestra. On May 18, 1931, he wrote again, inquiring about the status of the engraved printing plates. Evidently the work was being set in type as fast as individual movements were completed, because on September 19 Stravinsky advised Strecker that he had come to realize that each movement of the concerto should have a title, so that audiences would have some idea of the character of each movement. Stravinsky may have felt some pressure for completion because of the approaching premiere in October, but it is also clear that he had become immersed in the project and enjoyed working with the younger musician. The success of the venture with Dushkin subsequently led Stravinsky to compose his *Duo Concertant* for violin and piano as a work he and Dushkin could perform together. To the finished manuscript of the Violin Concerto he added an inscription that eloquently acknowledged his indebtedness to the violinist: "This work has been created under my direction . . . by Samuel Dushkin for whom I maintain a profound gratitude and a great admiration for the high artistry of his playing."

The finished concerto consists of four movements. Both central movements carry the title *Aria*, while the outside movements are identified by titles more frequently associated with earlier music. These titles and some of the passagework have elicited comparison with works by Sebastian Bach, a comparison that Stravinsky did not entirely reject. Each movement opens with a wide-spaced motto chord typical of much of Stravinsky's writing, but one that at first dismayed Dushkin. During one of their frequent luncheons, Stravinsky jotted a three-note chord on a scrap of paper and asked whether it could be played. Dushkin replied that it could not, to which the composer responded with obvious disappointment. Returning to his quarters, Dushkin tried the chord on the violin and discovered that it could, indeed, be played because of its unusual register, and immediately telephoned Stravinsky that it was possible. When the concerto was completed, he came to realize the reason for Stravinsky's disappointment at his original response, because he could see that the motto chord generated the opening measure of each movement and had become a musical signature for the concerto as a whole. In Stravinsky's own words, the chord was his "passport" to the concerto.

The *Toccata* opens with the "passport" chord played by the solo violin, followed by a figure in the trumpets that becomes a basic motive for the remainder of the movement. A second subject in A major and a reprise of the opening motive about midway in the movement suggest a sonata design, but the continuing expansion of motivic material and the interplay between soloist and orchestra play more important roles than any traditional structural plan. The motivic expansion and passagework end abruptly with an emphatically tonal cadence on D major.

The two *Arias* stand in as much contrast to each other as they do to the energetic outer movements of *Toccata* and *Capriccio*. *Aria I* opens with the "passport" chord, then proceeds in the character of a dignified scherzo movement. It is punctuated about two thirds of the way through by two sustained and interruptive diminished-seventh harmonies that seem designed to bring events to a halt, before the whole operation finally closes on another clearly defined cadence on D. In contrast, *Aria II* serves as the true slow movement for the concerto. The solo violin plays the by-now-familiar motto chord before widely spaced harmonies assume the task of providing resonance for the florid embellishments of the soloist. Two subsequent references to the opening measure divide the movement into three different sections, maintaining the tradition of three-part division for an aria but offering little suggestion of a return to the opening or any reference to an arch design.

The *Capriccio* lives up to its title in the exuberant figuration of the solo part. The general plan resembles a rondo design before it reaches a final tutti, introduced by a virtuoso dialogue between the concerto soloist and one solo violin (presumably the concert master) from the orchestra. This, too, reaches its conclusion on an emphatic cadence on D, designed, it seems, to be a closing affirmation of the tonic center that, for much of the concerto, has served mostly as a point of departure.

Dushkins's account of the premiere described it as a great success at the same time that it offered a pungent comment on Stravinsky, man and artist:

> Discussions were plentiful during the days following the perfor-mance as always after a new Stravinsky work. The press was divided, as usual. Some critics were enthusiastic. Some criticisms were vicious, as usual. Stravinsky was very angry. "Why are you so upset"? I asked him. . . . "No one can please everyone." Knowing him to be religious, I risked adding, "Even God doesn't please everyone." He jumped up and shouted, "*Especially* God!"[13]

The violinist Jascha Heifitz refused to learn the concerto because of the "unviolinistic" motto chord, while other violinists maintained and have consistently proved that it was perfectly playable. George Balanchine used the concerto for his ballet *Balustrade* in 1940, a chore-ographic setting that Stravinsky regarded as the most satisfactory visual realization of any of his works. The frequent performances of Stravinsky's Violin Concerto eloquently verify that the work has assumed its place in the repertory of 20th-century violin concertos.

Symphony of Psalms

[Prelude]—

[Double Fugue]—

[Symphonic Allegro]

Stravinsky began work on the Symphony of Psalms *early in 1930, completing the score in August. It was first performed in Brussels on December 13, 1930, by the Philharmonic Society of Brussels, Ernst Ansermet conducting.*

> **Ensemble**: *mixed chorus, five flutes (the fifth doubling piccolo), four*
> *oboes, English horn, three bassoons, contrabassoon, four horns, piccolo*
> *trumpet in D, four trumpets in C, three trombones, tuba, timpani, bass*
> *drum, two pianos, harp, cellos, and double basses.*

Since its first appearance, the *Symphony of Psalms* has been regarded as one of the masterpieces of 20th-century choral music. It should be understood that the title *Symphony* here refers to the element of ensemble performance rather than to the established genre of the symphony as it is recognized in the traditions of classical instrumental music. Stravinsky at first titled the work *Symphonie psalmodique*. When questioned about the meaning of *psalmodique*, he posed the alternative *Symphonie psalmique*, but that, also, failed to reflect precisely his thinking:

> To me the word "psalmique" indicates only that the Symphony contains some psalms sung by soloists or choirs; that is all. I was looking for a brief title which would seize the special character of my *Symphony*. In short, this is not a symphony into which I have put some psalms which are sung, but on the contrary, it is the singing of the psalms which I symphonize. . . .[14]

Apparently Stravinsky had some difficulties with titles for the individual movements as well. When the score was published, these were identified by metronomic tempo indications, numerical distinctions that have often been repeated as titles of movements in lieu of the more normal character words. In correspondence with the conductor Ansermet prior to the first performance and in the program accompanying that European premiere, Stravinsky applied the movement titles *Prelude*, *Double Fugue*, and *Symphonic Allegro*, maintaining that these terms accurately reflected the substance of the individual movements.

The *Symphony* was brought to fruition through a commission from the conductor Serge Koussevitzky for a work to celebrate the fiftieth anniversary of the Boston Symphony Orchestra and bore a title to that effect: "*Cette symphonie composée à la gloire de DIEU est dédiée au 'Boston Symphony Orchestra' à l'occasion du cinquantenaire de son existence.*" The contract with Boston, in which Stravinsky asked for $6,000, was signed on December 12, 1929. Prior to that, he had responded to his publisher's request for something popular with a decision to create a work that would be universally admired. It remains unclear whether the discussion between publisher and composer grew out of the possibility of a major commission, or whether Stravinsky had already entertained thoughts about such a work and allowed the Boston commission to serve as a catalyst for his plans. He must have had some plans for the work beyond its performance in Boston, because he asked that the contractual stipulations addressing Boston's claim to the first performance be modified to allow him to present the *Symphony* elsewhere if the Boston Symphony did not perform the work by November 15, 1930. This did indeed come about, because the first American performance in Boston did not take place until December 19, six days after the European premiere in Brussels.

Winds prevail in the orchestral ensemble, violins and violas are absent, and Stravinsky indicated that the chorus should include children's voices, although these could be replaced by female sopranos and altos if a children's choir were unavailable. At one point he considered the organ as an accompanying instrument but dismissed it because, in his own terms, "the monster never breathes," referring to the organ's idiomatic characteristic of unremitting sostenuto. At several times in his career Stravinsky voiced a fondness for wind instruments because of their natural breathing qualities, a characteristic that found a pronounced expression in his articulation of the instrumental fugue in the second movement, where breath marks separate the first five notes of each subject.

By his own account, Stravinsky turned to psalm texts for their universality, or popular access, and to Psalm 150 in particular for its dictum of praising the Lord through music. This became the basis for the third movement, the first he composed, and in turn suggested Psalm 38: 13–14 and Psalm 39: 2–4 for the first and second movements. The despair of the sinner who cannot hear (*Prelude*) is followed by a supplication for guidance (*Double Fugue*), the whole concluded by an admonition to praise the Lord with instruments (*Symphonic Allegro*). Stravinsky began with Slavic texts but later, presumably because of his wish for wide accessibility, turned to the Latin texts of the Vulgate. These texts offer an element of continuity throughout the work, as does the musical texture of the mixed chorus. Beyond that, many of the musical materials derive from series of major and minor thirds found in the trumpet and harp accompaniment at the *Allegro* sections of the third movement. This was the first part of the work Stravinsky composed, and as the preceding movement developed he expanded the pattern of thirds to become a germinal figure for the entire work.

The second movement is an ingeniously constructed double fugue, one for instruments and another for voices, which the composer described as one of his most overt uses of musical symbolism:

> An upside-down pyramid of fugues, it begins with a purely instrumental fugue of limited compass and employs only solo instruments. The restriction to treble range was the novelty of this initial fugue, but the limitation to flutes and oboes proved its most difficult compositional problem. The subject was developed from the sequence of thirds used as an ostinato in the first movement. The next and higher stage of the upside-down pyramid is the human fugue, which does not begin without instrumental help for the reason that I modified the structure as I composed and decided to overlap instruments and voices to give the material more development; but the human choir is heard *a capella* after that. The human fugue also represents a higher level in the architectural symbolism by the fact that it expands into the bass register. The third stage, the upside-down foundation, unites the two fugues.[15]

What Stravinsky does not tell us is that the human fugue at its beginning is accompanied by the instrumental fugue, and the opening motive of the instrumental subject returns a number of times in rhythmic and intervalic expansion. The entire ensemble is thereby closely integrated, and fulfills the composer's stated intent that instruments and voices were to be equally important.

The third movement drew on some of Stravinsky's established procedures and, as it was the first to be completed, generated materials that appear in the preceding movements as well. In retrospect, it stands as something of a matrix for the entire work. The setting of the opening *Alleluia, Laudate* DOMINUM returns approximately midway in the movement and again at the end, functioning as a unifying point of reference. The *Laudate* is set to a pattern of a rising semitone and falling fourth that several years later would become the germinal motive for the Symphony in C; here it becomes a musical signature for *Laudate* (praise), the main thrust of the text in Psalm 150. Stravinsky described the following *Allegro*, the main body of the movement, as the result of an inspired vision of Elijah's chariot climbing to the heavens, and claimed that never before had he written anything so literal as the rapid triplets played by piano and winds, representing the galloping of horses. The music unfolds with high energy, interrupted at one point by the opening *Alleluia* and supported at several points by ostinatos. The most extended of these, played by harp and piano, begins midway in the coda and extends to the concluding *Alleluia*; as with so many other structural features in the *Symphony of Psalms*, it shows a carefully conceived design of its own. A four-measure ostinato divides into two subordinate phrases of two measures each that, in essence, mirror each other. The effect is one of wheels working inside of wheels, with textural references for guideposts along the way. But for Stravinsky these texts are more important for the sounds of the syllables than for their literary prosody. In the final analysis, sonorous considerations lie at the heart of this musical edifice.

Few works by Stravinsky have met with comparable success. Even his usual detractors were muted by the *Symphony of Psalms*. One of the most eloquent tributes came from the French composer Francis Poulenc:

> Stravinsky has never deceived us, but rarely, also, has he offered such a beautiful surprise. . . . What is particularly to my taste in this new masterpiece is the absence of grandiloquence. . . . It is a work of peace. . . . One can only marvel at Stravinsky's powers of renewal. I salute you, Jean-Sebastian Stravinsky.[16]

Orchestral Works Derived from Music for the Theater

Stravinsky's first pronounced impact on music was through his ballet scores, and most of those have been performed in the concert hall as independent works, divorced from the original choreography. Part of what seems to be his innate talent for ballet may have come from his Russian heritage and its tradition of ballet, but beyond that he was particularly adept at expressing the dramatic core of a stage situation by musical means, creating highly focused scores of clearly defined dramatic intensity. Musical considerations prevail, the composer's knowledge of choreography and its coordination with the music notwithstanding. In an interview taken from a radio broadcast of 1938, the composer made it clear that he designed his theater music to be able to be performed independent of the stage:

> When I am writing for the theatre, my first anxiety is to make certain my music has an independent existence and to guard it from the danger of subjecting itself to the demands of the other theatrical elements involved. In my view the relationship between music and these extra-musical elements can be presented only in parallel, or in association. . . . If in earlier works like *The Firebird* I did not always follow the precepts I am now preaching, I quickly realized the vital need of doing so; and as early as *Petrushka* it will be found that the music is constructed on symphonic lines. My later scores are conceived and constructed as separate musical entities, independent of their scene purpose; and because of that I attach as much importance to their concert performance as to their stage presentation.[17]

By the end of the 20th century, several of these ballet scores have come to be among his most frequently performed creations, some transferred to the concert hall nearly in their original format, others in both ballet score and suite form, and at least one known almost exclusively as a *divertimento* drawn from the original ballet score.

Divertimento: Symphonic Suite from *Le baiser de la fée*

Sinfonia—

Danses suisses

Scherzo

Pas de deux: Adagio—Variation—Coda

Stravinsky prepared the score for Le baiser de la fée *(The Fairy's Kiss) between April and October 1928. It was first performed in Paris by Ida Rubinstein's company on November 27, 1928, with Stravinsky conducting. Excerpts from that ballet assembled as a concert suite were performed in Geneva in February 1931 with Ernst Ansermet conducting, and Stravinsky established the final shape of the suite in 1934, revising the score in 1949.*

Instrumentation: *piccolo, two flutes, two oboes, English horn, three
clarinets (the third doubling bass clarinet), two bassoons, four horns,
three trumpets, three trombones, tuba, timpani, bass drum, harp, and
strings.*

The ballet took shape in 1928 in response to a commission from Ida
Rubinstein for a ballet designed for her dance company. Late in 1927
Alexander Benois, with whom Stravinsky had collaborated in previous
ballets, had suggested a production that would honor the music of
Tchaikovsky and even provided a list of nonorchestral works that could
serve as a basis for the undertaking. Responding to both stimuli,
Stravinsky produced a score based on a number of piano works and
solo songs by Tchaikovsky, conceiving the whole as a tribute to the
most famous composer of Imperial Russia on the 35th anniversary of
his death. The plot came from Hans Christian Andersen's *The Ice
Maiden*, the tale of a fairy who marks a young boy with a kiss. She then
returns years later on the eve of his wedding—presumably the happiest
day of his life—to mark him once more with a kiss, claiming him for her
own and drawing him into the depths of icy waters to preserve his happiness forever. Stravinsky compressed the story, retitled it *Le baiser de la
fée*, and prefaced the score with a dedication to Tchaikovsky that drew
on the substance of the scenario: "I dedicate this ballet to the memory
of Peter Tchaikovsky by allying his muse to the fairy, and in this manner the ballet becomes an allegory. The muse has marked him with the
fatal kiss, whose mysterious imprint is felt in all the work of the great
artist."

   More than thirty years after the ballet had been written, Stravinsky
attempted to distinguish between those portions of the score that were
his own and those based on music by Tchaikovsky. Time, faulty memory, and intruding assumptions combined to render that list both
incomplete and inaccurate, but later studies by Lawrence Morton and
Richard Taruskin have identified the extensive list of Tchaikovsky
melodies Stravinsky assimilated into the score. Broadly considered, the
element of artistic sympathy between the composer and his model is
more important than literal quotation; Tchaikovsky's melodies provide
much of the substance, but Stravinsky gives all of them his own stamp
without losing the essence of the earlier composer's spirit.

   The result differs from Stravinsky's earlier essay into borrowed materials in *Pulcinella*, a score based on themes attributed to the 18th-century Italian composer Giovanni Battista Pergolesi. There, the music was arranged in a manner to preserve its 18th-century character; here, the borrowed materials are recomposed in a style that, in the opinion of many, improves upon the original source. Further, Stravinsky acknowledged that he was unfamiliar with most of the music of Pergolesi before he began that project, but he knew the works of Tchaikovsky thoroughly and reveled in this music that had been dear to his heart from childhood. *Le baiser de la fée* emerges as a pastiche that assimilates works by Tchaikovsky into a substantially different soundscape.

Stravinsky created the *Divertimento* from the larger ballet score through a process of selection rather than revision; he assembled sections in their entirety without rescoring them, cutting portions to achieve the desired balance, a process most clearly described in the following outline.

Divertimento	*Le baiser de la fée*
Sinfonia	Prologue and Scene One, minus 93 measures between 27 and 40
Danses suisses	Scene Two, "A Village Fête," minus the last 108 measures
Scherzo	Scene Three, "By the Mill," Introduction, followed by deletion of the material between rehearsal numbers 131 and 140, 141 and 154, and 155 and 157
Pas de deux	Dances two through four (B–D) from the *Pas de deux* of the ballet score, with a new ending

Through cross-reference it is possible to identify the musical sources for most sections of the *Divertimento*, but as an independent orchestral work the connection with Tchaikovsky is more tenuous than in the ballet score. Stravinsky often conducted the *Divertimento* on his concert tours. He enjoyed conducting the piece because in it he had approached composition and orchestration differently for the purpose of creating music that could be readily grasped by audiences on first hearing. The new style was presumably the expansion on melodies of another composer, and the clarity of orchestration reflects the relatively sparse scoring that pervades the *Divertimento*; in spite of a large ensemble, there are few places where all instruments play simultaneously.

Most of the opening *Sinfonia* expands on some portion of Tchaikovsky's *Berceuse pendant l'orage* (Lullaby during the Storm), a melody that opens both works and, in the ballet, returns near the end as the fairy makes her final claim on her chosen one. The *Danses suisses*, originally music in support of a Swiss village festival, incorporates as one of several high points a waltz based on Tchaikovsky's *Natha-valse* of 1882. Certainly a dance is appropriate to a festival scene, although Swiss villagers might be expected to engage in something more rustic than a waltz. The *Scherzo*, assembled from several disjunct sections of the original ballet score, offers a musical balance to the preceding movements through its characteristically quick tempo and thin scoring. Everything progresses quickly and clearly to the closing *Pas de deux*, in which the second, third, and fourth virtuoso dances of the original proceed to a decisive close.

As music drawn from a ballet, the *Divertimento* expands upon distinct sections marked by rhythmic vitality more than through the development or reprise of those materials. Stravinsky elaborates on Tchaikovsky's melodies in a manner that comes forth as his own. This work is less ascetic than many of his scores, but consistently efficient and thoroughly imaginative.

Jeu de cartes: Ballet en trois donnes

Deal I: Introduction—Pas d'action—Dance of the Joker—Little Waltz—

Deal II: Introduction—March—Variations of the Four Queens— Variations of the Jack of Hearts and Coda—March and Ensemble—

Deal III: Introduction—Waltz—Combat between Spades and Hearts—Triumph of the Hearts

According to Stravinsky's retrospective account, he began work on Jeu de cartes *in December 1935, completing it in late November 1936. It was first performed at New York's Metropolitan Opera House on April 27, 1937, by the American Ballet, Stravinsky conducting, with choreography by George Balanchine, William Dollar in the role of the Joker.*

Instrumentation: two flutes (the second doubling piccolo), two oboes (the second doubling English horn), two clarinets, two bassoons, four horns, two trumpets, three trombones, tuba, timpani, bass drum, and strings.

The impetus for *Jeu de cartes* came from a commission by Lincoln Kirsten and Edward Warburg in June 1936 for the newly formed American Ballet, later to become the New York City Ballet. Stravinsky invited Jean Cocteau to collaborate in the venture, but Cocteau declined, and the scenario that emerged was Stravinsky's own. His plan grew from a childhood experience during a visit to a German spa with his parents: the instrumental fanfare that opens each "Deal" representing the croupier's cry of *"Ein neues Spiel, ein neues Glück,"* as Stravinsky recalled the experience many years later.

Comparing this scenario with Stravinsky's other ballets will reveal one common dramatic feature: a discordant character who is evil (Kaschey), mischievous (Pulcinella), or at least pitiable (Petrushka) discomfits the others but finally gets his just deserts. Here it is the Joker who disrupts the normal progress of the game, but his fate remains unresolved on the stage and in the music. The score presents the title in French (*Jeu de cartes*), English (*A Game of Cards*), and German (*Kartenspiel*), and on at least one occasion a performance was advertised as *A Poker Game*, based on the play of cards represented in the scenario. To this Stravinsky objected strenuously, but otherwise he indicated no preference for a title other than his consistent reference to *Jeu de cartes* in his correspondence and conversation books.

It was in discussing this ballet that Stravinsky declared most emphatically that musical elements should prevail in his theater compositions, even though they had roots in the choreography. Describing *Jeu de cartes* to the conductor Ernst Ansermet more than a year later, he continued to maintain that the music was thoroughly symphonic, offering no descriptive elements that would hinder orchestral development. Stravinsky would later describe *Jeu de cartes* as his most "German" work, possibly referring to the childhood experience that served as inspiration for the scenario, but more likely thinking about the symphonic development that, in his perception, drew on musical traditions of 19th-century Germany.

His focus on the musical structure of *Jeu de cartes* came to the fore in a protracted disagreement with Ansermet over cuts the conductor proposed in concert performances. Stravinsky maintained that cuts were totally unnecessary and forbade Ansermet to delete any material. In subsequent correspondence, Stravinsky continued to reinforce his stance, maintaining that the proposed cuts would cripple his little *March*, which had its own unique design within the total work. Evidently Ansermet persisted, because Stravinsky wrote to his publisher that, because of Ansermet's action, the orchestra parts would have to be recalled. He followed with another letter to the concert societies of Winterthur and Zurich stating that he would allow *Jeu de cartes* to be performed only in its entirety or as separately identified fragments. Beyond the frustrations of a composer who saw one of his creations altered by what he perceived as an unsympathetic conductor, it is clear that Stravinsky considered the work an organic entity defined by its musical materials and structure, independent from the original choreography. It is that quality as much as any other that has contributed to the success of the work in the concert hall.

The music is continuous throughout, but a repeated introductory fanfare—the invocation of the croupier's cry recalled from Stravinsky's childhood—announces the beginning of each new shuffle of the cards and returns at the close in distorted guise, representing in a dramatic sense the defeat of the Joker and in a musical context a return to a central theme. The final harmony and unresolved seventh chord will pique any listener's curiosity, and appropriately so, for who knows what awaits the Joker! Within this framework, Stravinsky created a number of short, self-contained sections of witty music marked by their pronouncedly different character.

A generous repertory of allusions to well-known works from the concert hall adds a touch of ironic whimsy to the whole undertaking, reminding one at times of the musical eclecticism of Charles Ives. The first variation of Deal II recalls Beethoven's Eighth Symphony, the fourth refers to Johann Strauss's *Die Fledermaus*. The *Waltz* in Deal III was surely inspired by Ravel's *La Valse*, and most pronounced of all is the famous theme from Gioachino Rossini's *Il barbiere di Siviglia* as it appears in the following section. Careful scrutiny shows other references to familiar fare, all bearing Stravinsky's own trenchant musical stamp. One needs to keep in mind that this clever score originated as musical illumination for a choreographic game of chance in which the Joker, at times, runs wild.

The premiere of *Jeu de cartes* was coupled with *Apollo Musagetes* and *Le baiser de la fée*, the whole program being a celebration of Stravinsky as both conductor and composer at the end of his third and very successful American tour. The review in the *New York Times* of April 28, 1937, acknowledged that Stravinsky received an ovation, as was to be expected, but concluded that it was difficult to remember that these relatively smaller ballets were created by the same composer who had written *Petrushka* and *Les Noces*. In subsequent decades, the musical integrity of the score, the clever allusions to other familiar works, and the always colorful orchestration have combined to establish *Jeu de cartes* as a popular success in the context of Stravinsky's music for the theater.

Suites from *L'oiseau de feu*

Suite Taken from the Story of *L'oiseau de feu* (1910)

Introduction—Kashchey's Enchanted Garden—Appearance and Dance of the Firebird—Supplication of the Firebird—The Princesses' Game with the Golden Apples—The Princesses' Round Dance—Infernal Dance of all Kashchey's Subjects

Stravinsky composed the music for the ballet L'oiseau de feu *between November 1909 and May 1910. It was first performed by the Ballets Russes at the Opera House in Paris on June 25, 1910, conducted by Gabriel Pierné, with Mikhail Fokine, Tamara Karsavina, and Alexis Bulgakov in the principal roles.*

Instrumentation: *four flutes (the third and fourth doubling piccolo), three oboes, English horn, three clarinets (the third doubling piccolo clarinet in D), bass clarinet, three bassoons (the third doubling contrabassoon II), contrabassoon I, four horns, three trumpets, three trombones, tuba (also three trumpets, two tenor tubas, two bass tubas on stage), timpani, bass drum, cymbals, tam-tam, triangle, tambourine, glockenspiel, xylophone, celesta, three harps, piano, and strings*

Suite from *L'oiseau de feu* (1919)

Introduction—The Firebird and Its Dance—Variations—Round Dance of the Princesses—Infernal Dance of King Kashchey—Berceuse—Finale

*The Second Suite was first conducted by Ernst Ansermet in April 1919
with reduced instrumentation: two flutes (one doubling piccolo), two
oboes (the second doubling English horn), two clarinets, two bassoons,
four horns, two trumpets, three trombones, tuba, bass drum, cymbals,
triangle, xylophone, piano, harp, and strings.*

Firebird Ballet Suite (1945)

Introduction—Prelude and Dance of the Firebird—Variations—

Pantomime I—Pas de deux: Firebird and Ivan Tsarevich—

Pantomime II—Pantomime III—Rondo—Infernal Dance—
Lullaby—

Final Hymn

*The Third Suite, prepared in April 1945, was first performed at New
York's Metropolitan Opera House on October 24, 1945, with Jascha
Horenstein conducting and the same instrumentation as the 1919 suite
but without the English horn and with the addition of a snare drum.*

*Since 1945, the complete ballet music has frequently been per-
formed as a concert piece, thereby making available four different versions of L'oiseau de feu. Of the three suites drawn from that original
score, the 1919 version is the best known. The differences among the
suites lie in the orchestration, and to a lesser degree in the musical
materials. For the most part, changes to the original ballet score lie in
the realm of compression or reorchestration.*

The scenario of the ballet derives from a Russian fairy tale adapted by
Mikhail Fokine as a contrast between two magical characters: the brilliant firebird, here in the form of the wood fairy, and the evil monster,
represented by Kashchey. The monster overpowers all who enter his
kingdom, imprisoning the women and turning the men to stone.
Prince Ivan Tsarevich wanders into the magical kingdom in pursuit of
the firebird; catching it, he demands a magic feather in return for its
release. He soon encounters a group of captive maidens, falls in love
with one of them, but is dismayed to learn that all are under Kashchey's
spell and must return to his palace at dawn. He bravely breaks into the
palace in pursuit of his beloved, is captured by Kashchey's monsters
and doomed to petrifaction, but brings forth the magic feather from

the firebird who, upon his summons, reappears and tells him that Kashchey's immortality is preserved in the form of an egg. Prince Ivan finds and destroys the egg, the ogre and all his evil enchantments expire, and Ivan and his beloved are solemnly betrothed.

Diaghilev had assembled stage designers and choreographers who had worked together as a team in the successful 1909 season of the Ballets Russes. Nikolay Tcherepnin, father of Alexander Tcherepnin, who later became a close personal friend to Stravinsky, was originally to have composed the score for the proposed ballet. For reasons that remain unclear, the score that he produced ultimately became an independent orchestral work (*The Enchanted Kingdom*) and Tcherepnin amicably withdrew from the project. Diaghilev next turned to Anatoly Lyadov, writing to him on September 4, 1909, that he needed a Russian ballet, as there was yet no ballet score that could match parallel achievements in Russian opera, song, and symphony. The work was to be *L'oiseau de feu*, for which Fokine had already prepared a libretto. Lyadov did not produce a score, and Diaghilev at one point mentioned Alexander Glazanov, director of the St. Petersburg conservatory, as the next likely candidate. Exactly how Stravinsky got the job remains unclear. Contrary to his own account, it was not the result of Diaghilev's encounter with the tone poem *Feu d'artifice*, for that was not performed publicly until early in 1910.

Many years later another report, containing some inconsistencies, was attributed to Stravinsky:

> I had already begun to think about *The Firebird* when I returned to St. Petersburg from Ustilug in the fall of 1909, though I was not yet certain of the commission (which, in fact, did not come until December, more than a month after I had begun to compose; I remember the day Diaghilev telephoned me to say go ahead, and I recall his surprise when I said that I had already started.) Early in November I moved from St. Petersburg to a *dacha* belonging to the Rimsky-Korsakov family about seventy miles south-east of the city. I went there for a vacation in birch forests and snow-fresh air, but instead began to work on *The Firebird*. . . . I returned to St. Petersburg in December and remained there until March, when the composition was finished. The orchestral score was ready a month later, and the complete music was mailed to Paris by mid-

April. (The score is dated May 18th, but by that time I was merely
retouching details). . . . Diaghilev, the diplomat, arranged everything. He came to call on me one day, with Fokine, Nijinsky,
Bakst, and Benois. When the five of them had proclaimed their
belief in my talent, I began to believe, too, and accepted.[18]

But according to his *Autobiography*, Stravinsky received a telegram from
Diaghilev at the end of the summer, asking him to compose the music
for the new ballet. The inconsistencies between these reports might be
explained as faulty memory in the retelling of events several decades
after the fact, might derive from inaccuracies in the transmission of
information between Stravinsky and his littérateurs, or might represent
some combination of both. Without completely resolving the conflicting details, it seems probable that Stravinsky was aware of Diaghilev's
need for a ballet score and began work on the score in October or
November of 1909, optimistically anticipating that the commission
would come his way.

Once the commission was in hand, Stravinsky worked quickly and
in close collaboration with Fokine, apparently following the ballet master's choreographic conception. Descriptions of this working relationship by Fokine, written sometime before 1942, and recorded by
Stravinsky in the 1950s, offer interesting differences in perception.
Fokine's version is quite detailed and reflects the dancer's view that the
music was subordinate to his plans for the choreography:

I have staged many ballets since *The Firebird*, but never again,
either with Stravinsky or any other composer, did I work so
closely as on this occasion. . . . I did not wait for the composer to
give me the finished music. Stravinsky visited me with his first
sketches and basic ideas, he played them for me, I demonstrated
the scenes to him. At my request, he broke up his national themes
into short phrases corresponding to the separate movements of a
scene, separate gestures and poses.[19]

Stravinsky's description, recorded several years later, offers a different
emphasis:

Fokine is usually credited as the librettist of *The Firebird*, but I
remember that all of us . . . contributed ideas to the plan of the
scenario. . . . To speak of my own collaboration with Fokine

means nothing more than to say that we studied the libretto together, episode by episode, until I knew the exact measurements required of the music. In spite of his wearying homiletics, repeated at each meeting, on the role of music as *accompaniment* to dance, Fokine taught me much. . . .[20]

Without doubt, unusual care was given to the coordination of dance and music, and a comparable degree of attention was lavished on rehearsals involving this unusual music, not familiar to dancers in 1910. All this care was appropriate, perhaps needed, because *L'oiseau de feu* fulfilled Diaghilev's wish for a new type of ballet, Russian in its story, music, and choreography.

Stravinsky met the musical needs of the project by producing an imaginative score marked by the colorful orchestral techniques for which he later became famous. Music for those characters who are part of the fantasy world—Kashchey and the firebird—exploits the interval of a tritone embracing alternately major and minor thirds, a chromatic harmony that stands in contrast to the basic diatonic lines associated with the human characters: Prince Ivan and his beloved. Chromatic and diatonic elements contrast in the same degree as do fantasy and reality. Beyond the story line, Stravinsky identifies two Russian folk tunes that appear in the *Round Dance of the Princesses,* and a third in the finale. These melodies expand through permutations that would be familiar to those who either were thoroughly familiar with them through experience or were seeking to identify such materials. Their significance lies in the degree to which they contributed to the Russian character of the venture.

The colorful extravagance of both plot and music was matched by orchestration that has contributed significantly to the enduring popularity of *L'oiseau de feu* in its ballet and concert hall formats. Stravinsky later described the instrumental score as wastefully large, but claimed that he was more proud of some facets of the orchestration than of the music itself. At a time when the art of orchestration was reaching an apex in the works of Richard Strauss, Debussy, and Ravel, Stravinsky continued in the path he had established with *Feu d'artifice*, meeting the competition as he sustained the traditions established by his former teacher, Rimsky-Korsakov.

L'oiseau de feu was one of the most auspicious new musical works of its era. Both dancers and orchestral musicians were confounded by the music, but careful and exacting rehearsals with both Fokine and Stravinsky produced a brilliant performance. Both Ravel and Debussy were present at the premiere in Paris, and Stravinsky was introduced to Debussy at the conclusion of the performance, an honor for a young and relatively unknown composer. If any of the critics sustained any reservation about the production, it seems that they did not apply to the music, which met with general favor for all of its novelty. In later years, Stravinsky described the score as his "audience lollipop," and ultimately came to think that the six-movement orchestral suite made better music for dance than the original ballet score.

The success of this early work reflected a convergence of forces bearing on the emerging Ballets Russes under the leadership of Serge Diaghilev. Their 1909 season in Paris had been a commercial and artistic success and, perhaps more important, had capitalized on a prevailing interest in Russian culture to create an even greater appetite among the Parisians for more works that were truly Russian, however that quality might be defined. Fokine developed a ballet around the Russian fairy tale of the wood fairy, and Diaghilev persevered in his search for a Russian composer. When Stravinsky's extraordinary score was combined with the stage talents assembled, presented to an audience with a growing appetite for Russian art, heightened by Diaghilev's facile propaganda, the success, if not assured, was at least well prepared. But beyond all this, it was the compatibility of dance, staging, and music that caught the attention of many who were knowledgeable in the arts. Stravinsky had the good fortune to be at the center of an emerging success story and the musical talent to exploit the opportunity.

Much as *Feu d'artifice* had established Stravinsky's reputation in Russia, *L'oiseau de feu* confirmed that reputation internationally. The enduring popularity of the music has led some to regard the score as Stravinsky's most conventional work, primarily because it became the familiar item to which all his other works have been compared. It also played an important role in his career as a conductor of his own works; his debut as a conductor in Paris in 1915 at a Red Cross benefit concert featured this score, as did his last recording session of his own works, in Chicago in 1967.

Petrushka

I. The Shrovetide Fair—The Magic Trick—Russian Dance

II. Petrushka's Room

III. The Moor's Room—Dance of the Ballerina—The Ballerina and the Moor Waltz

IV. The Shrovetide Fair at Evening—Dance of the Nursemaids— Dance of the Coachmen and Stable Boys—The Mummers

Stravinsky composed the music for the ballet Petrushka *between August 1910 and May 1911, followed by a revision for smaller orchestra in 1946. It was first performed in Paris on June 13, 1911, by the Ballets Russes, Pierre Monteux conducting, with Tamara Karsavina, Alexander Orlov, Enrico Cecchetti, and Vaslav Nijinsky in the leading roles.*

Instrumentation *(1911): two piccolos, two flutes, four oboes (the fourth doubling English horn), four clarinets (the fourth doubling bass clarinet), four bassoons (the fourth doubling contrabassoon), four horns, two cornets, two trumpets (the first doubling piccolo trumpet in D), three trombones, tuba, timpani, bass drum, snare drum, cymbals, tam-tam, triangle, snare drum and long drum offstage, tambourine, xylophone, glockenspiel, celesta, piano, two harps, and strings.*

Revised instrumentation *(1946): three flutes (the third doubling piccolo), two oboes, English horn, three clarinets (the third doubling bass clarinet), two bassoons, contrabassoon, four horns, three trumpets, three trombones, tuba, timpani, bass drum, snare drum, triangle, cymbals, tambourine, tam-tam, xylophone, celesta, harps, piano, and strings.*

The success of *L'oiseau de feu* generated plans for a sequel, and Stravinsky proposed to Diaghilev another scenario that would eventually become *Le sacre du printemps*. Diaghilev urged him to proceed immediately, with plans for production in the spring of 1911, but as an interim composition project Stravinsky turned first to a concert piece for piano and orchestra. His frequently quoted account, recorded in his autobiography several years later, described his own recollection of the genesis of the score that would become the music for *Petrushka*:

In composing the music, I had in my mind a distinct picture of a
puppet, suddenly endowed with life, exasperating the patience of
the orchestra with diabolical cascades of arpeggios. The orchestra
in turn retaliates with menacing trumpet blasts. The outcome is a
terrific noise which reaches its climax and ends in the sorrowful
and querulous collapse of the poor puppet. Having finished this
bizarre piece, I struggled for hours, while walking beside the Lake
of Geneva, to find a title which would express in a word the character of my music and, consequently, the personality of this crea-
ture.

   One day I leapt for joy. I had indeed found my title—*Petrushka*,
the immortal and unhappy hero of every fair in all countries.
Soon afterwards Diaghilev came to visit me at Clarens, where I
was staying. He was much astonished when, instead of sketches of
the *Sacre*, I played him the piece I had just composed and which
later became the second scene of *Petrushka*. He was so much
pleased with it that he would not leave it alone and began per-
suading me to develop the theme of the puppet's sufferings and
make it into a whole ballet.[21]

Diaghilev offered his own view of events, relating that Stravinsky
played for him his piano concerto without the slightest thought about
use of the music for *Petrushka*. According to Diaghilev, it was he who
perceived the music as well suited for a ballet and that the story of
Petrushka was the perfect scenario. A more specific account by Serge
Lifar, Diaghilev's associate and biographer, states the case even more
strongly:

   The concerto for piano became *Petrushka*, the most grand of
   Stravinsky's creations. . . . It is important to note that at the time,
   Petrushka was an absolute musical novelty which set a model and
   revolutionized the treatment of the orchestra. No less important
   is the fact that the composer himself did not grasp the true
   importance of his concerto for piano; the prophetic insight of
   Diaghilev was wholly responsible.[22]

The self-serving accounts of two creative personalities should probably
be regarded for what they are, but later correspondence makes it clear
that the creation of the ballet was very much a collaborative effort

between Stravinsky the composer, Alexander Benois the stage designer and librettist (whom Stravinsky recognized on the original title page of the score), and Michael Fokine the choreographer. In their respective autobiographies, all written more than 25 years after the ballet's premiere, each claimed the major share of credit for the work. In truth, the final version of *Petrushka* reflected influences from a wide range of theatrical and literary sources that were actually enhanced by the often contradictory views of its three creators.

The work is divided into four tableaux that tell the ballet's story:

First Tableau: At the Shrovetide fair, the three-day carnival preceding Lent, people of various sorts stroll about. Street musicians accompanied by dancers appear and compete for the crowd's attention. When they retire, the master Showman emerges from a small theater with three puppets: Petrushka, the Ballerina, and the Moor. He brings them to life with the magic of his flute and they dance, at first on their small stage as puppets, but later out among the crowd as living creatures.

Second Tableau: The scene is Petrushka's cell. The Showman's magic has given human feeling to all three puppets, but Petrushka is the most sensitive and suffers painfully from his own limitations and the domination of his master. He seeks some comfort in the love of the Ballerina, and for a moment thinks he has won her, but, disturbed by his crude antics, she flees as Petrushka curses the Showman and hurls himself at his portrait.

Third Tableau: The Moor occupies a very different room, its colorful decorations reflecting the Moor's own flamboyant costume. In spite of his brutishness, the Ballerina finds him attractive and uses all her wiles to entice him. As they dance and progress toward love, Petrushka interrupts, wildly jealous, but the powerful Moor throws him out.

Fourth Tableau: The revelry of the Shrovetide fair has reached its height. A commotion in the Showman's theater heralds a dramatic turn of events. Petrushka rushes into the street, pursued by the Moor. Undeterred by the Ballerina's efforts to restrain him, the Moor strikes his rival with his scimitar and poor Petrushka dies in the snow, surrounded by the revelers, now very quiet. The Showman appears and through his magic touch returns Petrushka to his puppet state. Satisfied that the shattered figure is indeed only a figure of straw and wood, the crowd disperses. But as the Showman drags the puppet off the stage, he is terrified when the specter of Petrushka appears above the theater, derisively thumbing his nose at the Showman and jeering at all who have been fooled by the deception.

The character represented by Petrushka was a stock theatrical figure in Russian popular culture, comparable to Punchinello of "Punch and Judy" fame in England, Pulcinella in Italy, Polichinelle in France, and Hanswurst in Germany, figures who shared misshapen physical features, a squeaky voice, and a pointed hat. The traditional tale of Petrushka in Russian literature pits him against a number of wily adversaries who try to best him in some scheme of trade or barter, all of whom he beats or kills before he himself is dragged off to some sort of purgatory to pay for his deeds. The character endures as tragic and slightly unreal, one whose common passions drive him to yearn for unattainable human life, his frustrations representing the unfulfilled aspirations of all people. Puppet shows offering variations on this theme and Petrushka's tragicomic adventures were common at popular street fairs through the late 19th century and would have been known to the creators of the ballet by reputation or possibly through personal experience. The ballet scenario draws on these traditions but gives them a twist that was the fruit of the collaboration among Benois, Stravinsky, and Fokine, the claims of the individual artists notwithstanding.

Much of the dancing in the ballet follows nontraditional patterns; it develops around crowd scenes or narrative pantomime for the soloists rather than set dances. Unusual dancing called for unusual musical effects and structures, and Stravinsky's score offered a wide variety of scales, chords with added notes, altered chords, tone clusters, rhythmic patterns, melodic materials (some of them borrowed), and orchestral effects—a veritable compendium of early-20th-century techniques—all closely associated with events on the stage.

The most famous musical event, one that derives from the portrayal of the main character and that appears in different guises throughout the work, is the famous "Petrushka chord" resulting from the simultaneous sounding of two chords a tritone apart, usually C major and F-sharp major. This first appears near the beginning of the *Second Tableau,* when Petrushka becomes aware of his grotesque appearance. Initially played by two clarinets as an arpeggio, it returns a number of times, most prominently at the end of the ballet, when Petrushka's ghost appears above the theater, threateningly insulting the Showman and the audience in general. This juxtaposition of harmonies permeates much of the piano part and reflects the composer's habit of composing at the keyboard, in this instance with one hand playing on the white keys, the other on the black keys. Stravinsky conceived the sound as Petrushka's insult to the public and claimed to be more proud of the idea and its manifestation in the closing pages than of anything else in the score. As a harmonic gesture, the sonority has received exhaustive attention from theorists because of the antipodal nature of two harmonies a tritone apart, an interval that, in its pervasiveness, has become a musical hallmark of this score.

Other passages are more obvious but no less effective. When the first street musician appears with his dancer, the trumpets play the parallel fifths of his hurdy-gurdy, and the Showman's magic flute, which brings the puppets to life, then comes to life itself through a cadenza for solo flute in the orchestra. As a contemporary reference, the Moor and Ballerina dance to two waltzes by Joseph Lanner, a popular Viennese composer of dance music whose waltzes were still current in the late 19th century. When the bear trainer leads his animal across the stage, his pipe is represented by the orchestral flute while the bear "dances" to an inconclusive phrase played by the tuba, framed in the by-now-familiar interval of a tritone. All of these musical references might be explained as nothing more than good theater music or musical events closely allied to stage action, but the ingenious expressiveness of Stravinsky's orchestration elevates them far above the ordinary.

More subtle and significant were quotations from Rimsky-Korsakov, Tchaikovsky, a popular Parisian song by Émile Spencer (*La jambe en bois*), and other musical references familiar at the time. A number of Russian folk tunes appear in part, if not in their entirety. The *Shrovetide Fair* opens with peddler's street cries comparable to those appearing in a collection of such materials published in Moscow in 1906. It is followed fourteen measures later by a fragment from the *Song of the Volochobniki*, traditionally sung by beggars at Easter in the province of Smolensk, and the same tune, in a more complete statement, soon returns as the basis for the dancing of the merrymakers. As the collective dancing of the opening scene reaches a peak, the piano plays a version of the song of St. John's Eve, a melody long associated with the summer solstice throughout much of Europe. Other folk tunes appear, in whole or in part, throughout the first, third and fourth *Tableaux*. A

complete study of quoted materials in *Petrushka* can become an absorb-
ing bit of detective work, and it is probable that there are musical fragments yet to be identified. Their significance lies in the genuinely
Russian flavor they impart to the work and in the multiple threads of
musical recognition they may have woven among the score, stage
action, and audiences of 1911.

These materials, or musical inspiration derived from them, played
a significant role in Stravinsky's departure from the regularity of four-
measure phrases that form the basis for much music in the Western tradition. Rhythmic groups of five or seven and phrases of uneven length
lent a rhythmic vitality to the music that comprised one of its many
iconoclastic elements. That same quality created problems for the
dancers; Fokine, specifically, described the difficulties in remembering
the rapid changes in the counting. The dancers had no access to the
score, and would possibly have been unable to benefit from any such
opportunity. It was necessary that they remember all the music by ear
and memorize the arithmetical patterns defining the choreography. By
all accounts, rehearsals were tedious, with much learning by rote. Those
same rhythms posed problems for the orchestral conductor and players
more accustomed to patterns of regular and recurring lengths, a condition by no means lessened by the unusual effects in Stravinsky's orchestration and the instrumental virtuosity required for their execution.
After several decades, the score has been mastered and incorporated
into the standard repertory, but in 1911 it was a challenge.

In its artistic impact, *Petrushka* was one of the greatest successes of
the season and, for the most part, continued to be hailed as a major
achievement when performances spread beyond Paris. One review of
the premiere set the tone:

> *Pétrushka* is a marvel. The scenario of these "scenes burlesques" is
> of no consequence. The important thing is what the composer,
> co-author with Benois of this scenario, has retained of it. It does
> not seem possible to achieve a stronger, richer, and more intense
> evocation of the story. It is simply astonishing. Apart from an
> abundance of musical themes, original and "classical" and a pro-
> fusion of fantastic rhythms, Igor Stravinsky's orchestral scoring is
> extraordinary. Instrumental timbres flow in a stream in a most
> novel fashion. These sonorities engender among the audience a

sense of inexpressible exhilaration. Not a single measure remains indifferent. And what boldness in the handling of the instruments! What eloquence! What life! What youthfulness![23]

It was the imaginative and colorful score by Stravinsky that attracted the most comment, even from Benois, the stage designer and librettist. It was generally considered the greatest artistic achievement of the Ballets Russes under Diaghilev.

One of relatively few dissenting opinions came from André Rimsky-Korsakov, erstwhile personal friend of Stravinsky and son of his early mentor. He wrote that the ballet reflected the current infatuation with the 1830s but that it was by no means a faithful portrayal of the Shrovetide celebrations of that period, largely because of excessive French influence. He recognized the technical skill represented in both the music and stage action, as well as the talents of Benois and Stravinsky, but queried, "might not *Petrushka* be the prelude to some sort of musical futurism? If so, then perhaps 'twere better it had never been born."[24] The review pained Stravinsky deeply and ruptured a personal friendship of many years. Many of the comments from the younger Rimsky-Korsakov apparently stemmed from personal antipathy more than from artistic conviction.

In *Petrushka*, the music overwhelms the dance. This may derive from the original conception of the score as a concert piece for piano and orchestra to which choreography was added. But more important, it grows from the significant incorporation of Russian folk tunes and other materials current at the time, all carrying their attendant connotations and cast in the most imaginative orchestral setting. The work was successful as an artistic endeavor drawing on many sources, in the process setting a new standard for ballet as an art form equal to drama and opera.

Pulcinella

Stravinsky prepared the music for Pulcinella *between the fall of 1919 and April 1920 from works attributed to the Italian composer Giovanni Batista Pergolesi (1720–1736). The ballet was first performed at the Paris Opera on May 15, 1920, by the Ballets Russes, Ernst Ansermet conducting, Zoia Rosowska, soprano, Aurelio Anglado, tenor, and Gino*

*de Vecchi, bass, with Leonide Massine and Tamara Karsavina dancing
the principal roles of Pulcinella and Pimpenella.*

Instrumentation: *soprano, tenor, and bass voices, two flutes (the second doubling piccolo), two oboes, two bassoons, two horns, trumpet,
trombone, and strings, plus a solo group of first and second violin, viola,
cello, and double bass.*

Suite from *Pulcinella*

Sinfonia

Serenata—

Scherzino

Tarantella—

Toccata

Gavotta con due variazioni

Vivo

Tempo di minuetto

*The suite was assembled in 1922; it was first performed in Boston on
December 22, 1922 by the Boston Symphony Orchestra, Pierre
Monteux conducting. The instrumentation of the ballet score remains
largely intact except that instruments assume those parts originally written as vocal solos.*

The music of *Pulcinella* was long known best through the eight-movement suite, but in the last decades of the 20th century, and particularly
with the advent of compact disc recordings, the complete ballet score
has come into its own, and both versions appear in the concert hall.

The precise circumstances leading to the creation of *Pulcinella* have
been variously described. In the story most frequently encountered,
Stravinsky related that Diaghilev suggested that he look at some 18th-
century music with the idea of orchestrating it for a ballet:

When he said that the composer was Pergolesi, I thought he must
be deranged. I knew Pergolesi only by the *Stabat Mater* and *La
Serva Padrona*, and though I had just seen a production of the lat-

ter in Barcelona, Diaghilev knew I wasn't in the least excited by it. I did promise to look, however, and to give him my opinion.[25]

But in his autobiography, Stravinsky claimed that Diaghilev's suggestion was particularly appealing to him, as Pergolesi was a composer he liked and admired immensely! In an interview published in *Coemedia* on January 31, 1920, Stravinsky offered a still different version, claiming that the score was indeed based on themes by Pergolesi, and, because he was in Italy, he and Diaghilev explored libraries in search of Pergolesi material. In yet another version of the story, the dancer-choreographer Leonide Massine claimed that it was *he* who suggested to Diaghilev a ballet based on the *commedia dell'arte*. In response, Diaghilev suggested the music of Pergolesi, leading to a search through the library of the Conservatorio of San Pietro by Massine and Diaghilev for suitable works by Pergolesi, of which they selected fifteen items.

It seems probable that the idea originated with Diaghilev, who was seeking to capitalize on the current success of another ballet, *The Good-Humored Ladies,* based on music of Domenico Scarlatti, with a comparable work founded on Pergolesi, enhanced by the choreography of Leonide Massine and stage decor by Pablo Picasso. This was under way as early as June 1919. Stravinsky did not become involved with the project until the fall, at which time he was interrupted in his work on *Les noces* by what he described as a rush-order commission for *Pulcinella.*

The scenario of this light farce derives from an 18th-century Neapolitan manuscript containing a number of comedies involving Pulcinella, the traditional character of popular stage works in Naples. All the young women of the play love Pulcinella, while their young men, driven by jealousy, want to kill him. The men disguise themselves as Pulcinella in order to impress their sweethearts, but Pulcinella, crafty fellow that he is, has changed places with a double who pretends to die under the blows of his enemies. Pulcinella, in the garb of a magician, comes to revive his double. When the young men think they have finally dispatched him, the real Pulcenella appears and arranges marriages for all. Pulcinella himself weds Pimpenella with the blessings of his double, who has now assumed the role of the magician.

Much of the music Stravinsky adapted, believing it to be by Pergolesi, was in fact the work of several other composers, reflecting the long-standing problems of authenticity then encumbering Pergolesi's works. Seven items were by Domenico Gallo, a Venetian composer active during the mid-18th century; two more came from Carlo Ignazio Monza (d. 1739); and others were by Alessandro Parisotti (1835–1913) and Wilhelm Graf von Wassenaer. Those sources by Pergolesi came from three operas, one chamber cantata, and a sinfonia for cello and bass.

Stravinsky restructured the music for an orchestra of 33 players cast in three groups: winds (without clarinets), five-part strings, and a group of solo strings, approximating an ensemble that might be assembled for an 18th-century concerto grosso. For the most part, his changes to the original materials consisted of shortening the second half of binary movements, adding some of his own touches to the supporting parts, and expanding the chord structures. The vocal solos for soprano, tenor, and bass are included as part of the orchestral score, designed to be sung from the orchestra pit. With these traits, the music is not to be confused with an 18th-century score, nor does it reflect the expansive orchestral effects of Stravinsky's earlier ballets. He did not project the score as a satire, as some early critics claimed; he was in essence responding to Diaghilev's wish for a stylish orchestration, although the result was much reduced from what most parties associated with the ballet had expected. The music might be considered a "parody" in the same sense that some sacred music of the 16th century was based on popular secular works. These and similar debates that attempt to define this score as either a modern reproduction or a recomposition of Pergolesi's music are perhaps best answered by literally interpreting the straightforward description on the original program booklet from 1920: "*Pulcinella / Musique de Pergolesi / arrangée et orchestrée par Igor Stravinsky.*"

Pulcinella was Stravinsky's first substantial contact with music of earlier times. At the same time that he moved from Switzerland to France, he turned away from his Russian background in favor of 18th-century materials. In that context, *Pulcinella* represents one of his early steps toward neoclassicism, a turn of events he later verified. The criticisms of Stravinsky's borrowings overlooked many precedents that were at that time, and remain, accepted facts of musical life. The turn to materials associated with earlier times was in fact one more step forward in the growth of Stravinsky's creative faculties, a development that came to greater fulfillment in his works written between 1919 and 1951.

Le sacre du printemps

The Adoration of the Earth: Introduction—Augurs of Spring (Dance of the Young Girls)—Dance of Abduction—Spring Rounds—Games of Rival Cities—Procession of the Sages— Dance of the Earth

The Sacrifice: Introduction—Mystical Circles of the Young Girls— Glorification of the Chosen One—Evocation of the Ancestors— Ritual of the Ancestors—Sacrificial Dance of the Chosen One

Stravinsky composed this famous score between the summer of 1911 and March 1913. The ballet was first performed in Paris on May 29, 1913, by the Ballets Russes, Pierre Monteux conducting, the solo role of the Chosen One danced by Marie Piltz.

Instrumentation*: two piccolos, four flutes, four oboes, English horn, four clarinets (including clarinet in E-flat), two bass clarinets, four bassoons, two contrabassoons, eight horns, piccolo trumpet in D, four trumpets in C, bass trumpet in E-flat, three trombones, two tubas, timpani (two players and five drums), bass drum, cymbals, antique cymbals, tambourine, tam-tam, rasp (guero), triangle, and strings.*

Le sacre du printemps stands as one of the major landmarks of the modern era for music and dance. Both made a quantum leap forward; the score, at least, set forth many techniques that have come to be hallmarks of modern music. Rarely has one work attracted so much attention, so quickly, on such an international scale, confronting audiences with music so different from the prevailing soundscape.

Audience reaction to the first performance has been enshrined in the literature in a manner to assure notoriety for *Le sacre*, no matter what its musical style or substance. Its introduction in May 1913 will likely stand as the most famous premiere in the history of music, certainly the most heavily documented, even though few of the reports agree on all points. Although embellished by the encrustation of rumor, exaggeration, and journalistic hyperbole, multiple eyewitness accounts verify that the orchestra, large as it was, became drowned in a cacophony of whistling, yelling, and catcalls. The writer-photographer Carl van Vechten reported that his neighbor became so excited that, standing for a better view, he began to beat upon Vechten's head in time with the music, and Vechten's own immersion in the performance was such that he did not notice the blows for some time! The scene backstage was equally riotous, because the dancers could not hear the orchestra over the din created by the audience. According to Stravinsky's account, Vaslav Nijinsky, the famous dancer-turned-choreographer, was standing on a chair counting loudly for the dancers, while Diaghilev requested that the auditorium lights be flashed in an attempt to quiet the audience.

A review in *L'Echo de Paris* on the day following the first performance offers a description reflecting the substance of many comments that appeared in the press. After describing the choreography in a derisive tone, the writer turned to the music:

> The music of Stravinsky is disconcerting and disagreeable. Without doubt it is proposed to resemble the barbaric choreography. One regrets that the composer of *The Firebird* has allowed himself to fall into such errors.
>
> Certainly one finds, in *The Rite of Spring*, an incontestable virtuosity in orchestration, a certain rhythmic power, a facile invention of melodic fragments or representative sonorities combined for the purpose of accompanying, providing contrast, or characterizing the movements on stage. Here there is a musician happily gifted, ingenious, subtle, capable of form and emotion, as he has already proven.
>
> But in the desire . . . *to produce primitive*, prehistoric [effects] he has *brought his music to brutism*. To that end he has attempted to destroy all impression of tonality. One would like to follow in the score (which I have not received) this eminently *amusical* work. You can get an idea which corresponds to my impression: play on two pianos, with four hands, and transpose one part a tone but not the other. . . . It is simply a question of almost never obtaining one of those harmonies which formerly passed for consonance.[26]

This and other appraisals that appeared in the following months recognized Stravinsky's fertile imagination and skill as an orchestrator but revealed a nearly complete lack of comprehension of the musical substance of the score.

Stravinsky's music was not solely responsible for this *cause célèbre*. Diaghilev had carefully primed the public for an extraordinary event through prior publicity and an open dress rehearsal, leading one reporter to announce on the day of the performance that the ballet was one of the most astonishing creations he had witnessed by the Ballets Russes. The Parisian press had been alerted to a newsworthy event in a city famous for its wars of words over music. Further, the choreography of Nijinsky accounted for at least as much of the disturbance as did Stravinsky's music. Correspondence between the dancer and composer suggests that they maintained a thoroughly compatible personal relationship, but in musical matters Stravinsky found Nijinsky abysmally lacking in even a rudimentary understanding. The dancer had never played a musical instrument, knew nothing of musical notation, and, according to Stravinsky, had no concept of the coordination between dance and music except in his own, admittedly brilliant, dancing ability. The result was a long series of difficult rehearsals, dance steps that bore only fortuitous coordination with the music, and movements for the dancers that were at odds with normal physical capabilities. Diaghilev was quite satisfied with the public's initial response and the publicity it generated, commenting at a postconcert gathering that the whole affair was just what he had wanted. And what an affair it became! One correspondent observed that if all the people who later claimed to have witnessed the event had indeed been present, the seating capacity of the theater would have needed to be doubled.

At a second performance the audience was much less abusive, although there were still interruptions. *Le sacre* was performed as a concert work in Moscow and St. Petersburg in February 1914, to mixed reviews, and on April 5, 1914, Pierre Monteux conducted a concert performance in Paris that Stravinsky later described as a triumph. *Le sacre* was on its way to the fame it has since enjoyed, in spite of initial performances in musical centers throughout Europe and North America that continued to be met with a mixture of acclamation and bewilderment.

The story of the conception of *Le sacre* lies entangled in a web of memoirs and personal correspondence. Twenty years after the first appearance of *Le sacre*, at a time when the work had become world-famous, Stravinsky described his inspiration in an account that has become part of the canon surrounding this composition. He envisioned a pagan rite with wise elders, seated in a circle as they watch a young girl dance herself to death as an offering to the god of spring. He reportedly shared the idea with Diaghilev, who was enthusiastic about the potential of the story, and then consulted the painter Nicholas Roerich, a stage designer whom he knew from *L'oiseau de feu* but also an archeologist and self-taught authority on early Slavic history. Roerich had already conceived of a similar idea, based on a vision of a festival near the shore of a lake, carried out by ancient people in veneration of the earth. Composer and painter met during the summer of 1911 and worked out the general course of action and the order of different episodes. In later accounts, Stravinsky minimized the contributions of Roerich, but as further evidence has become available it seems more than likely that most of the story was indeed developed by Roerich. He countered Stravinsky's account with one of his own in which he claimed that *Le sacre* was one of two librettos he suggested to Stravinsky; contemporaries who knew both parties described the story as Roerich's, as have modern researchers who have had access to contemporary documentary evidence.

Controversy over the matter of priority of authorship in this search for origins does little to define the work's stature. The two artists together produced a Neolithic fantasy about sacrificial rites among the Slavs celebrating the revival of nature in the spring, the council of old and wise members of the tribe, and the regeneration of life itself through the sacrifice of one chosen as an offering, all sustained by awe over the primal forces of nature. Stravinsky later reported that the original title for this scenario was "Sacred Spring" or "Holy Spring"; the latter became "The Festival of Spring," which served as the prototype for the Gallicized *Le sacre du printemps*. Roerich and Stravinsky here conceived a work wherein dance, music, and set designs were to represent a single concept, the whole growing from a fusion of their creative fecundity.

The subject matter represented a facet of Slavic nationalism. Both artists felt that only a scrupulous adherence to ethnological authenticity would validate the stylistic innovations to which they aspired. To this end, Stravinsky produced a score in which the initial impression is one of overwhelming volume and diversity of sound. He acknowledged in later years that Diaghilev had encouraged him to write for a large orchestra in *Le sacre*, as expanded forces would be available, but he noted at the same time that he was not sure he otherwise would have written for an ensemble so large. The expanded resources were well used in the service of stage effects. The Introduction to Part I was assigned, by Roerich, to *dudki* (ancient reed pipes), here represented by the bassoon, a double reed instrument playing in a register so high that it loses its characteristic orchestral timbre. Double-tonguing by the winds and harmonics played by the strings further expand the orchestral palette. Both the size of the orchestra and the unusual effects it produced were assimilated into a broader texture of layered sound, the simultaneous presentation of multiple strata of orchestral activities in which different sections play against each other in autonomously cohesive patterns of harmony and rhythm. This was not new with Stravinsky, but few composers had expanded upon the technique as extensively as in *Le sacre*, where it became a prevailing feature of the musical texture.

Without diminishing the importance of the orchestral sound itself, it is rhythm that makes the most lasting impact. Two salient processes emerge: a constant, driving ostinato pattern, so insistent that it becomes hypnotic, often becoming a point of reference in itself; and a series of irregularly spaced accents, requiring constantly variable metric barring. Of the second, which prevails in the closing *Sacrificial Dance*, Stravinsky said that he could play the music as he conceived it but at first did not know how to commit it to paper in a manner to be grasped by others. The result is that the rhythm departs from the regularity of metric patterns and bar lines. The apparent dislocation of the beat came to be regarded as a main feature of Stravinsky's works, and from there moved into the canon of 20th-century music to be expanded in the works of many younger composers.

Much of the harmony radiates from the accumulation of pitches formed by the combination of two chords, usually traditional harmonies if heard independently but sounding more complex when played simultaneously. The stomping chord that dominates the *Augurs of Spring*, so distinctive that it is often identified as "The Rite of Spring chord," illustrates this structure through its combination of two chords separated by only a semitone. This and other harmonies in *Le sacre* likely grew from Stravinsky's practice of composing at the piano, where one hand could play in one key, the second hand in another or, at least as frequently, one hand could play on the white keys, the other on the black.

Many of the melodic materials result from the close approximation of folk song traditionally associated with Slavic festivals. These first appear as simple tunes of narrow compass, then often expand through repetition so insistent that it can become unnerving to a listener nurtured on music from Western European courts or concert halls. Yet this repetition varies through changes in rhythmic accent and orchestral colors sufficiently that what at first seems mundane becomes exciting, even exuberant. Stravinsky identified the opening bassoon solo as a quotation from a book of Lithuanian folk songs published in 1900, implying that this was the only true folk song in the work, but subsequent examination has identified a number of other derivative melodies, often changed in the specifics of their structure. More important than the exactitude of these quotations is the inherently Slavic character they lend to music intended to depict a ceremony of early Slavic people.

Some consideration of the activities spawned by *Le sacre du printemps* illustrates the work's pervasiveness on the 20th-century soundscape. It has become the subject of scholarly studies so extensive that they comprise an autonomous field of endeavor. Academic courses have been formed around the study of the score in all its ramifications, and the title has been borrowed for other activities ranging from traditional stage plays to popular outings. The 1939 film *Fantasia* adopted various parts of the ballet score for part of its sound track, a production that carried Stravinsky's music to the far corners of the globe; few listeners today can hear the *Augurs of Spring* without accompanying visions of dinosaurs rumbling across the cinematic screen. *Le sacre* has truly become part of a broadly shared musical heritage.

In 1913 music was suffering from a surfeit of oversophistication. The refined sonorities of Debussy deteriorated to tedium in the works of those attempting to imitate and sustain his style. Maurice Ravel, Debussy's most logical successor, turned toward more classic principles in both form and melody, and Gustav Mahler, Max Reger, and Richard Strauss represented the culmination of 19th-century traditions more than a new path. The time was ripe for an effective stroke of musical innovation. For many listeners, *Le sacre* represented that stroke, introducing an era of modern music. Audience expectations for contemporary music have not been the same since the first appearance of *Le sacre* in 1913 and Schoenberg's *Pierrot lunaire* a year later. It was a turning point for Stravinsky as well, for although he drew heavily on his

Russian heritage for the work, with its success he began to turn away from Mother Russia.

One can hardly consider *Le sacre* an unqualified modern work after all that has happened in music since 1913. The enduring achievement of this score, far better known as a concert work than as a ballet score, is its synthesis of Russian folklore, folk music elements, creative pantomime, and musical techniques that have come to identify the 20th century, a synthesis transcending the sources from which it grew.

Ralph Vaughan Williams

b. Down Ampney, United Kingdom, October 12, 1872;
d. London, August 26, 1958

The first mature works of Ralph Vaughan Williams emerged shortly before World War I. His reputation continued to grow throughout his long career, only to fall under a shadow after his death. In part this temporary decline reflected the slump in reputation that often follows a composer's demise, but it also reflected the shifting musical influences following World War II. With the return to favor of tonality and a greater interest in composers who could and would speak for a broader society, Vaughan Williams came into his own once again as the 20th century moved toward its close. The short list of works addressed here, determined by frequency of performance during the last decade of the century, represents a minute portion of his oeuvre, and all were written during his early years. If interest in his works continues to rise, the best days for Vaughan Williams's music may lie ahead.

This composer's family name has generated as much discussion following his death as it did during his lifetime. Ursula Vaughan Williams, the composer's widow, addressed the subject in the prefatory matter to her biography of the composer: "Ralph's grandfather, Sir Edward Vaughan Williams, seems to have been the first member of the family to use the double-barreled but unhyphenated name. All his sons were so named and though occasionally . . . Ralph was called Williams it is not correct. Ralph's name was pronounced Rafe, any other pronunciation used to infuriate him."[1]

Vaughan Williams came from a background of scholars, jurists, and other professional people, among them Charles Darwin. This distinguished family heritage led him to study with private tutors and exclusive schools, until he arrived at Cambridge University, where he earned a B.Mus., B.A., and D.Mus. He supplemented this formal education with two sessions at the Royal College of Music plus private studies with Max Bruch in Berlin and Maurice Ravel in Paris. In sum, he spent most of his first 29 years in schooling of one sort or another.

Composing was Vaughan Williams's consuming passion, but he also became involved in folk song research, church music, film music, conducting (particularly his own works), and various facets of the many music festivals that sprang up in England after 1918. In all of these activities, he was a champion of music for the people, maintaining that he could not successfully address the musical world at large until he had established a musical rapport with his own heritage. For Vaughan Williams, music was "a reaching out to the ultimate realities by means of ordered sound."[2]

In the early years of the century, Vaughan Williams embarked on a project of collecting and editing English folk songs that matched, at least in spirit, the efforts of Bartók and Kodály on the continent. Between 1903 and 1908, he transcribed more than eight hundred melodies, convinced that he was preserving a body of music on the verge of extinction. He rarely reverted to literal quotation of folk tunes in his compositions, but drew on their musical traits throughout his life. These native tunes awakened in him an abiding interest in music of common people, hymns in particular. He spent 1904 to 1906 preparing an edition of the *Church of England Hymnal*, claiming in his autobiography that the intimate acquaintance with some of the best (and worst) tunes of the world offered a better musical education than any amount of prescribed studies of traditional concert literature.

Above all, Vaughan Williams sustained a musical outlook that championed independent thought. He maintained that originality was less important than finding the right musical statement for the right moment, no matter that the material at hand might have been presented many times before. Thus it was that he could create in his own works a genuinely English flavor by drawing on the character of folk song and hymnody rather than on literal quotations. These traits prevail in his compositions originating before World War I. After 1918 his energies expanded to embrace a wider range of expression and imagery, but it was his pre-1914 works that were performed most frequently during the later part of the 20th century.

For his many achievements, Vaughan Williams was offered, but declined, many honors, although he did accept the Order of Merit in 1935. As a final tribute to his Englishness, his ashes were interred in Westminster Abbey near the tomb of Henry Purcell and Charles Villiers Stanford, an enduring tribute befitting a composer who, in the estimation of his countrymen, spoke with a singularly English voice.

A London Symphony

Lento—Allegro risoluto

Lento

Scherzo (Nocturne): Allegro vivace

Andante con moto—Maestoso alla marcia—Allegro—Maestoso alla marcia—

Epilogue: Andante sostenuto

Vaughan Williams completed the original version of A London Symphony *by the end of 1913. The first performance was given in London on March 27, 1914, by the Queen's Hall Orchestra, Geoffrey Toye conducting. Subsequent revisions were performed in London on March 18, 1918, by the New Queen's Hall Orchestra, Adrian Boult conducting; on May 4, 1920, by the London Symphony Orchestra, Albert Coates conducting; and on February 22, 1934, by the London Philharmonic Orchestra, Sir Thomas Beecham conducting.*

Instrumentation: *three flutes (the third doubling piccolo), two oboes, English horn, two clarinets, bass clarinet, two bassoons, contrabassoon, four horns, two trumpets, two cornets, three trombones, tuba, timpani, bass drum, snare drum, triangle, tam-tam, jingles (sleigh bells), cymbals, glockenspiel, harp, and strings (with many cues for the optional distribution of parts).*

By Vaughan Williams's own account, *A London Symphony* came about through the urging of his friend George Butterworth, to whom the completed work was dedicated. In his autobiography, Vaughan Williams related that Butterworth casually advised him that he should write a symphony:

I answered . . . that I never had written a symphony and never intended to. This was not strictly true, for I had in earlier years sketched three movements of one symphony and the first movement of another, all now happily lost. I suppose that Butterworth's words stung me, and, anyhow, I looked at some sketches I had made for what I believe was going to have been a symphonic poem (!) about London and decided to throw it into symphonic form.[3]

The result was Vaughan Williams's first purely instrumental symphony and the second of nine he would produce over a span of 48 years between 1910 and 1958. Shortly after the first performance in 1914, the score was sent to Germany. Vaughan Williams told his wife, Ursula, that he had submitted it to the publishers Breitkopf & Härtel in Leipzig for review and publication; to Michael Kennedy, his biographer, he reported that he had sent the score to the conductor Fritz Busch in Berlin. Either way, the manuscript was lost in the confusion surrounding the outbreak of World War I. George Butterworth entered the picture once again when he and others assisted in preparing from band parts a score for a second performance in 1915. When Butterworth was killed in action, it was only fitting that he become the dedicatee of the work that he had instigated and subsequently helped to preserve.

Responding to congenial criticism from friends following the first performance, Vaughan Williams revised the score a number of times, deleting material from movements two through four; only the first movement escaped major revisions. The extensive editing, the title, and the quotations of themes from the London soundscape generated protracted discussions concerning the level of its programmatic content, inspiring Vaughan Williams to address the matter in a program note:

> The title *A London Symphony* may suggest to some hearers a descriptive piece, but this is not the intention of the composer. A better title would perhaps be "Symphony by a Londoner," that is to say, the life of London (including, possibly, its various sights and sounds) has suggested to the composer an attempt at musical expression; but it would be no help to the hearer to describe these in words. The music is intended to be self-expressive, and must stand or fall as "absolute" music. Therefore, if listeners recognize suggestions of such things as the "Westminster Chimes" or the

"Lavender Cry" they are asked to consider these as accidents, not essential of the music.[4]

It seems clear that the symphony is programmatic, but in a vein different from most other orchestral works of the period. The writing of program music is a conscious procedure, usually preceded by a plan to portray something extramusical in musical terms. *A London Symphony* deals with the character of the city more than specific elements, and in that context it could well be a reflection of the composer's subconscious. Vaughan Williams many times claimed that a composer should speak from the basis of his own heritage, and by 1913 London was very much a part of his life. Therefore it seems more accurate to regard the music as an evocation of the London soundscape through subtle inference rather than through literal portrayal.

The initial *Lento* serves as an introduction to the first movement as well as to the entire symphony, to be answered in the final *Epilogue*. The basses quietly introduce the motto theme, two rising fourths separated by a whole tone, setting the pattern for a gradual accumulation of sound that concludes with an evocation of the chimes of Westminster at the half hour, represented by harp harmonics supported by clarinets. The *Allegro risoluto* offers most of the trappings of a large sonata design, but the main thrust comes more from an abundance of thematic material than from defined harmonic operations or structural designs. The first theme is a chromatic wail that jolts the listener out of the contemplative mood of the introduction. Several lively episodes lead to a second-theme section marked by a fanfare from the winds as they introduce a sprightly march. These materials return in varied shapes, enlivened by the interjection of new themes ranging from bombastic to lyrical, until the coda arrives. Themes first heard at the close of the exposition now blaze forth from the full orchestra, resolving the preceding tonal ambiguity with a dramatic G major.

In contrast, the following *Lento* opens with muted strings quietly supporting a melancholy lament played by the English horn. This contemplative mood continues throughout the first section of a broad three-part design. Solos by viola and clarinet introduce the midsection, marked more prominently by the clarinets' representation of a snatch from the lavender seller's cry, which the composer cited in his program note. Arpeggios by harp and strings contribute to an accumulation of sound in preparation for the return of the principal section, again identified by muted strings supporting the haunting English horn solo.

Vaughan Williams described the third movement as a nocturne in the form of a scherzo. Certainly the character of a scherzo emerges through the rapid triple meter that prevails throughout the movement. Some listeners hear references to street instruments, but it is the rapid dance rhythm that prevails, interrupted and freshened by sudden interpolations of duple meter and sometimes chordal textures. The thick scoring dissipates at the coda, leaving violins, violas, and cellos to sustain chords in support of fragmentary dialogue between basses and woodwinds.

The juncture between the first and second movements is marked by a pronounced change in dynamics from the full orchestra playing *ff* to muted strings playing *ppp*; that pattern is reversed between the third and fourth movements, when the muted strings playing *pppp* are followed by the full orchestra playing *f* and *appassionato*. This pattern of dynamics, along with other traits, adds to the balance between the first and last movements. The concluding rondo gets under way with a dignified march. Themes come and go in abundance, much as in the first movement, closing with another reference to the Westminster chimes, this time sounding three quarters past the hour and played only by the harp. In the final *Epilogue*, one of Vaughan Williams's most telling additions to the symphonic tradition, the basses and trombones play the basic motto from the introductory *Lento* against a continuous warbling from the strings and flute. The strings continue the motto in a reflective manner, gradually dropping away to leave the final statement to the solo violin.

In a letter of September 30, 1957, to his biographer, Michael Kennedy, Vaughan Williams advised that for a grasp of the coda, the writer should consult the end of H. G. Wells's *Tono-Bungay*, thereby initiating a discussion that has carried the question of program elements beyond his earlier comments. Wells's autobiographical novel ends with a chapter titled "Night and the Open Sea," in which he relates his thoughts as he takes a newly completed warship down the River Thames in a test run. He describes the passing scenery as a metaphor for the whole of England, all of which passes behind him as he enters the open sea and the future it represents:

To run down the Thames so is to run one's hand over the pages in the book of England from end to end. . . . And then the traditional and ostensible England falls from you altogether. The third movement begins, the last great movement in the London symphony, in which the trim scheme of the old order is altogether dwarfed and swallowed up. . . . And now behind us is blue mystery and the phantom flash of unseen lights, and presently even these are gone, and I and my destroyer tear out to the unknown across a great grey space. We tear into the great spaces of the future and the turbines fall to talking in unfamiliar tongues. Out to the open we go, to windy freedom and trackless ways. Light after light goes down. England and the Kingdom, Britain and the Empire, the old prides and the old devotions, glide abeam, astern, sink down upon the horizon, pass—pass. The river passes—London passes, England passes. . . .[5]

Tono-Bungay first appeared in 1908, so the substance of Wells's narrative may have lurked in the back of Vaughan Williams's mind as he assembled the musical sketches that became *A London Symphony*. It remains an open question whether he considered the work a musical transition from the past to the unknown future, but his brief reference to Wells's text should not be dismissed.

A review of the purely musical elements suggests a large arch form extending from the introductory *Lento* to the closing *Epilogue*. The sequence of the basic motto and Westminster chimes as they first appeared is mirrored in the close of the fourth movement and following *Epilogue*; the first and fourth movements resemble each other in their abundance of thematic material, and the two inner movements both proceed from a basic three-part design. These observations come after the fact and may or may not reflect the composer's intent. The perception of the score as a traditional symphonic structure, as a work of programmatic connotations, or as a broadly conceived arch can be left to personal choice and musical inclinations. All three approaches offer the listener a satisfying musical experience.

The symphony was a success with both audiences and critics from the time of its first performance. The first movement, in particular, was much applauded amid general agreement that a significant English symphony had emerged. Some of its success after 1918 grew from a sense of musical patriotism, a loyalty to all things English as a gesture of respect for all those lost on the battlefields of World War I. Gustav Holst, best known as composer of *The Planets*, wrote to Vaughan Williams: "You have really done it this time. Not only have you reached the heights but you have taken your audience with you. Also you have proved the musical superiority of England to France. I wonder if you realize how futile and tawdry Ravel sounded after your Epilogue."[6] *A London Symphony* was not an iconoclastic work, breaking down musical traditions at the time of its introduction or in the years following, but it was and remains an eloquent statement by a thoroughly English composer who spoke with a voice reflecting the cumulative musical experiences of the place and time in which he lived.

The Lark Ascending, Romance for Violin and Orchestra

Andante—Allegro tranquillo (quasi andante)—Allegro tranquillo—Allegro molto tranquillo

Vaughan Williams composed The Lark Ascending *in 1914, followed by a revision in 1920. It was first performed in a version for violin and piano at Shirehampton Public Hall on December 15, 1920, by Marie Hall, violin, and Geoffrey Mendham, piano; the first orchestral performance was given in London on June 14, 1921, by the British Symphony Orchestra, with Marie Hall as violin soloist, Adrian Boult conducting.*

Instrumentation: two flutes, oboe, two clarinets, two bassoons, two horns, triangle, solo violin, and strings.

Vaughan Williams took the title of *The Lark Ascending* from George Meredith's collection, *Poems and Lyrics of the Joys of the Earth*, and included an extract from that text along with the published score:

> He rises and begins to round,
> He drops the silver chain of sound,
> Of many links without a break,
> In chirrup, whistle, slur and shake.
>
> For singing till his heaven fills,
> 'Tis love of earth that he instils,

And ever winging up and up,
Our valley is his golden cup
And he the wine which overflows
To lift us with him as he goes.

Till lost on his aerial rings
In light, and then the fancy sings.[7]

Meredith's lines find musical realization in the solo violin as it characterizes both the bird's song and its flight. It was probably the textual association that gave rise to the descriptive title Romance. That term carries no implication for any established structural design, usually referring to the character of a lyric, strophic poem, often addressing an amorous topic. Vaughan Williams wrote another Romance for harmonica and strings, and used the title for the slow movements of his piano concerto (1926–1931) and Fifth Symphony (1938–1943). These and works by other composers under the title Romance offer a pervasive lyricism and include flights of fancy requiring graceful facility from the soloist, traits well represented in *The Lark Ascending*.

Two cadenzas, both based upon the same figuration over one extended harmony, open and close the work; a shorter cadenza based on the same material introduces an extended midsection. Regarded in this context alone, the music resembles a large arch, anchored by two comparable passages for the solo violin. This arrangement is more sophisticated than a common three-part design, because the first of the two longer cadenzas appears at the beginning to introduce the principal thematic material; the second returns at the end as a conclusion of that material, offering at least the suggestion of a symmetrical design. The shorter cadenza introducing the midsection serves as a point of reference, reinforcing the suggestion of the lark and its cries. All three cadenzas expand upon a warbling motive that takes flight, ascending to a point three octaves higher than the initial pitch, where, in one manner or another, they conclude with a series of descending thirds.

Tranquility prevails, as indicated by the performance directions. Temporary departures in the midsection disrupt this only slightly when, at the first *Allegro tranquillo*, the flutes introduce a theme that could well be an English folk dance in its sprightly but straightforward rhythm and narrow compass. Above this the solo violin adds trills and arpeggiated passagework, simple at first, later in double-stops. Much of the melodic writing embraces pentatonic patterns, a trait common to the *Tallis Fantasia* and *London Symphony* as well. In this quality Vaughan Williams may have been responding to music by many of his contemporaries on the continent, particularly Debussy and Ravel, but at no point do his efforts reflect anything other than his own style. All of this draws on modal harmonies that shift imperceptibly from the opening E minor to centers on A, C, D, C, A, and back to E, lending support to the impression of tonal symmetry.

Vaughan Williams created *The Lark* for the English violinist Marie Hall, to whom the work is dedicated. She worked with the composer in preparing the version for violin and piano, and may have influenced the creative process to some degree. The composer likely responded to her individual performance strengths, much as he did in his other concerted works created for specific soloists: the Viola Suite for Lionel Tertis; the Oboe Concert for Leon Goosens; and the Romance for Harmonica for Larry Adler. Vaughan Williams's own background as a string player shows in the dominance of melody in *The Lark*, a prevailing lyricism that sustained the popularity of the work through the century.

The Lark Ascending was an unusual work from an age dominated by Stravinsky and Debussy. A review of the first performance praised the work because it "showed serene disregard of the fashions of today or yesterday. It dreams its way along."[8] Any reverie induced in the listener by the beauty of the music should not overlook the subtle design and consistency of thematic material that mark the score as a miniature masterpiece.

Fantasia on a Theme by Thomas Tallis

Vaughan Williams completed the Fantasia on a Theme by Thomas Tallis *in June 1910, followed by revisions in 1913 and 1919. It was first performed at Gloucester Cathedral on September 6, 1910, by personnel of the London Symphony Orchestra, Vaughan Williams conducting.*

Instrumentation: *a solo quartet of two violins, viola, and bass; orchestra I of massed strings; orchestra II of two first violins, two second violins, two violas, two cellos, and bass.*

The *Tallis Fantasia* has aroused at least as much interest in the musical community as any of Vaughan Williams's works, owing to the invocation of Thomas Tallis, the musical heritage of 16th-century England, and the unique musical traits the work projects. After the death of Henry Purcell, the English musical scene had been dominated by musicians from abroad, starting with Handel in 1710 and extending through the presence of Mendelssohn and Wagner in the 19th century. Vaughan Williams was one of several composers associated with a revival of English music, and his *Tallis Fantasia* was one of the most eloquent reminders of England's musical past. Moreover, the resonant acoustic qualities of multiple string choirs created a sonic aura refreshingly different from the homogenization of orchestral timbres that prevailed in most contemporary orchestral works. Listeners drew comparisons with antiquity, ecclesiastical architecture, vocal church music, and the singing voice in general. For many observers, the music was either very old or very new; for some it was both.

The title *Fantasia* opened many possibilities for any composer in the early 20th century. In the distant past it had implied a work free from a vocal model. That concept later expanded to include freedom from the strictures of established designs and their attendant expectations. It then became a work in one movement, but with contrasting sections sharing some logical musical connection. In all of these, composers enjoyed an element of freedom to follow inspirations of the moment, but not to the extent that "anything goes." Vaughan Williams eventually produced several works titled *Fantasia on . . .* (*English Folk Song, Christmas Carols, "Greensleeves," "Old 104th" Psalm Tune,* and *"Linden Lea"*), but the *Fantasia on a Theme by Thomas Tallis* has endured as his most popular effort in this genre.

Vaughan Williams composed the work in response to a commission from the Three Choirs Festival, an annual event combining the choral resources of cathedrals in Gloucester, Worcester, and Hereford. These events drew heavily on sacred vocal music, but abstract instrumental works were also included. The long traditions of the festival clearly influenced the composer's choice of material, because Tallis was one of the great names among Tudor composers, producing works for both Catholic and Protestant services. The prospect of performance in a stone cathedral, with all of its attendant acoustic properties, also bore upon the score in the division of the ensemble into three distinct performing bodies. Vaughan Williams took pains to assure the musical autonomy of orchestra I and II plus the solo quartet through detailed instructions in the score concerning distribution of parts, doublings, and his intended seating plan. The acoustic effects produced by these three instrumental groups in their original venue comprise a prominent feature of the music in both conception and performance.

It was from 1904 to 1906, while he was engrossed in editing the *English Hymnal*, that Vaughan Williams became aware of the metrical psalm tunes Thomas Tallis had written for the Psalter of Matthew Parker in the 16th century. He was particularly taken with the music for Psalm 2, the third of nine hymnlike settings Tallis prepared, written in the third (Phrygian) mode. The melody lies in the tenor, each line of text ending with a long note and bar line. Vaughan Williams adapted this as No. 92 in the *English Hymnal*, placed the melody in the soprano, and regularized the rhythm for the text by Joseph Addison, "When rising from the bed of death, O'erwhelmed with guilt and fear." That same musical setting continued as No. 424 in *The Hymnal of the Protestant Episcopal Church in the United States of America 1940*, now with a text by Horatius Bonar, "I heard the voice of Jesus say." In a more recent version included as No. 692 in *The Hymnal 1982 According to the Use of the Episcopal Church*, Bonar's text has been retained, but the note values have been reduced by half, and Tallis's original barring and rhythmic structure have been restored. In the orchestral score at hand, Tallis and the traditions of 16th-century church music became a generating factor underlying a work intended for the cathedral in the same way English folk song served for many compositions by Vaughan Williams intended for the concert hall.

The broad musical qualities of the *Tallis Fantasia* are dominated by the consistent timbre of strings, the polychoral effects created by multiple groupings of those instruments, and the modal harmonies echoing the Tallis original. It remains a matter of conjecture whether Vaughan Williams chose a body of strings alone in emulation of the single timbre of the choral groups that prevailed at the Three Choirs Festival, but his sensitivity to sound suggests that the parallel was more than coincidental. The contrasts between four different string textures (solo string quartet, orchestra I, orchestra II, and passages for solo instruments) playing in the acoustic environment of a cathedral have been mentioned earlier; even a casual perusal of the music shows this to be a fundamental impetus in the score. These groups are distinguished by different thematic materials, different and carefully notated dynamics, and, sometimes, distinctions between pizzicato and bowed passages. The modal qualities reflect the Phrygian mode of the Tallis original, most of the time preserving the characteristic semitone above the tonic. Transposition of the original melody from E to G entails considerable chromatic alteration, and opens up harmonic flexibilities that contribute much to the haunting beauty of the work.

Vaughan Williams cast these basic materials in three large sections, all drawing on different features of the Tallis theme. The chordal invocation in the opening measures sets the tone. Following this brief introduction, the lower strings, playing pizzicato, present fragments of the theme, punctuated by a series of parallel chords that seem to wander in inconsequential fashion. This dialogue continues until the first full statement of the theme is played in unison by second violins, violas, and cellos. The first violins soar with a second statement of the theme, accompanied by an active countermelody. With the full theme presented and reinforced, Vaughan Williams expands on elements of its second phrase and the characteristic chords from the introduction.

The midsection arrives with a solo viola playing a passage drawn from the third phrase of Tallis's theme. The solo quartet expands on this through imitation, with interjections from the larger groups, and the three groups of strings continue with an elaboration on different fragments of the theme. The music builds to an intense climax before subsiding to thinner textures that in turn lead directly into the closing section. Here the initial phrase of the Tallis theme is played pizzicato, much as in the beginning, but the solo first violin soon assumes the theme, accompanied by solo viola and sustained tremolos from Orchestras I and II. In a much-compressed answer to the opening section, the ensemble arrives at a luxurious and concluding G major chord, *fortissimo*, which gradually fades away to infinity.

By the end of the 20th century, most audiences regarded the *Fantasia on a Theme by Thomas Tallis* as Vaughan Williams's first masterpiece, the work that presaged his later symphonic achievements. But reactions to the first performance in Gloucester Cathedral were not all enthusiastic, as indicated by an unidentified critic for the *Gloucester Journal*:

The "theme" on which the *Fantasia* is founded is not familiar to us, and the impression left on the mind by the whole composition was one of unsatisfaction (if we may use such a word). We had short phrases repeated with tiresome iteration, and at no time did the *Fantasia* rise beyond the level of an uninteresting exercise. The band played the piece as well as it could be played, and we had some nice contrasts in light and shade. But there was a feeling of relief when the *Fantasia* came to an end, and we could get to something with more colour and warmth.[9]

The critic offers no indication of what works might offer more color and warmth, but possibly he was anticipating some of the large sacred choral works for which the Three Choirs Festival was famous. Vaughan Williams may have taken to heart comments like this made by critics following early performances, because in his revisions of 1913 and 1919 he consistently deleted material, reducing the number of full statements of the Tallis theme.

On the other hand, the critic for the *Times* thought the work particularly appropriate to the environment in which it was introduced:

The work is wonderful because it seems to lift one into some unknown region of musical thought and feeling. Throughout its course one is never quite sure whether one is listening to something very old or very new. . . . We can recall no piece of pure instrumental music produced at a Three Choirs Festival which has seemed to belong to its surrounding so entirely as does this *Fantasia*. It could never thrive in a modern concert-room, but in the quiet atmosphere of the cathedral the mind falls readily into the reflective attitude necessary for the enjoyment of every unexpected transition from chord to chord. . . .[10]

Contrary to the contemporary assessment, the *Fantasia* has endured very well in the concert hall. But most listeners will agree that the acoustic aura of a cathedral, for which it was designed, is indeed sympathetic to the string writing. Nonetheless, this is music that transcends its environment.

William Walton

❧

*b. Oldham, United Kingdom, March 29, 1902; d. Forio d'Ischia, Italy,
March 18, 1983*

William Walton's creative life was marked by a quality of independence different from the nonconformity that was the custom for many of his contemporaries. He was not identified with any school or musical system; he therefore had to find his own way and develop his own style. He was largely self-taught at a time when much modern music was entering an era of technical complexity. He was not tied to any geographic locale, nor was his music championed by an identified performing group. He was of limited means and came from humble beginnings, but through most of his life there were patrons who supplied funds allowing him to live and work independently. In his later years, honored by a knighthood and the Order of Merit, and thereby presumably confirmed within the establishment in his native land, he chose to spend most of his time on Ischia, an island off the coast of Italy. This same independence comes forth in his music as he assimilates traditional materials and designs but treats them in a style unique to his own creative muse.

Both of Walton's parents were singers, and at an early age he exhibited a strong sense of melody and pitch. These talents enabled him to win a scholarship as chorister in the Christ Church Cathedral Choir at Oxford, where he remained from 1912 to 1918. When his family's income declined during World War I, Dr. Thomas Strong, dean of Christ Church and the first of William's many benefactors, paid the fees not covered by the scholarship. Here Walton began to compose a miscellany of vocal works, without instruction, but did not receive a degree because of repeated deficiencies in academic studies.

Through associations at Oxford, which turned out to be another stroke of good fortune, the young Walton became the musical protégé of Osbert, Edith, and Sacheverell Sitwell. This extraordinary family of literati had not yet achieved the renown it would later enjoy, but in its home Walton found much intellectual stimulation and a security that enabled him to pursue his own musical study. *Façade*, a collection of pieces for chamber ensemble designed to accompany Edith Sitwell's reading of her own poetry, attracted much attention in 1921 as an English response to Arnold Schoenberg's *Pierrot lunaire*, a work then very much the center of discussion in the musical community. Walton's witty score introduced him to the general public and marked the beginning of a career that would be sustained by a relatively short list of masterpieces.

Walton gained international attention with performances of his works at meetings of the International Society for Contemporary Music. His string quartet was presented at that group's meeting in 1923, and in spite of a desultory performance, Alban Berg regarded it as the work of the leading British modernist. Walton proved to be a slow and careful composer, producing scores that were meticulously crafted and thoroughly considered in all facets of their construction. His reputation rests on the enduring success of *Belshazzar's Feast*, the Symphony No. 1, and two concertos. He wrote other orchestral works, but his interests later expanded to include chamber music, opera, and music for films. His film scores, written between 1934 and 1970, are regarded by many as some of the most important work in that genre.

In England, Walton proved to be the premier young composer in the generation between Ralph Vaughan Williams and Benjamin Britten. On the international scene, he has been compared to Jean Sibelius and Sergei Prokofiev in both the character of some thematic materials and his structural designs. His independence surfaces again in his own musical credo, offered while still a young composer: "When I sit down to write music, I never trouble about modernism or anything else. I certainly never try to write for today or even for tomorrow, but to compose something which will have the same merit whatever time it is performed."[1]

Symphony No. 1

Allegro assai

Presto, con malizia

Andante con malinconia

Maestoso—Brioso ed ardentemente—Vivacissimo—Maestoso

Walton worked on his First Symphony from early 1932 until the late summer of 1935. The first three movements were performed in London on December 3, 1934, by the London Symphony Orchestra, Sir Hamilton Harty conducting; the complete symphony was performed in London on November 6, 1935, by the British Broadcasting Corporation Symphony Orchestra, Harty again conducting.

Instrumentation: *two flutes (the second doubling piccolo), two oboes, two clarinets, two bassoons, four horns, three trumpets, three trombones, tuba, timpani (two players), snare drum, tam-tam, cymbals, and strings.*

The success of *Belshazzar's Feast* in 1931 drew much attention to Walton as one of Britain's most promising musical talents. Either the publisher, Hubert Foss, or the conductor, Sir Hamilton Harty, or perhaps both acting in collaboration, suggested that Walton turn his talents to a symphony in order to sustain his recent success with the public. Work began in late February 1932, but progress was slow and erratic. In May, Walton mentioned in correspondence that events in his personal life had pushed his work far into the background, but optimistically referred to a planned performance date of March 27, 1933. Work continued slowly; that date passed without a finished score, and in September Walton wrote to Harty about his progress:

> I'm sorry I've been so slow in producing my symphony, but actually I don't think it is any the worse for it; in fact, I hope and think that it promises to be better than any work I've written hitherto, but that may be only an optimistic reaction to the months of despair I've been through when I thought I should never be able to write another note. However, the 1st movement is finished and the second ought to be in another ten days or so. But having disappointed you once, I feel chary about fixing any date for its ultimate completion, but it ought to be ready sometime for next season (1934).[2]

Based on the composer's projection, and perhaps some wishful thinking, Harty included the symphony in the prospectus for the 1933-to-

1934 season of the London Symphony Orchestra. Early in 1934, Walton wrote again, this time to the British Broadcasting Corporation (BBC), announcing further delays:

> Having been ill, I wrote to Sir Hamilton Harty telling him that it had put me so much behind with my symphony that it would be best not to announce it for performance on March 19th. In his reply he says amongst other things: "As for me, I must look forward to the first performance of this work whenever it is finished and I take it for granted that you will reserve it for me. If not ready in time for this season [early 1934], it could be produced early in the next, etc." So you will see that the May Festival performance hangs on whether I can finish in time for March 19th. I'm not in complete despair about doing so, but I just want to warn you in time, in case I don't.[3]

Walton followed that with a letter to the conductor Adrian Boult in February, saying there was no hope of completing the work in time for a performance on March 19. He then interrupted work on the symphony in order to compose music for the film *Escape Me Never* during the summer of 1934. At the end of August, he telephoned Hubert Foss that he had finished the symphony but was not sure about the last movement. A month later, Harty, in what must have been a mood of great resignation, repeated his willingness to produce the symphony whenever it was completed. Through machinations that would later become the topic of much discussion in British music circles, the first three movements of the long-anticipated symphony were performed on December 3, 1934 to high praise from both audience and critics. Two further performances of these movements followed in April 1935, as Walton again turned his attention to the last movement. By August 30 he had finished the score, to the delight and relief of his sponsors. He played the complete work for friends on October 13, slightly more than three weeks before the first full orchestra performance on November 6.

The symphony was written at a time when there was much experimentation with ways of achieving cohesion in a musical work without relying on traditional harmony. Walton's score is firmly tonal but expands on existing procedures within that context. Harmonic and thematic material interact and often develop independently; of the two, harmony usually emerges as the more important. To resolve conflicting musical activities, Walton often relies on pedal points, simply stated and sustained without ambiguity by the full orchestra, producing a thick texture of overpowering effect.

The *Allegro assai* opens with a quiet pedal point on B-flat, the first of several scattered throughout the movement. The melancholy first theme, played by the oboe over an agitated supporting figure from the second violins, marks the beginning of an orchestral crescendo that reaches its climax at the arrival of a new pedal point on C. The music progresses through other, similarly constructed orchestral crescendos founded on contrasts between a lyric line and supporting fragmentary material, or between melodies placed in the top and bottom of the ensemble (flute versus cello, for example). A unison B-flat closes the movement, offering no commitment to either major or minor mode.

The *Presto, con malizia* is a propulsive scherzo involving the whole orchestra in an aura of rhythmic vehemence. Misplaced accents, rapid exchanges between full orchestra and small groups, and a variety of special effects from the instruments (mutes, open and closed horn notes) combine to create a virtuoso exercise in orchestral playing. Walton's descriptive title, *con malizia*, invites speculation: with malice toward what, one wonders. Did this reflect his own mood at the time of composition, or a quality he wanted to evoke? What is malice in music? The relentless rhythmic drive of this movement suggests neither kindness nor gentility, but considering the speed of events, neither a performer nor a listener immersed in the score will have much time to reflect on such matters. This is music projecting a "take no prisoners" attitude, and that alone may sufficiently fulfill the title.

Portions of the third movement were among the first composed. A quick theme originally intended for the first movement did not work out and was subsequently incorporated into the opening of the *Andante con malinconia*. Contrast with the preceding movement could hardly be more pronounced. The unusual tonal center of C-sharp, not further defined by implied major or minor, lies midway between the B-flat of the first movement and the E of the second. The melancholy mood suggested by the *con malinconia* title comes about through the designation *dolorosa molto espress[ivo]* for the flutes' presentation of the parent theme, along with the accompaniment in muted horns and strings. Melody and pedal points become the most pronounced musical elements. Similar to the first movement, the music unfolds through thematic expansion more than through a division into sections that are developed and restated.

Walton's decision to incorporate a fugue in the middle of the last movement resolved many musical problems but introduced others. The pedal points that underlie much of the symphony are less compatible with fugal writing, so this section assumes a character different from the rest of the work. The counterpoint produces an increasing tension not released until it explodes in the whirlwind *Vivacissimo* that follows.

Delays in completing the symphony, exacerbated by what proved to be preemptory announcements of its introduction, fueled a mixed critical reaction to the finished work. Following the first full performance, some stylish critics pretended to find the last movement insufficient to balance those heard in earlier performances. In later years, Walton complained that the introduction of the incomplete symphony had taken place against his will, lending substance to the comments by those who chose to consider the finale an afterthought, which it definitely was not. There were substantive problems on both sides of the issue. Walton had allowed the symphony to be included in the prospectus of the London Symphony Orchestra for two consecutive years. Interest in his music ran high following the success of the Viola Concerto and *Belshazzar's Feast*; thus the parties managing the concert probably thought it wise to respond to that public interest by presenting the work when announced. They were weighing further delay and possible loss of interest against an incomplete performance and a risk of anticlimax when the finale was completed. With the perspective of time, these questions have become less pressing, as we now perceive the symphony as a whole. There are countless other works that have been written piecemeal, undergoing revision, rearrangement, or recomposition to reach a final state that we hear without knowledge of the creative struggles involved.

While Walton might complain about the pressures exerted on him to perform the symphony before it was finished, he could not complain about the review in the *Times* following the performance in November 1935:

> What we wanted to know was how Walton would resolve the complex situation which the earlier movements develop. . . . The success of the *finale* lies in the avoidance of anything like a return to

the manner of the first movement. It is the most "classical" in style of the four since its strongly defined subject matter is handled mainly contrapuntally. Indeed it might be described as a prelude and double fugue. It makes an exceedingly brilliant ending to the scheme, and its brilliance is enhanced by its clear B-flat major tonality. . . . This symphony, full of invention and containing passages of great beauty, especially in the *Adagio*, has a remarkable eloquence from first to last.[4]

Concerto for Violin and Orchestra

Andante tranquillo

Presto capriccioso alla napolitana

Vivace

Walton dated the end of his autograph score June 2, 1939, but revised the work during October and November 1943. It was first performed in Cleveland on December 7, 1939, by the Cleveland Orchestra conducted by Artur Rodzinski, with Jascha Heifetz as soloist.

Instrumentation: *two flutes (the second doubling piccolo), two oboes (the second doubling English horn), two clarinets, two bassoons, four horns, two trumpets, three trombones, timpani, snare drum, cymbals, tambourine, xylophone, harp, solo violin, and strings.*

Walton wrote one concerto each for violin, viola, and cello, all three created with a specific performer in mind as the result of a commission or specific request. The Violin Concerto was composed at a time when his previous successes had created a demand for his compositions. Jascha Heifetz—responding to a recommendation from the violist, William Primrose, and the success of Walton's Viola Concerto—approached Walton in 1936 about a concerto for his own use. Walton was pleased to accept the commission, because Heifetz was a violinist of great stature who could assure a public hearing and, pending a successful response, the possibilities of a recording.

Other matters prevented Walton from starting the concerto until January 1938, a time when he had traveled to Italy to facilitate his recovery from surgery in December 1937. On January 26, 1938, he wrote to his personal friend and publisher, Hubert Foss, that the "morning sickness" was beginning—meaning he was beginning the work—but otherwise there had been little progress. In that same letter, he reported that his hostess, Alice Wimborne, was making him work, and even became cross when he procrastinated. The following April, Walton received an invitation from the British Council to write a violin concerto that would be performed at concerts associated with the New York World Fair, to be held from April to October 1939. In Walton's view, the proposal fit his own plans very well, provided that Heifetz could be the soloist and would agree to the premiere being administered by the British Council. Walton described some of the details in a letter to Foss:

> Terms being £250 for a first performance only. No other rights being asked for, except maybe the dedication. Also a £100 extra for a trip to New York. I replied in the affirmative, stipulating that Heifetz should play the first performance. The British Council's terms not clashing with Heifetz's, I could try and kill two birds with one stone, for he can do whatever he likes about the work after the first performance.[5]

Always a careful and cautious worker, Walton soon was wrestling with doubts about the unfinished work, as he often did, and described his concerns in a letter to Foss:

> What . . . seems to me the greatest drawback is the nature of the work itself. It seems to be developing in an extremely intimate way, not much show and bravura, and I begin to have doubts (fatal for the work, of course) of this still small voice getting over at all in a vast hall holding 10,000 people. . . .[6]

Moreover, Walton worried that he didn't know how to make the solo part sufficiently elaborate to meet Heifitz's renown as a virtuoso. By June 1938, he had completed the first two movements and showed these to the violinist Antonio Brosa, a colleague from film work:

> He had written two movements, the first and second, and he lent it to me and I practised it, and he came home and played it with me and I made a few suggestions and so on, and he wrote to Heifetz telling him about this and sent him as samples the two

movements. Heifetz replied that he was not quite sure he liked
them as Walton wanted them and he suggested that he went [*sic*]
to America and worked it out with him. . . . Together they worked
out the third movement.[7]

By early 1939, Walton was still dissatisfied with the last movement
and sustained doubts whether Heifetz would perform the work. His
fears were allayed early in March when Heifetz cabled that he accepted
the concerto enthusiastically. At the end of May, Walton traveled to the
United States to discuss the concerto with Heifetz in detail, only to find
the violinist relatively unconcerned about such matters. He later commented that Heifetz had "jazzed up" the last movement a bit, but as
Heifetz's edited score was subsequently lost in a wartime shipping dis-
aster, the violinist's influence on the musical substance of the finished
score remains unclear. Considering the technical demands of the solo
part in the second and third movements and the stature the concerto
has come to enjoy in the repertory, it is difficult to grasp how either
composer or performer could have questioned its sufficiency in matters
of brilliance and virtuosity. The demanding writing calls for a masterful technique, but one that serves the substance of the music more than
bravura display.

In its broadest outlines, the Violin Concerto follows a design similar to those for viola and cello: an opening sonata design in moderate
tempo; a fast and brilliant scherzo; and a closing movement in moderate to quick tempo that incorporates thematic materials from earlier
movements into its own reprise.

The *Andante tranquillo* opens with background material very typical
of Walton: a wavering line played by the clarinet over a sustained tone
in horns and basses. The principal theme is in two parts, a long-
breathed melody played by solo violin and a slower countermelody
added by the bassoon. The violin expands on this material, until the
orchestral violins and flute introduce the second theme in the unusual
key of E-flat minor, in traditional harmonic practice far removed from
the original B minor. A cadenza placed midway in the development
offers respite from the concentration on the principal theme, and a
shorter cadenza functions as a bridge to the recapitulation. At this
point, the opening materials return, but in different timbres: the clarinet's undulating theme is now played by muted violins, the flute

assumes the principal melody, and the solo violin takes the bassoon's countermelody. In an imaginative orchestral gesture, Walton recasts the opening accompaniment for bassoon, harp, and timpani. In its two parts, the principal theme has dominated most of the movement until, almost as an afterthought, the bassoon interjects a quiet reference to the second theme in the last ten measures.

The second movement combines the outlines of a scherzo and trio, enhanced by references to Walton's experience of Italy. In the late spring of 1938, he reported that he had been bitten by a tarantula spider, an unpleasant incident that he commemorated by writing a movement in the spirit of a tarantella, the vigorous dance that folk wisdom has long considered a cure for such maladies. He described it as "presto capricciosamente alla napolitana—quite gaga, I may say, and of doubtful propriety after the 1st movement."[8] The full orchestra plays a brief fanfare that becomes a recurring point of reference throughout the movement, punctuating demanding passagework for the solo violin. The trio, qualified by the Italianate subtitle *Canzonetta*, offers a brief lyrical contrast in themes by the solo horn and oboe before the return of the opening material and further brilliant passages for the solo violin.

Three themes cast in a modified sonata design form the closing *Vivace*. Low strings introduce the first and most important melody, a furtive march in triple meter that dominates the movement. The full orchestra plays a jerky, contrasting bit before the flute introduces the second theme proper. In a poignant summation, the solo violin recalls the main theme from the opening *Andante tranquillo* as the bassoon plays the main theme from the *Vivace*, much changed in character, as a countermelody. Extending this spirit of reverie, the soloist soon returns with the second theme, now marked "Slow, dreamily with much expression." The mood does not last, because the cellos and basses return with their furtive theme in a gradual accelerando leading toward a concluding and emphatic march.

The salient features of Walton's Violin Concerto are his inspired adaptation of traditional designs and his skillful avoidance of clearly defined key centers as major constructive elements. Beyond those observations, we find here a solo part whose difficulty has earned for the concerto a reputation as a virtuoso vehicle, so well written for the violin that it challenges critics who maintain that a composer must master any instrument for which he proposes to write a concerto. For all of its technical demands, the concerto is not an empty showpiece. It is more appropriately described as a well-integrated, sometimes contemplative musical expression in which the solo violin exerts the greatest energy in exploring the potential of the materials at hand.

Concerto for Viola and Orchestra

Andante comodo

Vivo, con molto preciso

Allegro moderato

Walton composed the Viola Concerto in a relatively short time between late 1928 and March 1929. The first performance was given in London on October 3, 1929, by the Henry Wood Symphony Orchestra, conducted by Walton, with Paul Hindemith as soloist.

Instrumentation: *two flutes, piccolo, two oboes, English horn, two clarinets, bass clarinet, two bassoons, contrabassoons, four horns, three trumpets, three trombones, timpani, and strings.*

Walton revised the orchestration in 1961; this version, which has largely replaced the original, was introduced in London on January 18, 1962, by the London Philharmonic, Sir Malcolm Sargent conducting, with John Coulling as soloist.

Instrumentation: *Two flutes (the second doubling piccolo), two oboes (the second doubling English horn), two clarinets (the second doubling bass clarinet), two bassoons, four horns, two trumpets, three trombones, timpani, harp, and strings.*

Aside from its musical qualities, Walton's Viola Concerto rode on a wave of string concertos by English composers (Elgar, Rubbra, Rawsthorne, Britten), of which it formed a major part. In addition, the efforts of the famous British violist, Lionel Tertis, had done much to bring that instrument to the fore. Through his earlier works, particularly *Façade*, Walton had become known as a young English composer of facile talent, but the Viola Concerto showed him to be a composer who could speak with a style and substance equal to others of his generation anywhere.

It was the conductor Sir Thomas Beecham who suggested to Walton that he write a viola concerto for Lionel Tertis. In a letter of December 5, 1928, addressed to the poet Siegfried Sassoon, Walton referred to his work on the concerto and offered that it was his best effort up to that time. In further correspondence with Sassoon, he reported on February 2 that he had completed the second movement the previous day and that he continued to view it as his best work, concerns about the last movement notwithstanding.

When the score was completed, Walton duly forwarded it to Tertis but was dismayed when it came back by return post. In his autobiography, Tertis later referred to the incident with some chagrin:

> One work of which I did *not* give the first performance was Walton's masterly concerto. With shame and contrition I admit that when the composer offered me the first performance I declined it. I was unwell at the time; but what is also true is that I had not learnt to appreciate Walton's style. The innovations in his musical language, which now seem so logical and so truly in the main-stream of music, then struck me as far-fetched. It took me time to realize what a tower of strength in the literature of the viola is this concerto, and how deep the gratitude that we who play the viola should feel towards the composer. . . . I remember that, when Walton came to me with it and I refused the honour, he was generous enough not to seem to take it too much amiss but asked me to suggest someone else to undertake the performance. I immediately thought of Paul Hindemith, a well-known and much-talked-of composer and a viola-player too.[9]

In Walton's account, it was Edward Clark of the BBC rather than Tertis who suggested Hindemith. Either way, Hindemith was approached, and early in July he agreed to play the concerto. Walton was a bit surprised, because he felt that some portions of the score resembled Hindemith's own style, and he was also intimidated by the more famous German composer, well known as teacher and performer in addition to his creative works. Hindemith accepted the invitation because he liked the concerto, and he saw in the conductor Henry Wood a musician who, like himself, was interested in making music without undue fuss and bother or involvement in the public glitter of promotion and personality. Hindemith's publisher, Willi Strecker of B.

Schotts Söhne, had planned to promote Hindemith and his works with a big career as a solo violist, capitalizing on Hindemith's performance skills. However, he was less than pleased when he learned that Hindemith would be playing Walton's work. He complained to Gertrud Hindemith, the composer's wife, that her husband should be more discerning in selecting where and when he would perform:

> An appearance with Wood to play a concerto by a moderately gifted English composer . . . is not a fitting debut. Wood's promenade concerts are, like the conductor himself, a worthy institution at which the playing is so-so and never a sensation of the sort I am hoping for.[10]

Walton conducted the premiere. By his own account, the first rehearsal was a shambles. The orchestral parts contained many errors, requiring him to stay up all night before the performance to correct missing bars and wrong notes. The performance must have been much more successful; Lionel Tertis attended and was captivated by the music, although not by Hindemith's playing.

The Viola Concerto reflects a late Romantic spirit in its lyricism and relaxed formal designs. Walton himself was aware of the lyrical quality, because during the concerto's preparation he wrote to his friend the pianist Angus Morrison that "my style is changing—it is becoming more melodious and mature."[11] Much of the work's success derives from the happy match between musical materials and the writing for the solo instrument. Walton replaced the traditional fast–slow–fast order of movements with a sequence of moderate–fast–moderate tempos. He linked the two outer movements by recalling the main theme of the first shortly before the close of the last, a master stroke reflecting his own concept of the concerto as a single entity. Some observers have considered this a stratagem borrowed from Prokofiev's Violin Concerto No. 1, which offers a similar procedure formed around a comparable theme. Walton had probably heard Prokofiev's concerto, and sometimes he was glibly described as the "English Prokofiev." But at this writing there is no firm evidence that he consciously borrowed from Prokofiev in this matter. Any question of priority should not be allowed to obscure the artifice of this stroke which, along with several others, makes the last movement such an eloquent close to the concerto.

The violins introduce the main theme of the *Andante comodo* straight-away, soon followed by the viola. Solo passagework develops into a series of parallel sixths, played while the woodwinds recall a derivative head-motive in a series of false relations (a type of fluctuation between major and minor harmony). A portion of that material accompanies the viola's introduction of the second theme, and this too leads into passagework to accompany the woodwinds' extension of their three-note motive. In much of the following, the solo viola frequently returns to double-stop sixths before a long orchestral tutti leads to the recapitulation.

The second movement does not lend itself to stereotypical classifi-cation. It combines the character of a scherzo with a theme that returns in the manner of a rondo, all presented with speed and detachment. Viola and bassoon play the parent theme, a series of ascending fourths that quickly extend into rapid solo passagework. Intervening episodes cast this jocose motive into vivid relief as the music moves through lively contrasts between soloist, strings, brass, and woodwinds. The opening motive retains its identity until the soloist plays it one last time before expanding it into a series of wide leaps, concluded by one last fillip from clarinet and flute.

Most concertos end with a brilliant finale that expands on the tech-nical brilliance of the soloist. The finale of Walton's Viola Concerto offers much space to the soloist, but it is more important as a reflective summary of materials from the preceding movements. The music begins with a basic motive incorporating the same notes as the opening of the second movement, but in reverse order. This motive soon returns in dotted rhythms, in both original and inverted contours. A second theme, introduced by the violins, is taken up by the viola before it moves into a passage of double-stop sixths, a familiar sound from the first movement. The development expands on exchanges between the second theme and basic motive, until a fugue develops over a pedal point in the timpani. The tension thus generated finds release in the relaxed tempo of the reprise, where the parent theme from the first movement returns as a counterpoint to the motive of fifths. The violins recall a series of false relations from the first movement, and these wavering major-minor inferences occupy the solo viola in the closing measures, its ultimate A major clashing gently with the A minor of the violins. In this manner, Walton gathers the principal musical materials of the concerto into quiet repose.

Audiences have responded to these subtle operations with enthusiasm. One performance in Scotland was greeted with such favor that both soloist and conductor, Lionel Tertis and Adrian Boult, felt compelled to repeat the entire concerto as an encore, a very rare event in the modern concert hall. A more telling commentary is the number of violinists who have temporarily taken up the viola in order to perform this concerto, among them Yehudi Menuhin and, more recently, Nigel Kennedy. The prevailing view was expressed eloquently in a review by Peter Pirie: "Yet, if music be musical at all, how lovely a thing is Walton's Viola Concerto! How its perfectly calculated effects and completely unstrained technique serve with grace the poignant beauty of its content. Its ending is a stroke of genius. . . ."[12] At the close of the 20th century, those sentiments endured for devotees of this unusual concerto.

Belshazzar's Feast

Walton began work on Belshazzar's Feast *in December 1929. It was first performed in Leeds on October 8, 1931, by the Leeds Festival Chorus, the London Symphony Orchestra conducted by Sir Malcolm Sargent, and Dennis Noble, baritone.*

Ensemble: *double mixed chorus, baritone soloist, two flutes, piccolo, two oboes (the second doubling English horn in the absence of a saxophone), three clarinets (the second doubling clarinet in E-flat, the third doubling bass clarinet), two bassoons, contrabassoon, alto saxophone, four horns, three trumpets, three trombones, tuba, timpani, bass drum, snare drum, tenor drum, triangle, tambourine, castanets, cymbals, gong, wood block, slapsticks, anvil, xylophone, glockenspiel, two harps, piano (ad* libitum*), organ, and strings. Optional: two brass groups, each consisting of three trumpets, three trombones, and tuba, to be placed to the right and left of the conductor.*

By the close of the 20th century, *Belshazzar's Feast* was firmly established as one of the great choral works of the age, along with Stravinsky's *Symphony of Psalms* and Britten's *War Requiem*. The long tradition of choral music in England provided a fertile background for the conception, performance, and appreciation of a work that demands much from the singers. Walton's early musical training as a choirboy at

Oxford provided fertile soil for the blossoming of his talents in a choral work of expanded dimensions. Together with the Viola Concerto and First Symphony, *Belshazzar's Feast* confirmed earlier successes and has carried Walton's name to audiences around the world.

The published score appeared under the title *Belshazzar's Feast for mixed choir, baritone solo, and orchestra.* Several others have described it as a "cantata," "dramatic cantata," "theatrical cantata," or "oratorio," all attempts to categorize the work within traditional parameters not suggested by the composer. Michael Kennedy, one of the most eloquent Walton scholars, has offered the term "choral symphonic poem," a term encompassing most of the salient musical traits but still carrying an unnecessary aura of formalism. As a major choral work, *Belshazzar's Feast* is one of a kind, and there should be no substantial need to define it beyond the nomenclature offered by the composer's title.

The BBC asked three composers, including Walton, to produce works of limited proportions consisting of a small chorus, an orchestra of not more than fifteen players, and a soloist. Edward Clark of the BBC first approached Walton in August 1929, and by December, work was under way. Walton spent the period from December 1929 to May 1930 with Osbert Sitwell, the librettist, in Amalfi, Italy, presumably working on the BBC commission. At the end of May, Clark reported that Walton had returned from abroad with a completed *Belshazzar* score for two soloists, small chorus, and small orchestra. Walton later acknowledged that at one point he had envisioned the work for this small performing group, but the work Clark described was clearly different from the score that finally emerged. It seems likely that *Belshazzar* was still a work in progress in the late spring of 1930.

Early in the fall, R. J. F. Howgill of the BBC wrote to Hubert Foss of Oxford University Press about the emergence of a larger work:

> It seems to have been agreed between Edward Clark and William Walton that *Belshazzar's Feast* has grown to such proportions that it cannot be considered as a work specially written for broadcasting, and the latter therefore proposes to write something else as his commissioned work.[13]

Referring to this period of gestation several years later, Walton reported that during most of 1930, or at least from May to December, he had been unable to progress beyond the word "gold." Some parts of the score must still have been in a state of flux as late as the spring of 1931, because in a later interview Walton reported that the addition of the two brass bands at about this time was in response to a caustic witticism from Sir Thomas Beecham, who was originally scheduled to conduct the premiere. Whether the brass groups were added out of spite or from purely musical considerations we do not know, but either way, they remained in the score. Stories about the choristers' objections to the difficulty of their parts have surfaced from time to time, but these have not been reliably documented and should probably be included among the fables that grew up around an unusual and, later, very famous work.

Osbert Sitwell was one of Walton's close friends and benefactors during his poststudent days, and by 1929 was recognized as one of the Oxford literati who exercised considerable influence in England's progressive literary circles. The text he produced for Walton's work reflected his own interests at the time as well as his belief that, as a familiar story, "the hand that wrote upon the wall" would attract wide attention. He took material directly from the books of Daniel and Revelation, and parts of Psalms 81 and 137, to which he added a few words to assist in the poetic flow. The dramatic substance of the text deals with divine punishment for the sacrilege of defiling holy vessels and all they represent, followed by a cry of vindication from the oppressed but ultimately victorious Jews. These events are depicted in a scenario of three sections: the prophecy of Isaiah and the lament of the Jews; the feast at Belshazzar's court and the mysterious hand writing upon the wall; and a closing hymn of exaltation following the release of the Jews from captivity.

Walton reflects the three-part scenario in three large sections separated by two recitatives for the baritone. He uses the expanded performing resources sparingly, reserving the full ensemble for points of dramatic climax. In this process he establishes three sonorous units of voices alone, instruments alone, and voices and instruments together. On a smaller scale, he frequently turns to word-painting, creating harmonies or melodic contours to support specific texts. For example, grating dissonances in the unaccompanied chorus at the beginning lend pungency to the words of Isaiah as he prophesies the abduction and imprisonment of the Israelites. A few moments later, an undulating melodic contour enhances the words "By the waters of Babylon."

More dramatically, the baritone declamation that "In that night was Belshazzar slain" is answered by a choral shout of "Slain!" in which the individual pitches are only approximated. The orchestra offers its own textual enhancement, as in "Praise ye the god of silver" (answered by flute, piccolo, and harp harmonics), "Praise ye the god of iron" (followed by brass instruments and gong), "Praise ye the god of wood" (echoed by xylophone and wood block), and "Praise ye the god of brass" (another response from trumpets and trombones).

Thematic materials support the musical identity of the larger sections. Following the dissonant choral prophecy at the beginning, cellos and basses play a mournful theme that is assumed by the chorus and later returns as a close to the first section. A vigorously syncopated four-note motive, similar to the opening of the second movement of the Violin Concerto, introduces the second section describing the Babylonian feast, and peppers much of the music to follow. Most references link three statements over a span of three octaves, but the motive also appears as a separate item, and in that form closes the second section.

The following Grand Pause abruptly interrupts what has been headlong forward motion, and the music reaches its climax as the baritone recitative describes the writing that appears on the wall. Tremolos in harp and strings *sul ponticello* create an otherworldly atmosphere as the baritone intones the prophetic *Mene, mene, tekel upharsin* (Thou art weighed in the balance and found wanting). The trombone fanfare from the opening measures responds, the chorus follows with its own declamation, and the baritone concludes with the pronouncement of Belshazzar's death, emphasized by the hair-raising choral shout of "Slain!" The release of energy that follows continues through most of the concluding section, as the joy of the freed prisoners works itself out in a series of choral alleluias.

Most of the musical impact of *Belshazzar's Feast* derives from fundamentally conventional procedures. Walton proved himself a master of choral writing in passages ranging from ethereal peace to bitter rage. In other qualities he moves between extremes as abrupt changes in combination of performing resources produce sharp shifts in dynamics and texture. His silences are as effective and as important as his sonorous climaxes. Dissonances usually serve to enhance the text, and are built around traditional triadic structures rather than a contrived harmonic system.

This highly dramatic music was immediately successful following its introduction at the Leeds Festival in 1931. Early technical problems for the chorus were soon mastered, and the work was subsequently presented at the Festival of the International Society for Contemporary Music in Amsterdam in 1933, where it was regarded as a conventional work. It seems that the only objections were directed against the text, which some church authorities considered inappropriate for performance in a cathedral setting, the venue for most large choral performances. Those reservations may have been sparked by portions of the *Times* article following the first performance. An unidentified writer reviewed both Walton's work and Bach's Mass in B minor, performed the following day, in one article under the title "Leeds Music Festival: A Contrast of Religions—'Belshazzar's Feast' and Bach":

> Let not the three choirs of Worcester, Gloucester, and Hereford think that because this finale begins with "Sing aloud to God" and ends in antiphonal alleluias they may find here a suitable novelty for their cathedrals. *Belshazzar's Feast* is stark Judaism from first to last. It culminates in ecstatic gloating over the fallen enemy, the utter negation of Christianity. Its power as a dramatic oratorio compels admiration, but it is no more a "sacred" oratorio than is Handel's on the same subject. By comparison with it the other novelties of this festival and of many others appear merely decorative. In *Belshazzar's Feast* Mr. Walton has pursued his themes relentlessly, refusing all external decoration, and has produced a work of intense energy and complete sincerity. . . . This morning we have returned to the Christian civilization with Bach's Mass in B minor.[14]

The comments about the "utter negation of Christianity" in *Belshazzar's Feast* should be considered in light of the writer's clear preference for Bach's Mass. Had the review dealt only with Walton's work, the tone surely would have been different and subsequent clerical reactions less negative. After all, the substance of Sitwell's text had been in circulation for centuries before Walton set it to music!

Anton Webern

b. Vienna, Austria, December 2, 1883; d. Mittersill, Austria, September 15, 1945

The works of Anton Webern represented some of the most important influences on music in the middle of the 20th century. He was only one year younger than Stravinsky and two years younger than Bartók, but it was his musical aesthetic that most of the younger composers extended to create dramatically new sounds and procedures. When tonality became less important as an organizing feature of music, something had to replace it. The twelve-tone row process was the most important of several systems to emerge, and Webern was the first major composer to dedicate himself fully and without reservation to this technique. Starting with his Opus 17 (1924), it became as basic to his creative operation as tonality had been for the composers of the classical era. Webern extended the serial process to include elements other than pitch, offering to younger composers a model through which they could establish a comprehensive and consistent context for the projection of nontonal ideas. The breadth of his influence was recognized by an international Webern festival in Seattle in 1962 and another in Mittersill in 1969. Both events reflected a musical stature not matched by frequent performances of his works in the concert hall until later in the century.

When Webern completed his studies at the gymnasium in Klagenfurt, his family rewarded him with a trip to the Beyreuth Festival of 1902. That experience of Wagner's music sparked Webern's first major attempt at composition, a ballad for soprano and orchestra titled *Young Siegfried*. In the fall of 1902, he entered the University of Vienna to study musicology with the renowned scholar Guido Adler. His doctoral dissertation, a study of the *Choralis Constantinus* by the Renaissance master Heinrich Isaac, was completed in 1906 and included a description of the contrapuntal devices permeating Isaac's score that reads like a precis of the canonic techniques that later prevailed in Webern's mature works. He began supplemental studies in composition with Arnold Schoenberg in 1904 and, as was true of many Schoenberg students, came to revere his mentor with an intensity approaching idolatry. After 1908, the aspiring composer embarked on a conducting career that took him through a succession of appointments in provincial theaters, most of the engagements marked by musical success but personal frustration. In 1920, he settled in Mödling as conductor of a male chorus and private teacher of composition.

In the following two decades, Webern composed most of the music now associated with his name. He expanded on Schoenberg's premise of serialism with a consistency not followed by Schoenberg himself. Musical elements not drawn from the tone row were eliminated to the extent that a broadening circle of musical parameters fell within the influence of an established series. His artistic goal was "to develop everything else from *one* principal idea! That's the strongest unity—when everybody does the same, as with the Netherlanders, where the theme was introduced by each individual part, varied in every possible way. . . ."[1] Webern eventually became recognized as part of the Second Viennese School, a group of composers that saw itself as a continuation of the great Germanic musical tradition extending from Bach through Haydn, Mozart, and Beethoven and on to the triumvirate of Schoenberg, Berg, and Webern.

Passacaglia for Orchestra, Opus 1

Webern's Passacaglia *reached its final form in the spring of 1908. The first performance took place in Vienna on November 4, 1908, with members of the Vienna Tonkünstler Orchestra, Webern conducting.*

Instrumentation: *piccolo, two flutes, two oboes, English horn, two clarinets, bass clarinet, two bassoons, contrabassoon, four horns, three trumpets, three trombones, bass tuba, timpani, bass drum, cymbals, triangle, tam-tam, harp, and strings.*

Although designated as his first opus, the *Passacaglia* was by no means Webern's first composition. It was written as an informal graduation piece to mark the end of his regularly scheduled study with Schoenberg and probably represented the first work Webern was willing to place before the public. His choice of a *passacaglia*, a form based on extended variation of a minimal theme, was both an exemplar of Schoenberg's dictum of continuing variation and a gesture through which Webern could establish his roots in the great German tradition of the past at a time when he was moving into a new world of musical experiences. Beyond those considerations, admittedly speculative, the designation of a first opus indicated that he felt some degree of confidence in a public demonstration of his own technique as a composer.

Basses playing pizzicato introduce the *Passacaglia* theme: eight notes separated by rests of equal number and value. This bare-bones outline has reminded many listeners of a comparable theme in the Finale of Beethoven's *Eroica* Symphony. The harmonic implications of the first variation suggest another link with the past: the last movement of Brahms's Fourth Symphony. There, as in Webern's score, the harmonic relationship between the first and last measures creates a closed circle that propels the music forward through aural expectation. As would be true of Webern's later atonal works, his basic material—in this instance an eight-measure theme—shows a carefully conceived design full of latent possibilities.

The variations built on this simple yet fertile theme fall into three groups: variations 1-11, 12-15, and 16-23. Each group ends with a fermata. The midsection (variations 12-15) is further distinguished by a change to D major from the prevailing D minor tonality and a much subdued level of activity, *Sehr ruhig* (*very restful*) and *ppp*. Thus on a large scale the body of the *Passacaglia* suggests a broad arch, the whole linked by the underlying theme or some manifestation of it.

The first variation introduces the underlying harmonization of the theme and a countertheme in the flute. These elements become the basic materials in most of the musical exposition that follows. In subsequent variations, the countertheme is recast by clarinet, then strings, as the theme itself becomes more and more obscure. The music builds to a climax in variation 8 when the violins play the original form of the main theme against a transformation of another countertheme in the basses. The accrued orchestral density declines rapidly in variations 9-11 in order to arrive at the quiet fermata marking the close of the first section.

Variation 12 establishes D major and introduces a character that quickly sets this section apart from its musical surroundings. Trumpets play the *Passacaglia* theme in sustained notes, as motives drawn from

468   *Anton Webern*

earlier counterthemes are developed by the woodwinds. The last variation of the group closes on a harmony that prepares for the return of
the closing section in the original key and tempo.

As with the preceding groups, the closing section begins with a
quiet statement of the *Passacaglia* theme, this time by the trombones,
and the variations that follow expand through tightly knit injections of
motivic imitation. The last variation reaches a peak of intensity before
subsiding to a quiet fermata in preparation for the coda, which draws
on materials from variations 7 and 8 to close the work.

Webern's *Passacaglia* is one of those compositions that appeal to a
listener on several levels. One can follow the permutations of the basic
theme, the loosely configured A–B–A design of the three groups of variations, or, with repeated exposure, the references in later variations to
those heard near the beginning. Any one of these perceptions leaves the
impression of a cohesive artistic statement.

Most works identified with Schoenberg and his students were assured
of an initially harsh reception by critics for whom the delicate shades of
French impressionism still represented modernity. Webern's *Passacaglia* was
no exception. One Viennese critic claimed that Webern had written "a passacaglia which hardly justifies the name any longer. Respect for form,
without content."[2] But another writer heard much more in Webern's score:

> The composition, surprising in its curiosities of tonal combina-
> tions and their progressions, nevertheless convinces through the
> depth of the moods evoked. Nothing appears accidental, nothing
> forced by a mania for originality; least of all is anything conven-
> tionally imitated. The moods are *felt*, the sounds *heard*.[3]

Webern's growing recognition as a conductor offered him more
opportunities to introduce his works, and starting in 1923, the conductor Alexander von Zemlinsky began to perform the *Passacaglia* with
considerable success. Attitudes changed, and Webern's first opus was
described as "a work full of warmth and enterprise. . . . One regrets that
this first work remained an opus 1, that not six or twelve such works
followed it: Webern would have been in a leading position."[4] By this
time Webern had completed several other important works, but it
would take another thirty years before the musical world would accord
him the prominence prophesied for him by the prescient critic in 1923.

Notes

JOHN ADAMS

1. John Adams, interview by Robert Schwartz, in "Process *vs*. Intuition in the Recent Works of Steve Reich and John Adams," *American Music* 8 (Fall 1990): 247.
2. Adams, *The Chairman Dances* (New York: Associated Music Publishers, 1986): Preface.
3. Adams, interview by Edward Strickland, in *American Composers: Dialogues on Contemporary Music* (Bloomington, IN: Indiana University Press, 1991): 181–182.

SAMUEL BARBER

1. Samuel Barber, interview by John Gruen, in "And Where Has Samuel Barber Been?" *New York Times*, October 3, 1971, sec. 2, p. 21.
2. Olin Downes, "Rodzinsky Directs Barber Symphony," *New York Times*, March 26, 1937, p. 24.
3. Frank Granville Barker, Virtuoso Night Out," *Music and Musicians* 13 (August 1965), as quoted in Don A. Hennessee, *Samuel Barber: A Bio-Bibliography* (Westport, CT: Greenwood Press, 1985), 254.
4. Barber, undated program note, Philadelphia Orchestra Archives, in Barbara B. Heyman, *Samuel Barber: The Composer and His Music* (New York: Oxford University Press, 1992): 195–196.
5. Irving Fine, "English in Boston," *Modern Music* 23 (Summer 1946): 210.
6. Ross Lee Finney, "Orchestral Music," *Music Library Association Notes* 11 (December 1953): 146–147.
7. Samuel Barber, *Medea's Dance of Vengeance*, study score (New York: G. Schirmer, 1956): Preface.
8. Heyman, *Samuel Barber*, 275.

BÉLA BARTÓK

1. Olin Downes, "Bartók Concerto Introduced Here," *New York Times*, January 11, 1945, p. 18.
2. Béla Bartók, "Concerto for Orchestra," *Boston Symphony Orchestra Program*, December 1, 1944, in David Cooper, *Bartók: Concerto for Orchestra* (Cambridge, UK: Oxford University Press, 1996): 85.
3. Ibid.
4. Ibid
5. Bartók, "Analysis of the Second Concerto for Piano and Orchestra," in *Béla Bartók Essays*, ed. Benjamin Suchoff (New York: St. Martin's Press, 1976): 419.

6. Ralph Hawkes to Bartók, August 22, 1940, in Benjamin Suchoff, "Some Observations on Bartók's Third Piano Concerto," *Tempo* 65 (Summer 1963): 8.

7. Primrose to Bartók, January 22, 1945, in László Somfai, "Commentary" to *Béla Bartók: Viola Concerto, Facsimile Edition of the Autograph Draft* (Homosassa, FL: Bartók Records, 1995): 24.

8. Bartók to Primrose, August 2, 1945, in Somfai, "Commentary," 24–25.

9. Bartók to Primrose, September 8, 1945, in Somfai, "Commentary," 25.

10. See *Béla Bartók Essays,* ed. Benjamin Suchoff (New York: St. Martin's Press, 1976), 396.

11. Bartók, lecture notes, in Tibor Tallián, *Béla Bartók: The Man and His Work*, trans. Gyula Gulyás (Budapest: Szemtöl szemben Gondolat, 1981): 133.

12. Bartók to Octavian Beu, January 10, 1931, in *Béla Bartók Letters*, ed. János Deményi, trans. Peter Balabán and István Farkas (New York: St. Martin's Press, 1971): 201.

13. Bartók to his elder son, Béla, August 18, 1939, in *Bartók Letters*, 278.

14. Bartók to Zoltán Székely, October 17, 1936, in Claude Kenneson, *Székely and Bartók: The Story of a Friendship* (Portland, OR: Amadeus Press, 1994): 159.

15. *Kölner Stadt-Anzeiger*, November 29, 1926, in John Vinton, "The Case of *The Miraculous Mandarin*," *Musical Quarterly* 50 (January 1964): 13.

ALBAN BERG

1. Louis Krasner, report of a conversation with Berg, in "The Origins of the Alban Berg Violin Concerto," *Alban Berg Studien*, ed. Frank Grasberger and Rudolf Stephan (Vienna: Universal Edition, 1981). 2;110.

2. Berg, letter to Louis Krasner, July 1935, in *Alban Berg Studien*, 2;112.

3. Berg to Arnold Schoenberg, July 9, 1913, in *The Berg-Schoenberg Correspondence*, ed. Julian Brand, Christopher Hailey, and Donald Harris (New York: W. W. Norton, 1987): 182.

4. See Robert Falck, "Two *Reigen*: Berg, Schnitzler, and Cyclic Form," in *Encrypted Messages in Alban Berg's Music* (New York: Garland Publishing, 1998): 92–93.

5. George Perle, *The Operas of Alban Berg: Wozzeck* (Berkeley and Los Angeles, CA: University of California Press, 1980): 18.

LEONARD BERNSTEIN

1. Bernstein, "Program Note" accompanying study score of the *Serenade* ([United States]: Jalhi Publications), 1956.

2. *Chicago Daily Tribune*, quoted in Humphrey Burton, *Leonard Bernstein* (New York: Doubleday and Co., 1994): 258.

3. Leonard Bernstein, "Notes Struck at 'Upper Dubbing,' California," *New York Times*, May 30, 1954, sec. 2, p. 5.

4. Mstislav Rostropovich, interview by William Westbrook Burton, in *Conversations about Bernstein* (New York: Oxford University Press, 1995): 137.

BENJAMIN BRITTEN

1. Britten to Ralph Hawkes, October 1939, in Donald Mitchell and Philip Reed, eds., *Letters from a Life: The Selected Letters and Diaries of Benjamin Britten* (Berkeley and Los Angeles, CA: University of California Press, 1991): 2;703.

2. "Leading European Composers Writing Symphonic Work for 26th Centenary," *Japan Times*, February 25, 1940, in Mitchell and Reed, *Letters*, 2;805.

3. Britten to his sister, Beth Welford, April 28, 1940, in *Letters*, 2;803.

4. Prince F. Konoye, to the Director of the Cultural Bureau of the Japanese Foreign Office in Tokyo, in *Letters*, 2;881.

5. Britten to Tomio Mori, Japanese Vice-Consul, November 27, 1940, in *Letters*, 2;890–891.
6. Britten to Beth Welford, May 12, 1941, in *Letters*, 2;919.
7. Britten, letter to *Radio Times* (January 18, 1946), in *Letters*, 2;883.
8. "N. S.," *New York Times*, March 30, 1941, sec. 1, p. 47.
9. Britten to Beth Welford, May 12, 1941, in *Letters*, 2;919–920.
10. J. A. Westrup, "The Virtuosity of Benjamin Britten," *Listener* (July 16, 1941), p. 93, in *Letters*, 1;530.
11. Britten, interview with Donald Mitchell, February 1969, "Mapreading: Benjamin Britten in Conversation with Donald Mitchell," *The Britten Companion*, ed. Christopher Palmer (Cambridge, UK: Cambridge University Press, 1984): 96.

AARON COPLAND

1. Copland, interview by Vivian Perlis, in Aaron Copland and Vivian Perlis, *Copland Since 1943* (New York: St. Martin's Press, 1989): 66.
2. Ibid., 68.
3. Leonard Bernstein, address to a young people's audience in 1958, in Howard Pollack, *Aaron Copland: The Life and Work of an Uncommon Man* (New York: Henry Holt and Company, 1999): 417.
4. Copland to Victor Records, October 4, 1947, in Copland and Perlis, *Copland Since 1943*, 87.
5. Ibid., 93.
6. Douglas Watt, "Music About Town," *New Yorker* 26 (December 9, 1950): 140.
7. Peter Tranchell, "Music Review," *Music and Letters* 33 (October 1952): 366.
8. Aaron Copland and Vivian Perlis, *Copland 1900 Through 1942* (New York: St. Martin's Press, 1984): 245.
9. Copland, *El Salón México*, study score (New York: Boosey & Hawkes, 1939), preface.
10. Elizabeth Sprague Coolidge, in Copland and Perlis, *Copland Since 1943*, 30.
11. Copland, 1981 narrative in Pollack, *Aaron Copland*, 402.
12. Edward D. Andrews, *The Gift to Be Simple* (New York: J. J. Augustin, 1940): 136.
13. *American Ballads and Folk Songs*, comp. John A. Lomax and Alan Lomax (New York: Macmillan Co., 1934): 138.

JOHN CORIGLIANO

1. Corigliano, interview by Allan Kozinn, in "The 'Unfashionably Romantic' Music of John Corigliano," *New York Times*, April 27, 1980, sec. D, p. 24.

PETER MAXWELL DAVIES

1. From the composer's Web site for *An Orkney Wedding*, http://www.maxopus.com/works/wedding.htm.

MANUEL DE FALLA

1. Manuel de Falla, narrative in John Brande Trend, *Manuel de Falla and Spanish Music* (1929; New York: Alfred A. Knopf, 1934): 66–67.

GEORGE GERSHWIN

1. A photocopy of the contract appears in Robert Kimball and Alfred Simon, *The Gershwins* (New York: Atheneum, 1973): 50.
2. Gershwin, *New York Tribune*, November 29, 1925, in Edward Jablonski and Lawrence Stewart, *The Gershwin Years: George and Ira* (1973; New York: Da Capo Press, 1996): 105.

3. Walter Damrosch, comments preceding the first performance of the Concerto in F, December 3, 1925, in John Tasker Howard, *Our American Music*, 4th ed. (New York: Thomas Y. Crowell Company, 1965): 427.

4. Carl Engel, "Views and Reviews," *Musical Quarterly* 12 (April 1926): 304.

5. Gershwin, narrative to Isaac Goldberg, in Isaac Goldberg, *George Gershwin: A Study in American Music* (1931; New York: Frederick Ungar Publishing Co., 1958): 139.

6. Olin Downes, "A Concert of Jazz," *New York Times*, February 13, 1924, p. 16.

7. G. W. Gabriel, review of the first performance in the *Sun and Globe* (New York), in Goldberg, *George Gershwin*, 150.

8. Lawrence Gilman, *Tribune* (New York), in Goldberg, *George Gershwin*, 152.

9. Gershwin, advance notice for publication in *Musical America*, August 18, 1928, in Charles Schwartz, *Gershwin: His Life and Music* (Indianapolis, IN: Bobbs-Merrill Co., 1973): 164.

10. Olin Downes, *New York Times*, December 14, 1928, p. 37.

11. Oscar Thompson, *New York Evening Post*, in Nicholas Slonimsky, *Lexikon of Musical Invective*, 2nd ed. (New York: Coleman-Ross Co., 1965): 105.

12. Leonard Bernstein, in Alan Kendall, *George Gershwin* (London: Harrap, 1987): 94.

13. Gershwin, "Program Note," *Facsimile Edition of Cuban Overture* (NP: Warner Bros. Publications, 1987): 7.

ALBERTO GINASTERA

1. Ginastera, in Lillian Tan, "An Interview with Alberto Ginastera," *American Music Teacher* 33 (January 1984): 8.

2. Ginastera, in Gilbert Chase, "Remembering Alberto Ginastera," *Latin American Music Review* 6 (Summer 1985): 82–83.

HENRYK GÓRECKI

1. Górecki, from a talk given in 1977 published as "Powiem państu szczerze" ("I Shall Tell You Frankly"), *ViVO* 1 (1994): 48, quoted in Adrian Thomas, *Górecki* (Oxford: Clarendon Press, 1997): 91.

PAUL HINDEMITH

1. Paul Hindemith, *A Composer's World: Horizons and Limitations* (Cambridge, MA: Harvard University Press, 1953): 218.

2. Hindemith to his wife, Gertrud, March 15, 1940, in Luther Noss, *Paul Hindemith in the United States* (Chicago, IL: University of Illinois Press, 1989): 77.

3. Olin Downes, "Rodzinski Offers Hindemith Music," *New York Times*, January 21, 1944, p. 20.

GUSTAV HOLST

1. Holst to Herbert Thompson, April 7, 1922, in Richard Green, *Gustav Holst and a Rhetoric of Musical Character* (New York: Garland Publishing, 1994): 353–354.

2. Imogen Holst, *The Music of Gustav Holst*, 3rd rev. ed. (London: Oxford University Press, 1986): 39.

CHARLES IVES

1. Elliott Carter, interview with Vivian Perlis, June 20, 1969, in *Charles Ives Remembered* (New Haven, CT: Yale University Press, 1974): 138.

2. *Charles E. Ives: Memos*, ed. John Kirkpatrick (New York: W. W. Norton & Co., 1972; reprint, New York: W. W. Norton & Co., 1991): 98.

3. Ibid., 96.

4. Ives, *Postface to Washington's Birthday*, ed. James B. Sinclair (New York: Associated Music Publishers, 1991): 31.
5. Ives, *Essays Before a Sonata*, ed. Howard Boatwright (1961: New York: W. W. Norton & Co., 1970): 30.
6. *Ives: Memos*, 104, n. 1.
7. Ives, note to his copyist, in *A Temporary Mimeographed Catalogue of the Music Manuscripts and Related Material of Charles Edward Ives*, compiled by John Kirkpatrick (1960; New Haven, CT: Library of the Yale School of Music, 1976): 11.
8. *Ives: Memos*, 123.
9. Boris de Schloezer, *Les Dernière Nouvelles*, March 11, 1932, p. 5, in Frank R. Rossiter, *Charles Ives and his America* (New York: Liveright, 1975): 230–231.
10. Ives, reported conversation with the conductor Nicolas Slonimsky, in Larry Starr, *A Union of Diversities: Style in the Music of Charles Ives* (New York: Schirmer Books, 1992): 111.
11. *Ives: Memos*, 138.
12. Ibid., 87.
13. Warren S. Smith, "Slonimsky Orchestra Makes Bow," *Boston Post*, January 26, 1931, p. 5.
14. Henry Prunières, "American Compositions in Paris," *New York Times*, July 12, 1931, sec. 8, p. 6.
15. Paul Rosenfeld, "Charles E. Ives," *New Republic* 71 (July 20, 1932): 262–263.
16. Ralph Waldo Emerson, "The Sphinx," in *Oxford Book of American Verse*, ed. F. O. Matthiesen (New York: Oxford University Press, 1950): 86.

ZOLTÁN KODÁLY

1. Kodály, "Introduction to the Performance of the 'Peacock Variations,'" in *The Selected Writings of Zoltán Kodály*, trans. L. Halápy and F. Macnicol (London: Boosey & Hawkes, 1964): 222.
2. Heinrich Jalowetz, in János Breuer, *A Guide to Kodály*, trans. Maria Steiner (Budapest, Hungary: Corvina Books, 1990): 133.
3. Kodály, program notes for *Háry János*, in Martin Bookspan, "Kodály's Háry János Suite," *Stereo Review* 34 (February 1975): 59.

WITOLD LUTOSŁAWSKI

1. Lutosławski, interview by Douglas Rust, in "Conversation with Witold Lutosławski," *Musical Quarterly* 79 (Spring 1995): 213.
2. Lutosławski, interview by Bogdan Gieraczynski, in "Witold Lutosławski in Interview," *Tempo* 170 (September 1989): 6.
3. The principal folk tune sources can be found in the monograph by Steven Stuckey, *Lutosławski and His Music* (Cambridge, UK: Cambridge University Press, 1981): 50.

DARIUS MILHAUD

1. Milhaud, *My Happy Life*, trans. Donald Evans, George Hall, and Christopher Palmer (New York: Marion Boyars, 1995): 98. Milhaud's biography exists in several iterations, all still in circulation. As *Notes sans musique* (1949) it addressed Milhaud's life up to the time he returned to France from a wartime sojourn in the United States. An English translation of that work by Donald Evans appeared under the title *Notes without Music* (1952). A text addressing all of the composer's life was published shortly after his death with a new title, *Ma vie heureuse* (1974) and forms the basis for the translation cited here and in subsequent references.

2. Ibid., 110.
3. Milhaud, "The Jazz Band and Negro Music," *Living Age* 323 (October 18, 1924): 171.
4. Milhaud, *Life*, 118.
5. Émile Vuillermoz, *"Chroniques et notes,"* *Revue Musicale* 5 (December 1923): 167.
6. Milhaud, *Life*, 120.

CARL NIELSEN

1. Carl Nielsen, *Living Music*, trans. Reginald Spink (London: J. & W. Chester, 1953): 42.
2. Ibid., 34.
3. Nielsen, Symphony No. 4, study score (Leipzig, Germany: Wilhelm Hansen, 1916): Preface.
4. Nielsen to Emil Holm, July 24, 1914, in *The Nielsen Companion*, ed. Mina Miller (Portland, OR: Amadeus Press, 1994): 627.
5. Nielsen to Julius Röntgen, April 4, 1915, in *The Nielsen Companion*, 628.
6. Nielsen, interview by Ludwig Dolleris, in *Carl Nielsen: A Musical Biography* (Odense, Denmark: Viggo Madsen, 1949): 261.
7. Nielsen, interview by Axel Kjerulf, January 23, 1922, in David Fanning, *Nielsen: Symphony No. 5* (Cambridge, UK: Cambridge University Press, 1997): 97–8.

FRANCIS POULENC

1. Princess Edmond de Polignac to Poulenc, August 24, 1931, in Emmanuel Reibel, *Les Concertos de Poulenc* (Bourg-a-Reine, France: Zurfluh, 1999): 39.
2. Poulenc to Marguerite Long, October 6, 1931, in Carl B. Schmidt, *The Music of Francis Poulenc (1899–1963): A Catalogue* (Oxford, UK: Clarendon Press, 1995): 196.
3. Ibid., 197.
4. Poulenc, *Entretiens avec Claude Rostand* (Paris, France: Juilliard, 1954): 83, in Keith W. Daniel, *Francis Poulenc: His Artistic Development and Musical Style* (Ann Arbor, MI: UMI Research Press, 1982): 149.
5. Poulenc to Paul Collaer, October 1, 1932, in Sidney Buckland, trans. and ed., *Francis Poulenc: Selected Correspondence 1915–1963* (London, UK: Victor Gollancz, Ltd., 1991): 97.
6. Henry Prunières, *"La festival de musique à Venise,"* *Revue Musicale* 13 (November 1932): 316.
7. F. Bonovia, *New York Times*, February 26, 1933, sec. 9, p. 6.
8. Poulenc to André Schaeffner, 1942, in Buckland, *Selected Correspondence*, 130.

SERGEI PROKOFIEV

1. Quoted in Nicolas Slonimsky, *Music since 1900*, 4th ed. (New York: Charles Scribner's Sons, 1971): 1359–1360.
2. Sergei Prokofiev, *Soviet Diary 1927 and Other Writings*, trans. and ed. Oleg Prokofiev (London, UK: Faber and Faber, 1991): 258–259.
3. From *Vecherneye Slovo*, April 22, 1918, in Israel Nestyev, *Prokofiev*, trans. Florence Jonas (Stanford, CA: Stanford University Press, 1960): 158.
4. V. Kolomyitsev, from *Nory Den*, April 19, 1918, in Nestyev, *Prokofiev*, 158.
5. Olin Downes, "Prokofieff's Fifth Played Here Again," *New York Times*, February 14, 1946, p. 33.
6. Prokofiev, *Soviet Diary*, 247.
7. Vernon Duke, in David Gutman, *Prokofiev* (London, UK: The Alderman Press, 1988): 46–47.
8. Prokofiev, *Soviet Diary*, 242–243.

9. Nicolai Miaskovsky to the editor Derzhanovsky, April 16, 1913, in Nestyev, *Prokofiev*, 73.
10. From the *St. Petersburg Gazette*, September 7, 1913, in Slonimsky, *Music*, 228.
11. From *Rech*, 7 September 1913, ibid.
12. Prokofiev, *Soviet Diary*, 272–273.
13. Ibid., 277.
14. Prokofiev to Soëtens, April 10, 1936, in Edward Sainati, "Desperately Seeking Soëtens," *Strad* 107 (June 1996): 619.
15. "A.M.C.," in Sainati, "Desperately Seeking Soëtens," 614.
16. Prokofiev, "Music for *Alexander Nevsky*," February 16, 1939, in Vladimir Blok, comp., *Sergei Prokofiev: Materials, Articles, Interviews* (Moscow: Progress Publishers, 1978): 35.
17. Sergei Eisenstein, narrative in Harlow Robinson, *Serge Prokofiev: A Biography* (New York: Viking Press, 1987): 351.
18. Galina Ulanova, "The Author of My Favourite Ballets," April 16, 1954, in Prokofiev, *Materials, Articles, Interviews*, 236.

MAURICE RAVEL
1. Ravel to Hélène Jourdan-Morhange, in Arbie Orenstein, *Ravel: Man and Musician* (New York: Columbia University Press, 1976): 108.
2. Ravel, "Contemporary Music," *Rice Institute Pamphlet* 15 (April 1928): 141.
3. Ravel to M. D. Calvocoressi, July 16, 1931, in "Ravel's Letters to Calvocoressi," *Musical Quarterly* 27 (January 1941): 17.
4. Ravel to an unidentified friend, March 19, 1931, in Victor Seroff, *Maurice Ravel* (New York: Henry Holt and Company, 1953): 260.
5. Ravel to M. D. Calvocoressi, "Ravel's Letters," 17.
6. Ravel to Jelly d'Aranyi, March 13, 1924, in Arbie Orenstein, comp. and ed., *Ravel Reader* (New York: Columbia University Press, 1990): 252–253.
7. *Times* (London), April 28, 1924, in Rollo H. Myers, *Ravel: Life and Works* (Westport, CT: Greenwood Press, 1960): 67.
8. Manuel de Falla, "*Notes sur Ravel*," *Revue Musicale* 189 (March 1939): 82.
9. From *Era* (London), December 21, 1909, in Nicolas Slonimsky, *Music since 1900*, 4th ed. (New York: Charles Scribner's Sons, 1971): 124.
10. Pierre Lalo, *Le Temps* (Paris), in Myers, *Ravel*, 54.
11. Interview with "C. v. W.," *De Telegraf*, September 30, 1922, in Orenstein, *Ravel Reader*, 423.
12. Ravel to Calvocoressi, in "Ravel's Letters," 17–18.
13. Ravel, "*Esquisse autobiographique*," *Revue Musicale* 187 (December 1938): 215.
14. Ravel to Arthur Honegger, in H. H. Stuckenschmidt, *Maurice Ravel: Variations on His Life and Work*, trans. S. R. Rosenbaum (1966; London, UK: Calder and Boyars, 1969): 230.
15. Roland-Manuel, *Maurice Ravel* (London, UK: A. and E. Walter, 1947), 55–56.
16. Colvocoressi's account is reproduced in Roger Nichols, *Ravel Remembered* (New York: W. W. Norton, 1987), 187.
17. Michel Fokine, *Memoirs of a Ballet Master*, trans. V. Fokine (Boston: Little, Brown and Co., 1962), 195, 199.
18. Ravel, "*Esquisse autobiographique*," 213.
19. Ravel to Mme. René de Saint-Marceaux, June 27, 1909, in Orenstein, *Ravel Reader*, 107.
20 Ravel, "*Esquisse autobiographique*," 214.
21. Ravel to Ralph Vaughan Williams, June 7, 1914, in Orenstein, *Ravel Reader*, 146–147.
22. Ravel, "*Esquisse autobiographique*," 213.

DMITRI SHOSTAKOVICH

1. See Boris Schwarz, *Music and Musical Life in Soviet Russia* (London, UK: Barrie & Jenkins, 1972), 123 and Elizabeth Wilson, *Shostakovich: A Life Remembered* (Princeton, NJ: Princeton University Press, 1994), 108–112.
2. The full text of the *Resolution of the Central Committee of the All-Union Communist Party (Bolsheviks) of Februry 10, 1948* is reprinted in Nicolas Slonimsky, *Music since 1900*, 4th ed. (New York: Charles Scribner's Sons, 1971): 1358–1362.
3. Shostakovich, memoirs, in *Testimony: The Memoirs of Dmitri Shostakovich*, ed. Solomon Volkov, trans. Antonina W. Bouis (New York: Harper and Row, 1979): 183.
4. Shostakovich, *Testimony*, 154, 155, 156.
5. Hugh Ottoway, *Shostakovich Symphonies* (Seattle, WA: University of Washington Press, 1978): 34.
6. Shostakovich, conversation with Mstislav Rostropovich, in Wilson, *Shostakovich: A Life Remembered*, 326.
7. Lev Lebedinsky, interview by Elizabeth Wilson, in *Shostakovich: A Life Remembered*, 265.

IGOR STRAVINSKY

1. Igor Stravinsky, *Poetics of Music in the Form of Six Lessons*, trans. Arthur Knodel and Ingolf Dahl (New York: Vintage Books, 1947): 68.
2. Igor Stravinsky and Robert Craft, *Themes and Episodes* (New York: Alfred A. Knopf, 1966): 43.
3. Stravinsky, program book of the New York Philharmonic Orchestra, January 24, 1946, in William Austin, *Music in the 20th Century* (New York: W. W. Norton & Co., 1966): 339–340.
4. Igor Stravinsky and Robert Craft, *Dialogues* (1961; Berkeley and Los Angeles, CA: University of California Press, 1982): 50–51.
5. Olin Downes, "Stravinsky Leads the Philharmonic," *New York Times*, January 25, 1946, p. 26.
6. Vera Stravinsky and Robert Craft, *Stravinsky in Pictures and Documents* (New York: Simon and Schuster, 1978): 339.
7. Robert Craft, ed., *Stravinsky: Selected Correspondence* (New York: Alfred A. Knopf, 1985): 3;264, n. 77.
8. Ibid., 3;268.
9. Igor Stravinsky, *An Autobiography* (New York: W. W. Norton, 1962): 119.
10. Nikolai Medtner to Sergei Rachmaninoff, May 28, 1924, in Richard Taruskin, *Stravinsky and the Russian Traditions* (Berkeley and Los Angeles, CA: University of California Press, 1996): 2;1516.
11. Prokofiev to Nikolai Myaskovsky, June 1, 1924, in Taruskin, *Russian Traditions*, 2;1607.
12. From Eugene Goosens, *Overture and Beginners*, 247, in Charles M. Joseph, *Stravinsky and the Piano* (Ann Arbor, MI: UMI Research Press, 1983): 159.
13. Samuel Dushkin, "Working with Stravinsky," *Igor Stravinsky*, ed. Edwin Corle (New York: Duell, Sloan and Pierce, 1949; reprint, New York: Books for Libraries Press, 1969): 189 (page citation is to reprint edition).
14. Craft, *Selected Correspondence*, 1; 215–216, n. 273.
15. I. Stravinsky and Craft, *Dialogues*, 45.
16. Francis Poulenc in *Le Mois*, February-March 1931, in V. Stravinsky and Craft, *Pictures and Documents*, 297.
17. I. Stravinsky, interview by Georges Auric, June 3, 1938, in Eric Walter White, *Stravinsky: The Composer and His Works* (Berkeley and Los Angeles, CA: The University of California Press, 1966): 360.

18. Igor Stravinsky and Robert Craft, *Expositions and Developments* (Garden City, New York: Doubleday and Company, 1962): 145–146.

19. Michel Fokine, *Memoirs of a Ballet Master*, trans. Vitale Fokine (Boston: Little Brown and Company, 1961): 161.

20. I. Stravinsky and Craft, *Expositions and Developments*, 146–147.

21. Igor Stravinsky, *An Autobiography*, trans. unknown (1936; New York: W. W. Norton & Co., 1962): 31–32.

22. Serge Lifar, *Serge de Diaghilev: sa vie, son oeuvre, sa legende* (Monaco: Rocher, 1954): 226 n.

23. *Comoedia*, June 14, 1911, in Nicolas Slonimsky, *Music since 1900*, 4th ed. (New York: Charles Scribner's Sons, 1971): 190.

24. Andrei Rimsky-Korsakov, *Russian Intelligencer* 45 (January 25–February 7, 1913), in Taruskin, *Russian Traditions*, 1;764.

25. I. Stravinsky and Craft, *Expositions and Developments*, 126–127.

26. Adolphe Boschot, "Le 'Sacre du printemps,'" *L'Echo de Paris* May 30, 1913, in *Igor Stravinsky: Le Sacre du printemps, dossier de presse* (Geneva, Switzerland: Minkoff, 1980): 16.

RALPH VAUGHAN WILLIAMS

1. Ursula Vaughan Williams, *R. V. W.: A Biography of Ralph Vaughan Williams* (London, UK: Oxford University Press, 1964): xv.

2. Ralph Vaughan Williams, "What Is Music," *National Music and Other Essays*, 2nd ed. (Oxford, UK: Oxford University Press, 1987): 206.

3. Vaughan Williams, "A Musical Autobiography," *National Music*, 193.

4. Vaughan Williams, "Composer's Programme Notes," 1920, in Michael Kennedy, *A Catalogue of the Works of Ralph Vaughan Williams*, 2nd. ed. (London, UK: Oxford University Press, 1996): 71.

5. Herbert George Wells, *Tono-Bungay* (New York: Duffield and Company, 1929): 453, 457–458.

6. Gustav Holst to Vaughan Williams, March 29, 1914, in Ursula Vaughan Williams and Imogen Holst, eds., *Heirs and Rebels: Letters Written to Each Other and Occasional Writings on Music by Ralph Vaughan Williams and Gustav Holst* (London, UK: Oxford University Press, 1959): 43.

7. George Meredith, excerpt from "The Lark Ascending," in Ralph Vaughan Williams, *The Lark Ascending*, study score (London, UK: Oxford University Press, 1925): Preface.

8. *Times* (London), in Michael Kennedy, *The Works of Ralph Vaughan Williams* (London, UK: Oxford University Press, 1964): 154.

9. From the *Gloucester Journal*, in Kennedy, *Works*, 94.

10. [J. A. Fuller Maitland?], "Three Choirs Festival," *Times* (London), September 7, 1910, p. 11.

WILLIAM WALTON

1. "Meteoric Rise: Career of Mr. W. T. Walton," *Oldham Chronicle*, May 1, 1926, in Michael Kennedy, "William Walton: A Critical Appreciation," in *William Walton: A Thematic Catalog of His Musical Works*, compiled by Stewart R. Craggs (London, UK: Oxford University Press, 1977): 32.

2. Walton to Sir Hamilton Harty, September 1933, in Susan Walton, *William Walton: Behind the Façade* (New York: Oxford University Press, 1988): 76.

3. Walton to the BBC, January 1934, in Michael Kennedy, *Portrait of Walton* (New York: Oxford University Press, 1989): 74.

4. "William Walton's Symphony," *Times* (London), November 7, 1935, p. 12.

5. Walton to Hubert Foss, in S. Walton, *Behind the Façade*, 88.

6. Walton to H. Foss, May 11, 1938, in Kennedy, *Portrait*, 98.

7. Antonio Brosa, *Royal College of Music Magazine* 65 (Easter 1969): 10, in *William Walton: A Catalogue*, compiled by Stewart Craggs (New York: Oxford University Press, 1990): 71.

8. Walton to H. Foss, in Kennedy, *Portrait*, 99.

9. Lionel Tertis, *My Viola and I* (London: Paul Elek, 1974): 36.

10. Willi Strecker to Gertrud Hindemith, in S. Walton, *Behind the Façade*, 69.

11. Walton to Angus Morrison, February 12, 1929, in Kennedy, *Portrait*, 48.

12. Peter J. Pirie, "Broadcasting," *Musical Times* 104 (December 1963): 889.

13. R. J. F Howgill to H. Foss, September 4, 1930, in Kennedy, *Portrait*, 57.

14. *Times* (London), October 10, 1931, p. 10.

ANTON WEBERN

1. Anton Webern, *The Path to the New Music*, trans. Leo Black, ed. Willi Reich (Bryn Mawr, PA: Theodore Presser Company, 1963): 35.

2. From the *Wiener Illustriertes Extrablatt*, November 5, 1908, in Hans and Rosaleen Moldenhauer, *Anton Webern: A Chronicle of His Life and Works* (New York: Alfred A. Knopf, 1979): 97.

3. Ibid.

4. Ibid., 252.

Glossary

a capella: Literally, "in the style of the chapel"; in contemporary musical discourse, to sing or play without instrumental accompaniment.

adagio: Slow.

ad libitum: At the liberty (or discretion) of the performer, often abbreviated as *ad lib*.

allargando: Large, broad, thus a term designating something to be performed in an expansive manner.

allegretto: Moderately fast, but slower than allegro.

allegro: Fast.

amoroso: In a tender, loving manner.

andante: In a moving or walking tempo.

andantino: With a little movement; less rapid than allegro.

antecedent: The first of two complementary phrases or segments of musical activity which together comprise a more complete musical statement. See **consequent**.

antiphonal: Music drawing upon the effects produced by contrasting performing groups, often involving spatial separation of those units.

aria: Air, or song, most frequently applied to a solo section of an opera; by extension, an instrumental passage in the style of such a vocal work.

aria da capo: An aria of two sections, the ending of the second marked *da capo* (to the head, or beginning), indicating that the first section is to be repeated in performance, creating a balanced (A-B-A) structural plan.

arioso: In the manner of an aria, melodious; a movement or section of a musical work written in such a style.

arpeggio: To play consecutively, in ascending or descending order, the notes of a chord.

atonality: The absence of a central key or tonal point of reference. The term sometimes applies to that technique of composition known as the **twelve-tone method**, owing to its theoretical lack of a tonal center.

augmentation: A process of increasing note durations, usually in a specified proportion to the original notation, e.g., 1:2, 2:3, etc., leading to a decrease in rhythmic activity.

augmented fourth: 1) An interval of three whole-tones, in contrast to the perfect fourth, which consists of two and a half whole-tones. 2) That interval which acoustically divides the octave.

bar: One complete rhythmic unit defined by bar-lines. See **measure**.

bel canto: Literally "beautiful singing," or a melodic line written in the style of a broadly projected vocal melody.

binary: A structural design consisting of two sections, usually separated by a double bar-line.

cadence: The melodic or harmonic close at the end of a phrase.

cadenza: An elaborated cadence, sometimes quite extended, intended for a soloist, most frequently found in concertos and operatic arias.

canon: Music written according to a specific rule or process.

cantus firmus: "Fixed song," or a melody, usually borrowed from a prior source and adapted to serve as a structural foundation for a composition.

celesta: An instrument of the percussion section operated by a traditional keyboard, which in turn causes small hammers to strike metal bars.

chaconne: In early music the term is often interchangeable with *passacaglia*, q.v. In modern music some theorists identify the *chaconne* as a repeated harmonic pattern that recurs throughout a work or, more frequently, throughout one movement of a multimovement work.

chimes: See **tubular bells**.

choir: Any group of like-sounding instruments or voices.

chorale: A melody usually identified by its initial association with a sacred text and syllabic melodic style, traditionally intended for congregational singing.

chromatic: A note "colored" by an inflection up or down a half-step, or half-tone, by one of several notation signs. By extension, "chromaticism" refers to the extended application of that process to multiple notes within a passage or section. The **chromatic scale** consists of a series of half-steps.

coda: A closing section, usually short.

col legno: "With the wood," a term directing string players to strike the strings with the wood of the bow.

color: A term referring to the sound characteristics of one or more instruments or voices, as in "tone color."

coloratura: A highly elaborated melodic style, or a voice capable of singing fluently in that style, usually in the higher registers.

concertante: A style of music expanding on the contrasts between different performing media or music of different timbres. See **concerto**.

concertino: Literally, a small concerto.

concerto: A work based on the contrast between multiple units of one or more instruments. In the orchestral tradition, concertos usually consist of three movements in fast-slow-fast order, with one or more prominent cadenzas or solo sections featuring the solo instrument. **Solo concertos** featuring one instrument in contrast to a supporting group are most common.

concerto grosso: A concerto in which a solo instrument is replaced by a solo group.

consequent: A second or answering phrase that complements, melodically and harmonically, an opening or antecedent phrase, q.v. See **antecedent**.

conservatory: An institution designed for the training of musicians with a highly focused specialization in one area of musical endeavor, usually performance.

contrapuntal: A musical texture resulting from counterpoint, q.v., or music formed by two or more relatively independent lines.

counterpoint: A technique of writing based upon the coordination of two or more relatively independent musical lines.

crescendo: To increase in volume.

critic: One who comments on, writes about, or in some way describes musical literature or its performance in a manner intended for public consumption.

diatonic: Referring to the notes occurring naturally within a given key or pitch system.

diminuendo: Diminishing in volume of sound, becoming quieter.

diminution: A process of decreasing note values, usually by a specified proportion in relation to the original notation, producing an increase in rhythmic activity.

dissonance: In traditional styles, a sound produced by two or more tones, or harmonies, which in its musical context leads the hearer to expect some resolution to a more stable sound.

divertimento: A composition intended primarily for diversionary entertainment; in the 20th century, a work comprising any number of movements, usually shorter than movements of a symphony and often bearing dance titles.

dodecaphony, dodecaphonic: Referring to music of twelve tones, q. v.; or serial music based on a twelve-tone row, or a basic series of pitches established by the composer.

dominant: The fifth and, acoustically, the strongest note of a scale other than the tonic; often used as a synonym for the chord built on that note of the scale.

double-stop: In music for strings, a sound produced by bowing on two or more strings simultaneously on the same instrument.

downbeat: The first pulse in a measure, normally receiving the strongest accent in that rhythmic unit, named after the traditional downward motion of a conductor's hand or baton in designating that pulse.

English horn: A double-reed instrument sounding five notes (or a fifth) below its written pitch, often described as an alto oboe and physically identified by its onion-shaped bell.

enharmonic, enharmonicism: That condition in Western notation whereby one tone can be designated by different pitch names, e.g., A-sharp and B-flat are represented by the same key on traditional keyboards.

exposition: That section of a movement or larger work in which the principal material first appears, usually in the context of a sonata design. In a fugue, those sections that are given over to a statement of the full subject.

fantasie, fantasia: In music from the 18th through the 20th centuries, a work following the composer's fancy (creative imagination) rather than one of many traditional formal patterns; in early music (pre-1700), an instrumental work not based on a vocal model. See **rhapsody.**

f, ff, fff: Common abbreviations for the Italian words *forte* (loud), *fortissimo* (more loudly), and *fortississimo* (most loudly), placed within the musical text to indicate the dynamic level for an instrumental part or larger section of the music.

fluttertonguing: In music for wind instruments, a technique for the rapid articulation of notes through a fibrillation of the tongue, as in a rolled "r."

folk music: Music derived from the common practice of large cultural groups, often associated with uncomplicated harmonic structures and a text of indeterminate origin.

forte: See *f, ff, fff.*

fugue: A contrapuntal procedure wherein the theme, called a subject, appears successively in all parts of the musical texture and is continuously expanded and reaffirmed through imitative restatement. Frequently the term, as a title, identifies a work or a movement following the fugal process more or less consistently.

glissando: A rapid gesture, rising or descending, which sounds all the pitches available on an instrument; a slide.

Golden Section: The division of a work (or a movement, or other defined unit) into unequal parts in a manner that the proportion of the small part to the larger is the same as the proportion of the larger part to the whole. "Golden Section" often appears in art and architecture, and finds various applications in the music of Bartók and Ravel, among others.

grave: Solemn, serious, therefore usually implying slower tempos.

half cadence: A cadence ending deceptively on a harmony other than the tonic, usually the **dominant.**

harmonics: Overtones, or tones in the overtone series, which through special notations and operations on an instrument, usually one of the string family, produce a pure tone color as a special effect.

head-motive: A well-defined motive appearing at the beginning of a work, or movement of a work, usually returning in its original or altered form at some point later in the composition. See **motive.**

homophonic: A texture consisting of a principal melodic line or level of activity supported by a subordinate chordal accompaniment.

imitation: The presentation of a motive or melody by two or more parts successively, each continuing as other parts enter.

intermezzo: "In between," thus a work or movement between two others of contrasting character. By extension, the term usually applies to a relatively short or lyrical movement.

interval: The distance between two tones described by the number of notes encompassed. Thus A–B (two notes) is a second; A–C (three notes), is a third, etc.

inversion: The process of turning upside down, or inverting, any unit of music; thus the inversion of a rising melody will descend, or the inversion of an ascending interval will descend by the same distance.

Jew's harp: A folk instrument of indeterminate origin consisting of a freely vibrating metal tongue fixed within a metal frame; the frame is held against the player's mouth, the free end of the tongue strummed as the oral cavity provides a resonating chamber.

key: In traditional harmony, the system of whole- and half-steps (scales) that establishes one note as a central point of reference, such as the key of C, the key of D, etc.

langsam: Slow.

larghetto: A little slow, but less slow than **largo**.

largo: Slow.

lebhaft: Lively.

leitmotiv: A musical fragment (leading motive) or phrase that recurs throughout the course of an extended work, traditionally opera, which refers by association to some facet of the drama. The term most frequently appears in association with the music dramas of Richard Wagner, although it can be found in many works before and after Wagner.

maestoso: Majestic, in a majestic manner.

massig: German word meaning moderate, medium.

measure: One complete unit of rhythm in traditional notation, contained between adjacent bar lines. See **bar**.

melisma: A melodic flourish centered around one pitch or harmonic interval.

melismatic: A text setting incorporating more than one melisma.

minuet: A graceful court dance of the 18th and early 19th centuries in moderate triple meter. Also, a movement written in the style of that dance, *ergo*, the dance movement frequently incorporated in symphonies. See **principal song and trio**.

meter: The system by which rhythmic pulses are grouped into units called measures, thus triple (groups of three beats) or duple (groups of two beats) meter.

mezzo: Middle, or medium.

modal: Most commonly, music that is characterized by one of the scales other than those traditionally identified as major or minor.

mode: A scale based on one of several patterns of whole- and half-step intervals; most frequently a reference to such systems as they were established in Western ecclesiastical music. See **modal**.

modulation: In tonal music, q.v., the process of change from one to another key or tonic center, usually, but not always, through a gradual process.

monothematic: The condition of having only one significant theme in a composition.

morendo: Dying away.

motive: A short, distinctive bit of melody sufficiently well defined to retain its identity through any number of restatements or transformations. See **head-motive**.

night music: A musical texture of multiple small motives or melodic gestures that collectively give the impression of sounds of nature at night. The term probably originated with the fourth movement of Bartók's piano suite *Out of Doors*, which bears the title *Musique nocturne*.

non troppo: Not too much.

note: A single unit of notation indicating one tone of specified pitch and duration.

obbligato: Necessary, must be played; a part, a section, or a style of execution that is specified by the compose and not left to the discretion of the performer.

opus: "Work," a number assigned to a piece of music by the composer or publisher to identify the chronological order of composition or publication.

orchestral bells: See **tubular bells.**

ostinato: A consistently repeated figure, either rhythmic (most common), melodic, or harmonic, which through its repetition comprises a stable reference or an element of continuity.

passacaglia: A musical design based upon a melodic pattern, traditionally in triple meter, which is repeated consistently throughout a composition as a structural element. In early music the *passacaglia* was a dance, and the term may appear as the title of a movement that follows this procedure. See **chaconne**.

pedal point: A sustained note, group of notes, or chord forming a static point of reference, theoretically (although rare in practice) independent from the prevailing musical fabric.

perpetuum mobile: "Perpetual motion," sometimes designated by the Italian *moto perpetuo*. A composition or extended passage marked by constant motion from beginning to end in a fast tempo, usually based on notes of a single value.

pesante: Heavy, heavily.

piano: See *p, pp, ppp*

pitch: The number of vibrations per second, which identifies a specific tone; a higher number of vibrations produces a relatively "higher" pitch, a lower number a "lower" pitch.

pizzicato: To pluck the strings of an instrument that is usually played with a bow.

polyphonic: A musical texture of two or more independent melodies sounding at the same time.

polytonal: A harmonic quality of music that expands upon more than one tonal center, or key, simultaneously.

ponticello: Usually *sul ponticello*, a descriptive term applied to bowed string instruments calling for players to bow very near the bridge, producing a nasal tone lacking in resonance.

p, pp, ppp: Common abbreviations for the Italian words *piano* (quiet), *pianissimo* (more quietly), and *pianississimo* (most quietly).

presto: Quick, fast.

prestissimo: Faster than *presto*; literally, as fast as possible.

principal song and trio: A collective term encompassing the principle of a broad three-part design (A–B–A) which in turn derives from the classic minuet and trio in which the minuet is restated following the trio section. The generic term "principal song" is designed to include those applications in which the main sections may be something other than a traditional minuet.

program music: Music that illustrates or portrays through musical means an extra-musical element.

quarter-tone: One half of a **semitone**. An interval not available on instruments of fixed pitch; violins and some wind instruments can produce quarter-tones by playing a written pitch slightly higher or lower than written.

rallentando: Slowing, decreasing in speed.

rhapsody: A work presumed, often erroneously, to follow no predetermined or traditionally recognized structural design.

ritard: Gradually slower.

ritornello: A section of music or musical material that returns in the same or nearly the same manner throughout a composition, separated by intervening episodes of contrasting materials. See **rondo.**

rondo: A musical design founded on the restatement of a principal section or theme (ritornello) separated by intervening sections of contrasting materials. See **ritornello.**

scherzando: Playful.

scherzo: Traditionally, a dance movement of three-part design, usually fast and often something of a display piece for the orchestra.

schnell: Fast.

semitone: One half of a full-tone, or the smallest interval between two adjacent notes as they are represented on a traditional keyboard; the smallest interval in the intonation system of Western music.

semplice: Simply, in a simple manner.

short score: A compressed score in which multiple parts are condensed on relatively few staffs, usually three or four. When writing for orchestra, most composers will create a short score as a matter of ease and efficiency before arranging the music for full ensemble in a score with a staff assigned to each independent instrument of the ensemble. Conductors of wind ensembles often work from a short score; orchestral conductors rarely do so.

sonata: One of the most frequently encountered forms (structural plans) of instrumental music in the Western tradition. It traditionally consists of three major sections, one in which basic materials are presented, usually in different keys (see **exposition**), a second, contrasting section in which opening materials may be expanded through several procedures (a **development**), and a third section in which materials from the opening return, now all in the same key (a **recapitulation**). Sometimes identified as "sonata-allegro design" because of its frequent association with quick tempos, or as "first-movement form," because of its prevalence in the first of multimovement instrumental works.

sonorism: A term coined in the mid-20th century referring to that quality of music in which timbre, texture, register, and similar sound characteristics become the primary focus of a composition.

sordino: Mute, or with mutes.

sostenuto: Sustained.

staccato: Notes played in a short, detached manner.

stop time: A style of accompaniment associated with American popular music in which the basic melody and harmony are compressed into a regular pattern of attacks separated by silences, originally in support of tap dancing or other stage activity.

suite: Traditionally, a work consisting of several movements, frequently stylized dances in contrasting meter and tempo. In the 20th century the term may apply to any collection of separate and autonomous movements or to a collection of excerpts from a ballet.

sul tasto: To bow a string instrument over the fingerboard in order to produce a less resonant tone.

symphonic poem: A one-movement work for orchestra, usually but not always designed to portray some extramusical element or story.

symphony: Usually a multimovement work written for an ensemble of contrasting choirs of instruments in which the string choir traditionally plays the most important role; through common use, an ensemble that performs such works.

syncopation: A temporary displacement of normal patterns of rhythmic accent.

tam-tam: A percussion instrument consisting of a circular metal plate, slightly convex, with the edges bent inward, the whole suspended vertically and struck with (usually) a soft-headed beater. Sometimes called a gong.

tempo: The "time" or relative frequency of rhythmic pulses of music, thus the rhythmic speed of a given work, sometimes specified as a given number of beats per minute.

ternary: In three parts, usually referring to a structural design of three sections.

tessitura: That part of a performer's range that encompasses the major portion of musical activity in a piece. By extension, a high or low *tessitura* describes the location of melody within the range of the medium performing it.

texture: A descriptive term addressing the relationship between musical lines or musical parts. See **homophonic, polyphonic.**

timbre: That quality of sound that distinguishes one instrument or voice from another.

tom-tom: A drum, usually with two heads, no snares, played with various beaters.

tonality: A system of composition in which the pitch materials are ordered around one central tone. Through practice this has led to a hierarchy of tones within a key and a comparable hierarchy of harmonies based on those tones.

tone: 1) A sound of definite pitch. 2) An interval encompassing two half tones, q.v., such as C to D or A-flat to B-flat; a whole-tone. 3) The quality of sound (**timbre**) produced by an instrument or voice, as in "a rasping tone."

tonic: The central or most important note in music written in a tonal system; in practical application, the chord or harmony based upon that note.

transposing instruments: Those instruments of the orchestra that, for convenience of notation on a musical staff, sound a pitch different from the written note. Instruments in B-flat sound that pitch (lower) when playing C; instruments in F sound that pitch in response to a written C, etc.

transposition: The presentation of music at a pitch or in a key other than that which is written.

tremolo: A rapid, nonmeasured repetition of a single note, most frequently encountered in orchestral string writing. The term is sometimes applied to a rapid alternation of notes more than a whole-tone apart, as in a harmonic trill.

tripartite: Three-part. See **ternary.**

tritone: An interval of three whole-tones, acoustically dividing the octave into two equal parts. Its particular qualities within the traditional tonal system have led composers to both avoid and emphasize its presence, depending on the desired tonal orientation.

tubular bells: Metal tubes of varying lengths suspended in a frame in a pattern similar to a piano keyboard and struck on the top end with a small hammer, originally of wood, today made of rawhide. The aggregate instrument is also called chimes, orchestral chimes, and orchestral bells.

tutti: "All," or full ensemble; a section played by the full ensemble.

twelve-tone music: A technique of composition founded on the premise that all twelve tones of the chromatic scale are equal and, in any given work, generally appear in a designated sequence. See **dodecaphony, atonality.**

unison: That point where two or more musical lines or instrumental parts come together on one pitch in the same octave.

vibraphone: A percussion instrument consisting of metal bars, graduated in length and arranged in a pattern similar to a piano keyboard. A resonating tube below each bar contains in its top a circular disc, which, when rotated by electric motor, alternately opens and closes the resonator, producing the distinctive vibrato for which the instrument is named. The player may use mallets of different consistency, may play with the vibrators on or off, and has access to a damper pedal acting on all the bars.

vibrato: A repeated small fluctuation in pitch executed as a decorative ornament.

virtuoso: Referring to an unusually high degree of technical skill in any musical activity, but most frequently applied to performance, thus a virtuoso violinist, a virtuoso pianist, et al.

vivace: Vivacious.

vivo: Lively.

whole-tone: See **tone**.

whole-tone scale: A scale of six tones per octave, consisting entirely of whole steps.

xylophone: A percussion instrument consisting of pitched wooden bars that are struck with any one of several kinds of small mallets. The bars are arranged in the manner of a piano keyboard and suspended over circular tubes of graduated lengths to accommodate the pitch and enhance the resonance.

Recommended Reading

These references have been chosen for their widespread availability to the interested layperson who wishes further information on the composers and music addressed in the main text. *The New Grove Dictionary of Music and Musicians, 2nd Edition (2000)* is the standard English-language reference work in music, offering encyclopedic information on composers, the salient traits of their music, comprehensive bibliographies, and a list of works.

JOHN ADAMS
Smith, Geoff and Nicola Walker Smith. *New Voices: American Composers Talk about Their Music*. Portland, OR: Amadeus Press, 1995.
Strickland, Edward. *American Composers: Dialogues on Contemporary Music*. Bloomington, IN: Indiana University Press, 1991.

SAMUEL BARBER
Hennessee, Don A. *Samuel Barber: A Bio-Bibliography*. Westport, CT: Greenwood Press, 1985.
Heyman, Barbara. *Samuel Barber: The Composer and His Music*. New York: Oxford University Press, 1992.
Pollack, Howard. "Samuel Barber, Jean Sibelius, and the Making of an American Romantic." *Muscial Quarterly* 84 (2000): 175–205.

BÉLA BARTÓK
Gillies, Malcolm, ed. *The Bartók Companion*. Portland, OR: Amadeus Press, 1994.
Stevens, Halsey. *The Life and Music of Béla Bartók*. 3rd ed. prepared by Malcolm Gillies. Oxford: Clarendon Press, 1993.

ALBAN BERG
Jarman, Douglas. *The Music of Alban Berg*. Berkeley: University of California Press, 1978.
Simms, Bryan R., ed. *Schoenberg, Berg, and Webern: A Companion to the Second Viennese School*. Westport, CT: Greenwood Press, 1999.

LEONARD BERNSTEIN
Burton, Humphrey. *Leonard Bernstein*. New York: Doubleday, 1994.
Peyser, Joan. *Bernstein: A Biography*. Rev. and updated. New York: Billboard Books, 1998.

BENJAMIN BRITTEN

Carpenter, Humphrey. *Benjamin Britten: A Biography*. New York: Charles Scribner's Sons, 1992.

Mitchell, Donald and Philip Reed, eds. *Letters from a Life: The Selected Letters and Diaries of Benjamin Britten*. 2 vols. Berkeley: University of California Press, 1991.

Palmer, Christopher, ed. *The Britten Companion*. Cambridge: Cambridge University Press, 1984.

AARON COPLAND

Copland, Aaron and Vivian Perlis. *Copland: 1900 through 1942*. New York: St Martin's / Marek, 1984.

——. *Copland since 1943*. New York: St. Martin's Press, 1989.

Pollack, Howard. *Aaron Copland: The Life and Work of an Uncommon Man*. New York: Henry Holt and Co., 1999.

JOHN CORIGLIANO

Holland, Bernard. "Highbrow Music to Hum." *New York Times Magazine*, January 31, 1982, pp. 25, 56–57, 65, 67, 70.

PETER MAXWELL DAVIES

Griffiths, Paul. *Peter Maxwell Davies*. London: Robson Books, 1982.

Seabrook, Mike. *Max: The Life and Music of Maxwell Davies*. London: Victor Gollancz, Ltd., 1994.

MANUEL DE FALLA

Armero, Gonzalo and Jorge de Persia, eds. *Manuel de Falla: His Life and Works*. Trans. Tom Skipp. London: Omnibus Press, 1990.

James, Burnett. *Manuel de Falla and the Spanish Musical Renaissance*. London: Victor Gollancz, Ltd., 1979.

GEORGE GERSHWIN

Jablonski, Edward and Lawrence Stewart. *The Gershwin Years: George and Ira*. New York: Da Capo Press, 1996.

Kimball, Robert and Alfred Simon. *The Gershwins*. New York: Atheneum, 1973.

Schwartz, Charles. *Gershwin: His Life and Music*. Indianapolis: The Bobbs-Merrill Company, Inc., 1973.

ALBERTO GINASTERA

Chase, Gilbert. "Alberto Ginastera: Argentine Composer." *Musical Quarterly* 43 (October 1957): 439–460.

HENRYK GÓRECKI

Thomas, Adrian. *Górecki*. Oxford: Clarendon Press, 1997.

PAUL HINDEMITH

Hindemith, Paul. *A Composer's World: Horizons and Limitations*. Cambridge, MA: Harvard University Press, 1953.

——. *The Craft of Musical Composition*. Trans. Arthur Mendel. 3 vols. Mainz, Germany: B. Schotts Söhne, 1945.

Kemp, Ian. *Hindemith*. London and New York: Oxford University Press, 1970.

Neumeyer, David. *The Music of Paul Hindemith*. New Haven, CT: Yale University Press, 1986.

GUSTAV HOLST
Greene, Richard. *Gustav Holst and a Rhetoric of Musical Character*. New York: Garland Publishing, Inc, 1994.
Holst, Imogen. *The Music of Gustav Holst and Holst's Music Reconsidered*. 3rd rev. ed. Oxford: Oxford University Press, 1986.

CHARLES IVES
Burkholder, J. Peter. *All Made of Tunes: Charles Ives and the Uses of Musical Borrowing*. New Haven, CT: Yale University Press, 1995.
Hitchcock, Wiley. *Ives*. London: Oxford University Press, 1977.
Starr, Larry. *A Union of Diversities: Style in the Music of Charles Ives*. New York: Schirmer Books, 1992.

ZOLTÁN KODÁLY
Breuer, János. *A Guide to Kodály*. Trans. Maria Steiner. Budapest, Hungary: Corvina Books, 1990.

WITOLD LUTOSŁAWSKI
Rae, Charles Bodman. *The Music of Lutosławski*. 3rd ed. London: Omnibus Press, 1999.
Stucky, Steven. *Lutosławski and his Music*. New York: Cambridge University Press, 1981.

DARIUS MILHAUD
Collaer, Paul. *Darius Milhaud*. Trans. and ed. Jane Hohfeld Galante. San Francisco: San Francisco Press, 1988.
Milhaud, Darius. *My Happy Life*. Trans. Donald Evans, George Hall, and Christopher Palmer. London: Marian Boyars, 1995.

CARL NIELSEN
Lawson, Jack. *Carl Nielsen*. London: Phaidon Press, 1997.
Miller, Mina, ed. *The Nielsen Companion*. Portland, OR: Amadeus Press, 1994.
Simpson, Robert. *Carl Nielsen: Symphonist 1865–1931*. Rev. 2nd. ed. New York: Taplinger Publishing Co., 1979.

CARL ORFF
Liess, Andreas. *Carl Orff: His Life and Music*. Trans. A. and H. Parkin. London: Caldar and Boyars, 1966.

FRANCIS POULENC
Ivry, Benjamin. *Francis Poulenc*. London: Phaidon Press, 1996.
Poulenc, Francis. *Selected Correspondence 1915–1963*. Trans. and ed. Sidney Buckland. London: Victor Golancz, Ltd., 1991.

SERGEI PROKOFIEV
Minturn, Neil. *The Music of Sergei Prokofiev*. New Haven, CT: Yale University Press, 1997.
Prokofiev, Sergei. *Soviet Diary 1927 and other Writings*. Trans. and ed. Oleg Prokofiev. London: Faber and Faber, 1991.
Robinson, Harlow. *Sergei Prokofiev*. New York: Viking Press, 1987.

MAURICE RAVEL

Orenstein, Arbie. *Ravel: Man and Musician*. New York: Columbia University Press, 1975.
——, ed. *A Ravel Reader: Correspondence, Articles, Interviews*. New York: Columbia University Press, 1990.

DMITRI SHOSTAKOVICH

Fay, Laurel E. *Shostakovich: A Life*. Oxford: Oxford University Press, 2000.
Wilson, Elizabeth. *Shostakovich: A Life Remembered*. Princeton, NJ: Princeton University Press, 1994.

IGOR STRAVINSKY

Craft, Robert. *Stravinsky: Chronicle of a Friendship*. Rev. exp. ed. Nashville, TN: Vanderbilt University Press, 1994.
Taruskin, Richard. *Stravinsky and the Russian Traditions*. 2 vols. Berkeley, CA: University of California Press, 1996.
White, Eric Walter. *Stravinsky: The Composer and his Works*. Berkeley, CA: University of California Press, 1966.

RALPH VAUGHAN WILLIAMS

Kennedy, Michael. *The Works of Ralph Vaughan Williams*. London: Oxford University Press, 1964.
Mellers, Wilfred. *Vaughan Williams and the Vision of Albion*. London: Barrie & Jenkins, 1989.
Vaughan Williams, Ralph. *National Music and Other Essays*. 2nd ed. Oxford: Oxford University Press, 1987.

WILLIAM WALTON

Kennedy, Michael. *Portrait of Walton*. Oxford: Oxford University Press, 1989.
Walton, Susan. *William Walton: Behind the Façade*. Oxford: Oxford University Press, 1988.

ANTON WEBERN

Bailey, Kathryn. *The Life of Webern*. Cambridge: Cambridge University Press, 1998.
Kolneder, Walter. *Anton Webern: An Introduction to His Works*. Trans. Humphrey Searle. Berkeley, CA: University of California Press, 1968.
Simms, Bryan R., ed. *Schoenberg, Berg, and Webern: A Companion to the Second Viennese School*. Westport, CT: Greenwood Press, 1999.

Index